DICTIONARY *of* ANCIENT RABBIS

DICTIONARY *of* ANCIENT RABBIS

Selections from The Jewish Encyclopaedia

Edited by

JACOB NEUSNER

HENDRICKSON PUBLISHERS

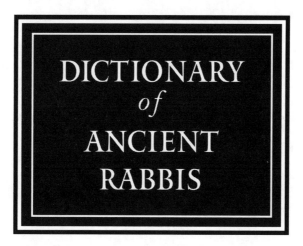

Dictionary of Ancient Rabbis: Selections from *The Jewish Encyclopaedia*
Edited by Jacob Neusner

Hendrickson Publishers, Inc.
P. O. Box 3473
Peabody, Massachusetts 01961-3473

Articles reproduced from the first edition of:
Singer, Isadore, ed. *The Jewish Encyclopaedia.* New York: Funk and Wagnall, 1901–1906.

Printed in the United States of America.

First Printing—August 2003

Library of Congress Cataloging-in-Publication Data

Dictionary of ancient rabbis : selections from the Jewish encyclopaedia / edited by Jacob Neusner.
p. cm.
ISBN 1-56563-932-4 (hardcover : alk. paper)
1. Rabbis—Biography—Dictionaries—English. 2. Hasidim—Biography—Dictionaries—English. I. Neusner, Jacob, 1932–
BM750.D53 2003
296.1′2′00922—dc21
2003051137

DICTIONARY OF ANCIENT RABBIS

SELECTIONS FROM *THE JEWISH ENCYCLOPAEDIA*

EDITED BY JACOB NEUSNER

PREFACE

This dictionary of ancient rabbis sets forth the entries, originally published in *The Jewish Encyclopaedia*,[1] that are devoted to the sages of the Mishnah, Tosefta, Talmuds, and midrash compilations of late antiquity. That classic exercise of a century ago, the first major statement of Judaic learning to appear in the United States,[2] encompassed numerous entries on rabbinic Judaism in its formative age, its sages and their lives, its theology and institutions, its history and its literature. Most rabbinic sages mentioned in the classical documents of Judaism receive an entry that summarizes the references and sayings attributed to them and stories told about them in those documents. The stress throughout rests on Talmudic narratives treated as historical facts, not on legal philosophy or theology.

More than a mere curiosity out of a dead past, these entries retain considerable interest, even though learning has moved beyond them at many points. Of what use are exercises now a century old? While, as I shall explain, scholarship has progressed, the entries on named sages of ancient times contain valuable and dependable facts. Specifically, they assemble the more important bits and pieces of information attached to specified names of persons deemed rabbinic sages. A handbook of the data scattered across rabbinic compilations of late antiquity makes for ready reference. The precision and comprehensive character of the collection provide a convenient starting point for systematic, critical research: a checklist of what should be addressed.

But these entries do not qualify as biographies, and the narratives to which they refer, as history. Indeed, the data in these pages do not comprise what the scholars who collected them supposed they did, which is biographical sketches of the life and times of the named figures. Nor do they necessarily tell us much, if anything, about the times in which the specified sages lived. Until shown otherwise, the fact that a story is told about a given sage or a saying attributed to him tells us only that at the closure of the document, someone made such an allegation. Thus the picture we may derive from the rabbinic writings portrays

[1] Isadore Singer, ed. New York: Funk and Wagnall, 1901–1906.

[2] The editor of the rabbinic department was Louis Ginzberg, whose many entries present us with models of erudition and clarity. It was produced from 1900 to 1903 when he resigned to accept a position in the Department of Talmud at the Jewish Theological Seminary of America, where he taught for the next half-century until his death in 1953.

the state of opinion in the times and circles in which those writings came to closure. Nevertheless from the beginnings of the academic study of Judaism (die Wissenschaft des Judenthums) to the second third of the twentieth century, scholars thought they could recover the historical Aqiba or the historical Yohanan ben Zakkai, not simply the documentary record of what later sages thought they knew about the prior masters. Now, efforts at biography fall to pieces and prove rare in academic scholarship.[3]

Much has changed in scholarly approaches to the study of the rabbis of the Mishnah and the Talmud. A clearer picture of the character of the rabbinic references to named sages and their standing as cultural artifacts will place into perspective the valuable reference-work assembled for the study of rabbinic Judaism in the *Jewish Encyclopaedia* and reproduced in these pages.

THE RABBINIC COUNTERPART TO BIOGRAPHY: "EPISODES" AS PARADIGMS

It is best to commence with a positive proposition, only then turning to the negative one. Let us therefore begin with the present state of the question: if not biography, then what?

About no single rabbinic sage of late antiquity, the first six centuries C.E., do we have the materials that sustain anything like a serviceable biography.[4] That is not merely because the sources do not serve for critical history in the conventional sense, but because they do intend

[3] The most current "biography" is: Alon Goshen-Gottstein. *The Sinner and the Amnesiac: The Rabbinic Invention of Elisha ben Abuya and Eleazar ben Arach.* Stanford, Cal.: Stanford University Press, 2000.

[4] I originally addressed the problem of rabbinic biography in the following works, after which I dismissed the possibility of a critical-historical "life" of any rabbinic sage of antiquity. *A Life of Yohanan ben Zakkai.* Leiden: Brill, 1962, was awarded the Abraham Berliner Prize in Jewish History by the Jewish Theological Seminary of America in 1962, and the second edition was completely revised in 1970 and translated into French, Italian, and Japanese. *Development of a Legend: Studies on the Traditions Concerning Yohanan ben Zakkai.* Leiden: Brill, 1970. *The Rabbinic Traditions about the Pharisees before 70.* 3 vols. Leiden: Brill, 1971. Repr., *The Masters.* Vol. 1 of *The Rabbinic Traditions about the Pharisees before 70.* Atlanta: Scholars Press, 1999. *The Houses.* Vol. 2. of Ibid. *Conclusions.* Vol. 3. of Ibid. *Eliezer ben Hyrcanus: The Tradition and the Man.* 2 vols. Leiden: Brill, 1973. After my *Eliezer ben Hyrcanus*, so far as I know, not a single biography of a rabbi was written in any Western language or—more significantly—accepted for a dissertation in any Western university. The Israeli academic journals—*Tarbiz, Zion, Sinai*, for example—have continued to publish articles on rabbinic personalities and characters, their philosophy and legal theory and the like, but, significantly, none of this is now translated into English. I should claim responsibility, therefore, for ending research in rabbinic biography, which, in the conventional framework, I showed to be uncritical. Monographs that argue in favor of the authenticity of attributions of sayings to particular rabbis have not been succeeded by "lives" of those same rabbis, which confirms the utter collapse of biography as a significant system of thought for rabbinic Judaism.

a different kind of treatment of lives of persons. Paradigmatic episodes in place of distinctive and individual biography yield the model of the life framed by the Torah: a life lived within the rules of nature, but facing outward toward supernature, a life transcending the natural world, measured by moments of transcendence. Hence "lives" are not recounted, but paradigmatic events of rabbinic Judaism are. These comprise only four topics: (1) advent into the Torah, (2) the active and complex realm of negotiation within the Torah, (3) virtue measured by the Torah and responding to the special vices that the Torah can nurture, and (4) death in the supernatural setting that overcomes nature: not dirt to dirt, but soul to Heaven, along with the Torah.

Linear and sustained narrative of the events of the social entity ("nation," in general, "Israel" in particular) corresponds to biography, in the present context, lives of sages.[5] Just as the historical mode of thought generates the composition of sustained narratives, so practitioners of history will also write lives of persons, e.g., Moses, or at least continuous tales of a biographical character, with some sort of connected narrative, real or contrived, to give the impression of personal history. Practitioners of the historical sciences—Josephus for instance—give us not only biography but also autobiography, just as much as philosophers or theologians of history, Augustine being the best example, will supply a biographical counterpart to a history. It obviously follows that where history leads biography follows close behind.

But among the sages, who engaged in not historical but paradigmatic thinking, what place can we define for the counterpart to biography? The answer: exemplary anecdotes, the counterpart to singular events, not biographies as the counterpart to sustained historical narrative. That answer is obvious. The real question becomes: What is the character of those exemplary, one-time anecdotes? Knowing that they are going to exemplify paradigmatic concerns or realize the model through the medium of persons, rather than public events, does not guide us to a theory of the particular character of the personal anecdotes that the model generates. Paradigmatic thinking about the social order not only yields anecdotes instead of continuous history. It also attends to the representation of persons, but solely for paradigmatic purposes and in a manner calculated to yield, not continuous narrative, but a restatement, in individual terms, of the paradigm. And that is to be expected. For once time loses its continuity and sequential quality, marking time calls upon other indicators of order and division than those demanded by the interplay of nature's telling time and humanity's interposing its rhythms. Lives of persons, beginning to end, need not be told, indeed,

[5] In this context, see my *Why No Gospels in Talmudic Judaism?* Atlanta: Scholars Press, 1988.

cannot be told, for the same reason that sequential, continuous narrative also cannot be constructed.

The paradigm, formed out of the congruence of humanity's and nature's time, rather than their incongruity, will identify, out of the moments presented by a human life, those that gain importance by appeal to the paradigm itself; the natural course of a human life, from death to birth, bears no more meaning in the amplification of the paradigm than the passage of empires, viewed as singular, or the story of a reign or a dynasty, viewed in its own terms. These matter, for paradigmatic thinking, when the pattern or model determines; otherwise, they do not register at all. Of the many empires of antiquity, four counted to the paradigm of rabbinic Judaism, Babylonia, Media, Greece, and Rome. What of Parthians, what of Sasanians, certainly weighty as Greece and Rome and for long centuries quite able to hold their own (with their huge Jewish populations) against Greece and Rome? They did not count, so were not counted.

We know, of course, why they did not matter: they never intersected with the natural life of the holy people, Israel, in the holy land, the land of Israel; they never threatened Jerusalem in the way in which Babylonia, Greece (in Seleucid times), and Rome did. That principal part of the paradigm points to one main principle of selection in the range of events. Working back from events to the principle of selection that operates within the model governing rabbinic Judaism's disposition of time (past, present, future), we are able to define out of what is selected the operative criterion: the congruence of the selected model to nature's time, not its contrast in conjunction therewith. Then what is to be said about the paradigm's points of interest in human lives? Since, we must anticipate, the paradigm will not elicit interest in a continuous life and so will not produce biography, let alone autobiography, at what points will the model encompass episodes in human lives? To state the question more simply: where, when, and why will individual persons make a difference, so as to warrant the writing down of details of personal lives?

Asked in this way, the question produces a ready answer, in three parts, two of which take but a moment for their exposition. First, does the paradigm before us take an interest in the lives of persons? It does. Second, if it does, then at what point in a human life will anecdotes preserve the model for exemplary conduct, defining the principle of selection, out of a human life as much as out of the happenings of the social world, of what counts? The principle of selection, at each point, somehow relates to the Torah. And, third, how does the paradigm emerge, having received a richer and more nuanced definition, out of the encounter with individual lives?

The answer is that the model that governs the formation of the rabbinic writings examined here certainly does narrate episodes in personal lives, not only events in the social order. Second, the points of special interest are (1) how an individual studies the Torah; (2) remarkable deeds of virtue in the individual's life; (3) how the individual dies. Learning, virtue, and a dignified death—these form the paradigmatic points of interest. Only after reviewing a few instances of the way in which the writings set forth their paradigms of Torah-study on the one side and virtue on the other shall we address the third question. This review will yield questions of a still deeper order than has yet been suggested here, questions that concern the interplay of nature, the Torah, and truth. The stakes grow higher.

THE PARADIGMATIC PERSON

The function of—not biography but—exemplary *episodes* in named individuals' lives is to show the union of nature and social order through the person of the sage. That union takes place within the medium of the Torah, which corresponds to nature and lays out the governing rules thereof, but also encompasses the social order and defines its laws as well. Anecdotes about masters of Torah then serve to convey principles of Torah, with the clear proviso that anecdotes about events may equally set forth precisely those same principles. So the paradigm describes regularities without regard to considerations of scale, whether social or private, any more than matters of earlier or later, past or present or future, make any difference.

That fact, by the way, also explains why the paradigm in play really excludes not only biography but also personality in any form. Individuals make a difference, so as to warrant the writing down of components of personal lives, at the point at which they lose all individuality and serve in some way or other to embody and exemplify a detail of the paradigm best set forth in the dimensions of private life. We then identify no difference between the social entity and the private person because the paradigm works out indifferent to matters of scale or context and says what it says wherever it says it. How does the paradigm emerge out of the encounter with individual lives? The answer is now clear. A paradigm that proposes to present a single, coherent, and cogent picture of the life of Israel under the aspect of the timeless Torah has to make its statement about not only the social order viewed whole, but the individuals who comprise that order. The paradigm requires the counterpart to biography, as much as the counterpart to history, for its own reasons; it cares about individuals for the same reason that it cares about the social entity Israel.

Personal anecdotes do for the paradigm at hand what biography does for history. Just as biography renders the large conclusions of history manageable and in human scale, so the anecdotes express the statements of the paradigm in a form accessible to human imitation and identification. But anecdotes about people also deepen our perception of the paradigm. For the issue of time is recast as the span of a human life enters consideration. Paradigm in place of history yields a narrative of the cult and a story of the temple, not the history of the people and the life of the sage.[6]

IF PARADIGM, THEN WHY NOT BIOGRAPHY? THE UNWRITTEN GOSPELS OF JUDAISM: STORIES TOLD BUT NOT COMPILED

Having set forth a positive proposition, let me now turn to the negative. First, why are there no gospels[7] in rabbinic Judaism? The answer *cannot* be that there were no data. On the contrary there were ample data, as the work of rabbinic biography with which scholarship occupied itself for a century demonstrates. Indeed, the final organizers of the Bavli, the Talmud of Babylonia, who, it is commonly alleged, flourished circa 500–600 C.E., had a tripartite corpus of inherited materials awaiting composition into a final, closed document.[8]

The first type of material, in various states and stages of completion, addressed the Mishnah or took up the principles of laws that the Mishnah had originally brought to articulation. These the framers of the Bavli organized in accord with the order of those Mishnah tractates that they selected for sustained attention.

Second, they had in hand received materials, again in various conditions, pertinent to Scripture, both as Scripture related to the Mishnah and also as Scripture laid forth its own narratives. These they set forth

---

[6] I amplify these matters in *The Presence of the Past, the Pastness of the Present: History, Time, and Paradigm in Rabbinic Judaism.* Bethesda, Md.: CDL Press, 1996.

[7] I use the word "gospel" with a small G as equivalent to "didactic life of a holy man, portraying the faith." Obviously, the Christian usage, with a capital G, must maintain that there can be a Gospel only about Jesus Christ. Claims of uniqueness are, of course, not subject to public discourse. In the present context, I could as well have referred to lives of saints, since Judaism of the dual Torah produced neither a gospel about a central figure nor lives of saints. Given the centrality of Moses "our rabbi," for example, we should have anticipated a "Gospel of Moses" parallel to the Gospels of Jesus Christ, and, lacking that, at least a "life of Aqiba," scholar, saint, martyr, parallel to the lives of various saints. We also have no autobiographies of any kind, beyond some "I"-stories, which themselves seem to me uncommon.

[8] I compared Bavli and Yerushalmi tractates Sukkah, Sanhedrin, and Sotah, showing the proportion of what I call Scripture units of thought to Mishnah units of thought. See my *Judaism: The Classic Statement; The Evidence of the Bavli.* Chicago: University of Chicago Press, 1986.

as Scripture commentary. In this way, the penultimate and ultimate redactors of the Bavli laid out a systematic presentation of the two Torahs, the oral, represented by the Mishnah, and the written, represented by Scripture.

And, third, the framers of the Bavli also materials focused on sages. In the received form and attested in the Bavli's pages, these were framed around twin biographical principles, either as strings of stories about great sages of the past or as collections of sayings and comments drawn together solely because the same name stood behind all the collected sayings. These can easily have been composed into biographies. In the context of Christianity and of Judaism, it is appropriate to call the biography of a holy man or woman, meant to convey the divine message, a gospel.

Hence the question raised here: why no gospels in Judaism? The question is an appropriate one, because there could have been. The final step—assembling available stories into a coherent narrative, with a beginning, middle, and end, for example—is what was not taken. No document was devoted to the life of a given sage and his teachings, and none to lives of sages and their teachings grouped together.

Take the Talmud of Babylonia for example. The Bavli as a whole lays itself out as a commentary to the Mishnah. So the framers wished us to think that whatever they wanted to tell us would take the form of Mishnah commentary. But a second glance indicates that the Bavli is made up of enormous composites, themselves closed prior to inclusion in the Bavli. Some of these composites—around thirty-five to forty percent of Bavli, if my sample is indicative—were selected and arranged along lines dictated by a logic other than that deriving from the requirements of Mishnah commentary. The components of the canon of Judaism of the dual Torah prior to the Bavli had encompassed amplifications of the Mishnah, in the Tosefta and in the Yerushalmi, as well as the same for Scripture, in such documents as Sifré to Leviticus, Sifré to Numbers, and another Sifré to Deuteronomy, Genesis Rabbah, Leviticus Rabbah, and the like.

But there was no entire document, now extant, organized around the life and teachings of a particular sage. Even The Fathers According to Rabbi Nathan, which contains a good sample of stories about sages, is not so organized as to yield a life of a sage or even a systematic biography of any kind. Where events in the lives of sages do occur, they are thematic and not biographical in organization, e.g., stories about the origins; as to Torah-study, of diverse sages; and death-scenes of various sages. Never in that document does the sage, whether Aqiba or Yohanan ben Zakkai or Eliezer b. Hyrcanus, define the appropriate organizing principle for sequences of stories or sayings. And there is no other in which the sage forms an organizing category for any material purpose.

Accordingly, the decision that the framers of the Bavli reached was to adopt the two redaction principles inherited from the antecedent century or so and to reject the one already rejected by their predecessors, even while honoring it. They organized the Bavli around the Mishnah. But they adapted and included vast tracts of antecedent materials organized as scriptural commentary. These they inserted whole and complete, not at all in response to the Mishnah's program.

And, finally, while making provision for small-scale compositions built upon biographical principles, preserving both strings of sayings from a given master (and often a given tradent of a given master) as well as tales about authorities of the preceding half millennium, they never created redaction compositions, of a sizable order, that focused on given authorities. Nevertheless sufficient materials certainly lay at hand to allow doing so. In the three decisions, two of what to do and one of what not to do, the final compositors of the Bavli indicated what they proposed to accomplish: to give final form and fixed expression, through their categories of the organization of all knowledge, to the Torah as it had been known, sifted, searched, approved, and handed down, even from the remote past to their own day. So in our literary categories, the compositors of the Bavli were encyclopedists. Their creation turned out to be the encyclopedia of Judaism, its summa, its point of final reference, its court of last appeal, its definition, it conclusion, its closure—so they thought, and so say those that followed, to this very day.

Shall we then draw so grand a conclusion from so modest a fact as how people sorted out available redaction categories? Indeed so, if we realize that the modes by which thinkers organized knowledge leads us deep into the theses by which useful knowledge rises to the surface while what is irrelevant or unimportant or trivial sinks to the bottom. If we want to know what people thought and how they thought it, we can do worse than begin by asking about how they organized what they knew, on the one side, and about how they made their choices in laying out the main lines of the structure of knowledge, on the other.

THE DOCUMENTARY COMPOSITIONS NO ONE MADE: COLLECTIONS OF WISE SAYINGS AND BIOGRAPHIES

The Yerushalmi and the collections of scriptural exegeses comprise compositions made up of already-worked-out units of discourse focused upon the Mishnah and Scripture, respectively. Other completed units of thought, such as we might call paragraphs or even short chapters, deal with individual sages. Midrash compilations and Mishnah commentaries, both the Yerushalmi and the Bavli, contain a sizable quantity of sage units of discourse. These surely coalesced in yet a third type of book. Specifically, sayings and stories about sages could have been organized into collections of wise sayings attributed to various authorities (like Avot), on the one side, or sequences of tales, e.g., brief snippets of biographies or lives of the saints, on the other. Let me spell out what we do find, which will underline the noteworthy character of the fact at hand: materials not used for their obvious purpose, in the way in which materials of a parallel character were used for their purpose.

Let me define more fully the character of the discourse that focuses upon the sage. In this type of composition—e.g., a paragraph of thought, a story—things that a given authority said are strung together or tales about a given authority are told at some length. Whoever composed and preserved units of discourse on the Mishnah and on Scripture ultimately preserved the same for the sage in the two Talmuds. What that fact means is simple. In the circles responsible for making up and writing down completed units of discourse, three distinct categories of interest defined the task: (1) exegesis of the Mishnah, (2) exegesis of Scripture, and (3) preservation and exegesis, in exactly the same reverential spirit, of the words and deeds of sages. Not only so, but the kind of analysis to which Mishnah and Scripture exegeses were subjected also applied to the exegesis of sage stories.

That fact may be shown in three ways. First, just as Scripture supplied proof texts, so deeds or statements of sages provided proof texts. Second, just as a verse of Scripture or an explicit statement of the Mishnah resolved a disputed point, so what a sage said or did might be introduced into discourse as ample proof for settling a dispute. And third, it follows that just as Scripture or the Mishnah laid down Torah, so what a sage did or said laid down Torah. In the dimensions of the applied and practical reason by which the law unfolded, the sage found a comfortable place in precisely the taxonomic categories defined by both the Mishnah and Scripture. Let us examine a few substantial examples of the sorts of sustained discourse in biographical materials turned out by circles of sages. What we shall see is an important fact. Just as these circles composed units of discourse about the meaning of a Mishnah passage, a larger theoretical problem of law, the sense of scriptural verse, and the sayings and doings of scriptural heroes seen as sages, so they did the same for living sages themselves.

In the simplest example we see that two discrete sayings of a sage are joined together. The principle of conglomeration, therefore, is solely the name of the sage at hand. One saying has to do with overcoming the impulse to do evil, and the other has to do with the classifications of sages' program of learning. What the two subjects have in common is slight. But to the framer of the passage, that fact meant nothing. For he thought that compositions joined by the same tradent and authority—Levi and Simeon—should be made up.

B. BERAKHOT 4B.XXIII.

A. Said R. Levi bar Hama said R. Simeon b. Laqish, "A person should always provoke his impulse to do good against his impulse to do evil,
B. "as it is said, 'Provoke and do not sin' (Ps. 4:5).
C. "If [the good impulse] wins, well and good. If not, let him take up Torah study,
D. "as it is said, 'Commune with your own heart' (Ps. 4:5).
E. "If [the good impulse] wins, well and good. If not, let him recite the Shema,
F. "as it is said, 'upon your bed' (Ps. 4:5).
G. "If [the good impulse] wins, well and good. If not, let him remember the day of death,
H. "as it is said, 'And keep silent. Sela' (Ps. 4:5)."
I. And R. Levi bar Hama said R. Simeon b. Laqish said, "What is the meaning of the verse of Scripture, 'And I will give you the tables of stone, the law and the commandment, which I have written, that you may teach them' (Exod. 24:12)?
J. "'The tables' [here] refers to the Ten Commandments.
K. "'Torah' refers to Scripture.
L. "'Commandment' refers to Mishnah.
M. "'Which I have written' refers to the Prophets and the Writings.
N. "'That you may teach them' refers to the Gemara.
O. "This teaches that all of them were given to Moses from Sinai."

The frame of the story at hand links A–H and I–O in a way unfamiliar to those accustomed to the principles of conglomeration in legal and biblical-exegetical compositions. In the former, a given problem or principle of law will tell us why one item is joined to some other. In the latter, a single verse of Scripture will account for the joining of two or more otherwise discrete units of thought. Here one passage, A–H, takes up Ps. 4:5; the other, I–O, Exod. 24:12. The point of the one statement hardly goes over the ground of the other. So the sole principle by which one item has joined the other is biographical: a record of what a sage said about topics that are, at best, contiguous, if related at all.

A second way of stringing together materials illustrative of the lives and teachings of sages is to join incidents involving a given authority or (as in the following case) two authorities believed to have stood in close relationship with one another, disciple and master, for instance. Often these stories go over the same ground in the same way. In the following, the two farewell stories make essentially the same point but in quite different language. What joins the stories is not only the shared theme but the fact that Eliezer is supposed to have studied with Yohanan b. Zakkai.

B. SANHEDRIN 68A.II.

A. Our rabbis have taught on Tannaite authority:
B. When R. Eliezer fell ill, his disciples came in to pay a call on him. They said to him, "Our master, teach us the ways of life, so that through them we may merit the world to come."
C. He said to them, "Be attentive to the honor owing to your fellows, keep your children from excessive reflection, and set them among the knees of disciples of sages, and when you pray, know before whom you stand, and on that account you will merit the life of the world to come."
D. And when R. Yohanan b. Zakkai fell ill, his disciples came in to pay a call on him. When he saw them, he began to cry. His disciples said to him, "Light of Israel! Pillar at the right hand! Mighty hammer! On what account are you crying?"
E. He said to them, "If I were going to be brought before a mortal king, who is here today and tomorrow gone to the grave, who, should he be angry with me, will not be angry forever, and, if he should imprison me, will not imprison me forever, and if he should put me to death, whose sentence of death is not for eternity, and whom I can appease with the right words or bribe with money, even so, I should weep.
F. "But now that I am being brought before the King of kings of kings, the Holy One, blessed be he, who endures forever and ever, who, should he be angry with me, will be angry forever, and if he should imprison me, will imprison me forever, and if he should put me to death, whose sentence of death is for eternity, and whom I cannot appease with the right words or bribe with money,
G. "and not only so, but before me are two paths, one to the Garden of Eden and the other to Gehenna, and I do not know by which path I shall be brought,
H. "and should I not weep?"
I. They said to him, "Our master, bless us."
J. He said to them, "May it be God's will that the fear of Heaven be upon you as much as the fear of mortal man."
K. His disciples said, "Just so much?"
L. He said to them, "Would that it were that much. You should know that, when a person commits a transgression, he says, 'I hope no man sees me.'"
M. When he was dying, he said to them, "Clear out utensils from the house, because of the uncleanness [of the corpse, which I am about to impart when I die], and prepare a throne for Hezekiah king of Judah, who is coming."

The links between B–C and D–M are clear. First, we have stories about sages' farewells. Second, people took for granted, because of the lists of *m. Abot* 2:2ff., that Eliezer was disciple of Yohanan b. Zakkai. Otherwise, it is difficult to explain the joining of the stories, since they scarcely make the same point, go over the same matters, or even share a common literary or rhetorical form or preference. But a framer of a composition of lives of saints, who is writing a tractate on how saints die, will have found this passage a powerful one indeed.

Yet another approach to the utilization of tales about sages was to join together stories on a given theme but told about different sages. A tractate or a chapter of a tractate on a given theme, for example, suffering and its reward, can have emerged from the sort of collection that follows. The importance of the next item is that the same kinds of stories about different sages are strung together to make a single point.

B. BERAKHOT 5B.XXXI.

A. R. Hiyya bar Abba got sick. R. Yohanan came to him. He said to him, "Are these sufferings precious to you?"
B. He said to him, "I don't want them. I don't want their reward."
C. He said to him, "Give me your hand."
D. He gave him his hand, and [Yohanan] raised him up [out of his sickness].
E. R. Yohanan got sick. R. Hanina came to him. He said to him, "Are these sufferings precious to you?"
F. He said to him, "I don't want them. I don't want their reward."
G. He said to him, "Give me your hand."
H. He gave him his hand and [Hanina] raised him up [out of his sickness].
I. Why so? R. Yohanan should have raised himself up.
J. They say, "A prisoner cannot get himself out of jail."

B. BERAKHOT 5B.XXXII.

A. R. Eliezer got sick. R. Yohanan came to see him and found him lying in a dark room. [The dying man] uncovered his arm, and light fell [through the room]. [Yohanan] saw that R. Eliezer was weeping. He said to him, "Why are you crying? Is it because of the Torah that you did not learn sufficiently? We have learned: 'All the same are the ones who do much and do little, so long as each person will do it for the sake of heaven.'
B. "Is it because of insufficient income? Not everyone has the merit of seeing two tables [Torah and riches, as you have. You have been a master of Torah and also have enjoyed wealth].
C. "Is it because of children? Here is the bone of my tenth son [whom I buried, so it was no great loss not to have children, since you might have had to bury them]."
D. He said to him, "I am crying because of this beauty of mine which will be rotting in the ground."
E. He said to him, "For that it certainly is worth crying," and the two of them wept together.
F. He said to him, "Are these sufferings precious to you?"
G. He said to him, "I don't want them. I don't want their reward."

H. He said to him, "Give me your hand."
I. He gave him his hand, and [Yohanan] raised him up [out of his sickness].

B. BERAKHOT 5B.XXXIII.

A. Four hundred barrels of wine turned sour on R. Huna. R. Judah, brother of R. Sala the Pious, and rabbis came to see him (and some say it was R. Ada bar Ahba and rabbis). They said to him, "The master should take a good look at his deeds."
B. He said to them, "And am I suspect in your eyes?"
C. They said to him, "And is the Holy One, blessed be he, suspect of inflicting a penalty without justice?"
D. He said to them, "Has anybody heard anything bad about me? Let him say it."
E. They said to him, "This is what we have heard: the master does not give to his hired hand [the latter's share of] vine twigs [which are his right]."
F. He said to them, "Does he leave me any! He steals all of them to begin with."
G. They said to him, "This is in line with what people say: 'Go steal from a thief but taste theft too!' [Simon: If you steal from a thief, you also have a taste of it.]"
H. He said to them, "I pledge that I'll give them to him."
I. Some say that the vinegar turned back into wine, and some say that the price of vinegar went up so he sold it off at the price of wine.

The foregoing composite makes the same point several times: "Not them, not their reward." Sufferings are precious, but sages are prepared to forego the benefits. The formally climactic entry at XXXIII makes the point that, if bad things happen, the victim has deserved punishment. In joining these several stories about sages—two involving Yohanan, the third entirely separate—the compositor of the passage made his point by juxtaposing two like biographical snippets to a distinct one. Collections of stories about saints can have served quite naturally when formed into tractates on pious virtues, expressing these virtues through strong and pictorial language such as we have before us.

The foregoing sources have shown two important facts. First, a principle of composition in the sages' circles was derived from interest in the teachings associated with a given sage, as well as in tales and stories told about a sage or groups of sages. The first of the passages shows us the simplest composition of sayings, the latter, an equivalent conglomeration of related stories. Up to this point, therefore, the reader will readily concede that biographical materials on sages, as much as Mishnah exegesis and Scripture exegesis, came forth out of circles of sages. But I have yet to show that such materials attained sufficient volume and cogency from large-scale compilations—conglomerates so substantial as to sustain entire books.

CHAPTERS AND TRACTATES ON LIVES OF SAGES: WHAT MIGHT HAVE BEEN

At the risk of taxing the reader's patience, I shall now demonstrate that, had the framers of large-scale rabbinic compositions wished, they could readily have made up tractates devoted to diverse sayings of a given authority (or, tradent-and-authority, that is, "Rabbi X says Rabbi Y says"). What follows to demonstrate the possibility are two enormous compositions, which together can have made up as much as half of a Talmud chapter in volume. If anyone had wanted to compose a chapter around rabbinic authorities' names, he is thus shown to have had the opportunity.

The first shows us a string of sayings, not only in a single set of names, but also on discrete subjects. We also see how such a string of sayings could form the focus of critical analysis and secondary amplification to which any other Talmudic passage was subjected. There could have been, not only a Talmud based on the Mishnah and a midrash composition based on the Scripture, but also a life of a saint (a gospel?) based on a set of rabbis's sayings. Here is the Talmud that could have served a collection of sayings of Yohanan-in-the-name-of-Simeon b. Yohai.

B. BERAKHOT 7B–8A.LIX.

A. [7B] Said R. Yohanan in the name of R. Simeon b. Yohai, "From the day on which the Holy One, blessed be he, created the world, there was no man who called the Holy One, blessed be he, 'Lord,' until Abraham came along and called him Lord.

B. "For it is said, 'And he said, O Lord, God, whereby shall I know that I shall inherit it' (Gen. 15:8)."

C. Said Rab, "Daniel too was answered only on account of Abraham.

D. "For it is said, 'Now therefore, O our God, hearken to the prayer of your servant and to his supplications and cause your face to shine upon your sanctuary that is desolate, for the Lord's sake' (Dan. 9:17).

E. "'For your sake' is what he should have said, but the sense is, 'For the sake of Abraham, who called you Lord.'"

B. BERAKHOT 7B–8A.LX.

A. And R. Yohanan said in the name of R. Simeon b. Yohai, "How do we know that people should not seek to appease someone when he is mad?

B. "As it is said, 'My face will go and then I will give you rest' (Exod. 33:14)."

B. BERAKHOT 7B–8A.LXI.

A. And R. Yohanan said in the name of R. Simeon b. Yohai, "From the day on which the Holy One, blessed be he, created his world, there was no one who praised the Holy One, blessed be he, until Leah came along and praised him.

B. "For it is said, 'This time I will praise the Lord' (Gen. 29:35)."
C. As to Reuben, said R. Eleazar, "Leah said, 'See what is the difference [the name of Reuben yielding reu (see) and ben (between)] between my son and the son of my father-in-law.
D. "'The son of my father-in-law, even knowingly, sold off his birthright, for it is written, "And he sold his birthright to Jacob" (Gen. 25:33).
E. "'See what is written concerning him: "And Esau hated Jacob" (Gen. 27:41), and it is written, "And he said, is he not rightly named Jacob for he has supplanted me these two times?" (Gen. 27:36).
F. "'My son, by contrast, even though Joseph forcibly took away his birthright, as it is written, "But for as much as he defiled his father's couch, his birthright was given to the sons of Joseph" (1 Chron. 5:1), did not become jealous of him, for it is written, "And Reuben heard it and delivered him out of their hand" (Gen. 37:21).'"
G. As to the meaning of the name of Ruth, said R. Yohanan, "It was because she had the merit that David would come forth from her, who saturated (RWH) the Holy One, blessed be he, with songs and praises."
H. How do we know that a person's name affects [his life]?
I. Said R. Eleazar, "It is in line with the verse of Scripture: 'Come, behold the works of the Lord, who has made desolations in the earth' (Ps. 46:9).
J. "Do not read 'desolations' but 'names' [which the same root yields]."

B. BERAKHOT 7B–8A.LXII.

A. And R. Yohanan said in the name of R. Simeon b. Yohai, "Bringing a child up badly is worse in a person's house than the war of Gog and Magog.
B. "For it is said, 'A Psalm of David, when he fled from Absalom, his son' (Ps. 3:1), after which it is written, 'Lord how many are my adversaries become, many are they that rise up against me' (Ps. 3:2).
C. "By contrast, in regard to the war of Gog and Magog it is written, 'Why are the nations in an uproar? And why do the peoples mutter in vain?' (Ps. 2:1). D."But it is not written in that connection, 'How many are my adversaries become.'"
E. "A Psalm of David, when he fled from Absalom, his son (Ps. 3:1):
F. "'A Psalm of David'? It should be, 'A lamentation of David'!
G. Said R. Simeon b. Abishalom, "The matter may be compared to the case of a man against whom an outstanding bond was issued. Before he had paid it, he was sad. After he had paid it, he was glad.
H. "So too with David, when he the Holy One had said to him, 'Behold, I will raise up evil against you out of your own house,' (2 Sam. 2:11), he was sad.
I. "He thought to himself, 'Perhaps it will be a slave or a bastard child, who will not have pity on me.'
J. "When he saw that it was Absalom, he was happy. On that account, he said a psalm."

B. BERAKHOT 7B–8A.LXIII.

A. And R. Yohanan said in the name of R. Simeon b. Yohai, "It is permitted to contend with the wicked in this world.

B. "For it is said, 'Those who forsake the Torah praise the wicked, but those who keep the Torah contend with them' (Prov. 28:4)."
C. It has been taught on Tannaite authority along these same lines:
D. R. Dosetai bar Matun says, "It is permitted to contend with the wicked in this world, for it is said, 'Those who forsake the Torah praise the wicked, but those who keep the Torah contend with them' (Prov. 28:4)."
E. And if someone should whisper to you, "But is it not written, 'Do not contend with evildoers, nor be envious against those who work unrighteousness' (Ps. 37:1)," say to him, "Someone whose conscience bothers him thinks so.
F. "In fact, 'Do not contend with evildoers' means do not be like them; 'nor be envious against those who work unrighteousness' means do not be like them.
G. "And so it is said, 'Let your heart not envy sinners, but fear the Lord all day' (Prov. 23:17)."
H. Is this the case? And lo, R. Isaac has said, "If you see a wicked person for whom the hour seems to shine, do not contend with him, for it is said, 'His ways prosper at all times' (Ps. 10:5).
I. "Not only so, but he wins in court, as it is said, 'Your judgments are far above, out of his sight' (Ps. 10:5).
J. "Not only so, but he overcomes his enemies, for it is said, 'As for all his enemies, he farts at them' (Ps. 10:5)."
K. There is no contradiction. The one [Isaac] addresses one's own private matters [in which case one should not contend with the wicked], but the other speaks of matters having to do with Heaven [in which case one should contend with them].
L. And if you wish, I shall propose that both parties speak of matters having to do with Heaven. There is, nonetheless, no contradiction. The one [Isaac] speaks of a wicked person on whom the hour shines, the other of a wicked person on whom the hour does not shine.
M. And if you wish, I shall propose that both parties speak of a wicked person on whom the hour shines, and there still is no contradiction.
N. The one [Yohanan, who says the righteous may contend with the wicked] speaks of a completely righteous person, the other [Isaac] speaks of someone who is not completely righteous.
O. For R. Huna said, "What is the meaning of this verse of Scripture: 'Why do you look, when they deal treacherously, and hold your peace, when the wicked swallows up the man that is more righteous than he' (Hab. 1:13)?
P. "Now can a wicked person swallow up a righteous one?
Q. "And lo, it is written, 'The Lord will not leave him in his hand' (Ps. 37:33). And it is further written, 'No mischief shall befall the righteous' (Prov. 12:21).
R. "The fact therefore is that he may swallow up someone who is more righteous than he, but he cannot swallow up a completely righteous man."
S. And if you wish, I shall propose that, when the hour shines for him, the situation is different.

B. BERAKHOT 7B–8A.LXIV.

A. And R. Yohanan said in the name of R. Simeon b. Yohai, "Beneath anyone who establishes a regular place for praying do that person's enemies fall.
B. "For it is said, 'And I will appoint a place for my people Israel, and I will plant them, that they may dwell in their own place and be disquieted no more, neither shall the children of wickedness afflict them any more as at the first' (2 Sam. 7:10)."
C. R. Huna pointed to a contradiction between two verses of Scripture: "It is written, 'To afflict them,' and elsewhere, 'To exterminate them' (1 Chron. 17:9).
D. "To begin with, merely to afflict them, but, at the end, to exterminate them."

B. BERAKHOT 7B–8A.LXV.

A. And R. Yohanan said in the name of R. Simeon b. Yohai, "Greater is personal service to Torah than learning in Torah [so doing favors for a sage is of greater value than studying with him].
B. "For it is said, 'Here is Elisha, the son of Shaphat, who poured water on the hands of Elijah' (2 Kings 3:11).
C. "It is not said, 'who learned' but 'who poured water.'
D. "This teaches that greater is service to Torah than learning in Torah."

In a moment we shall see the context, in the Bavli tractate, in which this composite is located.

It is not difficult to pick up the main beams of the foregoing construction, since they are signified by Yohanan-Simeon sayings, LIX.A, LX.A, LXI.A, LXII.A, LXIII.A, LXIV.A, and LXV.A—seven entries in line. The common theme is not prayer; no other topic is treated in a cogent way either. The sort of inner coherence to which any student of the Bavli is accustomed does not pass before us. Rather we have a collection of wise thoughts on diverse topics, more in the manner of Proverbs than in the style of the great intellects behind the sustained reasoning in passages of the Bavli and much of the Yerushalmi as well.

What is interesting is that, at a later stage, other pertinent materials have been inserted, for example, Rab's at LIX.C–E, and so on down. There is no reason to imagine that these sayings were made up in response to Yohanan-Simeon's statement. Quite to the contrary, framed in their own terms, the sayings were presumably tacked on at a point at which the large-scale construction of Yohanan-Simeon was worked over for a purpose beyond the one intended by the original compositor. For what he wanted to do he did, which is, compose a collection of Yohanan-Simeon sayings. If he hoped that his original collection would form part of a larger composition on Yohanan, he surely was disappointed. But even if he imagined that he would make up material for compositions of lives and sayings of saints, he cannot have expected his little collection to end up where and how it did, as part of a quite different corpus of writing from one in which a given authority had his say or in which stories were told in some sort of sensible sequence about a particular sage. The type of large-scale composition, for which our imagined compositor did his work, never came into being in the rabbinic canon.

In the following, still longer example I begin with the passage to which the entire composition, organized in the name of a tradent and a sage, is attached. At B. Berakhot 6B/1:1 XLI, we have a statement that a synagogue should have a regular quorum. Then the next passage, 1:1 XLII, makes the secondary point that a person should pray in a regular place—a reasonable amplification of the foregoing. That is, just as there should be a quorum routinely organized in a given location, so should an individual routinely attach himself to a given quorum. This statement is given by Helbo in Huna's name. What follows is a sizable set of sayings by Helbo in Huna's name, all of them on the general theme of prayer but none of them on the specific point at hand. Still more interesting, just as in the foregoing, the passage as a whole was composed so that the Helbo-Huna materials themselves are expanded and enriched with secondary accretions. For instance, at XLIII the base materials are given glosses of a variety of types. All in all, we see what we may call a little tractate in the making. But, as we shall hardly have to repeat, no one in the end created a genre of rabbinic literature to accommodate the vast collections of available compositions on sages' sayings and doings.

B. BERAKHOT 6B.XLI.

A. Said R. Yohanan, "When the Holy One, blessed be he, comes to a synagogue and does not find ten present, he forthwith becomes angry.

B. "For it is said, 'Why when I came was there no one there? When I called, there was no answer' (Isa. 50:2)."

B. BERAKHOT 6B.XLII.

A. Said R. Helbo said R. Huna, "For whoever arranges a regular place for praying, the God of Abraham is a help, and when he dies, they say for him, 'Woe for the humble man, woe for the pious man, one of the disciples of Abraham, our father.'

B. "And how do we know in the case of Abraham, our father, that he arranged a regular place for praying?

C. "For it is written, 'And Abraham got up early in the morning on the place where he had stood' (Gen. 19:27).

D. "'Standing' refers only to praying, for it is said, 'Then Phinehas stood up and prayed' (Ps. 106:30)."

E. Said R. Helbo to R. Huna, "He who leaves the synagogue should not take large steps."

F. Said Abbayye, "That statement applies only when one leaves, but when he enters, it is a religious duty to run [to the synagogue].
G. "For it is said, 'Let us run to know the Lord' (Hos. 6:3)."
H. Said R. Zira, "When in the beginning I saw rabbis running to the lesson on the Sabbath, I thought that the rabbis were profaning the Sabbath. But now that I have heard what R. Tanhum said R. Joshua b. Levi said,
I. "namely, 'A person should always run to take up a matter of law, and even on the Sabbath, as it is said, "They shall walk after the Lord who shall roar like a lion [for he shall roar, and the children shall come hurrying]" (Hos. 11:10),'
J. "I too run."

B. BERAKHOT 6B.XLIII.

A. Said R. Zira, "The reward for attending the lesson is on account of running [to hear the lesson, not necessarily on account of what one has learned.]"
B. Said Abbayye, "The reward for attending the periodic public assembly [of rabbis] is on account of the crowding together."
C. Said Raba [to the contrary], "The reward for repeating what one has heard is in reasoning about it."
D. Said R. Papa, "The reward for attending a house of mourning is on account of one's preserving silence there."
E. Said Mar Zutra, "The reward for observing a fast day lies in the acts of charity one performs on that day."
F. Said R. Sheshet, "The reward for delivering a eulogy lies in raising the voice."
G. Said R. Ashi, "The reward for attending a wedding lies in the words [of compliment paid to the bride and groom]."

B. BERAKHOT 6B.XLIV.

A. Said R. Huna, "Whoever prays behind the synagogue is called wicked,
B. "as it is said, 'The wicked walk round about' (Ps. 12:9)."
C. Said Abbayye, "That statement applies only in the case of one who does not turn his face toward the synagogue, but if he turns his face toward the synagogue, we have no objection."
D. There was a certain man who would say his prayers behind the synagogue and did not turn his face toward the synagogue. Elijah came by and saw him. He appeared to him in the guise of a Tai Arab.
E. He said to him, "Are you now standing with your back toward your master?" He drew his sword and killed him.
F. One of the rabbis asked R. Bibi bar Abbayye, and some say, R. Bibi asked R. Nahman bar Isaac, "What is the meaning of the verse, 'When vileness is exalted among the sons of men' (Ps. 12:9)?"
G. He said to him, "This refers to matters that are exalted, which people treat with contempt."
H. R. Yohanan and R. Eleazar both say, "When a person falls into need of the help of other people, his face changes color like the kerum, for it is said, 'As the kerum is to be reviled among the sons of men' (Ps. 12:9)."

I. What is the meaning of kerum?
J. When R. Dimi came, he said, "There is a certain bird among the coast towns, called the kerum. When the sun shines, it turns many colors."
K. R. Ammi and R. Assi both say, "[When a person turns to others for support], it is as if he is judged to suffer the penalties of both fire and water.
L. "For it is said, 'When you caused men to ride over our heads, we went through fire and through water' (Ps. 66:12)."

B. BERAKHOT 6B.XLV.

A. And R. Helbo said R. Huna said, "A person should always be attentive at the afternoon prayer.
B. "For lo, Elijah was answered only at the afternoon prayer.
C. "For it is said, 'And it came to pass at the time of the offering of the late afternoon offering, that Elijah the prophet came near and said, "Hear me, O Lord, hear me" ' (1 Kings 18:36–37)."
D. "Hear me" so fire will come down from heaven.
E. "Hear me" that people not say it is merely witchcraft.
F. R. Yohanan said, "[A person should also be attentive about] the evening prayer.
G. "For it is said, 'Let my prayer be set forth as incense before you, the lifting up of my hands as the evening sacrifice' (Ps. 141:2)."
H. R. Nahman bar Isaac said, "[A person should also be attentive about] the morning prayer.
I. "For it is said, 'O Lord, in the morning you shall hear my voice, in the morning I shall order my prayer to you, and will look forward' (Ps. 5:4)."

B. BERAKHOT 6B.XLVI.

A. And R. Helbo said R. Huna said, "Whoever enjoys a marriage banquet and does not felicitate the bridal couple violates five 'voices.'
B. "For it is said, 'The voice of joy and the voice of gladness, the voice of the bridegroom and the voice of the bride, the voice of those who say, "Give thanks to the Lord of hosts"' (Jer. 33:11)."
C. And if he does felicitate the couple, what reward does he get?
D. Said R. Joshua b. Levi, "He acquires the merit of the Torah, which was handed down with five voices.
E. "For it is said, 'And it came to pass on the third day, when it was morning, that there were voices [thus two], and lightnings, and a thick cloud upon the mount, and the voice of a horn, and when the voice of the horn waxed louder, 'Moses spoke and God answered him by a voice.' (Exod. 19:16, 19) [thus five voices in all]."
F. Is it so [that there were only five voices]?
G. And lo, it is written, "And all the people saw the voices" (Exod. 20:15). [So this would make seven voices.]
H. These voices came before the giving of the Torah [and do not count].
I. R. Abbahu said, "It is as if the one [who felicitated the bridal couple] offered a thanksgiving offering.
J. "For it is said, 'Even of them that bring thanksgiving offerings into the house of the Lord' (Jer. 33:11)."

K. R. Nahman bar Isaac said, "It is as if he rebuilt one of the ruins of Jerusalem.
L. "For it is said, 'For I will cause the captivity of the land to return as at the first, says the Lord' (Jer. 33:11)."

B. BERAKHOT 6B.XLVII.

A. And R. Helbo said R. Huna said, "The words of any person in whom is fear of Heaven are heard.
B. "For it is said, 'The end of the matter, all having been heard: fear God and keep his commandments, for this is the whole man' (Qoh. 12:13)."
C. What is the meaning of the phrase, "For this is the whole man" (Qoh. 12:13)?
D. Said R. Eleazar, "Said the Holy One, blessed be he, 'The entire world has been created only on account of this one.'"
E. R. Abba bar Kahana said, "This one is worth the whole world."
F. Simeon b. Zoma says, "The entire world was created only to accompany this one."

B. BERAKHOT 6B.XLVIII.

A. And R. Helbo said R. Huna said, "Whoever knows that his fellow regularly greets him should greet the other first.
B. "For it is said, 'Seek peace and pursue it' (Ps. 34:15).
C. "If he greeted him and the other did not reply, the latter is called a thief.
D. "For it is said, 'It is you who have eaten up the vineyard, the spoil of the poor is in your houses' (Isa. 3:14)."

What we noted in connection with the Yohanan-Simeon collection needs no restatement here. The scope and dimensions of the passage prove impressive. Again we must wonder for what sort of composition the framer of the Helbo-Huna collection planned his writing. Whatever it was, it hardly fit the ultimate destination of his work.

To show that fact, I now reproduce the outline of the entire composite of the Bavli in which the sets of compositions take their place. There we see how names of authorities provided the organizing principle for collecting sayings and stories. But these same composites formed around named sages prove miscellaneous in the context of the entire construction. I have abbreviated the outline by focusing on the main units of discourse. At issue is the exegesis of Mishnah tractate Berakhot 1:1. That is cited in bold face type and defines the principal, but not the only, rubrics for sustained exposition-bearing letters. To abbreviate matters, I omit the secondary and tertiary extensions and refinements, except where they bear upon our issue.

MISHNAH TRACTATE BERAKHOT 1:1

A. FROM WHAT TIME DO THEY RECITE THE SHEMA IN THE EVENING? FROM THE HOUR THAT THE PRIESTS WHO HAD

IMMERSED AFTER UNCLEANNESS AND AWAITED SUNSET TO COMPLETE THE PROCESS OF PURIFICATION ENTER A STATE OF CLEANNESS, THE SUN HAVING SET, SO AS TO EAT THEIR HEAVE OFFERING.

1. I:1: On what basis does the Tannaite authority stand when he begins by teaching the rule, "From what time . . . ," in the assumption that the religious duty to recite the Shema has somewhere been established? In point of fact, it has not been established that people have to recite the Shema at all. Furthermore, on what account does he teach the rule concerning the evening at the beginning? Why not start with the morning?

B. **"UNTIL THE END OF THE FIRST WATCH," THE WORDS OF R. ELIEZER:**

1. II:1: What is R. Eliezer's view about the division of the night-watches? If he takes the view that the night is divided into three watches, let him say, "Until four hours have passed in the night." If he takes the view that the night is divided into four watches, let him say, "Until three hours have passed in the night."
2. II:2: What is R. Eliezer's reckoning? If he is reckoning from the beginning of the several watches, then what need is there to give a sign for the beginning of the first watch? It is twilight. If he is reckoning from the end of the several watches, then what need is there to give a sign for the end of the third watch? It is marked by the coming of the day.

To this point, the Talmudic compositors have simply expounded the opening statement of the Mishnah tractate at hand, A–B, citing and glossing the rule. Now we come to our first topical appendix.[9]

C. **TOPICAL APPENDIX ON THE DIVISION OF THE NIGHT**

1. II:3: Said R. Isaac bar Samuel in the name of Rab, "The night is divided into three watches, and over each watch, the Holy One, blessed be he, sits and roars like a lion. He says, 'Woe to the children, on account of whose sins I have wiped out my house and burned my palace, and whom I have exiled among the nations of the world.'"
   a. II:4: Story that goes over the same point in a larger framework of narrative.
   b. II:5: Secondary expansion on a subordinate theme of the foregoing.

3. II:6: Our rabbis have taught on Tannaite authority: "The night has four watches," the words of Rabbi. Rabbi Nathan says, "Three."
   a. II:7: Gloss of a detail of the foregoing.
      1) II:8: Reverting to the statement that David got up at midnight: "At midnight I rise to give thanks to you because of your righteous ordinances" (Ps. 119:62), Did David get up at midnight? He got up at dusk of the evening.

[9] For a systematic account of composites of an anomalous character within the Talmud of Babylonia, see my *Rationality and Structure: The Bavli's Anomalous Juxtapositions*. Atlanta: Scholars Press, 1997.

2) II:9: Continuation of the foregoing. Did David really know exactly when it was midnight?
3) II:10: "A prayer of David: Keep my soul, for I am pious" (Ps. 86:1–2).
   a) II:11: Gloss of a detail of the foregoing.
4) II:12: Now did David really call himself "pious"? And has it not been written, "I am not sure to see the good reward of the Lord in the land of the living" (Ps. 27:13). How could David have been unsure, if he knew he was pious?

D. AND SAGES SAY, "UNTIL MIDNIGHT."

1. III:1: Since Eliezer holds that the time of "lying down" is when one goes to bed, on which account Eliezer has the Shema recited only until the end of the first watch, and since Gamaliel allows the Shema to be recited until dawn, understanding "lying down" to refer to the entire period of sleep, we ask: Which view did sages adopt?
   a. III:2: Gloss of a detail subordinate in the foregoing.

Now we commence with a sequence of miscellaneous composites, not serving as Mishnah commentary at all.

E. COMPOSITE ON PSALM 145

1. III:3: Said R. Eleazar bar Abina, "Whoever says the Psalm, 'Praise of David' (Ps. 145) three times a day may be assured that he belongs to the world to come."
2. III:4: Referring to Ps. 145, said R. Yohanan, "On what account is there no verse beginning with an N is Psalm 145? It is because the N starts the verse referring to the fall of (the enemies of) Israel."

F. MISCELLANEOUS ITEM, OUT OF PHASE WITH ITS CONTEXT

1. III:5: Said Eleazar bar Abina, "What is said about Michael is greater than what is said about Gabriel."

G. RECITING THE SHEMA ON ONE'S BED

1. III:6: Said R. Joshua b. Levi, "Even though a person has recited the Shema in the synagogue, it is a religious duty to recite it in bed."
   a. III:7: Said R. Levi bar Hama said R. Simeon b. Laqish, "A person should always provoke his impulse to do good against his impulse to do evil."
2. III:8: Said R. Isaac, "Whoever recites the Shema on his bed is as if he holds a two-edged sword in his hand to fight against demons." And R. Isaac said, "From whoever recites the Shema on his bed demons stay away." Said R. Yohanan to him, "Lo, even children in kindergarten know that, for it is written, 'And he said, If you will diligently hearken to the voice of the Lord your God and will do that which is right in his eyes and will give ear to his commandments and keep all his statutes, I will put none of the diseases upon you which I have put upon the Egyptians, for I am the Lord who heals you' (Ex. 15:26). Rather, phrase the matter in this way: 'Upon whoever has the possibility of taking up the study of Torah and does not do so, the Holy One, blessed be he, brings ugly and troubling suffering, as it is said,

'I was dumb with silence. I kept silence from the good thing, and so my pain was stirred up' (Ps. 39:3). 'The good thing' speaks only of the Torah, as it is said, 'For I give you a good doctrine, do not forsake my teaching' (Prov. 4:2)."

a. III:9: Secondary expansion on a proof-text in the foregoing.

H. IF A PERSON SEES THAT SUFFERINGS AFFLICT HIM, LET HIM EXAMINE HIS DEEDS.

a. III:10: Secondary development of the concluding proposition of III:8: Said Raba, and some say, R. Hisda, "If a person sees that sufferings afflict him, let him examine his deeds."

b. III:11: R. Jacob bar Idi and R. Aha bar Hanina differed. One of them said, "What are sufferings brought on by God's love? They are any form of suffering which does not involve one's having to give up studying Torah."

c. III:12: It has been taught on Tannaite authority: R. Simeon b. Yohai says, "Three good gifts did the Holy One, blessed be he, give to Israel, and all of them he gave only through suffering. These are they: Torah, the Land of Israel, and the world to come."

d. III:13: A Tannaite authority repeated the following statement before R. Yohanan: "Whoever devotes himself to study of the Torah or acts of loving kindness, or who buries his children, is forgiven all his sins."

e. III:14: Said R. Yohanan, "The suffering brought by skin-ailments such as are listed at Lev. 13–14 and by the burial of one's children are not sufferings that are brought by God's love."

f. III:15: R. Hiyya bar Abba got sick. R. Yohanan came to him. He said to him, "Are these sufferings precious to you?"

g. III:16: R. Eliezer got sick. R. Yohanan came to see him and found him lying in a dark room. The dying man uncovered his arm, and light fell through the room. Yohanan saw that R. Eliezer was weeping. He said to him, "Why are you crying? Is it because of the Torah that you did not learn sufficiently? We have learned: 'All the same are the ones who do much and do little, so long as each person will do it for the sake of heaven.'"

h. III:17: Four hundred barrels of wine turned sour on R. Huna. R. Judah, brother of R. Sala the Pious, and rabbis came to see him (and some say it was R. Ada bar Ahba and rabbis). They said to him, "The master should take a good look at his deeds."

i. III:18: It has been taught on Tannaite authority: Abba Benjamin says, "I have been particularly attentive to two matters for my entire life, first, that my prayer should be said before my bed, second, that my bed should be placed on a north-south axis."

Abba Benjamin in fact forms the focus of four compositions, shaped into a composite around his name.

1) III:19: Other sayings of Abba Benjamin: It has been taught on Tannaite authority: Abba Benjamin says, "If two people go

in to say a prayer, and one of them finished saying a prayer sooner than the other and did not wait for his fellow but left, in Heaven the angels tear up his prayer in his very presence and it is rejected.

2) III:20: It has been taught on Tannaite authority: Abba Benjamin says, "If the eye had the power to see them, no creature could withstand the demons."
3) III:21: It has been taught on Tannaite authority: Abba Benjamin says, "A prayer of a person is heard only if it is said in the synagogue."

I. THE TEFILLIN OF THE HOLY ONE, BLESSED BE HE. GOD'S PRESENCE IN THE SYNAGOGUE

1. III:22: Said R. Abin bar Ada said R. Isaac, "How do we know on the basis of Scripture that the Holy One, blessed be he, puts on phylacteries? As it is said, 'The Lord has sworn by his right hand, and by the arm of his strength' (Is. 62:8)."
2. III:23: Said R. Nahman bar Isaac to R. Hiyya bar Abin, "As to the phylacteries of the Lord of the world, what is written in them?"
3. III:24: Said Rabin bar R. Ada said R. Isaac, "About anyone who regularly comes to the synagogue, but does not come one day, the Holy One, blessed be he, inquires."
4. III:25: Said R. Yohanan, "When the Holy One, blessed be he, comes to a synagogue and does not find ten present, he forthwith becomes angry."

Helbo-Huna statements now are collected. They cohere around the name of the authority and therefore formed a composite before they were inserted in the present setting by reason of the relevance of the first of the sayings to the topic at hand.

5. III:26: Said R. Helbo said R. Huna, "For whoever arranges a regular place for praying, the God of Abraham is a help, and when he dies, they say for him, 'Woe for the humble man, woe for the pious man, one of the disciples of Abraham, our father.'" Said R. Helbo to R. Huna, "He who leaves the synagogue should not take large steps."
   a. III:27: Said R. Zira, "The reward for attending the lesson is on account of running to hear the lesson, not necessarily on account of what one has learned."
6. III:28: Said R. Huna, "Whoever prays behind the synagogue is called wicked."
   a. III:29: Other sayings of Huna on Prayer and Piety: And R. Helbo said R. Huna said, "A person should always be attentive at the afternoon prayer."
   b. III:30: Other sayings of Huna: And R. Helbo said R. Huna said, "Whoever enjoys a marriage banquet and does not felicitate the bridal couple violates five 'voices.'"
   c. III:31: Other sayings of Huna: And R. Helbo said R. Huna said, "The words of any person in whom is fear of Heaven are heard."

   d. III:32: Other sayings of Huna: And R. Helbo said R. Huna said, "Whoever knows that his fellow regularly greets him should greet the other first."
7. III:33: Said R. Yohanan in the name of R. Yosé, "How do we know that the Holy One, blessed be he, says prayers?"
8. III:34: It has been taught on Tannaite authority: Said R. Ishmael b. Elisha, "One time I went in to offer up incense on the innermost altar, and I saw the Crown of the Lord, enthroned on the highest throne, and he said to me, 'Ishmael, my son, bless me.'"
   a. III:35: Other sayings of Yohanan in the name of Yosé: And said R. Yohanan in the name of R. Yosé, "How do we know that one should not placate a person when he is angry?"
      1) III:36: Gloss of foregoing.
   b. III:37: Other sayings of Yohanan in the name of Yosé: And R. Yohanan said in the name of R. Yosé, "Better is one self-reproach that a person sets in his own heart on account of what he has done than a great many scourgings."
   c. III:38: And R. Yohanan said in the name of R. Yosé, "There were three things that Moses sought from the Holy One, blessed be he, and he gave them to him."
      1) III:39: Secondary development of the foregoing.
      2) III:40: As above.
   d. III:41: Other sayings of Yohanan in the name of Yosé: And R. Yohanan said in the name of R. Yosé, "Every word containing a blessing that came forth from the Mouth of the Holy One, blessed be he, even if stated conditionally, was never retracted."

Now we come to the Yohanan-Simeon composite that we considered earlier. What we see is that the composite is parachuted down whole and complete, a topical miscellany held together only by the names of the authorities to whom the sayings are attributed.

J. COMPOSITE OF SAYINGS OF YOHANAN IN THE NAME OF SIMEON B. YOHAI

1) III:42: Sayings of Yohanan in the name of Simeon b. Yohai: Said R. Yohanan in the name of R. Simeon b. Yohai, "From the day on which the Holy One, blessed be he, created the world, there was no man who called the Holy One, blessed be he, 'Lord,' until Abraham came along and called him Lord.
2) III:43: And R. Yohanan said in the name of R. Simeon b. Yohai, "How do we know that people should not seek to appease someone when he is mad?"
3) III:44: And R. Yohanan said in the name of R. Simeon b. Yohai, "From the day on which the Holy One, blessed be he, created his world, there was no one who praised the Holy One, blessed be he, until Leah came along and praised him."

4) III:45: And R. Yohanan said in the name of R. Simeon b. Yohai, "Bringing a child up badly is worse in a person's house than the war of Gog and Magog."
5) III:46: And R. Yohanan said in the name of R. Simeon b. Yohai, "It is permitted to contend with the wicked in this world."
6) III:47: And R. Yohanan said in the name of R. Simeon b. Yohai, "Beneath anyone who establishes a regular place for praying do that person's enemies fall."
7) III:48: And R. Yohanan said in the name of R. Simeon b. Yohai, "Greater is personal service to Torah than learning in Torah, so doing favors for a sage is of greater value than studying with him."
8) III:49: R. Yohanan said in the name of R. Simeon b. Yohai, "What is the meaning of that which is written, 'But as for me, let my prayer be made to you, O Lord, in an acceptable time' (Ps. 69:14)? When is an acceptable time? It is the time that the community is saying its prayers."
   a) III:50: Expansion of the foregoing. Said R. Simeon b. Laqish, "Whoever has a synagogue in his town and does not go in there to pray is called a bad neighbor."
   b) III:51: As above.
   c) III:52: As above.

Another composite formed around the names of authorities and tradents is now inserted, whole and complete.

K. COMPOSITE OF SAYINGS OF HIYYA BAR AMMI IN THE NAME OF ULLA

1) III:53: Said Raba to Rafram bar Papa, "Let the master tell us some of those excellent sayings having to do with the synagogue which were said in the name of R. Hisda." He said to him, "This is what R. Hisda said: 'What is the meaning of the verse of Scripture, "The Lord loves the gates of Zion (SYN) more than all the dwellings of Jacob" (Ps. 87:2)? The Lord loves the gates that are distinguished (SYN) in law more than synagogues and school-houses.'" That is in line with what R. Hiyya bar Ammi said in the name of Ulla, "From the day on which the house of the sanctuary was destroyed, the Holy One, blessed be he, has had in his world only the four cubits of the law alone."
2) III:54: And R. Hiyya bar Ammi said in the name of Ulla, "Greater is the status of one who derives benefit from his own labor than one who fears heaven."
3) III:55: And R. Hiyya bar Ammi said in the name of Ulla, "A person should always live in the place in which his master lives."

L. PROPER CONDUCT IN SYNAGOGUE WORSHIP; PROPER CONDUCT WHEN THE TORAH IS READ

1. III:56: Said R. Huna bar Judah said R. Menahem said R. Ammi, "What is the meaning of the verse that follows: 'And they who forsake the

Lord shall be consumed' (Is. 1:28)? This refers to one who leaves the scroll of the Torah when it is read and goes out of the synagogue."

2. III:57: Said R. Huna bar Judah said R. Ammi, "A person should always complete the reading of his passage of Scripture along with the congregation studying the same lection from the Pentateuch as is read in the synagogue, following the practice of repeating the verse of Scripture two times, with one reading from the translation of the same verse into Aramaic."
   a. III:58: Complement to a detail of the foregoing.
      1) III:59: Secondary continuation of the foregoing.

The picture is clear. Biographical materials were redacted into sizable compositions, yielding composites of some volume. What I said earlier about the availability of collections of sayings assigned to a given authority—a composite comparable to the Synoptic Gospels's "Q"—has now been amply instantiated.

Not only so, but the Talmudic counterpart to "Q" materials—collections of sources assigned to a given authority—found a rational position within the Bavli's larger program. Readers should not suppose that the Bavli is comprised by a set of miscellanies, lacking proposition, exposition, or argument. The opposite is the case. The collection of sayings and stories that cohere around a given authority's name is uncommon, and most of the compositions of the Bavli expound propositions in a philosophical and coherent manner. But what we now see in some detail is that materials for biographies did circulate and reach penultimate stages of redaction. What did not happen was the formation out of such composites of large-scale biographical exercises. These we do not find in rabbinic literature, not complete documents, not in combination to form biographical or historical documents.

Now let us turn to the situation of biographies in the counterpart foundation writings of Christianity. The comparison with the literary situation of rabbinic Judaism affords perspective on the facts just now surveyed. The difference is documentary: the very character of the writing-down of the religious systems and structures contains within itself a theological statement.

COMPARISON AND CONTRAST: THE GOSPELS AND THE MISHNAH, THE CHURCH FATHERS AND THE TALMUD

IF CHRISTIANITY WERE WRITTEN DOWN BY RABBIS . . .

If Christianity were written down in the way in which Judaism is, what should we know about Christianity, and how should we know it? In order for New Testament scholars to find out what they need to know about the rabbinic literature to use it for New Testament studies, they require a clear picture of the character of rabbinic literature. What better way to provide such a picture than to translate "Judaic" into "Christian"? As a kind of bilingual interpreter, I mean to give a picture of the kind of evidence scholars of earliest Christianity would face, if the New Testament and patristic writings were truly comparable to the Mishnah and rabbinic literature.

What I wish to do is to paint a picture of our problem in studying early Christianity, if the sources of early Christianity had reached us in the way and in the condition, in which those of early rabbinic Judaism come down to us. That is to say, what should we know, and how should we know it, if the records of early Christianity were like the rabbinic literature of late antiquity?

(1) What could we know, if all the literature of early Christianity had reached us in a fully homogenized and intellectually seamless form? Not only the New Testament, but all the works of the church fathers, from Justin to Augustine, now would be represented as expressions of one communal mind, dismembered and built into a single harmonious logical structure on various themes. True, they would be shown constantly to disagree with one another. But the range of permissible disagreement would define a vast area of consensus on all basic matters, so that a superficial contentiousness would convey something quite different: one mind on most things, beginning to end. The names of the fathers would be attached to some of their utterances. But all would have gone through a second medium of tradents and redactors—the editors of the compendium, the "Patristic Talmud," so to speak—and these editors would have picked and chosen what they wanted of Justin, and what of Origen, what of Tertullian, and what of Augustine, in line with what the editors themselves found interesting. In the end, the picture of the first six centuries of early Christianity would be the creation of people of the sixth century, out of the shards and remnants of people of the first five. Our work then would be to uncover what happened before the end through studying a document that portrays a timeless world.

Not only would the document be so framed as implicitly to deny historical development of ideas, but the framers would also gloss over diverse and contradictory sources of thought. I do not mean only that Justin, Irenaeus, and Tertullian would be presented as individual authors in a single, timeless continuum. I mean that all gnostic and Catholic sources would be broken up into sense-units and their fragments rearranged in a structure presented as representative of a single Christianity, with a single, unitary theology. This synthesized ecumenical body of Christian thought would be constructed so as to set out judgments on the principal theological topics of the day, and these judgments would have been accepted as normative from that day to this. So the first thing we must try to imagine is a Christianity which reaches us fully harmonized and whole—a Christianity of Nicaea and Chalcedon, but not of Arians, Nestorians, monophysites and the rest, so there is no distinctive Justin, nor Augustine, no Irenaeus, and no gnostics, and surely no Nag Hammadi, but all are one "in Christ Jesus," so to speak.

(2) Let me emphasize that this would be not merely a matter of early Christian literature's reaching us without the names of the authors of its individual documents. The thing we must try to imagine is that there would be no individual documents at all. Everything would have gone through a process of formation and redaction that obliterated the marks of individuality. Just as the theology would be one, so would the form and style of the documents which preserved it. Indeed, what would be striking about this picture of Christianity would not be that the tractate of Mark lacks the name of Mark, but that all of the tractates of the Gospels would be written in precisely the same style and resort to exactly the same rhetorical and redaction devices. Stylistic unity so pervasive as to eliminate all traces of individual authorship, even of most preserved sayings, would now characterize the writings of the first Christians. The sarcasm of Irenaeus, the majesty of Augustine, the exegetical ingenuity of Origen, and the lucid historicism of Aphrahat—all would be homogenized. Everyone would talk in the same way about the same things—one uniform rhetoric, a single topical agendum serving nearly everybody.

(3) And now to come to a principal task of the study of early Christianity: what should we know about Jesus, and how should we know it, if sayings assigned to Jesus in one book were given to Paul in a second, to John in a third, and to "They said," or, "He said to them," in a fourth? Can we imagine trying to discover the historical Jesus on this turf? If even the provenance of a saying could not be established on the basis of all those to whom it is attributed, if, often, even a single *Vorlage* and *Urtext* could not be postulated then what sort of work on the biography and thought of any of the early figures of Christianity would be credible?

(4) This brings me to the most difficult act of imagination, which I must ask readers to perform: a supererogatory work of social imagination. Can we imagine a corner of the modern world in which this state of interpretation—of total confusion, of harmonies, homologies, homogenies—is not found confusing but reassuring? Can we mentally conjure up a social setting for learning in which differentiation is avoided and credulity rewarded, in which analysis is heresy, dismissed as worthless or attacked as "full of mistakes"? Can we conceive of a

world in which repetition, in one's own words, of what the sources say is labeled scholarship, and anthologizing is labeled learning? In New Testament scholarship, we must imagine, the principal task now is to write harmonies of the Gospels and in patristic studies, to align the Catholic with the gnostic, the second century with the fifth, the Arian and the Athanasian, monophysite and Nestorian.[10] In a word, we speak of a world in which the Diatesseron is the last word in scholarship, and in which contentiousness about trivial things masks a firm and iron consensus. In this imagined world, scholars further hold that all the sources are historical, and merely alluding to them suffices to establish facts of history.

If readers can envision such a state of affairs, then we have entered the world of sources and scholarly orthodoxies confronted by us who study the ancient Judaism emergent from the rabbinic literature. And, it follows, scholars of New Testament history and exegesis will grasp the fact that rabbinic literature is simply not homologous to the writings on which they work and cannot be used in anything like the same way. Not only so, but that literature deals with different types of problems and answers altogether different questions with the result that we cannot present to rabbinic literature questions deemed appropriate for address to another kind of writing. A life of Jesus or of Augustine is plausible; a life of Aqiba or Hillel is not. An account of the intellectual biography of Paul and his theology is entirely a propos, the sources answering precisely the questions that are asked. A counterpart picture of Judah the Patriarch, who wrote up the Mishnah, or of Rabbah, Abbayye, or Raba, the greatest geniuses of the Talmud, is not. Then to use one type of writing to address questions appropriate to another type of writing is surely a dubious operation, or it would be, if it were not entirely routine, as the entries on sages in the *Jewish Encyclopaedia* show.

The Rabbis

(1) I can spell out matters now very simply and very rapidly. First, as to the axioms of scholarship, all the rabbinic sources are treated as

[10] I wrote this in 1979 and could not foresee that E. P. Sanders would present precisely such a picture of a single, homogeneous Judaism, joining the Judaic counterpart of monophysites and Nestorians into a single conflation. In chapter six, I show that he has done precisely that. Sanders exhibits an infirm grasp of the entire critical agenda in the study of the Judaic sources, and an examination of his presentation of them in his *Judaism: Practice and Belief, 63 BCE–66 CE*. London: SCM/Philadelphia: Trinity Press International, 1992, and in his *Jewish Law from Jesus to the Mishnah: Five Studies*. London: SCM/Philadelphia: Trinity Press International, 1990, shows them to be uninformed or half-informed. My reply to him is in *Judaic Law from Jesus to the Mishnah: A Systematic Reply to Professor E. P. Sanders*. Atlanta: Scholars Press, 1993. To my knowledge Sanders did not respond publicly to my reply.

representatives of a single, seamless world view and as expressions of a single, essentially united group, either the views as a whole, or, among the enlightened, *the* rabbis as a group. While some more critical souls concede there may have been distinctions between the first century rabbis' thought and that of the fourth, the distinctions make no material difference in accounts of "the rabbis" and their thought. Whether anthologies or anthological essays (Moore, Montefiore and Loewe, Bonsirven, Urbach), *the* rabbis are represented in their views on God, world, and redemption, as though all rabbis for seven hundred years had the same thing to say as all others.

Now this representation of *the* rabbis is subject to an important, commonplace qualification. Everyone knows that the Talmuds abound in the recognition of differences between the teachings of different rabbis in different periods on different points in discussions of which traditions or source was followed by the proponent of this or that opinion. But the recorded differences are about particular, trivial points. The Talmudic discussion, moreover, is directed normally towards reconciling them. What is particularly lacking in available accounts of "the rabbinic mind" is, first, recognition and delineation of different general positions or basic attitudes, of the characteristic makeup, and backgrounds of different schools; second, what is lacking is anything like adequate reporting of the change of teachings over the course of time and in relation to historical changes. Obviously, there is plenty of speculation on how an individual or group reacted to a particular historical situation or event. But these random speculations are unsystematic and appear to be made up for the occasion. So these apparent exceptions to what I say have to be recognized—because they prove the accuracy of my description of the prevailing consensus that governed until the final quarter of the twentieth century.

(2) Second, as to the sources, the documents of earlier rabbinic Judaism exhibit an internally uniform quality of style. So the scholars who represent a seamless world accurately replicate the literary traits of the sources of the portrait. It is exceedingly difficult to differentiate on formal or stylistic grounds among the layers of the Mishnah, which is the document of rabbinic Judaism first brought to redaction. The two Talmuds then so lay matters out as to represent themselves as the logical continuity from the Mishnah. They do so by breaking up the Mishnah into minute units and then commenting on those discrete units of thought. Consequently, the Mishnah as a document, a document that presents its own worldview and its own social system, is not preserved and confronted. Nor do the Talmuds present themselves as successive layers, built upon, but essentially distinct from the Mishnah. Rather, the Talmuds aim at completely harmonizing their own materi-

als both with the Mishnah and among themselves, despite the self-evidently contradictory character of the materials. Once more we observe, there are limits to disagreement. The continuing contentiousness of the documents, their preservation of diverse viewpoints on single issues, both underline the rigidly protected limits of permissible disagreement. Intense disagreement about trivialities powerfully reinforces basic unities and harmonies. The fact that, out there, were Jews who decorated synagogues in ways the Talmuds cannot have led us to anticipate, is mentioned only in passing, as if it is of no weight or concern. What matters to this literature is not how the Jews lived, nor even how they worshipped, but only the discussions of the rabbinic schools and courts. What the documents say is what we are supposed to think, within the range of allowed difference. Consequently, the intellectually unitary character of the sources is powerfully reinforced by the total success of the framers and redactors of the sources in securing stylistic unity within documents and in some measure even among them.

(3) These facts have not prevented scholars from writing about history and biography, upon the basis of the unanalyzed and unchallenged allegations of the rabbinic sources. Just as people had arguments about what Jesus really said and did before the rise of form criticism, so the rage and secure contentiousness of scholars in this field mask the uncertainty of their entire structure. It is as if by arguing on essentially minor points, as in the Talmuds themselves, the colleagues may avoid paying attention to the epistemological abyss beneath them all. Instead of analysis and argument, dogma took over. There were two: (a) "Believe unless you have to doubt," and, by way of settling all doubts, (b) "Would our holy rabbis lie?"—there being no substantive difference between the two theological dogmas. The one was promulgated at the Hebrew University of Jerusalem, the other at Bar Ilan University, the one under secular, the other under Orthodox auspices. There is no difference between them.

So there are agreed-upon solutions to the problems of diverse authorities behind the same saying and amplification and variation of details in a single story. These commonly lead to very felicitous conclusions. If the same saying is in three mouths, it is because they agreed to say it. True, "we cannot be sure that they were not talking simultaneously in different places (thanks to the holy spirit)." Or, if there are three versions of essentially the same story, like the Sermon on the Mount and the Sermon on the Plain, it is because, in the wonderful ways of Providence, it happened two times. Every time the text says, "One time," that was, indeed, one event.

(4) Finally, as I have already hinted, these serendipitous facts, these happy agreements, these assured and unquestioned results of a

hundred years of critical scholarship following upon fifteen hundred years of uncritical scholarship, which produced the same results, enjoy the powerful support of the three great communities that read the rabbinic literature at all. I mean, Orthodox Jews in Yeshivas, scholarly Jews in rabbinic seminaries and Israeli universities, and the generality of Christian scholars of New Testament. To the Orthodox, the rabbinic sources are part of the whole Torah of Moses our rabbi, the revealed word of God. For them, "our holy rabbis" cannot deceive. To the scholars in American and European rabbinic schools and Institutes of Judaic Studies and Israeli universities, the critical program of scholarship on early Christianity is perceived from a distance. In their books and articles they settle complex questions of literary analysis and historical epistemology with an array of two assumptions, three logical arguments, and four "probative" examples. They do not perceive the immense, detailed work, which stands, for example, behind debates on Q and the Synoptic Problem. Indeed, the work of analysis of sources bores them. Whether work is original or dull, the bulk of it simply dismisses as settled, questions that would be deemed urgent in biblical and patristic literature and in the history of early Christianity. As to the New Testament scholars, their view is that things go better when we read rabbinic literature as a set of facts, which speak for themselves, rather than complex problems requiring solutions. For them, the rabbinic literature as it stands, unanalyzed and un-criticized, tells us all about Jerusalem and Galilee in the time of Jesus. Billerbeck is a dictionary of facts, and the beginning of sound exegesis. Or, to put matters in a more theological way, in Gospels research, salvation is of the Jews.

That scholarly edifice lies in ruins, and has been replaced by a different structure of thought altogether. The contrast between the treatment of Judaism in *The Jewish Encyclopaedia* and the presentation of that same subject in the *Encyclopaedia of Judaism*, which I organized and edited with Alan J. Avery-Peck and William Scott Green, tells the tale.[11] But to articulate that difference would require only reproducing side-by-side the titles of the principal entries in the two encyclopedias as these treat the same topic. What has shifted then is blatant. But for the collection of facts, no one has done a better job than *The Jewish Encyclopaedia*, which is why the relevant entries for named sages are reproduced here.

[11] Six volumes form a statement of method and result in response to the approaches to history, including biography, religion, literature, and theology that I have framed in the past four decades: *The Encyclopaedia of Judaism*. 3 vols. Leiden: Brill/New York: Continuum, 1999; *The Encyclopaedia of Judaism: Supplement One*. Leiden: Brill/New York: Continuum, 2002; *The Encyclopaedia of Judaism: Supplement Two*. Leiden: Brill/New York: Continuum, 2003; and *The Encyclopaedia of Judaism: Supplement Three*. Leiden: Brill/New York: Continuum, 2004.

A

ABAYE (called also **Abayi**, **Abaya**, **Abbaye**): Babylonian amora; born about the close of the third century; died 339 (see ACADEMIES IN BABYLONIA). His father, Kaylil, was the brother of Rabbah bar Naḥmani, a teacher at the Academy of Pumbedita. Abaye's real name was Naḥmani, after his grandfather; but being left an orphan at an early age, he was adopted by his uncle, Rabbah bar Naḥmani, who nicknamed him Abaye ("Little Father"), to avoid confusion with his grandfather of the same name, and thenceforth he was known as Abaye, without any other title. It is a curious fact that he perpetuated the memory of his foster-mother, probably a slave in Rabbah's household, by mentioning her name in many popular recipes and dietetic precepts, some of which seem to be based on superstitious notions. He introduced each recipe with the phrase, "My mother told me." Abaye's teachers were his uncle Rabbah and Joseph bar Ḥama, both of whom successively became presidents of the Pumbedita Academy. When Joseph died (333), this dignity was conferred upon Abaye, who retained it until his death some five years later. Rabbah trained him in the application of the dialectic method to halakic problems, and Joseph, with his stores of traditional lore, taught him to appreciate the value of positive knowledge.

Superior as Abaye no doubt was in his dialectic analysis of halakic sentences, he was, nevertheless, surpassed in this regard by Raba, with whom he had been closely associated from early youth. To the disputations between these amoraim we owe the development of the dialectic method in the treatment of halakic traditions. Their debates are known as the "Hawayot de-Abaye we-Raba" (Debates of Abaye and Raba), the subjects of which were then considered such essential elements of Talmudic knowledge that by an anachronism they were thought to be known to Johanan ben Zakkai, who lived some centuries before (Suk. 28*a*). Their halakic controversies are scattered throughout the Babylonian Talmud. With the exception of six of his decisions, the opinions of Raba were always accepted as final. Abaye was never so happy as when one of his disciples had completed the study of a Mishnah treatise. On such occasions he always gave a feast to his pupils (Shab. 118*b*), though his circumstances were needy, and wine never appeared upon his table. His peace-loving disposition and his sincere piety are well exhibited in his maxims (Ber. 17*a*), among which occur the following: "Be mild in speech; suppress your wrath; and maintain good-will in intercourse with your relatives as well as with others, even with strangers in the market-place."

Abaye urged his disciples to conduct themselves in such a way as to lead others to the love of God (Yoma, 86*a*). In Biblical exegesis he was one of the first to draw a distinct line between the evident meaning of the text (*peshaṭ*) and the sense ascribed to it by midrashic interpretation. He formulated the following rule, of great importance in Talmudic exegesis (Sanh. 34*a*): "One Bible verse can be referred to different subjects, but several different Bible verses can not refer to one and the same subject." He defended the Apocryphal book Ecclesiasticus against his teacher Joseph. By quoting from it a number of edifying passages he showed that it did not belong to the heretical books which are forbidden, and even compelled his teacher to admit that quotations might with advantage be taken from it for homiletical purposes (Sanh. 100*b*). Possessing an extensive knowledge of tradition, Abaye became a most eager disciple of Dimi, the Palestinian amora, who had brought to Babylonia a perfect treasury of interpretations by Palestinian amoraim. Abaye considered Dimi, as a representative of the Palestinian school, a qualified Bible exegete, and used to ask him how this or that Bible verse was explained in "the West," or Palestine. Of his own interpretations of Biblical passages only a few, of a haggadic nature, are preserved; but he often supplements, elucidates, or corrects the opinions of older authorities.

BIBLIOGRAPHY: Lampronti, *Paḥad Yiẓḥaḳ*, s.v.; Heilprin, *Seder ha-Dorot*, pp. 22–25; Hamburger, *R. B. T.*, 1883, part ii., s.v.; Kohut, *Aruch*, s.v. (in which is found an enumeration of all the passages of the Talmud containing Abaye's name); Bacher, *Ag. Bab. Amor.* s.v.; Weiss, *Dor*; M. S. Antokolski in *Ha-Asif*, 1885, ii. 503–506, with Straschun's notes.

W. B.

ABBA BAR ABBA: A Babylonian amora of the second and third centuries, distinguished for piety, benevolence, and learning. He is known chiefly through his son Mar Samuel, principal of the Academy of Nehardea, and is nearly always referred to as "Samuel's father." Abba traveled to Palestine, where he entered into relations with R. Judah I., the patriarch, with whose pupil Levi bar Sisi he was on terms of intimate friendship. When Levi died Abba delivered the funeral oration and glorified the memory of his friend.

BIBLIOGRAPHY: *Midr. Samuel*, ed. Buber, 1893, x. 3; *Yer. Peah*, viii. 21*b*; *Ket.* 51*b*; Frankel, *Mebo*, pp. 56*a et seq.*; Heilprin, *Seder ha-Dorot*, 1882, ii. 3.

W. B.

ABBA B. ABINA: An amora who flourished in the third century. He was a native of Babylonia and a pupil of Rab. He emigrated to Palestine, where he became well known in tradition, particularly through his various haggadic sayings. The confession which he composed for the Day of Atonement deserves special mention. It reads:

"My God, I have sinned and done wicked things. I have persisted in my bad disposition and followed its direction. What I have done I will do no more. Be it Thy will, O Everlasting God, that Thou mayest blot out my iniquities, forgive all my transgressions, and pardon all my sins" (Yer. Yoma, end 45*a*).

Bibliography: Bacher, *Ag. Pal. Amor.* iii. 526, 527; Heilprin, *Seder ha-Dorot*, ii. 15.

W. B.

ABBA ARIKA (usually called **RAB**): Celebrated Babylonian amora and founder of the Academy of Sura; flourished in third century; died at Sura in 247. His surname, "Arika" (Aramaic, אריכא; Hebrew, ארך; English, "Long"—that is, "Tall"; it occurs only once—Ḥul. 137*b*), he owed to his height, which, according to a reliable record, exceeded that of his contemporaries. Others, reading "Areka," consider it an honorary title, "Lecturer" (Weiss, "Dor," iii. 147; Jastrow, "Dict." *s.v.*). In the traditional literature he is referred to almost exclusively as Rab the Master (both his contemporaries and posterity recognizing in him a master), just as his teacher, Judah I., was known simply as Rabbi. He is called Rabbi Abba only in the tannaitic literature (for instance, Tosefta, Beẓah, i. 7), where a number of his sayings are preserved. He occupies a middle position between the Tannaim and the Amoraim, and is accorded the right, rarely conceded to one who is only an amora, of disputing the opinion of a tanna (B. B. 42*a* and elsewhere).

Rab was a descendant of a distinguished Babylonian family which claimed to trace its origin to Shimei, brother of King David (Sanh. 5*a*; Ket. 62*b*). His father, Aibo, was a brother of Ḥiyya, who lived in Palestine, and was a highly esteemed scholar in the collegiate circle of the patriarch Judah I. From his associations in the house of his uncle, and later as his uncle's disciple and as a member of the academy at Sepphoris, Rab acquired such an extraordinary knowledge of traditional lore as to make him its foremost exponent in his native land. While Judah I. was still living, Rab, having been duly ordained as teacher—though not without certain restrictions (Sanh. *l.c.*)—returned to Babylonia, where he at once began a career that was destined to mark an epoch in the development of Babylonian Judaism.

In the annals of the Babylonian schools the year of his arrival is recorded as the starting-point in the chronology of the Talmudic age. It was the 530th year of the Seleucidan and the 219th year of the common era. As the scene of his activity, Rab first chose Nehardea, where the exilarch appointed him *agoranomos*, or market-master, and Rabbi Shela made him lecturer (amora) of his college (Yer. B. B. v. 15*a*; Yoma, 20*b*). Thence he removed to Sura, on the Euphrates, where he established a school of his own, which soon became the intellectual center of the Babylonian Jews. As a renowned teacher of the Law and with hosts of disciples, who came from all sections of the Jewish world, Rab lived and worked in Sura until his death. Samuel, another disciple of Judah I., at the same time brought to the academy at Nehardea a high degree of prosperity; in fact, it was at the school of Rab that Jewish learning in Babylonia found its permanent home and center. Rab's activity made Babylonia independent of Palestine, and gave it that predominant position which it was destined to occupy for several centuries.

The method of treatment of the traditional material to which the Talmud owes its origin was established in Babylonia by Rab. That method takes the Mishnah of Judah ha-Nasi as a text or foundation, adding to it the other tannaitic traditions, and deriving from all of them the theoretical explanations and practical applications of the religious Law. The legal and ritual opinions recorded in Rab's name and his disputes with Samuel constitute the main body of the Babylonian Talmud. His numerous disciples—some of whom were very influential and who, for the most part, were also disciples of Samuel—amplified and, in their capacity as instructors and by their discussions, continued the work of Rab. In the Babylonian schools Rab was rightly referred to as "our great master." Rab also exercised a great influence for good upon the moral and religious conditions of his native land, not only indirectly through his disciples, but directly by reason of the strictness with which he repressed abuses in matters of marriage and divorce, and denounced ignorance and negligence in matters of ritual observance.

Rab, says tradition, found an open, neglected field and fenced it in (Ḥul. 110*a*). Especial attention was given by him to the liturgy of the Synagogue. He is reputed to be the author of one of the finest compositions in the Hebrew prayer-book, the Musaf service of the New Year. In this noble prayer are evinced profound religious feeling and exalted thought, as well as ability to use the Hebrew language in a natural, expressive, and classical manner (Yer. R. H. i. 57*a*). The many homiletic and ethical (haggadistic) sayings recorded of him show similar ability. As a haggadist Rab is surpassed by none of the Babylonian Amoraim. He is the only one of the Babylonian teachers whose haggadistic utterances approach in number and contents those of the Palestinian haggadists. The Palestinian Talmud has preserved a large number of his halakic and haggadistic utterances; and the Palestinian Midrashim also contain many of his Haggadot. Rab delivered homiletic discourses, both in the college (*bet ha-midrash*) and in the synagogues. He especially loved to treat in his homilies of the events and personages of Biblical history; and many beautiful and genuinely poetic embellishments of the Biblical record, which have become common possession of the Haggadah, are his creations. His Haggadah is particularly rich in thoughts concerning the moral life and the relations of human beings to one another. A few of these utterances may be quoted here:

"The commandments of the Torah were only given to purify men's morals" (Gen. R. xliv.). "Whatever may not properly be done in public is forbidden even in the most secret chamber" (Shab. 64*b*). "It is well that people busy themselves with the study of the Law and the performance of charitable deeds, even when not entirely disinterested; for the habit of right-doing will finally make the intention pure" (Pes. 50*b*). "Man will be called to account for having deprived himself of the good things which the world offered" (Yer. Ḳid. end). "Whosoever hath not pity upon his fellow man is no child of Abraham" (Beẓah, 32*b*). " It is better to cast oneself into a fiery furnace than publicly to put to shame one's fellow creature" (B. M. 59*a*). "One should never betroth himself to a woman without having seen her; one might subsequently discover in her a blemish because of which one might loathe her and thus transgress the commandment: 'Thou shalt love thy neighbor as thyself'" (Ḳid. 41*a*). "A father should never prefer one child above another; the example of Joseph shows what evil results may follow therefrom" (Shab. 10*b*).

Rab loved the Book of Ecclesiasticus (Sirach), and warned his disciple Hamnuna against unjustifiable asceticism by quoting advice contained therein—that, considering the transitoriness of human life ('Er. 54*a*), one should not despise the good things of this world. To the celestial joys of the future he was accustomed to refer in the following poetic words:

"There is naught on earth to compare with the future life. In the world to come there shall be neither eating nor drinking, neither trading nor toil, neither hatred nor envy; but the righteous shall sit with crowns upon their heads, and rejoice in the radiance of the Divine Presence" (Ber. 17*a*).

Rab also devoted much attention to mystical and transcendental speculations which the rabbis connect with the Biblical account of creation (Gen. i., Ma'aseh Bereshit), the vision of the mysterious chariot of God (Ezek. i., Ma'aseh Merkabah), and the Divine Name. Many of his important utterances testify to his tendency in this direction (Ḥag. 12*a*, Ḳid. 71*a*).

Concerning the social position and the personal history of Rab we are not informed. That he was rich seems probable; for he appears to have occupied himself for a time with commerce and afterward with agriculture (Ḥul. 105*a*). That he was highly respected by the Gentiles as well as by the Jews of Babylonia is proved by the friendship which existed between him and the last Parthian king, Artaban ('Ab. Zarah, 10*b*). He was deeply affected by the death of Artaban (226) and the downfall of the Arsacidan dynasty, and does not appear to have sought the friendship of Ardeshir, founder of the Sassanian dynasty, although Samuel of Nehardea probably did so. Rab became closely related, through the marriage of one of his daughters, to the family of the exilarch. Her sons, Mar Ukba and Nehemiah, were considered types of the highest aristocracy. Rab had many sons, several of whom are mentioned in the Talmud, the most distinguished being the eldest, Ḥiyya. The latter did not, however, succeed his father as head of the academy: this post fell to Rab's disciple Huna. Two of his grandsons occupied in succession the office of exilarch (*resh galuta*, Ḥul. 92*a*).

Rab died at an advanced age, deeply mourned by numerous disciples and the entire Babylonian Jewry, which he had raised from comparative insignificance to the leading position in Judaism (Shab. 110*a*, M. Ḳ. 24*a*).

BIBLIOGRAPHY: I. H. Weiss, in *Kokbe Yiẓḥaḳ*, No. 8, pp. 22–30; No. 9, pp. 49–55; No. 10, pp. 16–21; the same, *Dor*, iii. 147–161; Abr. Lewysohn, in Kobak's *Jeschurun* (Hebrew part), vi. 114–120 and vii. 6–16; Jos. Umanski, in Gräber's *Oẓar ha-Sifrut*, v. 159–212: M. I. Mühlfelder, *Rabh, Ein Lebensbild*, 1871; Bacher, *Ag. Bab. Amor.* pp. 1–33; Reifmann, in *Ha-Maggid*, 1871, No. 12; D. Kahana, in *Ha-Shiloaḥ*, 1898, pp. 432–440; I. S. Antokolski, in *Ha-Asif*, ii., with notes by Straschun.

W. B.

ABBA BAR BENJAMIN BAR ḤIYYA, (called also **Abba b. Minyomi** or **Minyomin b. Ḥiyya**): A Palestinian scholar of the third and fourth centuries, contemporary of R. Abbahu. While the country of his birth can not be named with certainty, he was probably born in Babylonia; for he is found there (Ḥul. 80*a*) seeking halakic information from Rab Huna b. Ḥiyya, the son-in-law of R. Jeremiah b. Abba, who lived in Babylonia (Bek. 31*a*) and who was probably the brother of Benjamin b. Ḥiyya, the father of Abba and disciple of Rab Ḥisda, who also lived in Babylonia. Hence, it may be assumed that Abba b. Benjamin was a native of the same country and that he removed to Palestine, where he established himself at Arbela. Here R. Abbahu once visited him (Yer. Shebi'it, vi. 36*d*). In the Palestinian Talmud he is always referred to as Abba b. Benjamin. Twice (Yer. Ber. v. 9*d*, and Yer. Giṭ. v. 47*b*) he is quoted by the name of Abaye b. B.; this, however, is the result of a clerical error, as clearly appears from the reading of the manuscript Syrileio (Yer. Ber. *ad loc.*) and of the parallel passages in the Babylonian Talmud (R. H. 35*a*; Soṭah, 38*b*). In the latter Talmud he is sometimes quoted by the appellation of b. Benjamin, and sometimes as b. Minyomi or Minyomin (a dialectic form of Benjamin). Hence he should not be confounded with the Abba bar Minyomi who is identical with Abba b. Martha. The Babylonian Talmud, in quoting him, generally adds to his name that of his grandsire Ḥiyya (Ḥul. 80*a*; Yeb. 122*b*), and he may also be recognized by the character of the traditions cited in his behalf, which usually refer to Baraitot.

BIBLIOGRAPHY: Heilprin, *Seder ha-Dorot*, ii. 17; Bacher, *Ag. Pal. Amor.* i. 117.

S. M.

ABBA B. BIZNA: A Palestinian amora of the fourth century, who is occasionally mentioned as a haggadist, and as having handed down certain halakic opinions (Yer. B. Ḳ. v. 5*a*).

BIBLIOGRAPHY: Heilprin, *Seder ha-Dorot*, ii. 17; Bacher, *Ag. Pal. Amor.* iii. 647.

W. B.

ABBA COHEN OF BARDELA: A scholar of the last tannaitic generation (about the beginning of the third century). The few Halakot emanating from him refer to the rabbinical civil law. In Biblical homiletics several of his expositions have been preserved (Sifre, Deut. 2; Gen. R. 23, 76, 93). The last-mentioned passage runs as follows: "Wo to mankind, because of the day of judgment; wo, because of the day of trial! Balaam, the wisest among the Gentiles, was confounded at the reproof of his ass (Num. xxii. 30). Joseph, one of the youngest of Jacob's sons, silenced his elder brethren (Gen. xlv. 3). How will man be able to endure the judgment of the omniscient Lord?" (B. M. 10*a*; Yer. Giṭ. viii. 49*c*; Yer. B. M. i. 7*d*; Yer. B. B. viii. 16*b*).

S. M.

ABBA GORION OF SIDON: A tanna, who flourished in the second century. He handed down to posterity a saying of Abba Saul (Mishnah, Ḳid. iv. 14, Yerushalmi version) and one of Rabban Gamaliel II. That of Gamaliel, quoted in the introduction to Esther R., forms the beginning to a Midrash on the Book of Esther, for which reason the latter is called Midrash Abba Gorion.

BIBLIOGRAPHY: Bacher, *Ag. Tan.* i. 95, ii. 368.

W. B.

ABBA ḤANIN and his son, ABBA JOSE. See ḤANIN, ABBA, and JOSE, ABBA.

ABBA BAR ḤIYYA B. ABBA: A Palestinian amora, who flourished at the beginning of the fourth century. He was the son of Ḥiyya bar Abba, the well-known pupil of Johanan, and transmitted to his generation the sayings of Johanan, which in their turn had been delivered to him by his father (Yer. Soṭah, ix. 24*c*). He was on terms of intimate friendship with Zeira (Ḥul. 86*b*).

BIBLIOGRAPHY: Frankel, *Mebo*, p. 57*a*; Bacher, *Ag. Pal. Amor.* iii. 648.

W. B.

ABBA JOSE BEN DOSITAI. See JOSE, ABBA, BEN DOSITAI.

ABBA JOSE BEN ḤANIN. See JOSE, ABBA, BEN HANIN.

ABBA JOSE OF MAḤUZA. See JOSE, ABBA, OF MAḤUZA.

ABBA JUDAH. See ABBA JUDAN.

ABBA JUDAN (or **JUDAH**): A philanthropist who lived in Antioch in the early part of the second century. As an example of his generosity, it is recorded that once he sold half of his property, already considerably reduced by the demands of charity, to avoid turning away empty-handed Rabbis Eliezer, Joshua, and Akiba, who were collecting donations for educational purposes. The record adds that the blessings conferred upon him by these rabbis bore fruit, for shortly afterward, by a happy accident, he discovered a treasure (Yer. Hor. iii. 48*a*, Lev. R. v. 4). His name was not permitted to fall into oblivion, and for centuries later the name "Abba Judan" seems to have been applied in Palestine to every unusually benevolent man (Lev. R. *l.c.*, Deut. R. iv. 8). It is thus the Jewish parallel to the name Mæcenas which is still applied, two thousand years after the life of its original bearer, to every great patron of art.

L. G.

ABBA ḲOLON: A mythical Roman mentioned in a Talmudic legend concerning the foundation of Rome, which, according to the Haggadah, was a result of the impious conduct of the Jewish kings. According to the legend, the first settlers of Rome found that their huts collapsed as soon as built, whereupon Abba Ḳolon said to them, "Unless you mix water from the Euphrates with your mortar, nothing that you build will stand." Then he offered to supply such water, and for this purpose journeyed through the East as a cooper, and returned with water from the Euphrates in wine-casks. The builders mixed this water with the mortar and built new huts that did not collapse. Hence the proverb, "A city without Abba Ḳolon is not worthy of the name." The newly built city was therefore called "Babylonian Rome" (Cant. R. i. 6).

Probably this legend was intended to show the dependence of the Roman empire upon the natural resources of the East; but it contains a number of points that still remain unexplained. The above-mentioned Roman, or, more properly, Greco-Roman, proverb is just as obscure as the name "Abba Ḳolon," which, originating in some classic word, was distorted by the Jews into "a father of a colony," not without the mental reservation that "Ḳolon" is the Aramaic equivalent of "shame." An attempt has been made to identify the name with that of Deucalion (Krauss, "Lehnwörter," ii. *s.v.*), to which it bears no philological or historical relation. The most probable identification is that by Brüll, who refers to a legend in John Malalas' "Chronicles," p. 301, of a magician named Ablaccon, under the emperor Tiberius. This Ablaccon protected the city of Antioch, by the aid of a rampart of stone, against the overflow of the mountain streams.

BIBLIOGRAPHY: Brüll, in Kobak's *Jeschurun*, vi. 3; Krauss, *Griechische und Lateinische Lehnwörter im Talmud*, etc., ii. s.v. Berlin, 1899; Vogelstein and Rieger, *Gesch. d. Juden in Rom*, i. 86.

L. G.

ABBA BEN MARI. See RABBA BEN MARI.

ABBA B. MARTHA (identical with **ABBA B. MINYOMI,** and generally quoted with both appellations; very rarely as **Abba b. Martha** alone, or **Abba b. Minyomi alone**; Beẓah, 22*a*; Git. 29*b*): A Babylonian scholar of the end of the third century and beginning of the fourth. He seems to have been in poor circumstances. Once he incurred a debt to the *resh galuta* (exilarch), which he could not repay, and only by disguising himself did he at the time escape arrest for it (Yeb. 120*a*). Later he was apprehended and sorely pressed for payment; but when the exilarch discovered that his debtor was a rabbinical scholar, he released him (Shab. 121*b*). His mother, Martha, seems to have been in easy circumstances; for, when Abba was bitten by a rabid dog and, in accordance with contemporary therapeutics, was obliged to drink through a tube of copper (compare Brecher, "Das Transcendentale im Talmud," p. 219, note), Martha substituted one of gold (Yoma, 84*a*). Notwithstanding his pecuniary straits, Abba did not take advantage of the Biblical and Talmudic law (Mishnah, Sheb. x. 1), according to which the Sabbatical year cancels all debts. He once owed some money to Rabbah, and paid it in the year of release, using the form of a donation (Giṭ. 37*b*).

S. M.

ABBA BAR MEMEL: A Palestinian amora, who lived toward the end of the third century. He belonged to the circle of Ammi at Tiberias, and enjoyed the reputation of a great halakist. In three propositions he limited and rendered practically harmless the application of the Gezerah Shawah, the second of the thirteen hermeneutic rules of R. Ismael, which otherwise might easily have led to arbitrary ritual decisions (Yer. Pes. vi. 33*a*). His proposed reforms were never carried into practise, no other amora having joined him to form a valid legislative body (Yer. M. Ḳ. ii. 81*b*). Among his haggadic passages the most significant is one on the names of God (Ex. R. iii.):

"God spake to Moses: 'Thou desirest to know My name, I AM THAT I AM (Ex. iii. 14). That is, I am called according to my revealed activities. When I am judging mankind, I am called *Elohim*; when I am going out to war against the wicked, I am called *Zebaot*; when I am holding judgment in suspense over the sins of men, I am called *El Shaddai*; when showing mercy to the world, I am called YHWH, because this name denotes the quality of mercy in God' (Ex. xxxiv. 6)."

W. B.

ABBA BAR PAPPAI (or **PAPA**): A Palestinian amora, of the fourth century who died 375. As the second link in the transmission by tradition of Levi's haggadic sayings, he is generally mentioned together with Joshua of Siknin, who was the first link (Yer. Ber. iv. 7*b*; Yer. Bik. ii. 64*c*; Yer. Yoma, iv. 41*b*). He addressed halakic questions to Jose and Mani the son of Jonah, who in turn placed halakic problems before him (Yer. Shab. iii. 5*d*).

BIBLIOGRAPHY: Bacher, *Ag. Pal. Amor.* iii. 650, 651; Frankel, *Mebo*, p. 58*a*.

W. B.

ABBA SAḲḲARA (or **SIḲRA***): Insurrectionary leader; lived in the first century in Palestine. According to Talmudic accounts (Giṭ. 56*a*), he took a very prominent part in the uprising against Rome in 70, being then at the head of the Zealots at Jerusalem. He was the nephew of Johanan ben Zakkai, at that time leader of the Peace party. After the Zealots had destroyed all storehouses, thus causing a famine in the besieged city, Johanan ben Zakkai invited Abba to an interview and asked him: "Why do you act in such a manner? Will you kill us by famine?" Abba replied: "What shall I do? If I tell them anything of the kind, they will slay me." Thereupon Johanan said to him: "Try and invent for me some possibility of escape so that I may be able to save something out of the general wreck." Abba complied with the request; and the Talmud gives a full account of the device by which he enabled his uncle to flee to the Romans.

The historical character of this account is not beyond doubt, and it is especially surprising that Josephus knows nothing of Abba as leader of the Zealots. The fact that Josephus does not mention him, can not, however, be accepted as a sufficient proof against the Talmudic account, for he ignores also Johanan ben Zakkai, one of the most important and influential men at the time of the destruction of the Second Temple. Purely personal motives may have actuated the vainglorious historian to ignore both uncle and nephew. There exists, however, a Midrash which tends to show that there is at least a grain of truth in his account. In Eccl. R. vii. 11 it is related: "There was at Jerusalem a certain Ben Baṭiaḥ, a nephew of Johanan ben Zakkai, who was in charge of the storehouses, which he destroyed by fire" (see also Kelim, xvii. 12; Tosef., Kelim, vii. 2, and the article BEN BAṬIAḤ).

This account is quite independent of that in the Talmud, since they differ not only with regard to the names, but also materially for, whereas the Talmudic account states that Johanan escaped from Je-

* With regard to the appellation Saḳḳara, which means "the dyer," it may be remarked that both the first edition and the Benveniste edition of the Talmud have the word without י (*yod*), which seems to forbid the reading "Sikra" and the connecting of this name with the revolutionary party name of the Sicarii.

rusalem by the aid of his nephew, it is related in the Midrash that he barely escaped death at the hands of his nephew. It might, therefore, be assumed that there existed a third and older source from which both the Talmudic and midrashic accounts were derived, and also that the traditions thus handed down underwent some change in the course of transmission.

BIBLIOGRAPHY: Rapoport, *'Erek Millin*, pp. 1–2, 257; Derenbourg, *Essai*, p. 280; *Lam. R.*, ed. Buber, p. 66. All three hold that "Abba Sakkara" of the *Bab. Talmud* is a misinterpretation of the Palestinian "Rosh Kisrin" or "Rosh Sikrin" (Head of the Sicarii). But Abba can not be used in this sense in Aramaic. Besides, the *Bab. Talmud* itself renders "Rosh Sikrin" with "Resh Baryone."

L. G.

ABBA SAUL BEN BOTNIT. See SAUL, ABBA B. BATNIT.

ABBA SAUL. See SAUL, ABBA.

ABBA OF SIDON: A Palestinian amora of the latter part of the third century or the early part of the fourth. He is mentioned only once, as a transmitter of a haggadic saying of Samuel b. Naḥman (Midr. Sam. xxiii.; Eccl. R. vii. 1).

W. B.

ABBA THE SURGEON (UMANA): Mentioned in the Talmud as an example of genuine Jewish piety and benevolence (Ta'anit, 21*b* *et seq.*). Although dependent upon his earnings, he was so unselfish and considerate that, in order to avoid embarrassing the poor among his patients, he would never accept pay directly from any one, but instead attached to a certain part of his house a box in which each might place what he pleased. Abba's confidence in humanity was once tested by two young disciples in a remarkable manner. Having lodged with him one night, in the morning they took the mattresses upon which they had slept and offered them to him for sale at his own price. He recognized his own property, but, rather than abash the young men by reclaiming it, he excused their peculiar conduct in his mind on the plea that they certainly must need the money for a benevolent object. When the joke was explained to him, he refused to take back the amount paid, on the ground that, in his heart, he had dedicated it to a charitable purpose. Of Abba the legend is told (Talmud, *l.c.*) that he daily received greetings from heaven, whereas Abaye, 280–339, the greatest Talmudic authority of that age, was deemed worthy of divine notice once a week only.

L. G.

ABBA (BA) BAR ZABDAI: A Palestinian amora, who flourished in the third century. He studied in Babylonia, attending the lectures of Rab and Huna, and subsequently settled at Tiberias, where he occupied a respected position by the side of Ammi and Assi. Mention is made of his custom of saying his prayers in a loud voice (Yer. Ber iv. 7*a*). Of his haggadic productions there exists, among others, a sermon for a public fast-day, on Lam. iii. 41 (Yer. Ta'anit, ii. 65*a*), from which the following may be quoted: "Is it, then, possible to 'lift up our heart with our hands'? This verse is intended to advise us 'to put pur heart—our bad inclinations—in our hands,' in order to remove them, and then to turn to God in heaven. As long as a man holds an unclean reptile in his hand, he may bathe in all the waters of creation, but he can not become clean: let him throw it away and he is purified."

BIBLIOGRAPHY: Bacher, *Ag. Pal. Amor.* iii. 533, 535; Frankel, *Mebo*, pp. 66a, 67.

W. B.

ABBA BAR ZEBINA (or **ZEMINA**): A Palestinian amora of the fourth century. He was a pupil of R. Zeira, in whose name he transmitted many sayings. He was employed in Rome as a tailor in the house of a Gentile who, under the threat of death, tried to force him to break the dietary laws. Abba, however, steadfastly refused to yield to this, and showed so much courage that the Roman admiringly exclaimed: "If you had eaten, I should have killed you. If you be a Jew, be a Jew; if a heathen, a heathen!" (Yer. Sheb. iv. 35*a et seq.*).

Tanḥuma b. Abba relates another anecdote concerning a pious tailor at Rome (Gen. R. xi.), who bought the most expensive fish; this anecdote may refer to our Abba bar Zebina (but see Shab. 119*a*, where the same story is told of Joseph, "the reverer of the Sabbath").

BIBLIOGRAPHY: Bacher, *Ag. Pal. Amor.* iii. 651, 652; Frankel, *Mebo*, pp. 56*a*, 57.

W. B.

ABBAHU: A celebrated Palestinian amora of the third amoraic generation (about 279–320), sometimes cited as R. Abbahu of Cæsarea (Ḳisrin). His rabbinic education was acquired mainly at Tiberias, in the academy presided over by R. Johanan, with whom his relations were almost those of a son (Yer. Ber. ii. 4*b*; Giṭ. 44*b*; B. B. 39*a*). He frequently made pilgrimages to Tiberias, even after he had become well known as rector of the Cæsarean Academy (Yer. Shab. viii. 11*a*; Yer. Pes. x. 37*c*). He was an authority on weights and measures (Yer. Ter. v. 43*c*). He learned Greek in order to become useful to his people, then under the Roman proconsuls, that language having become, to a considerable extent, the rival of the Hebrew even in prayer (Yer. Soṭah, vii. 21*b*); and, in spite of the bitter protest of Simon b. Abba, he also taught his daughters Greek (Yer. Shab. vi. 7*d*; Yer. Soṭah, ix. 24*c*; Sanh. 14*a*). Indeed, it was said of Abbahu that he was a living illustration of the maxim (Eccl. vii. 18; compare Targum), "It is good that thou shouldest take hold of this [the study of the Law]; yea, also from that [other branches of knowledge] withdraw not thine hand: for he that feareth God shall come forth of them all" (Eccl. R. to vii. 18).

Being wise, handsome, and wealthy (B. I. 84*a*; Yer. B. M. iv. 9*d*), Abbahu became not only popular with his coreligionists, but also influential with the proconsular government (Ḥag. 14*a*; Ket. 17*a*). On one occasion, when his senior colleagues, Ḥiyya b. Abba, Ammi, and Assi, had punished a certain woman, and feared the wrath of the proconsul, Abbahu was deputed to intercede for them. He had, however, anticipated the rabbis' request, and wrote them that he had appeased the informers but not the accuser. The witty enigmatic letter describing this incident, preserved in the Talmud (Yer. Meg. iii. 74*a*), is in the main pure Hebrew, and even includes Hebrew translations of Greek proper names, to avoid the danger of possible exposure should the letter have fallen into the hands of enemies and informers (compare 'Er. 53*b*). After his ordination he declined a teacher's position, recommending in his stead a more needy friend, R. Abba of Acre (Acco), as worthier than himself (Soṭah, 40*a*). He thereby illustrated his own doctrine that it is a divine virtue to sympathize with a friend in his troubles as well as to partake of his joys (Tan., Wa-yesheb, ed. Buber, 16). Later he assumed the office of rector in Cæsarea, the former seat of R. Hoshaya I., and established himself at the so-called Kenishta Maradta (Insurrectionary Synagogue; Yer. Naz. vii. 56*a*; Yer. Sanh. i. 18*a*; compare Josephus, "B. J." ii. 14, § 5; Jastrow, "Dict." p. 838), whence some of the most prominent teachers of the next generation issued. He did not, however, confine his activity to Cæsarea, where he originated several ritualistic rules (Yer. Dem. ii. 23*a*, R. H. 34*a*), one of which—that regulating the sounding of the *shofar*—has since been universally adopted, and is referred to by medieval Jewish casuists as "Takkanat R. Abbahu" (the Enactment of R. Abbahu; compare "Maḥzor Vitry," Berlin, 1893, p. 355). He also visited and taught in many other Jewish towns (Yer. Ber. viii. 12*a*; Yer. Shab. iii. 5*c*).

While on these journeys, Abbahu gathered so many Halakot that scholars turned to him for information on mooted questions (Yer. Shab. viii. 11a; Yer. Yeb. i. 2*d*). In the course of these travels he made a point of complying with all local enactments, even where such compliance laid him open to the charge of inconsistency (Yer. Ber. viii. 12*a*; Yer. Beẓah, i. 60*d*). On the other hand, where circumstances required it, he did not spare even the princes of his people (Yer. 'Ab. Zarah, i. 39*b*). Where, however, the rigorous exposition of laws worked hardship on the masses, he did not scruple to modify the decisions of his colleagues for the benefit of the community (Shab. 134*b*; Yer Shab. xvii. 16*b*; Yer. M. Ḳ. i. 80*b*). As for himself, he was very strict in the observance of the laws. On one occasion he ordered some Samaritan wine, but subsequently learning that there were no longer any strict observers of the dietary laws among the Samaritans, with the assistance of his colleagues, Ḥiyya b. Abba, Ammi, and Assi, he investigated the report, and, ascertaining it to be well founded, did not hesitate to declare the Samaritans, for all ritualistic purposes, Gentiles (Yer. 'Ab. Zarah, v. 44*d*; Ḥul. 6*a*).

R. Abbahu's chief characteristic seems to have been modesty. While lecturing in different towns, he met R. Ḥiyya b. Abba, who was lecturing on intricate halakic themes. As Abbahu delivered popular sermons, the masses naturally crowded to hear him, and deserted the halakist. At this apparent slight, R. Ḥiyya manifested chagrin, and R. Abbahu hastened to comfort him by comparing himself to the pedler of glittering fineries that always attracted the eyes of the masses, while his rival was a trader in precious stones, the virtues and values of which were appreciated only by the connoisseur. This speech not having the desired effect, R. Abbahu showed special respect for his slighted colleague by following him for the remainder of that day. "What," said Abbahu, "is my modesty as compared with that of R. Abba of Acre (Acco), who does not even remonstrate with his interpreter for interpolating his own comments in the lecturer's expositions." When his wife reported to him that his interpreter's wife had boasted of her own husband's greatness, R. Abbahu simply said, "What difference does it make which of us is really the greater, so long as through both of us heaven is glorified?" (Soṭah, 40*a*). His principle of life he expressed in the maxim, "Let man ever be of the persecuted, and not of the persecutors; for there are none among the birds more persecuted than turtle-doves and pigeons, and the Scriptures declare them worthy of the altar" (B. Ḳ. 93*a*).

R. Abbahu, though eminent as a halakist, was more distinguished as a haggadist and controversialist. He had many interesting disputes with the Christians of his day (Shab. 152*b*; Sanh. 39*a*; 'Ab. Zarah, 4*a*). Sometimes these disputes were of a jocular nature. Thus, a heretic bearing the name of Sason (= Joy) once remarked to him, "In the next world your people will have to draw water for me; for thus it is written in the Bible (Isa. xii. 3), 'With joy shall ye draw water.'" To this R. Abbahu replied, "Had the Bible said 'for joy' [*le-sason*], it would mean as thou sayest; but since it says 'with joy' [*be-sason*], it means that we shall make bottles of thy hide and fill them with water" (Suk. 48*b*). These controversies, though forced on him, provoked resentment; and it is even related that his physician, Jacob the Schismatic (*Minaah*), was slowly poisoning him, but R. Ammi and R. Assi discovered the crime in time ('Ab Zarah, 28*a*).

Abbahu had two sons, Zeira and Ḥanina. Some writers ascribe to him a third son, Abimi (Bacher, "Ag. Pal. Amor."). Abbahu sent Ḥanina to the academy at Tiberias, where he himself had studied; but the lad occupied himself with the burial of the dead, and on hearing of this, the father sent him a reproachful message in this laconic style: "Is it because there are no graves in Cæsarea (compare Ex. xiv. 11) that I have sent thee off to Tiberias? Study must precede practise" (Yer. Pes. iii. 30*b*). Abbahu left behind him a number of disciples, the most prominent among whom were the leaders of the fourth amoraic generation, R. Jonah and R. Jose. At Abbahu's death the mourning was so great that it was said, "Even the statues of Cæsarea shed tears" (M. Ḳ. 25*b*; Yer. 'Ab. Zarah, iii. 42*c*).

There are several other Abbahus mentioned in the Talmudim and Midrashim, prominent among whom is Abbahu (Abuha, Aibut) b. Ihi (Ittai), a Babylonian halakist, contemporary of Samuel and Anan ('Er. 74*a*), and brother of Minyamin (Benjamin) b. Ihi. While this Abbahu repeatedly applied to Samuel for information, Samuel in return learned many Halakot from him (Naz. 24*b*; B. M. 14*a*, 75*a*).

BIBLIOGRAPHY: Grätz, *Gesch. d. Juden*, 2d ed., iv., 304, 307–317; Jost, *Gesch. des Judenthums und seiner Sekten*, ii. 161–164; Frankel, *Mebo*, pp. 58*a*–60; Weiss, *Dor*, iii. 103–105; Bacher, *Ag. Pal. Amor.* ii. 88–142.

S. M.

["When does your Messiah come?" a Christian (Minaah) once asked Abbahu in a tone of mockery; whereupon he replied: "When you will be wrapped in darkness, for it says, 'Behold, darkness shall cover the earth, and gross darkness the nations; then shall the Lord rise upon thee and His glory shall be seen on thee' [Isa. lx. 2]," (Sanh. 99*a*). A Christian came to Abbahu with the quibbling question: "How could your God in His priestly holiness bury Moses without providing for purificatory rites, yet oceans are declared insufficient?" (Isa. xl. 12). "Why," said Abbahu, "does it not say, 'The Lord cometh with fire'?" (Isa. lxvi. 15). "Fire is the true element of purification, according to Num. xxi. 23," was his answer (Sanh. 39*a*). Another question of the same character: "Why the boastful claim: 'What nation on earth is like Thy people Israel' (II Sam. vii. 23), since we read, 'All the nations are as nothing before Him'?" (Isa. xl. 17), to which Abbahu replied: "Do we not read of Israel, he 'shall not be reckoned among the nations'?" (Num. xxiii. 9, Sanh. as above). Abbahu made a notable exception with reference to the Tosefta's statement that the Gilionim (Evangels) and other books of the Mineans are not to be saved from a conflagration on Sabbath: "the books of those at Abidan may be saved" (Shab. 116*a*). Of special historical interest is the observation of Abbahu in regard to the benediction "Baruk Shem Kebod Malkuto" (Blessed be the Name of His glorious Kingdom) after the "Shema' Yisrael," that in Palestine, where the Christians look for points of controversy, the words should be recited aloud (lest the Jews be accused of tampering with the unity of God proclaimed in the Shema'), whereas in the Babylonian city of Nehardea, where there are no Christians, the words are recited with a low voice (Pes. 56*a*). Preaching directly against the Christian dogma, Abbahu says: "A king of flesh and blood may have a father, a brother, or a son to share in or dispute his sovereignty, but the Lord saith, 'I am the Lord thy God! I am the first; that is, I have no father, and I am the last; that is, I have no brother, and besides me there is no God; that is, I have no son'" (Isa. xliv. 6; Ex. R. 29). His comment on Num. xxiii. 19 has a still more polemical tone: "God is not a man that he should lie; neither the son of man, that he should repent. If a man say, 'I am God,' he lieth, and if he say, 'I am the son of man,' he will have to repent, and if he say, 'I shall go up to heaven,' he will not do it, nor achieve what he promises" (Yer. Ta'anit, ii. 65*b*).

Some of his controversies on Christian theological subjects, as on Adam (Yalḳ., Gen. 47), on Enoch (Gen. R. 25), and on the resurrection (Shab. 152*b*), are less clear and direct (see Bacher, "Ag. Pal. Amor." ii. 97, 115–118). K.]

ABBAYE: An amora. See ABAYE.

ABDAN or **ABIDAN** (contraction of **ABBA YUDAN**): A Palestinian scholar of the first amoraic generation, who lived about the beginning of the third century. As a disciple and clerk (amora) of Rabbi (Judah I.) he seems at times to have been too officious in his bearing toward the members of the rabbinical college. Thus, when R. Ishmael ben Yose, who was very corpulent, seemed to be forcing his way into the college in a manner contrary to the college rules, Abdan exclaimed, "Who is he that strides over the heads of the holy people?" When the innocent man replied, "It is I, Ishmael ben Yose, who am come to learn the Law from Rabbi," Abdan retorted, "Art thou worthy to learn from Rabbi?" Piqued by this insolence, Ishmael asked, "Was Moses worthy to learn from the Almighty?" Thereupon Abdan inquired, "And art thou Moses?" To which Ishmael made the reply, "And is thy master the Almighty?"

On that very occasion, however, after Rabbi had entered the college hall, an opportunity presented itself for Ishmael to prove himself an expert in halakic knowledge, while Abdan, who, coming back from an errand, attempted to force his way through the assembled crowd, was ordered by Rabbi to remain at the door. Legend adds that Abdan was severely punished for his arrogance. He himself was visited with an attack of eczema, and two of his sons were drowned. His memory, however, was revered as that of a good man, for R. Naḥman b. Isaac, in referring to this legend, thanked God for abasing Abdan in this world and not reserving his punishment for the world to come.

BIBLIOGRAPHY: *Yeb.* 105*b*; *Yer. Ber.* iv. 7, v. 8*d*; *Bab. ibid.* 27*b*; *Niddah*, 66*a*; *Gen. R.* x. 8.

S. M.

ABDIMA (called also **Abdimi, Abudma, Abudmi**, all equivalent to **Ebdimus** = **Eudemus**—compare Jastrow, "Dict." p. 3; and in the Babylonian Talmud frequently contracted to **Dimi**): Name of several Palestinian amoraim, known also in Babylonia. One of them is mentioned in the Palestinian Talmud simply as R. Abdimi or R. Abudmi, without any cognomen. He flourished in the fourth century, contemporaneously with R. Jose II., who survived him, and with R. Eliezer II. See Yer. Er. x. 26*a*; Yer. B. B. ix. 16*d*; doubtful, Yer. Ket. xi. 34*b*.

The Palestinian Talmud and the midrashic literature mention several more amoraim by the name of Abdima or one of its variants, some of whom will be found under DIMI.

S. M.

Abdima (Dimi) of Ḥaifa: A Palestinian amora of the third generation (third and fourth centuries). He was a recognized authority in halakic matters, prominent contemporaries as well as successors citing his views in support of their own; nor was he less distinguished in the field of the Haggadah. According to him, this rule of etiquette should be observed: When a scholar (*ḥakam*) passes to take his seat at college, one should rise in his honor within a distance of four cubits, and remain standing till he has passed to a like distance. In honor of a vice-president of the Sanhedrin (*ab bet din*), one should rise as soon as one perceives him coming, and remain standing until he has passed to a distance of four cubits; but when the president of the Sanhedrin (*nasi*) passes, one should rise as soon as one observes him approaching, and remain standing long enough for him to reach his place and be seated; for thus the Bible (Ex. xxxiii. 8) says, "All the people stood up . . . and looked after Moses, until he was gone into the tent" (Ḳid. 33*b*). Commenting on Eccl. xii. 7, "And the spirit shall return to God who gave it," the famous haggadist, R. Samuel b. Naḥman, remarks that R. Abdima of Ḥaifa thus illustrates this passage: "A priest who belonged to the order known as Ḥaberim [see ḤABER], the members of which were very strict in all observances of Levitical cleanliness, entrusted a sacred loaf of *terumah* to one less strict ('Am ha-Areẓ), saying, 'Behold, I am clean, and my house is clean, and my utensils are clean, and this loaf is clean: if thou wilt return it to me in the condition in which I hand it to thee, well and good; if not, I shall burn it in thy presence.' Thus says the Holy One—blessed be He!—to man, 'Behold, I am pure, and My mansion is pure, and My ministers are pure, and the soul which I give into thy keeping is pure: if thou wilt return it to Me as I give it to thee, it shall be well; otherwise, I shall burn it in thy presence'" (Eccl. R. *ad loc.*). One of Abdima's aphorisms is: "With the destruction of the First Temple the gift of prophecy was taken from the prophets and bestowed upon the learned" (B. B. 12*a*). Another: "Before man eats and drinks he has two hearts; after he eats and drinks he has but one" (B. B. 12*b*; Yalḳ., Job, § 906).

BIBLIOGRAPHY: *Yer. Meg.* iii. 74*b*; *Bab. Meg.* 29*b*; *Yer. M. Ḳ.* iii. 82*c*; *Yer. Niddah,* ii. 50*a*; *Lam. R.* to i. 1; *Midr. Teh.* to Ps. xxxi. 6, and lxviii. 10; *Yalḳ. Teh.* 717; Bacher, *Ag. Pal. Amor.* iii. 536–538.

S. M.

Abdima (Dimi) bar Hamar (sometimes with the addition **b. Ḥasa**): A Palestinian who immigrated into Babylonia; senior contemporary of Raba and Joseph, of the fourth century. His name is connected with but a small number of Halakot, and only few of his Haggadot are preserved. Commenting on the words of Moses (Deut. xxx. 11–13), "This commandment is not in the heaven. . . Neither is it beyond the sea," he observes: "And were it even so: were the Law in heaven, it would be man's duty to ascend to obtain it; were it beyond the seas, he would be obliged to cross them in quest of it" ('Er. 55*a*). In using Biblical texts for homiletic purposes he follows the usual method of straining the text, or playing upon similarities of expression or even of sound; for example, the Biblical statement (Ex. xix. 17), "They stood at the base (*betaḥtit*) of the mount," he construes as implying that "the Holy One—blessed be He!—had bent the mountain over the Israelites, saying to them, 'If you accept the Law it will be well; otherwise here will be your grave'" (Shab. 88*a*; 'Ab. Zarah, 2*b*). Elsewhere he is reported as interpreting the term "Taanath" in the passage (Josh. xvi. 6), "And the border went about eastward unto Taanath-shiloh," as if it were related to *taaniyah* (sorrow) or to *anaḥ* (to sigh); and, therefore, he understands by Taanath-shiloh the spot at the sight of which man is reminded of the sacrificial rites once practised in Shiloh, and sighs at their discontinuance (Zeb. 118*a et seq.*; compare "Diḳduḳe Soferim," *l.c.*, and Yalḳ., Deut. § 881). In Yer. Meg. i. 72*d* a different interpretation of the same text, but also taking Taanath in the sense of sorrow, is reported in the name of R. Abdima of Sepphoris.

S. M.

Abdima b. Hamdure or **Hamdude**: An amora of the third century. He is probably identical with (Mar) Bar Hamdure, the disciple of Samuel (Shab. 107*b*; compare "Diḳduḳe Soferim," *ad loc.* 125*a*; Yoma, 87*b*; Suk. 20*a*; Men. 38*b*).

S. M.

Abdima Naḥota: A Palestinian amora of the fourth century; contemporary of the Babylonian amoraim Rab Ḥisda and Rab Joseph. He was senior to R. Assi II., who delivered halakic decisions in his name. Like

Abin III., he was wont to travel and to disseminate traditions among the academies of his native country and of Babylonia; hence his surname Naḥota, which means one who is wont to go down to Babylonia. See DIMI.

BIBLIOGRAPHY: *Yer. Shab.* viii. 11*b*; *Yer. ʻEr.* i. 19*b*; *Yer. Ḳid.* i. 60*d*; *Yer. B. B.* iii. 13*d*.

S. M.

Abdima (Abdimi) of Sepphoris: A Palestinian amora of the fifth century; disciple of R. Mana III. and of R. Huna II. He was a distinguished scholar in his age, as is evident from his father being quoted as Immi, the father of Abdima of Sepphoris (Yer. Beẓah, i. 60*d*).

BIBLIOGRAPHY: *Yer. Ber.* iv. 8*a*; *Yer. Ta'anit,* ii. 65*c*; *Yer. Ket.* i. 25*b*; *Yer. Niddah,* ii. 50*b*.

S. M.

Abdimi Mallaḥa ("The Sailmaker"): A contemporary of R. Ḥiyya b. Abba and Jacob b. Aḥa, who was one of the numerous class of scholars engaged in handicraft (Yer. B. M. iv. 9*d*; Yer. Suk. ii. 53*a*).

S. M.

Abdimus ben R. Jose: One of the variants of the popular name of R. Menahem ben R. Jose. The other forms are Abirodimus, Avradimus, Vradimas, and Vradimus. For the etymology of the name see Jastrow, "Dict." i. 375.

BIBLIOGRAPHY: *Yer. Yeb.* i. 2*b*; *Yer. Sheb.* viii. 38*b*; *Sifra, Emor,* 10, 13; *Shab.* 118*b*; *Ned.* 81*a*.

S. M.

ABIMI B. ABBAHU: A scholar of the third century. Abimi's native country and parentage are doubtful. He is always cited as Abimi, the son of R. Abbahu; he was as fond of quoting Baraitot as was R. Abbahu of Cæsarea of collecting them; and once he applied to a R. Abbahu for legal advice (Ket. 85*a*). These circumstances point to Palestine as his native country and to R. Abbahu of Cæsarea as his father; hence Bacher ("Ag. Pal. Amor." ii. 101) so describes him. On the other hand, it is a remarkable fact that his name does not appear in the Palestinian Talmud, and that even where the latter quotes Abbahu as illustrating filial piety, the filial piety of Abimi, praised by his father in the Babylonian Talmud, is not mentioned. Moreover, Abimi never refers to Abbahu, and settles debts in Babylonia through Ḥama b. Rabbah b. Abuha (Ket. *l.c.*). who never was in Palestine. Frankel (Mebo, p. 60*a*), holding the two names Abbahu and Abuha to be identical, believes Abimi to have been a Babylonian, and a brother of Rabbah b. Abuha. Abimi is often mentioned as reporting Baraitot. One of these, treating of the honor due to parents, says "One man feeds his father on pheasants and yet tires him of this world; while another yokes his father to the treadmill and yet prepares him for the enjoyments of the world to come" (Ḳid. 31*a*). Elsewhere this paradox is thus explained: The first case is that of one who was in the habit of furnishing his father with stuffed birds, and who, when the father once inquired, "Son, whence dost thou get all this?" replied, "Old man, eat and be silent as dogs do." The second is the case of one who was engaged in turning a millstone when his father was drafted to do public service. The son exchanged places with his father, remarking that he was more able to bear the abuses incident to such service than was his aged father (Yer. Peah, i. 15*c;* Yer. Ḳid. i. 61*c*.; compare Rashi to Babli Ḳid. *l.c.*). Abimi himself was cited by his own father as an example of filial piety. Though blessed with five learned sons, all of whom had been found worthy of ordination, he would not permit them to take his place in waiting on their grandfather. Once his father called for water to drink. Abimi hastened to bring it, and, finding his father asleep, remained reverently standing over him until he awoke. It is said that Abimi then and there conceived an ingenious explanation of the Seventy-ninth Psalm (see Lam. R. on iv. 11; Midr. Teh. *l.c.*). According to another Baraita cited by Abimi, the Messianic epoch of Israel will extend over a period of seven thousand years: for the Scripture says (Isa. lxii. 5), "As the bridegroom rejoiceth over the bride, so shall thy God rejoice over thee"; and as the bridal feast lasts seven days, and the Lord's day is equal to a thousand of man's years, it follows that the bridal feast between the Lord and Israel is to continue for seven thousand years (Sanh. 99*a*, Rashi *ad loc.*; see Shab. 119*b*; Ket. 85*a*; Shebu. 42*a*; 'Ab. Zarah, 34*b*; Ḥul. 63*b*).

S. M.

ABIMI OF HAGRONIA (possibly Agranum; see Neubauer, "Géographie du Talmud," p. 347): A Babylonian amora of the fourth century, disciple of Raba b. Joseph and teacher of Rab Mordecai, the colleague of Rab Ashi. One of his aphorisms reads: "For the man whom women have slain there is no law and no judge" (B. M. 97*a*); that is, where a man suffers injury through his own weakness, he can not invoke the protection of the law (see Yeb. 64*b*; B. M. 77*b*; B. B. 174*b*; Mak. 13*b*).

S. M.

ABIN R. (called also **Abun**, **Abuna**, **Bun**, **Rabin**, variant forms of the same name of Talmudic authorities and used promiscuously): Rabin is a contraction of R. Abin, and appears more frequently in the Babylonian than in the Palestinian Talmud. R. Abin and R. Abun, on the contrary, occur in the latter more frequently than in the former; while the abbreviated form, Bun, is peculiar to the Palestinian Talmud. Among the twoscore or more of amoraim cited in rabbinic literature by one or the other form of the name, the most prominent are the following:

1. A teacher of the second amoraic generation, some of whose halakic deliverances are preserved in the Palestinian Talmud through R. Eleazar ben Pedat (Yer. Ta'anit, i. 64*c et passim*). He is probably identical with Rabin Saba (R. Abin the Elder) of the Babylonian Talmud, who sat at the feet of Rab, and with the one who is said to have died about the time his son of like name was born (compare 3 below).

2. A Palestinian amora, junior contemporary of the preceding (Yer. Sheḳ. iv. 48*c*). He is mentioned, together with R. Measha and R. Jeremiah, as carrying on a halakic controversy with R. Abbahu II., R. Ḥanina ben Papa, and R. Isaac Nappaḥa (the Smith). R. Abbahu calls all of the opposition "youngsters"; he nevertheless manifests special regard for the intelligence of R. Abin, to whose approval he refers with satisfaction (B. B. 142*b*). The same compliment is paid to R. Abin by R. Zeira (Niddah, 42*a*).

3. An amora of the fourth and fifth generations, very frequently mentioned in both Talmuds and in contemporary rabbinic literature. Born in Palestine, where he was educated under R. Jeremiah (Shab. 63*b et passim*), Babylonian academies could nevertheless claim him as their disciple; for he frequently traveled between the two countries, from each of which he conveyed halakic decisions and exegetical remarks of his predecessors and contemporaries. Occasionally he transmitted to Babylon by letter Palestinian decisions (Ket. 49*b*; Niddah, 68*a*); but generally he delivered them orally, for he considered it one of the great distinctions of the Jewish nation that most of its laws were unwritten (Yer. Peah, ii. 17*a*). But, whether written or oral, his communications were treated with great respect, the most prominent Babylonian teachers of the fourth generation, Abaye and Raba, placing more reliance upon them than upon those of other learned rivals. R. Abin knew neither of his parents; his father having died shortly before, and his mother soon after his birth (Yer. Peah, i. 15*c*; compare Gen. R. lviii.). As his children died at an early age (Pes, 70*b*; Ḥul. 110*a*), there were no natural ties to bind him to his native country; and when, in the reign of Constantius, persecutions of the Jews occurred in Palestine, R. Abin, with a considerable number of scholars, deserted his native land and settled in Babylonia (Ḥul. 101*b*; compare Graetz, "History of the Jews," ii. 567). In his old age, however, he returned to Palestine, where he died, and where R. Mana ordered general mourning for his death (Yer. M. Ḳ. iii. 83*b*, top).

The following may serve as specimens of Abin's homiletic observations:

Referring to Ps. xv. 4, "He that sweareth to his own hurt, and changeth not," R. Abin says: "That is, he who reduces his purse to the extent of self-deprivation, in order to do a good deed" (Midr. Teh. *ad loc.*).

"Great is the power of the benevolent: they need not seek protection under the shadow of the wings of the earth or of any heavenly beings; but can take refuge under the shadow of the Holy One, blessed be He! Thus it is written (Ps. xxvi. 7), 'How excellent is Thy loving kindness, O God! therefore the children of men [practising it] take refuge under the shadow of Thy wings'" (Pesiḳ. xvi. 124*a*; compare Ruth R. to ii. 12).

BIBLIOGRAPHY: Bacher, *Ag. Pal. Amor.* iii. 397–403, where fuller details are given.

S. M.

ABIN or **ABUN:** An eminent cabalist of Le Mans (about 1040), a descendant of R. Simon of Le Mans, and grandfather of R. Simon the Great, the contemporary of R. Gershom ben Judah of Metz.

BIBLIOGRAPHY: Michael, *Or ha-Ḥayyim*, No. 25 and note; Zunz, *Z. G.* p. 565, reads *Abun*, as does also Gross, *Gallia Judaica*, p. 363.

K.

ABIN BEN ADDA: A Babylonian amora of the fourth century, disciple of Rab Judah ben Ezekiel and senior contemporary of Raba ben Joseph. Although no original thinker, he served the cause of both the Halakah and the Haggadah, by storing up in his mind and transmitting decisions and observations of his eminent predecessors, particularly those of R. Isaac. Among these is the following:

"Whence do we learn that the Holy One—blessed be He!—is with those assembled in synagogues? It is said (Ps. lxxxii. 1), 'God standeth in the congregation of God' [A.V. "the mighty"]. And whence do we learn that, when ten persons are engaged in prayer, the Divine Presence [Shekinah] is with them? It is said, 'God standeth in the congregation of God' [*edah* signifying in rabbinic lore an assembly of ten persons]. And whence do we learn that the Divine Presence is with three persons sitting in judgment? It is said (Ps. *l.c.*), 'He judgeth among the judges' [A.V. "gods"]. And whence do we know that, when only two persons are engaged in the study of the Torah, the Divine Presence is with them? It is said (Mal. iii. 16), 'Then they that feared the Lord spake often one to another; and the Lord hearkened and heard it.' And whence do we learn that, even when a single individual occupies himself with the study of the Torah, the Divine Presence is with him? It is said (Ex. xx. 24), 'Wherever I cause my name to be remembered, there will I come to thee and bless thee'" (Ber. 6*a*).

S. M.

ABIN B. RAB ḤISDA (Ḥasdi): A Palestinian amora, a disciple of R. Johanan (Giṭ. 5*b*). In addition to some halakic opinions, a few exegetical remarks by him are preserved in the midrashic literature, from which it appears that he was a linguist and tried to define the meaning of Hebrew Biblical words by reference to cognate languages (Tan. Ki Tissa, ed. Buber; Pesiḳ. R. x.; Cant. R. to vii. 3 and 9).

S. M.

ABIN B. ḤIYYA: A Palestinian amora of the fourth generation, and a colleague of R. Jeremiah. His teachers, R. Zeira I. and R. Hila, were among the greatest authorities of the third generation, and his younger contemporaries recognized him as an authority in halakic matters. After a short life of diligent study and earnest teaching he died, mourned by his contemporaries; and R. Zeira II. thus applied to him and illustrated the Scriptural passage (Eccl. v. 12):

"The sleep of a laboring man is sweet, whether he eat little or much." "A king had hired many laborers, among whom there was one who accomplished more than was expected of him. The king, noticing this, often invited the man to accompany him on his leisurely walks. When the time came to pay the laborers, this one received as much as any of the rest; and when the laborers complained of partiality, the king replied, 'This man has accomplished in a couple of hours more than you have in a whole day.' So, R. Bun accomplished in the eight and twenty years which he devoted to the study of the Law what no other distinguished scholar could accomplish in a century" (Eccl. R. to v. 11).

S. M.

ABIN B. KAHANA: A Palestinian amora, one of the teachers of R. Abun ben Ḥiyya (Tem. 20*b*), and junior colleague of R. Hoshaya II. (Yer. Ter. viii. 45*c*). R. Jonah, of the fourth amoraic generation, transmits a halakic discussion in his name (Yer. Hor. ii. 46*d*).

S. M.

ABIN B. NAḤMAN: A beloved disciple of R. Judah ben Ezekiel (B. M. 107*a*). He is mentioned as a transmitter of Baraitot (Yeb. 84*b*; B. B. 94*b*).

S. M.

ABINA (called also **Abuna** or **Buna**): An amora of the third and fourth centuries, always cited without any cognomen. He was a Babylonian by birth, a disciple of Rab Huna I., and befriended by Geniba (Giṭ. 65*b*; Yer. Giṭ. vi. 48*a*), in whose name he reports a Halakah (Ḥul. 50*b*). Most of his knowledge, however, he seems to have acquired from R. Jeremiah b. Abba, who is likewise often cited in the Palestinian Talmud without patronymic (compare Shab. 12*b*; Yer. Shab. i. 3*b*); for it is in R. Jeremiah's name that he most frequently transmits decisions (Shab. 137*b*; Yer. Shab. xix. 17*b*). In Babylonia he had halakic controversies with Rab Ḥisda and Rab Sheshet (Ket. 24*b*, 43*a*); but in his later years he migrated to Palestine, where R. Zeira I. (Zera) and R. Jacob b. Aḥa became his friends. They and other amoraim of the third generation frequently reported Halakot they had learned from him

(Yer. Pes. v. 32*c*; Yer. 'Er, iv. 21*d*; Yer. Yeb. iii. 4*c*; Yer. Ket. xiii. 36*a*; Yer. Shebu. vi. 37*a*). The rabbinic rule on the pronunciation of the Tetragrammaton (written YHWH and pronounced Adonai) he bases on the passage in Ex. iii. 15, "This is my name forever, and this is my memorial unto all generations," applying the first to the written form (*ketib*), and the second to the reading (*ḳeri*) (Pes. 50*a*, Ḳid. 71*a*). A heretic once remarked to R. Abina (a variant reading attributes it to Abbahu): "It is written (II Sam. vii. 23), 'What one nation is like thy people, even like Israel,' an only nation on earth? Wherein consists your distinction? Ye also are included among us; for the Bible says (Isa. xl. 17), 'All nations before him are as nothing.'" To this R. Abina replied: "By one of your own people it has been established concerning us, as it is written (Num. xxiii. 9), 'He [Israel] shall not be reckoned among the nations'" (Sanh. 39*a*). The assumption that there were two scholars of the name of Abina unaccompanied by a cognomen has resulted from confounding R. Jeremiah b. Abba, when cited without his patronymic, with a later amora.

A R. Abuna Zeira (the younger) is mentioned in connection with his enforced violation of the Sabbath as a consequence of religious persecutions (Yer. Sheb. iv. 35*a*), but nothing more is known of him.

BIBLIOGRAPHY: Bacher, *Ag. Pal. Amor.* iii. 539, 540.

S. M.

ABLAT: A Gentile sage and astrologer in Babylonia. The close friendship which existed between him and Mar Samuel (died 254) shows that the legal restrictions of their religion did not prevent the Babylonian Jews from social communication with their heathen neighbors. An anecdote given in 'Ab. Zarah (30*a*) illustrates the kind consideration and courtesy which prevailed on both sides. Ablat was a guest in the house of Mar Samuel on an occasion when wine was usually served. The rabbinic law forbids Jews to use wine that has come in contact with idolaters. Knowing this, Ablat declined to take his wine before Mar Samuel, whom he called "the wisest of the Jews." But Mar Samuel, anticipating this very difficulty, had met it by ordering mulled wine, which was not under the ban; and he thus overcame a restriction that practically prevented his friend from partaking of his hospitality (Shab. 129*a*).

Ablat enjoyed great popularity among the Jews, as is shown by the fact that the Jerusalem Talmud (Shab. iii. 6*a*) cites a question respecting a rabbinical precept put by him to a Jewish scholar and the latter's answer.

L. G.

ABTALION, POLLION, or **PTOLLION:** A leader of the Pharisees in the middle of the first century B.C. and by tradition vice-president of the great Sanhedrin of Jerusalem. He was of heathen descent (Bab. Yoma, 71*b*; 'Eduy. v. 6; Giṭ. 57*b*; Yer. M. Ḳ. iii. 81*b*; see Weiss, "Dor Dor we-Dorshaw," i. 1, and Landau, p. 319). Despite this fact, Abtalion, as well as his colleague, Shemaiah, the president of the Sanhedrin, was one of the most influential and beloved men of his time. Once, when the high priest was being escorted home from the Temple by the people, at the close of a Day of Atonement, the Talmud (Yoma, 71*b*) relates that the crowd deserted him upon the approach of Abtalion and his colleague and followed them. Abtalion used his influence with the people in persuading the men of Jerusalem, in the year 37 B.C., to open the gates of their city to Herod. The king was not ungrateful and rewarded Abtalion, or, as Josephus calls him, "Pollion," with great honors (Josephus, "Ant." xv. 1, § 1). Although there is no doubt that, in this passage of Josephus, Abtalion is meant by this name Pollion (the original form of the name is presumably "Ptollion," which explains both the prefixed *A* in the Talmud and the omission of the *t* in Josephus), in another place ("Ant." xv. 10, § 4), where this name recurs, it is doubtful whether Abtalion is intended or not. Josephus relates there how Herod exacted the oath of allegiance under penalty of death, and continues: "He desired also to compel Pollion, the Pharisee, and Sameas, together with the many who followed them, to take this oath; they, however, refused to do this, but nevertheless were not punished as were others who had refused to take it, and this indeed out of consideration for Pollion." Since this episode took place in the eighteenth year of Herod's reign (20 or 19 B.C.), this Pollion can not have been Abtalion, who died long before, as we learn from authoritative Talmudic sources, according to which Hillel, the pupil and successor of Abtalion, was the leader of the Pharisees about 30 B.C. It is probable, therefore, that Josephus was misled by the similarity of the names Shemaiah and Shammai, and so wrote "Pollion and Sameas" instead of "Hillel and Shammai."

Very little is known concerning the life of Abtalion. He was a pupil of Judah ben Ṭabbai and Simon ben Sheṭaḥ, and probably lived for some time in Alexandria, Egypt, where he and also his teacher Judah took refuge when Alexander Jannæus cruelly persecuted the Pharisees. This gives pertinence to his well-known maxim (Ab. i. 12), "Ye wise men, be careful of your words, lest ye draw upon yourselves the punishment of exile and be banished to a place of bad water (dangerous doctrine), and your disciples, who come after you, drink thereof and die, and the name of the Holy One thereby be profaned." He cautions the rabbis herein against participation in politics (compare the maxim of his colleague) as well as against emigration to Egypt, where Greek ideas threatened danger to Judaism. Abtalion and his colleague Shemaiah are the first to bear the title *darshan* (Pes. 70*a*), and it was probably by no mere chance that their pupil Hillel was the first to lay down hermeneutic rules for the interpretation of the Midrash; he may have been indebted to his teachers for the tendency toward haggadic interpretation. These two scholars are the first whose sayings are recorded in the Haggadah (Mek., Beshallaḥ, iii. 36, ed. Weiss.). The new method of *derush* (Biblical interpretation) introduced by Abtalion and Shemaiah seems to have evoked opposition among the Pharisees (Pes. 70*b*. Compare also Josephus, *l.c.*, *Πολλίων ὁ Φαρισαῖος*, where a title is probably intended). Abtalion and Shemaiah are also the first whose Ḥalakot (legal decisions) are handed down to later times. Among them is the important one that the paschal lamb must be offered even if Passover fall on a Sabbath (Pes. 66*a*). Abtalion's academy was not free to every one, but those who sought entrance paid daily a small admission fee of one and a half tropaika; that is, about twelve cents (Yoma, 35*b*). This was no doubt to prevent overcrowding by the people, or for some reasons stated by the Shammaites (Ab. R. N. iii. [iv.] 1).

BIBLIOGRAPHY: *Monatsschrift*, i. 118–120; Grätz, *Gesch. d. Juden*, 2d ed., iii. 187 *et seq.*, 617–618; Landau, in *Monatsschrift*, vii 317–329; Herzfeld, *ibid.* iii. 227; idem, *Gesch. d. Volkes* Israel, ii. 253; Derenbourg, *Essai*, pp. 116, 117, 149, 463; Weiss, *Dor*, i. 148 *et seq.*, 152, 153; Brüll, *Mebo*, pp. 25–27; Hamburger, *R. B. T.* ii., s.v. *Semaya*, Lehman, in *Rev. Ét. Juives*, xxiv. 68–81.

L. G.

ABUN BEN SAUL: An elegist who was probably a pupil of Isaac Alfasi and, most likely, is the one whose death Moses ibn Ezra deplores in a poem. Two of his elegies are found in the Maḥzor of Avignon.

BIBLIOGRAPHY: Zunz, *Literaturgesch.* p. 343; Luzzatto, in *Kerem Ḥemed*, iv. 31, 32, 85, 86.

M. B.

ACADEMIES IN BABYLONIA: The Jews of Babylonia, no doubt, shared in the changes and movements that Ezra and his successors, who came from Babylonia, introduced into Palestine. But for the four centuries covering the period from Ezra to Hillel there are no details; and the history of the succeeding two centuries, from Hillel to Judah I., furnishes only a few scanty items on the state of learning among the Babylonian Jews. Sherira Gaon, in his famous letter (the chief source of information on the Babylonian schools) referring to those dark centuries, wrote: "No doubt, here in Babylonia public instruction was given in the Torah; but besides the exilarchs there were no recognized heads of schools until the death of Rabbi [Judah I.]." The principal seat of Babylonian Judaism was NEHARDEA, where there certainly was some institution of learning. A very ancient synagogue, built, it was believed, by King Jehoiachin, existed in Nehardea. At Huẓal, near

Nehardea, there was another synagogue, not far from which could be seen the ruins of Ezra's academy. In the period before Hadrian, Akiba, on his arrival at Nehardea on a mission from the Sanhedrin, entered into a discussion with a resident scholar on a point of matrimonial law (Mishnah Yeb., end). At the same time there was at Nisibis, in northern Mesopotamia, an excellent Jewish college, at the head of which stood Judah ben Betera (Bathyra), and in which many Palestinian scholars found refuge at the time of the persecutions. A certain temporary importance was also attained by a school at Nehar-Peḳod, founded by the Palestinian immigrant Hananiah, nephew of Joshua ben Hananiah, which school might have been the cause of a schism between the Jews of Babylonia and those of Palestine, had not the Palestinian authorities promptly checked Hananiah's ambition.

Among those that helped to restore Palestinian learning, after Hadrian, was the Babylonian scholar Nathan, a member of the family of the exilarch, who continued his activity even under Judah I. Another Babylonian, Ḥiyya, belonged to the foremost leaders in the closing age of the Tannaim. His nephew, ABBA ARIKA, afterward called simply Rab, was one of the most important pupils of Judah I. Rab's return to his Babylonian home, the year of which has been accurately recorded (530 of the Seleucidan, or 219 of the common era), marks an epoch; for from it dates the beginning of a new movement in Babylonian Judaism—namely, the initiation of the dominant role which the Babylonian Academies played for several centuries. Leaving Nehardea to his friend Samuel, whose father, Abba, was already reckoned among the authorities of that town, Rab founded a new academy in Sura, where he held property. Thus, there existed in Babylonia two contemporary academies, so far removed from each other, however, as not to interfere with each other's operations. Since Rab and Samuel were acknowledged peers in position and learning, their academies likewise were accounted of equal rank and influence. Thus both Babylonian rabbinical schools opened their lectures brilliantly, and the ensuing discussions in their classes furnished the earliest stratum of the scholarly material deposited in the Babylonian Talmud. The coexistence for many decades of these two colleges of equal rank originated that remarkable phenomenon of the dual leadership of the Babylonian Academies which, with some slight interruptions, became a permanent institution and a weighty factor in the development of Babylonian Judaism.

When Odenathus destroyed Nehardea in 259—twelve years after Rab's death, and five years after that of Samuel—its place was taken by a neighboring town, PUMBEDITA, where Judah ben Ezekiel, a pupil of both Rab and Samuel, founded a new school. During the life of its founder, and still more under his successors, this school acquired a reputation for intellectual keenness and discrimination, which often degenerated into mere hair-splitting. Pumbedita became the other focus of the intellectual life of Babylonian Israel, and retained that position until the end of the gaonic period.

Nehardea once more came into prominence under Amemar, a contemporary of Ashi. The luster of Sura (also known by the name of its neighboring town, Mata Meḥasya) was enhanced by Rab's pupil and successor, Huna, under whom the attendance at the academy reached unusual numbers. When Huna died, in 297, Judah ben Ezekiel, principal of the Pumbedita Academy, was recognized also by the sages of Sura as their head. On the death of Judah, two years later, Sura became the only center of learning, with Ḥisda (died 309) as its head. Ḥisda had in Huna's lifetime rebuilt Rab's ruined academy in Sura, while Huna's college was in the vicinity of Mata Meḥasya (Sherira). On Ḥisda's death Sura lost its importance for a long time. In Pumbedita, Rabbah bar Naḥmani (died 331), Joseph (died 333), and Abaye (died 339) taught in succession. They were followed by Raba, who transplanted the college to his native town, Maḥuza. Under these masters the study of the Law attained a notable development, to which certain Palestinian scholars, driven from their own homes by the persecutions of Roman tyranny, contributed no inconsiderable share.

After Raba's death, in 352, Pumbedita regained its former position. The head of the academy was Naḥman bar Isaac (died 356), a pupil of Raba. In his method of teaching may be discerned the first traces of an attempt to edit the enormous mass of material that ultimately formed the Babylonian Talmud. Not Pumbedita, however, but Sura, was destined to be the birthplace of this work. After Raba's death, Papa, another of his pupils, founded a college in Naresh, near Sura, which, for the time being, interfered with the growth of the Sura school; but after Papa's death, in 375, the college at Sura regained its former supremacy. Its restorer was ashi, under whose guidance, during more than half a century (Ashi died 427), it attained great prominence, and presented such attractions that even the exilarchs came there, in the autumn of each year, to hold their customary official receptions. The school at Pumbedita recognized the preeminence of that of Sura; and this leadership was firmly retained for several centuries.

The unusual length of Ashi's activity, his undeniable high standing, his learning, as well as the favorable circumstances of the day, were all of potent influence in furthering the task he undertook; namely, that of sifting and collecting the material accumulated for two centuries by the Babylonian Academies. The final editing of the literary work which this labor produced did not, it is true, take place until somewhat later; but tradition rightly names Ashi as the originator of the Babylonian Talmud. Indeed, Ashi's editorial work received many later additions and amplifications; but the form underwent no material modification. The Babylonian Talmud must be considered the work of the Academy of Sura, because Ashi submitted to each of the semiannual general assemblies of the academy, treatise by treatise, the results of his examination and selection, and invited discussion upon them. His work was continued and perfected, and probably reduced to writing, by succeeding heads of the Sura Academy, who preserved the fruit of his labors in those sad times of persecution which, shortly after his death, were the lot of the Jews of Babylonia. These misfortunes were undoubtedly the immediate cause of the publication of the Talmud as a complete work; and from the Academy of Sura was issued that unique literary effort which was destined to occupy such an extraordinary position in Judaism. Rabina (R. Abina), a teacher in Sura, is considered by tradition the last amora; and the year of his death (812 of the Seleucidan, or 500 of the common era) is considered the date of the close of the Talmud. The three centuries in the course of which the Babylonian Talmud was developed in the academies founded by Rab and Samuel were followed by five centuries during which it was zealously preserved, studied, expounded in the schools, and, through their influence, recognized by the whole diaspora. Sura and Pumbedita were considered the only important seats of learning: their heads and sages were the undisputed authorities, whose decisions were sought from all sides and were accepted wherever Jewish communal life existed. In the words of the haggadist (Tan., Noah. iii.), "God created these two academies in order that the promise might be fulfilled, that the word of God should never depart from Israel's mouth" (Isa. lix. 21). The periods of Jewish history immediately following the close of the Talmud are designated according to the titles of the teachers at Sura and Pumbedita; thus we have "the time of the Geonim and that of the Saboraim. The Saboraim were the scholars whose diligent hands completed the Talmud in the first third of the sixth century, adding manifold amplifications to its text. The title "gaon," which originally belonged preeminently to the head of the Sura Academy, came into general use in the seventh century, under Mohammedan supremacy, when the official position and rank of the exilarchs and of the heads of the academy were regulated anew. But in order to leave no gaps between the bearers of the title, history must either continue the Saboraim into the seventh century or accept an older origin for the title of gaon. In point of fact, both titles are only conventionally and indifferently applied; the bearers of them are heads of either of the two academies of Sura and Pumbedita and, in that capacity, successors of the Amoraim. The inherited higher standing of Sura endured until the end of the eighth century, after which Pumbedita came into greater importance. Sura will always occupy a prominent place in Jewish history; for it was there that Saadia gave a new impulse to Jewish lore, and thus paved the way for the intellectual regeneration of Judaism. Pumbedita, on the other hand, may boast that two of its teachers, Sherira and his son Hai (died 1038), terminated in most glorious fashion the age of the Geonim and with it the activities of the Babylonian Academies.

The official designation of the Babylonian Academies was the Aramaic *metibta* (Hebrew, *yeshibah*), session, meeting. The head of the academy was accordingly called *resh metibta* (Hebrew, *rosh yeshibah*). There is a tradition that Huna, the second principal of Sura, was the first to bear the title. Before him the usual appellation in Babylonia was *resh sidra*; *resh metibta* remained the official designation for the head of the academy till the end of the gaonic period, and was by no means displaced by the title gaon, which, in fact, signifies merely "Highness" or "Excellency."

At the side of the *resh metibta*, and second to him in rank, stood the *resh kallah* (president of the general assembly). The *kallah* (general assembly) was a characteristic feature of Babylonian Judaism altogether unknown in Palestine. Owing to the great extent of Babylonia, opportunities had to be furnished for those living far from the academies to take part in their deliberations. These meetings of outside students, at which of course the most varying ages and degrees of knowledge were represented, took place twice a year, in the months Adar and Elul. An account dating from the tenth century, describing the order of procedure and of the differences in rank at the kallah, contains details that refer only to the period of the Geonim; but much of it extends as far back as the time of the Amoraim. The description given in the following condensed rendering furnishes, at all events, a curious picture of the whole institution and of the inner life and organization of the Babylonian Academies:

"In the kallah-months, that is, in Elul, at the close of the summer, and in Adar, at the close of the winter, the disciples journey from their various abodes to the meeting, after having prepared in the previous five months the treatise announced at the close of the preceding kallah-month by the head of the academy. In Adar and Elul they present themselves before the head, who examines them upon this treatise. They sit in the following order of rank: Immediately next to the president is the first row, consisting of ten men; seven of these are reshe kallah; three of them are called 'ḥaberim' [associates]. Each of the seven reshe kallah has under him ten men called 'allufim' [masters]. The seventy allufim form the Sanhedrin, and are seated behind the above-mentioned first row, in seven rows, their faces being turned toward the president. Behind them are seated, without special locations, the remaining members of the academy and the assembled disciples.

"The examination proceeds in this wise: They that sit in the first row recite aloud the subject-matter, while the members of the remaining rows listen in silence. When they reach a passage that requires discussion they debate it among themselves, the head silently taking note of the subject of discussion. Then the head himself lectures upon the treatise under consideration, and adds an exposition of those passages that have given rise to discussion. Sometimes he addresses a question to those assembled as to how a certain Halakah is to be explained: this must be answered only by the scholar named by the head. The head adds his own exposition, and when everything has been made clear one of those in the first row arises and delivers an address, intended for the whole assembly, summing up the arguments on the theme they have been considering. . . .

"In the fourth week of the kallah-month the members of the Sanhedrin, as well as the other disciples, are examined individually by the head, to prove their knowledge and capacity. Whoever is shown to have insufficiently prepared himself is reproved by the head, and threatened with the withdrawal of the stipend appropriated for his subsistence. . . . The questions that have been received from various quarters are also discussed at these kallah assemblies for final solution. The head listens to the opinions of those present and formulates the decision, which is immediately written down. At the end of the month these collective answers [responsa] are read aloud to the assembly, and signed by the head."

BIBLIOGRAPHY: *Letter of Sherira Gaon*; Zacuto, *Sefer Yuḥasin*; Grätz, *Gesch. d. Juden*, 2d ed., v. 429–434; idem, Hebrew trans., iii. 490–492; Is. Halevy, *Dorot ha-Rishonim*, iii. 214–229; Weiss, *Dor*, iii. 42, 145; iv. see index, p. 361; Ad. Schwarz, *Hochschulen in Palästina und Babylonien*, in *Jahrb. f. Jüd. Gesch. und Lit.* 1899.

W. B.

ACADEMIES IN PALESTINE: According to an oft-quoted tradition of Hoshayah (a collector of Tannaite traditions, who lived in Cæsarea in the first half of the third century), there existed in Jerusalem 480 synagogues, all of which were destroyed with the Temple. Each of these synagogues was provided with a school for Biblical instruction, as well as one for instruction in the oral law. Besides these schools of the lower and middle grades mentioned by the tradition (which is not to be too readily discredited, though it may have exaggerated their number for the sake of a good round figure), there existed in Jerusalem a sort of university or academy—an institution composed of the scribes (sages and teachers), whose pupils, having outgrown the schools, gathered around them for further instruction and were called, therefore, *talmide ḥakamim* ("disciples of the wise"). There is, however, no certain information as to the organization of this institute, or of the relation in which it stood to the Great Sanhedrin, whose Pharisee members certainly belonged to it. The most important details of its activity are afforded by the accounts concerning the schools ("houses") of HILLEL and SHAMMAI, whose controversies and debates belong to the last century of the period of the Second Temple, and relate not only to the Halakah, but also to questions of Biblical exegesis and religious philosophy. For example, it is said that the schools of Shammai and Hillel occupied two and a half years in discussing the question whether it had been better for man not to have been created ('Er. 13*b*).

The destruction of Jerusalem put as abrupt an end to the disputes of the schools as it did to the contests between political parties. It was then that a disciple of Hillel, the venerable JOHANAN BEN ZAKKAI, founded a new home for Jewish Law in JABNEH (JAMNIA), and thus evoked a new intellectual life from the ruins of a fallen political existence. The college at Jabneh, which at once constituted itself the successor of the Great Sanhedrin of Jerusalem by putting into practise the ordinances of that body as far as was necessary and practicable, attracted all those who had escaped the national catastrophe and who had become prominent by their character and their learning. Moreover, it reared a new generation of similarly gifted men, whose task it became to overcome the evil results of still another dire catastrophe—the unfortunate Bar Kokba war with its melancholy ending. During the interval between these two disasters (56–117), or, more accurately, until the "War of Quietus" under Trajan, the school at Jabneh was the recognized tribunal that gathered the traditions of the past and confirmed them; that ruled and regulated existing conditions; and that sowed the seeds for future development. Next to its founder, it owed its splendor and its undisputed supremacy especially to the energetic Gamaliel, a great-grandson of Hillel, called GAMALIEL II., or Gamaliel of Jabneh, in order to distinguish him from his grandfather, Gamaliel I. To him flocked the pupils of Johanan ben Zakkai and other masters and students of the Law and of Biblical interpretation. Though some of them taught and labored in other places—Eliezer ben Hyrcanus in Lydda; Joshua ben Hananiah in Beḳiin; Ishmael ben Elisha in Kefar Aziz, Akiba in Bene Beraḳ; Hananiah (Ḥanina) ben Teradyon in Siknin—Jabneh remained the center; and in "the vineyard" of Jabneh, as they called their place of meeting, they used to assemble for joint action.

In the fertile ground of the Jabneh Academy the roots of the literature of tradition—Midrash and Mishnah, Talmud and Haggadah—were nourished and strengthened. There, too, the way was paved for a systematic treatment of Halakah and exegesis. In Jabneh were held the decisive debates upon the canonicity of certain Biblical books; there the prayer-liturgy received its permanent form; and there, probably, was edited the Targum on the Pentateuch, which became the foundation for the later Targum called after Onkelos. It was Jabneh that inspired and sanctioned the new Greek version of the Bible—that of Akylas (Aquila). The events that preceded and followed the great civil revolution under Bar Kokba (from the year 117 to about 140) resulted in the decay and death of the school at Jabneh. According to tradition (R. H. 31*b*), the Sanhedrin was removed from Jabneh to Usha, from Usha back to Jabneh, and a second time from Jabneh to Usha. This final settlement in Usha indicates the ultimate spiritual supremacy of Galilee over Judea, the latter having become depopulated by the war of Hadrian. Usha remained for a long time the seat of the academy; its importance being due to the pupils of Akiba, one of whom, Judah ben Ilai, had his home in Usha. Here was undertaken the great work of the restoration of Palestinian Judaism after its disintegration under Hadrian. The study of the Law flourished anew; and Simon, a son of Gamaliel, was invested with the rank that had been his father's in Jabneh. With him the rank of patriarch became hereditary in the house of Hillel, and the seat of the academy was made identical with that of the patriarch.

In the time of Simon ben Gamaliel the seat of the Sanhedrin was frequently changed; its first move being from Usha to Shefar'am (the modern Shef'a 'Amr, a village about twelve miles eastward of Haifa); thence, under Simon's son and successor, Judah I., to Bet Shearim; and finally to SEPPHORIS (Zipporin), the modern Sefoorieh, where a celebrated disciple of Akiba, Jose ben Ḥalafta, had been teaching. Only with great difficulty could Simon ben Gamaliel establish his authority over this pupil of Akiba, who far outshone him in learning. Simon's son, Judah I., however, was fortunate enough to unite with his inherited rank the indisputable reputation of a distinguished scholar, a combination of great importance under the circumstances. JUDAH, in whom "Torah and dignity" were combined, was the man appointed to close an important epoch and to lay the foundation of a new one. The academy at Sepphoris, to which eminent students from Babylonia also flocked, erected an indestructible monument to itself through Judah's activity in editing the Mishnah, which attained to canonical standing as the authentic collection of the legal traditions of religious practise. In the Mishnah, the completion of which was accomplished soon after the death of its author or editor (about 219), the schools both of Palestine and of Babylonia received a recognized text-book, upon which the lectures and the debates of the students were thenceforward founded. The recognition of Rabbi Judah's Mishnah marks a strong dividing line in the history of the Academies and their teachers: it indicates the transition from the age of the TANNAIM to that of the AMORAIM.

After Judah's death Sepphoris did not long remain the seat of the patriarch and the Academy. Gamaliel III., the unpretentious son of a distinguished father, became patriarch; but Ḥanina ben Ḥama succeeded him as head of the school, and introduced the new order of things that commenced with the completion of the Mishnah. In Ḥanina's lifetime the last migration of the Sanhedrin occurred. His pupil, JOHANAN B. NAPPAḤA, settled in TIBERIAS, and the patriarch Judah II. (grandson of Judah I.) soon found himself compelled to remove to that city. The imposing personality and unexampled learning of Johanan rendered Tiberias for a long period the undisputed center of Palestinian Judaism, the magnet which attracted Babylonian students.

When Johanan died in 279—this is the only settled date in the whole chronology of the Palestinian amoraim—the renown of the Tiberias Academy was so firmly established that it suffered no deterioration under his successors, although none of them equaled him in learning. For a time, indeed, CÆSAREA came into prominence, owing solely to the influence of HOSHAYA, who lived there in the first half of the third century, and exercised the duties of a teacher contemporaneously with the Church father, Origen, with whom he had personal intercourse. After Johanan's death the school at Cæsarea attained a new standing under his pupil Abbahu; and throughout the whole of the fourth century the opinions of the "sages of Cæsarea" were taken into respectful account, even in Tiberias. Sepphoris also resumed its former importance as a seat of learning; and eminent men worked there in the fourth century, long after the disaster to the city wrought by the forces of the emperor Gallus. From the beginning of the third century there had been an academy at LYDDA in Judea, or "the South," as Judea was then called. This academy now gained a new reputation as a school of traditional learning. From it came the teacher to whom Jerome owed his knowledge of Hebrew and his insight into the "Hebræa Veritas." But neither Cæsarea, Sepphoris, nor Lydda could detract from the renown of Tiberias.

Tiberias accordingly remained the abode of the official head of Judaism in Palestine and, in a certain sense, of the Judaism of the whole Roman empire, as well as the seat of the Academy, which considered itself the successor of the ancient Sanhedrin. The right of ordination which, since Simon ben Gamaliel, the patriarch alone had exercised (either with or without the consent of the Council of Sages), was later on so regulated that the degree could only be conferred by the patriarch and council conjointly. The patriarchal dignity had meanwhile become worldly, as it were; for exceptional learning was by no means held to be an essential attribute of its possessor. The Academy of Tiberias, whose unordained members were called *ḥaberim* (associates), never lacked men, of more or less ability, who labored and taught in the manner of Johanan. Among these may be mentioned Eleazar b. Pedat, Ami and Assi, Ḥiyya bar Abba, Zeira, Samuel b. Isaac, Jonah, Jose, Jeremiah, Mani, the son of Jonah, and Jose b. Abin, who constitute a series of brilliant names in the field of the Halakah. In the department of the Haggadah—always highly prized and popular in Palestine—the renown of Tiberias was also greatly augmented by many prominent and productive workers, from the contemporaries and pupils of Johanan down to Tanḥuma b. Abba, who was illustrious as a collector and an editor of haggadic literature.

The imperishable monument to the school of Tiberias is the Palestinian or, as it is commonly called, the Jerusalem Talmud, of which Johanan b. Nappaḥa laid the foundation; for which reason he is generally styled, although erroneously, its redactor or author. In point of fact, however, this work was not completed until nearly a century and a half after Johanan's death; and its close is undoubtedly connected with the extinction of the patriarchal office (about 425). But Tiberias did not therefore cease to be a seat of learning, although very little of its subsequent activity is known. According to a Babylonian legend, a scion of the Babylonian exilarch's house fled to Tiberias in the first third of the sixth century, and there became a *resh pirḳa* (ἀρχιφερεχιτης = head of the school); a hundred years later a Syrian bishop made an appeal to the sages of Tiberias for the purpose of inducing Du Nuwas, the Jewish king of South Arabia, to cease his persecution of the Christians there.

Further importance was gained by Tiberias as the seat of the Masoretic traditions and innovations; for there in the seventh century was introduced that system of punctuation which was destined to aid so efficiently in the proper reading and understanding of the Biblical text. This system, which achieved universal recognition, is called the "Tiberian punctuation." At Tiberias flourished, about the middle of the eighth century, the Masorite Phinehas, called also Rosh Yeshibah ("Head of the Academy"), and Asher the Ancient, or the Great, forefather of five generations of Masorites (Nehemiah, Moses, Asher, Moses, and Aaron), was to a certain extent his contemporary. The last-named Aaron ben Moses ben Asher (briefly called Ben Asher), a contemporary of Saadia, brought the Tiberian school of Masorites to a distinguished end. Tiberias thereafter ceased to play any part in Jewish learning, until, in the twelfth century, it emerged for a brief period, and again in the sixteenth century, when it became the object of the pious ambition of Don Joseph Nasi of Naxos.

W. B.

ADDA: The name of two amoraim, neither of whom had a distinguishing patronymic or cognomen. The elder was a Palestinian, and lived in the first generation (third century). He was a colleague of R. Jonathan (Yer. Ter. x. 47*b*). The younger was a disciple of Raba, and a contemporary of R. Ashi (Men. 43*a*, 59*b*).

S. M.

ADDA B. ABIMI (BIMI): A Palestinian amora of the fourth generation, disciple of R. Ḥanina b. Pappi, and contemporary of R. Hezekiah. It is surmised that his patronymic Abimi was changed into Ukmi or Ikkuma, that is, "the Dark," because his memory was not retentive enough to guard him against the misquoting of traditions (Yer. Ber. ix. 14*a*; Yer. Ta'anit, iii. 64*b*; 'Er. 9*b*, 12*a*; Beẓah, 26*b*).

S. M.

ADDA B. AHABAH (AḤWAH): 1. A Babylonian amora of the second generation (third and fourth centuries), frequently quoted in both the Jerusalem and the Babylonian Talmud. He is said to have been born on the day that Rabbi (Judah I.) died (Ḳid 72*a*, *b*; Gen. R. lviii). He was one of the disciples of Abba Arika (Rab), at whose funeral he rent his garments twice in token of his mourning for the great scholar (Yer. B. Ḳ. ii. 3*a*; Ber. 42*b et seq.*). In Pumbedita R. Adda gathered about him a great many pupils, whom he taught sometimes in the public thoroughfares (Yeb. 110*b*). He lived to a very old age, and when interrogated on the merits that entitled him to be so favored of heaven, he gave the following sketch of his life and character:

> "No one has ever preceded me to the synagogue, nor has any one ever remained in the synagogue after my departure. I never walked as much as four cubits without meditating on the Law, and never thought of its contents at places not scrupulously clean. Nor did I prepare a bed for myself to enjoy regular sleep, nor did I disturb my colleagues by walking to my seat at college among them. I never nicknamed my neighbor nor rejoiced at his fall. Anger against my neighbor never went to bed with me, and I never passed the street near where my debtor lived: and while at home I never betrayed impatience, in order to observe what is said (Ps. ci. 2), 'I will walk within my house with a perfect heart'" (Yer. Ta'anit, iii. 67*a*; somewhat different in Babli, *ibid.* 20*b*).

Yet where sanctity of life and the glory of heaven were concerned, he lost his patience and risked much. Thus, on one occasion, when he observed on the street a woman named Matun dressed in a manner unbecoming a modest Jewess, he violently rebuked her. Unfortunately for him the woman was a Samaritan, and for the attack on her he was condemned to pay a fine of 400 zuz (about $60 actual value, or ₤12), and thereupon he repeated a popular saying, "*Matun, matun* [waiting, patience] is worth 400 zuz!" (Ber 20*a*).

Such a character is generally surrounded by a halo of legend, and later ages supplied this. It is said that R. Adda's piety was so highly valued in the sight of heaven that no favor asked by him was ever refused. In times of drought, for example, when he pulled off but one shoe (preparatory to offering prayer), an abundance of rain descended; but if he pulled off the other, the world was flooded (Yer Ta'anit, *l.c.*). Even his teacher, the famous Rab, realized Adda's protective influence. On one occasion when he and Samuel, accompanied by Adda, came to a tottering ruin, and Samuel proposed to avoid it by taking a circuitous route, Rab observed that just then there was no occasion for fear, since R. Adda b. Ahabah, whose merits were very great, was with them; consequently no accident would befall them. Samuel's great colleague R. Huna I. also believed in and availed himself of R. Adda's supposed miraculous influence with heaven. This rabbi had a lot of wine stored in a building that threatened to collapse. He was anxious to save his property, but there was danger of accident to the laborers. Therefore he invited Rab Adda into the building, and there engaged him in halakic discussions until the task of removing its contents was safely accomplished; hardly had the rabbis vacated the premises when the tottering walls fell (Ta'anit, 20*b*).

Of Rab Adda's numerous noteworthy observations on Biblical texts, the following may be quoted: "The man who is conscious of sin and confesses it, but does not turn away from it, is like the man who holds a defiling reptile in his hand; were he to bathe in all the waters of the world, the bath would not restore him to cleanness. Only when he drops it from his hand, and bathes in but forty seahs (= about 100 gallons) of water he is clean." This follows from the Biblical saying (Prov. xxviii. 13), "Whoso confesseth and forsaketh them shall have mercy"; and elsewhere it is said (Lam. iii. 41), "Let us lift up our heart as well as our hands unto God in the heavens" (Ta'anit, 16*a*; compare Tosef. *ibid.* i. 8).

2. A disciple of Raba, addressed by the latter as "my son." In a discussion the elder rabbi once rebuked him as devoid of understanding (Ta'anit, 8*a*, Yeb. 61*b*; Sanh. 81*a*, *b*). Subsequently he studied under R. Papa ana waited on R. Naḥman b. Isaac (B. B. 22*a:* see version in Rabbinowicz, "Diḳduḳe Soferim," *ad loc.*, note 6; Ḥul. 133*b*, where some manuscripts read "bar Ḥana" or "Ḥanah").

S. M.

ADDA B. ḤUNYA: The homiletic observation on Eccl. i. 4 ("One generation passeth away, and another generation cometh: but the earth abideth forever") has thus been transmitted by him: "Consider the present generation as good as the generation that is passed and gone. Say not, 'Were R. Akiba living I would study the Bible under him; were R. Zerah and R. Johanan living, I would read Mishnah before them.' But consider the generation that has arisen in thy days, and the wise men of thy time, as good as the previous generations and as the earlier wise men that have been before thee" (Eccl. R. *ad loc.*; compare Midr. Sam. § 15).

S. M.

ADDA B. MATNA: A Babylonian amora of the fourth century, disciple of Abaye and of Raba. He appears to have obtained some halakic information from Rabina I., and in his later years to have associated with Rabina II. To satisfy his thirst for knowledge, he felt obliged to leave his home, and when his wife asked, "What will thy little ones do?" he laconically replied, "Are the water-plants in the marshes all gone?" (Shab. 48*a*; Ket. 28*a*, 77*b*, 85*a*; Shebu, 18*a*; Meg. 28*b*; 'Er. 22*a*).

S. M.

ADDA, MESHOḤAAH (משוחאה "Surveyor"): A disciple of R. Judah b. Ezekiel, who instructed Raba how to measure city limits for the regulation of Sabbath walks ('Er. 56*b*, B. M. 107*b*).

S. M.

ADDA B. MINYOMI: A Babylonian amora of the third century, junior contemporary of Rabina I. and of Huna Mar b. Iddi. He is sometimes quoted anonymously as "The Court of Nehardea" (B. Ḳ. 31*b*, Ḥul. 49*a*, Sanh. 17*b*).

S. M.

ADDA B. SIMON: A Palestinian amora, who is known chiefly for ethical rules quoted in the name of his predecessors (Yer. Ber. ii. 4*d*; Yer. Meg. 1, 71*c;* Eccl. R. iv. 17).

S. M.

AḤA OR AḤAI: The name of nearly fourscore rabbis quoted in the Talmud and in midrashic literature. Some of these are misnamed through the errors of copyists; others appear but once or twice, and, consequently, can not be identified with any degree of certainty. Those mentioned below embrace the most prominent teachers of their respective generations; and the foremost of them are the following three sages, who are always quoted by that name, alone, without any patronymic or cognomen.

S. M.

AḤA (AḤAI) I.: A tanna of the second century, junior contemporary of Simon ben Yoḥai, with whom, as well as with others of the fourth and fifth tannaitic generations, he appears in halakic disputations. While he is, therefore, best known as a halakist, he is occasionally met also in the field of the Haggadah. Thus, commenting on Ex. xiv. 15, "Wherefore criest thou unto me? speak unto the children of Israel, that they go forward," he quotes Ps. cvi. 23, "Therefore he said that he would destroy them, had not Moses, his chosen, stood before him in the breach, to turn away his wrath, lest he should destroy them"; and remarks, "The Lord said to Moses, 'Why criest thou unto me? For thy sake I will save Israel. Had it not been for thy prayers I should have destroyed them ere this, because of their idolatry' " (Mek., Beshallah, 3). Elsewhere he derives from Deut. vi. 7 ("And thou shalt talk of them [the commandments] when thou sittest in thine house, and when thou walkest by the way") the duty of man to have set hours for the study of the Torah, and not to make it subject to opportunity (Yoma, 19*b*; Tosef., Ber. 2, 2; Tosef., Shab. 15, 17; Bab. Shab. 127*a*; Tosef., Yeb. 14, 4; Tosef., Giṭ. 3,. 1; Tosef., Niddah, 6, 13; Bab. Niddah, 21*b*).

S. M.

AḤA (AḤAI) II.: A Palestinian amora of the first amoraic generation (third century), surnamed Berabbi, Ha-Gadol or Roba ("the Great"). He systematized Baraitot at the Academy of Ḥiya ha-Gadol, and was teacher of Samuel ha-Zaḳen (Ber. 14*a*; Yer. Ber. ii. 5*a*; Yer. Sanh. ii. 20*c*, iv. 22*b*, v. 22*c*; Bek. 24*b*). The Midrash preserves the following homily of his on Num. xiii. 2: "Send thou men, that they may search the land of Canaan, which I give unto the children of Israel," the last clause of which appears to be superfluous. Prefacing this homily with a quotation from Isa. xl. 8, "The grass withereth, the flower fadeth; but the word of our God shall stand forever," he illustrates his subject with the following simile:

"A king once had a friend with whom he made a covenant saying, 'Follow me and I will bestow a gift upon thee.' The friend obeyed the royal summons, but soon after died. Then the king spoke to his friend's son, saying, 'Although thy father is dead, I shall not cancel my promise of a gift to him; come, thou, and receive it.'. The king is the Holy One—blessed be He! and the friend is Abraham, as it is said in Isa. xli. 8, 'the seed of Abraham my friend.' To him the Holy One had said, 'Follow me,' as we read in Gen. xii. 1, 'Get thee out of thy country unto a land that I will show thee.' And to him the Lord promised a gift; as it is said [Gen. xiii. 17], 'Arise, walk through the land; for I will give it unto thee'; and again [Gen. xiii. 15], 'All the land which thou seest, to thee I will give it, and to thy seed forever.' Abraham, Isaac, and Jacob were dead; but the Lord said to Moses, 'Although I promised to give the land to Israel's fathers, who are now dead, I shall not cancel my promise, but fulfil it to their children': thus we understand the text, 'The word of our God shall stand forever' " (Tan., Shelaḥ, 3; Num. R. xvi.).

S. M.

AḤA (AḤAI) III.: A Palestinian amora of the fourth century and associate of the most prominent teachers of the fourth amoraic generation, R. Jonah and R. Yose II. He was a native of Lydda in southern Palestine, but settled in Tiberias, where Huna II., Judah bar Pazi, and himself eventually constituted a bet din, or court of justice (Yer. Ter. ii. 41*d*; Yer. Shab. vi. 8*a*; Yer. B. B. viii. 16*a*; Yer. Sanh. i. 18*c*, end). Like his elder namesakes, he was a recognized authority on Halakah; but in Haggadah he surpassed them, "being by far the most frequently-quoted by haggadists of his own times and of subsequent generations. Commenting on Abraham's attempt to sacrifice Isaac, Aḥa tries to prove that the patriarch misunderstood the divine call. He refers to Ps. lxxxix. 35 [A. V. 34], "My covenant will I not break, nor alter the thing that is gone out of my lips," which he construes thus:

"My covenant will I not break, even that covenant in which I have assured Abraham: 'In Isaac shall thy seed be called' [Gen. xxi. 12], nor alter the thing which is gone out of my lips, when I said to him, 'Take now thy son' [Gen. xxii. 2]. This may be compared to a king, who expressed to his friend a wish to see a tender child put on his table. His friend immediately went forth, and returned with his own child, whom he placed on the table before the king. He again went forth, and returned with a sword to slay the child, whereupon the king exclaimed, 'What art thou doing?' 'Sire,' replied the anxious friend, 'didst thou not express a desire for a tender child on thy table? ' To which the king answered, 'Have I asked for a dead child? It is a live one I desire.' Even so, said the Holy One—blessed be He!—to Abraham: 'Take now thy son, and offer him there for a burnt offering;' whereupon Abraham built an altar, and placed his son upon it. But when he stretched forth his hand for the knife, the angel cried out, 'Lay not thine hand upon the youth.' And when Abraham inquired, 'Didst thou not tell me to offer my son? the angel retorted, 'Did I tell thee to kill him?' " (Tan., Wayera, ed. Buber, 40; Gen. R. lvi.).

One of Aḥa's epigrams reads, "The Jew needs privations to lead him back to God" (Cant. R. i. 4; Lev. R. xiii.). His gratitude to the defenders of his people he expressed by saying, "To him who speaks a good word for Israel, the Lord will assign an exalted station in the world; for it is written [Isa. xxx. 18], 'He will exalt him who has pity on you' " (Pesiḳ. R. 32, 196*a*). For other homiletic observations, see Pesiḳ. R. 4, 39*b*, xiii. 111*b*, xvii. 131*a*, 133*b*, xxi. 145*a*, xxx. 191*b*; Tan., ed. Buber, index of authors; Midr. Teh., ed. Buber, index; Pesiḳ. R., ed. Friedmann, index; see also a full account in Bacher, "Ag. Pal. Amor." iii. 106–163.

S. M.

AḤA: Brother of Abba, the father of Jeremiah b. Abba; a contemporary of Abba Arika (third century). The latter said that in the history of the world there never had been a man so penitent as King Josiah, and after him came Aḥa, the brother of Abba (Shab. 56*b*).

S. M.

AḤA B. ADDA: An amora of the fourth century; born and educated in Palestine. He emigrated to Babylonia, where he became a disciple of Rab Judah ben Ezekiel and of Rab Hamnuna II. He frequently reported decisions of his Palestinian teachers. He survived all his associates of the third amoraic generation. As he grew old he became weak and his hands trembled; and it is related that, to imitate his signature in a judicial document, a forger made his own hand tremble like that of the aged scholar (Ḳid. 30*a*; Sanh. 90*b*; Suk. 21*b*, 26*a*; B. B. 167*a*). That Aḥa loved virtue for virtue's sake may be inferred from the construction he put on Mal. iii. 18. He says: " 'Then shall ye return, and discern between the righteous and the wicked.' This means between the believer and the unbeliever. 'Between him that serveth God for God's sake and him that serveth Him not for His sake;' that is, man should not use his knowledge of the Law as an ax to cut with or as a crown wherewith to crown himself" (Midr. Teh. to Ps. xxxi., ed. Buber; compare Ab. iv. 5).

S. M.

AḤA AREKA. See AḤA (AḤAI) B. PAPA.

AḤA B. AWYA or **'AWA:** A Babylonian halakist of the third generation of Amoraim. He once visited Palestine, where he attended the lectures of Rab Assi (Yasa I.), and seems to have met Rabbi Johanan. He was a disciple of Rab Ḥisda in Babylonia, and appears frequently in controversy with Rab Ashi I. (Pes. 33*b*; Yeb. 117*a*; B. B. 3*a*, 46*b*, 56*a*; Ḥul. 31*a*, 50*b*).

S. M.

AḤA BARDALA: A Babylonian amora of the first generation, a contemporary of Abba Areka (Suk. 26*a*; Beẓah, 14*a*; Giṭ. 14*a*).

S. M.

AḤA OF DIFTI: A Babylonian amora of the sixth generation (fifth century), frequently found in halakic discussion with Rabina II. For a time he acted as counselor (ḥakam) of the exilarch (*resh galuta*) Mar Zuṭra I. (441–450). After the death of Naḥman b. Huna he would have been elected to the position of rector of the academy at Sura (once held by Ashi) but for the strategy of his friend Mar b. Ashi (Ṭabyomi), who considered himself entitled to the honor of filling the seat formerly occupied by his own father. While the members of the academy, resolved to elect Aḥa, were within, awaiting the appointed hour for voting, Mar had himself elected outside the academy (B. B. 12*b*, Yeb. 8*a*; Ned. 23*a*; Naz. 42*a*; Sanh. 42*a*; Men. 5*b*; Grätz, "Gesch. d. Juden," iv. 465, n. 68).

S. M.

AḤA (AḤAI) B. ḤANINA: A Palestinian amora of the third and fourth centuries. He collected rare Baraitot among the leading scholars of Daroma in southern Judea, which he communicated to his colleagues elsewhere, even as far as the Babylonian academies. Often he reports Halakot on behalf of Joshua b. Levi (Ber. 8*b;* Suk. 54*a*; Yeb. 57*a*; Soṭah, 24*b*; Ḥul. 132*b*); also many Haggadot (see Bacher, "Ag. Pal. Amor." iii. 540–546). R. Levi, the famous haggadist of the second and third amoraic generations, received from Aḥa b. Ḥanina the reason for the collocation of the ninth and tenth benedictions in the Prayer of Benedictions, known by the name of "Shemoneh 'Esreh" (Yer. Ber. ii. 5*a*). He recommends visiting the sick as a means of facilitating a cure, declaring that every one who calls on a patient relieves him of one sixtieth part of his suffering (Ned. 39*b*).

S. M.

AḤA BAR HUNA: A Babylonian amora of the fourth generation, disciple of Rabbah b. Naḥmani and of Sheshet. Ḥisda, another teacher of Aḥa, employed him for his halakic correspondence with Raba ben Joseph, who recognized in him a great and wise man (Pes. 47*a*, Yeb. 89*b*, Ned. 90*a*, B. B. 70*a*, Sanh. 43*a*, Shebu. 36*b*). It happened in his days that Ifra-Ormuzd, the queen-mother of Sapor II. of Persia, sent to Raba an animal to be sacrificed to the Jewish God and according to ancient Jewish rites; but as the sacrifices had ceased with the destruction of Jerusalem, Raba deputized Aḥa b. Huna, together with Rab Safra, to burn the proffered sacrifice on a sand-bank by the sea, on a pyre prepared of newly felled wood (Zeb. 116*b*).

S. M.

AḤA B. IḲA: A Babylonian amora of the fourth century, junior contemporary of Raba, and nephew of Aḥa b. Jacob. He is frequently quoted in halakic discussions by his contemporaries and successors, and received the title of Bar be-Rab (Fellow of the Academy) from his uncle Aḥa, with whom he carried on halakic controversies ('Er. 63*a*, Ket. 74*a*, Sanh. 42*a*, Naz. 42*a*).

S. M.

AḤA OF IRAK: A Babylonian, who is alleged to have invented the Assyrian or Babylonian (super-linear) system of vowel-points and accents (נקוד). He is known only from Karaite sources, which are somewhat unreliable. Pinsker ("Liḳḳuṭe Ḳadmoniyot") thinks Aḥa is identical with Nissi ben Noah, the contemporary of Anan; and Graetz partly follows that opinion. But later investigators have proved that Nissi (if he existed at all) must have lived in the thirteenth century; his identity with Aḥa is, therefore, out of the question. Fürst places Aḥa in the first half of the sixth century, and thinks he may be identical with the Saborean Aḥa bar Abbuhu, who died in 511.

BIBLIOGRAPHY: Fürst, *Gesch. d. Karäert, i.* 15, 133; Gottlober, לתולדות הקדאים בקודת; Frankl, *Concerning Simḥa Pinsker*, in *Ha-Shaḥar*, viii.; Harkavy, *Notes to the Hebrew edition of Grätz, Gesch. d. Juden*, iii.; *Jew. Quart. Rev.* i. 243.

P. WI.

AḤA B. ISAAC: A Palestinian amora of the third generation (fourth century), junior contemporary of Zeira I., Ami I., and Abba (Ba) b. Mamel (Yer. Shab. iii. 6*a*, vi. 8*a*). Speaking of the glories of Solomon's Temple, he relates that when King Solomon constructed the sacred edifice he placed in it all kinds of trees made of gold; and whenever any kind of tree blossomed outside, the corresponding one inside blossomed also. In proof of this, Aḥa quotes the Biblical passage (Isa. xxxv. 2), "It shall blossom abundantly, and rejoice even with joy and singing: the glory of Lebanon shall be given unto it, the excellency of Carmel and Sharon." Lebanon was the symbolic name of the Temple (Yer. Yoma, iv. 41*d*).

S. M.

AḤA B. JACOB: A Babylonian amora, senior contemporary of Abaye and Raba (B. Ḳ. 40*a*), and a disciple of Huna, head of the academy at Sura. So incessant was his application to study that it undermined his health, and brought on a serious illness, from which, however, he recovered. Seeing some of his former schoolmates, who had contracted similar ailments and had become chronic sufferers, he applied to himself the Scriptural saying (Eccl. vii. 12), "Wisdom giveth life to them that have it" (Yeb. 64b). Nor did he long remember the warning of his early experience. He devoted all his days to the study of the Law; and when worldly avocations compelled him to "borrow" part of the day, he would "repay" it by studying at night ('Er. 65*a*). After his ordination as teacher he established himself at Paphunia (Epiphania; supposed to be on the Euphrates), where he became an authority on ritual matters, as well as a distinguished haggadist. By degrees he earned the reputation of being one of the foremost men of his age ('Er. 63*a*). He is also reported to have been a skilful writer of Torah scrolls (B. B. 14*a*; Ḳid. 35*a*; B. Ḳ. 54*b*; Niddah, 676; Sanh. 46*b*). Fragments of his homiletic sayings are preserved in Shab. 85*a*; 'Er. 54*a*; Pes. 3*a*; Yoma, 19*b*, 75*b*; Ḥag. 13*a*; Ḳid. 40*a*. In halakic discussion he is quoted in Yer.

Sheb. vi. 36*b*; Pes. 116*b*, 117*b*; Yoma, 76*a*; Ḳid. 35*a*; Sanh. 36*b*; Hor. 5*b*, 6*b*; Ker. 5b.

In addition to his diligent pursuit of halakic and haggadic studies Aḥa appears to have applied himself to philosophy and mysticism (Ber. 59*a*, Shab. 66*b*, B. B. 75*a*), and legend represents him as an adept in the occult sciences. It relates that a demon had established himself in the neighborhood of Abaye's academy, and greatly harassed the frequenters of the school, even when they walked together in daylight. No one seemed able to dislodge him. When Abaye was informed that Aḥa bar Jacob was on his way to Pumbedita, he arranged with the inhabitants of the city to refuse to accommodate him, so that he should be compelled to lodge in the academy. Aḥa arrived, and no sooner had he completed his arrangements for his night's rest than the demon appeared to him in the shape of a seven-headed hydra. Aḥa immediately betook himself to prayer; and at each genuflection one of the heads of the hydra dropped off. In the morning Aḥa reproachfully said to Abaye, "Had not heaven seen fit to work a miracle, my life would have been endangered" (Ḳid. 29*b*; see Bacher, "Ag. Bab. Amor." pp. 137–139).

S. M.

AḤA B. JOSEPH: A Babylonian amora who flourished in the fourth and fifth centuries. His life was an unusually long one; for in his youth he attended Ḥisda's lectures (306), and in his old age discussed halakic matters with Ashi II. (died 427). It is stated that he was afflicted with asthma, for which Mar Ukba prescribed three ounces of asafetida to be taken in the course of three days. During another severe attack, he was treated medically by Kahana (Shab. 110*b*, 140*a*; B. M. 87*a*, 109*b*; Men. 35*b*; 'Er. 29*b*; Yeb. 31*b*; B. M. 109*b*; Ḥul 105*a*).

S. M.

AḤA (AḤAI) B. MINYOMI: A Babylonian amora of the fourth generation (fourth century), disciple of Naḥman b. Jacob, and contemporary of Abaye. Aḥa b. Minyomi was probably a brother of Adda b. Minyomi (Yeb. 94*a*; Ḳid. 66*a*; B. Ḳ. 106*a*; B. B. 148*b*, 159*b*; 'Ab. Zarah, 7*b*).

S. M.

AḤA (AḤAI) B. PAPA or **PAPI:** A Palestinian amora of the third generation (fourth century). He was the contemporary of Abbahu ("Die Ag. der Pal. Amor." iii. 546), Zeira I., and Abba II. He was surnamed Arika, an appellation of disputed meaning (compare Jastrow, "Dict." under אריכא, and ABBA ARIKA; Shab. 111*a*, 113*a*; Yer. R. H. iv. 59*b*; Yer. Yeb. viii. 9*b*). Referring to repentance, Aḥa is quoted as saying, "Great indeed is the power of repentance! It counteracts heavenly decrees, and even annuls heavenly oaths!" The same sentence is attributed to Abba

b. Papa (Pesiḳ. xxv. 163*a*, Buber's note; see Bacher, "Ag. Pal. Amor." iii. 651). That repentance counteracts heavenly decrees, he proves from the life of Jeconiah, "Write ye this man [Coniah] childless" (Jer. xxii. 30); yet we find (I Chron. iii. 17) that Jeconiah was the father of no less than eight sons, among them Shealtiel. That repentance annuls heavenly oaths he deduces from the same message by Jeremiah (xxii. 24), "As I live, saith the Lord, though Coniah, the son of Jehoiakim king of Judah, were the signet upon my right hand, yet would I pluck thee thence"; but at a later date Haggai (ii. 23) says, "In that day, saith the Lord of hosts, will I take thee, O Zerubbabel, my servant, the son of Shealtiel, saith the Lord, and will make thee as a signet" (Cant. R to viii. 6).

S. M.

AḤA B. RAB: A Babylonian amora of the third and fourth generations (fourth century). He was a contemporary of Rabina I. and the senior of Aḥa b. Jacob. His opinions were supported by his grandson, Mesharsheya (Sanh. 76*b*, 77*a*; Ḥul. 33*a*).

S. M.

AḤA (**AḤAI**) **B. RABA:** A Babylonian amora, son of Raba b. Joseph, and a contemporary of Amemar II. and of Ashi; died in 419. During the last five years of his life he filled the rectorate of the academy at Pumbedita (Shab. 93*b*; Yeb. 46*a*; B. B. 124*b*; Men. 3*b*; "Letter of Sherira"; Grätz, "Gesch. d. Juden," 2d ed., iv. 379).

S. M.

AḤA B. SHILA OF KEFAR TAMRATA or **TEMARTA:** A haggadist of the second amoraic generation (third century). Commenting on Esth. ii. 23, "And it was written in the book of the chronicles before the king," he is reported to have pointed out therein a lesson of encouragement to the Godfearing. If the chronicles written by mortals assure rewards for good deeds, how much more ought we to be assured that the pious will be duly rewarded, when the Holy One—blessed be He!—shall produce His book, concerning which it is said (Mal. iii. 16), "And the Lord hearkened and heard it, and a book of remembrance was written before him" (Esther R. to ii. 23; compare Meg. 16*a*).

S. M.

AḤA B. TAḤLIFA: Babylonian amora of the fourth and fifth centuries; disciple of Raba, friend of Aḥa b. Ika, and senior colleague of Rabina II. (Sanh. 24*a*, 'Er. 63*a*, Giṭ. 73*a*).

S. M.

AḤA B. ZEIRA. See Ahabah (Ahawah) B. Zeira.

AHABAH (AHAWAH, AḤA, AḤWA) B. ZEIRA (**ZERA**)**:** Palestinian amora of the fourth century, who taught at Cæsarea (Yer.

Ḥal. i. 57*a*; Yer. Pes. ii. 29*b*), son of R. Zeira (Zera) I. His fame as a halakist spread beyond his native land, even reaching Babylonia, and sages consulted him on the ritual. Inquiries concerning his father's decisions were made of him (Yer. Ber. 3*d*), and even during his father's lifetime Ahaba transmitted the paternal Halakot to his colleagues ('Er. 96*b*, R. H. 305). He is also favorably known in midrashic literature. Commenting on Ps. xxviii. 3, he points out a characteristic difference between Joseph's brothers and Absalom. He remarks that the good qualities of the sons of Israel may be gathered from the mention of their faults. Thus, it is said of them (Gen. xxxvii. 4), "And they hated him [Joseph], and could not speak peaceably unto him," which shows that what they felt in their hearts they expressed with their mouths. Of Absalom, however, it is said (II Sam. xiii. 22), "Absalom spoke to Amnon neither good nor bad," hiding his feelings in his heart (Midr. Teh. xxviii.; Gen. R. lxxxiv.; Yalḳ., Gen. § 141). On Solomon's comparison of his beloved to the apple-tree (Song Sol. ii. 3) he remarks: "as the apple-tree sends forth its buds before the appearance of its leaves, so Israel expressed faith before hearing the purport of the divine message. Thus it is written (Ex. iv. 31), 'And the people believed and heard.' Also at Sinai (Ex. xxiv. 7), they promised first to do all the Lord should command and then to hearken to His voice" (Cant. R. ii. 3). Other homiletic remarks of his occur in Yer. Ber. v. 8*d*; Gen. R. lxxxiv; Lam. R. ii. 17; Eccl. R. iii. 11, ix. 11.

BIBLIOGRAPHY: Frankel, *Mebo*, 63*a*; Bacher, *Ag. Pal. Amor.* iii. 656–659.

S. M.

AḤADBOI: Babylonian amora of the sixth and seventh generations. He was president of the academy of Sura in its declining days, but filled the office for only six months. His death was then caused by an earthquake on the Day of Atonement in the year 822 of the Seleucidan era = 511. The name is a contraction of Aḥa de-Abba or De-Abboi ("Father's Brother") and corresponds with Ahab of the Bible.

BIBLIOGRAPHY: *Letter of Sherira*, ed. Neubauer, in *Mediæval Jew. Chron.* i.; Brüll's *Jahrb.* ii. 38; Jastrow, *Dict.* s. v.

S. M.

AḤADBOI B. AMMI: Babylonian amora of the fourth generation (fourth and fifth centuries), a disciple of Rab Ḥisda and Rab Sheshet (Pes. 75*a*; B. M. 91*a*; Sanh. 55*a*; Bek. 39*a*; Niddah, 37*b*). While the latter was discussing some intricate point of ritual, Aḥadboi, by facetious remarks, confused his teacher. The teacher felt grieved, and the disciple suddenly lost his power of speech. This was considered as a visitation from heaven for putting his master to shame. Thereupon Aḥadboi's mother, who had been Rab Sheshet's nurse, appealed, on behalf of her afflicted son, to her former foster-child to pardon the indiscretion of his pupil and pray for his recovery. At first Rab Sheshet refused her petition; but after she had pointed to her breasts, which formerly nourished him, and entreated him to be merciful on their account, he complied, and soon afterward Aḥadboi recovered his speech. His colleagues then stigmatized Aḥadboi as "the babe that confounded his mother's ways" (B. B. 9*b*; see Tos. *ad loc.* According to Rashi it was Rab Sheshet's own mother who interceded in behalf of Aḥadboi). Aḥadboi reports in R. Eleazar's name an observation calculated to encourage beneficence toward the poor. Quoting the prophet's metaphor (Isa. lix. 17), "He put on righteousness [*ẓedaḳah*—used in later Hebrew for "charity"] as a breastplate," he says: "That coat is composite in its nature; scale being joined to scale till the armor is completed. Similarly, with regard to ẓedaḳah, farthing is added to farthing; and ultimately there is a large amount to the giver's credit in heaven's register" (B. B. 9*b*).

S. M.

AḤAI: An appellation given to several rabbis who ordinarily bear the prænomen Aḥa, under which name they are grouped; while others better known by the name of אחי (or אחאי) are as follows: **1.** A Palestinian amora of the third century, contemporary of R. Ammi and R. Assi. He was judge of a divorce court (Giṭ. 5*b*). **2.** A distinguished Babylonian teacher who flourished during the closing days of the amoraic period and at the beginning of the saboraic epoch. During his time the compilation and editing of the Babylonian Talmud, begun by Rab Ashi, gradually neared completion. His fame was not confined to his birthplace, Be-Ḥatim, or to his native country; for even in Palestine he was recognized as a great authority. Thus when the substance of a ritualistic controversy between him and Samuel b. Abbahu was submitted to a Palestinian academy for final adjudication, the rabbis decided in favor of the latter's opinion; but they added the significant warning, "Be careful of the views of R. Aḥai, for he is the light of the diaspora" (Ḥul. 59*b*). So, while but few of the sayings and teachings of his contemporaries are quoted in the Talmud, not less than ten distinct opinions of Rab Aḥai are incorporated in its pages (Yeb. 24*a*, 46*a*; Ket. 2*b*, 10*a*, 47*a*; Ḳid. 13*a*; Shebu. 41*b*; Zeb. 102*b*; Ḥul. 65*b*; Bek. 5*a*, 6*a*; Niddah, 33*a*). Rab Aḥai died in 506 ("Letter of Sherira"; Grätz, "Gesch. d. Juden," 1st ed., iv. 473). Brüll, "Jahrb." ii. 25 *et seq.*, identifies him with Rab Aḥai b. Ḥanilai; but the great majority of ancient and modern rabbinical chronicles identify him with Rab Aḥai b. Huna.

S. M.

AḤAI B. JOSIAH: Tanna of the fourth and fifth generations (second century). His father, Josiah, was probably the well-known tanna

R. Josiah, a pupil of R. Ishmael. The following legend, intended to demonstrate the consciousness of the dead, and citing a conversation between an amora of the fourth century and Aḥai's ghost, incidentally points out the place of Aḥai's sepulcher:

Grave-robbers engaged in digging in soil belonging to Rab Naḥman suddenly heard a groan issuing from the ground. They hastened to report this to R. Naḥman ben Isaac [see MS. M. in "Diḳduḳe Soferim," *ad loc.*], who immediately repaired to the scene. The following dialogue tells the rest: *Naḥman:* Who art thou, sir? *Ghost:* I am Aḥai ben Josiah. *N.* Did not Rab Mari declare that the bodies of the pious dead returned to dust? *Gh.* Who is Mari? I know him not. *N.* Well, then, it is written in the Bible [Eccl. xii. 7]: The dust shall return to the earth as it was. *Gh.* Evidently he who hath taught thee the Book of Ecclesiastes did not teach thee the Book of Proverbs. There it is stated [xiv. 30]: Envy is rottenness of the bones. Whoever cherishes envy in his breast, his bones will become rotten; but he who doth not nourish envy in his breast, his bones shall not rot. [Here Naḥman touched the ghost, and finding it substantial, addressed it]: Arise, my master! and come into my house. *Gh.* Thou betrayest thy ignorance even of the Books of the Prophets; for there it is said [Ezek. xxxvii. 13]: Ye shall know that I am the Lord, when I have opened your graves, O my people, and brought you out of your graves. Until then the dead can not rise. *N.* But is it not written [Gen. iii. 19]: Dust thou art and unto dust shalt thou return? *Gh.* That will come to pass shortly before the Resurrection [Shab. 152*b*].

Now, as Naḥman ben Isaac (compare "Diḳduḳe Soferim" to *l.c.*) was a Babylonian, and his land lay in Babylonia, Aḥai's body, resting in Naḥman's ground, was also in Babylonia. Moreover, there is other evidence of Aḥai's having been in Babylonia during the course of his life. Judah I. states that there were some fishermen who violated the Sabbath by plying their trade on that day; and that Aḥai b. Josiah, observing this, excommunicated them. This happened in Birta de-Saṭia, in Babylonia (Ḳid. 72*a*). Further, we are informed that he had some personal property in Babylonia, while he himself was in Palestine; for the Talmud relates: R. Aḥai b. Josiah owned a vessel of silver which was in Nehardea. He commissioned Dositai ben Jannai and Jose ben Kippar to reclaim it and, on their return to Palestine, to bring it to him (Giṭ. 14*a*). From all these data it is evident that Aḥai ben Josiah was buried in Babylonia, where he had spent his last days; that he had been in that country before the death of Judah I., and that he had some personal property in Babylonia, even while he himself was in Palestine. There is, in fact, little doubt that Ahai spent his riper years on Babylonian soil and with Babylonian scholars. This accounts for the failure to find him mentioned in the Palestinian Talmud or the Palestinian Midrashim; while he is referred to in the Babylonian Talmud and in the halakic Midrashim compiled by the disciples of Rab (Be-Rab) in Babylonia ('Er.

13*a*, Giṭ. 45*a*, Mek. Bo, 3—twice; *ibid.*, Baḥodesh, § 7; compare *ibid.* Ki Tissa; Sifre, Num. 106, 126).

As an ethical teacher, Ahai tried to impress the strictest morality on the people. "Whoever eyes woman will eventually fall into sin; and whoever watches her step will rear unworthy children" (Ned. 20*a*). On domestic economy he observed:

> "Whoso purchases breadstuff in the market is like the infant whose mother is dead, and who is therefore carried from door to door to suckle at strangers' breasts, never getting its fill. Whoso purchases bread in the market is like one interred. But whoso eats of his own store is like the child raised on its own mother's breasts." He also remarked, "As long as a man supports himself he enjoys peace of mind; but when he is dependent, even on his own parents or on his own children, he has no peace of mind; still less so when he depends on strangers" (Ab. R. N. xxxi. [ed. Schechter, xxx.]; compare Men. 103*b*, Yer. Shek. iii. 51*a*, and parallels).

BIBLIOGRAPHY: Bacher, *Ag. Tan.* ii. 393, 394.

S. M.

AḤER. See ELISHA BEN ABUYAH.

AIBU (IBU): By this name, unaccompanied by patronymic or cognomen, are known four amoraim, three of whom were members of the famify of Abba Arika (Rab) in Babylonia, and the remaining one was a distinguished Palestinian. **1.** The father of Rab, and elder half-brother of Ḥiyya the Great, a lineal or lateral descendant of the royal house of David (Ket. 62*b*; Yer. Ta'anit, iv. 68*a*; Gen. R. xcviii.). After the birth of Aibu, his father, having become a widower, married a widow who had a daughter, and from that union came Ḥiyya. Aibu married his stepsister, and was thus related to Ḥiyya as both half-brother and brother-in-law (Sanh. 5*a*, Pes. 4*a*). Aibu was a disciple of Eleazar b. Zadok (Suk. 44*b*); and Ḥiyya, speaking to Rab, often addressed him as Bar Paḥate (Son of Nobles; Ber. 13b), thus testifying to the noble gifts of his elder half-brother. **2.** A son of Rab, who inherited his name from his grandfather, but not his scholarly capacity. His father, seeing that Aibu was not endowed with great mental gifts, advised him to turn his attention to secular pursuits, and furnished him with a number of practical rules of conduct. Aibu became a farmer; and some had occasion to criticize him for not observing a rabbinical enactment (Pes. 113*a*; B. M. 93*b*; 'Ab. Zarah, 35*b*). **3.** A grandson of Rab (Suk. 44*b*). So little was he known as an authority on the Halakah, that the name of his Palestinian contemporary Abbahu was sometimes substituted for his (Pes. 46*a*, Ḥul. 122*b et seq.*). **4.** See following article.

S. M.

AIBU (IBU): A prominent haggadist of the fourth amoraic generation (fourth century), contemporary of Judah (Judan) b. Simon

(b. Pazzi; Midr. Teh. to viii. 2, cxiii. 1). He was versed in the Halakah, in which he often reported opinions in "behalf of Rabbi Yannai (Ket. 54*b*, 104*b*; Ḳid. 19*a*, 33*a*; Zeb. 103*a*); but no original decisions have come down from him. In the field of the Haggadah, on the contrary, while we find him repeating observations of his predecessors (Gen. R. xliv., lxxxii.; Midr. Teh. to ci. 8), he is generally original in his remarks. Commenting on Jacob's order to Joseph, "Go and see whether it be well with thy brethren and well with the flock" (Gen. xxxvii. 14), the question is raised, Do flocks of sheep appreciate human greetings? Whereunto Aibu replies: "It is man's duty to pray for and look after the well-being of the dumb animal that contributes to his welfare" (Tan., Wayesheb, 13, ed. Buber; see Gen. R. lxxxiv.). In specifying the number of men that escorted Abraham on his journey to Moriah (Gen. xxii. 3), and Saul on his visit to the witch of En-dor (I Sam. xxviii. 8), Scripture, according to R. Aibu, intends to convey the practical lesson, that man when traveling should be accompanied by at least two servants, or else he may himself become his servant's servant (Lev. R. xxvi.).

In his Biblical exegesis, he aims to reconcile variations in Scriptural expressions. Thus, Aibu explains the reason assigned for God's mercies in the passage, "The Lord will not forsake his people for his great name's sake" (I Sam. xii. 22), and the omission of that reason in the similar message, "The Lord will not cast off his people" (Ps. xciv. 14), by applying the latter to the times of the people's piety, and the former to the days of heedlessness. God is always good: when the people are deserving of His goodness He showers it upon them for their own sake; when, on the contrary, they are not deserving, He forsakes them not for His great name's sake (Ruth R. to i. 6). Similarly, he explains the variation in the version of the Fourth Commandment, "Remember the Sabbath day" (Ex. xx. 8), and "Keep the Sabbath day" (Deut. v. 12). According to Aibu (on behalf of Resh Laḳish) the term "remember" applies to cases when one is not able to rest on the Sabbath day, as, for instance, when one is on a sea voyage, and only remembering is possible; the term "keep" applies to ordinary circumstances, when "keeping" is obligatory (Pesiḳ. R. xxiii.).

Dwelling on the verse (Ps. viii, 4 [A. V. 3]), "When I consider thy heavens, the work of thy fingers," etc., Aibu remarks:

> "There are three classes of men: (1) those who are contented with admiring the grandeur of the sky, with the moon and stars and planets; (2) those who pray to God to reserve all the good due to them for heaven in the hereafter; and (3) a class of lazy workingmen who say, 'Whatever thou wilt give us, give us now, both what may be our due and whatever may be bestowed upon us through our fathers' merits: give us whatever thy fingers have wrought' " (Midr. Teh. to Ps. viii. 4).

Elsewhere he says: "No man departs from this world having realized even half of his desires. When a man has acquired a hundred pieces of gold, he longs to increase them to two hundred; and when he has two hundred, he is anxious to double these again" (Eccl. R. i. 13, iii. 10). Aibu's homiletic observations are numerous, both those related in his own name and those reported in his behalf by the haggadists of his own and subsequent generations (compare Pesiḳ. i., iii., v., xvii., xxv., xxvii.; Pesiḳ. R. ed. Friedman, index; Tan., ed. Buber, index; Midr. Teh. ed. Buber, index; Bacher, "Ag. Pal. Amor." iii. 63–79).

S. M.

AIBU (IBU) B. NAGGARI: A Palestinian amora of the fourth generation (fourth century), disciple of Hila, and contemporary of Judah b. (Simon b.) Pazzi. He reports Halakot in behalf of many of his predecessors (Yer. Sheḳ. iv. 48*c*, Yer. Meg. i. 70*a*, Yer. Yeb. i. 2*c*), and also advances opinions of his own. Several of his homiletic observations are preserved. One of these makes the scriptural verse "When he shall be judged, let him be condemned" (Ps. cix. 7) the basis for the often-cited rabbinic doctrine that Satan is always ready to accuse at a man's critical moment (Yer. Shab. ii. 5*b*; Yalḳ., Gen. § 31). Another, and the one most frequently quoted, is that which exonerates David from the imputation that he really "sat before the Lord" (compare II Sam. vii. 18), whereas sitting in the Temple was strictly prohibited. Aibu interprets the Hebrew term *wayesheb* ("he sat") as if it were *wayasheb* ("he settled," or "prepared himself"), and interprets it as signifying that David composed himself for praying before the Lord (Yer. Pes. v. end, 32*d et al.*; the reading Bun b. Nagdi, in Midr. Sam. xxvii., is obviously a copyist's error). That Aibu received instructions directly from Johanan, as seems to be intimated in the Babylonian Talmud (R. H. 21*a*), is doubtful, since he was known to have been a disciple of Hila (see Frankel, "Mebo," pp. 63*a*, 75*b*; Bacher, "Ag. Pal. Amor." iii. 559–560).

S. M.

'AKABIA BEN MAHALALEL: A religious teacher, probably of the second tannaitic generation (first and second centuries). Of his early history nothing is known; his teachers are nowhere named; and of his sayings comparatively few have been preserved (Mishnah 'Eduy. v. 6, 7; Mishnah Bek. v. 4; Mishnah Niddah, ii. 6; Mishnah Neg. i. 4, v. 3). The Mishnah portrays him as a man who, even in cases where different traditions were held by the majority of his colleagues, fearlessly and persistently maintained opinions on some Halakot, because those opinions were founded on traditions he had received from his learned predecessors. On one occasion the majority demanded that he renounce his divergent opinions, but he refused. It was even intimated to him that, in the event of his compliance, he would be elevated to the dignity of AB BET DIN (president of the court); but 'Akabia rejected the proposition, remarking, "I would rather be called a fool all my lifetime than be a sinner for one moment."

In the course of the discussion of the Halakah concerning the administration of "the water of jealousy" (Num. v. 11–31), 'Akabia declared that, if the subject of the test was not a free-born Jewess, the test-water was not to be administered; while the majority declared a proselyte or an emancipated slave to be the equal of a free-born daughter in Israel. In support of their view the majority cited a case in point, where the former associate presidents of the Sanhedrin, Shemaiah and Abtalion, had the test made on a freed woman; whereupon 'Akabia disdainfully exclaimed, "Dugma hishḳuha." This might mean "To one like themselves they gave to drink," and may be construed as an allusion to an old rumor to the effect that these associate presidents were themselves lineal descendants of proselytes (Giṭ. 57*b*); or it might mean "They gave her a sham to drink." The memory of those chiefs being held in esteem, 'Akabia's insinuation gave offense; wherefore the sentence of *nidduy* (isolation, excommunication) was passed on him. This he bore to the end of his days rather than violate his convictions. However, before his death, he admonished his son to submit to the views of the majority, even in the cases where he himself had shown such persistent opposition. His son expressing surprise at so apparent an inconsistency, the dying sage replied: "I have received my tradition from a majority of a school in my days, and so have my opponents. I was bound to conform to the tradition I had received; and so are they bound by their tradition. But thou hast heard the traditions both from myself and from my opponents; from a minority and from a majority, and it is proper for thee to reject the opinions of the individual and adopt the views of the majority" ('Eduy. v. 7).

Another characteristic trait of 'Akabia was the great stress he laid on personal merit. When, on his deathbed, he was requested by his son to recommend him to the sages, he declined to do so. His son inquired whether his father had discovered in him any trait which rendered him unworthy of such recommendation; and 'Akabia's reply was, "No! but thine own deeds will make thee welcome, or thine own deeds will make thee obnoxious" ('Eduy. v. 7).

'Akabia's motto in life was: "Remember whence thou hast come, whither thou goest, and before whom thou must be prepared to render an account of thy doings" (Ab. iii.. 1; compare Ab. R. N. xix; Yer. Soṭah, ii. 18*a*; Derek Ereẓ R. iii). Beyond this maxim and the Halakot enumerated above, nothing from him has been transmitted. As to his epoch scholars are divided. While some place him in the patriarchate of Hillel I. (30 B.C. to 10 of the present era), and even somewhat earlier, others bring him down to the first tannaitic generation (10–80); still others believe that he flourished during the patriarchate of GAMALIEL II. (80–117). The circumstances and scholastic achievements of the second tannaitic generation render ʻAkabia's excommunication more reasonable.

The decree of excommunication failed to obscure ʻAkabia's merited fame; for his name reached subsequent generations surrounded by such a halo of glory as to throw doubt on the decree itself. "God forbid," exclaims JUDAH B. ILAI, one of the tannaim of the fourth generation (139–165), "that we should think that ʻAkabia was excommunicated, for the Temple gates were never closed behind a man in Israel so great in wisdom and in the fear of sin as was ʻAkabia ben Mahalalel" (ʻEduy. *l.c.*). This expression, which is based on the law forbidding an excommunicated person to enter the Temple court, was in later days taken literally, and gave rise to forced halakic discussions and comments (Ber. 19*a*, Pes. 64*b*), as well as to hypothetical speculations about the age of ʻAkabia. Elsewhere (Sifre, Num. 105) it is said, "Whoever asserts that ʻAkabia was ever excommunicated will have to answer before the tribunal of heaven." This observation is wrongly attributed to Judah b. Betera I. (compare Shab. 97*a*); and conclusions as to ʻAkabia's early age are erroneously deduced therefrom.

BIBLIOGRAPHY: Brüll, *Mebo ha-Mishnah*, i. 49; Frankel, *Darke ha-Mishnah*, pp. 56 *et seq.*; Grätz, *Gesch. d. Juden*, 2d ed., iv. 39; Jost, *Gesch. des Judenthums und seiner Sekten*, ii. 34; Weiss, *Dor*, i. 176; Hamburger, *R. B. T.* ii. 32; Derenbourg, *Essai sur l' Histoire de la Palestine*, p. 483; Mendelsohn, *Rev. Ét. Juives*, xli. 31–44.

S. M.

AKIBA BEN JOSEPH: Palestinian tanna; born about 50; martyred about 132. A full history of Akiba, based upon authentic sources, will probably never be written, although he, to a degree beyond any other, deserves to be called the father of rabbinical Judaism (Yer. Shek. iii 47*b*, R. H. i. 56*d*). Legend, which delights in embellishing the memory of epoch-marking personages, has not neglected Akiba (see AKIBA BEN JOSEPH IN LEGEND); but, despite the rich mass of material afforded by rabbinical sources, only an incomplete portrait can be drawn of the man who marked out a path for rabbinical Judaism for almost two thousand years.

Akiba ben Joseph (written עקיבא in the Babylonian style, and עקיבה in the Palestinian—another form for עקביה), who is usually called simply Akiba, was of comparatively humble parentage (Yer. Ber. iv. 7*d*, Bab. *ibid.* 27*b*).* Of the romantic story of Akiba's marriage with the daughter

* A misunderstanding of the expression "Zekut Abot" (Ber. *l.c.*), joined to a tradition concerning Sisera, captain of the army of Hazor (Giṭ. 57*b*, Sahh. 96*b*), is the source of another tradition (Nissim Gaon to Ber. *l.c.*), which makes Akiba a descendant of Sisera.

of the wealthy Jerusalemite, Kalba Sabu'a, whose shepherd he is said to have been (see AKIBA BEN JOSEPH IN LEGEND), only this is true, that Akiba was a shepherd (Yeb. 86*b*; compare *ibid.* 16*a*). His wife's name was Rachel (Ab. R. N. ed. Schechter, vi. 29), and she was the daughter of an entirely unknown man named Joshua, who is specifically mentioned (Yad. iii. 5) as Akiba's father-in-law. She stood loyally by her husband during that critical period of his life in which Akiba, thitherto the mortal enemy of the rabbis, an out-and-out *'am ha-areẓ* (ignoramus) (Pes. 49*b*), decided to place himself at the feet of those previously detested men. A reliable tradition (Ab. R. N. *l.c.*) narrates that Akiba at the age of forty, and when he was the father of a numerous family dependent upon him, eagerly attended the academy of his native town, Lydda, presided over by Eliezer ben Hyrcarnus. The fact that Eliezer was his first teacher, and the only one whom Akiba later designates as "rabbi," is of importance in settling the date of Akiba's birth. It is known that in 95–96 Akiba had already attained great prominence (Grätz, "Gesch. d. Juden," 2d ed., iv. 121), and, further, that he studied for thirteen years before becoming a teacher himself (Ab. R. N. *l.c.*). Thus the beginning of his years of study would fall about 75–80. Earlier than this, Johanan ben Zakkai was living; and Eliezer, being his pupil, would have been held of no authority in Johanan's lifetime. Consequently, if we accept the tradition that Akiba was forty when beginning the study of the Law, he must have been born about 40–50. Besides Eliezer, Akiba had other teachers—principally Joshua ben Hananiah (Ab. R. N. *l.c.*) and Nahum of Gimzo (Hag. 12*a*). With Rabban Gamaliel II., whom he met later, he was upon a footing of equality. In a certain sense, Ṭarphon was considered as one of Akiba's masters (Ket. 84*b*); but the pupil outranked his teacher, and Ṭarphon became one of Akiba's greatest admirers (Sifre, Num. 75). Akiba probably remained in Lydda (R. H. i. 6), as long as Eliezer dwelt there, and then removed his own school to Bene Beraḳ, five Roman miles from Jaffa (Sanh. 32*b*; Tosef., Shab. iii. [iv.] 3). Akiba also lived for some time at Ziphron (Num. xxxiv. 9), the modern Zafrân (Z. P. V. viii. 28), near Hamath (see Sifre, Num. iv., and the parallel passages quoted in the Talmudical dictionaries of Levy and Jastrow). For another identification of the place, and other forms of its name, see Neubauer, "Géographie," p. 391, and Jastrow, *l.c.*

The greatest tannaim of the middle of the second century came from Akiba's school, notably Meir, Judah ben Ilai, Simeon ben Yoḥai, Jose ben Ḥalafta, Eleazar b. Shammai, and Nehemiah. Besides these, who all attained great renown, Akiba undoubtedly had many disciples whose names have not been handed down, but whose number is variously stated by the Haggadah at 12,000 (Gen. R. lxi. 3), 24,000 (Yeb. 62*b*), and 48,000 (Ned. 50*a*). That these figures are to be regarded merely as haggadic exaggerations, and not, as some modern historians insist, as the actual numbers of Akiba's political followers, is evident from the passage, Ket. 106*a*, in which there are similar exaggerations concerning the disciples of other rabbis. The part which Akiba is said to have taken in the Bar Kokba war can not be historically determined. The only established fact concerning his connection with Bar Kokba is that the venerable teacher really regarded the patriot as the promised Messiah (Yer. Ta'anit, iv. 68*d*); and this is absolutely all there is in evidence of an active participation by Akiba in the revolution. The numerous journeys which, according to rabbinical sources, Akiba is said to have made, can not have been in any way connected with politics. In 95–96 Akiba was in Rome (Grätz, "Gesch. d. Juden," iv. 121), and some time before 110 he was in Nehardea (Yeb. xvi. 7); which journeys can not be made to coincide with revolutionary plans. In view of the mode of traveling then in vogue, it is not at all improbable that Akiba visited en route numerous other places having important Jewish communities (Neuburger in "Monatsschrift," 1873, p. 393); but information on this point is lacking. The statement that he dwelt in Gazaka in Media rests upon a false reading in Gen. R. xxxiii. 5, and 'Ab. Zarah, 34*a*, where for "Akiba" should be read " 'Uḳba," the Babylonian, as Rashi on Ta'anit, 11*b*, points out. Similarly the passage in Ber. 8*b* should read "Simon b. Gamaliel" instead of Akiba, just as the Pesiḳta (ed. Buber, iv. 33*b*) has it. A sufficient ground for refusing credence in any participation by Akiba in the political anti-Roman movements of his day is the statement of the Baraita (Ber. 61*b*), that he suffered martyrdom on account of his transgression of Hadrian's edicts against the practise and the teaching of the Jewish religion, a religious and not a political reason for his death being given.

Akiba's death, which, according to Sanh. 12*a*, occurred after several years of imprisonment, must have taken place about 132, before the suppression of the Bar Kokba revolution; otherwise, as Frankel ("Darke ha-Mishnah," p. 121) remarks, the delay of the Romans in executing him would be quite inexplicable. That the religious interdicts of Hadrian preceded the overthrow of Bar Kokba, is shown by Mek., Mishpaṭim, 18, where Akiba regards the martyrdom of two of his friends as ominous of his own fate. After the fall of Bethar no omens were needed to predict evil days. Legends concerning the date and manner of Akiba's death are numerous; but they must all be disregarded, as being without historical foundation (see AKIBA BEN JOSEPH IN LEGEND).

Before proceeding to a consideration of Akiba's teaching, a word or two as to his personal character will be in place. According to the customary conception of the Pharisees, one would imagine him as being a typically proud and arrogant rabbi, looking down with contempt upon the common people. How modest he was in reality is shown by his funeral address over his son Simon. To the large assembly gathered on the occasion from every quarter, he said:

> "Brethren of the house of Israel, listen to me. Not because I am a scholar have ye appeared here so numerously; for there are those here more learned than I. Nor because I am a wealthy man; for there are many more wealthy than I. The people of the south know Akiba; but whence should the people of Galilee know him? The men are acquainted with him; but how shall the women and children I see here be said to be acquainted with him? Still I know that your reward shall be great, for ye have given yourselves the trouble to come simply in order to do honor to the Torah and to fulfil a religious duty" (Sem. viii., M. Ḳ. 21*b*).

Modesty is a favorite theme with Akiba, and he reverts to it again and again. "He who esteems himself highly on account of his knowledge," he teaches, "is like a corpse lying on the wayside: the traveler turns his head away in disgust, and walks quickly by" (Ab. R. N., ed. Schechter, xi. 46). Another of his sayings, quoted also in the name of Ben 'Azzai (Lev. R. i. 5), is specially interesting from the fact that Luke, xiv. 8–12, is almost literally identical with it: "Take thy place a few seats below thy rank until thou art bidden to take a higher place; for it is better that they should say to thee 'Come up higher' than that they should bid thee 'Go down lower' " (see Prov. xxv. 7). Though so modest, yet when an important matter and not a merely personal one was concerned Akiba could not be cowed by the greatest, as is evidenced by his attitude toward the patriarch Gamaliel II. Convinced of the necessity of a central authority for Judaism, Akiba became a devoted adherent and friend of Gamaliel, who aimed at constituting the patriarch the true spiritual chief of the Jews (R. H. ii. 9). But Akiba was just as firmly convinced that the power of the patriarch must be limited both by the written and the oral law, the interpretation of which lay in the hands of the learned; and he was accordingly brave enough to act in ritual matters in Gamaliel's own house contrary to the decisions of Gamaliel himself (Tosef., Ber. iv. 12).

Concerning Akiba's other personal excellences, such as benevolence, and kindness toward the sick and needy, see Ned. 40*a*, Lev. R. xxxiv. 16, and Tosef., Meg. iv. 16. In this connection it may be mentioned that Akiba filled the office of an overseer of the poor (Ma'as. Sh. v. 9, and Ḳid. 27*a*).

Eminent as Akiba was by his magnanimity and moral worthiness, he was still more so by his intellectual capacity, by which he secured an enduring influence upon his contemporaries and upon posterity. In the first place, Akiba was the one who definitely fixed the canon of the Old Testament books. He protested strongly against the canonicity of certain of the Apocrypha, Ecclesiasticus, for instance (Sanh. x. 1, Bab. *ibid.* 100*b*, Yer. *ibid.* x. 28*a*), in which passages קורא is to be explained according to Ḳid. 49*a*, and חיצונים according to its Aramaic equivalent ברייתא; so that Akiba's utterance reads, "He who reads *aloud* in the synagogue from books not belonging to the canon as if they were canonical," etc. He has, however, no objection to the private reading of the Apocrypha, as is evident from the fact that he himself makes frequent use of Ecclesiasticus (Bacher, "Ag. Tan." i. 277; Grätz, "Gnosticismus," p. 120). Akiba stoutly defended, however, the canonicity of the Song of Songs, and Esther (Yad. iii. 5, Meg. 7*a*). Grätz's statements ("Shir ha-Shirim," p. 115, and "Ḳohelet," p. 169, respecting Akiba's attitude toward the canonicity of the Song of Songs are misconceptions, as Weiss ("Dor," ii. 97) has to some extent shown. To the same motive underlying his antagonism to the Apocrypha, namely, the desire to disarm Christians—especially Jewish Christians—who drew their "proofs" from the Apocrypha, must also be attributed his wish to emancipate the Jews of the Dispersion from the domination of the Septuagint, the errors and inaccuracies in which frequently distorted the true meaning of Scripture, and were even used as arguments against the Jews by the Christians.

Aquila was a man after Akiba's own heart; under Akiba's guidance he gave the Greek-speaking Jews a rabbinical Bible (Jerome on Isa. viii. 14, Yer. Ḳid. i. 59*a*). Akiba probably also provided for a revised text of the Targums; certainly, for the essential base of the so-called Targum Onkelos, which in matters of Halakah reflects Akiba's opinions completely (F. Rosenthal, "Bet Talmud," ii. 280).

Akiba's true genius, however, is shown in his work in the domain of the Halakah; both in his systematization of its traditional material and in its further development. The condition of the Halakah, that is, of religious praxis, and indeed of Judaism in general, was a very precarious one at the turn of the first Christian century. The lack of any systematized collection of the accumulated Halakot rendered impossible any presentation of them in form suitable for practical purposes. Means for the theoretical study of the Halakah were also scant; both logic and exegesis—the two props of the Halakah—being differently conceived by the various ruling tannaim, and differently taught. According to a tradition which has historical confirmation, it was Akiba who systematized and brought into methodic arrangement the MISHNAH, or Halakah codex; the MIDRASH, or the exegesis of the Halakah; and the HALAKOT,* the logical amplification of the Halakah (Yer. Sheḳ. v. 48*c*, according to the correct text given by Rabbinowicz, "Diḳduḳe Soferim," p. 42;

* For this meaning of Halakah, see especially Tosef., Zab.i. 5. מסדר הלכות means to find logical foundation for the Halakot.

compare Giṭ. 67*a* and Dünner, in "Monatsschrift," xx. 453, also Bacher, in "Rev. Ét. Juives," xxxviii. 215.)

The *δευτερώσεις τοῦ καλουμένου* 'Ραββὶ 'Ακιβά * mentioned by Epiphanias ("Adversus Hæreses," xxxiii. 9, and xv., end), as well as the "great Mishnayot of Akiba" in the Midr. Cant. R. viii. 2; Eccl. R. vi. 2, are probably not to be understood as independent Mishnayot (*δευτερώσεις*) existing at that time, but as the teachings and opinions of Akiba contained in the officially recognized Mishnayot and Midrashim. But at the same time it is fair to consider the Mishnah of Judah ha-Nasi (called simply "the Mishnah") as derived from the school of Akiba; and the majority of halakic Midrashim now extant are also to be thus credited. Johanan bar Nappaḥa (199–279) has left the following important note relative to the composition and editing of the Mishnah and other halakic works: "Our Mishnah comes directly from Rabbi Meir, the Tosefta from R. Nehemiah, the Sifra from R. Judah, and the Sifre from R. Simon; but they all took Akiba for a model in their works and followed him" (Sanh. 86*a*). One recognizes here the threefold division of the halakic material that emanated from Akiba: (1) The codified Halakah (which is Mishnah); (2) the Tosefta, which in its original form contains a concise logical argument for the Mishnah, somewhat like the "Lebush" of Mordecai Jafe on the "Shulḥan 'Aruk"; (3) the halakic Midrash. The following may be mentioned here as the halakic Midrashim originating in Akiba's school: the Mekilta of Rabbi Simon (in manuscript only) on Exodus; Sifra on Leviticus; Sifre Zuṭṭa on Numbers (excerpts in Yalḳ. Shim'oni, and a manuscript in Midrash ha-Gadol, edited for the first time by B. Koenigsberger, 1894); and the Sifre to Deuteronomy, the halakic portion of which belongs to Akiba's school.

Admirable as is the systematization of the Halakah by Akiba, his hermeneutics and halakic exegesis—which form the foundation of all Talmudic learning—surpassed it. The enormous difference between the Halakah before and after Akiba may be briefly described as follows: The old Halakah was, as its name indicates, the religious practice sanctioned as binding by tradition; to which were added extensions, and, in some cases, limitations, of the Torah, arrived at by strict logical deduction. The opposition offered by the Sadducees—which became especially strenuous in the last century B.C.—originated the halakic Midrash, whose mission it was to deduce these amplifications of the Law, by tradition and logic, out of the Law itself. It might be thought that with

* In the second passage Rabbi Akiba has been corrupted into Barakiban, as also in Jerome's "Epistola ad Algasiam," 121, where, instead of Barachibas, Rab Achibas should be read. The statement in Epiphanius's "Adversus Hæreses," xlii. (ed. Migne, p. 744), that Akiba was born shortly before the Babylonian exile, is based upon the confusion of Akiba with Ezra, who was considered toy Jewish authorities the founder of tradition (Suk. 20*a*), and as whose successor Akiba is designated (Sifre, Deut. 48).

the destruction of the Temple—which event made an end of Sadduceeism—the halakic Midrash would also have disappeared, seeing that the Halakah could now dispense with the Midrash. This probably would have been the case had not Akiba created his own Midrash, by means of which he was able "to discover things that were even unknown to Moses" (Pesiḳ., Parah, ed. Buber, 39*b*). Akiba made the accumulated treasure of the oral law—which until his time was only a subject of knowledge, and not a science—an inexhaustible mine from which, by the means he provided, new treasures might be continually extracted. If the older Halakah is to be considered as the product of the internal struggle between Phariseeism and Sadduceeism, the Halakah of Akiba must be conceived as the result of an external contest between Judaism on the one hand and Hellenism and Hellenistic Christianity on the other. Akiba no doubt perceived that the intellectual bond uniting the Jews—far from being allowed to disappear with the destruction of the Jewish state—must be made to draw them closer together than before. He pondered also the nature of that bond. The Bible could never again fill the place alone; for the Christians also regarded it as a divine revelation. Still less could dogma serve the purpose, for dogmas were always repellent to rabbinical Judaism, whose very essence is development and the susceptibility to development. Mention has already been made of the fact that Akiba was the creator of a rabbinical Bible version elaborated with the aid of his pupil, Aquila, and designed to become the common property of all Jews; thus Judaizing the Bible, as it were, in opposition to the Christians. But this was not sufficient to obviate all threatening danger. It was to be feared that the Jews, by their facility in accommodating themselves to surrounding circumstances—even then a marked characteristic—might become entangled in the net of Grecian philosophy, and even in that of Gnosticism. The example of his colleagues and friends, ELISHA BEN ABUYAH, BEN 'AZZAI and BEN ZOMA strengthened him still more in his conviction of the necessity of providing some counterpoise to the intellectual influence of the non-Jewish world.

Akiba sought to apply the system of isolation followed by the Pharisees (פרושים—those who "separate" themselves) to doctrine as they did to practise, to the intellectual life as they did to that of daily intercourse, and he succeeded in furnishing a firm foundation for his system. As the fundamental principle of his system, Akiba enunciates his conviction that the mode of expression used by the Torah is quite different from that of every other book. In the language of the Torah nothing is mere form; everything is essence. It has nothing superfluous; not a word, not a syllable, not even a letter. Every peculiarity of diction, every particle, every sign, is to be considered as of higher importance, as having a wider relation and as being of deeper meaning than it seems to have. Like Philo (see Siegfried, "Philo," p. 168), who saw in the Hebrew construction of the infinitive with the finite form of the same verb—which is readily recognizable in the Septuagint—and in certain particles (adverbs, prepositions, etc.) some deep reference to philosophical and ethical doctrines, Akiba perceived in them indications of many important ceremonial laws, legal statutes, and ethical teachings (compare Hoffmann, "Zur Einleitung," pp. 5–12, and Grätz, "Gesch." iv. 427). He thus gave the Jewish mind not only a new field for its own employment, but, convinced both of the unchangeableness of Holy Scripture and of the necessity for development in Judaism, he succeeded in reconciling these two apparently hopeless opposites by means of his remarkable method. The following two illustrations will serve to make this clear: (1) The high conception of woman's dignity, which Akiba shared in common with most other Pharisees, induced him to abolish the Oriental custom that banished women at certain periods from all social intercourse. He succeeded, moreover, in fully justifying his interpretation of those Scriptural passages upon which this ostracism had been founded by the older expounders of the Torah (Sifra, Meẓora', end, and Shab. 64*b*). (2) The Biblical legislation in Ex. xxi. 7 could not be reconciled by Akiba with his view of Jewish ethics: for him a "Jewish slave" is a contradiction in terms; for every Jew is to be regarded as a prince (B. M. 113*b*). Akiba therefore teaches, in opposition to the old Halakah, that the sale of a daughter under age by her father conveys to her purchaser no legal title to marriage with her, but, on the contrary, carries with it the *duty* to keep the female slave until she is of age, and then to marry her (Mek., Mishpaṭim, 3). How Akiba endeavors to substantiate this from the Hebrew text is shown by Geiger ("Urschrift," p. 187). How little he cared for the letter of the Law whenever he conceives it to be antagonistic to the spirit of Judaism, is shown by his attitude toward the Samaritans. He considered friendly intercourse with these semi-Jews as desirable on political as well as on religious grounds; and he permitted—in opposition to tradition—not only eating their bread (Sheb. viii. 10) but also eventual intermarriage (Ḳid. 75*b*). This is quite remarkable, seeing that in matrimonial legislation he went so far as to declare every forbidden union as absolutely void (Yeb. 92*a*) and the offspring as illegitimate (Ḳid. 68*a*). For similar reasons Akiba comes near abolishing the Biblical ordinance of Kilaim; nearly every chapter in the treatise of that name contains a mitigation by Akiba. Love for the Holy Land, which he as a genuine nationalist frequently and warmly expressed (see Ab. R. N. xxvi.), was so powerful with him that he would have exempted agriculture from much of the rigor of the Law. These examples will suffice to justify the opinion that Akiba was the man to whom Judaism owes preeminently its activity and its capacity for development.

Goethe's saying, that "in self-restraint is the master shown," is contradicted by Akiba, who, though diametrically opposed to all philosophical speculation, is nevertheless the only tanna to whom we can attribute something like a religious philosophy. A tannaitic tradition (Ḥag. 14*b*; Tosef., Ḥag. ii. 3) mentions that of the four who entered paradise, Akiba was the only one that returned unscathed. This serves at least to show how strong in later ages was the recollection of Akiba's philosophical speculation (see ELISHA B. ABUYA). Akiba's utterances (Abot, iii. 14, 15) may serve to present the essence of his religious conviction. They run: "How favored is man, for he was created after an image; as Scripture says, 'for in an image, Elohim made man'" (Gen. ix. 6). "Everything is foreseen; but freedom [of will] is given to every man." "The world is governed by mercy... but the divine decision is made by the preponderance of the good or bad in one's actions." Akiba's anthropology is based upon the principle that man was created בצלם, that is, not in the image of God—which would be בצלם אלהים—but after an image, after a primordial type; or, philosophically speaking, after an Idea—what Philo calls in agreement with Palestinian theology, "the first heavenly man". Strict monotheist that Akiba was, he protested against any comparison of God with the angels, and declared the traditional interpretation of כאחד ממנו (Gen. iii 22) as meaning "like one of us" to be arrant blasphemy (Mek., Beshallaḥ, 6). It is quite instructive to read how a contemporary of Akiba, Justin Martyr, calls the old interpretation—thus objected to by Akiba—a "Jewish heretical one" ("Dial. cum Tryph." lxii.). In his earnest endeavors to insist as strongly as possible upon the incomparable nature of God, Akiba indeed lowers the angels somewhat to the realms of mortals, and, alluding to Ps. lxxviii. 25, maintains that manna is the actual food of the angels (Yoma, 75*b*). This view of Akiba's, in spite of the energetic protests of his colleague Ishmael, became the one generally accepted by his contemporaries, as Justin Martyr, *l.c.*, lvii., indicates.

Against the Judæo-Gnostic doctrine ("Recognit." iii. 30; Sifre, Num. 103; Sifra, Wayikra, 2), which teaches that angels—who are spiritual beings—and also that the departed pious, who are bereft of their flesh, can see God, the words of Akiba, in Sifra, *l.c.*, must be noticed. He insists that not even the angels can see God's glory; for he interprets the expression in Ex. xxxiii. 20, "no man can see me and live" (וחי), as if it read "no man or any living immortal can see me." Next to the transcendental nature of God, Akiba insists emphatically, as has been mentioned, on the freedom of the will, to which he allows no limitations. This insistence is in opposition to the Christian doctrine of the sinfulness and depravity of man, and apparently controverts his view of divine predestination. He derides those who find excuse for their sins in this supposed innate depravity (Ḳid. 81*a*). But Akiba's opposition to this genetically Jewish doctrine is probably directed mainly against its Christian correlative, the doctrine of the grace of God contingent upon faith in Christ, and baptism. Referring to this, Akiba says, "Happy are ye, O Israelites, that ye purify yourselves through your heavenly Father, as it is said (Jer. xvii. 13, *Heb.*), 'Israel's hope is God' " (Mishnah Yoma, end). This is a play on the Hebrew word מקוה ("hope" and "bath"). In opposition to the Christian insistence on God's love, Akiba upholds God's retributive justice elevated above all chance or arbitrariness (Mekilta, Beshallaḥ, 6). But he is far from representing justice as the only attribute of God: in agreement with the ancient Palestinian theology of the מדת הדין ("the attribute of justice") and מדת הרחמים ("the attribute of mercy") (Gen. R. xii., end; the *χαριστική* and *κολαστική* of Philo, "Quis Rer. Div. Heres," 34, Mangey, i. 496), he teaches that God combines goodness and mercy with strict justice (Ḥag. 14*a*). The idea of justice, however, so strongly dominates Akiba's system that he will not allow God's grace and kindness to be understood as arbitrary. Hence his maxim, referred to above, "God rules the world in mercy, but according to the preponderance of good or bad in human acts."

As to the question concerning the frequent sufferings of the pious and the prosperity of the wicked—truly a burning one in Akiba's time—this is answered by the explanation that the pious are punished in this life for their few sins, in order that in the next they may receive only reward; while the wicked obtain in this world all the recompense for the little good they have done, and in the next world will receive only punishment for their misdeeds (Gen. R. xxxiii.; Pesiḳ. ed. Buber, ix. 73*a*). Consistent as Akiba always was, his ethics and his views of justice were only the strict consequences of his philosophical system. Justice as an attribute of God must also be exemplary for man. "No mercy in [civil] justice!" is his basic principle in the doctrine concerning law (Ket. ix. 3); and he does not conceal his opinion that the action of the Jews in taking the spoil of the Egyptians is to be condemned (Gen. R. xxviii. 7). From his views as to the relation between God and man he deduces the inference that he who sheds the blood of a fellow man is to be considered as committing the crime against the divine archetype (דמות) of man (Gen. R. xxxiv. 14). He therefore recognizes as the chief and greatest principle of Judaism the command, "Thou shalt love thy neighbor as thyself" (Lev. xix. 18; Sifra, Ḳedoshim, iv.). He does not, indeed, maintain thereby that the execution of this command is equivalent to the performance of the whole Law; and in one of his polemic interpretations of Scripture he protests strongly against the contrary opinion of the Christians, according to whom Judaism is "simply morality" (Mek., Shirah, 3, 44*a*, ed. Weiss). For, in spite of his philosophy, Akiba was an extremely strict and national Jew. His doctrine concerning the Messiah was the realistic and thoroughly Jewish one, as his declaration that Bar Kokba was the Messiah shows. He accordingly limited the Messianic age to forty years, as being within the scope of a man's life—similar to the reigns of David and Solomon—against the usual conception of a millennium (Midr. Teh. xc. 15). A distinction is, however, to be made between the Messianic age and the future world (עולם הבא). This latter will come after the destruction of this world, lasting for 1,000 years (R. H. 31*a*). To the future world all Israel will be admitted, with the exception of the generation of the Wilderness and the Ten Tribes (Sanh. xi. 3, 110*b*). But even this future world is painted by Akiba in colors selected by his nationalist inclinations; for he makes Messiah (whom, according to Ezek. xxxvii. 24, he identifies with David) the judge of all the heathen world (Ḥag. 14*a*).

A man like Akiba would naturally be the subject of many legends (see Akiba ben Joseph in Legend). The following two examples indicate in what light the personality of this great teacher appeared to later generations. "When Moses ascended into heaven, he saw God occupied in making little crowns for the letters of the Torah. Upon his inquiry as to what these might be for, he received the answer, 'There will come a man, named Akiba ben Joseph, who will deduce Halakot from every little curve and crown of the letters of the Law.' Moses' request to be allowed to see this man was granted; but he became much dismayed as he listened to Akiba's teaching; for he could not understand it" (Men. 29*b*). This story gives in naive style a picture of Akiba's activity as the father of Talmudical Judaism. The following account of his martyrdom is on a somewhat higher plane and contains a proper appreciation of his principles: When Rufus—"Tyrannus Rufus," as he is called in Jewish sources—who was the pliant tool of Hadrian's vengeance, condemned the venerable Akiba to the hand of the executioner, it was just the time to recite the "Shema'." Full of devotion, Akiba recited his prayers calmly, though suffering agonies; and when Rufus asked him whether he was a sorcerer, since he felt no pain, Akiba replied, "I am no sorcerer; but I rejoice at the opportunity now given to me to love my God 'with all my life,' seeing that I have hitherto been able to love Him only 'with all my means' and 'with all my might,' " and with the word "One!" he expired (Yer. Ber. ix. 14*b*, and somewhat modified in Bab. 61*b*). Pure monotheism was for Akiba the essence of Judaism: he lived, worked, and died for it. See also Akiba ben Joseph in Legend.

Bibliography: Frankel, *Darke ha-Mishnah*, pp. 111–123; J. Brüll, *Mebo ha-Mishnah*, pp. 116–122; Weiss, *Dor*, ii. 107–118; H. Oppenheim, in *Bet Talmud*,

ii. 237–346, 269–274; I. Gastfreund, *Biographie des R. Akiba*, Lemberg, 1871; J. S. Bloch, in *Mimizraḥ u-Mima'arab*, 1894, pp. 47–54; Grätz, *Gesch. d. Juden*, iv. (see index); Ewald, *Gesch. d. Volkes Israel*, vii. 367 *et seq.*; Derenbourg, *Essai*, pp. 329–331, 395 *et seq.*, 418 *et seq.*; Hamburger, *R. B. T.* ii. 32–43; Bacher, *Ag. Tan.* i. 271–348; Jost, *Gesch. des Judenthums und Seiner Sekten*, ii. 59 *et seq.*; Landau, in *Monatsschrift*, 1854, pp. 45–51, 81–93, 130–148; Dünner, *ibid.* 1871, pp. 451–454; Neubürger, *ibid.* 1873, pp. 385–397, 433–445, 529–536; D. Hoffmann, *Zur Einleitung in die Halachischen Midraschim*, pp. 5–12; Grätz, *Gnosticismus*, pp. 83–120; F. Rosenthal, *Vier Apokryph. Bücher... R. Akiba's*, especially pp. 95–103, 124–131; S. Funk, *Akiba* (Jena Dissertation), 1896; M. Poper, *Pirke R. Akiba*, Vienna, 1808; M. Lehmann, *Akiba, Historische Erzählung*, Frankfort-on-the-Main, 1880; J. Wittkind, *Ḥuṭ ha-Meshulash*, Wilna, 1877; Braunschweiger, *Die Lehrer der Mischnah*, pp. 92–110.

L. G.

——**In Legend:** Akiba, who sprang from the ranks of the "plain people," loved the people; and they testified their admiration of his extraordinary accomplishments in the language of the people—in legend. The Haggadah, embodying the rabbinical legend—beginning with that all-important change in Akiba's life when, in the prime of life, he commenced to study—dwells upon every phase of his career and does not relinquish him even in death. Legendary allusion to that change in Akiba's life is made in two slightly varying forms, of which the following is probably the older:

Akiba, noticing a stone at a well that had been hollowed out by drippings from the buckets, said: "If these drippings can, by continuous action, penetrate this solid stone, how much more can the persistent word of God penetrate the pliant, fleshly human heart, if that word but be presented with patient insistency" (Ab. R. N. ed. Schechter, vi. 28).

According to another legend, it would appear that Akiba owed almost everything to his wife. Akiba was a shepherd in the employ of the rich and respected Kalba Sabu'a, whose daughter took a liking to him, the modest, conscientious servant. She consented to secret betrothal on the condition that he thenceforth devote himself to study. When the wealthy father-in-law learned of this secret betrothal, he drove his daughter from his house, and swore that he would never help her while Akiba remained her husband. Akiba, with his young wife, lived perforce in the most straitened circumstances. Indeed, so poverty-stricken did they become that the bride had to sell her hair to enable her husband to pursue his studies. But these very straits only served to bring out Akiba's greatness of character. It is related that once, when a bundle of straw was the only bed they possessed, a poor man came to beg some straw for a bed for his sick wife. Akiba at once divided with him his scanty possession, remarking to his wife, "Thou seest, my child, there are those poorer than we!" This pretended poor man was none other than the prophet Elijah, who had come to test Akiba (Ned. 50*a*).

By agreement with his wife, Akiba spent twelve years away from her, pursuing his studies under Eliezer ben Hyrcanus and Joshua ben Ḥananiah. Returning at the end of that time, he was just about to enter his wretched home, when he overheard the following answer given by his wife to a neighbor who was bitterly censuring him for his long absence: "If I had my wish, he should stay another twelve years at the academy." Without crossing the threshold, Akiba turned about and went back to the academy, to return to her at the expiration of a further period of twelve years. The second time, however, he came back as a most famous scholar, escorted by 24,000 disciples, who reverently followed their beloved master. When his poorly clad wife was about to embrace him, some of his students, not knowing who she was, sought to restrain her. But Akiba exclaimed, "Let her alone; for what I am, and for what we are, to this noble woman the thanks are due" (Ned. 50*a*, Ket. 62*b et seq.*).

Akiba's success as a teacher put an end to his poverty; for the wealthy father-in-law now rejoiced to acknowledge a son-in-law so distinguished as Akiba. There were, however, other circumstances which made a wealthy man of the former shepherd lad. It appears that Akiba, authorized by certain rabbis, borrowed a large sum of money from a prominent heathen woman—a *matrona*, says the legend. As bondsmen for the loan, Akiba named God and the sea, on the shore of which the matrona's house stood. Akiba, being sick, could not return the money at the time appointed; but his "bondsmen" did not leave him in the lurch. An imperial princess suddenly became insane, in which condition she threw a chest containing imperial treasures into the sea. It was cast upon the shore close to the house of Akiba's creditor; so that when the matrona went to the shore to demand of the sea the amount she had lent Akiba, the ebbing tide left boundless riches at her feet. Later, when Akiba arrived to discharge his indebtedness, the matrona not only refused to accept the money, but insisted upon Akiba's receiving a large share of what the sea had brought to her (Commentaries to Ned. *l.c.*).

This was not the only occasion on which Akiba was made to feel the truth of his favorite maxim ("Whatever God doeth He doeth for the best"). Once, being unable to find any sleeping accommodation in a certain city, he was compelled to pass the night outside its walls. Without a murmur he resigned himself to this hardship; and even when a lion devoured his ass, and a cat killed the cock whose crowing was to herald the dawn to him, and the wind extinguished his candle, the only remark he made was, "This, likewise, must be for a good purpose!"

When morning dawned he learned how true his words were. A band of robbers had fallen upon the city and carried its inhabitants into captivity, but he had escaped because his abiding place had not been noticed in the darkness, and neither beast nor fowl had betrayed him (Ber. 60*b*).

Akiba's many journeys brought numerous adventures, some of which are embellished by legend. Thus in Ethiopia he was once called upon to decide between the swarthy king and the king's wife; the latter having been accused of infidelity because she had borne her lord a white child. Akiba ascertained that the royal chamber was adorned with white marble statuary, and, basing his decision upon a well-known physiological theory, he exonerated the queen from suspicion (Num. R. ix. 34). It is related that during his stay in Rome Akiba became intimately acquainted with the Jewish proselyte Keṭia' bar Shalom, a very influential Roman—according to some scholars identical with Flavius Clemens, Domitian's nephew, who, before his execution for pleading the cause of the Jews, bequeathed to Akiba all his possessions ('Ab. Zarah, 10*b*). Another Roman, concerning whose relations with Akiba legend has much to tell, was Tinnius Rufus, called in the Talmud "Tyrannus" Rufus. One day Rufus asked: "Which is the more beautiful—God's work or man's?" "Undoubtedly man's work is the better," was Akiba's reply; "for while nature at God's command supplies us only with the raw material, human skill enables us to elaborate the same according to the requirements of art and good taste." Rufus had hoped to drive Akiba into a corner by his strange question; for he expected quite a different answer from the sage, and intended to compel Akiba to admit the wickedness of circumcision. He then put the question, "Why has God not made man just as He wanted him to be?" "For the very reason," was Akiba's ready answer, "that the duty of man is to perfect himself" (Tan., Tazri'a, 5, ed. Buber 7).

A legend according to which the gates of the infernal regions opened for Akiba is analogous to the more familiar tale that he entered paradise and was allowed to leave it unscathed. (Ḥag. 14*b*). There exists the following the tradition: Akiba once met a coal-black man carrying a heavy load of wood and running with the speed of a horse. Akiba stopped him and inquired: "My son, wherefore dost thou labor so hard? If thou art a slave and hast a harsh master, I will purchase thee of him. If it be out of poverty that thou doest thus, I will care for thy requirements." "It is for neither of these," the man replied; "I am dead and am compelled because of my great sins to build my funeral pyre every day. In life I was a tax-gatherer and oppressed the poor. Let me go at once, lest the demon torture me for my delay." "Is there no help for thee?" asked Akiba. "Almost none," replied the deceased; "for I understand that my sufferings will end only when I have a pious son. When I died, my wife was pregnant; but I have little hope that she will give my child proper training." Akiba inquired the man's name and that of his wife and her dwelling-place; and when, in the course of his travels, he reached the place, Akiba sought for information concerning.the man's family. The neighbors very freely expressed their opinion that both the deceased and his wife deserved to inhabit the infernal regions for all time—the latter because she had not even initiated her child into the Abrahamic covenant. Akiba, however, was not to be turned from his purpose; he sought the son of the tax-gatherer and labored long and assiduously in teaching him the word of God. After fasting forty days, and praying to God to bless his efforts, he heard a heavenly voice (*bat ḳol*) asking, "Wherefore givest thou thyself so much trouble concerning this one?" "Because he is just the kind to work for," was the prompt answer. Akiba persevered until his pupil was able to officiate as reader in the synagogue; and when there for the first time he recited the prayer, "Bless ye the Lord!" the father suddenly appeared to Akiba, and overwhelmed him with thanks for his deliverance from the pains of hell through the merit of his son (Kallah, ed. Coronel, 4*b*, and see quotations from Tan. in Aboab's "Menorat ha-Maor," i. 1, 2, § 1, ed. Fürstenthal, p. 82; also Maḥzor Vitry, p.112). This legend has been somewhat elaborately treated in Yiddish under the title, "Ein ganz nue Maase von dem Tanna R. Akiba," Lemberg, 1893 (compare Tanna debe Eliyahy Zuṭṭa, xvii., where Johanan b. Zakkai's name is given in place of Akiba).

Akiba's martyrdom—which is an important historical event—gave origin to many legends. The following describes his supernatural interment:

Contrary to the vision (Men. 29*b*), which sees Akiba's body destined to be exposed for sale in the butcher's shop, legend tells how Elijah, accompanied by Akiba's faithful servant Joshua, entered unperceived the prison where the body lay. Priest though he was, Elijah took up the corpse—for the dead body of such a saint could not defile—and, escorted by many bands of angels, bore the body by night to Cæsarea. The night, however, was as bright as the finest summer's day. When they arrived there, Elijah and Joshua entered a cavern which contained a bed, table, chair, and lamp, and deposited Akiba's body there. No sooner had they left it than the cavern closed of its own accord, so that no man has found it since (Jellinek, "Bet ha-Midrash," vi. 27, 28; ii. 67, 68; Braunschweiger, "Lehrer der Mischnah," 192–206).

L. G.

AMMI, AIMI, or **IMMI**: The name of several amoraim. In the Babylonian Talmud the first form only is used; in the Palestinian Talmud all three forms appear promiscuously, Immi predominating, and sometimes

R. Ammi is contracted into "Rabmi" or "Rabbammi" (Yer. 'Ab. Zarah, v. 45*a*, *b*). The most distinguished of these is a Palestinian amora of the third generation (third century). His native country is not named, but it is generally assumed to be Babylonia. It seems probable that the lifelong friendship existing between R. Ammi and R. Assi had its origin in ties of blood. R. Assi is identical with R. Assi (Jose) b. Nathan, and R. Ammi's full name, as given by himself, is Ammi b. Nathan (Giṭ. 44*a*); both of them, moreover, were of priestly descent (Meg. 22*a*, Ḥul. 107*b*), so that they seem to have been the sons of the same father; and as R. Assi is a native Babylonian, there is reason for assuming R. Ammi's Babylonian nativity. In his early age Ammi attended the college at Cæsarea, presided over by R. Hoshaiah I. (Yer. Shab. iii. 5*d*), and later he went to Tiberias and became the disciple of R. Johanan, at whose death he voluntarily observed the ritual period of mourning prescribed on the death of nearest relatives only (M. Ḳ. 25*b*). When he once heard that his Babylonian contemporary, R. Naḥman, had expressed himself disrespectfully of a misapplied opinion of R. Johanan, he indignantly exclaimed, "Does Naḥman think that because he is the son-in-law of the exilarch, he may speak disparagingly of R. Johanan's opinions?" (Ḥul. 124*a*). In Tiberias he became the center of a large circle of learned friends, among whom were R. Abbahu, R. Ḥanina (Ḥinena) b. Pappi, R. Isaac, and R. Samuel b. Naḥmani (M. Ḳ. 17*a*, 20*a*; Yeb. 48*b*); but the closest and most enduring friendship existed between him and R. Ḥiyya b. Abba and R. Assi (Ber. 16*a*, Yer. Pes. iii. 30*b*), both of whom were Babylonian immigrants.

Although R. Ammi had been in Palestine long before R. Assi, they were both ordained at the same time, and received a warm greeting from the students, who sang, "Such men, such men ordain for us! Ordain for us not those who use words like 'sermis' and 'sermit,' or 'hemis' and 'tremis' " (Ket. 17*a*, Sanh. 14*a*; see the explanation of these expressions in Bacher, "Ag. Pal. Amor." ii. 145, note 1; Krauss, "Lehnwörter," ii. 276; Jastrow, "Dict." p. 477; *idem*, "Future of Talmudic Texts," p. 15), which was an allusion to the simple language used by these rabbis as contrasted with the admixtures of foreign terms employed by other teachers. These two, together with R. Ḥiyya, constituted a court of justice, the administration of which at one time endangered their liberty, if not their lives. For a certain offense they had passed a severe sentence on a woman named Tamar, whereupon she preferred charges against them before the proconsular government for interfering with the Roman courts. Fearing the consequences of this denunciation they requested R. Abbahu to exert his influence with the government in their behalf; but he had anticipated the request, and nothing more was heard of the case (Yer. Meg. iii. 74*a*). Among their Babylonian contemporaries, Ammi and Assi were known as "the Palestinian judges," or as "the distinguished priests of Palestine" (Giṭ. 59*b*, Sanh. 17*b*). On the other hand, when R. Ammi quoted a doctrine of Rab or of Samuel, he introduced it with the expression, "Our masters in Babylonia say" (Shebu. 47*a*; compare Sanh. *l.c.*). Eventually R. Ammi succeeded to the rectorate of the college at Tiberias (Ḥul. 134*b*); but that did not prevent him from attending to his judicial functions, in conjunction with Assi. Indeed, it is reported that they interrupted their studies hourly, and, rapping at the college door, announced their readiness to hear causes if required (Shab. 10*a*). They would offer their prayers in the college building, preferring for that purpose the spaces between the pillars to all the thirteen synagogues in the city (Ber. 8*a*, 30*b*). Besides filling these offices, they, together with R. Ḥiyya, acted as inspectors and, where necessary, as organizers of schools for children and for adults. One of the instructions given by Ammi to the schoolmasters was to accommodate itinerant scholars in the schoolrooms (Yer. Meg. iii. 74*a*). In connection with one of the tours of inspection, the following characteristic anecdote is related:

> They came to a place where there were neither primary schools for children nor advanced schools for adults, and requested that the guardians of the city be summoned. When the councilmen appeared before them, the rabbis exclaimed, "Are these the guardians of the city? They are the destroyers of the city!" When asked who were the guardians, they replied, "The instructors of the young and the masters of the old; for thus the Scripture says (Ps. cxxvii. 1), 'Except the Lord keep the city, the watchman waketh but in vain' " (Yer. Ḥag. i. 76*c*, Midr. Teh. on *l.c.*).

Besides their familiarity with Halakah and Haggadah, Ammi and Assi also possessed some knowledge of the sciences of their time. They prescribed remedies in cases of sickness ('Ab. Zarah, 28*a*), and studied the habits of animals (Lev. R. xix. 1, Midr. Sam. v.). Much as they valued the study of the Law, they prized pious deeds still higher. Therefore they and R. Ḥiyya did not scruple to absent themselves from college and to miss a lecture by R. Eleazar; when the interment of a stranger required their attention (Yer. Pes. iii. 30*b*); and when once a considerable sum of money was presented to the college, Ammi took possession of it in the name of the poor, among whom it was subsequently distributed (Ḥul. 134*b*). Once R. Ammi, accompanied by R. Samuel b. Naḥmani, undertook a journey to the court of Zenobia, queen of Palmyra (267–273), to intercede for Zeir b. Ḥinena, who had been seized by her orders. Zenobia refused to liberate him, remarking, "Your God is accustomed to work miracles for you," when a Saracen, bearing a sword, entered and reported, "With this sword has Bar Nazar killed his brother"; this incident saved Zeir b. Ḥinena (Yer. Ter. viii. 46*b*). On another occasion he was ready to ransom a man who had repeatedly sold himself to the Ludi (lanistæ, procurers of subjects for gladiatorial contests—Jastrow, "Dict." p. 695). He argued that although the Mishnah (Giṭ. iv. 9) exempted a Jew from the duty of ransoming a man who repeatedly sells himself to non-Israelites, still it was his duty to ransom the children (to save them from sinking into idolatry); so much the greater was this obligation in a case where violent death was imminent. Ammi's colleagues, however, convinced him that the applicant for his protection was totally unworthy of his compassion, and he finally refused to interfere (Giṭ. 46*b* *et seq.*).

R. Ammi and R. Assi are very frequently cited in both Talmuds and in the Midrashim, and often together, either as being of the same opinion or as opposed to each other. Owing to this circumstance, the same doctrines are quoted sometimes in the name of one and sometimes in that of the other (compare Ber. 9*b*; Pes. 119*a*; Suk. 34*a*; Ta'anit, 3*a*; Suk. 44*a*; M. Ḳ. 3*b*). The same uncertainty manifests itself even where the reporter had probably received the tradition directly from one of them (Ḥul. 84*b*; Ber. 20*b*; Soṭah, 4*b*; Giṭ. 7*a*).

Following are some specimens of R. Ammi's exegetics: Commenting on Lam. iii. 41, "Let us lift up our heart with our hands unto God in the heavens," he observes, "No man's prayer is heard of heaven unless he carry his soul in the hands which he raises in prayer." "The prayer for rain is granted only for the sake of the men of faith." In support of this remark, Ammi, by means of an exegetical substitution of synonymous Hebrew words, quotes the verse (Ps. lxxxv. 11), "When Faith springeth forth from the earth, Beneficence looketh down from heaven" (Ta'anit, 8*a*). In Moses' designation of Israel as "a stiff-necked people" (Ex. xxxiv. 9), Ammi sees not so much a reproach as a praise of its firmness in religion, even in the face of persecution: "The Jew would either live as a Jew or die on the cross" (Ex. R. xlii.)· According to R. Ammi, death is the consequence of sin, and suffering the penalty of wrongdoing; the first observation he derives from the Scriptural saying (Ezek. xviii. 4), "The soul that sinneth, it shall die"; the second from Ps. lxxxix. 33, "I will visit their transgressions with the rod (of chastisement), and their iniquity with stripes" (Shab. 55*a*, Eccl. R. on v. 4).

BIBLIOGRAPHY: Grätz, *Gesch. d. Juden*, 2d ed., iv. 300–307; Frankel, *Mebo*, p. 63*a*; Weiss, *Dor*, iii. 96; Bacher, *Ag. Pal. Amor.* ii. 143–173.

S. M.

AMORA (plural, **Amoraim,** אמראים): A word signifying "the speaker," or "the interpreter," derived from the Hebrew and Aramaic verb *amar* ("to say," or "to speak"). It is used in the Talmud in a twofold sense:

(1) In a limited sense, it signifies the officer who stood at the side of the lecturer or presiding teacher in the academy and in meetings for public instruction, and announced loudly, and explained to the large assembly in an oratorical manner, what the teacher had just expressed briefly and in a low voice. While the lecturer generally pronounced his sentences in the academic language, which was chiefly Hebrew, the Amora gave his explanations in Aramaic, the popular idiom (see Rashi on Yoma, 20*b*). The original term for such an office was *meturgeman* ("the translator," or "the interpreter"), which term, even later on, was often interchanged with that of Amora (M. Ḳ. 21*a*, Sanh. 7*b*, Ḳid. 31*b*). Some of these officers are mentioned by name, as R. Ḥuẓpit, the interpreter at the academy of Rabban Gamaliel II. (Ber. 27*b*); Abdon, the interpreter appointed by the patriarch R. Judah (Yer. Ber. iv. 7*c*); R. Pedat, the interpreter of R. Jose; Bar Yeshita, the interpreter of R. Abbahu (Yer. Meg. iv. 75*c*); Judah bar Naḥmani, the interpreter of R. Simeon b. Laḳish (Ket. 8*b*). On his return from Palestine the celebrated teacher Rab (Abba Areka), while still unknown in Babylonia, in the absence of the regular Amora acted on one occasion as Amora in the academy of R. Shila (Yoma, 20*b*). It having been discovered that younger incumbents of this responsible office, in their endeavors to shine as orators (Soṭah, 40*a*), often failed to interpret the ideas of the presiding teacher correctly, R. Abbahu established the rule that no one under the age of fifty should be appointed to the position (Ḥag. 14*a*).

(2) In a wider sense the term Amora was applied, in Palestine as well as in Babylonia, to all the teachers that flourished during a period of about three hundred years, from the time of the death of the patriarch R. Judah I. (219) to the completion of the Babylonian Talmud (about 500). The activity of the teachers during this period was devoted principally to expounding the Mishnah—the compilation of the patriarch R. Judah—which became the authoritative code of the oral law. This activity was developed as well in the academies of Tiberias, Sepphoris, Cæsarea, and others in Palestine, as in those of Nehardea, Sura, and later of Pumbedita, and in some other seats of learning in Babylonia. In these academies the main object of the lectures and discussions was to interpret the often very brief and concise expression of the Mishnah, to investigate its reasons and sources, to reconcile seeming contradictions, to compare its canons with those of the Baraitot, and to apply its decisions to, and establish principles for, new cases, both real and fictitious, not already provided for in the Mishnah. The teachers that were engaged in this work—which finally became embodied in the Gemara—were properly called Amoraim; *i.e.*, interpreters or expounders (of the Mishnah). They were not as independent in their legal opinions

and decisions as their predecessors, the Tannaim and semi-Tannaim, as they had not the authority to contradict decisions and principles unanimously accepted in the Mishnah itself or in the Baraitot. The Palestinian Amoraim, having been ordained, as a general rule, by the *nasi*, had the title of "rabbi"; while the Babylonian teachers of that period had only the title of "rab" or of "mar."

The Palestinian Amoraim are distinguished by their simple method of teaching and expounding the Mishnah. The Babylonians indulged more in dialectical discussions. This was especially the case in the Academy of Pumbedita, where the dialectical method reached its highest development. The hair-splitting dialectic prevailing in that academy is satirized in the proverb: "In Pumbedita they know how to pass an elephant through a needle's eye"; that is, by their dialectical argumentation they can prove even that which is absolutely impossible (B. M. 38*b*).

The period of the Babylonian Amoraim is generally divided into six minor periods or generations, which are determined by the beginning and the end of the activity of their most prominent teachers. The period of the Palestinian Amoraim, being much shorter than that of the Babylonian, ends with the third generation of the latter. Frankel, in his "Mebo Yerushalmi," treating especially of the Palestinian Amoraim, divides them also into six generations.

The Chief Amoraim: The Amoraim mentioned in the Talmud number many hundreds. The names of the most distinguished among them, especially those that presided over the great academies, are given here in chronological order.

I P. First generation of Palestinian Amoraim (from the year 219–279):
Jannai, the Elder; Jonathan, the Elder.
Oshay'a, the Elder; Levi bar Sisi.
Ḥanina bar Ḥama; Hezekiah.
Johanan bar Nappaḥa; Simon b. Laḳish.
Joshua ben Levi; Simlai.

I B. First generation of Babylonian Amoraim (219–257):
Shila, in Nehardea.
Rab (Abba Areka), in Sura.
Mar Samuel, in Nehardea.
Mar 'Uḳba, chief-justice in Kafri.

II P. Second generation of Palestinian Amoraim (279–320):
Eleazar ben Pedat, in Tiberias.
Ammi and Assi, in Tiberias.
Ḥiyya bar Abba; Simeon bar Abba.
Abbahu, in Cæsarea.
Zera (or Zeira).

II B. Second generation of Babylonian Amoraim (257–320):
Huna, in Sura.
Judah ben Ezekiel, in Pumbedita.
Ḥisda, in Sura.
Sheshet, in Shilhi.
Naḥman ben Jacob, in Nehardea.

Other distinguished teachers belonging to this generation were Rabba bar Bar-Ḥana and ‘Ulla ben Ishmael.

III P. Third generation of Palestinian Amoraim (320–359):
Jeremiah,
Jonah, } in Tiberias.
Jose bar Zabda,

These three Amoraim were the last authorities in Palestine. The compilation of the Palestinian Talmud was probably accomplished in their time.

III B. Third generation of Babylonian Amoraim (320–375):
Rabbah bar Huna, in Sura.
Rabbah bar Naḥman,
Joseph bar Ḥiyya, } in Pumbedita.
Abaye (Naḥmani),
Raba, son of Joseph bar Ḥama, in Maḥuza.
Naḥman ben Isaac, in Pumbedita.
Papa bar Ḥanan, in Narash.

IV B. Fourth generation of Babylonian Amoraim (375–427):
Ashi, in Sura, compiler of the Babylonian Talmud.
Amemar, in Nehardea.
Ẓebid bar Oshay‘a,
Dimi bar Ḥinena,
Rafram I., } in Pumbedita.
Kahana bar Taḥlifa,
Mar Zuṭra,
Judah Mani b. Shalom.
Eliezer b. Jose.
Jose b. Abin.
Tanḥuma.

V B. Fifth generation of Babylonian Amoraim (427–468):
Mar Yemar (contracted to Maremar), in Sura.
Idi bar Abin,
Mar bar Ashi, } in Sura.
Aḥa of Difta,
Rafram II., in Pumbedita.

VI B. Sixth generation of Babylonian Amoraim (468–500):
Rabbina bar Huna, the last Amora of Sura
Jose, the last Amora of Pumbedita and the first of the Saboraim.

The Amoraim were followed by the Saboraim, who gave to the Talmud its finishing touch.

For particulars of the life and work of each of the above-mentioned Amoraim see articles under their respective names.

BIBLIOGRAPHY: For the older literature on the Amoraim: Sherira Gaon, in his *Iggeret*; Zacuto, in his *Yuḥasin*; Heilprin, in his *Seder ha-Dorot*. Modern literature: Fürst, *Kultur- und Literaturgesch. d. Juden in Asien*, which treats especially of the Babylonian academics and teachers during the period of the Amoraim, Leipsic, 1849; Rapoport, *'Erek Millin*, 1852, article Amora; Frankel, *Mebo ha-Yerushalmi*, Breslau, 1870; Grätz, *Gesch, d. Juden*, il., chaps, xviii.–xxii.; Weiss, *Dor*, iii.; Hamburger, *Realencyklopädie*, ii.; Mielziner, *Introduction to the Talmud*, chap, iv., Cincinnati, 1894; Strack, *Einleitung in den Talmud;* Bacher, *Ag. Bab. Amor.*; idem, *Ag. Pal. Amor.*

M. M.

ASHI: A celebrated Babylonian amora; born 352; died 427; reestablished the academy at Sura, and was the first editor of the Babylonian Talmud. According to a tradition preserved in the academies (Ḳid. 72*b*), Ashi was born in the same year that RABA, the great teacher of MAḤUZA, died, and he was the first teacher of any importance in the Babylonian colleges after RABA' s death. Simai, Ashi's father, was a rich and learned man, a student of the college at Naresh, near Sura, which was directed by Papa, Raba's disciple. Ashi's teacher was Kahana, a member of the same college, who afterward became president of the academy at Pumbedita.

While still young Ashi became the head of the Sura Academy, his great learning being acknowledged by the older teachers. It had been closed since Ḥisda's death (309), but under Ashi it regained all its old importance. His commanding personality, his scholarly standing and wealth are sufficiently indicated by the saying then current, that since the days of Judah I., the Patriarch, "learning and social distinction were never so united in one person as in Ashi" (Sanh. 36*a*). Indeed, Ashi was the man destined to undertake a task similar to that which fell to the lot of Judah I. The latter compiled and edited the MISHNAH; Ashi made it the labor of his life to collect after critical scrutiny, under the name of "GEMARA," those explanations of the Mishnah that had been handed down in the Babylonian academies since the days of Rab, together with all the discussions connected with them, and all the halakic and haggadic material treated in the schools.

Conjointly with his disciples and the scholars who gathered in Sura for the "Kallah" or semi-annual college-conference, he completed this task. The kindly attitude of King Yezdegerd I., as well as the devoted and respectful recognition of his authority by the academies of Nehardea and Pumbedita, greatly favored the undertaking. A particularly important element in Ashi's success was the length of his tenure of office as head of the Sura Academy, which must have lasted fifty-two years, but which tradition, probably for the sake of round numbers, has exaggerated into sixty. According to the same tradition, these sixty years are said to have been so symmetrically apportioned that each treatise required six months for the study of its Mishnah and the redaction of the traditional expositions of the same (Gemara), thus aggregating thirty years for the sixty treatises. The same process was then repeated for thirty years more, at the end of which period the work was considered complete.

The artificiality and unreality of this legendary account are made clear by the facts that the treatises are of different degrees of length and difficulty, and that a large number of them possess no Gemara whatever. Probably all that is historical in this statement is that Ashi actually revised the work twice—a fact that is mentioned in the Talmud (B. B. 157*b*). Beyond this, the Talmud itself contains not the slightest intimation of the activity which Ashi and his school exercised in this field for more than half a century. Even the question as to whether this editorial work was written down, and thus, whether the putting of the Babylonian Talmud into writing took place under Ashi or not, can not be answered from any statement in the Talmud. It is nevertheless probable that the fixation of the text of so comprehensive a literary work could not have been accomplished without the aid of writing. The work begun by Ashi was continued by the two succeeding generations, and completed by Rabina, another president of the college in Sura, who died in 499. To the work as the last-named left it, only slight additions were made by the Saboraim. To one of these additions—that to an ancient utterance concerning the "Book of Adam, the first man"—the statement is appended (B. M. 86*a*), "Ashi and Rabina are the last representatives of independent decision [horaah]," an evident reference to the work of these two in editing the Babylonian Talmud, which as an object of study and a fountainhead of practical "decision" was to have the same importance for the coming generations as the Mishnah had had for the Amoraim.

Ashi not only elevated Sura till it became the intellectual center of the Babylonian Jews, but contributed to its material grandeur also. He rebuilt Rab's academy and the synagogue connected with it; sparing no expense, and personally superintending their reconstruction (Shab. 11*a*). As a direct result of Ashi's renown, the exilarch came annually to Sura in the month after the New-Year to receive the respects of the assembled representatives of the Babylonian academies and congregations. To such a degree of splendor did these festivities and other conventions in Sura attain, that Ashi expressed his surprise that some of the Gentile residents of Sura were not tempted to accept Judaism (Ber. 17*b*).

Sura retained the prominence conferred on it by Ashi for several centuries; and only during the last two centuries of the Gaonic period did Pumbedita again become its rival. Ashi's son Tabyomi—always spoken of as "Mar (Master), the son of Rab Ashi," was a recognized scholar; but it was not until 455, twenty-eight years after his father's death, that he was invested with the position which his father had so successfully filled for more than half a century.

BIBLIOGRAPHY: *Letter of Sherira Gaon*; Heilprin, *Seder ha-Dorot;* Zacuto, *Yuḥasin*; Weiss, *Dor*, iii. 208 *et seq.*; Bacher, *Agada der Babyl. Amoräer*, p. 144.

J. SR. W. B.

ASSI (Assa, Issi, Jesa, Josah, Jose, sometimes דבסי, a contraction of Rab or Rabbi Assi): A prænomen of several amoraim, which, with its variants, is a modification or diminutive of "Joseph" (compare Bacher, "Ag. Tan." ii. 371; "Ag. Pal. Amor." ii. 151, 8). "Assi" is of Babylonian origin, while other forms are Palestinian. Hence in the Babylonian Talmud, except in cases of clerical error, "Assi" is the only form used; whereas in the Palestinian Talmud and Midrashim all forms are used indifferently, two or even more appearing in a single passage (for instance, Yer. Kil. ix. 32*b*) or in parallel passages (compare Yer. 'Er. vi. 23*d*; Yer. Sheḳ. ii. 46d, vii. 50*c*; Yer. Naz. iv. 53*b*). As to the bearers of the name, most of those having additional patronymics or cognomens are better known by the appellation of "Jose." The two that are best known by their simple prænomen, without further designation, are considered here. Great care is requisite in determining the authorship of doctrines and sayings bearing the above name. Both the Assis are halakic authorities, are native Babylonians, and are cited in both Talmudim, and they flourished within about half a century of each other. They can therefore be distinguished only by observing the persons with whom they are associated or who transmit their opinions. Thus, where Assi appears in company with Rab, with Samuel, or with their contemporaries, Assi I. is meant; but where the associates are members of a later generation, it is Assi II. Again, where Huna I., Judah b. Ezekiel, or their contemporaries or predecessors cite the name, it is Assi I.; but where their disciples, or their younger contemporaries or successors (particularly in the Palestinian Talmud and Midrashim) report, it is most frequently Assi II. Where, finally, none of these landmarks is present, a positive determination is well-nigh impossible, nor can the presence or absence of the titles Rab and Rabbi, on which (according to Tos. Ḥul. 19*a*, *s.v.* Amar) many rely, be accepted as a clue.

Assi (Assa, Issi) I., Rab: A Babylonian amora of the first generation, third century; contemporary of Rab (ABBA ARIKA) and his equal in dialectics, though inferior to him in general knowledge of the Halakah (Sank. 36*b*). But even in the latter branch Rab manifested great deference for Assi's opinions, often adopting these in preference to his own (Meg. 5*a*; Ḳid. 45*b*; Sanh. 29*b*; B. B. 62*a*). Socially, also, Rab treated Assi as an equal (Shab. 146*b*). Mar Samuel, also, treated Assi with great respect (B. Ḳ. 80*a et seq.*). Rab Assi is better known in the field of the Halakah than in that of the Haggadah, where he is found in association with Kahana and putting questions to Rab (Giṭ. 88*a*; compare Lam. R., Introd. 33; Yoma 10*a*).

According to a Talmudic narrative combining fact and fiction, Assi's end was precipitated by grief. Commissioned by his dying teacher and friend, Rab, to bring about Shela b. Abuna's retraction of a certain decision on the ritual, Assi visited the latter, when the following conversation took place: Assi: "Retract thy decision because Rab has retracted his opinion on which thy decision was based." Shela: "Had Rab renounced his opinion he would have told me so himself." Assi, misunderstanding the instructions of Rab, thereupon excommunicated his colleague. Shela: "Does the master not fear the fire for abusing a scholar?" (compare Ab. ii. 10.) Assi: "I am a mortar [" Asita," a play on his name] of brass, over which decay has no power." Shela: "And I am an iron pestle that may break the brass mortar." Assi soon after sickened and died; whereupon Shela, to prevent his adversary from carrying evil reports of him to Rab, prepared his own shroud and died also. At the double funeral it was observed that the myrtle branches which lay on the two biers leaped from one to the other, whence it was inferred that the departed spirits had become reconciled (Niddah 36*b et seq.*; the names Isi b. Judah, etc., used in Assi's reply to Shela are a glossator's interpolation borrowed from Pes. 113*b*). Of Assi's last hours the Midrash relates the following: As Rab Assi was about to depart from this world, his nephew entered the sick-room and found him weeping. Said the nephew: "My master, why weepest thou? Is there any part of the Torah which thou hast not learned or taught? Look at the disciples before thee. Is there any one good deed that thou hast not practised? And does not above all thy noble traits stand the fact that thou hast never acted as judge and hast never permitted thyself to be appointed to public office?" Then answered Rab Assi: "My son, this is just the reason why I am weeping. Perhaps I shall be required to answer for being able to administer justice and not doing so, thus exemplifying in myself what the Scripture means by saying (Prov. xxix. 4), 'The king by judgment establisheth the earth; but the man that holdeth himself aloof ["terumah" = separation] overthroweth it'" (Tan., Mishpaṭim, *2*). Some writers regard this scene as occurring at the death of Assi II.; but the concluding words of the visitors address, as well as the dying teacher's reason for his anxiety, are entirely inconsistent with the career of Assi II., whose activity as judge is a prominent feature of his life. (Yer. Shab. i. 3*a*; Yer. Sheḳ. vi: 50*b*; Yer. Suk. i. *52a*; Yeb. 16*b*; Ned. 21*b*; Yer. Ned. iii. 37*d*; Yer. Giṭ. ix. 50*d*; B. B. 126*a*; Shebu. 26*a*, 41*a*; Ḥul. 19*a*, *20a*).

Bibliography: Heilprin, *Seder ha-Dorot*, ii. *s.v.*; Weiss, *Dor*, iii. 97, *ib.* 154; Halevy, *Dorot ha-Rishonim*, ii. 228.

Assi (Assa, Issi, Jesa, Josah, Jose) II., R.: A Palestinian amora of the third generation, third and fourth centuries; one of the two Palestinian scholars known among their Babylonian contemporaries as "the Palestinian judges" and as "the distinguished priests of Palestine," his companion being R. Ammi (Giṭ. 59*b*; Sanh. 17*b*). Assi was born in Babylonia, where he attended the college of Mar Samuel (Yer. Ter. i. 40*a*; Yer. 'Er. vi. 23*d*), but later emigrated in consequence of domestic trouble. On his arrival in Tiberias, Assi had an adventure with a ruffian, which ended disastrously for the latter. Assi was making his way toward the baths, when he was assaulted by a "scorner." He did not resent the assault, except by remarking, "That man's neck-band is too loose," and continued on his way. It so happened that an archon was at that very hour trying a thief, and the scoffer, still laughing at the adventure with Assi, came to witness the trial just when the judge interrogated the culprit as to accomplices. The culprit, seeing the man laughing, thought that it was at his discomfiture, and to avenge himself pointed to the ruffian as his accomplice. The man was apprehended and examined. He confessed to a murder he had committed, and was sentenced to be hanged with the convicted thief. Assi, on returning from the baths, encountered the procession on its way to the execution. His assailant on seeing him exclaimed, "The neck-band which was loose will soon be tightened"; to which Assi replied, "Thy fate has long since been foretold, for the Bible says (Isa. xxviii. 22), 'Be ye not scorners lest your bands be made strong' " (Yer. Ber. ii. 5*c*).

Assi became a disciple of R. Johanan, and so distinguished himself that R. Eleazar called him "the prodigy of the age" ("mofet ha-dor"; Ḥul. 103*b*), and as such legend pictures him. Concerning the futile longings of many to communicate with the departed spirit of R. Hiya the Great, legend relates that R. Jose fasted eighty days in order that a glimpse of R. Hiya might be granted him. Finally the spirit of the departed appeared; but the sight so affected R. Jose that his hands became palsied and his eyes dim. "Nor must you infer from this," the narrator continues, "that R. Josah was an unimportant individual. Once a weaver came to R. Johanan and said, 'In a dream I have seen the skies fall, but one of thy disciples held them up.' When asked whether he knew that disciple, the weaver replied that he would be able to recognize him. R. Johanan thereupon had all his disciples pass before the weaver, who pointed to R. Josah as the miraculous agent" (Yer. Kil. ix. 32*b*; Eccl. R. ix. 10). Another adventure, which, however, bears the impress of fact, is related of him, wherein he was once abducted in a riot and given up as lost, but R. Simon ben Lakish, the former gladiator, rescued him at the risk of his own life (Yer. Ter. viii. 46*b*).

Assi's professional career in Palestine is so closely intertwined with that of R. Ammi that the reader may be referred to the sketch of the latter for information on that subject. R. Assi was very methodical in his lectures, making no digressions to answer questions not germane to the subject under discussion; and whenever such were propounded to him, he put off reply until he reached the subject to which they related (Yer. Shab. xix. 16*d*; Yer. 'Er. vi. 24*a*),

R. Assi is frequently quoted in both Talmudim and in the Midrashim. Profound is his observation: "At first the evil inclination is like a shuttle-thread (or spider-web), but eventually it grows to be like a cart rope, as is said in the Scriptures (Isa. v. 18), 'Wo unto them that draw iniquity with cords of vanity, and sin as if it were with a cart rope' " (Suk. 52*a*). An anecdote characteristic of rabbinical sympathy for inferiors and domestics is thus related: The wife of R. Jose had a quarrel with her maid, and her husband declared her in the wrong; whereupon she said to him, "Wherefore didst thou declare me wrong in the presence of my maid?" To which the rabbi replied, "Did not Job (xxxi. 13) say, 'If I did despise the cause of my manservant or of my maidservant, when they contended with me, what then shall I do when God riseth up? And when He visiteth, what shall I answer Him?' " (Gen. R. xlviii. 3). When Assi died, R. Hiya b. Abba, who had been his associate as judge and as teacher, went into mourning as for a relative (Yer. Ber. iii. 6*a*). The day of his death is recorded as coincident with a destructive hurricane (M. Ḳ. 26*b*).

The suggestion may here be offered that R. Assi, before his emigration to Palestine, was known as Assi (Issi, Jose) b. Nathan, the one that is met with in an halakic controversy with Ulla (b. Ishmael, Ber. 63*a*), propounding a ritual question to Hiya b. Ashi (Shab. 53*a*), and seeking an interpretation of a Baraita from the mouth of Rab) Sheshet (Ned. 78*a*; B. B. 121*a*).

BIBLIOGRAPHY: Grätz, *Gesch. der Juden*, iv. 300–307, 2d ed.; Frankel, *Mebo*; 100*a* (here some of the references undoubtedly point to Assi I.); Weiss, *Dor*, iii. 97; Bacher, *Ag. Pal. Amor.* ii. 143–173 (here some sayings of Assi I. are attributed to Assi II.); Halevy *Dorot ha-Rishonim*, ii. 232.

J. SR. S. M.

B

BABA BEN BUṬA: Teacher of the Law at the time of Herod, and perhaps a member of the prominent family known as "The Sons of Baba" "Bene Baba"), who, at the time of the siege of Jerusalem by Herod (37 B.C.), resisted its surrender, and whom Costobarus protected from the wrath of Herod for ten years, until they were discovered and put to death (Josephus, "Ant." xv. 7, § 10). But, according to a tradition preserved in the Babylonian Talmud (B. B. 3*b* *et seq.*), Baba ben Buṭa was the only teacher of the Law who was spared by Herod. According to this tradition it was Baba b. Buta, deprived of his eyesight by Herod, who advised the latter to rebuild the Temple in expiation of his great crimes. The following conversation between the king and the blind teacher, with its haggadic embellishments, forms the principal part of this tradition, and it probably rests upon a historical foundation:

"One day Herod came to visit the blind teacher and, sitting down before him, said, 'See how this wicked slave [Herod] acts.' Said he [Baba] to him, 'What can I do to him?' Said he, 'Curse him, sir.' Said he, 'It is written (Eccl. x. 20), "Curse not the king; no, not in thy thought."' 'But,' said Herod, 'he is no king.' Upon which Baba said, 'Let him be only a man of wealth, it is written (*ib.*), " And curse not the rich in thy bedchamber"; or let him be merely a chief, it is written (Ex. xxii. 27 [A.V. 28]), "Curse not a ruler of thy people."' 'But,' said Herod, 'this is interpreted to mean a ruler that acts according to the customs of thy people; but that man [Herod] does not act according to the customs of thy people.' Said he, 'I am afraid of him,' to which Herod replied, 'There is no man here to go and tell him; for I and thou sit here alone.' Said he, 'It is written (Eccl. *l.c.*), "For a bird of the air shall carry the voice, and that which hath wings shall tell the matter."'

"Herod now disclosed himself, and said, 'Had I known that the rabbis were so discreet, I should not have put them to death. What, now, can a man like me do to repair this wrong?' 'He,' said Baba, 'has extinguished the light of the world [put to death the teachers], as it is written (Prov. vi. 23), "For the commandment is a lamp; and the Law is light"; let him busy himself with the light of the world [the Temple], of which it is written (Isa. ii. 2), "All nations shall flow unto it"' [a play on *nahar*, which also means "light "]. Said Herod, 'I am afraid of the [Roman] government.' To which Baba replied, 'Send a messenger; he will be one year in going to Rome, will be detained there one year, and make his home voyage in one year, and in the mean while thou shalt have torn down and built'; and Herod did accordingly."

In halakic tradition Baba b. Buṭa is recorded as a disciple of Shammai; and it is said that he prevented an opinion of Shammai concerning a question of sacrifices from becoming a rule, because he was convinced of the correctness of Hillel's opposing opinion (Beẓah 20*a* *et seq.*). Baba was so scrupulous in his religious observances that he brought a free-will offering every day, for fear that he might have committed a sin requiring atonement. These sacrifices were called "sin-ofterings of the pious" "ḥasidim"). Baba was a member of the "bet din" and always saw that justice was done, particularly to women (Git. 57*a*; Ned. 66*b*).

BIBLIOGRAPHY: Grätz, *Gesch. der Juden*, 2d ed., iii. 166, 208; Weiss, Dor, i. 177 *et seq.*

J. SR. W. B.

BAR DALA, BARDALA, BAB DALIA, BARDALIA: A place near Lydda, which once harbored a rabbinic seat of learning (B. M. 10*a* *et seq.*; see Rabbinowicz, "Diḳduḳe Soferim," *ad loc.*; Beẓah 14*a*, see Rabbinowicz, *ib.*; Yer. 'Er. vi. 24*a*; Yer. Kil. i. 27*a*; Yer. Sheb. ii. 33d). It is supposed to be identical with Bet-Deli ('Eduy. viii. 5; Yeb. xvi. 7, in Yer. Mish. and Gemara 16*a*, "Badla"), which is recognized by some in Wady Ed-Dalia, between Tibnin and Safed in Galilee; by others, in Bet-Ulia (Dulia) on the road from Hebron to Jaffa. As the place was not far from Lydda—so that a Bardalian was sometimes considered as a Lyddan (Yer. Sanh. i. 18c)—the latter conjecture is the more probable. The local name is used in rabbinical literature as a surname, designating several scholars who hailed from that place (ABBA COHEN OF BARDALA, AHA BARDALA), and is occasionally employed as a prænomen; *e.g.*, Bardala b. Ṭabyome (Ḥag. 5*a*; see also Zeb. 33*b*).

BIBLIOGRAPHY: Schwarz, Das *Heilige Land*, p. 89; Neubauer, *G. T.* p. 263; Z. Frankel, *Mebo*, p. 70*a*; Jastrow, *Dict.* p. 190*a*; Kohut, *Aruch Completum*, ii. 185*b*, *ib.* 67*a*; Hirschensohn, *Meḥḳere Areẓ*, p. 75.

J. SR. S. M.

BAR GIORA, SIMON (called also **Simon Giora**): Jewish leader in the revolt against Eome; born about the year 50, at Gerasa. To judge from his Dame he was the son of a proselyte. The date of his birth is determined by the fact that he was very young at the time of the war with Nero. He was distinguished for bodily strength and reckless courage. After Cestius had been put to flight he surrounded himself with a band of men and devastated the lands of the Idumeans about Akrabattene; but, being pursued by troops from Jerusalem, he threw himself into the fortress of Masada (Josephus, "B. J." ii. 22, § 2; iv. 9, § 3). He kept up his guerrilla warfare, however, gradually increasing his troops until they numbered many thousand Sicarii; and, after fortifying Nain, he encamped in the valley of Paran. Having conquered the Idumeans and mastered Hebron, he swept up to the very gates of Jerusalem. Here an ambush was laid by the Jews of the city, and his wife and some of his soldiers were seized; but Bar Giora compelled them to be delivered up to him (*ib.* iv. 9, §§ 8, 10). In the mean time the Idumeans and the Zealots in Jerusalem came into conflict (April, 68); and the Idumeans, suffering defeat, called Bar Giora into the city. Though Matthias, high priest at the time, had been instrumental in summoning him, Bar Giora later put him to death (*ib.* iv. 9, § 11; v. 13, § 1), henceforth considering himself lord of the city, and maintaining constant strife with John of Gischala, leader of the Zealots, the latter being outdone in their frenzy by Bar Giora's followers, the Sicarii.

The Idumeans, though formerly oppressed by Bar Giora, now joined their forces to his. From his strong fortification at Phaselis—in which he garrisoned his ten thousand soldiers—he could command the whole of Jerusalem (*ib.* v. 3, § 1; 6, § 1). When Titus moved up to the walls of Jerusalem, Bar Giora made peace with John and the Zealots, and in a number of sallies inflicted serious losses on the Romans (*ib.* v. 2, § 4; vi. 1, § 7). After Jerusalem had been almost entirely taken and the Temple had been burned down (on the Ninth of Ab), Bar Giora and other fearless men withdrew to the upper city, from which they negotiated with Titus, offering to surrender on condition that they should be allowed to go free under oath not to draw their weapons. The Romans refused, and the struggle broke out afresh. On the eighth of Elul the upper city also fell a prey to the flames. John surrendered, but Bar Giora, resisting to the last, took flight through subterranean passages. Hunger, however, drove him to come forth. He startled the Roman soldiers by his sudden appearance in a white shroud; but they quickly recovered from their fright, seized him, and led him to Titus. He was kept for the emperor's triumph at Rome, where he was dragged through the streets and then hurled from the Tarpeian rock (Josephus, "B. J." vii. 2, § 1; vii. 5, § 6; 8, § 1).

BIBLIOGRAPHY: Dio Cassius, lxvi. 7; Tacitus, *Hist.* v. 12; Egesippus, iv. 22, v. 49; Schurer, *Gesch.* i. 521 *et seq.* A passage in *Pesiḳ. R.* seems to refer to the subiect (*Monatsschrift*, xli. 563), also a passage m Ab. R. N., B, c. vii. (Jerusalem vi. 15).

G. S. KR.

BAR ḲAPPARA (Aramaic; Hebrew, "Ben ha-Ḳappar"): Palestinian scholar of the beginning of the third century, occupying an intermediate position between tanna and amora. His real and complete name was Eleazar (there seems to be no ground for the form "Eliezer") ben Eleazar ha-Ḳappar. This is the form appearing in the tannaite sources, Tosefta (Beẓah i. 7; Ḥullin vi. 3) and Sifre (Num. 42, ed. Friedmann, p. 12*b*): the usual Talmudic form, "Bar Ḳappara," and the frequent appellation, "Eleazar ha-Ḳappar Berabbi", are abbreviations of this.

Like nearly all those who occupied the intermediate positions between tannaim and amoraim (called "semi-tannaim" for convenience' sake), Bar Cappara was a pupil of Judah I. ha-Nasi; but he seems to have counted among his teachers, in addition, K. Nathan the Babylonian (Midr. Teh. xii. 4, ed. Buber; other editions and MSS. read "Jonathan") and R. Jeremiah ben Eleazar, probably identical with the Jeremiah mentioned in the Mekilta and Sifre (Pesiḳ. xxvii. 1726; Tan., Aḥare Mot, vi. [ed. Buber, vii.]; and parallel passages cited by Buber). The strained relations between Bar Ḳappara and the patriarchal house, of which mention will shortly be made, induced him to withdraw to the south of Palestine. Bar Cappara set up his academy at Cæsarea (concerning פרוד or פארוד, the alleged residence of Bar Ḳappara, in the passage 'Ab. Zarah 31*a*, nothing further is known; according to Bacher, "Agada der Tannaiten," ii. 505, it may have been a suburb of Cæsarea); and his school came to be a serious rival of Rabbi's. Among the most important of its scholars were Hoshayah, "the father of the Mishnah" (Ker. 8*a*), and Joshua b. Levi, the distinguished haggadist, who to a large extent transmitted the Haggadali of Bar Ḳappara (Shab. 75*a*). The greatest admirers of Rabbi and the best supporters of the patriarchal house, Ḥanina b. Ḥama and Johanan b. Nappaḥa, could not refrain from acknowledging Bar Ḳappara's greatness (Niddah 20*a*; 'Ab. Zarah *l.c.*). It is related of him that once while walking on the mole of Cæsarea and seeing a Roman that had escaped from shipwreck in utter destitution, he took him to his house and provided him with clothing and all necessaries, including money. Later this castaway became proconsul of Cæsarea, and occasion soon offered itself to show his gratitude to his rescuer, when Jews involved in a political disturbance were arrested, and he released them on Bar Ḳappara's intervention (Eccl. R. xi. 1, on "Cast thy bread upon the waters").

Of more interest than liis contemporaries' recognition of his greatness as a halakist and a humanitarian, are the many characteristic utterances of his that mark him as a phenomenal personality in his day. Some examples may be given. He said: "He who can calculate the solstices and movements of the planets [that is, understands astronomy] and fails to pay attention to these things, to him may be applied the verse [Isa. v. 12] 'They regard not the works of the Lord, nor the operation of his hands" (Shab. 75*a*). This statement about the duty of studying astronomy and physics gains in significance if placed in juxtaposition with Bar Ḳappara's totally different opinion in regard to the study of the Torah. According to him, if a Jew read only two portions from the Torah daily—one in the morning and one in the evening—he fulfils the precept to meditate in God's law by day and night (Ps. i. 2; Midr. Teh. *ad loc.*). Bar Ḳappara not only admired natural science, proscribed though it was by most Jews of the time, who considered it "Greek learning," but he also appreciated the Hellenic love of the beautiful;

and probably he was the sole Palestinian who judged the literary activity of the Alexandrian Jews favorably. A truly liberal exposition of his on Gen. ix. 27 was: "The words of the Torali shall be recited in the speech of Japheth [Greek] in the tents of Shem" (in the synagogues and schools) (Gen. R xxxvi. 8).

Bar Ḳappara's respect for the exact sciences was equaled by his aversion for metaphysical speculation, which just at his time flourished in the form of Gnosis among Jews and Christians. Referring to Deut. iv. 32, "Ask now of the days that are past, which were before thee," Bar Ḳappara says, "Seek to know only of those days that followed the Creation; but seek not to know what went before" (Gen. R. i. 10), meaning to say that the world and the history of man in the world provide sufficient matter for the mind's employment without subtle investigations into hidden mysteries.

Highly characteristic of Bar Ḳappara's conception of life and its ideals is his opinion concerning self-abnegation: "The Scriptures [Num. vi. 11] say: 'The priest shall... make an atonement for him [the Nazarite] for that he sinned by the soul' " [A. V. "dead"; Hebrew text, "nefesh," means also "soul "]. By what soul did he sin? He denied himself wine. Now, if the Nazarite who denied himself wine only is called a sinner, how much more is he a sinner who has denied himself everything?" (B. Ḳ. 91*b*; Ta'anit 11*a* and parallels; compare Rab's similar saying in Yer. Ḳid., end; see ABBA ARIKA). It required not a little courage and self-confidence to declare asceticism sinful at a time when fasting and abstemiousness of all kinds were held to be the greatest virtues.

A comparison of this view of Bar Ḳappara concerning abstinence with Rabbi's declaration before his death that he had not experienced the slightest sensual gratification in his life (Ket. 104*a*), reveals the striking contrast in the conceptions of the two men. This difference was true no less in regard to the affairs of daily life than to matters of the intellect. No greater dissimilarity is possible than was presented by the majestic repose and princely grandeur of Rabbi, and the poetic abandon and gay address of Bar Ḳappara. Since Rabbi's mere presence sufficed to put a check upon Bar Ḳappara, it is possible that a breach between the two men might not have come to pass had their personal relations alone been concerned. But the members of the patriarch's family, especially Simon, his son, and Ben Elasah, his son-in-law, rich but unlettered (Ned. 51*a*), were frequently subjected to Bar Ḳappara's biting satire. A somewhat irreverent remark about Rabbi, which he let slip in Simon's presence, was reported by Simon to Rabbi, who informed Bar Ḳappara of his firm resolve never to grant him ordination (M. Ḳ. 16*a*).

According to the Yerushalmi, however, the final rupture was induced by the following incident: During a gathering at Rabbi's house Bar Ḳappara remarked to Rabbi's unlearned son-in-law that it was conspicuous in him to maintain complete silence while all others present were asking Rabbi for opinions on subjects of learning. Ben Elasah was at a loss as to what question to put to his father-in-law, but Bar Ḳappara prompting him by whispers in his ear, he propounded to Rabbi the following riddle:

"High from Heav'n her eye looks down;
Constant strife excites her frown;
Winged beings shun her sight;
She puts youth to instant flight;
The aged, too, her aspect scout;
Oh! oh! the fugitive cries out.
And by her snares whoe'er is lured
Shall never more from sin be cured!"

(Translation by A. Sekles, in "The Poetry of the Talmud," pp. 87, 88, New York, 1880.)

When Rabbi turned round after hearing the riddle of his son-in-law, he discovered Bar Ḳappara smiling, and exclaimed: "I do not recognize you, old one!" (meaning also, "I do not recognize you *as an* elder, a sage!"). Bar Cappara now understood that he would never receive ordination (Yer. M. Ḳ. iii. 81*c*).

What the riddle really signifies is not known, despite many attempts to explain it. The most probable view is the one taken by Abraham Krochmal that Bar Ḳappara intended it as a criticism of Rabbi's unrelenting severity toward young and old. The verse is extremely valuable as a specimen of Neo-Hebraic poetry in Talmudic times; its few lines furnish, perhaps, the sole testimony to the activity of the Jews of that time in secular poetry. Its language is classic, but not slavishly so; forceful and pure, yet easy and flowing. It is a curious coincidence that the one othei specimen of Bar Ḳappara's poetry which has been preserved in the sources should be the eloquent words in which he proclaimed Rabbi's death to the assembled people of Sepphoris. They are: "Brethren of the house of Jedaiah [an epithet of the inhabitants of Sepphoris], harken unto me! Mortals and angels have long been wrestling for the possession of the holy tablets of the Law; the angels have conquered. They have captured the tablets " (Yer. Kil. ix. 32*b*; Yer. Ket. xii. 35*a*; Bab. Ket. 104*a*, Eccl. R vii. 11, ix. 10, with many variants of the text, which is here given according to Eccl. R. *l.c.*). Bar Ḳappara's presence in Sepphoris at Rabbi's death shows that, despite Rabbi's unjust attitude toward him, he duly appreciated his great obligations to his teacher; and there is no cause to doubt the sincerity of his grief for Rabbi's death.

Bar Ḳappara was especially known to the Amoraim as the author of a Mishnah called the Mishnah of Bar Ḳappara (Pesiḳ. xv. 122*a*; Yer. Hor. iii. 48*c*; and many other places). This Mishnah compilation has not been preserved, and probably at the final redaction of the Talmud it was no longer extant (Meïri, in commentary on Abot, ed. Wilna, p. 14, does not mention the fact of having had such a Mishnah collection [thus Schorr, "He-Ḥaluẓ," *i.* 44, and A. Krochmal, *ib.* iii. 118], but a Baraita cited in Bar Ḳappara's name in the Talmud). Nevertheless, the numerous passages from his Mishnah that found their way into the Talmud suffice for judgment upon its character.

Meïri (*l.c.*) quite correctly designates it as a supplement to the Mislmah of Rabbi, intended chiefly to explain it, and, on rare occasions, to give differing opinions. Bar Ḳappara 's Mishnah also presented variants to Rabbi's Mishnah, and later on became occasionally so interwoven in the text of the latter that doubt arose whether the Mishnah in question belonged to the one or to the other (Yer. Pes. x. 37d). The Mislmah of Bar Ḳappara was also used by the redactor of the Tosefta, who derived many decisions from it (for instances, see Weiss, "Dor Dor we-Dorshaw," ii. 219). Whether Bar Ḳappara's Mishnah ever reached Babylonia has not been definitely ascertained, the one passage in the Babli referring to it having originated with Simon b. Laḳish, a Palestinian (B. B. 154*b*). [Compare also Is. Halevy, "Dorot ha-Rishonim," ii. 123–125, who, without sufficient reason, denies the existence of Bar Ḳappara's Mishnah.]

Bar Ḳappara is the last one in Talmudic times who is stated to have had knowledge of fables. The Midrash (Lev. R. xxviii. 2) relates that because Rabbi did not invite Bar Ḳappara to the wedding of his son, Bar Ḳappara revenged himself in the following way: At the feast which Rabbi subsequently gave in Bar Ḳappara's honor, the latter told a vast number of fox fables–300, it is reported—and the guests left the food untouched in order to listen to him.

BIBLIOGRAPHY: Bacher, *Agada der Tannaiten*, ii. 503–520 (for other passages in the same, see the Index); Brull. *Mebo na-Mishnah*, i. 244, 289–392; Frankel, *Darke ha-Mishnah*, p. 313; idem, *Mebo*, 20*a et seq.*, 71*a*; Gratz, *Gesch. der Juden*. 4th ed., iv. 198,199, 211; Hamburger, Supplement to *R. B. T.* pp. 36–38; Kohan, in *Ha-Asif*, iii. 330–333 (Kohan here first pointed out the identity of Bar Ḳappara with Eleazar ben Eleazar ha-Ḳappar); Abraham Krochmal, in *He-Ḥaluẓ*, ii. 84; Rapoport, in *Literaturblatt des Orients*, I. 38, 39'; Reifmann, *Pesher Dabar*; Weiss, *Dor Dor we-Dorshaw*, ii. 191, 219.

J. SR. L. G.

BEBAI (ביבי; Biblical form בבי. The readings ביבוב, ביבין are copyists' mistakes for ביב״י; and the variant ביבא is a clerical error for ביבאי): The Palestinian and the Babylonian Talmudim, as also the Palestinian Midrashim, frequently cite an amora named Bebai, sometimes as "Rabbi" and sometimes as "Rab," but without further designation; and as all the data relating to the name refer to the same age, rabbinic chronologists have always considered them as applying to one person. What is remarkable in this connection, but has been overlooked, is the fact that out of nearly fifty subjects treated in connection with the name, only one appears in both Talmudim (Yer. Sheḳ. iii. 47*c* and parallels; Men. 103*b*); from which it may be inferred that the doctrines and sayings appearing under the name of Bebai in the Palestinian sources do not emanate from the Babylonian Bebai, and vice versa. Probably it was this fact which first aroused Frankel's suspicion as to the identity of the Palestinian Bebai with the Babylonian, and accordingly both Frankel ("Mebo," 68*b*) and Bacher ("Ag. Pal. Amor." iii. 667 *et seq.*) refer to two Bebais, of Palestine and Babylonia respectively.

Bebai I., R.: Palestinian amora of the third generation (third century). R. Zeira I., on his first arrival in Palestine, heard Bebai repeating a Halakah in the name of Malluk (Ḥul. 49*a*); and the same Zeira refers to a time when he and Bebai sat at the feet of R. Johanan (Nid. 25*b*, where the patronymic "b. Abaye " is undoubtedly a clerical error, inasmuch as Abaye himself could scarcely have been born before the death of R. Johanan, in 279). Bebai subsequently became a disciple of R. Assi II. (Yer. Ta'an. ii. 66*b*; Mak. 21*b*; Yalḳ., Deut. 932), although he also addresses R. Abbahu as his teacher (Yer. Ḳid. iv. 66*b*). He seems to have been outranked, however, by his former colleague, R. Zeira, for he is often found before the latter in the rôle of a reciter (Yer. Ma'as. Sh. v. 56*a*; Yer. Ḳid. iii. 64*d*); and it is known that he was once commissioned by Zeira to procure some cloth from the Saturnalian fair at Beshan ("Bethshean," Yer. 'Ab. Zarah i. 39*c*). Probably this was done with the purpose of affording Bebai some emolument; for he was poor, as is evident from the following anecdote: R. Bebai was engaged in explaining a Baraita, when R. Isaac b. Bisna interrupted him with a question on the subject, to which Bebai gave a peevish reply. R. Zeriḳan remonstrated with him; remarking, "Because he asks thee a question thou scoldest him!" Thereupon Bebai excused himself; pleading, "I am not master of myself; for, as R. Ḥanan has said, 'The Biblical dictum (Deut. xxviii. 66), "Thy life shall hang in doubt before thee," is realized in the one who purchases liis yearly supplies from the market, he having no fields of liis own; "Thou shalt fear day and night," represents the condition of him who draws his provisions for the week from the huckster in the marketplace; "Thou shalt have no assurance of thy life," may be said of him who is obliged to procure provisions by the day from the shopkeeper,' as I do" (Yer. Shab. viii. 11*a*; Yer. Sheḳ. iii. 47*c*, viii. 51*a*; Men. 103*b*).

This Bebai is known in the Haggadah as well as in the Halakah; and while lie often transmits the views of others, he as often advances his own. According to him, the sin of hypocrisy is alluded to earliest in the Decalogue. Seeing, he argues, that perjury is explicitly prohibited by the command (Lev. xix. 12), "Ye shall not swear by my name falsely," the prohibition (Ex. xx. 7), "Thou shalt not take the name of the Lord thy God in vain," must refer to one who leads a sinful life while parading such ceremonies of holiness as Tefillin and Ṭallit (Pesiḳ. R. 22). The divine order to number the Israelites (Ex. xxx. 12) lie explains by the following illustration: "A king once had numerous flocks. Wolves attacked them and killed many; whereupon the king ordered the herdsman to number the remainder, that he might discover how nrnny were missing. Thus, after the catastrophe of the golden calf, did the Lord say to Moses, 'Number the Israelites, and find out how many are missing' " (Pesiḳ. ii. 18*a*; Tan., Ki Tissa, 9). Bebai, it seems, never visited Babylonia, since we see him silting at the feet of R. Johanan (who died about 279), studying under Assi II., and attending Zeira I.; and Dimi, who emigrated to Babylonia about fifty years after R. Johanan's death, reports (Shab. 74*a*), in illustration of a Halakah, an act of Bebai at a reception tendered to Ammi and Assi (Yer. Ber. i. 3*b*; *ib*. viii. 12*a*, Yer. Kil. v. 30*a*; Yer. Sheb. i. 33*b*; Yer. Ter. viii. 45*c*; Yer. Sheḳ. ii. 46*c*; Yer. Giṭ. v. 47*b*; Yer. Sanh. i. 18*a*; Yer. Nid. iii. 50*d*; Pesiḳ. R. 15; Pesiḳ., Haḥodesh, 50*a*; Midr. Teh., ed. Buber, Index; Frankel, "Mebo," 68*b*; Bacher, "Ag. Pal. Amor." iii. 66 *et seq*.).

Bebai II., Rab: Babylonian amora of the third generation (third and fourth centuries). He was a disciple of R. Naḥman (Hag. 22*b*; Yeb. 12*b*; B. M. 23*b*), and, it seems, a fellow-pupil ("talmid-ḥaber") of R. Joseph ('Er. 23*b*, 75*b*). Adda b. Ahaba's host, a proselyte, and Bebai had some litigation about a certain public office to which both laid claim. They personally appealed to R. Joseph; and he decided that, as Bebai was a great scholar, he was entitled to the superintendence of the religious affairs of the community, leaving the management of the municipal affairs to the other (Ḳid. 76*b*). Elsewhere it is stated that to settle a scholastic dispute between Bebai and others as to whether Rab (Abba Arika) had indorsed or disapproved a decision of R. Muna, R. Joseph threw the weight of his opinion on the side of Bebai (Meg. 18*b*).

Of his private life an interesting incident is preserved in the Talmud (Shab. 80*b*; M. Ḳ. 9*b*). Bebai was in the habit of using wine or beer at his meals—a luxury rarely indulged in by the Babylonian Jews—and he is also reported to have employed a certain paste to improve his daughters complexion. A Gentile neighbor of Bebai tried the same experiment on his own daughter with a fatal result; whereupon he said, "Bebai has slain my daughter." R. Nahman, hearing of the case, remarked, "Bebai indulges in strong drinks; therefore, his daughter needs skin-improving pastes: we are more abstinent; consequently we need no such cosmetics for our daughters" (Ket. 39*a*; Ḳid. 81*a*; B. B. 36*b*).

J. SIT. S. M.

BEBAI B. ABAYE: A Babylonian scholar of the fourth and fifth amoraic generations (fourth century), son of the celebrated ABAYE Naḥmani, and presiding judge in Pumbedita (Yeb. 75*b*; Ket. 85*a*), where his father had directed the academy. Some rabbinic chronologists (J. Schorr, "Wa'ad Ḥakamim," 24*b*; Bacher, "Ag. Pal. Amor." iii. 667, note 5) suggest his identity with Bebai II., which, however, is chronologically incorrect (compare Heilprin, "Seder ha Dorot," ii., *s.v.* "Bebai b. Abin"), the latter having been a fellow-pupil of Rab Joseph, whereas Bebai b. Abaye was a contemporary of Naḥman b. Isaac, Kahana III. (Ber. 6*b*; 'Er. 90*a*), Pappi, and Huna b. Joshua. As Abaye was a scion of the priestly house of Eli, which was doomed to premature death (I Sam. ii. 33; see R. H. 18*a*), both Pappi and Huna b. Joshua frequently taunted Bebai with being descended from frail (short-lived) stock, and therefore with uttering frail, untenable arguments ('Er. 25*b*; compare "Diḳduḳe Soferim" *a.l.*; B. M. 109*a*; B. B. 137*b*, 151*a*; compare Jastrow, "Dict." 794*a*, *s.v.* "Mammulaë"). Bebai b. Abaye seems to have led a contemplative life; and legend relates some curious stories about him (Hag. 4*b*; Ber. 6*a*; Ber. 8*b*; 'Er. 8*a*; Shab. 3*a*, 4*a*; Hul. 43*b*; Ker. 3*b*, Zeb. 107*a*.).

J. SU. S. M.

BEBAI B. ABBA, R.: A Palestinian haggadist, of uncertain date and rarely cited, whose name appears also as "Bebai Rabbah," "Beba Raba," and "Beba Abba " (Lev. R. xxix. 9; Yer. Ta'an. ii. 65*d*; Pesiḳ. Baḥodesh, 154*a*; Yalk., Lev. 645). He is cited (Lev. R. iii.) as having commended the following form of confession for the Day of Atonement, which is partly adopted in the ritual for the evening service of that day: "I confess before Thee all the evil I have committed. I have indeed stood in the path of evil; but as I have done, I shall do no more. May it please Thee, O my God, to forgive all my sins, pardon all my iniquities, and remit all my errors." This Bebai states, is in accordance with what the prophet teaches in saying (Isa. Iv. 7), "Let the wicked forsake his way, and the unrighteous mao his thoughts," etc. (compare Yer. Yoma viii. end, 45*c*).

In the Wilna (1878) edition of the Midrash the patronymic is "Abia"; in the ed. Warsaw (1850) it is "Abaye." "Yuḥasin" and "Sed. ha-Dor.," however, read "Abba"; and Heilprin ("Seder ha-Dor.," *s.v.*) suggests the identity of Bebai b. Abba with Bebai b. Abin, identifying the latter with the Bebai generally cited without patronymic. But "Abin" seems to be a misreading of "Abaye."

J. SR. S. M.

BEBAI, BEN: A priestly family or gild having charge of the preparation of wicks for the Temple lamps (Sheḳ. v. 1; Yer. Sheḳ. v. 48*d*; Yer. Peah viii. 21*a*). The name is derived from the first person appointed to that office after the return from the Babylonian captivity (Tiḳlin Hadtin to Yer. Sheḳ.). At a later time, owing to the double meaning of the word "peḳi'a," used in the Mishnah, an erroneous opinion was set forth that the family Ben Bebai had the supervision of the straps used for the chastisement of negligent priests (Yoma 23*a*).

J. SR. S. M.

BEN 'AZZAI: A distinguished tanna of the first third of the second century. His full name was Simon b. 'Azzai, to which sometimes the title "Rabbi" is prefixed. But, in spite of his great learning, this title did not rightfully belong to him; for he remained all his life in the ranks of the "talmidim" or "talmide hakamim" (pupils or disciples of the wise). Ben 'Azzai and Ben Zoma were considered in the tannaitic school-tradition as the highest representatives of this degree in the hierarchy of learning (Tosef., Ḳid. iii. 9; Bab. Ḳid. 49*b*; Ber. Ḳid. 57*b*; Yer. Ma'as Sh. ii. 53d; Bab. Sanh. 17*b*). Ben 'Azzai is especially named as an eminent example of a "pupil who is worthy of the hora'ah,"of the right of independent judgment in questions of religious law (Hor. 2*b*). Ben 'Azzai stood in close relation to the leaders of the school of Jabneh. He handed down, "from the mouth of two-and-seventy elders," who were present on the occasion, a halakic decision, which was accepted in Jabneh on the day when Eleazar b. Azariah was elected president in the place of Gamaliel II. (Yad. iv. 2; Zeb. i. 3); also another resolution of the same day, declaring the books Kohelet and Shir ha-Shirim to be as sacred as the other Scriptures, whereby the collection of the Biblical writings, or the canon, was officially closed (Yad. iii. 5).

Chief among Ben 'Azzai's teachers was Joshua b. Hananiah, whose opinions he expounded (Parah i. 1), proved to be correct (Yeb. iv. 13), or defended against Akiba (Yoma ii. 3; Ta'anit iv. 4; Tosef., Sheb. ii. 13) Akiba himself was not really Ben 'Azzai's teacher, although the latter occasionally calls him so, and once even regrets that he did not stand in closer relation as pupil to Akiba (Ned. 74*b*); and he expressed the same regret in regard to Ishmael b. Elisha (Ḥul. 71*a*). In his halakic opinions and Biblical exegesis, as well as in other sayings, Ben 'Azzai follows Akiba; and, from the tone in which he speaks of Akiba in the discourses that have been handed down, the Amoraim concluded that his relations with Akiba were both those of pupil and of colleague (Yer. B. B. ix. 17*b*; Bab. *ib.* 158*b*; Yer. Shek. iii. 47*b*; Yer. R. H. i. 56*d*).

Ben 'Azzai's most prominent characteristic was the extraordinary assiduity with which he pursued his studies. It was said of him afterward,

"At the death of Ben 'Azzai the last industrious man passed away" (Soṭah ix. 15). A later tradition (Midr. Hallel) says of the zealous studies of Ben 'Azzai and Akiba—by way of reference to Ps. cxiv. 8—that in their perceptive faculty both had been as hard as rock; but, because they exerted themselves so greatly in their studies, God opened for the man entrance into the Torah, so that Ben 'Azzai could explain even those things in the Halakah that the schools of Shammai and Hillel had not understood. His love of study induced Ben 'Azzai to remain unmarried, although he himself preached against celibacy, and even was betrothed to Akiba's daughter, who waited for years for him to marry her, as her mother had waited for Akiba (Ket. 63*a*). When Eleazar b. Azariah reproved him for this contradiction between his life and his teachings, he replied: "What shall I do? My soul clings lovingly to the Torah; let others contribute to the preservation of the race" (Tos. Yeb. viii. 4; Bab. *ib.* 63*b*; Gen. R. xxxiv.; compare Soṭah 4*b*).

Another characteristic of Ben 'Azzai was his great piety. It was said, "He who has seen Ben 'Azzai in his dreams is himself on the way to piety" (Ber. 57*b*) Thanks to this piety he could, without injury to his soul, devote himself to theosophic speculations, when he, like Ben Zoma, Elisha b. Abuyah, and Akiba, entered, as tradition has it, into the garden ("pardes") of the esoteric doctrine. Tradition (Ḥag. 14*b*) says of him: "He beheld the mysteries of the garden and died; God granted him the death of His saints" (Ps. cxvi. 15). With reference to this verse, Ben 'Azzai himself had taught that God shows to the pious, near the hour of their death, the le wards awaiting them (Gen. R. lxii). Other sayings of his concerning the hour of death have been handed down (Ab. R. N. xxv.). According to a tradition not entirely trustworthy, Ben 'Azzai was among the first victims of the persecutions under Hadrian; his name, therefore, is found on a list of the "ten martyrs" (Lam. R. ii. 2).

Ben 'Azzai's posthumous fame was extraordinare. The greatest amora of Palestine, Johanan, and the greatest amora of Babylonia, Rab, each said, in order to mark their authority as teachers of the Law: "Here I am a Ben 'Azzai" (Yer. Bik. ii. 65*a*; Yer. Peah vi. 19*c*). The name of Ben 'Azzai is applied in the same sense by the great Babylonian amora Abaye (Soṭah 45*a*; Kid. 20*a*; 'Ar. 30*b*) and Raba ('Er. 29*a*) A haggadic legend of Palestine relates of Mm the following: "Once, as Ben 'Azzai was expounding the Scriptures, flames blazed up around him, and being asked whether he was a student of the mysteries of the 'Chariot of God,' he replied: 'I string together, like pearls, the words of the Torah with those of the Prophets, and those of the Prophets with those of the Hagiographers; and therefore the words of the Torah rejoice as on the day when they were revealed in the flames of Sinai' " (Lev. R xvi.; Cant. R. i. 10).

Under Ben 'Azzai's name, traditional literature has preserved many sentences, with and without Biblical foundation. Two of these have been taken over into the sayings of the Fathers (Ab. iv. 2, 3). After a saying of Ben 'Azzai, at the beginning of the third chapter of "Derek Ereẓ Rabbah," this little book—which began originally with that chapter—is called "Pereḳ Ben 'Azzai" (Rashi to Ber. 22*a*; Tos. to 'Er. 53*b*). In a sentence that recalls a fundamental thought of Akiba, Ben 'Azzai gives the characteristic features of a kind of deterministic view of the world: "By thy name they shall call thee, at the place where thou belongest shall they see thee, what is thine they shall give to thee; no man touches that whicù is destined for his neighbor; and no government infringes even by a hair's breadth upon the time marked for another government" (Yoma 38*a et seq.*). Following Hillel, Akiba had declared the commandment "thou shalt love thy neighbor as thyself " (Lev. xix. 18) to be the greatest fundamental commandment of the Jewish doctrine; Ben 'Azzai, in reference to this, said that a still greater principle was found in the Scriptural verse," This is the book of the generations of Adam [origin of man]. In the day that God created man [Adam], in the likeness of God made he him" (Gen. v. 1; Sifra, Ḳedoshim, iv.; Yer. Ned. ix. 41c; Gen. R. xxiv.). The commandment to love God with all the soul (Deut. vi. 5), Ben 'Azzai explained in the same manner as Akiba: "Love him even to the last breath of the soul!" (Sifre, Deut. 32). Several of Ben 'Azzai's haggadic sentences, having been called forth by those of Akiba, are introduced by the words, "I do not wish to oppose the interpretation of my master, but will only add to his words" (Sifra, Wayiḳra, ii; Mek., Bo, Introd).

Ben 'Azzai's observations on sacrifices (Sifre, Num. 143) are obviously directed against Gnosticism. As against the doctrine of the Gnostics, that the part of the Law containing the rules of sacrifice could have originated only with a secondary god, the demiurge, who is merely just, not beneficent, Ben 'Azzai maintains, that in connection with the sacrificial laws, not any one of the various names of God is there used, but precisely the distinctive name, the Tetragrammaton, in which especially the goodness of God is emphasized, in order that the "minim" (disbelievers) might not have an opportunity to prove their views by the Bible. Ben 'Azzai's symbolic interpretation of the first word of Lamentations (אֵיכָה) is also polemical and probably directed against Pauline Christianity. He holds that in the numerical value of the four letters of this word is indicated that the Israelites did not go into exile until after they had denied the *one* God (אֹ), the *ten* commandments (י), the law of circumcision, given to the *twentieth* generation after Adam (כֹ), and the *five* (הֹ) books of the Torah (Lam. B. i. 1).

J. SR. W. B.

BEN BAG-BAG: An early tanna. At the end of the Mishnah Abot (v. 22, 23) two sentences are given concerning the study of the Torah; one by Ben Bag Bag, the other by Ben He-He Both sentences are also ascribed to Hillel (Ab. R N. xii); as indeed in their pithy language as well as Aramaic wording they are similar to the well-known Aramaic sentences of Hillel. Tradition reports two exegetical questions, which Ben He-He asked of Hillel (Ḥag 9*b*) Ben Hê Hê and Ben Bag Bag may, therefore, be considered disciples of Hillel; or, as is even more likely, both names represent one and the same person.

The peculiarity of these names may be explained by the following anecdote (Shab. 31*a*). Hillel once convinced a proselyte of the truth of the oral law by proving to him, in a lesson on the Hebrew alphabet, that even a knowledge of the phonetic value and of the order of the letters of the alphabet is not possible without a belief in their oral transmission from age to age. If this proselyte is identical with the disciple of Hillel quoted under the above pseudonyms, then the one name, "Ben Hê-Hê," may have been chosen to indicate that "He" is always pronounced "He," as the tradition shows; and the other name, "Ben BG-BG," to show that in the alphabet the sequence bet gimel is fixed by tradition. That Ben Hê-Hê and Ben Bag-Bag are identical is apparently an old tradition, mentioned by Abraham Zacuto in "Yuḥasin."

In Tos. to Ḥag. 9*b* Ben Bag-Bag and Ben Hê-Hê are also considered to be proselytes, although the symbolic meaning of their names is differently accounted for. Several halakic interpretations of Scriptural passages by Ben Bag-Bag have been transmitted: of Ex. xiii. 13 (Bek. 12*a*); of Lev. xix. 11 (Sifra, Ḳedoshim, ii. 2; Toset, B. Ḳ. x. 38, Bab. B. Ḳ. 27*b*); of Num. xxviii. 2 (Pes. 96*a*; Men. 49*b*; 'Ar. 13*b*; anonymously stated in Sifre, Num. 142, and in the name of 'Akiba in Meg. Ta'anit i.); of Deut. xiv. 26 (Sifre, Deut. 107; 'Er. 27*b*).

There is another rabbi distinct from this elder Ben Bag-Bag who was never cited with a given name. He is Johanan ben Bag-Bag, possibly the son of the former. Nothing is known about him except that he sent to Nisibis a halakic question to Judah b. Betera, a contemporary of Akiba, who in his reply referred to Ben Bag-Bag as one noted for being "familiar with the chambers of the Law" (Tosef., Ket. v. 1; Yer. Ket. v. 29*d*; Bab. Ḳid. 10*b*; Sifre, Num. 117).

J. SR. W. B.

BEN-BAṬIAḤ: 1. A man, at the time of the teachers of the Mishnah (" 'Aruk," *s.v.* אגרוף), whose fist, being about the size of an adult's head, was used as a standard of measurement (Kelim xvii, Bek. 37*b*; compare hip-bone of the giant king Og, Tosef., Oh. ixv. 4).

2. The son of the sister of Johanan b. Zakkai, who, as one of the ringleaders of the Zealots, burned the granaries at Jerusalem in order that the Jews should have to fight more desperately (Lam. R. i. 5; Eccl. R. vii 11; Yalḳ., Eccl. 975). In Git. 56*a* the name "Abba Saḳḳara" (or, as others read, "Abba Siḳra" = leader of the Sicarii) occurs. Many think that the two persons are identical (see ABBA SAḲḲARA).

J. SR. S. KR.

BEN DAMA (or **DAMAH;** full name, **ELEAZAR B. DAMA[H]**): Tanna of the beginning of the second century; a nephew of ISHMAEL B. ELISHA. His inclination toward Hellenism and the Judæo-Christians contrasted with the attitude of his uncle, whom he once asked if he should study "Greek Wisdom," since he had finished the study of the Torah. The answer of Ishmael was: "Study the Torah day and night and 'Greek Wisdom' when it is neither day nor night." Ben Dama died of a snake's bite, and the following account is given of his last moments:

Jacob of Kefar Sama (Sakonya), a Judæo-Christian, wanted to charm away the deadly effects of the bite by formulas in the name of Jesus; but Ishmael did not believe in such charms and would not allow him to come in. Just as Ben Dama essayed to prove to his uncle that there could be no objection to the cure from a Jewish standpoint, he died, and Ishmael exclaimed, "God has shown thee mercy in that thou didst depart in peace and didst not transgress the law of the sages" (Tosef., Hul. ii. 22, 23; 'Ab. Zarah 27*b*; Yer. 'Ab. Zarah ii. 40*d*).

It is not improbable that Ben Dama's inclination toward the Judæo-Christians was the reason that nothing written by him was transmitted either by the Halakah or by the Haggadah, and that neither the Babylonian nor the Palestinian Talmud gives him the title "Rabbi." His title and full name have been preserved by the Tosefta (Ḥul. *l.c.*), which contains a balakic controversy between Ben Dama and Ishmael (Sheb. iii. 4).

BIBLIOGRAPHY: Heilprin, *Seder ha-Dorot*, ed. Warsaw, 1882, ii. 84; Grätz, *Gesch. der Juden*, 3d ed., iv. 81.

K. L. G.

BEN HÊ HÊ. See BEN BAG-BAG.

BEN KALBA SABBUA': A rich and prominent man of Jerusalem who flourished about the year 70. According to the Talmud (Git. 56*a*), he obtained his name from the fact that any one that came to his house hungry as a dog (Kalba), went away satisfied (Sabbua'). He was one of the three rich men of Jerusalem (the other two being Naḳdimon ben Goryon and Ben Ẓiẓit ha-Keset), each of whom had in his storehouses enough to provide the besieged city with all the necessaries of life for ten years. But as these three favored peace with Rome, the Zealots burned their hoards of grain, oil, and wood, thus causing a dreadful famine in Jerusalem (Giṭ. *ib.*; Lam. R i. 5; Eccl. R. vii. 11; Ab. R. N., ed.

Schechter, vi. 31, 32, in which Ben Kalba Sabbua''s wealth is described as still greater).

Although the details of this account are hardly supported by historical evidence, there is no reason to doubt the existence of the three rich men. But the account in the Babylonian Talmud, according to which Akiba ben Joseph was the son-in-law of Ben Kalba Sabbu'a, is probably without any historical foundation; nor is there any reference to it in the Palestinian sources. It tells of the secret marriage of Ben Kalba's daughter; that she was turned away by her father; and that he finally became reconciled to her (Ned. 50*a*; Ket. 62*b* *et seq.*). Compare AKIBA IN LEGEND.

A grave, alleged to be that of Ben Kalba Sabbua', to which the Jews pay great respect, is pointed out about half a mile north of Jerusalem. It is mentioned by Benjamin b. Elijah, a Karaite who traveled in Palestine (compare T. Gurland, "Ginze Yisrael," i. 53). Recent excavations show that there actually are graves on this spot; but the statement that an inscription bearing Ben Kalba Sabbua''s name was found there has not been proved (Gurland, *ib.* p. 68; "Ha-Maggid," viii. 28).

BIBLIOGRAPHY: Derenbourg, *Essai sur l'Histoire de la Palestine*, p. 281, note; Grätz, *Gesch. der Juden*, 3d ed., iii. 527, 528; Luncz, *Jerusalem*, pp. 92, 93.

J. SR. L. G.

BEN ZAKKAI. See JOHANAN B. ZAKKAI.

BEN ZOMA: Tanna of the first third of the second century. His full name is Simon b. Zoma without the title "Rabbi"; for, like Ben 'Azzai, he remained in the grade of "pupil," and is often mentioned together with Ben 'Azzai as a distinguished representative of this class (see BEN 'AZZAI). Like Ben 'Azzai, also, he seems to have belonged to the inner circle of Joshua b. Hananiah's disciples; and a halakic controversy between them is reported in which Ben Zoma was the victor (Naz. viii. 1).

His erudition in the Halakah became proverbial; for it was said, "Whoever sees Ben Zoma in his dream is assured of scholarship" (Ber. 57*b*). He was, however, specially noted as an interpreter of the Scriptures, so that it was said (Soṭah ix. 15), "With Ben Zoma died the last of the exegetes" ("darshanim"). Yet only a few of his exegetic sayings have been preserved. The most widely known of these is his interpretation of the phrase, "that thou mayest remember the day when thou earnest forth out of Egypt" (Deut. xvi. 3), to prove that the recitation of the Biblical passage referring to the Exodus (Num. xv. 37–41) is obligatory for the evening prayer as well as for the morning prayer. This interpretation, quoted with praise by Eleazar b. Azariah (Ber. i. 5), has found a place in the Haggadah for the Passover night. In a halakic interpretation Ben Zoma explains the word "naḳi" (clean) in Ex. xxi. 28 by referring to the usage of the word in every-day life (B. Ḳ. 41*a*; Kid. 56*b*; Pes. 22*b*).

The principal subject of Ben Zoma's exegetic research was the first chapter of the Torah, the story of Creation. One of his questions on this chapter, in which he took exception to the phrase "God made" (Gen. i. 7), has been handed down by the Palestinian haggadists (though without the answer), with the remark, "This is one of the Biblical passages by which Ben Zoma created a commotion all over the world" (Gen. R. iv.). An interpretation of the second verse of the same chapter has been handed down in a tannaitic tradition (Tosef., Hag. ii. 5, 6; compare Ḥag. 15*a*), together with the following anecdote: Joshua b. Hananiah was walking one day, when he met Ben Zoma, who was about to pass him without greeting. Thereupon Joshua asked: "Whence and whither, Ben Zoma?" The latter replied: "I was lost in thoughts concerning the account of the Creation." And then he told Joshua his interpretation of Gen. i. 2. When speaking to his disciples on the matter, Joshua said, "Ben Zoma is outside," meaning thereby that Ben Zoma had passed beyond the limit of permitted research.

As a matter of fact, Ben Zoma was one of the four who entered into the "garden" of esoteric knowledge (see BEN 'AZZAI). It was said of him that he beheld the secrets of the garden and "was struck" with mental aberration (Ḥag. 14*b*). The disciples of Akiba applied to the limitless theosophic speculations, for which Ben Zoma had to suffer, the words of Prov. xxv. 16, "Hast thou found honey? eat so much as is sufficient for thee, lest thou be filled therewith, and vomit it" (Tosef., Ḥag. *l.c.*, Bab. Ḥag. *l.c.*, compare Midr. Mishle on xxv. 16).

Even the few sentences of Ben Zoma that have come down to us show the depth of his thoughts; as, for instance, his reflections on seeing large crowds of people (Tosef., Ber. vii. [vi.] 2; Ber.

"Ben Zoma, seeing the crowds on the Temple mount, said, 'Blessed be He who created all these to attend to my needs. How much had Adam to weary himself with! Not a mouthful could he taste before he plowed and sowed, and cut and bound sheaves, and threshed and winnowed and sifted the grain, and ground and sifted the flour, and kneaded and baked, and then he ate; but I get up in the morning and find all this ready before me. How much had Adam to weary himself with! Not a shirt could he put on before he sheared and washed the wool, and hatcheled and dyed and spun and wove and sewed, and then he clothed himself; but I rise in the morning and find all this ready before me. How many trades are anxiously busy early in the morning; and I rise and find all these things before me!' "

Also his reflections on man as the guest of God in this world (*ib.*):

"A grateful guest says, " That host be remembered for good! How many wines he brought up before me; how many portions he placed before me; how many cakes he offered me! All that he did, he did for my sake.' But the ill-willed guest says, 'What did I eat of his? A piece of bread, a bite of meat. What did I drink? A cup of wine. Whatever he did, he did for the sake of his wife and bis children.' Thus the Scripture says [Job xxxvi. 24], 'Remember that thou magnify His work, whereof men have sung.' "

Again, take bis fourfold motto (Ab. iv. 1) on the truly wise, the truly rich, the truly powerful, and the truly esteemed. In the closing words of Ecclesiasles, "for this is the whole man," he finds the thought expressed, that the pious man is the crown and end of mankind; the whole race ("the whole world") was created only to be of service to him who fears God and respects His commandments (Ber. 6*b*; Shab. 30*b*; see 'Aruk, *s.v.* צוות, 5). Ben Zoma is also the originator of the beautiful sentence, "Hast thou, in repentance, been ashamed in this world, thou wilt not need to be ashamed before God in the next" (Ex. R. xxx. 19).

BIBLIOGRAPHY: Bacher, *Agada der Tannaiten*, i. 429; Frankel. *Darke ha-Mishnah*, pp. 134–136: Graetz, *History of the Jews*, ii. 358, 381; Weiss, Dor, ii. 126; Braunschweiger, *Lehrer der Mischnah*, pp. 257–259.

J. SR. W. B.

BENAIAH (Hebrew, "Benayahu" or "Benayah," "the Lord hath built").—**Biblical Data: 1.** One of the Bene Parosh who took foreign wives (Ezra x. 25); in I Esd. ix. 26 he is called "Baanias."

2. One of the Bene Pahath-moab in the same list (Ezra x. 30), called "Naidus" in I Esd. ix. 31.

3. One of the Bene Bani in the same list (Ezra x. 35); he is called "Mabdai" in I Esd. ix. 84.

4. One of the Bene Nebo in the same list (Ezra x. 48); he is called "Banaias" in I Esd. ix. 35.

5. A Simeonite chief (I Chron. iv. 36).

6. Son of Jeiel, and grandfather of the Jahaziel who brought a message of encouragement to Jehoshaphat (II Chron. xx. 14).

7. Father of Pelatiah, the prince of the people denounced by Ezekiel (Ezek. xi. 1, 13).

8. The Pirathonite, one of the thirty valiant men of David (I Chron. xi. 31; II Sam. xxiii. 30), commanding the army in the eleventh month (I Chron. xxvii. 14).

9. A Levite singer (I Chron. xv. 18), who also played in the Temple service (I Chron. xv. 20, xvi. 5).

10. A priest, one of those who "did blow with the trumpets before the ark" (I Chron. xv. 24, xvi. 6).

11. A Levite in the reign of Hezekiah, who assisted in keeping the offerings brought to the Temple (II Chron. xxxi. 13).

12. Son of Jehoiada, a priest (I Chron. xxvii. 5) who distinguished himself in military affairs under David, and later on in Solomon's reign.

Three of his exploits are particularly mentioned: (1) the slaughter of the two Ariels of Moab; (2) the killing of a lion that had been trapped in a pit: Benaiah descended into the pit and there battled with the beast; (3) the overthrow of an Egyptian or a Miẓri, from whom he wrenched his weapon and slew him with it (II Sam. xxiii. 20–22 = I Chron. xi. 22–25). Officially Benaiah held various positions. He commanded the Cherethites and Pelethites (II Sam. viii. 18, xx. 23); was placed by David over the guard (I Chron. xi. 25; II Sam. xxiii. 23); and commanded the army in the third month (I Chron. xxvii. 5). In Adonijah's attempt at the kingship, Benaiah sided with Solomon (I Kings i. 8 *et seq.*) and took part in proclaiming the latter king. On the death of David, Benaiah, by order of Solomon, put Joab and Adonijah to death (I Kings ii. 25). Later Benaiah succeeded to the supreme command of the army (I Kings ii. 35). Along with the other priest Abiathar, Benaiah acted as one of the counselors of King David (I Chron. xxvii. 34; the reading "Jehoiada ben Benaiah" is evidently wrong).

J. JR. G. B. L.

——**In Rabbinical Literature:** The Rabbis taught that Benaiah was president of the Sanhedrin under David (Ber. 4*a*). His position as leader of the Jewish scholars is declared to be indicated in II Sam. xxiii. 20, the verse being expounded as follows: Benaiah was a man, בן איש חי ("son of a valiant man," A. V.; Hebr., "son of a man living"), who could be called "alive" even after his death; "who had done many acts"; of "Kabzeel," *i.e.*, he was very active in behalf of the Torah ("kabaẓ," he collected; "el," for God). "He slew two sons of Ariel." There was no one like him either at the time of the first or of the second Temple, Ariel, "lion of God," being a symbolic name for Temple. "He went down and slew a lion in the midst of a pit in the time of snow," may be interpreted either that he broke the ice in order to perform prescribed ablutions, or, figuratively, that he studied on a winter's day the great and abstruse book, Sifra (Ber. 18*b*; Targ. II Sam. *l.c.*).

Benaiah also occupied an eminent position under Solomon, being his chancellor and best friend. When the queen of Sheba was coming to visit Solomon, the latter sent Benaiah, whose beauty resembled the morning star, to meet her; he shone among his companions like Venus among the other stars (Targ. Sheni on Esther i. 2; ed. Munk, p. 9). When the queen saw him, she thought him Solomon, and was about to fall on her knees before him; when he told her who he was, she said to her companions: "Although ye have not seen the lion, ye have seen his den; judging by Benaiah, ye may form for yourselves an idea of Solomon" (*l.c.* p. 10). When Solomon returned to Jerusalem after his long wanderings, he at once went to Benaiah and reminded him of the times past, giving such details that the latter could not doubt that be was talking with Solomon (Midrash "Shir ha-Shirim," ed. Grünhut, p. 30*a*; compare Giṭ. 68*b*; see also Jellinek, "B. H." vi. 124–126). In the cabalistic literature Benaiah is counted among the thirty pious ones who exist in every generation in order that the world may continue (Zohar i. 105*b*; compare i. 6*b*).

J. SR. L. G.

BENJAMIN (or **MINYOMI**) **ASYA** ("Physician"): A Babylonian rabbinic scholar of the third and fourth amoraic generations (fourth century), contemporary of Rab Joseph and Raba, and founder of a school named after him, Debe Minyomi Asya. It is reported that the disciples of his school spoke disrespectfully of the Rabbis, saying, "Of what benefit are the rabbis to us? They have never proved it to be lawful for us to eat the raven, or to be unlawful to eat the pigeon!" (meaning to say that, in spite of their disputations and hair-splitting arguments, the Rabbis have no authority to alter or abrogate a Biblical precept [Sanh. 99*b* *et seq.*]). Raba obtained from Benjamin some medical information; and when on one occasion he publicty lectured on the subject before the people of Maḥuza, Benjamin's sons or disciples, who seem to have formed a medical gild, resented this publication of their professional secrets (Shab. 133*b*; 'Ab. Zarah 28*b*). Benjamin Asya is probably identical with Minyomi b. Niḥumi, the contemporary of Amemar I. (Ket. 69*a*), to whom Abaye appealed from a decision of Rab Joseph (*ib.* 81*b*). Brüll identifies Benjamin Asya with Bar Nathan Asya, who once manifested his disregard for rabbinic enactments by traveling on the second day of the Feast of Weeks from Beram (some read "Be Rab" = school) to Pumbedita, on which account Rab Joseph excommunicated him (Pes. 52*a*; see Diḳduḳe Soferim, *ad loc.*). Brüll discovers in this school the origin of Karaism ("Jahrb." i. 225).

J. SR. S. M.

BENJAMIN B. LEVI, R.: A Palestinian amora of the fourth century (third or fourth generation), junior contemporary of R. Ammi and R. Isaac (Yer. Peah i. 15a), and senior to Abin II. (Yer. Pes. vii. 34c; Yer. Hor. i. 46a). His name is connected with several Halakot (Yer. Ter. i. 40b; Yer. Pes. ii. 28d; Yer. 'Ab. Zarah ii. 42a, where his patronymic reads "Levaï"), but more frequently with homiletic remarks. On God's message by Jeremiah (xxiii. 24), "Can one hide himself in secret places that I shall not see him ["er'ennu"]?" he observes, "When one sitteth in a corner and occupieth himself with the study of the Law, I show him ["ar'ennu"] to the public, or when he hides himself for sinful purposes of apostasy, I expose him to public gaze" (Ex. R. viii.; Tan., Wa'era, 9; compare Num. R. ix. 9). According to him, when the time for Israel's restoration shall come, there will be a change in the order of nature; at present when the north wind blows no south wind prevails, and when the south wind prevails there is no north wind; but when God shall restore the exiled, He shall produce an "argestes" (see Jastrow, "Dict." p. 115b), when both winds shall do service, as it is written (Isa. xliii. 6), "I will say to the north, Give up, and to the south, Keep not back: bring my sons from far," etc. (Esther R. to i. 8; Cant. R. to iv. 16; Lev. R. ix.; Num. R. xiii.).—[Gen. R. lxxxvii.; Midr. Teh. lxxxvii. 2; Pesik. xiii. 112a, xviii. 137a; Pesik. R. xviii.; Lev. R. xxviii.; compare Eccl. R. to i. 3.]

Bibliography: Frankel, *Mebo*, 69b; Bacher, *Ag. Pal. Amor.* iii. 661 *et seq.*

J. SR. S. M.

BERECHIAH I., R.: A Palestinian scholar of the second amoraic generation (third century), always cited without the accompaniment of patronymic or cognomen. Once only (Lev. R. i. 4) is he quoted as **Berechiah Saba** (the Elder), by R. Abin III., the contemporary of Berechiah II.; and in this instance the designation "Saba" is used to distinguish between the namesakes. Nothing is known of Berechiah's life, and comparatively little preserved of his teachings, though it is quite probable that some of his sayings are attributed to his later and more renowned namesake (compare Frankel, "Mebo," 69b). A discussion of his with R. Ḥiyya of Kefar Teḥumin is reported on the merit of the study of the Torah. One of them teaches that the whole of this world does not equal the value of a single passage of the Law; and the other argues, "Even the discharge of all the Biblical commandments is not equal to the merit of mastering a single passage of the Law" (Yer. Peah i. 15d). Rabbah b. Naḥman, a contemporary of Rabbah b. Huna, transmits in the name of Berechiah a homily on the continuance of the protective influence of patriarchal merit ("zekut abot"; Yer. Sanh. x. 27d; compare Lev. R. xxxvi. 6, where the names of the rabbis are badly corrupted). R. Tanhum b. Ḥanilaï, the disciple of R. Joshua ben Levi (B. Ḳ. 55a), too, reports Haggadot in the name of Berechiah (Tan., Tazria', 9; Pesiḳ. R. xxi. 110a). Bacher denies the existence of this Berechiah, and to sustain his opinion changes the chronological order in the passages quoted ("Ag. Pal. Amor." iii. 351, 354, note 3; 628, note 7).

Bibliography: Frankel, *Mebo*, 69b; Weiss, *Dor*, iii. 91, note 17.

J. SR. S. M.

BERECHIAH II., R.: A Palestinian amora of the fourth century. In the Talmud he is invariably cited by his prænomen alone; but in the Midrashim he is frequently cited with the addition of "ha-Kohen," and sometimes with the further addition of the title "Berebi" (compare Pesiḳ. ii. 21a, xii. 107b; Pesiḳ. 3 [ed. Friedmann, p. 8a]; Num. R. xiv. 3; Pesiḳ. R. 3 [ed. Friedmann, p. 9a]; Num. R. *l.c.*; Tan., Beha'aloteka, 5;

Num. R. xv. 7); and according to at least one Midrash (Lev. R. xxx. 1), his father's name was Ḥiyya (see also Tan., ed. Buber, Ḥayye Sarah, 6, note 35).

While Palestine may justly claim him as a citizen, Berechiah is probably a Babylonian by birth, since he not only cites teachings of Babylonian scholars ("Rabbanan de-Tamman," Gen. R. lvi. 11, xcviii. 3; Esther R. i. 1; compare Gen. R. xxxvii. 3, where this expression is converted into "Rabbi Ḥanin," and Mid. Teh. cv., beginning, where "de-Tamman" is omitted), but also shows himself quite familiar with the private history of Babylonian families (Yer. Ḳid. iii. 64c; Lev. R. xxxii. 7). Judging, however, from the insignificant number of his sayings recorded in the Babylonian Talmud as compared with his almost innumerable teachings preserved in the Palestinian Talmud and the Palestinian Midrashim, and considering also that his acknowledged masters were Palestinians, it is safe to say that he was in Palestine at an early age. Berechiah's acknowledged master in the Haggadah was R. Ḥelbo (Yer. Kil. ix. 32c; Lam. R. on iii. 23; Cant. R. on i. 2); but it seems that he personally knew R. Ḥelbo's predecessors, Levi and Abba b. Kahana, and witnessed a heated exegetical controversy between them (Gen. R. xlvii. 9). If this be so, Berechiah must have lived to an advanced age, for he was in a legal controversy with R. Mana (the Younger) (Yer. Ḳid. iii. 64d). Rapoport ("Briefe," ed. Gräber, p. 80) makes him a teacher of Jerome.

Berechiah is cited in both the Babylonian Talmud (Ber. 55a; Yoma 71a; Ta'anit 4a; Soṭah 13b) and the Palestinian, in the field of the Halakah (Yer. Ber. vii. 11b; Yer. Peah i. 15a; Yer. Ma'as. v. 52a; Yer. Suk. ii. 53a; Yer. Soṭah vii. 21b; Yer. Ḳid. iii. 64d; Yer. Sanh. xi. 30b) and in that of the Haggadah; but it is the latter which he cultivated mainly. Few names appear in the Midrashic literature as frequently as does Berechiah's. In Pesiḳta alone he is cited sixty-eight times, either as originator or as transmitter; in Pesiḳta Rabbati sixty-one times (see Friedmann, Introduction, p. 18), in Tan. (ed. Buber) seventy-three times (Buber's Introduction, p. 46), in Mid. Teh. eighty-five times (Buber's Introduction, p. 28), and correspondingly numerous are his remarks preserved in the other Midrashim. Some specimens of his teachings are here subjoined.

In accordance with the oneirological views of his days, he asserts that dreams, though realized partly, are never realized fully. "Whence do we learn this? From Joseph, who dreamed (Gen. xxxvii. 9), 'Behold, the sun, and the moon, and eleven stars made obeisance to me'; and at that time his mother, typified in his vision by the moon (*ib.* 10), was no more among the living" (Ber. 55a). He thus construes the Psalmist's saying, "The Lord knoweth the way of the righteous, but the way of the ungodly perisheth" (Ps. i. 6): "When the Holy One—blessed be He!—came to create man, He foresaw that pious and impious men would descend from him, and He said, 'If I create him, the impious will descend from him; if I create him not, how will the pious descend from him? ' What did the Holy One—blessed be He!—do? He removed the ways of the impious out of His sight, and by means of His attribute of mercy ["middat ha-Raḥamim"] He created man. This is the meaning of the Scripture, 'God knoweth ["holdeth in view"] the way of the righteous '" (Mid. Teh. on *l.c.*; Gen. R. viii. 4). In commenting on Eccl. vii. 17, "Be not overmuch wicked," he says: "The Bible does not mean to teach that it is permitted to sin a little; but it means to say, if thou didst sin a little, say not, 'I am under the wrath of God on account of this little, and can be no worse off for sinning more '" (Eccl. R. on *l.c.*; Mid. Teh. on i. 1; compare Shab. 31b). With reference to the Scriptural saying (Ps. xxxii. 1), "Happy is he whose transgression is forgiven" (literally, "who is lifted above transgression"), he cites R. Simon [Samuel?] b. Ammi as remarking, "Happy is the man who is master over sin, that sin be not master over him" (Gen. R. xxii. 6). In the same strain is Berechiah's remark on Solomon's saying, "There is a time to be born, and a time to die" (Eccl. iii. 2): "Happy is he whose hour of death is like his hour of birth; who, as he was pure and innocent in the hour of his birth, is also innocent at the hour of his death" (Yer. Ber. ii. 4d; Eccl. R. on *l.c.*; Deut. R. vii. 6).

BIBLIOGRAPHY: Bacher, *Ag. Pal. Am.* iii. 344–396.

J. SR. S. M.

BERURIAH (=probably **Valeria):** Daughter of the martyr R. Hananiah ben Teradion, and wife of R. Meïr; born in the first quarter of the second century, she lived at Tiberias after the Hadrianic persecutions. Her traits of character, gleaned from Talmudic passages, show her to have been a helpmate worthy of her great husband, and to have possessed a personality corresponding to the emergencies of the troublous times following upon the failure of Bar Kokba's insurrection. They betray intellectual qualities and attainments as well as womanly tenderness and stanch virtues. It is said that she studied three hundred Talmudic subjects daily (Pes. 62b), and R. Judah endorsed a decision of hers, on a question about clean and unclean, in which she went counter to the view of "the wise" ("ḥakamim") (Tosef., Kelim, B. M. i. 6).

Her womanly tenderness is shown by a Biblical interpretation (Ber. 10a): Her husband, grievously vexed by wicked neighbors, prayed for their extermination. Beruriah exclaimed: "What! do you dare pray thus because the Psalmist says: 'Let ḥaṭaïm be consumed out of the earth'? (Ps. civ. 35) Observe that he does not say ḥoṭeïm ["sinners"], but ḥaṭaïm ["sins"]. And then look to the end of the verse: 'And the wicked will be no more.' Once sins are rooted out, there will be no more evil-doers." Of her ready wit the following is a specimen (*ib.*): In a dispute between Beruriah and a sectary, the latter quoted Isa. liv. 1: "Sing, O barren, thou that didst not bear," and mockingly asked whether barrenness is cause for singing. Beruriah directed him to look to the end of the verse: "More are the children of the desolate than the children of the married wife." The principle upon which both interpretations rest, "Look to the end of the verse" (לסיפיה דקרא שפיל), became an exegetical rule current among the later Talmudical sages.

In 'Er. 53b *et seq.* there are other examples of her knowledge of Jewish Scriptures and her almost coquettish playfulness, coexisting in her with a capacity for righteous indignation, displayed when it was proposed, for her father's sake, to pay funeral honors to her scapegrace brother. Father, mother, and sister alike denounced his conduct, the last applying to him Prov. xx. 17 (R. V.), "Bread of falsehood is sweet to a man; but afterward his mouth shall be filled with gravel" (Sem. xii.; Lam. R. iii. 16).

Beruriah's life fell in calamitous times. Not only did she lose her father through the Hadrianic persecutions, but her mother at the same time suffered a violent death, and her sister was carried off to Rome, or perhaps Antioch, to lead a life of shame under coercion. At Beruriah's instance, R. Meïr set out to save her sister's honor, and succeeded ('Ab. Zarah 18a; Sifre, Deut. 307; Eccl. R. vii. 11). In consequence he had to flee to Babylonia, and Beruriah accompanied him.

Beruriah is best known in connection with the touching story of the sudden death of her two sons on the Sabbath, while their father was at the house of study. On his return, at the conclusion of the Sabbath, he at once asked for them. Their mother replied that they had gone to the house of study, and, feigning to disregard her husband's rejoinder, that he had looked for them there in vain, she handed him the cup of wine for the Habdalah service. His second inquiry for them was evaded by a similar subterfuge. After R. Meïr had eaten his evening meal, Beruriah asked formally for permission to put a question to him. "Rabbi," she then said, "some time ago a deposit was left with me for safe-keeping, and now the owner has come to claim it. Must I return it?" "Can there be any question about the return of property to its owner?" said R. Meïr, half astonished and half indignant that his wife should entertain a doubt. "I did not care to let it go out of my possession without your knowledge," replied Beruriah, seemingly in excuse, and, taking him by the hand, led him into the room in which the bodies of their two sons were lying on the bed. When she withdrew the cover, R. Meïr broke out in tears and plaints. Gently Beruriah reminded him of his answer to her question about the return of a treasure entrusted to one for safe-keeping, adding the verse from Job (i. 21): "The Lord gave, and the Lord hath taken away; blessed be the name of the Lord." This story, which has found a home in all modern literatures, can be traced to no earlier source than the Yalkuṭ (Prov. 964, quotation from a Midrash).

With Beruriah's death is connected a legend mentioned by Rashi ('Ab. Zarah 18b). To explain R. Meïr's flight to Babylonia, the commentator relates the following:

"Once Beruriah scoffed at the rabbinical saying, 'Women are light-minded' (Kid. 80b), and her husband warned her that her own end might yet testify to the truth of the words. To put her virtue to the test, he charged one of his disciples to endeavor to seduce her. After repeated efforts she yielded, and then shame drove her to commit suicide. R. Meïr, tortured by remorse, fled from his home."

The historical kernel of this story can not be disengaged. As told, the narrative is wholly at variance with what is known of Beruriah's character and that of R. Meïr. Beruriah probably died at an early age.

BIBLIOGRAPHY: Adolf Blumenthal, *Rabbi Meïr*, pp. 108–111; M. Kayserling, *Die Jüdischen Frauen in der Geschichte, Literatur und Kunst*, pp. 120–124; Henry Zirndorf, *Some Jewish Women*, pp. 162–173; Bacher, *Ag. Tan.* i. 400, ii. 5.

J. SR. H. S.

BET HILLEL AND BET SHAMMAI: The "School (literally, "house") of Hillel" and the "School of Shammai" are names by which are designated the most famous antagonistic schools that flourished in Palestine during the first century (first tannaitic generation), and which more than others contributed to the development of the oral law.

Down to the advent of Hillel and Shammai, who were the founders of the great schools bearing their names, there were but few casuistic differences among the schools. Between Hillel and Shammai themselves three (or, according to some authorities, five) disputes are mentioned in the Talmud (Shab. 15a; Ḥag. ii. 2; 'Eduy. i. 2, 3; Niddah i. 1); but with the increase of their disciples disputations increased to such an extent as to give rise to the saying, "The one Law has become two laws" (Tosef., Ḥag. ii. 9; Sanh. 88b; Soṭah 47b).

The prevailing characteristics of the disputes are the restrictive tendency of the Shammaites and the moderation of the Hillelites. Three hundred and sixteen controversies between these two schools are preserved in the pages of the Talmud, affecting 221 Halakot, 29 halakic interpretations, and 66 guard-laws ("gezerot"); and out of the whole number only 55 (or about one-sixth) present the Shammaites on the side of leniency. Moreover, even where the characteristic tendencies appear to have changed masters, the practical result remains the same; being the logical and consistent resultants of some opinions expressed elsewhere, and in line with the natural tendencies of the respective schools; and some of their restrictive views the Hillelites subsequently rejected, adopting what were exceptionally the more moderate views of the Shammaites ('Eduy. i. 12 *et seq.*; compare Weiss, "Dor,"i. 179 *et seq.*). That the latter, as a school, ever receded from their standpoint to join the ranks of their more moderate antagonists is nowhere indicated; though individuals of that school, like Baba ben Buta, sometimes acknowledged the unreasonableness of their party by deserting its standard for that of Bet Hillel (Bezah 20a; Yer. Ḥag. ii. 78a). Hence it is that the Mishnah introduces some of their controversies with the remark, "These are of the lenient views of Bet Shammai and the restrictive views of Bet Hillel" ('Eduy. iv. 1; Tosef., 'Eduy. ii. 2).

The reason assigned for their respective tendencies is a psychological one. The Hillelites were, like the founder of their school (Ber. 60a; Shab. 31a; Ab. i. 12 *et seq.*), quiet, peace-loving men, accommodating themselves to circumstances and times, and being determined only upon fostering the Law and bringing man nearer to his God and to his neighbor. The Shammaites, on the other hand, stern and unbending like the originator of their school, emulated and even exceeded his severity. To them it seemed impossible to be sufficiently stringent in religious prohibitions. The disciples of Hillel, "the pious and gentle follower of Ezra" (Sanh. 11a), evinced in all their public dealings the peacefulness, gentleness, and conciliatory spirit which had distinguished their great master; and by the same characteristic qualities they were guided during the political storms which convulsed their country. The Shammaites, on the contrary, were intensely patriotic, and would not bow to foreign rule. They advocated the interdiction of any and all intercourse with those who either were Romans or in any way contributed toward the furtherance of Roman power or influences. Dispositions so heterogeneous and antagonistic can not usually endure side by side without provoking serious misunderstandings and feuds; and it was owing solely to the Hillelites' forbearance that the parties did not come to blows, and that even friendly relations continued between them (Tosef., Yeb. i. 10; Yeb. 14b; Yer. Yeb. i. 3b), for a time at least. But the vicissitudes of the period exerted a baneful influence also in that direction.

When, after the banishment of Archelaus (6 C.E.), the Roman procurator Coponius attempted to tax the Jews, and ordered a strict census to be taken for that purpose, both schools protested, and the new measure was stigmatized as so outrageous as to justify all schemes by which it might be evaded. The general abhorrence for the system of Roman taxation manifested itself in looking with distrust upon every Jew who was officially concerned in carrying it out, whether as tax-collector ("gabbai") or as customs-collector ("mokes"); these were shunned by the higher ranks of the community, and their testimony before Jewish courts had no weight (B. Ḳ. x. 1; *ib.* 113a; Sanh. iii. 3; *ib.* 25b). About this time the malcontents held the ascendency. Under the guidance of Judas the Gaulonite (or Galilean) and of Zadok, a Shammaite (Tosef., 'Eduy. ii. 2; Yeb. 15b), a political league was called into existence, whose object was to oppose by all means the practise of the Roman laws. Adopting as their organic principle the exhortation of the father of the Maccabees (I Macc. ii. 50), "Be ye zealous for the law, and give your lives for the covenant of your fathers," these patriots called themselves "Ḳanna'im," Zealots (Josephus, "B. J." iv. 3, § 9, and vii. 8, § 1; Raphall, "Post-Biblical History," ii. 364); and the Shammaites, whose principles were akin to those of the Zealots, found support among them. Their religious austerity, combined with their hatred of the heathen Romans, naturally aroused the sympathies of the fanatic league, and as the Hillelites became powerless to stem the public indignation, the Shammaites gained the upper hand in all disputes affecting their country's oppressors. Bitter feelings were consequently engendered between the schools; and it appears that even in public worship they would no longer unite under one roof (Jost, "Gesch. des Judenthums und Seiner Sekten," i. 261; Tosef., R. H., end). These feelings grew apace, until toward the last days of Jerusalem's struggle they broke out with great fury.

As all the nations around Judea made common cause with the Romans, the Zealots were naturally inflamed against every one of them; and therefore the Shammaites proposed to prevent all communication between Jew and Gentile, by prohibiting the Jews from buying any article of food or drink from their heathen neighbors. The Hillelites, still moderate in their religious and political views, would not agree to such sharply defined exclusiveness; but when the Sanhedrin was called together to consider the propriety of such measures, the Shammaites, with the aid of the Zealots, gained the day. Eleazar ben Ananias invited the disciples of both schools to meet at his house. Armed men were stationed at the door, and instructed to permit every one to enter, but no one to leave. During the discussions that were carried on under these circumstances, many Hillelites are said to have been killed; and there and then the remainder adopted the restrictive propositions of the Shammaites, known in the Talmud as "The Eighteen Articles." On account of the violence which attended those enactments, and because of the radicalism of the enactments themselves, the day on which the Shammaites thus triumphed over the Hillelites was thereafter regarded as a day of misfortune (Tosef., Shab. i. 16 *et seq.*; Shab. 13a, 17a; Yer. Shab. i. 3c).

Bet Shammai and Bet Hillel continued their disputes—probably interrupted during the war times—after the destruction of the Temple, or until after the reorganization of the Sanhedrin under the presidency of

Gamaliel II. (80 C.E.). By that time all political schemes and plans for the recovery of the lost liberty had become altogether foreign to the ideas of the spiritual leaders; and the characteristics of the Hillelites once more gained the ascendency. All disputed points were brought up for review (see 'AKABIA); and in nearly every case the opinion of the Hillelites prevailed (Tosef., Yeb. i. 13; Yer. Ber. i. 3b; Grätz, "Gesch. der Juden," 2d ed., iv. 424, note 4). Thenceforth it was said: "Where Bet Shammai is opposed to Bet Hillel, the opinion of Bet Shammai is considered as if not incorporated in the Mishnah" ("Bet Shammai bimeḳom Bet Hillel enah Mishnah"—Ber. 36b; Beẓah 11b; Yeb. 9a); that is, null and void.

Of the personnel of these schools there is no record, they being invariably cited collectively as "Bet Shammai" or "Bet Hillel." Nor can their number be stated with exactitude. In round figures, the Babylonian Talmud (Suk. 28a; B. B. 134a) gives the number of Hillel's disciples as eighty, while the Palestinian Talmud (Yer. Ned. v. 39b) makes of them as many pairs. Both sources mention two of them by name, Jonathan ben Uzziel and Johanan ben Zakkai; and it is added that Jonathan was the greatest and Johanan the least among the whole number. No such traditions are recorded of the Shammaites. Of their school three are mentioned by name; viz., Baba ben Buṭa (Beẓah 20a), Dositai of Kefar Yetma ('Orlah ii. 5), and Zadok (Tosef., 'Eduy. ii. 2); but they are mentioned simply because, though Shammaites, they sometimes upheld the views of the Hillelites. See HILLEL and SHAMMAI.

BIBLIOGRAPHY: Grätz, *Gesch. der Juden*, 3d ed., iii. 275–278, 500 *et seq.*, *ib.* notes 23, 26; Jost, *Gesch. des Judenthums und Seiner Sekten*, i. 261–270; Frankel, *Darke ha-Mishnah*, pp. 45–55; Weiss, *Dor Dor we-Dorshaw*, i. 177–187; idem, *Introd. to Mek.* v. *et seq.*; Brüll, *Mebo ha-Mishnah*, pp. 43–49; Bacher, *Agada der Tannaiten*, i. 14–25; Schwarz, *Die Controversen der Shammaiten und Hilleliten*, Carlsruhe, 1893.

J. SR. S. M.

BET HA-MIDRASH: High school; literally, "house of study," or place where the students of the Law gather to listen to the MIDRASH, the discourse or exposition of the Law. It is used in contradistinction to the Bet ha-Sefer, the primary school which children under thirteen attended to learn the Scriptures. Thus it is said in Gen. R. lxiii. 10: "Esau and Jacob went together to the bet ha-sefer until they had finished their thirteenth year, when they parted; the former entering the houses of idols, and the latter the batte ha-midrashot." Elsewhere it is stated, "There were 480 synagogues (batte kenesiot) in Jerusalem, each containing a bet ha-sefer, (primary school for the Scriptures), and abet Talmud (same as bet ha-midrash), for the study of the Law and the tradition; and Vespasian destroyed them all" (Yer. Meg. iii. 73d; Lam. R.,

Introduction 12, ii. 2; Pesiḳ. xiv. 121b; Yer. Ket. xiii. 35c, where "460" is a clerical error). The same tradition is given somewhat differently in Bab. Ket. 105a: Three hundred and ninety-four courts of justice were in Jerusalem and as many synagogues, "batte ha-midrashot" (high schools), and "batte soferim" (primary schools). According to Yer. Ta'anit iv. 7, p. 69a; Lam. R. ii. 2, iii. 51, there were 500 primary schools in Betar, the smallest of which had no less than 300 pupils (compare Soṭah 49b, Giṭ. 58a, which speak of 400 schools, each with 400 pupils). The number of schools (480) in Jerusalem besides the one in the Temple is derived by gemaṭria from the word מלאתי = 481 (Lam. R. *l.c.*).

The bet ha-midrash in the Temple hall (Luke ii. 46, xx. 1, xxi. 37; Matt. xxi. 23, xxvi. 55; John xviii. 20) is called the "bet ha-midrash ha-gadol," the great high school (Tanna debe Eliyahu R. ix. [x.], xvi., and elsewhere). It formed the center of learning, and was, of course, the oldest one, standing in close relation to the "Bet Din ha-Gadol," the high court of justice in the Temple. Its history can not well be traced. A "bet wa'ad," meeting-place of scholars, existed as early as the days of Jose ben Joezer of Zereda, the martyr of the Maccabean time, who teaches: "Let thy house be a bet wa'ad for the wise" (Ab. i. 4). The name "bet wa'ad" is met with also in Soṭah ix. 15; Yer. Ber. iv. 7c; Yer. Ta'anit iv. 67d, and elsewhere. The hearers or disciples were seated on the ground at the feet of their teachers (Ab. *l.c.*; Luke x. 39; Acts xxii. 3). In the first century, schools existed everywhere at the side of the synagogues (Acts. xix. 9, "the school of one Tyrannus"). The primary school, bet ha-sefer, was, however, instituted at a later time, first by Simeon ben Shetaḥ, about 100 B.C. at Jerusalem (Yer. Ket. viii. 32c), and later introduced generally, for the benefit of all children, by Joshua b. Gamla in the first century (B. B. 21a). The Haggadah reflects a later mode of life when speaking of a bet ha-midrash of Shem and Eber which was attended by Isaac, occasionally also by Rebekah, and regularly by Jacob (Targ. Yer. to Gen. xxii. 19, xxiv. 62, xxv. 22; Gen. R. lxiii.; Tanna debe Eliyahu R. v.); of that of Jacob at Sukkot, which Joseph frequented (Targ. Yer. to Gen. xxxiii. 17, xxxvii. 2; Num. xxiv. 5); of that which Judah was sent to build for Jacob in Egypt (Gen. R. xcv.; Tan., Wayiggush, xi.); or of that of Moses, where Moses and Aaron and his sons taught the Law (Targ. Yer. to Ex. xxxix. 33; compare Num. R. xxi.: "Joshua arranged the chairs for the scholars attending the bet wa'ad of Moses"). Similarly the prophet Samuel had his "bet ulphana" (Aramaic for "bet ha-midrash") in Ramah (Targ. to I Sam. xix. 19). Solomon built synagogues and schoolhouses (Eccl. R. ii. 4). King Hezekiah furnished the oil for lamps to burn in the synagogues and schools, and threatened to have killed by the sword any one who would not study the Law; so that soon there was no 'AM HA-AREẒ to be found in the land, nor a child or woman unfamiliar with all the precepts on Levitical purity (Sanh. 94b). Especially those of the tribe of Issachar devoted their time to the study of the Law in the bet ha-midrash, Zebulun the merchant furnishing them the means of support (I Chron. xii. 33; Deut. xxxiii. 18; Gen. R. lii., xcix.; Targ. Yer. *l.c.*).

Jethro was promised that his descendants would never see the schoolhouses (batte ha-midrashot) disappear from among them (Tanna debe Eliyahu R. v.; compare Mek., Yitro, 'Amaleḳ, 2).

In Mishnaic times (Shab. xvi. 1) it appears that public discourses were held in the bet ha-midrash; but Targ. Yer. on Judges v. 9 indicates that it was used later for the study of the Law, and the popular discourses were delivered at the synagogue.

The first bet ha-midrash of which there is authentic record is the one in which Shemaiah (Sameas) and Abtalion (Pollion) taught, and which Hillel, when a youth, could attend only after having paid admission-fee to the janitor (Yoma 35b). Whether or not this charge of a fee, so contradictory to the maxim of the men of the Great Synagogue (Abot i. 1), "Raise many disciples," was a political measure of the time, it seemingly stands in connection with a principle pronounced by the Shammaites (Ab. R. N., *A*, iii.; *B*, iv., ed. Schechter, p. 14), that "only those who are wise, humble, and of goodly, well-to-do parentage should be taught the Law." On the other hand, the Hillelites insisted that "all, without exception, should partake of the privilege, inasmuch as many transgressors in Israel, when brought nigh to the Law, brought forth righteous, pious, and perfect men." Against the Hillelite principle, R. Gamaliel wanted to exclude all those who had not stood the test of inner fitness. He was outvoted, with the result that 400 (or, according to some authorities, 700) chairs were necessarily added in order to seat the newcomers (Ber. 28a). The customary seating of the pupils on chairs marks an improvement, and this new feature gave to the schoolhouse the name"yeshibah" (Abot ii. 7) or "metibta" (B. M., 85a, b).

The bet ha-midrash of Jabneh was called "vineyard," either because it stood in a vineyard (Schürer, "Gesch." 3d ed., ii. 325, note 49) or, as rabbinical tradition asserts, because it was built in semicircular shape, thus resembling a vineyard (Ket. iv. 6; 'Eduy. ii. 4; Yer. Ber iv. 7d). At all events the name "vineyard" became the usual appellation for the bet ha-midrash; hence Song of Songs vii. 13 (A. V. 12), "Let us get up early to the vineyards," was applied to the bet ha-midrash ('Er. 21b).

It is frequently recommended as highly meritorious to be one of the first to come to the bet ha-midrash and the last to leave (Shab. 127a; Giṭ. 7a; Meg. 15b; Suk. 28a; Sanh. 3b).

It was believed to bring misfortune to sit at meals during the time that the discourse was being held in the bet ha-midrash (Giṭ. 38b).

It was forbidden to sleep in the bet ha-midrash (Tanna debe Eliyahu R. xiii., xiv.). In Babylonia, where scholars spent their whole time in the school, exception was made to this rule (Ber. 25a; Meg. 28a). Mothers won special merit by training their children to go to the bet ha-sefer, and wives by waiting for the return of their husbands from the bet ha-midrash (Ber. 17a). Every session at the bet ha-midrash was expected to offer some new idea to the student; hence the frequent question: "What new thing was offered at the bet ha-midrash to-day?" (Tosef., Soṭah, vii. 9; Ḥag. 3a; Yer. Giṭ. v. 47d; and elsewhere). The bet ha-midrash ranks higher than the synagogue; consequently a synagogue may be transformed into a bet ha-midrash; but the latter can not be changed into a house of worship (Meg. 26b, 27a). "He who goeth from the synagogue to the bet ha-midrash—that is, from the divine service to the study of the Law—will be privileged to greet the majesty of God; for so says Ps. lxxxiv. 8 [A. V. 7]. 'They go from strength to strength, every one of them appeareth before God in Zion'" (Ber. 64a). To the bet ha-keneset (synagogue) and the bet ha-midrash in Babylonia are referred the words of Ezek. xi. 16, Hebr: "I will be to them as a little sanctuary in the countries where they shall come" (Meg. 29a). The Haggadah finds allusions to the bet ha-midrash in Ps. xc. 1: "Thou hast been our dwelling-place in all generations"; and Ps. lxxxii. 1, Hebr.: "God standeth in the midst of the congregation of [those who seek] God" (*ib.*; Gen. R. xlviii.); and also in Balaam's words (Num. xxiv. 5): "How lovely are thy tents, O Jacob, thy tabernacles, O Israel" (Targ. Yer. to Num. *l.c.*; Sanh. 105b); likewise in Cant. viii. 10: "I am a wall and my breasts like towers" (Pes. 87a), and Cant. ii. 8, 9, refer to the synagogue and the schoolhouse: "The voice of my beloved! behold he cometh leaping...; my beloved is like a roe," meaning that God proceeds from one synagogue to the other, and from one bet ha-midrash to the other, to bless Israel (Pesiḳ. v. 48b).

God also has His bet ha-midrash in heaven, and teaches the Law to the righteous (Tanna debe Eliyahu R. i., iii., iv., v., viii., ix.); it is called the "upper yeshibah" or "metibta" (B. M. 86a; Ber. 18b; Ta'anit 21b). "He who accustoms himself to go to the bet ha-keneset and bet ha-midrash in this world shall also be admitted into the bet ha-keneset and bet ha-midrash of the world to come" (Joshua b. Levi, in Deut. R. vii.; Midr. Teh. to Ps. lxxxiv. 5 [A. V. 4]).

The name "bet ha-midrash" recurs in the Arabic "madrasah," for school; and Jews under the influence of Arabic life called the bet ha-midrash also midrash (Güdemann, "Gesch. des Erziehungswesens und der Kultur der Juden in Frankreich und Deutschland," i. 92 *et seq.*, 265; "Quellenschriften zur Gesch. des Unterrichts," p. 99). A systematic plan of education of the thirteenth century, published and translated by Güdemann, *l.c.*, proposes to impose on each member of a congregation in the whole country or district the old half-shekel tax for the maintenance of the great bet ha-midrash or high school to be built in the capital near the synagogue, and for primary schools to be in each town, where the disciples, together with the teachers, should live during the week, separated from their parents and removed from all contact with the outside world. During the Middle Ages the bet ha-midrash was open day and night for both public discourses and private studies. It contained usually a large library for the use of the students, and became an attractive center and meeting-place also for scholars of other cities. Inevitably this privilege was frequently abused, and the bet ha-midrash often became the resort of idlers and poor homeless strangers who spent their time in gossip rather than in study. The official name given by non-Jews to the bet ha-midrash in Nuremberg (1406) is "Judenschule" (see Güdemann, "Gesch. d. Erziehungswesens und der Kultur d. Abendländ. Juden," p. 67, note 10). Whether the same name, "Judenschule," for the synagogue, given to it by the Christian population (Güdemann, *l.c.* p. 94, note 2), originated from the use of the bet ha-midrash also as a place of worship by the students, customary as early as Talmudical times (Ber 8a), or from other causes, the proverbial "noise of the Judenschule" seems to refer to the lively discussions which took place in the bet ha-midrash (though at times the synagogue was used also for learned disputations), and not to any disorder in connection with the divine service.

The number of hearers or disciples at the bet ha-midrash was not limited as was the case in the ḤEDER, or primary school (Abrahams, "Jewish Life in the Middle Ages," p. 349). The rabbis or ordained teachers, as a rule engaged by the community to take charge of the studies in the bet ha-midrash, often dwelt in the same house; thus in Germany where the bet ha-midrash received the Latin name Clausa (Claus = cloister), also called "Claus Rabbis" or "Clausner." The synagogue and bet ha-midrash were often in the same building or adjoining each other. For the course of studies and other regulations concerning the bet ha-midrash, see the article ACADEMIES.

BIBLIOGRAPHY: Güdemann, *Jüdisches Unterrichtswesen Während der Spanisch-Arabischen Periode*, 1873, p. 791; idem, *Gesch. des Erziehungswesens und der Kultur der Abendländ. Juden*, I. 1880, III. 1888 (see Index); idem, *Quellenschriften zur Gesch. des Unterrichts und der Erziehung bei den Deutschen Juden*, 1891 (see Index); Abrahams, *Jewish Life in the Middle Ages*, 1896, pp. 34, 349 *et seq.*; Hamburger, *R. B. T.* ii., s.v. *Dehrhaus*; Weber, *System der Altsynagogalen Theologie*, 1880, pp. 34, 127–360; Schürer, *l.c.*; Jacobs, *Jews of Angevin England*, pp. 243–251, 343–344.

J. SR. K.

BUN: As a personal prenomen this name is a dialectic abridgment of "Abun" ("Abin," "Rabin"; see Jastrow, "Dictionary," 147a; compare Pesiḳ. xxx. 192b; Yer. ḥag. i. 76c; Yer. Suk. v. 55d), and appears exclusively in Palestinian literary sources (Yer. Ter. viii.45c; Yer. Pes.iii. 29d; Yer. Sheḳ. iv. 48b; Yer. Yeb. iii. 4c). Several amoraim so cited are mentioned under the full name as it appears in the Babylonian Talmud (see, for example, ABIN B. ḤIYYA, ABIN B. KAHANA); and a Palestinian scholar of the fourth century is cited once under the name of "Bun b. Bisna" (Yer. Yeb. iv. 7b), and once (*ib.* i. 2d) under that of "Abun b. Bizna."

J. SR. S. M.

D

DIMI (also called **Abdimi** and **Abudimi**): Amora of the fourth century who often carried Palestinian doctrinal and exegetical remarks to the Babylonian schools, and Babylonian teachings to Palestine (see ABDIMA NAḤOTA). In consequence of a decree of banishment issued by Constantius against the teachers of Judaism in Palestine, he finally settled in Babylonia (Ḥul. 106a; Grätz, "Gesch." 2d ed., iv. 338; against Grätz, however, see I. ha-Levi, "Dorot ha-Rishonim," ii. 468–473). Dimi was a perfect storehouse of diversified knowledge, which he diligently gathered and as freely disseminated; and he made the transmission of the teachings of his most prominent Palestinian predecessors his special mission. He reported in the names of Jannai, Ḥanina, Joshua ben Levi, Simeon ben Laḳish, Isaac, Eleazar, and, most frequently, R. Johanan; and almost as often he reported Palestinian observations with merely the introductory formula במערבא אמרי ("They say in the West"; Shab. 7a, 8b, 52a, 63b, 72a, 85b, 105a, 108b, 125b; 'Er. 3a; Yoma 55b; Ta'an. 10a; Ḥag. 15b; Meg. 18a; Yer. Ned. ix. 41b; B. Ḳ. 114b; B. M. 58b; B. B. 74b; Sanh. 7b, 56a, 63a; Men. 26b; Tem. 12b, 14a; 'Ar. 16a).

Abaye was the most appreciative recipient of Dimi's information, which ranged along the lines of the Halakah and the Haggadah, occasionally touching also physical geography, history, and ethics (Shab. 108a; Ket. 17a, 111b; Ber. 44a; Ḳid. 31a; 'Ab. Zarah 36b; B. M. 58b). When Abaye once inquired of him, "What do the Westerners [Palestinians] most strenuously avoid in their social intercourse?" Dimi replied, "Putting a neighbor to shame; for R. Ḥanina counts this sin among the three unpardonable ones" (the other two being adultery and calling nicknames) (B. M. 58b). Dimi was also opposed to the bestowal of overmuch praise, and thus illustrated the Biblical proverb (Prov. xxvii. 14), "He that blesseth his friend with a loud voice, rising early in the morning, it shall be counted a curse to him."

Usually Dimi communicated his knowledge personally; but where circumstances required it, he did so by messages. Thus, when on one occasion, having himself reported in Pumbedita a Halakah as construed by R. Johanan, he discovered on his arrival at Nehardea that he had been mistaken, he sent word to the misinformed, candidly confessing, "What I have told you is founded on an error" (Shab. 63b).

BIBLIOGRAPHY: Grätz, *Gesch.* 2d ed., iv., note 29; Bacher, *Ag. Pal. Amor.* iii. 691; Heilprin, *Seder ha-Dorot*, ii., *s.v.*

Dimi: Babylonian scholar of the fourth century; brother of Rab Safra. According to the testimony of his contemporary, R. Abba, Dimi was not endowed with worldly goods (Ket. 85b), but was blessed with a clear conscience. In his last hours he was visited by his learned brother, to whom he remarked, "May it come home to me ["I deserve God's mercy," Jastrow, "Dict." p. 132a], because I have observed all the rules prescribed by the Rabbis"; and when asked, "Didst thou also refrain from sounding thy neighbor's praises, for in continually talking of one's virtues, a man incidentally refers to his vices?" he replied, "I have never heard of such a precept; and had I heard it, I should have followed it" ['Ar. 16a]. Another version makes Dimi himself the transmitter of that very rule (*ib.*; B. B. 164b; compare DIMI; "Semag," Prohibition 9; "Diḳduḳe Soferim," in B. B. *l.c.*).

Dimi of Ḥaifa (Meg. 29b; compare "Sheiltot Ḥanukkah," end): See ABDIMA OF ḤAIFA.

Dimi b. Ḥama: See ABDIMA BAR ḤAMA.

Dimi b. Ḥinena: Babylonian amora of the fourth century; contemporary of Rab Safra ('Er. 61a) and of Ḥiyya b. Rabbah b. Naḥmani (R. H. 34b); also of Raba, before whom he and his brother Rabbah (Rabbin) b. Ḥinena once appeared as litigants (B. B. 13b). That he was prominent among the scholars of his age may be assumed from the fact that Rab Ḥisda cites a halakic decision of his (Zeb. 36b).

Dimi b. Huna of Damharia: Babylonian halakist of the sixth amoraic generation (fifth century); contemporary of Rabbina III. (Sanh. 29b; Men. 81a).

Dimi b. Isaac: Babylonian amora of the fourth generation; junior of Rab Judah b. Ezekiel, who gave him some lessons in comparative anatomy (Ḥul. 45b). Introducing a lecture on the Book of Esther, Dimi cites Ezra ix. 9, "Our God hath not forsaken us in our bondage, but hath extended mercy unto us in the sight of the kings of Persia." "When?" he asks; and answers, "In the days of Haman" (Meg. 10b; the Talmud manuscript in the Munich Library reads "Abudimi b. Isaac"; and instead of "Haman," some versions have "Mordecai and Esther"; see "Diḳduḳe Soferim" *ad loc.*).

Dimi b. Joseph: Babylonian scholar of the third amoraic generation (third century); disciple of Mar Samuel (Ket. 60a; Nid. 66a), and senior to Rab Ḥisda and Rab Sheshet (B. B. 53b). His sister sued him before Rab Naḥman for the restoration of a parcel of land which she had legally transferred to him in her illness. Probably because of Dimi's age and professional status, he refused to obey Naḥman's summons until he was threatened with excommunication (*ib.* 151a). When his son had the misfortune to lose a child within thirty days from its birth, and—contrary to the rabbinic rule, which does not impose mourning for an infant under thirty days of age—he had assumed ritualistic mourning, Dimi remonstrated with him, observing, "It is only because thou desirest to be regaled with delicacies that thou indulgest in ritualistic mourning for so young an infant" (Shab. 136a).

Dimi b. Levai: Babylonian scholar of the fourth century. On one occasion, the skies being overcast, he thought that the sun had set; and as the day was the eve of the Sabbath, he at once inaugurated the Sabbath. Subsequently the skies cleared, and he discovered his mistake. On his application for information on the law under such circumstances, Abaye declared that he might resume his daily occupations (Ber. 27b).

Dimi of Nehardea: Babylonian scholar of the fourth century; head of the Academy of Pumbedita (385–388). Prior to his elevation to the rectorate he was a produce-merchant; and the Talmud preserves an anecdote of that time which affords an insight into the economic laws of the age as well as an idea of Dimi's standing among the learned even in his youth. The law had provided that—except the dealer in spices or perfumes at any time, and the public generally while fairs were being held—no non-resident merchant might enter his wares in competition with local traders. A notable exception to this rule was the scholar. To him the market was always open; and to facilitate his sales and his return to study, the law gave him the rights of monopoly until he disposed of his goods. Now, Dimi once brought to Maḥuza a shipload of dried figs, when Raba was requested by the resh galuta (exilarch) "to tap Dimi's pitcher", *i.e.*, to examine him ascertain whether he was a scholar and consequently entitled to the special market privileges. Raba deputed Adda b. Abba (Ahaba) to examine Dimi; and Adda propounded to the newcomer a supposititious ritualistic question. Dimi thought that his interlocutor was Raba himself, and deferentially inquired, "Is not my master Raba?" The other, familiarly tapping him on the sandal, replied, "Between me and Raba there is a great difference.

At any rate, I am thy superior, and Raba is thy superior's superior." The privileges of the market were not granted to Dimi, and eventually the figs spoiled. He then applied to Rab Joseph for redress; and the latter, provoked at the discomfiture of the scholar, exclaimed, "He who hath not failed to avenge the disgrace of the Edomite king [see II Kings iii. 27; Amos ii. 1] will not fail to avenge thy disgrace." It is added that shortly afterward Rab Adda died suddenly, and several rabbis, including Dimi, who had some grievances against him, reproached themselves with having been indirectly instrumental in his punishment (B. B. 22a).

As an educator Dimi acted on the maxim, "Rivalry among scholars advances scholarship"; therefore he approved Raba's rule not to remove a teacher because his rival makes better progress with his pupils, arguing that rivalry will induce more strenuous efforts and produce better results. On the other hand, Raba, believing that "mistakes will correct themselves," showed preference for the teacher that succeeded in imparting much knowledge, even if not very exact. Dimi opposed this with his maxim, "Where error has once crept in, it stays"; and he therefore looked for precision rather than for quantity (B. B. 21a).

Dimi seems to have confined himself to the cultivation of the Halakah; for in the comparatively few instances where he is cited in the Talmud (besides those quoted see M. Ḳ. 12a; Yeb. 121a; B. B. 138b; Men. 35a; Ḥul. 51b) he appears in connection with some Halakah, while no Haggadah appears to bear his name.

Dimi b. Nehemiah (Nahman) b. Joseph: Babylonian amora of uncertain age, and but rarely cited in rabbinical literature (Sanh. 23b, 24a). He is probably identical with Abdimi b. Neḥuniah, by whom the Psalmist's effusion (Ps. cxxxix. 14), "I will praise thee; for I am fearfully and wonderfully made: marvelous are thy works; and that my soul knoweth right well," is illustrated thus: "Some things are beneficial to the liver and deleterious to the windpipe; others are beneficial to the latter and deleterious to the former. There are ten organs in man: the windpipe [larynx] produces voice; the gullet conducts the food; the liver is the seat of anger; the lungs promote thirst; the gall, jealousy; the stomach, sleep; the first stomach grinds the food; the spleen promotes laughter; the kidneys counsel; and the heart decides—therefore does David glorify, 'I will praise thee,' etc. Therefore, too, does he elsewhere [Ps. ciii. 1] exhort, 'Bless the Lord, O my soul: and all that is within me, bless his holy name'" (Midr. Teh. *ad loc.*; compare Eccl. R. vii. 19).

BIBLIOGRAPHY: Sherira, *Letter*, ed. Goldberg, 1845, p. 37; Zacuto, *Yuḥasin*, ed. Filipowski, p. 123; Heilprin, *Seder ha-Dorot*, ii., *s.v.*; Weiss, *Dor*, iii. 207.

L. G. S. M.

DOSA (or **DOSAI**; an abbreviated form of "Dosithai" or "Dositheos," *Δοσίθεος*): Father of the tannaite Ḥanina b. Dosa, famous for his piety.

S. S. W. B.

DOSA (also known as **Dosai**): Palestinian amora, probably of the fourth century. The Jerusalem Talmud has preserved two of his halakic decisions, and Midrashic literature several of his haggadic utterances. Among the latter is the assertion that the dangerous "snare" from which God will protect man (Prov. iii. 26) is the function of judging in matters of religious law. Dosa died on the new moon of Nisan. This date was especially recorded, because on that occasion refreshments were offered to the mourners (Yer. Mek., end), a custom not usually observed on semi-holidays.

Bibliography: Bacher, *Ag. Pal. Amor.* iii. 693.

S. S. W. B.

DOSETAI or **DOSITHEUS** (*Δοσίθεος*): A name, corresponding to the Hebrew "Mattaniah" or "Nethaneel," which seems to have been a favorite one both in Palestine and in Alexandria (Josephus, "Ant." xiii. 9, § 2; xiv. 10, § 18; xv. 6, § 2). It has been borne by the following:

Dosetai of Kefar-Yatma, a pupil of Shammai (Orlah ii. 5). **Dosetai b. Matun**, a tannaite mentioned in a Baraita (Ber. 7b; Meg. 6b) as the author of a haggadic sentence, which in another place (Derek Ereẓ, ii.) is ascribed to **Dosetai b. Judah**. According to Yoma 30b, an amora, Dosetai b. Matun, handed down a sentence of Johanan's; but the correct reading is "Justai b. Matun," which is found in the parallel passage, Zeb. 99a, and is confirmed by the Jerusalem Talmud (Yer. B. Ḳ. vii. 6a). On **Abba Jose b. Dosetai** see Bacher, "Ag. Tan." ii. 388.

Of those from the time of the Amoraim who have borne the name the following may be mentioned:

Dosetai, the father of Apotriḳi or Patriḳi. (Ḥul. 64b; compare B. M. 5a). He is perhaps the same Patriḳi or Patriḳ who is mentioned as the brother of Derosa (Yer. Yoma iv. 41d). **Dosetai the Elder** (Yer. Ned. x. 42b; Yer. Ḥag. i. 76d), mentioned with a younger Dosetai. He is probably the Dosetai frequently referred to in Midrashic literature as having handed down the sentences of Samuel b. Naḥman and of Levi (Bacher, "Ag. Pal. Amor." i. 488, 492, 503; ii. 431; iii. 695).

Dosetai b. Jannai: Tanna of the latter half of the second century, known especially as having handed down sentences of the tannaim Meïr, Jose b. Ḥalafta, and Eleazar b. Shammu'a. On a journey to Babylon he was ill-treated at Nehardea by the Jewish-Persian authorities, and took revenge by giving a satirical description of the latter. The account of the affair is preserved in two different versions (Giṭ. 14a, b; Yer. Giṭ. i. 43d; Yer. Ḳid. iii. 64a).

Examples of Dosetai's humor are to be found in his answers to his pupils' questions on the differences between man and woman (Niddah 31b), and in his reply to the question why Jerusalem did not have thermæ like Tiberias: "If Jerusalem had warm springs," he answered, "the pilgrims coming up for the feasts would have dwelt on the pleasures of the baths offered them, instead of considering how best to fulfil the regulations for the pilgrimage" (Pes. 8b). The words of Eccl. xi. 6 ("In the morning sow thy seed," etc.) he explained as a reminder to the farmer to be diligent in his sowing and planting (Ab. R. N. iii.). In another sentence (*ib.* xi.) he showed how the person who does not work during the six week-days will soon find himself compelled to work on the Sabbath. One of Dosetai's sermons praises almsgiving, interpreting Ps. xvii. 15 thus: "Through charity shall I see thy face, and enjoy thy sight on awakening" (B. B. 10a).

In a later Midrashic legend (Tan., Wayesheb, 2; Pirḳe R. El. xxxviii.) **Dosetai b. Jannai** is the name of one of the two teachers sent by the Assyrian king to convert the pagans who had settled to Israel (later on, the Samaritans). The name was probably suggested by its similarity to that of the Samaritan sect of the Dositheans (Bacher, "Ag. Tan." ii. 385–387).

Dosetai b. Judah: Tanna of the latter half of the second century. He was the author of several halakic sentences (see B. Ḳ. 83b; Ḳid. 69a, and parallels) and transmitted those of Simon b. Joḥai. On one occasion Dosetai's opinion was opposed to that of Judah I., the patriarch ('Ar. 30a). Four interpretations of Deut. xxxii. bear his name (Sifre, Deut. 306, 309, 318, 320; comp. Bacher, "Ag. Tan." ii. 390 *et seq.*).

Dosetai of Biri: Palestinian amora of the early part of the fourth century. 'Ulla, a native of Biri in Galilee, once addressed a halakic question to him ('Ab. Zarah 40a). The Babylonian Talmud contains three interpretations of Scripture from Dosetai's sermons, which were perhaps handed down in the schools of Babylon by 'Ulla, who had come up from Palestine. One of these refers to Num. x. 36 (B. Ḳ. 83a; compare Sifre to Num. lxxxiv., and the Baraita, Yeb. 64a); another, to I Sam. xxii. 1 *et seq.* ('Er. 45a); while the third is an original exposition showing how David in Ps. xix. 13 *et seq.* gradually begs forgiveness for his sins, like a Samaritan pedler unfolding his wares one after the other (Sanh. 107a). Palestinian sources do not mention Dosetai of Biri (Bacher, "Ag. Pal. Amor." iii. 695; Krauss, in "Monatsschrift," xli. 561).

Dosetai of Kokaba: Contemporary of the tanna Meïr. He asked the latter what was meant by the sentence, "The belly of the wicked shall want" (Prov. xiii. 25), and Meïr answered by relating an incident characteristic of the pagan's vain and intemperate love of pleasure (Pesiḳ. vi. 59b; Pesiḳ. R. xxvi. 82b; Midr. Mishle xiii. 25 [where instead of Kokaba,

Be-Yeshebab is mentioned as the home of Dosetai]; Tan., Pinḥas, 13; Num. R. xxi.). According to another version of this story, Meïr was the questioner and Dosetai the narrator. It is unnecessary to assume (compare Oppenheim in Berliner's "Magazin," i. 68, and Goldberg in "Ha-Maggid," xii. 62) that "Dosetai" is here a generic term, meaning a Dosithean (Bacher, "Ag. Tan." ii. 32).

J. SR. W. B.

E

ELA (HELA, ILAA, ILAI, ILI, LA, LEIA, YELA): Palestinian scholar of the third amoraic generation (third and fourth centuries). In one form or another, his name frequently appears in both Yerushalmi and Babli, mostly in the field of the Halakah. He was so distinguished that his contemporary and friend Zera I., admiring Ela's acumen, exclaimed, "The very air of Palestine imparts wisdom" (B. B. 158b). On two other occasions the same Zera applied to him the epithet "Bannaya d'Oraita" (Builder of the Law: establisher of fine legal points; Yer. Yoma iii. 40c; Yer. Giṭ. vii. 48d).

He carried his theoretical knowledge into actual life, so that the very appointments of his house afforded object-lessons in rabbinic rites (Yer. Yoma i. 38c; Yer. Meg. iv. 75c). It is related that when on a certain Friday his duties detained him at college till late into the night, and, returning home, he found the entrance barred and the people asleep, rather than desecrate the Sabbath by knocking at the gate for admission, he spent the night on the steps of his house (Yer. Beẓah v. 63a).

In halakic exegetics Ela laid down the guiding rule, "Every textual interpretation, must respect the subject of the context" (Yer. Yoma iii. 40c; Yer. Meg. i. 72a). Another and the most frequently cited of his exegetic rules is, "Wherever the Bible uses any of the terms 'beware,' 'lest,' or 'not,' a prohibitory injunction is involved" (Men. 99b, and parallels). Quite a number of exegetical observations applied to halakic deductions are preserved under Ela's name (Yer. Shab. i. 2b, etc.), and he reports like interpretations by his predecessors (Yer. Ma'as. Sh. v. 55d). In the field of the Haggadah, also, Ela is often met (Yer. Shab. ii. 5b, vi. 8c; Yer. Yoma v. 42b, etc.), but as a transmitter of the homilies of others he appears only rarely (Yer. Peah i. 16a; Sanh. 44a). That psychological test of human character as betrayed in the passions produced "by the cup, by cash, and by choler" (בכוסו בכיסו ובכעסו, Er. 65a; compare Derek Ereẓ Zuṭa, v.), which some ascribe to this Ela (Ilai), others ascribe to Ilai the tanna (second century).

Eulogizing R. Simon b. Zebid, Ela skilfully interweaves several verses from the Book of Job, to which he adds simply their application to Simon's death, thus: "'Where shall wisdom be found? and where is the place of understanding?' (Job xxviii. 12). 'The depth saith, It is not in me: and the sea saith, It is not with me' (*ib.* 14). 'It is hid from the eyes of all living, and kept close from the fowls of the air' (*ib.* 21). The four objects necessary to man, if lost, may be replaced; for 'there is a vein for the silver, and a place for gold where they fine it. Iron is taken out of the earth, and brass is molten out of the stone' (*ib.* 1–2); but when a scholar dies, who can take his place? We have lost Simon: whence shall we procure his like?" (Yer. Ber. iii. 5*c*, and parallels).

BIBLIOGRAPHY: Frankel, *Mebo*, p. 75*b*; Weiss, Dor, iii. 101; Brüll, *Mebo ha-Mishnah*, i. 139; Bacher, *Ag. Pal. Amor.* iii. 699.

S. S. S. M.

ELEAZAR I. (LAZAR) (Eleazar b. Shammua'): Mishnaic teacher of the fourth generation, frequently cited in rabbinic writings without his patronymic (Ab. iv. 12; Giṭ. iii. 8, incorrectly "Eliezer"; compare Gem. Giṭ. 31b; Yer. Giṭ. iii. 45a, Mishnah and Gem.). He was of priestly descent (Meg. 27b; Soṭah 39a) and rich (Eccl. R. xi. 1), and acquired great fame as a teacher of traditional law. He was a disciple of Akiba (Zeb. 93a, 110b), but owing to the Hadrianic proscriptions of Jewish observances, was not ordained by him. After Akiba's death, however, R. Judah b. Baba ordained Eleazar, together with Meïr, Jose b. Ḥalafta, Judah b. Ila'i, and Simon b. Yoḥai, at a secluded spot between Usha and Shefar'am. The ordainer was detected in the act and brutally slain; but the ordained escaped, and eventually became the custodians and disseminators of Jewish tradition (Sanh. 13b; 'Ab. Zarah 8b).

Mention is made of a controversy between Eleazar and R. Meïr at Ardiska (Tosef., Naz. vi. 1; see Neubauer, "G. T." p. 106). He also maintained halakic discussions with R. Judah b. 'Illai and R. Jose (Tosef., Zeb. v. 4, x. 10), and quite frequently with R. Simon b. Yoḥai (Sheḳ. iii. 1; Yoma v. 7); but he never appeared with them at the sessions of the Sanhedrin at Usha. Hence it may be assumed that he did not return to the scene of his ordination. Whereever he settled, he presided over a college to which large numbers of students were attracted ('Er. 53a; Yer. Yeb. viii. 9d; compare Mek., Beshallaḥ, Amalek, i.), among whom are named Joseph or Issi ha-Babli (Tosef., Zeb. ii. 17; Men. 18a), and the compiler of the Mishnah, R. Judah I. ('Er. 53a); and thus, while his name does not appear in rabbinic lore as often as the names of his colleagues at the ordination, Eleazar had an ineradicable influence on the development of the Talmud. Abba Arika styles him "the most excellent among the sages" (טובינא דחכימי, Ket. 40a; Giṭ. 26b), and R. Johanan expresses unbounded admiration for his large-heartedness ('Er. 53a).

Eleazar's motto was, "Let the honor of thy pupil be as dear to thee as that of thy colleague; that of thy colleague, as the reverence of thy master; and the reverence of thy master, as that of the Most High" (Ab. iv. 12; Ab. R. K xxvii. 4). His disciples once requested him to tell them whereby he merited unusual longevity, when he replied, "I have never converted the Synagogue into a passageway [for the sake of convenience]; have never trodden over the heads of the holy people [*i.e.*, corne late to college and stepped between the rows of attentive students; compare ABDAN]; and have never pronounced the priestly blessing before offering the benediction preceding it" (Meg. 27b; Soṭah 39a). When asked what merits will save man from the tribulations which are to precede the Messianic epoch, he replied, "Let him engage in the study of the Law and in deeds of benevolence" (Sanh. 98b). According to Eleazar, children as well as pious adults share in the glory of God (Midr. Teh. xxii. 31). He also taught that the world rests on a single pillar, the name of which is "Righteousness"; as the Bible says (Prov. x. 25, Hebr.), "The righteous is the foundation of the world" (Ḥag. 12b).

The following anecdote concerning Eleazar is twice told in the Midrashim (Lev. R. xxiii. 4; Cant. R. ii. 2): R. Eleazar visited a certain place where he was invited to lead the people in prayer, but he avowed inability to do so. "What!" cried the astonished people; "is this the celebrated R. Eleazar? Surely he deserves not to be called 'Rabbi'!" Eleazar's face colored with shame, and he repaired to his teacher Akiba. "Why art thou so crestfallen?" inquired Akiba; whereupon Eleazar related his unpleasant experience. "Does my master wish to learn?" asked Akiba; and, on receiving Eleazar's affirmative answer, Akiba instructed him. Later, Eleazar again visited the scene of his mortification, and the people again requested him to lead them in prayer. This time he readily complied with their request, whereupon the people remarked, "R. Eleazar has become unmuzzled" (איתחסם, from חסם = "to muzzle"), and they called him "Eleazar Ḥasma" (compare Geiger, "Schriften," iv. 343). The hero of this anecdote is doubtless the subject of the present article, and not, as is generally assumed, Eleazar Ḥisma. The latter was never Akiba's pupil. Indeed, he was Akiba's senior, and in the account of a halakic discussion between him and Eleazar b. Azariah and Akiba, his name precedes that of Akiba (Neg. vii. 2; Sifre, Deut. 16). Eleazar I. was an acknowledged disciple of Akiba, and the Midrashim explicitly state that he "went to Akiba, his teacher."

BIBLIOGRAPHY: Bacher, *Ag. Tan.* ii. 275 *et seq.*; Brüll, *Mebo ha-Mishnah*, i. 196 *et seq.*; Frankel, *Darke ha-Mishnah*, pp. 173 *et seq.*; Heilprin, *Seder ha-Dorot*, ii., *s.v.*; Weiss, *Dor*, ii. 164 *et seq.*; Zacuto, *Yuḥasin*, ed. Filipowski, pp. 45, 58.

S. S. S. M.

ELEAZAR II. (LAZAR): Palestinian amora of the third century (second and third generations). In the Midrashim he is frequently cited with his patronymic, **Eleazar b. Pedat,** but in the Talmudim only occasionally so. He was a Babylonian by birth (Yer. Ber. ii. 4b; Yer. Sheḳ. ii. 47a) and of priestly descent (Yer. Ber. v. 9d; M. Ḳ. 28a). In his native country he was a disciple of Samuel ('Er. 66a; B. B. 82b), and more especially of Rab (B. B. 135b; Ḥul. 111b), whom he in after years generally cited by the appellation "our teacher" (Giṭ. 9b; B. B. 152a), and whose college he revered above all others, recognizing in it the "lesser sanctuary" of the Diaspora, spoken of by Ezekiel (xi. 16) as promised to the exiles in Babylonia (Meg. 29a; Yalḳ., Ezek. 352). When and why he left his native country is not stated; but from the data extant it appears that his ardent love for "the land of Israel" (Ket. 111a), and the superior opportunities which Palestine afforded for religious practises (Yer. R. H. ii. 58b; Ket. 112a), impelled him to emigrate thither—and at a comparatively early age, since some of Rabbi's contemporaries were still alive and active (B. B. 87a; Ḥul. 110a). Indeed, it seems that for a time Eleazar even attended the lectures of R. Ḥiyyah (Yer. Ket, ix. 33b; Yer. B. M. x. 12c) and of R. Hoshaiah (Yer. Yeb. iv. 5d). This was for him a period of hard study, which gave rise to the homiletic remark that the Biblical saying (Prov. v. 19), "Be thou ravished always with her love," was well illustrated by Eleazar b. Pedat at Sepphoris, who was so absorbed in his studies as to be unconscious of all worldly needs ('Er. 54b).

Later, Eleazar became attached to the college founded by R. Johanan at Tiberias (Yer. Ber. ii. 4b; Tem. 25b; Ker. 27a), where his scholarship procured him great honors. In the city he was associated with Simon b. Eliakim in the office of judge (B.Ḳ. 117b), and at the college he occupied the position of colleague-disciple (חבר ותלמיד) of Johanan (Yer. Sanh. i. 18b), who himself repeatedly admitted that Eleazar had enlightened him (Yer. Meg. i. 72c; Yer. Sanh. iii. 21b), once declaring that "the son of Pedat sits and interperts the Law as did Moses at the direct inspiration from the Almighty" (Yeb. 72b). After the death of Simeon b. Laḳish, Eleazar was chosen to fill the position of assistant to Johanan (B. M. 84a). When Johanan became disabled through grief at Simeon's death, Eleazar presided over the college (Yer. Meg. i. 72b), and after the death of Johanan succeeded him in the office of head master.

The fame of Eleazar as an expert expounder of the Law having reached Babylonia, his most prominent contemporaries there addressed to him intricate halakic questions, to which he returned satisfactory answers (Beẓah 16b; Yer. Ḳid. i. 60c; B. B. 135b; Ḥul. 86b). This happened so often that he became known in his native country as the "master [*i.e.*, legal authority] of the land of Israel" (Yoma 9b; Giṭ. 19b; Niddah 20b); and anonymous decisions introduced in the Babylonian schools with the statement שלחו מתם ("They sent word from there"; Beẓah 41b; Giṭ. 73a) were understood, as a matter of course, to emanate from Eleazar b. Pedat (Sanh. 11b).

Eleazar was averse to the study of esoterics (Ḥag. 13a). With reference to this study, lie would cite the saying of Ben Sira (Ecclus. [Sirach] iii. 21), "Seek not things that are too hard for thee, and search not out things that are above thy strength" (Yer. Ḥag. ii. 77c). He prized knowledge above all things; therefore he remarked, "He who possesses knowledge is as great as if the Temple were rebuilt in his days" (Sanh. 92a); and from Job xx. 21 he teaches that he who does not contribute toward the support of scholars will not be blessed in his property (*ib.*). Eleazar was exceedingly poor, and often lacked the necessaries of life (Ta'an. 25a). He frequently sang the praises of charity. "The practise of charity," he was wont to say, "is more meritorious than all oblations; as the Bible says (Prov. xxi. 3), 'To do justice [Hebr. צדקה] and judgment is more acceptable to the Lord than sacrifice' [Suk. 49b]. He who practises charity secretly is greater [in the sight of God] than Moses himself; for Moses himself admitted (Deut. ix. 19), 'I was afraid of the anger,' while of secret charity the Bible says (Prov. xxi. 14), 'A gift in secret pacifieth anger'" (B. B. 9b). Benevolence and acts of loving-kindness, גמילות חסדים, extending to both rich and poor, are, according to Eleazar's interpretation, even greater than charity; as the Bible says (Hosea x. 12), "Sow to yourselves in righteousness [Hebr. לצדקה], reap in mercy [חסד]." With reference to צדקה, the Bible uses "sowing," indicating an operation that leaves it in doubt whether the sower will or will not enjoy the fruit; while with reference to mercy "reaping" is used, an occupation that renders the enjoying of the results very probable (Suk. 49b). From the same Scriptural expression Eleazar draws the lesson, "Charity is rewarded only in proportion to the kindness in it" (*ib.*); that is, the pleasant and thoughtful way in which it is given, and the personal sacrifice it involves.

Poor as he was, Eleazar would never accept any gifts, or even invitations to the patriarch's table. When any were extended to him, he would decline them with the remark, "It seems that ye do not wish me to live long, since the Bible says (Prov. xv. 27), 'He that hateth gifts shall live'" (Meg. 28a; Ḥul. 44b). His scant earnings he would share with other needy scholars; thus, he once purposely lost a coin in order that poverty-stricken Simon b. Abba, who was following him, might find it. When the latter did find it and offered to restore it, Eleazar assured him that he had renounced its ownership and forfeited all rights thereto, and that consequently it was the property of the finder (Yer. B. M. ii. 8c). It is also reported as his custom first to offer a mite to the poor, and then to offer prayer to God (B. B. 10a). Even to impostors he would never refuse charity. "Were it not for the existence of impostors, not a single refusal of charity could ever be atoned for; we therefore ought to show gratitude to them" (Yer. Peah viii. 21b.; Ket. 68a).

There are no data to show how long Eleazar survived R. Johanan, but the probability is that he died about 279 C.E.

BIBLIOGRAPHY: Bacher, *Ag. Pal. Amor.* ii. 1 *et seq.*; Frankel, *Mebo*, pp. 111b *et seq.*; Heilprin, *Seder ha-Dorot*, ii., *s.v.*; Weiss, *Dor*, iii. 85 *et seq.*; Zacuto, *Yuḥasin*, ed. Filipowski, pp. 113a *et seq.*

S. S. S. M.

ELEAZAR B. ABINA: Palestinian haggadist of the fourth amoraic generation (fourth century C.E.); junior contemporary of Aḥa III., in whose name he repeats some homiletic remarks (Pesiḳ. R. xiv. 60b, xxi. 109b), and senior of R. Yudan, who reports in his name (Midr. Teh. xxxi. 7).

One of the homilies bearing Eleazar's name argues that the observance of the Sabbath is tantamount to all other commandments combined, which he tries to prove from passages in each of the three divisions of the Bible—the Pentateuch (Ex. xvi. 28, 29), the Prophets (Ezek. xx. 13), and the Hagiographa (Neh. ix. 13, 14).

BIBLIOGRAPHY: Bacher, *Agada der Palestinensischen Amoräer*, iii. 696 *et seq.*

S. S. S. M.

ELEAZAR BEN AḤWAI (AḤBAI): Probably identical, according to Bacher ("Ag. Tan." ii. 553), with Eleazar b. Mahbai or Maḥbai, a tanna of the second century, contemporary of Judah b. Bathyra and Aḥa I. (Tosef., Yeb. xiv. 4). He is cited but twice under this name. His most important remark is with regard to the Pentateuchal expression לאמר ("saying"; literally, "to say"), which frequently follows the statement, "God spake to Moses," and which he explains as implying that God spake to Moses not in Moses' interest, but in that of Israel: He spake to Moses *to say* to the people (Sifra, Wayiḳra, ii. 13; compare Yalḳ., Lev. 431, where the patronymic is "Dehabai").

S. S. S. M.

ELEAZAR BEN ‘ARAK: Tanna of the second generation (first century C.E.). Being first among the disciples of R. Johanan ben Zakkai (Ab. ii. 8; Ab. R. N. xiv. 3), he delighted his master with his wisdom and penetration, so that the most extravagant encomiums were lavished upon him. It was said, "Were all the sages of Israel placed in one scale, and Eleazar b. ‘Arak in the other, he would outweigh them all" (Ab. *l.c.*; Ab. R. N. xiv. 4), while his great master styled him "Rising Well" or "Gushing stream" (מעין המתגבר, נחל שוטף, *ib.*). The master once propounded the question, "Which acquisition is best for man to strive after?" Several solutions were handed in, among them one from Eleazar, who suggested, "A good heart" (לב טוב); thereupon Johanan remarked, "I prefer Eleazar's solution to all of yours, since yours are included in his" (Ab. ii. 9; Ab. K K. xiv. 5). Again, the master propounded,

"Which is the worst characteristic that man should shun?" In this case, also, Eleazar's reply, "An evil heart," was accepted by the teacher (*ib.*). Compare BERURIAH.

In the mystical interpretation of the Scriptures, also, Eleazar distinguished himself, and to such an extent as to call forth his master's ecstatic exclamation, "Happy art thou, O father Abraham, from whose loins sprang Eleazar b. 'Arak" (Yer. Ḥag. ii. 77a). To his counsel, often sought and always beneficial, was applied the Biblical expression (Ps. i. 3), "Whatsoever he doeth shall prosper." Beneficiaries of his counsel in their admiration styled him "Prophet"; whereupon he remarked, "I am neither a prophet nor the son of a prophet, but my teachers have communicated to me the traditional verity that every counsel subserving the promotion of the glory of God realizes good results" (Midr. Teh. i. 3.). His motto was, "Be diligent in the pursuit of study; be prepared to answer the Epicurean, and realize for whom thou laborest and who thy employer is."

Eleazar's name is connected with but few halakot, and with only one halakic midrash. The reason for this disappointing paucity of doctrines and sayings is found in the story of the period immediately succeeding the death of Johanan b. Zakkai. The disciples chose Jabneh for their scene of activity, while Eleazar went to Emmaus, the residence of his wife—a particularly healthful place, blessed with good water, a pleasant climate, and warm baths.

Separated from his colleagues, his faculties became stunted; and he is said to have completely forgotten all he had ever learned (Ab. R. N. xiv. 6, Eccl. R. vii. 7). In later years he was pointed out as a warning to the self-opinionated; the Talmud applying to him the motto of R. Nehorai: "Inter thyself in a place where the Law is studied, and think not that it will seek thee; for only thy colleagues will perpetuate it in thy possession; rely not on thine own understanding" (Shab. 147b; Ab. iv. 14).

BIBLIOGRAPHY: Bacher, *Ag. Tan.*, i. 74 *et seq.*; Brüll, *Mebo ha-Mishnah*, i. 87; Fraenkel, *Darke ha-Mishnah*, p. 91; Hamburger, *R. B. T.* ii. 155; Heilprin, *Seder ha-Dorot*, ii. *s.v.*; Weiss, *Dor Dor we-Dorshaw*, ii. 80; Zacuto, *Yuḥasin.* ed. Filipowski, p. 35b.

S. S. S. M.

ELEAZAR B. AZARIAH: Mishnaic scholar of the second generation (first century C.E.); junior contemporary of Gamaliel II., Eliezer b. Hyrcanus, and Joshua b. Hananiah, and senior of Akiba (Sifre, Deut. 32; Sanh. 101a). He traced his pedigree for ten generations back to Ezra (Ber. 27b; Yer. Yeb. i. 3b), and was very wealthy (Shab. 54b; Beẓah 23a; compare Ḳid. 49b). These circumstances, added to his erudition, gained for him great popularity. When Gamaliel II., in consequence of his provoking demeanor, was temporarily deposed from the patriarchate, Eleazar, though still very young, was elevated to that office by the deliberate choice of his colleagues. He did not, however, occupy it for any length of time, for the Sanhedrin reinstated Gamaliel. He was retained as vice-president ("ab bet din"), nevertheless, and it was arranged that, Gamaliel should lecture three (some say two) Sabbaths, and Eleazar every fourth (or third) Sabbath (Ber. 27b *et seq.*; Yer. Ber. iv. 7c *et seq.*; Yer. Ta'an. iv. 67d).

In company with Gamaliel, Joshua, and Akiba, he journeyed to Rome (Kallah R. vii.; Derek Ereẓ R. v.). Neither the object of the journey nor the result of the mission is stated; but that affairs important as pressing were involved is apparent from the season at which the journey was undertaken: they celebrated the Feast of Booths aboard the ship (Sifra, Emor, xvi. 2; Suk. 41b). With the same companions Eleazar once visited the ruins of the Temple at Jerusalem (Sifre, Deut. 43). On a visit to the aged Dosa b. Harkinas the latter joyfully exclaimed, "In him I see the fulfilment of the Scriptural saying (Ps. xxxvii. 25): 'I have been young, and now am old; yet have I not seen the righteous forsaken, nor his seed begging bread'" (Yeb. 16a; Yer. Yeb. i. 3c *et seq.*), by which he probably alluded to Eleazar's great learning and his proverbial wealth. The latter was amassed by dealing in wine, oil (Tosef., 'Ab. Zarah, v. 1; B. B. 91a), and cattle (Shab. 54b; Beẓah 23a). Subsequent generations entertained the belief that dreaming of Eleazar b. Azariah presaged the acquisition of wealth.

With Eleazar's accession to the patriarchate the portals of the academy were opened wide to all who sought admittance. It is said that three hundred benches had to be added for the accommodation of the eager throngs which pressed into the halls of learning. Under his presidency, too, a review of undecided points of law was undertaken. To Eleazar rabbinic homiletics owes the introduction of the rule called סמוכין (="contiguous"), by which one Scriptural passage is explained or supplemented by another immediately preceding or succeeding it. Thus, Eleazar declares that the slanderer and the listener and the false witness deserve to be thrown to the dogs. He derives this idea from the juxtaposition of the expression (Ex. xxii. 30 [A. V. 31]), "Ye shall cast it to the dogs," and (*ib.* xxiii. 1) the prohibition against raising false reports, bearing false witness, and associating with the false witness (Pes. 118a; Mak. 23a).

In his homilies he generally aims to bring out some ethical or practical lesson. With reference to the Day of Atonement the Bible says (Lev. xvi. 30), "On that day... ye may be clean [Hebr. תטהרו = "ye shall cleanse yourselves"] from all your sins before the Lord." Therefrom Eleazar draws the lesson that the efficacy of the day extends only to sins against God, while sins against man are not forgiven unless the offended party has first been reconciled (Yoma viii. 9; Sifra, Aḥare Mot, viii. 2). The Bible says (Deut. xxiii. 8 [A. V. 7]), "Thou shalt not abhor an Egyptian... because thou wast a stranger in his land." Thereupon Eleazar remarks, "The Egyptians admitted the Israelites out of self-interest; nevertheless God accounts their act as one of merit. Now, if he who unintentionally confers a favor is accorded a token of merit, how much more so he who intentionally does a good deed" (Sifre, Deut. 252; compare Ber. 63b). Similar is his deduction from Deut. xxiv. 19, which says, "When thou cuttest down thine harvest in thy field, and hast forgot a sheaf in the field, thou shalt not go again to fetch it: it shall be for the stranger, for the fatherless, and for the widow: that the Lord thy God may bless thee in all the work of thine hands." "Here," argues Eleazar, "the Bible promises blessings to him by whom a good deed is done unintentionally; hence if one unwittingly loses money, and a needy one finds it and sustains life thereon, God will bless the loser for it" (Sifra, Wayiḳra [Ḥoba], xii. 13; Sifre, Deut. 183).

Eleazar was independent in his Biblical interpretations. He often rejected Akiba's opinions, remarking, "Even if thou persist the whole day in extending and limiting, I shall not harken to thee" (Sifra, Ẓaw, xi. 6; Men. 89a), or, "Turn from the Haggadah and betake thee to the laws affecting leprosy and the defilement of tents" (ואהלות נגעים; Ḥag. 14a; Sanh. 38b). Above all, he strove to be methodical. When one applied to him for information on a Biblical topic, he furnished that; was he called upon to explain a mishnah, a halakah, or a haggadah, he explained each point. Eleazar was opposed to frequent sentences of capital punishment. In his opinion a court that averages more than one execution in the course of seventy years is a murderous court (Mak. i. 10).

In the following few sentences is comprised Eleazar's practical philosophy:

"Without religion there is too true wisdom; without wisdom there is no religion. Where there is no wisdom there is no fear of God; where there is no fear of God there is no wisdom. Where there is no discernment there is no learning; without learning there is no discernment. Where there is a want of bread, study of the Torah can not thrive; without study of the Torah there is a lack of bread.

"With what is he to be compared who possesses more knowledge than good deeds? With a tree of many branches and but few roots. A storm comes and plucks it up and turns it over. Thus also Scripture says (Jer. xvii. 6), 'He shall be like the heath in the desert, and shall not see when good cometh; but shall inhabit the parched places in the wilderness, in a salt land and not inhabited.' But what does he resemble who can show more good deeds than learning? A tree of few branches and many roots. Even should all the winds of heaven rage against it, they could not move it from its place. Thus, the Bible says (*l.c.* 8), 'He shall be as a tree planted by the waters, that spreadeth out her roots by the river, and shall not see when heat cometh, but her leaf shall be green; and shall not be careful in the year of drought, neither shall cease from yielding fruit '" (Ab. iii. 17; Ab. R. N. xxii. 1).

While he lived he enjoyed the encomiums of his famous colleagues, who said, "That generation in which Eleazar b. Azariah flourishes can not be termed orphan" (Ḥag. 3b; Mek., Bo, xvi.); and when he died the learned said, "With the death of R. Eleazar b. Azariah was removed the crown of the sages" (Tosel, Soṭah, xv. 3; Soṭah 49b; Yer. Soṭah ix. 24c).

BIBLIOGRAPHY: Bacher, *Ag. Tan.* i. 219 *et seq.*; Brüll, *Mebo ha-Mishnah*, i. 88 *et seq.*; Frankel, *Darke ha-Mishnah*, pp. 91 *et seq.*; Grätz, *Gesch.* 2d ed., iv. 37 *et seq.*; Hamburger, *R. B. T.* ii. 156 *et seq.*; Heilprin, *Seder ha-Dorot*, ii., *s.v.*; Weiss, *Dor*, ii. 94 *et seq.*; Zacuto, *Yuḥasin*, ed. Filipowski, pp. 39b *et seq.*

S. S. S. M.

ELEAZAR OF BARTOTA. See ELEAZAR B. JUDAH OF BARTOTA.

ELEAZAR B. DAMA. See BEN DAMA.

ELEAZAR B. DINAI: Leader of the ZEALOTS (35–60, C.E.). When the Jews of Peræa had boundary disputes with the pagan population of Philadelphia, the procurator Fadus killed Annibas, one of the three leaders, and banished the other two, Amram and Eleazar. The latter may be identical with Eleazar b. Dinai. When Jewish pilgrims traversing Samaritan territory were killed by hostile Samaritans, the Jews in self-defense called Eleazar b. Dinai down from the mountains, and he ravaged Akrabatene.

The procurator Felix succeeded by cunning in capturing Eleazar and his band, sending him in chains to Rome (Josephus, "Ant." xx. 1, § 1; 6, § 1; 8, § 5; "B. J." ii. 12, § 4; 13, § 2).

Rabbinical sources also mention Eleazar. The Midrash to Cant. iii. 5 says that in the days of Amram and (Ben) Dinai the Jews prematurely attempted liberation. Mention is also made of a companion of Eleazar, Teḥina ben Perisha by name, probably the Alexander mentioned by Josephus. Through the example of these two men murders became so frequent that the sacrifice of atonement for an unknown murderer (Deut. xxi. 1–8) was abolished (Soṭah ix. 9; Tosef. xiv. 1; Bab. 47b; Yer. 24a; Sifre, Deut. 205). The wife of Eleazar b. Dinai is also mentioned (Ket. 27a).

BIBLIOGRAPHY: Grätz, *Gesch.* 4th ed., iii. 431, 436; Schürer, *Gesch.* 3d ed., i. 570; Büchler, Das *Grosse Synedrion in Jerusalem*, p. 143, Vienna, 1902.

G. S. KR.

ELEAZAR B. DURDAIA: A famous penitent, quoted both as a warning against debauchery, which leads to death, and as an encouragement to repentance, which leads to eternal happiness. It is related of him that, after leading a life of licentiousness, he at last bethought himself of his latter end. He mentally sought intercessors among the elements, beseeching them to appeal for his pardon and future peace; but none was found competent to act for him, they themselves being finite, and doomed to annihilation. Concluding that his future depended solely on himself, he prayed and wept until he died. Thereupon, legend adds, a BAT ḲOL announced that Eleazar was assured of happiness in the hereafter. When Rabbi (Judah I.) heard this story, he exclaimed, "Verily, some procure eternal happiness only after toiling many years, while others obtain the same result in a short time" ('Ab. Zarah 17a).

S. S. S. M.

ELEAZAR B. ELEAZAR HA-KAPPAR. See BAR ḲAPPARA.

ELEAZAR (ELIEZER) B. ENOCH: A scholarly contemporary of 'Aḳabia b. Mahalalel and Gamaliel II. According to the statement of Judah b. 'Illai, it was this Eleazar, and not 'Aḳabia, who was excommunicated by the Sanhedrin for the reason that he quibbled about the rabbinic regulations concerning "cleansing of hands" ('Eduy. v. 6). Nothing more is known of him; but the fact of his being cited in connection with 'Aḳabia, and the explicit declaration of the transgression which prompted the august tribunal to excommunicate him, evidence his prominence in his day. Probably because of excommunication, in which state he ended his earthly existence (*ib.*), none of his doctrines was discussed in the academies or recorded in rabbinic literature.

BIBLIOGRAPHY: Mein, *Introduction to Abot*, ed. Stern, 11b; Mendelsohn, in *Rev. Et. Juives*, xli. 39 *et seq.*

S. S. S. M.

ELEAZAR OF HAGRONIA: Babylonian scholar of the fourth amoraic generation (fifth century); junior of Aha b. Jacob and Raba (b. Joseph). He is mentioned twice in the Babylonian Talmud, and both times in connection with extraordinary circumstances. Once he incurs divine punishment for assuming rabbinic authority at a place over which extended the jurisdiction of Aḥa b. Jacob ('Er. 63a); and then again he is represented as having dreamed an ominous dream. It was a season of drought at Hagronia (Agranum; Neubauer, "G. T." p. 347) when Raba happened to visit the town. He ordained a day of fasting and prayer, but no rain came. Then he inquired, "Did any one have a dream last night?" Eleazar had had one, and at Raba's request he told it as follows: "There was said to me in my dream, 'Good greetings to the good teacher from the good Lord who, in His goodness, doeth good to His people.'" On hearing this Raba remarked, "This betokens that

Heaven will be propitious." Thereupon prayer was again offered, and soon rain descended (Ta'an. 24b).

S. S. S. M.

ELEAZAR (ELIEZER) B. HISMA: Tanna of the second and third generations (second century); disciple of Joshua b. Hananiah and Gamaliel II. (Ḥag. 3a; Hor. 10a). In their use of the word "ben" in connection with his cognomen "Ḥisma" or "Ḥasma" (see Geiger, "Schriften," iv. 343, and Strack, "Einleitung in den Thalmud," 2d ed., p. 81), the sources are inconsistent; its insertion, however, seems justifiable. "Ḥisma" is not an adjectival cognomen (see ELEAZAR I.), but a locative, the place probably being identical with Hizmeh (see Luncz, "Jerusalem," vi. 67; Hastings, "Dict. Bible," i., *s.v.* "Azmaveth"); hence "ben Ḥisma" means "son of [= "native of"] Ḥisma" (compare R. H. 17a; Meg. 19a; Ḳid. ii. 3).

Several halakot are preserved under Eleazar's name in the Mishnah (Ter. iii. 5; B. M. vii. 5), and he is met with in halakic controversies with Eleazar b. Azariah and Akiba (Neg. vii. 2; Sifra, Tazria', i. 2), and with Eliezer b. Jacob I. (Pes. 32a; Yalḳ., Lev. 638); and to him is ascribed the economic rule that the. employee is not entitled to a proportion of his employer's produce greater than the amount of his wages (B. M. vii. 5, 92a; Sifre, Deut. 266).

Some haggadot also are ascribed to him (Mek., Beshallaḥ, Wayassa', 4; *ib.*, Amalek, 1; Yoma 19b). Conjointly with R. Joshua, he gives an allegorical reason for Amalek's attack on Israel (Ex. xvii. 8 *et seq.*) just at the time it occurred. Citing. Job viii. 11, "Can a rush grow up without mire? Can the flag grow without water?" he remarks, "Even so is it impossible for Israel to flourish without the Law; and since they had neglected the Law [see Ex. xvii. 1–7], an enemy was ordered out to war against them" (compare Yalḳ. to Ex. *l.c.*, § 262; anonymous in Yalḳ. to Job *l.c.*, § 904). Again, he cites Isa. xliii. 22, "But thou hast not called on me, O Jacob," and applies it to those who are not devout in their prayers, but while reciting the "Shema'" communicate with their neighbors by sign language (compare Yalḳ. to Isa. *l.c.*, § 318).

Not only was he possessed of wide rabbinic learning, but he was also an adept in the sciences. Joshua, introducing him and Johanan b. (Gudgada) Nuri to the notice of Patriarch Gamaliel II., remarked of them that they could approximately calculate the number of drops contained in the ocean (Hor. 10a). As they were very poor, Gamaliel appointed them to remunerative offices in the academy (Sifre, Deut. 14; Yalḳ., Deut. 902; Hor. *l.c.*). Probably it was here—because the academicians sought from him instruction in secular science—that Eleazar remarked, "The laws concerning birds' nests and those concerning the incipient uncleanness of woman are elements of the Law, while astronomy and geometry are only condiments of wisdom" (Ab. iii. 18; Ab. R. N. xxvii. 2).

BIBLIOGRAPHY: Bacher, *Ag. Tan.* i. 374; Brüll, *Mebo ha-Mishnah*, i. 149; Frankel, *Darke ha-Mishnah*, p. 134; Geiger, *Schriften*, iv. 343; Heilprin, *Seder ha-Dorot*, ii., *s.v.*; Weiss, *Dor*, ii. 122; Zacuto, *Yuḥasin*, ed. Filipowski, p. 41b.

S. S. S. M.

ELEAZAR B. JAIR: Leader of the Sicarii, the remnant of whom, driven from Jerusalem about 70 by Eleazar b. Ananias, retired to MASADA. Eleazar was a descendant of Judah, the founder of the party of Zealots. Besieged by the Romans, Eleazar exhorted his fellow warriors to prefer death to slavery, and, when it became necessary, to kill first their families and then themselves. This speech, together with a dirge on the fall of Jerusalem ascribed to him, is found in Hebrew in Yosippon, ch. 97, though the hero is here erroneously called "Eleazar b. Ananias."

BIBLIOGRAPHY: Grätz, *Gesch.* 4th ed., iii. 460, 549; Schürer, *Gesch.* 3d ed., i. 639.

G. S. KR.

ELEAZAR (LAZAR) BEN JOSE I.: Tanna of the fourth and fifth generations (second century). He was second among the five learned sons of Jose b. Ḥalafta (Shab. 118b; Yer. Yeb. i. 2b); and the father repeatedly reports opinions which he had heard from Eleazar (Sifre, Deut. 148; Pes. 117a; Yoma 67a), while the latter transmits halakot in his father's name (Men. 54b; Pesiḳ. i. 4a). He is often cited in the Tosefta, though never in the Mishnah. He accompanied Simon b. Yoḥai on a visit to Rome, with the object of appealing to the government for the abrogation of the renewed Hadrianic decrees, which seriously impeded the religious life of the Jews. On the way Eleazar was attacked by a dangerous illness, but he recovered and proceeded on the journey (Me'i. 17b; see Rashi). The mission was successful (Me'i. 17a *et seq.*; see SIMEON B. YOḤAI), and at Rome Eleazar met the organizer of the first Roman Jewish academy, Mattai b. Ḥeresh, with whom he discussed halakic questions (Yoma 84b; Me'i. 17a).

Of this and other journeys Eleazar reports some experiences. In Rome he saw the curtain of the Holy of Holies and the high priest's golden headband, which Titus had carried thither from Jerusalem (Yoma 57a; Suk. 5a). In Alexandria he learned that the ancient Egyptians had filled in with Jewish bodies unfinished places in the walls: he is even said to have actually seen evidences of those cruelties (Sanh. 111a). Twice he reports controversies with Samaritans (Soṭah 33b [Yer. Soṭah vii. 21a reads "Eleazar b. Simon"]; Sanh. 90b).

Eleazar lays great stress on philanthropic works, saying, "Charity and benevolence are intercessors for Israel: they effect peace between God and the people" (Tosef., Pes. iv. 18; B. B. 10a). He further says, "Whoso sinneth and repenteth, and thereafter leadeth an upright life, obtaineth immediate pardon; but whoso saith, 'I shall sin and then repent,' three times will he be forgiven, but no more" (Ab. R. N. xl. 5).

BIBLIOGRAPHY: Bacher, *Ag. Tan.* ii. 412; Brüll, *Mebo ha-Mishnah*, i. 246; Heilprin, *Seder ha-Dorot*, ii., *s.v.*; Weiss, *Dor*, ii. 187; see also Grätz, *Gesch.* 2d ed., iv. 208; Vogelstein and Rieger, *Gesch. der Juden in Rom*, i. 31.

S. S. S. M.

ELEAZAR (LAZAR) B. JOSE II.: Palestinian amora of the fifth generation (fifth century); senior of Naḥman II. and Aḥa III. (Pesiḳ. v. 55a). Most of his utterances are remarks which he had directly or indirectly heard from Abbahu, Ḥanina b. Abbahu, Tanḥum b. Ḥiyya, and others (Yer. Ber. vii. 11d; Yer. Ma'as. i. 49a, ii. 49c; Yer. 'Er. iii. 23d; Lam. R. iii. 17); but he also expresses his own views, both doctrinal and homiletical (Yer. Shab. xvi. 15d; Yer. Kil. viii. 31a; Yer. Ḥallah, ii. 58b; Ex. R. xxiii. 5; Lev. R. xi. 6; Pesiḳ. *l.c.*). His father, Jose II., seems to have been his principal teacher, for frequently it was before him that Eleazar propounded his views (Yer. Ber. i. 3d, iv. 8a; Yer. Ned. iv. 38d); and it is related that his father often chided him for lack of zeal. Quoting the statement (I Chron. ix. 20), "In time past the Lord was with him [Phinehas]," he used to say, "As long as Phinehas was zealous for the Law, the Lord was with him; but when he ceased to be zealous the Lord forsook him" (Yer. Yoma i. 38d; Yer. Meg. i. 72a; Yer. Hor. iii. 47d).

S. S. S. M.

ELEAZAR (ELIEZER LAZAR) B. JUDAH OF BARTOTA (BIRIA, BIRTA, BIRTOTA): Scholar and philanthropist of the third tannaitic generation (first and second centuries); disciple of Joshua b. Hananiah, and contemporary of Akiba (Ṭ. Y. iii. 4, 5; Tosef., Bek. vii. 6). Sometimes the cognomen is omitted (compare Tosef., Zab. i. 5, and Zab. i. 1), and sometimes the patronymic (Ab. iii. 7). While his name is connected with but few halakot, and with still fewer midrashim, he has established for himself an indelible name in the list of the charitable. His motto was, "Give Him of His own: thyself and what thou possessest are His, as David says (I Chron. xxix. 14): 'All things come of thee, and of thine own have we given thee'" (Ab. iii. 7); and he lived up to his motto. It is related that he was so extravagant in his benevolence as to give away all that he possessed; wherefore the collectors for the poor would avoid meeting him (Ta'an. 24a). In illustration of this characteristic, the Talmud (*ib.*) cites the following instance:

"Eleazar's daughter was to be married. While making purchases for the occasion, he espied the collectors, who were hiding from him. He overtook them, and begged them to acquaint him with their mission. They informed him that they were soliciting for a marriage portion for a couple of orphans, whereupon he exclaimed, 'Verily, that couple takes precedence over my daughter'; and he gave them all that he had about him." Legend adds that he retained one zuz, and with that he bought wheat, which he carried home and put away in the storeroom. When his wife soon afterward tried to open the room in order to see what Eleazar had brought, it was found to be full to overflowing with grain. In the meantime Eleazar had repaired to the academy, and thither his daughter hastened with the joyful tidings, remarking, "Come and see what thy friend has done for thee"; but when he had heard her story, he consecrated the grain also to charity.

BIBLIOGRAPHY: Bacher, *Ag. Tan.* i. 443; Brüll, *Mebo ha-Mishnah*, i. 142; Frankel, *Darke ha-Mishnah*, p. 134; Heilprin, *Seder ha-Dorot*, ii., *s.v.*; Zacuto, *Yuḥasin*, ed. Filipowski, p. 56b.

S. S. S. M.

ELEAZAR (ELIEZER) HA-ḲAPPAR: Tanna of the fourth generation (second century); father of BAR ḲAPPARA, who is sometimes cited by the same name. Eleazar is quoted in the Mishnah (Ab. iv. 21), where he says, "Envy, lust, and ambition shorten man's life." From him the Mishnah (*ib.* 22) also preserves the following exhortation: "The born are to die, and the dead to revive, and the living to be judged; in order to know, and to notify, and that it may be known, that He is the Framer, and He the Creator, and He the Judge, and He the Witness, and He the Complainant, and He with whom there is no iniquity, nor forgetfulness, nor respect of persons, nor taking of a bribe, for all is His, is about to judge; and know that all is according to His plan. Let not thy 'yeẓer ' [evil inclinations] assure thee that the grave is an asylum; for perforce thou wast created (Jer. xviii. 6), and perforce thou wast born, and perforce thou livest, and perforce thou diest, and perforce thou art about to give account and reckoning before the King of Kings, the Holy One, blessed be He!" Elsewhere (Sifre, Num. 42; compare Num. R. xi. 7) he says, "Great indeed is peace: it is the end of all blessings" (see Num. vi. 26). For other ethical lessons from him see Ab. R. N. xxix. 4; Derek Ereẓ Zuṭa ix. 1. Some of his teachings are probably to be ascribed to his son.

BIBLIOGRAPHY: Bacher, *Ag. Tan.* ii. 500; Heilprin, *Seder ha-Dorot*, ii., *s.v.*; C. Taylor, *Sayings of the Jewish Fathers*, 2d ed., pp. 76 *et seq.*

S. S. S. M.

ELEAZAR B. MAHBAI. See ELEAZAR B. AḤWAI.

ELEAZAR B. MALAI: Palestinian scholar of the fourth century, whose name is mentioned but once, in the Babylonian Talmud, and then only as the reporter of a homily of Simeon b. Laḳish, which reproves the wickedness of the courts with the following words: "'Your hands are defiled with blood' (Isa. lix. 3) refers to the judges, whose hands are ever open to receive bribes; 'your fingers with iniquity' (*ibid.*) refers to the judiciary's scribes, who write false or specious documents; 'your lips have spoken lies' refers to the lawyers, who misconstrue the law, or instruct their clients how to plead; 'your tongue hath muttered perverseness' refers to the litigants, who plead falsehood" (Shab. 139a; Rashi *ad loc.*). It is not certain, however, that "Malai" was Eleazar's real patronymic, some editions reading "Simlai" instead (see Rabbinowicz, "Diḳduḳe Soferim" to Shab. *l.c.*).

S. S. S. M.

ELEAZAR B. MATTAI (MATTHIAS): Tanna of the third and fourth generations (second century); contemporary of Hananiah b. Ḥakinai, Ben 'Azzai, and Simon of Teman (Tosef., Ber. iv. 18). It is stated that, together with Ḥalafta and Hananiah, he examined the stones which, by order of Joshua, the Israelites brought up from the Jordan and pitched in Gilgal (Josh. iv.), and approximated their weight (Tosef., Soṭah, viii. 6). Eleazar was a disciple of R. Tarphon (Tosef., Ber. *l.c.*; compare Mek., Beshallaḥ, 5), and is met with in scholastic disputations with Judah b. 'Illai and Simon b. Yoḥai (Tosef., Pes. vi. 2; Pes. 79b *et seq.*). According to one report, he and Hananiah were "the disciples" present at the dispute between R. Meïr and the rabbis; (Yer. Ma'as, Sh. ii. 53d); according to another, they were among the four expert linguists of the Jamnian Sanhedrin (Yer. Sheḳ. v. 48d; compare Sanh. 17b). From the Scriptural dictum (Lev. v. 1), "If a soul sin, and hear the voice of swearing," he argues that one is subject to hear the voice of swearing because of his having sinned. Accordingly, the teaches, "Whoso witnesses a transgression was doomed to see it; and whoso witnesses a good-deed has deserved to see it" (Tosef., Shebu. iii. 4). He is mentioned once in the Mishnah (Yeb. x. 3), and several times in baraitot, in connection with halakic controversies.

BIBLIOGRAPHY: Brüll, *Mebo ha-Mishnah*, i. 141; Frankel, *Darke ha-Mishnah*, p. 183; Weiss, *Dor*, ii. 123.

S. S. S. M.

ELEAZAR B. MENAHEM: Palestinian scholar of the fourth amoraic generation (fourth century). No halakot and but few haggadot are connected with his name. Commenting on the Biblical expression (Ps. xxxvi. 9 [A. V. 8]), "Thou shalt make them drink of the river of thy pleasures" (עדניך, lit. "thy Edens"), he remarks, "Since the Bible says not 'thy Eden,' but 'thy Edens,' it implies that every pious soul has an [apartment in] Eden for itself" (Tan., Emor, ed. Buber, 9; Lev. R. xxvii. 1; Midr. Teh. xxxiv. 23 reads "Isaac b. Menahem"). From the expression (Gen. xiii. 8), "He [Abraham] went on his journeys," Eleazar infers that Abraham returned from Egypt by the way he had traveled thither, to liquidate the debts he had previously incurred (Gen. R. xli. 3).

Bibliography: Bacher, *Ag. Pal. Amor.* iii. 697; Heilprin, *Seder ha-Dorot,* ii., *s.v.*

S. S. S. M.

ELEAZAR OF MODI'IM (MODAIM): Scholar of the second tannaitic generation (first and second centuries); disciple of Johanan ben Zakkai (B. B. 10b), and contemporary of Joshua ben Hananiah and Eliezer ben Hyrcanus (Mek., Beshallaḥ, Wayassa', 3 *et seq.*). He was an expert haggadist, and frequently discussed exegetical topics with his distinguished contemporaries. Gamaliel II. often deferred to Eleazar's interpretations, admitting, "The Moda'i's views are still indispensable" (Shab. 55b).

As his life embraced the period of Hadrianic persecutions and of the Bar Kokba insurrection, many of his homilies refer, explicitly or impliedly, to existence under such conditions (Grätz, "Gesch." iv. 79, note). Eleazar expressed his confidence in Providence in this comment on the Scriptural statement (Ex. xvi. 4), "the people shall go out, and gather a certain rate every day" (lit. "the portion of the day on its day," דבר יום ביומו): "He who creates the day creates its sustenance." From this verse he also argued, "He who is possessed of food for the day, and worries over what he may have to eat the next day, is wanting in faith; therefore the Bible adds [*ib.*], 'that I may prove them, whether they will walk in my law, or no'" (Mek. *l.c.* 2).

Eleazar's last days fell in the dark period of the insurrection headed by. Bar Kokba, and he ended his life in the then besieged city of Bethar. Of these days rabbinic tradition relates as follows:

"During the Roman siege R. Eleazar of Modi'im fasted and prayed daily that God might not strictly judge the people that day nor surrender the city to the enemy, because of the sins of the inhabitants. The siege being protracted, and no immediate conquest being in prospect, the Roman commander meditated on withdrawing, when a Samaritan persuaded him to wait a while, and offered his services to aid in subduing the apparently unconquerable Jews by stratagem—by creating a suspicion of treachery among the besieged against Eleazar. 'For,' argued he, 'as long as this hen wallows in ashes [as long as Eleazar by his prayers encourages in the people the hope of God's protection], so long will Bethar remain impregnable.' Thereupon he smuggled himself into the city through some subterranean ducts, and, approaching Eleazar, who was engaged in prayer, pretended to whisper in to his ear a secret message. Those present, regarding this mysterious movement with suspicion, soon reported it to Bar

Kokba, and declared, 'Eleazar intends to establish peace between the city and Hadrian.' Bar Kokba had the Samaritan brought before him and interrogated him on the import of his conversation with the sage; but the Samaritan replied, 'If I reveal the royal secrets to thee, the commander will kill me; and if I refrain, thou wilt kill me. I would rather kill myself than betray my king's secrets.' Bar Kokba then summoned Eleazar and questioned him; but Eleazar protested that he had been absorbed in devotional exercises, and had heard nothing. This increased Bar Kokba's suspicion of meditated treason, and aroused him to such anger that he kicked Eleazar, in consequence of which the aged sage, enfeebled by fasting and prayer, fell dead."

The story adds that a "bat ḳol" thereupon pronounced the immediate doom of the chief of the insurrection and of the beleaguered city, which soon came to pass (Yer. Ta'an. iv. 68d; Lam. R. ii. 2).

BIBLIOGRAPHY: Bacher, *Ag. Tan.* i. 194: Brüll, *Mebo ha-Mishnah*, i. 130; Frankel, *Darke ha-Mishnah*, p. 127; Hamburger, *R. B. T.* ii. 161; Heilprin, *Seder ha-Dorot*, ii., *s.v.*; Weiss, *Dor*, ii. 130; Zacuto, *Yuḥasin*, ed. Filipowski, p. 33a.

S. S. S. M.

ELEAZAR BEN PEDAT. See ELEAZAR II. (LAZAR).

ELEAZAR BEN PERATA I.: Tanna of the third generation (second century); junior contemporary of Eleazar of Modi'im (Tosef., Sanh. iv. 8; Yer. Meg. i. 71c) and of Jose the Galilean (Mek., Yitro, Ba-ḥodesh, 2). He lived through the period when, according to a younger contemporary, the performance of circumcision was punished by the Romans with the sword; the study of the Jewish law, with the stake; the celebration of Passover, with crucifixion; and the observance of the Feast of Booths, with the scourge (Mek. *l.c.* 6; Lev. R. xxxii. 1). Still, Eleazar faithfully adhered to the teachings of his religion. Once he was arrested and cast into prison, where he met Hananiah ben Teradion. He tried to instil hope into his fellow prisoner's breast, because there was only one charge against him, that of teaching the Law, while himself he considered lost, because there were five counts against him. Hananiah, on the contrary, thought that Eleazar's chances of escape were better than his own; and the sequel proved that he was right. Hananiah was condemned to a terrible death, while Eleazar was acquitted ('Ab. Zarah 17b).

Eleazar's studies embraced both Halakah and Haggadah, mostly the latter. One of his homilies warns against calumny in these words: "Observe how mighty are the consequences of the evil tongue. Learn them from the fate of the spies [see Num. xiii. *et seq.*]. Of the spies it is related [*ib.* xiv. 37], 'Those men that did bring up the evil report upon the land, died by the plague before the Lord.' And of what had they spoken evil? Of trees and of stones [see *ib.* xiii. 32]. If, now, those who slandered dumb objects were punished so severely, how much greater must be the punishment of him who traduces his neighbor, his equal!" (Tosef., 'Ar. ii. 11; 'Ar. 15a).

He draws practical lessons also from Scriptural texts. On a certain Sabbath some prominent coreligionists, having just learned that the Romans were seeking them, applied to Eleazar for legal advice a to the permissibility of flight from danger on the Sab bath. Eleazar referred them to Scriptural history. "Why do you inquire of me?" said he. "Look at Jacob [see Hosea xii. 13 (A. V. 12)], at Moses [Ex. ii. 15], and at David [I Sam. xix. 10, 18], and see what they did under similar circumstances" (Tan., Masse'e, i.; Num. R. xxiii. 1).

S. S. S. M.

ELEAZAR BEN PERATA II.: Tanna of the second and third centuries; grandson of Eleazar ben Perata I.; sometimes designated as "Eleazar b. Perata, the grandson of Eleazar b. Perata ha-Gadol" (Ket. 100a; Giṭ. 33a; Yer. Meg. iv. 75b), and also without the addition of his grandfather's name (Yer. Suk. iii. 54a; Suk. 39a). He confined his studies mainly to the Halakah, and was a contemporary of R. Judah I. (see Suk. *l.c.*; Yer. Meg. *l.c.*).

BIBLIOGRAPHY: Bacher, *Ag. Tan.* i. 403; Brüll, *Mebo ha-Mishnah*, i. 140, 326; Heilprin, *Seder ha-Dorot*, ii., *s.v.*

S. S. S. M.

ELEAZAR B. SHAMMUA'. See ELEAZAR I (LAZAR).

ELEAZAR BEN SIMON: Tanna of the second century. He was the son of Simon b. Yoḥai, and since he participated in many of his father's adventures, history and legend have woven an almost interminable tissue of fact and fiction concerning him (see B. M. 83b *et seq.*; Pesiḳ. x. 88b *et seq.*). His youth he spent with his father in a cave, hiding from the Roman persecutors of the Jews, who sought his father's life; and there he devoted himself to the study of the Torah (Shab. 33b; Gen. R. lxxix. 6, and parallel passages; compare Yer. Sheb. ix. 38d). After the death of Hadrian, when events took a somewhat more favorable turn for the Jews, father and son left the cave and returned to the busy world. Eleazar, grown too zealous during his protracted hermitage, often cursed those who devoted their time to things secular, and his father found it necessary to interfere, appeasing them and mollifying him (Shab. *l.c.*).

After Simon's death Eleazar entered the academy of the Patriarch Simon b. Gamaliel II., and became the colleague of the patriarch's son, Judah I., the compiler of the Mishnah; but no great friendship seems to have subsisted between these two scholars.

Unlike his father, who hated the Romans and their rule, Eleazar accepted office under their government. In consequence thereof he grew very unpopular, and one of the rabbis remonstrated with him, saying, "Vinegar product of wine [="Degenerate scion of a distinguished sire"], how long wilt thou continue to deliver the people of God to the hangman?" Eleazar, however, continued in office, excusing himself with the averment, "I but weed out thistles from the vineyard," His mentor answered that the weeding ought to be left to the proprietor of the vineyard—that is, that God Himself would visit punishment on the idlers and evildoers.

Later in life he regretted the part he had taken under the hated government, and is said to have imposed on himself the most painful penance. Still, fearing that the aversion engendered in his people by the aid he had rendered their persecutors would prompt them to deny him the last honors after his death, he enjoined his wife not to bury him immediately after dissolution, but to suffer his remains ta rest under her roof. He died at Akbara, in northern Galilee, and his faithful wife carried out his injunction to the letter. Legend relates many miracles performed by the dead rabbi, one of which was that litigants plead their cases in the rabbi's house, and the verdict was pronounced from the mortuary chamber.

After many years his former colleagues resolved to bury him, but a new difficulty arose. The inhabitants of Akbara, believing that the sage's remains miraculously protected them against incursions of wild beasts, refused permission to remove the body. Ultimately, however, in compliance with the request of the rabbis people from the nearby town of Biria carried it off by stealth, and it was deposited at Meron beside that of his father (B. M. 84b). In consideration of his varied learning, his surviving colleagues cited the Scriptural verse (Cant. iii. 6), "Who is it that cometh out of the wilderness like pillars of smoke, perfumed with myrrh and frankincense, with all powders of the merchant?" and answered, "It is Eleazar b. Simon, who united in himself all noble qualities, he having been well versed in Scripture and in traditional law, and having been a [liturgical] poet, a leader in prayers, and a preacher" (Lev. R. xxx. 1; Cant. R. *l.c.*).

BIBLIOGRAPHY: Bacher, *Ag. Tan.* ii. 400 *et seq.*; Brüll, *Mebo ha-Mishnah*, i. 236; Frankel, *Darke ha-Mishnah*, p. 199; Hamburger, *R. B. T.* ii. 159; Jastrow, in *Monatsschrift*, 1882, pp. 195 *et seq.*; Weiss, *Dor*, ii. 185; Zacuto, *Yuḥasin*, ed. Filipowski, p. 52b.

S. S. S. M.

ELEAZAR B. ZADOK. See ELIEZER B. ZADOK.

ELIEZER ("God is help"): **1.** Servant of Abraham; mentioned by name only in Gen. xv. 2, a passage which presents some difficulties. Eliezer is described by Abraham as בן משק (R. V. "possessor of my house") and as דמשק (R. V. "Dammesek-Eliezer"). According to Eduard

König ("Syntax," § 306h) בן here, as frequently, has the force of an adjective or participle, and the phrase "ben meshek" (steward; comp. ממשק, Zeph. xi. 9, and משך, Job xxviii. 18) is the subject of the sentence, which reads "and the steward of my house is this Damascene [Onk. and Pesh.] Eliezer," "Damashek" being used intentionally for the adjective "Damashki" on account of the assonance with "meshek" (König, "Stilistik," 1900, p. 291). Holzinger ("Genesis") and Gunkel ("Genesis") think the Masoretic text of xv. 2 has no meaning, and Cheyne and Black ("Encyc. Bibl." col. 1269) condemn it as absurd and incorrect, but no satisfactory emendation has been suggested.

That Abraham, on his way from Haran, passed through Damascus is certainly not improbable. Naḥmanides connects him with that city, as do various traditions (Justinus, "Historiæ," xxvi. 2; Judith v. 6 *et seq.*; Josephus, "Ant." vii. 1, viii. 2; Eusebius, "Præparatio Evangelica," ix. 7 *et seq.*). He may there have acquired this servant, who is also spoken of in Gen. xxiv., though the name is not given, in connection with the commission to choose a wife for Isaac. Still, even the Rabbis felt the difficulties of the present text, as their various interpretations of דמשק show. According to Eleazar b. Pedath, it denotes Eliezer as one "that draws and gives others to drink" (דולה ומשקה)—that is, imparts to others the teachings of his master (Yoma 18b; comp. Rashi *ad loc.*). Others found in the word "meshek" an allusion to his coveting (שוקק) Abraham's possessions. In דמשק lies the indication that Abraham pursued the kings (Gen. xiv.) to Damascus, and the Targum Pseudo-Jonathan and Yerushalmi read: "through whom many miracles were wrought for me in Damascus" (comp. Gen. R. xliv.).

That Eliezer took part in that battle, or was, perhaps, the only combatant at Abraham's side, the Rabbis find indicated in the number (318) of the soldiers (Gen. xiv. 14), the numerical value of the letters in אליעזר being 1 + 30 + 10 + 70 + 7 + 200 = 318 (Gen. R. xliii., xliv.; Pesik. 70a, b; Ned. 32a; Shoḥer Ṭob to Ps. cx.; compare Ep. Barnabas ix.; it is the classical illustration of GEMAṬRIA under the twenty-ninth Exegetical Rule of Eliezer, the son of Jose the Galilean). Modern critics (Hugo Winckler and Gunkel) have held this "318" to refer to the number of days in the year that the moon is visible. The rabbinical cryptogram for "Eliezer" rests certainly on as solid grounds.

BIBLIOGRAPHY: Kittel. *Gesch. der Hebräer*, ii. 124; Holzinger, *Kurzer Handkommentar zur Genesis*, p. 144; H. Winckler, *Gesch. des Volkes Israel*, 1900, ii. 27; Gunkel. *Handkommentar zur Genesis*, pp. 164, 231, 259.

E. G. H.

——**In Rabbinical Literature:** Eliezer was presented to Abraham by Nimrod. Once Eliezer saved Abraham's life by disclosing to him the devices for his destruction prepared by Nimrod (Pirḳe R. El. xvi.). At Sodom Eliezer saw a native maltreating a stranger: taking the part of the wronged man, he was himself severely wounded. He brought suit against his aggressor, but the judge condemned Eliezer to pay to the native of Sodom a certain amount of money for having been bled. Thereupon Eliezer inflicted a severe wound upon the judge, saying: "Pay to the man who bled me the amount you owe me for having bled you." The men of Sodom used to place a guest on a bed, and if his length exceeded that of the bed they cut off the excess, but if the man was shorter than the bed he was stretched (comp. the Greek legend of Procrustes). Asked to lie in the bed, Eliezer replied that at the death of his mother he had vowed never to sleep in a bed. Another custom in Sodom was that he who invited a stranger to a wedding should forfeit his coat. Once Eliezer, being very hungry, entered a house where a wedding was being celebrated, but could get nothing to eat. He then sat down next one of the wedding guests; on being asked by him who had invited him, he replied: "By you." The latter, fearing to lose his coat, left the house precipitately. Eliezer then sat near another, on whom he played the same trick, with the same result, until at last he had succeeded in driving all the guests out of the house. He then secured the meal for himself (Sanh. 109b).

Eliezer is credited with having acquired all the virtues and learning of his master (Yoma 28b). It is even said that his features resembled so closely those of Abraham that Laban mistook him for his kinsman. When Abraham led Isaac to Mount Moriah to offer him as a sacrifice, Eliezer cherished the hope of becoming Abraham's heir, and a discussion on this subject arose between him and Ishmael (Pirḳe R. El. xxxi.). On completing the mission of selecting a wife for Isaac he was freed, and God rewarded him with the kingdom of Bashan, over which he reigned under the name of "Og." It was he who refused to allow the Israelites to go through his territory on their way to Palestine (Masseket Soferim, end). His size was so vast that from one of his teeth, which he had lost through fright when scolded by Abraham, the latter made a chair on which he used to sit. In the treatise Derek Ereẓ Zuṭa (i. 9) Eliezer is counted among the nine who entered paradise while still living.

S. S. I. BR.

2. The second son of Moses; mentioned in Ex. xviii. 4; I Chron. xxiii. 15, 17. The name is explained (Ex. *l.c.*) to mean "the God of my father was mine help" (the ב of the predicate; see Koenig, "Syntax," § 338). Rashi, quoting the Mekilta, relates a miraculous incident to account for the choice of the name, while Ibn Ezra makes it expressive of the joy of Moses upon hearing of the death of the Pharaoh who had proscribed him. The historical existence of this son has been doubted. Ex. ii. 22 and iv. 25 mention only one son—Gershom. Ibn Ezra felt the difficulty, but concluded that the one son mentioned in iv. 25 is Eliezer; while Naḥmanides argues that there was another son, but that there had been no occasion to mention him before. Ex. iv. 20 indicates that Moses, before leaving for Egypt, whether with his family (Ex. iv. 20) or without it (Ex. xviii. 2), had more than one son; and the reading בנה = "her son" (iv. 25) may be a miswriting for בניה = "her sons," agreeing with xviii. 3. Baentsch ("Exodus-Leviticus.") holds that "Eliezer" is a double for "Eleazar," the son of Aaron, while Holzinger ("Exodus," p. 7) accounts for the uncertainty by arguing that in view of Judges xviii. 30 P intentionally omitted all reference to the sons.

E. G. H. E. K.

3. A prophet, the son of Dodavah of Mareshah, who opposed the alliance of Jehoshaphat with Ahaziah (II Chron. xx. 37).

4. Son of Zichri, made captain of the Reubenites by King David (I Chron. xxvii. 16).

5. A priest who acted as trumpeter before the Ark when it was conveyed to Jerusalem by King David (I Chron. xv. 24).

6. One of the chief men sent by Ezra (Ezra viii. 16) to secure ministers for the Temple at Jerusalem.

E. G. H. E. I. N.

ELIEZER: Palestinian amora of the fifth century; contemporary of Abdimi (Yer. 'Er. x. 26a) and of Berechiah II. (Gen. R. lxxvii. 3; Yalḳ., Gen. 132). Conjointly with Abba Mari and Mattaniah, he permitted Jews to bake bread on the Sabbath for the Roman soldiers under Ursicinus (Yer. Beẓah i. 60c; compare Jastrow, "Dict." 124b, *s.v.* ארסקינס; Frankel, "Mebo," 55b *et seq.*). He was more of a halakist than a haggadist (see, in addition to passages cited, Yer. 'Orlah ii. 62b; Yer. Pes. viii. 36a).

S. S. S. M.

ELIEZER B. ḤISMA. See ELEAZAR B. ḤISMA.

ELIEZER (LIEZER) BEN HYRCANUS: One of the most prominent tannaim of the first and second centuries; disciple of R. Johanan ben Zakkai (Ab. ii. 8; Ab. R. N. vi. 3, xiv. 5) and colleague of Gamaliel II., whose sister he married (see IMMA SHALOM), and of Joshua b. Hananiah (Ab. *l.c.*; Ab. R. N. *l.c.*; B. B. 10b). His earlier years are wrapped in myths; but from these latter it may be inferred that he was somewhat advanced in life when a desire for learning first seized him, and impelled him, contrary to the wishes of his father, to desert his regular occupation and to repair to Jerusalem to devote himself to the study of the Torah. Here he entered Johanan's academy and for years studied diligently, notwithstanding the fact that he had to cope with great privations. It is said that sometimes many days elapsed during which he did not have a single meal. Johanan, recognizing Eliezer's receptive and retentive mind, styled him "a cemented cistern that loses not a drop" (Ab. *l.c.*). These endowments were so pronounced in him that in later years he could declare, "I have never taught anything which I had not learned from my masters" (Suk. 28a).

His father in the meantime determined to disinherit him, and with that purpose in view went to Jerusalem, there to declare his will before Johanan ben Zakkai. The great teacher, having heard of Hyrcanus' arrival and of the object of his visit, instructed the usher to reserve for the expected visitor a seat among those to be occupied by the élite of the city, and appointed Eliezer lecturer for that day. At first the latter hesitated to venture on Johanan's place, but, pressed by the master and encouraged by his friends, delivered a discourse, gradually displaying wonderful knowledge. Hyrcanus having recognized in the lecturer his truant son, and hearing the encomiums which Johanan showered on him, now desired to transfer all his earthly possessions to Eliezer; but the scholar, overjoyed at the reconciliation, declined to take advantage of his brothers, and requested to be allowed to have only his proportionate share (Ab. R. N. vi. 3; Pirḳe R. El. i. *et seq.*). He continued his attendance at Johanau's college until near the close of the siege of Jerusalem, when he and Joshua assisted in smuggling their master out of the city and into the Roman camp (see JOHANAN BEN ZAKKAI).

Subsequently Eliezer proceeded to Jabneh (Ab R. N. iv. 5; Giṭ. 56), where he later became a member of the Sanhedrin under the presidency of Gamaliel II. (Ab. R. N. xiv. 6; Sanh. 17b), though he had established, and for many years afterward conducted, his own academy at Lydda (Sanh. 36b). His fame as a great scholar had in the meantime spread, R. Johanan himself declaring that Eliezer was unequaled as an expositor of traditional law (Ab. R. N. vi. 3); and many promising students, among them Akiba (*ib.*; Yer. Pes. vi. 33b), attached themselves to his school.

Eliezer became known as "Eliezer ha-Gadol" (= "the Great"; Tosef., 'Orlah, 8; Ber. 6a, 32a; Soṭah 13b, 48b, 49a; generally, however, he is styled simply "R. Eliezer"), and with reference to his legal acumen and judicial impartiality, the Scriptural saying (Deut. xvi. 20), "That which is altogether just [lit. "Justice, justice"] shalt thou follow," was thus explained: "Seek a reliable court: go after R. Eliezer to Lydda, or after Johanan ben Zakkai to Beror Ḥel," etc. (Sanh. 32b). Once he accompanied Gamaliel and Joshua on an embassy to Rome (Yer. Sanh. vii. 25d; Deut. R. ii. 24).

Rabbi Eliezer was very severe and somewhat domineering with his pupils and colleagues (see Sifra, Shemini, i. 33; 'Er. 63a; Ḥag. 3b; Meg. 25b), a characteristic which led occasionally to unpleasant encounters. The main feature of his teaching was a strict devotion to tradition: he objected to allowing the Midrash or the paraphrastic interpretation to pass as authority for religious practise. In this respect he sympathized with the conservative school of Shammai, which was also opposed to giving too much scope to the interpretation. Hence the assertion that he was a Shammaite, though he was a disciple of R. Johanan ben Zakkai, who was one of Hillel's most prominent pupils. This brought Eliezer into conflict with his colleagues and contemporaries, who realized that such conservatism must be fatal to a proper development of the oral law. It was also felt that the new circumstances, such as the destruction of the Temple and the disappearance of the national independence, required a strong religious central authority, to which individual opinion must yield.

At last the rupture came. The Sanhedrin deliberated on the susceptibility to Levitical uncleanness of an 'aknai-oven (an oven consisting of tiles separated from one another by sand, but externally plastered over with cement). The majority decided that such an oven was capable of becoming unclean, but Eliezer dissented. As he thus acted in direct opposition to the decision of the majority, it was deemed necessary to make an example of him, and he was excommunicated. Still, even under these circumstances great respect was manifested toward him, and the sentence was communicated to him in a very considerate manner. Akiba, dressed in mourning, appeared before him and, seated at some distance from him, respectfully addressed him with "My master, it appears to me that thy colleagues keep aloof from thee." Eliezer readily took in the situation and submitted to the sentence (B. M. 59b; Yer. M. Ḳ. iii. 81a *et seq.*). Thenceforth Eliezer lived in retirement, removed from the center of Jewish learning; though occasionally some of his disciples, visited him and informed him of the transactions of the Sanhedrin (Yad. iv. 3).

During the persecutions of the Jewish Christians, in Palestine, Eliezer was charged with being a member of that sect, and was summoned before the penal tribunal. Being asked by the governor, "How can a great man like thee engage in such idle things?" he simply replied, "The judge is right." The judge, understanding thereby Eliezer's denial of all connection with Christianity, released him, while Rabbi Eliezer understood by "judge" God, justifying the judgment of God which had brought this trial upon him. That he should be suspected of apostasy grieved him sorely; and though some of his pupils tried to comfort him, he remained for some time inconsolable. At last he remembered that once, while at Sepphoris, he had met a sectary who communicated to him a singular halakah in the name of Jesus; that he had approved of the halakah. and had really enjoyed hearing it, and, he added, "Thereby I transgressed the injunction (Prov. v. 8), 'Remove thy way far from her, and come not nigh the door of her house,' which the Rabbis apply to sectarianism as well as to heresy" ('Ab. Zarah 16b; Eccl. R. i. 8). The suspicion of apostasy and the summons before the dreaded tribunal came, therefore, as just punishment. This event in his life may have suggested to him the ethical rule, "Keep away from what is indecent and from that which appears to be indecent" (Tosef., Ḥul. ii. 24). It is suggested that his sayings, "Instructing a woman in the Law is like teaching her blasphemy" (Soṭah iii. 4); "Let the Law be burned rather than entrusted to a woman" (*ib.*); and "A woman's wisdom is limited to the handling of the distaff" (Yoma 66b), also date from that time, he having noticed that women were easily swayed in matters of faith.

Separated from his colleagues and excluded from the deliberations of the Sanhedrin, Eliezer passed his last years of life unnoticed and in comparative solitude. It is probably from this melancholy period that his aphorism dates: "Let the honor of thy colleague [variant, "pupils"] be as dear to thee as thine own, and be not easily moved to anger. Repent one day before thy death. Warm thyself by the fire of the wise men, but be cautious of their burning coals [= "slight them not"], that thou be not, burned; for their bite is the bite of a jackal, their sting is that of a scorpion, their hissing is that of a snake, and all their words are fiery coals" (Ab. ii. 10; Ab. R. N. xv. 1). When asked how one can determine the one day before his death, he answered: "So much the more must one repent daily, lest he die to-morrow; and it follows that he must spend all his days in piety" (Ab. R. N. *l.c.* 4; Shab. 153a).

When his former colleagues heard of his approaching dissolution, the most prominent of them hastened to his bedside at Cæsarea. When they appeared before him he began to complain about his long isolation. They tried to mollify him by professing great and unabated respect for him, and by averring that it was only the lack of opportunity that had kept them away. He felt that they might have profited by his teaching. Thereupon they besought him to communicate to them traditions concerning certain moot points, particularly touching Levitical purity and impurity. He consented, and answered question after question until all breath left him. The last word he uttered was "ṭahor" (= "pure"), and this the sages considered as an auspicious omen of his purity; whereupon they all rent their garments in token of mourning, and R. Joshua revoked the sentence of excommunication.

Eliezer died on a Friday, and after the following Sabbath his remains were solemnly conveyed to Lydda, where he had formerly conducted his academy, and there he was buried. Many and earnest were the eulogies pronounced over his bier. R. Joshua is said to have kissed the stone on which Eliezer used to sit while instructing his pupils, and to have remarked, "This stone represents Sinai [whence the Law was revealed]; and he who sat on it represented the Ark of the Covenant" (Cant. R. i. 3). R. Akiba applied to Eliezer the terms which Elisha had applied to Elijah (II Kings ii. 12), and which Joash subsequently applied to Elisha himself (*ib.* xiii. 14), "O my father, my father, the chariot of Israel, and the horsemen thereof" (Ab. R. N. xxv. 3).

Though excommunicated, Eliezer is quoted in the Mishnah, the Baraita, and the Talmudim more frequently than any one of his colleagues. He is also made the putative author of Pirḳe de-R. Eliezer or Baraita of R. Eliezer, though internal evidence conclusively proves the late origin of the work.

Bibliography: Bacher, *Ag. Tan.* i. 100–160; Brüll, *Mebo ha-Mishnah*, i. 75–82; Frankel, *Darke ha-Mishnah*, pp. 75–83; Grätz, *Gesch.* 2d ed., iv. 43 *et seq.*; Hamburger, *R. B. T.* ii. 163–168; Heilprin, *Seder ha-Dorot*, ii., *s.v.*; Oppenheim, *Bet Talmud*, iv. 311, 332, 360; Weiss, *Dor*, ii. 81 *et seq.*; Wiesner, *Gibe'at Yerushalayim*,, pp. 61 *et seq.*; Zacuto, *Yuḥasin*, ed. Filipowski, pp. 50a *et seq.*; G. Deutsch, *The Theory of Oral Tradition*, pp. 30, 34, Cincinnati. 1896.

s. s. S. M.

ELIEZER B. JOSE HA-GELILI: Tanna of the fourth generation (second century); one of Akiba's later disciples (Ber. 68b; Cant. R. ii. 5; Eccl. R. xi. 6; see Eliezer b. Jacob). While he cultivated both the Halakah (Soṭah v. 3; Tosef., Sanh. i. 2; Sanh. 3b) and the Haggadah, his fame rests mainly on his work in the latter field. Indeed, with reference to his homiletics, later generations said, "Wherever them meetest a word of R. Eliezer b. R. Jose ha-Gelili in the Haggadali, make thine ear as a funnel (Ḥul. 89a; Yer. Ḳid. i. 61d; Pesiḳ. R. x. 38b; compare Jastrow, "Dict." *s.v.* אפרכסת). For, even where he touched on the Halakah, he always brought exegesis to bear upon the matter. Thus, arguing that after legal proceedings are closed the court may not propose a compromise, he says, "The judge who then brings about a settlement is a sinner; and he who blesses him is a blasphemer, of whom it may be said (Ps. x. 3) ובוצע ברך נאץ ה׳ ["The compromiser he blesseth: the Lord he contemneth"; A. V. "Blesseth the covetous, whom the Lord abhorreth"]. The Law must perforate the mountain (*i.e.*, must not be set aside under any considerations); for thus the Bible says (Deut. i. 17), 'Ye shall not be afraid of the face of man; for the judgment is God's'" (Tosef., Sanh. *l.c.*; Sanh. 6b; Yer. Sanh. i. 18b). He compiled a set of hermeneutic rules as guides in interpreting the Scriptures, some of which are adaptations of those of his predecessors, and in so far applicable to Halakah as well as to Haggadah. Those specifically homiletlcal are based on syntactical or phraseological or similar peculiarities of the Biblical texts which constitute the substance of the Midrashim.

Like his colleagues, at the close of the first academic session after the Bar Kokba insurrection, Eliezer publicly thanked the people of Usha. He said, "The Bible relates (II Sam. vi. 12), 'The Lord hath blessed the house of Obed-edom, and all that pertaineth unto him, because of the ark of God.' Is this not very significant? If, for merely dusting and cleaning the Ark, which neither ate nor drank, Obed-edom was blessed, how much more deserving of blessings are they who have housed the scholars, have furnished them with meat and drink, and have otherwise shared with them their goods!" (Ber. 63b). Elsewhere (Cant. R. ii. 5) this is attributed to another speaker, while Eliezer is credited with the following: "It is recorded (II Sam, xv. 6), 'Saul said unto the Kenites... Ye showed kindness unto all the children of Israel, when they came up out of Egypt.' "Was it not to Moses alone to whom Jethro ["the Kenite"; see Judges i. 16, iv. 11] had shown kindness? But the Bible, here implies the rule that whoso deals kindly with any one of the spiritual heads of Israel, to him it is accounted as if he had done so to the whole people" (compare Lev, B. xxxiv. 8). With reference to the Biblical statement (Josh. xxiv. 32), "The bones of Joseph, which the children of Israel brought up out of Egypt, buried they in Shechem," he remarks, "Was it not Moses who brought up those bones (Ex. xiii. 19)? But this teaches that where one starts a good deed and fails to bring it to a finish, another party performing the unfinished part, the whole deed is credited to the latter" (Gen. R. lxxxv. 3; compare Soṭah 13b; Tan., 'Ekeb. 6). He counsels that one should advance or postpone a journey in order to enjoy the company of a good man; and likewise to avoid the company of a bad one (Tosef., Shab. xvii. [xviii.] 2, 3; *ib.* 'Ab. Zarah i. 17, 18).

BIBLIOGRAPHY: Bacher, *Ag. Tan.* ii. 292 *et seq.*; Brüll, *Mebo ha-Mishnah*, i. 212; Frankel, *Darke ha-Mishnah*, p. 186; Heilprin, *Seder ha-Dorot*, ii., *s.v.*; Weiss, *Dor*, ii. 167; Zacuto, *Yuḥasin*, ed. Filipowski, p. 57a.

S. S. S. M.

ELIEZER B. TADDAI: Tanna of the second century; contemporary of Simon b. Eleazar (Tosef., 'Er. vii. [v.] 9); and quoted in some baraitot in connection with halakot and with haggadot (Tosef., Shab. xvi. fxvii.] 10; Mek., Beshallaḥ, Shirah, l.; Tan., Beshallaḥ, 11). Nothing is known of his history, and, as is the case with many others, the exact version of his prænomen can not be ascertained. The Tosefta (*l.c.*) reads "Eleazar," and so does Yerushalmi (Shab. iii. 5d.; 'Er. vi. 33c); while the Babylonian Talmud (Shab. 123a; 'Er. 71b) and the Midrashim (*l.c.*) read "Eliezer." See also Tosef., Shab. *l.c.*; Rabbinowicz, "Diḳduḳe Soferim" to Shab. and 'Er. *l.c.*

S. S. S. M.

ELIEZER (ELEAZAR) B. ZADOK: 1. Tanna of the first century; disciple of Johanan the Horonite (Tosef., Suk. ii. 3; Yeb. 1515). He traced his descent from Shinhab or Senaah of the tribe of Benjamin ('Er. 41a; Ta'an. 12a). In his youth he saw the Temple in its glory (Mid. iii. 8; Suk. 49a; Sanh. 52b; Men. 88b), and later witnessed its destruction by the Romans (Tosef., Ket. v. 9; Lam. R. i. 5). During his residence in Jerusalem he, in partnership with Abba Saul b. Baṭnit, conducted a wine and oil business (Tosef., Beẓah, iii. 8). He is reported to have acquired from some Alexandrian Jews a building formerly used as a private synagogue (Tosef., Meg. iii. [ii.] 6; Yer. Meg. iii. 72d). The partners were generally applauded for their fairness and piety (Tosef., Beẓah, *l.c.*).

After the destruction of Jerusalem, Eliezer is found at Acco (Acre), where, as he himself relates, he witnessed the distress of his vanquished people. There he saw the daughter of the once fabulously rich Nicodemus b. Gorion of Jerusalem risking her life at the hoofs of horses to pick up the grains which they had dropped (Ket. 67a; Lam. R. i. 16; compare Yer. Ket. v. 30b *et seq.*). Another prominent Jewish woman, Miriam, the daughter of Simon b. Gorion (perhaps Giora, the leader of the Zealots, who surrendered to Titus; see Josephus, "B. J." vii. 2), Eliezer saw tied by her tresses to the tail of a horse, and thus dragged behind the Roman horsemen (Yer. Ket. v. 80c; compare Lam. R. *l.c.*). Later he is found at Jabneh, a frequent visitor at the residence of Patriarch Gamaliel II. (Tosef., Beẓah, ii. 13 *et seq.*; Pes. 37a; Beẓah 22b), and a member of the Sanhedrin (Shab. 11a; Niddah 48b), where he frequently related personal observations which he had made in the days of Judea's independence (Tosef., Pes. vii. 13; compare Yer. Pes. viii. 36b; Tosef., Suk. ii. 10; Tosef., Meg. iii. 15; Tosef., Sanh. ix. 11; Tosef., Kelim, B. B. ii. 2); and on some of his reports the Sanhedrin founded halakot (Pes. x. 3, 116b; B. B. 14a; Men. 40a).

The frequency of his reminiscences in Talmudic literature forms the strongest argument for the assumption that he was the first compiler of a now lost treatise on mourning called "Ebel Zuṭarta" (see Brüll, "Jahrb." i. 16–26; Klotz, "Ebel Rabbati," pp. 3 *et seq.*). How long he remained in Jabneh is not stated; but he did not end his clays there. According to a Talmudic notice (M. Ḳ. 20a; Sem. xii.), he died at Ginzaḳ (Gazaca) in Media, far away from his family; and his son, Zadok II., learned of his death only after the lapse of three years.

2. Grandson of the preceding; flourished in the fourth tannaitic generation (second century). He is often met with in halakic controversies with the later disciples of Akiba (Kil. vii. 2; Kelim xxvi. 9; Miḳ. vi. 10). Like his grandfather, he spent many years in Babylonia, where Abba Arika's father studied under him (Suk. 44b; see AIBU, 1). Unlike his grandfather, in whose name no practical decisions are on record, he decided questions submitted to him (Suk. *l.c.*); and his own acts are cited as illustrations in ritualistic law (*ib.*; Tosef., Suk. ii. 2; Yer. Sanh. vii. 24h; the illustration of the Tosefta is anachronistically ascribed to the elder Eliezer b. Zadok).

BIBLIOGRAPHY: Bacher, *Ag. Tan.* i. 50–55; Brüll. *Mebo ha-Mishnah*, i. 91–93; Frankel, *Darke ha-Mishnah*, pp. 97–99, 178; Heilprin, *Seder ha-Dorot*, ed. Maskileison, ii. 59a, 68b; Weiss, *Dor*, ii. 121; Zacuto, *Yuḥasin*, ed. Filipowski, pp. 26a, 58a.

S. S. S. M.

ELISHA BEN ABUYAH (called also by the Rabbis **Aḥer,** "the other"): Born in Jerusalem before 70; flourished in Palestine at the end of the first century and the beginning of the second. At one time the Rabbis were proud to recognize him as of their number; but later their opposition to him grew so intense that they even refrained from pronouncing his name, and referred to him in terms used to designate some vile object ("dabar aḥer," lit. "another thing"). For this reason it is almost impossible to derive from rabbinical sources a clear picture of his personality, and modern historians have differed greatly in their estimate of him. According to Grätz, he was a Karpotian Gnostic; according to Siegfried, a follower of Philo; according to Dubsch, a Christian; according to Smolenskin and Weiss, a victim of the inquisitor Akiba.

Of Elisha's youth and of his activity as a teacher of the Law very little is known. He was the son of an esteemed and rich citizen of Jerusalem, and was trained for the career of a scholar. His praise of this method of education is the only saying that the Mishnah has found worth perpetuating. According to Abot iv. 25, his favorite saying was, "Learning in youth is like writing upon new paper, but learning in old age is like writing upon paper which has already been used." Elisha was a student of Greek; as the Talmud expresses it, "Aḥer's tongue was never tired of singing Greek songs" (Yer. Meg. i. 9), which, according to some, caused his apostasy (Ḥag. 16b, below). Bacher has very properly remarked that the similes which Elisha is reported to have used (Ab. R. N. xxiv.) show that he was a man of the world, acquainted with wine, horses, and architecture. He must have acquired a reputation as an authority in questions of religious practise, since in Mo'ed Ḳaṭan 20a one of his halakic decisions is recorded—the only one in his name, though there may be others under the names of different teachers. The Babylonian Talmud asserts that Elisha, while a teacher in the bet ha-midrash, kept forbidden books ("sifre minim") hidden in his clothes. This statement is not found in the Jerusalem Talmud, and if at all historical, may possibly mean that he also studied the writings of the Sadducees, who, owing to changes made by the censors, are sometimes called "minim."

The oldest and most striking reference to the views of Elisha is found in the following baraita (Ḥag. 14b; Yer. ii. 1):

"Four [sages] entered paradise—Ben 'Azzai, Ben Zoma, Aḥer, and Akiba. Ben 'Azzai looked and died; Ben Zoma went mad; Aḥer destroyed the plants; Akiba alone came out unhurt."

There can be no doubt that the journey of the "four" to paradise, like the ascension of Enoch (in the pre-Christian books of Enoch) and of so many other pious men, is to be taken literally and not allegorically. This conception of the baraita is supported by the use of the phrase נכנס לפרדס ("entered paradise"), since נכנס לג"ע ("entered the Garden of Eden"= paradise) was a common expression (Derek Ereẓ Zuṭa i.; Ab. R. N. xxv.). It means that Elisha, like Paul, in a moment of ecstasy beheld the interior of heaven—in the former's case, however, with the effect that he destroyed the plants of the heavenly garden.

The Talmud gives two different interpretations of this last phrase. The Babylonian Talmud says:

"What is the meaning of 'Aḥer destroyed the plants'? Scripture refers to him (Eccl. v. 5 [A. V. 6]) when it says: 'Suffer not thy mouth to cause thy flesh to sin.' What does this signify? In heaven Aḥer saw Meṭaṭron seated while he wrote down the merits of Israel. Whereupon Aḥer said: 'We have been taught to believe that no one sits in heaven, ... or are there perhaps two supreme powers?' Then a heavenly voice was heard: 'Turn, O backsliding children (Jer. iii. 14), with the exception of Aḥer.'"

The dualism with which the Talmud charges him has led some scholars to see here Persian, Gnostic, or even Philonian dualism. They forget that the reference here to Meṭaṭron—a specifically Babylonian idea, which would probably be unknown to Palestinian rabbis even five hundred years after Elisha—robs the passage of all historical worth. The story is of late origin, as is seen from the introductory words, which stand in no connection with the context, as they do in the parallel passage in the Jerusalem Talmud. This latter makes no mention of Elisha's dualism; but it relates that in the critical period following the rebellion of Bar Kokba, Elisha visited the schools and attempted to entice the students from the study of the Torah, in order to direct their energies to some more practical occupation; and it is to him, therefore, that the verse "Suffer not thy mouth to cause thy flesh to sin" (Eccl. v. 5) is to be applied. In connection with this the Biblical quotation is quite intelligible, as according to another haggadah (Shab. 34b; Eccl. R. v. 5) "flesh" here means children—spiritual children, pupils—whom Elisha killed with his mouth by luring them from the study of the Torah. The Babylonia amoraim must have known this story, from which they took the concluding part and attached it to another legend. The Jerusalem Talmud is also the authority for the statement that Elisha played the part of an informer during the Hadrianic persecutions, when the Jews were ordered to violate the laws of the Torah. As evidence of this it is related that when the Jews were ordered to do work on the Sabbath, they tried to perform it in a way which could be considered as not profaning the Sabbath. But Elisha betrayed the Pharisees to the Roman authorities. Thus it is probable that the antipathy of Elisha was not directed against Judaism in general, but only against Pharisaism. The reason given for his apostasy is also characteristic. He saw how one man had lost his life while fulfilling a law for the observance of which the Torah promised a long life (Deut. xxii. 7), whereas another man who broke the same law was not hurt in the least. This practical demonstration, as well as the frightful sufferings of the martyrs during the Hadrianic persecutions, strengthened his conviction that there was no reward for virtue in this life or the next. These statements of the Jerusalem Talmud are no doubt based on reliable tradition, as they are also confirmed by the Babylonian Talmud (Ḳid. 39b). Bearing in mind what is said about Elisha, there can be little doubt that he was a Sadducee.

The harsh treatment he received from the Pharisees was due to his having deserted their ranks at such a critical time. Quite in harmony with this supposition are the other sins laid to his charge; namely, that he rode in an ostentatious manner through the streets of Jerusalem on a Day of Atonement which fell upon a Sabbath, and that he was bold enough to overstep the "teḥum" (the limits of the Sabbath-day journey). Both the Jerusalem and the Babylonian Talmuds agree here, and cite this as proof that Elisha turned from Pharisaism to heresy. It was just such non-observance of customs that excited the anger of Akiba (Soṭah 27b). The mention of the "Holy of Holies" in this passage is not an anachronism, as Grätz thinks. For while it is true that Eliezer and Joshua were present as *the* geonim par excellence at Elisha's circumcision—which must, therefore, have occurred after the death of Johanan ben Zakkai (80 C.E.)—it is also true that the "Holy of Holies" is likewise mentioned in connection with Rabbi Akiba (Mak., end); indeed, the use of this expression is due to the fact that the Rabbis held holiness to be inherent in the place, not in the building (Yeb. 6b).

The same passage from the Jerusalem Talmud refers to Elisha as being alive when his pupil R. Meïr had become a renowned teacher. According to the assumption made above, he must have reached his seventieth year at that time. If Elisha were a Sadducee, the friendship constantly shown him by R. Meïr could be understood. This friendship would have been impossible had Elisha been an apostate or a man of loose morals, as has been asserted. Sadducees and Pharisees, however, lived in friendly intercourse with one another (for example, Rabban Gamaliel with Sadducees; 'Er. 77b). For legends concerning Elisha see JOHANAN BEN NAPPAḤA.

BIBLIOGRAPHY: Grätz, *Gnosticismus und Judenthum*, pp. 56–71; P. Smolenski, *Sämmtliche Werke*, ii. 267–278; A. Jellinek, *Elischa b. Abuja*. Leipsic, 1847: I. H. Weiss, *Dor*, ii. 140–143; M. Dubsch, in *He-Ḥaluẓ*, v. 66–72; Siegfried, *Philo von Alexandrien*, pp. 285–287; Bacher, *Ag. Tan.* i. 432–436; Hoffmann, *Toledot Elischa b. Abuja*, Vienna, 1880; S. Rubin, *Yalk.*, *Shelomoh*, pp. 17–28, Cracow, 1896; M. Friedländer, *Vorchristlich. Jüd. Gnosticismus*, 1898, pp. 100 *et seq.*; Bäck, *Elischa b. Abuja-Acher*, Frankfort-on-the-Main, 1891. Compare also M. Letteris' Hebrew drama *Ben Abuja*, an adaptation of Goethe's *Faust*, Vienna, 1865; B. Kaplan, in *Open Court*, Aug., 1902.

L. G.

'ENA, RAB: Babylonian scholar of the third amoraic generation (third century); contemporary of Rab Judah b. Ezekiel. The two were known as "sabe de Pumbedita" (elders of Pumbedita, Sanh. 17b; 'Er. 79B *et seq.*).

'Ena once pronounced at the house of the exilarch a halakic discourse which greatly displeased his younger contemporary Rabbah, and the latter declared his statement to be astounding and himself to deserve degradation by the removal of his "meturgeman" (Ḥul. 84b; see Rashi *ad loc.*).

Rab Naḥman, however, had a better opinion of 'Ena's learning. Twice 'Ena opposed Naḥman's views (Pes. 88a; Meg. 14b); and both times Naḥman, familiarly addressing him as "'Ena Saba" (Old 'Ena) or, according to some versions, "'Anya Saba" (= "Poor Old Man"; a play on his name, "'Ena"), points out that 'Ena's views as well as his own are right, their respective applications depending on circumstances. Both times he prefaces this with the remark, "From me and from thee will the tradition bear its name."

S. S. S. M.

G

GAMALIEL: Name which occurs in the Bible only as a designation of the prince of the tribe of Manasseh (Num. i. 10; ii. 20; vii. 54, 59; x. 23). In post-Biblical times the name occurs with special frequency in the family of Hillel. In a story in connection with a proselyte made to Judaism by Hillel, and which is supported by reliable tradition, it is said that the proselyte had two sous born to him after his conversion, whom he named in gratitude "Hillel" and "Gamaliel" (Ab. R. N. xv. [ed. Schechter, p. 62]; Midr. ha-Gadol, ed. Schechter, to Ex. xxviii.; see note *ad loc.*). Perhaps Hillel's father was called "Gamaliel," in which case the usual custom would have required the giving of this name to Hillel's first-born son. Besides the six patriarchs of the name of Gamaliel, tradition knows of others of the same name who lived in Palestine in the third and fourth centuries, and who are reckoned among the Palestinian amoraim.

Bibliography: Frankel, *Mebo Yerushalmi*, pp. 71a–72b.

S. S. W. B.

GAMALIEL I.: Son of Simon and grandson of Hillel; according to a tannaitic tradition (Shab. 15a), he was their successor as nasi and first president of the Great Sanhedrin of Jerusalem. Although the reliability of this tradition, especially as regards the title of "nasi," has been justly disputed, it is nevertheless a fact beyond all doubt that in the second third of the first century Gamaliel (of whose father, Simon, nothing beyond his name is known) occupied a leading position in the highest court, the great council of Jerusalem, and that, as a member of that court, he received the cognomen "Ha-Zaḳen." Like his grandfather, Hillel, he was the originator of many legal ordinances with a view to the "tiḳḳun ha-'olam" (= "improvement of the world": Giṭ. iv. 1–3; comp. also Yeb. xvi. 7; R. H. ii. 5). Gamaliel appears as the head of the legal-religious body in the three epistles which he at one time dictated to the secretary Johanan (account of Judah b. 'Illai: Tosef., Sanh. ii. 6; Sanh. 11b; Yer. Sanh. 18d; Yer. Ma'as. Sh. 56c). Two of these letters went to the inhabitants of Galilee and of the Darom (southern Palestine), and had reference to the tithes; the third letter was written for the Jews of the Diaspora, and gave notice of an intercalary month which Gamaliel and his colleagues had decided upon. That part of the Temple territory—a "stairway of the Temple mount"—where Gamaliel dictated these letters is also the place where he once ordered the removal of a Targum to Job—the oldest written Targum of which anything is known (report of an eye-witness to Gamaliel II., grandson of Gamaliel I.: Tosef., Shab. xiii. 2; Shab. 115a; Yer. Shab. 15a).

Gamaliel appears also as a prominent member of the Sanhedrin in the account given in Acts (v. 34 *et seq.*), where he is called a "Pharisee" and a "doctor of the law" much honored by the people. He is there made to speak in favor of the disciples of Jesus, who were threatened with death (v. 38–39): "For if this counsel or this work be of men, it will come to naught: but if it be of God, ye can not overthrow it." He is also shown to be a legal-religious authority by the two anecdotes (Pes. 88b) in which "the king and the queen" (Agrippa I. and his wife Kypris; according to Büchler, "Das Synhedrion in Jerusalem," p. 129, Agrippa II. and his sister

Berenice) go to him with questions about the ritual. Tradition does not represent Gamaliel as learned in the Scriptures, nor as a teacher, because the school of Hillel, whose head he undoubtedly was, always appears collectively in its controversies with the school of Shammai, and the individual scholars and their opinions are not mentioned. Hence Gamaliel is omitted in the chain of tradition as given in the Mishnah (Abot i., ii.), while Johanan b. Zakkai is mentioned as the next one who continued the tradition after Hillel and Shammai. Gamaliel's name is seldom mentioned in halakic tradition. The tradition that illustrates the importance of Johanan b. Zakkai with the words, "When he died the glory of wisdom [scholarship] ceased," characterizes also the importance of Gamaliel I. by saying: "When he died the honor [outward respect] of the Torah ceased, and purity and piety became extinct" (Soṭah xv. 18).

Gamaliel, as it appears, did most toward establishing the honor in which the house of Hillel was held, arid which secured to it a preeminent position within Palestinian Judaism soon after the destruction of the Temple. The title "Rabban," which, in the learned hierarchy until post-Hadrianic times, was borne only by presidents of the highest religious council, was first prefixed to the name of Gamaliel. That Gamaliel ever taught in public is known, curiously enough, only from the Acts of the Apostles, where (xxii. 3) the apostle Paul prides himself on having sat at the feet of Gamaliel. That the latter paid especial attention to study is shown by the remarkable classification of pupils ascribed to him, for which a classification of the fish of Palestine formed a basis (Ab. R. N. xl.). In this arrangement Gamaliel enumerates the following kinds of pupils: (1) a son of poor parents who has learned everything by study, but who has no understanding; (2) a son of rich parents who has learned everything and who possesses understanding; (3) a pupil who has learned everything, but does not know how to reply; (4) a pupil who has learned everything and knows also how to reply. These correspond to the following varieties of fishes: (1) an unclean, *i.e.* ritually uneatable fish; (2) a clean fish; (3) a fish from the Jordan; (4) a fish from the great ocean (Mediterranean).

Besides this dictum of Gamaliel's, which is no longer wholly intelligible, only that saying has been preserved which is related in the Mishnah Abot (i, 16) under the name of Gamaliel; for, in spite of Hoffmann's objections ("Die Erste Mischna," p. 26), it is probably right to hold with Geiger ("Nachgelassene Schriften," iv. 308) that Gamaliel I. is intended. The saying is in three parts, and the first clause repeats what Joshua b. Perahyah had said long before (Abot i, 5): "Secure a teacher for thyself." The other two parts agree very well with the impression which the above-mentioned testimonial gives of Gamaliel as a thoroughly conscientious "Pharisee": "Hold thyself [in religious questions] far from doubt, and do not often give a tithe according to general valuation." Tradition probably contains many sayings of Gamaliel I. which are erroneously ascribed to his grandson of the same name. Besides his son, who inherited his father's distinction and position, and who was one of the leaders in the uprising against Rome, a daughter of Gamaliel is also mentioned, whose daughter he married to the priest Simon b. Nathanael (Tosef., 'Ab. Zarah, iii. 10).

As a consequence of being mentioned in the New Testament, Gamaliel has become a subject of Christian legends (Schürer, "Geschichte," ii. 365, note 47). A German monk of the twelfth century calls the Talmud a "commentary of Gamaliel's on the Old Testament." Gamaliel is here plainly the representative of the old Jewish scribes (Bacher, " Die Jüdische Bibelexegese," in Winter and Wünsche, "Jüdische Literatur," ii. 294). Even Galen was identified with the Gamaliel living at the time of the Second Temple (Steinschneider, "Hebr. Uebers." p. 401). This may be due to the fact that the last patriarch by the name of Gamaliel was also known as a physician (see Gamaliel VI.).

BIBLIOGRAPHY: Frankel. *Darke ha-Mishnah*, p. 52; Weiss, Dor; Grätz, *Gesch.* 3d ed., iii. 373 *et seq.*; Derenbourg, *Hist.* pp. 239 *et seq.*; Schürer, *Gesch.* 2d ed., ii. 364; Bücbler, Das *Synhedrion in Jerusalem*, pp. 115–131.

S. S. W. B.

GAMALIEL II. (called also **Gamaliel of Jabneh,** to distinguish him from his grandfather, Gamaliel I.): The recognized head of the Jews in Palestine during the last two decades of the first and at the beginning of the second century. He continued with great energy and success the work of restoration begun by Johanan b. Zakkai. The tradition of the meeting between Johanan and Vespasian (Giṭ. 56b) relates that the former obtained the pardon of Gamaliel's family from the Roman emperor; and this part of the story may rest on a historical basis. Johanan probably retired from his position as president of the learned assembly at Jabneh, which took the place of the Sanhedrin at Jerusalem; and the office was given to Gamaliel, under whose leadership even those pupils of Johanan who excelled Gamaliel in scholarship willingly placed themselves. One of the greatest of these pupils, Eliezer b. Hyrcanus, married Gamaliel's sister, Imma Shalom (Shab. 116a; B. M. 59b). Perhaps it was Gamaliel II. to whom the title of "nasi" (prince; later replaced by "patriarch") was first given to raise him in public estimation and to revive the Biblical designation for the head of the nation. This title later became hereditary with his descendants. Gamaliel was officially recognized by the Roman authorities; and he journeyed to Syria for the purpose of being confirmed in office by the governor (*ἡγεμών*; 'Eduy. vii. 7; Sanh. 11b).

The guiding principle in all of Gamaliel's actions is set forth in the words which he spoke on the occasion of his quarrel with Eliezer

b. Hyrcanus (B. M. 59b): "Lord of the world, it is manifest and known to Thee that I have not done it for my own honor nor for that of my house, but for Thy honor, that factions may not increase in Israel." The ends which Gamaliel had in view were the abolition of old dissensions, the prevention of new quarrels, and the restoration of unity within Judaism. To attain these objects he consistently labored to strengthen the authority of the assembly at Jabneh as well as his own, and thus brought upon himself the suspicion of seeking his own glory. His greatest achievement was the termination of the opposition between the schools of Hillel and Shammai, which had survived even the destruction of the Temple. In Jabneh, says tradition (Yer. Ber. 3b; 'Er. 13b), a voice from heaven ("bat ḳol") was heard, which declared that, although the views of both schools were justifiable in principle (as "words of the living God "), in practise only the views of Hillel's school should be authoritative.

Gamaliel took care that the decisions reached by the assembly under his presidency should be recognized by all; and he used the instrument of the ban relentlessly against obstinate opposers of these decisions. He even placed his own brother-in-law, Eliezer b. Hyrcanus, under the ban (B. M. 59b). Gamaliel forced Joshua b. Hananiah, another famous pupil of Johanan b. Zakkai, to recognize the authority of the president in a most humiliating way, namely, by compelling Joshua to appear before him in traveler's garb on the day which, according to Joshua's reckoning, should have been the Day of Atonement, because Gamaliel would suffer no contradiction of his own declaration concerning the new moon (R. H. ii. 25a, b). Gamaliel, however, showed that with him it was only a question of principle, and that he had no intention of humiliating Joshua; for, rising and kissing him on the head, he greeted him with the words: "Welcome, my master and my pupil: my master in learning; my pupil in that thou submittest to my will." A story which is characteristic of Gamaliel's modesty is told of a feast at which, standing, he served his guests himself (Sifre to Deut. 38; Ḳid. 32b). But he manifested the excellence of his character most plainly upon the day on which he harshly attacked Joshua b. Hananiah, in consequence of a new dispute between them, and thereby so aroused the displeasure of the assembly that he was deprived of his position. Instead of retiring in anger, he continued to take part, as a member of the assembly, in the deliberations conducted by the new president, Eleazar b. Azariah. He was soon reinstated in office, however, after asking pardon of Joshua, who himself brought about Gamaliel's restoration in the form of a joint presidency, in which Gamaliel and Eleazar shared the honors (Ber. 27b–28a; Yer. Ber. 7c, d).

The most important outward event in Gamaliel's life that now followed was the journey to Rome, which he undertook in company with his colleague Eleazar and the two leading members of the assembly in Jabneh, Joshua b. Hananiah and Akiba. This journey was probably made toward the end of Domitian's reign (95), and had for its object the prevention of a danger which threatened on the part of the cruel emperor (Grätz, "Geschichte," 3d ed., iv. 109). This journey, together with the stay of the scholars in Rome, left many traces in both halakic and haggadic tradition (see Bacher, "Ag. Tan." i. 84). Especially interesting are the accounts of the debates which the scholars held with unbelievers in Rome, and in which Gamaliel was the chief speaker in behalf of Judaism (*ib.* p. 85). Elsewhere also Gamaliel had frequent opportunities to answer in controversial conversations the questions of unbelievers and to explain and defend the teachings of the Jewish religion (*ib.* p. 76). At times Gamaliel had to meet the attacks of confessors of Christianity; one of these was the "min," or philosopher, who maliciously concluded from Hosea v. 6 that God had completely forsaken Israel (Yeb. 102b; Midr. Teh. to Ps. x., end; most completely reproduced from the old source in Midr. ha-Gadol to Lev. *xxvi.* 9, in Bacher, "Ag. Tan." 2d ed., i. 83). There is a satirical point in a story in which Gamaliel with his sister brings a fictitious suit concerning an inheritance before a Christian judge and convicts him of having accepted bribes; whereupon Gamaliel quotes Jesus' words in Matt. v. 17 (Shab. 116a, b). The sect of believers in Jesus, which was ever separating itself more distinctly from all connection with Judaism, and which with other heretics was classed under the name of "minim," led Gamaliel, because of its tendencies dangerous to the unity of Judaism, to introduce a new form of prayer, which he requested Samuel ha-Ḳaton to compose, and which was inserted in the chief daily prayer, the eighteen benedictions (Ber. 28b; Meg. 17b). This prayer itself, which together with the Shema' forms the most important part of the Jewish prayer-book, likewise owes its final revision to Gamaliel (*ib.*). It was Gamaliel, also, who made the recitation of the "eighteen prayers" a duty to be performed three times a day by every Israelite (see "Monatsschrift," xlvi. 430).

Still another liturgical institution goes back to Gamaliel—that of the memorial celebration which takes the place of the sacrifice of the Passover lamb on the first evening of Passover. Gamaliel instituted this celebration (Pes. x. 5), which may be regarded as the central feature of the Pesaḥ Haggadah, on an occasion when he spent the first Passover night with other scholars at Lydda in conversing about the feast and its customs (Tosef., Pes. x. 112). The memory of the lost sanctuary, which the celebration of the Passover evening also served to perpetuate, was especially vivid in Gamaliel's heart. Gamaliel and his companions wept over the destruction of Jerusalem and of the Temple when they heard the noise of the great city of Rome, and at another time when they stood on the Temple ruins (Sifre, Deut. 43; Mak., end; Lam. R. v. 18).

Gamaliel's appreciation of the virtue of mercy is well illustrated by a saying of his in allusion to Deut. xiii. 18: "Let this be a token unto thee! So long as thou thyself art compassionate God will show thee mercy; but if thou hast no compassion, God will show thee no mercy" (Tosef., B. Ḳ. ix. 30; Yer. B. K. *l.c.*; comp. Shab. 151a). Gamaliel was touchingly attached to his slave Ṭabi (Suk. ii. 1), at whose death he accepted condolences as for a departed member of the family (Ber. ii. 7).

In his intercourse with non-Jews Gamaliel was unconstrained, for which he was sometimes blamed. A friendly conversation is recorded ('Er. 64b) which he had with a heathen on the way from Acre to Ecdippa (Achzib). On the Sabbath he sat upon the benches of heathen merchants (Tosef., M. Ḳ. ii. 8). Various details have been handed down by tradition concerning the religious practises of Gamaliel and his house (see the following Tosefta passages: Dem. iii. 15; Shab. i. 22, xii. [xiii.], end; Yom-Ṭob i. 22; ii. 10, 13, 14, 16). In Gamaliel's house it was not customary to say "Marpe'!" (Recovery) when any one sneezed, because that was a heathenish superstition (Tosef., Shab. vii. [viii.] 5; comp. Ber, 53a). Two concessions were made to Gamaliel' s household in the way of relaxing the severity of the rules set up as a barrier against heathendom: permission to use a mirror in cutting the hair of the head (Tosef., 'Ab. Zarah, iii. 5; comp. Yer. 'Ab. Zarah 41a), and to learn Greek (Tosef., Sotah, xv. 8; Soṭah, end). In regard to the latter, Gamaliel's son Simon relates (Sotah 49b) that many children were instructed in his father's house in "Greek wisdom."

Aside from his official position, Gamaliel stood in learning on an equal footing with the legal teachers of his time. Many of his halakic doctrinal opinions have been handed down. Sometimes the united opinion of Gamaliel and Eliezer b. Hyrearms is opposed to that of Joshua b. Hananiah (Ket. i. 6–9), and sometimes Gamaliel holds a middle position between the stricter opinion of the one and the more lenient view of the other (Sheb. ix. 8; Ter. viii. 8). Gamaliel assented to certain principles of civil law which have been transmitted in the name of Admon, a former judge in Jerusalem, and which became especially well known and were authoritative for ensuing periods (Ket. xiv. 3–5). Many of Gamaliel's decisions in religious law are connected with his stay in some place in the Holy Land. In Ecdippa the archisynagogue Scipio (שגביון) asked him a question which he answered by letter after his return home (Tosef., Ter. ii. 13). There are also records of Gamaliel's stay in Kafr 'Uthnai (Git. i. 5; Tosef., Git. i.4), in Emmaus (Hul. 91b), in Lydda (Tosef., Pes. ii. 10, x., end), in Jericho (Tosef., Ber. iv. 15), in Samaria (Tosef., Dem. v. 24), and in Tiberias (Tosef., Shab. xiii. 2).

In the field of the Haggadah should be especially mentioned the questions relating to biblical exegesis which Gamaliel liked to discuss in a circle of scholars, as had also his predecessor, Johanan b. Zakkai. There are records of four such discussions (on Prov. xiv. 34, see B. B. 10b; on Gen. xl. 10, see Ḥul. 92a; on Gen. xlix. 4, see Shab. 55b; on Esth. v. 4, see Meg. 12b), which all end with Gamaliel's expressed desire to hear the opinion of the eminent haggadist Eleazar of Modi'im. A part of Gamaliel's textual exegesis is found in the controversial conversations mentioned above. He portrays the distress and corruption of the times in a remarkable speech which concludes with an evident reference to the emperor Domitian. He says:

"Since lying judges have the upper hand, lying witnesses also gain ground; since evil-doers have increased, the seekers of revenge are also increasing; since shamelessness has augmented, men have lost their dignity: since the small says to the great, 'I am greater than thou,' the years of men are shortened; since the beloved children have angered their Father in heaven, He has placed a ruthless king over them [with reference to Job xxxiv. 20]. Such a king was Ahasuerus, who first killed his wife for the sake of his friend, and then his friend for the sake of his wife" (Introduction to Midr. Abba Gorion, beginning; Esther R., beginning).

Gamaliel uses striking comparisons in extolling the value of handiwork and labor (Tosef., Ḳid. i. 11), and in expressing his opinion on the proper training of the mind (Ab. R. N. xxviii.). The lament over his favorite pupil, Samuel ha-Ḳaṭon, which he made in common with Eleazar b. Azariah, is very touching: "It is fitting to weep for him; it is fitting to lament for him. Kings die and leave their crowns to their sons; the rich die and leave their wealth to their sons; but Samuel ha-Ḳaṭon has taken with him the most precious thing in the world—his wisdom—and is departed" (Sem. 8).

The Roman yoke borne by the Jewish people of Palestine weighed heavily upon Gamaliel. In one speech (Ab. R. N. *l.c.*) he portrays the tyranny of Rome that devours the property of its subjects. He reflects on the coming of the Messiah, and describes the period which shall precede His appearance as one of the deepest moral degradation and direst distress (Derek Ereẓ Zuṭa x.). But he preaches also of the fruitfulness and blessing which shall at some time distinguish the land of Israel (Shab. 30b). Gamaliel probably lived to see the beginning of the great movement among the Jews in Palestine and in other lands, under the emperors Trajan and Hadrian, which led to a final attempt under Bar Kokba to throw off the Roman yoke. Gamaliel's death, however, occurred in a time of peace. The pious proselyte Aquila honored his obsequies by burning valuables to the extent of seventy minæ, accordiag to an old custom observed at the burial of kings (Tosef., Shab. vii. [viii.] 18; 'Ab. Zarah 11a); and Eliezer b. Hyrcanus and Joshua b. Hananiah, the aged teachers of the Law, arranged the ceremonies for his funeral (M. Ḳ. 27a; Yer. M. Ḳ. 82a). Gamaliel insured the perpetuation of his memory by his order to be buried in simple linen garments, for the example which he thus set put an end to the heavy burial expenses which had come to be almost unbearable; and it subsequently became the custom to devote to the memory of Gamaliel one of the goblets of wine drunk in the house of mourning (Ket. 8b).

Of Gamaliel's children, one daughter is known, who answered in a very intelligent fashion two questions addressed to her father by an unbeliever (Sanh. 34a, 90b). Two of Gamaliel's sons are mentioned as returning from a certain feast (Ber. i. 2). Of these, Simon was called long after the death of Gamaliel to occupy his father's position, which became hereditary in his house. It can not be regarded as proved that the tanna Ḥaninah ben Gamaliel was a son of Gamaliel II. (Büchler, "Die Priester und der Cultus," p. 14); this is more likely to be true of Judah ben Gamaliel, who reports a decision in the name of Ḥaninah ben Gamaliel (Tosef., 'Ab. Zarah, iv. [v.] 12; 'Ab. Zarah 39b).

BIBLIOGRAPHY: Frankel, *Darke na-Mishnah*, pp. 69 *et seq.*; Weiss, *Dor*, ii. 71; Grätz, *Gesch.* 3d ed., iii., *passim*; Derenbourg, *Hist.* pp. 306–313, 314–346; Bacher, *Ag. Tan.* i. 78–100; Schürer, *Gesch.* 3d ed., ii. 369; Landau, in *Monatsschrift*, i. 283 *et seq.*, 323; Scheinin, *Die Hochschule zu Jamnia*, 1878.

S. S. W. B.

GAMALIEL III.: Son of Judah I., who before his death appointed him his successor as nasi (Ket. 103a). Scarcely anything has been handed down concerning his deeds or concerning the whole period of his activity (within the first third of the third century). The revision of the Mishnah, begun by his father, was without doubt concluded under him. Three sayings of Gamaliel III. are incorporated in the Mishnah (Abot ii. 2–4). The first deals with the study of the Torah and with devoting oneself to the general welfare, of the public. The second warns against the selfishness of the Roman rulers: "Beware of the government, because rulers attach a man to themselves for their own interests; they seem to be friends when it is to their advantage, but they abandon him when he is in need." The third saying recommends submission to the will of God: "Make His will thy will, so that He may make thy will like His own; make thy will of no account beside His, so that He may make the will of others of no account before thine." The Tosefta contains but one saying of Gamaliel (Soṭah vi. 8), a paraphrase of Num. xi. 22, in which Moses complains of the unreasonableness of the people's wishes; a baraita (Men. 84b) contains a halakic exegesis of Gamaliel. Hoshaiah asks Gamaliel' s son, Judah II., concerning a halakic opinion of his father's (Yer. Ber. 60d). Johanan tells of a question which Gamaliel III. answered for him (Hul. 106a). Samuel, the Babylonian amora, tells of differences of opinion between Gamaliel and other scholars (Niddah 63b; B. B. 139b; Yer. B. B. 10d).

BIBLIOGRAPHY: Grätz, *Gesch.* 3d ed., iv. 211; Weiss, *Dor*, iii. 42; Halevy, *Dorot ha-Rishorum*, ii. 20 *et seq.*; Bacher, *Ag. Tan.* ii. 554.

S. S. W. B.

GAMALIEL IV.: Son and successor of the patriarch Judah II., and father of the patriarch Judah III. The period of activity of these patriarchs can not be determined. Grätz puts Gamaliel IV. in the last third of the third century. According to Halevy, he was a contemporary of Hoshaiah, of whom it is related that he prevented Gamaliel from introducing into Syria an ordinance referring to tithing the fruits of the field (Yer. Ḥal. 60a). In the Jerusalem Talmud ('Ab. Zarah 39b) is mentioned a question of religious law addressed to Gamaliel by Abbahu. In answering it the teacher describes himself as an unimportant person and of little learning ("adam ḳaṭon") in comparison with Abbahu.

BIBLIOGRAPHY: Grätz, *Gesch.* 3d ed., iv. 449; Halevy, *Dorot ha-Rishonim*, ii. 257.

S. S. W. B.

GAMALIEL V.: Son and successor of the patriarch Hillel II.; celebrated in connection with the perfecting of the Jewish calendar in 359. From geonic sources ("Seder Tanna'im we-Amora'im") only his name and those of his two successors are known. But in a letter written in 393, Jerome mentions that the emperor Theodosius I. (379–395) had condemned to death the former consul Esychius, for obtaining, by fraud important papers belonging to the patriarch Gamaliel, who was much incensed against the culprit.

BIBLIOGRAPHY: Grätz, *Gesch.* 3d ed., iv. 356, 450.

S. S. W. B.

GAMALIEL VI.: The last patriarch. The decree of the emperors Honorius and Theodosius II. (Oct. 17, 415) contains interesting data concerning him. By this decree the patriarch was deprived of all the higher honors which had been given him, as well as of the patriarchate, because he had permitted himself to disregard the exceptional laws against the Jews, had built new synagogues, and had adjudged disputes between Jews and Christians. With his death the patriarchal office ceased, and an imperial decree (426) diverted the patriarchs' tax ("post excessum patriarchorum") into the imperial treasury. Gamaliel VI. appears to have been a physician. Marcellus, a medical writer of the fifth century, mentions a remedy for disease of the spleen which had been discovered not long before by "Gamalielus Patriarcha."

BIBLIOGRAPHY: Grätz, *Gesch.* 3d ed., iv. 360, 450.

S. S. W. B.

GARMU, BET: A family of skilled bakers employed in the Temple at Jerusalem as bakers of the show bread (Ex. xxv. 30). They kept secret their method of baking. Fearing the family might die out and the secret perish with them, the chiefs of the Temple replaced them with experts from Alexandria, but these could not compete with the Garmuites. The sages therefore summoned the latter back to their office; they, however, would not return until their original salary had been doubled, and for this they were ever after censured. When asked why they would not reveal the secrets of their art, they replied, "Our forebears communicated to us their premonition that the Temple would eventually be destroyed; should we instruct others in our art, it might come to pass that our pupils would exercise the art in the service of some idolatrous temple." The Garmuites are often mentioned with reverence as models of scrupulous honesty (Yoma iii. 11, 38a; Tosef., Yoma, ii. 5, and parallels).

E. C. S. M.

GEBINI (from Lat. "Gabinius"): Officer of the Second Temple, whose duty was at certain times of each day to announce the rite to be performed, and to remind the appointees of their respective parts in the performance of that rite. Thus he would cry out: "Priests, attend to the sacrifice; Levites, attune the hymn; Israelites, take your places" (Sheḳ. v. 1; Yer. Sheḳ. v. 48c). Gebini's voice is said to have been once heard by Agrippa at a distance of eight miles, whereupon the king richly rewarded him (Sheḳ. *l.c.*). Elsewhere it is said that his proclamations in the Temple were often heard at Jericho, a distance of ten miles (Tamid iii. 8; Yoma 20b; Yer. Suk. v. 55b, incorrectly גבי). It is believed that "Gebini" became an eponym for all successors in the office of Temple crier (see commentaries to Sheḳ. *l.c.*).

S. S. S. M.

H

HAGGAI: Judean prophet of the early post-exilic period; contemporary with Zechariah (Ezra v. 1; III Ezra [I Esd.] vi. 1, vii. 3).

חגי = "Aggeus" in I Esd.; "Aggæus," 'Αγγαῖος = "festal" (born on feast-day) or "feast of Yah" (Olshausen, "Grammatik," § 277b); Wellhausen, in Bleek, "Einleitung," 4th ed., p. 434, takes "Haggai" to be equivalent to "Hagariah" C = "God girdeth"). The name is found on Semitic inscriptions—Phenician, Palmyrene, Aramaic, Hebrew; comp. "C. I. S." lxviii. 1 and Lidzbarski, "Handbuch der Nordsemitischen Epigraphik," p. 270, Weimar, 1898; it occurs as "Ḥagga" on a tablet from Nippur (Hilprecht, in " Pal. Explor. Fund Quarterly," Jan., 1898, p. 55).

Very little is known of Haggai's life. Ewald ("Propheten des Alten Bundes," p. 178, Göttingen, 1868) concludes from Hag. ii. 3 that he had seen the first Temple, in which case he would have been a very old man at the time of Darius Hystaspes, in the second year of whose reign (520 B.C.) Haggai appears as a prophetic preacher to stir the people to the work of rebuilding the Temple (Hag. i. 1 *et seq.*).

It is not certain that Haggai was ever in Babylonia. He may have lived continuously at Jerusalem (comp. Lam. ii. 9). At all events, to judge by the extent of his book, his public ministry was brief. That Zechariah was the leading prophet of those times (Zech. vii. 1–4) lends plausibility to the assumption that Haggai was nearing death when he made his appeal to the people. According to tradition he was born in Chaldea during the Captivity, and was among those that returned under Zerubbabel. It has even been claimed that he was an angel of YHWH, sent temporarily to earth to move the indifferent congregation (see Hag. i. 13). He was remembered as a singer of psalms, and as the first to use the term "Hallelujah." In fact, his name is mentioned in the Septuagint superscriptions to Psalms cxii., cxlv.–cxlix., though not in all manuscripts alike (Köhler, "Die Weissagungen Haggais," p. 32; Wright, "Zechariah and His Prophecies," xix. *et seq.*; B. Jacob, in Stade's "Zeitschrift," xvi. 290; Cheyne and Black, "Encyc. Bibl." ii. 1935, note 2, in reference to Epiphanius, "Vitæ Prophetarum"). By Jewish historiography Haggai is numbered among the "men of the Great Synagogue" (B. B. 15a), or among those that "transmitted revelation" from their prophetic predecessors to the "men of the Great Synagogue" (Ab. R. N. i. [recension A, p. 2, ed. Schechter]; comp. Yoma 9b). In his days prophetic inspiration was growing less frequent (*ib.*).

Haggai is credited with having instituted certain practical decisions (taḳḳanot"). Among these were a provision for the intercalation of the month of Adar (R. H. 19b); a decision in favor of enlarging the altar; a decision permitting the bringing of sacrifices independently of the existence or presence of the Temple (Mid. iii. 1; Zeb. 62; Yer. Naz. ii. 7). The organization of the priestly service into twenty-four relays (Tosef., Ta'an. ii.; 'Ar. 12b), and the regulation of the wood-contributions (Tosef., Ta'an. iii.; Ta'an. 28; comp. Neh. x. 35), are traced to him. Other references to Haggai's legislative influence are given in R. H. 9; Yeb. 16a; Ḳid. 43a; Ḥul. 137b; Bek. 57; Naz. 53a. The "seat " (מדוכה) on which he sat as legislator is mentioned (Yeb. 16a).

E. G. H.

ḤALAFTA: Name of several tannaim and amoraim; frequently interchanged with **Ḥaifa, Ḥalifa, Ḥilfa, Ḥilfai, Ilfa**, and **Taḥlifa**.

ḤALAFTA: Scholar of the first and second centuries (second tannai tic generation), always cited without patronymic or cognomen; his descent is traced back to Jonadab the Rechabite (Yer. Ta'an. iv. 68a; Gen. R. xcviii. 4). He was a senior contemporary of Gamaliel II. and Johanan b. Nuri (Tosef., Shab. xiii. [xiv.] 2; *ib.* Ma'as. Sh. i. 13), and conducted a rabbinic school at Sepphoris. Here he introduced some ritual reforms (Ta'an. ii. 5; R. H. 27a). Tradition relates that, together with Hananiah b. Teradion and Eleazar b. Mattai, he saw the monuments which Joshua had placed in the Jordan (see ELEAZAR B. MATTAI). Halafta seems to have attained an advanced age. He communicated to Gamaliel II. an order given by his grandfather Gamaliel I., and which he had himself heard in the last years of Judea's independence (Shab. 115a); he subsequently participated in the 'Aḳabia controversy (see "R. E. J." xli. 41), and later he is met with in the company of Eleazar b. Azariah, Ḥuẓpit the interpreter, Yeshebab, and Johanan b. Nuri, when they were old (Tosef., Kelim, B. B. ii. 2). But few halakot are preserved in his name, and most of these were transmitted by his more famous son, R. Jose (Kil. xxvi. 6; Tosef., Ma'as. Sh. i. 13; *ib.* B. B. ii. 10; *ib.* Oh. v. 8; Bek. 26a).

BIBLIOGRAPHY: Brüll, *Mebe ha-Mishnah*, i. 139; Frankel, *Darke ha-Mishnah*, p. 132; Heilprin, *Seder ha-Dorot*, ii.; Weiss, *Dor*, ii. 122; Zacuto, *Yuḥasin*, ed. Filipowski, p. 64.

E. C. S. M.

ḤALAFTA OF HUNA (HUGA, HEWAH, ḤEFA): Palestinian amora of the third century; senior of R. Johanan. The latter communicates to Ḥalafta's sons a halakah in their father's name (Giṭ. 86b; Yer. Giṭ. ix. 50b).

BIBLIOGRAPHY: Frankel, *Mebo*, 85a.

E. C. S. M.

ḤALAFTA (ḤILFAI) B. ḲARUYA, ABBA (also known as **ḤALFA**): 1. Tanna of the second century, contemporary of Gamaliel II. Gamaliel once visited him at Ḳaruya (Kiryava; see Neubauer, "G. T." p. 277), and solicited his prayers; whereupon Ḥalafta pronounced over him the blessing of Psalm xx. 5 (A.V. 4) (Midr. Teh. *ad loc.*). As "Ḥilfa" or "Ḥilfai" he is cited in connection with some halakot (Tosef., Ma'as. Sh. iv. 5; Yer. Ma'as. Sh. iv. 54d), and it appears that one of his halakot was taught and practised in Rome (*ib.*).

2. Palestinian amora of the third century, contemporary of Ḥiyya b. Abba (B. B. 123a). They both endeavored to reconcile the apparent discrepancy between the statement of Gen. xlvi. 27, "All the souls of the house of Jacob, which came into Egypt, were threescore and ten," and the list preceding it (8–26), which contains one less. Ḥiyya would have it that the person unnamed in the list was a twin sister of Dinah. This view Ḥalafta rejects, arguing that a twin sister might as well be

ascribed to Benjamin. Finally, Ḥiyya quotes Ḥama b. Ḥanina as authority for the assumption that Jochebed was born soon after Jacob and his party entered Egypt, and is. therefore reckoned among the souls that originally came with Jacob; with her the full count of seventy is completed (B. B. 123a; see also Gen. R. lxxxii. 8). Bacher ("Ag. Pal. Amor." ii. 177) locates the meeting of these rabbis in Rome. It is nowhere shown, however, that the younger Ḥalafta ever visited Rome, and the context from which Bacher draws the inference speaks of Ḥalafta the elder. As to the prænomen, it appears variously as "Ilfa," "Ḥilfai," "Ḥalifa," "Taḥlifa." Once it is altogether omitted, leaving only the title and cognomen (Gen. R. xix. 3; comp. Pesiḳ. Zuṭarta to Gen. iii. 1). It is probable that to Ḥalafta b. Ḳaruya belongs the remark headed with the curious name of R. Barḳirya. Seeing a procession of coffins containing the remains of people who had died in foreign lands, R. Barḳirya remarked to Eleazar: "What benefit can they derive from being buried here? To them I apply the words: 'Ye made mine heritage an abomination [since ye did not choose to live here],' and 'when ye entered, ye defiled my land [since ye entered as corpses]' " (Jer. ii. 7). Eleazar, however, told him that as soon as such processions reach Palestine, clods of Palestinian earth are laid on the coffins, and that that makes atonement, as the Bible says, "His earth will atone for His people" (Deut. xxxii. 43, Hebr.; Yer. Kil. ix. 32d; comp. Pesiḳ. R. i. 3; Tan., Wayeḥi, 6 [ed. Buber, p. 214], where "Ḳaẓrah" occurs in place of "Barḳirya"). The custom of sprinkling Palestinian earth on the dead is still common.

E. C. S. M.

ḤALAFTA OF KEFAR HANANIAH, R. or **ABBA:** Tanna of the second century; junior of R. Meïr, in whose name he transmits the legal maxim: When the condition is expressed before an obligation depending on it, the condition is valid; but when the obligation precedes the condition, the condition is void. From him the Mishnah (Ab. iii. 6) preserves an interesting homily on the number of persons constituting a quorum for the study of the Law. In the treatise Abot, usually incorporated in the Jewish rituals, the name of the author of this mishnah is "R. Ḥalafta b. Dosa of Kefar Hananiah"; in Maḥzor Vitry (ed. Berlin, 1893, p. 508), however, the patronymic does not appear, but there are also some other variants.

Bibliography: Heilprin, *Seder ha-Dorot*, ii.; Zacuto, *Yuḥasin*, ed. Filipowski, p. 64.

E. C. S. M.

ḤAMA B. BISA (BISAI): Amora of the third century, who formed the middle link of a scholarly trio, and who exceeded his predecessor, as his successor in turn exceeded him, in the acquisition of knowledge. Like many other students, he left home and family, being gone twelve years. When he returned, fearing to startle his family, he went first to the local bet ha-midrash, whence he sent word to them of his arrival. While there his young son Hoshaiah soon engaged him in a discussion, neither knowing the other. Ḥama, admiring the logical bent of the young man's mind, sorrowfully reflected on his long absence from home, where he himself might have raised such a son. He at last went to his house, and there, while seated beside his wife, he saw enter his late interlocutor at the bet ha-midrash. Surmising that he had come to continue the discussion, Ḥama rose to receive him, whereupon his wife surprised him by exclaiming, "Does a father ever rise before a son?" (Ket. 72a). On another occasion father and son were discussing a point of civil law. They disagreed and submitted their views to Bisa, the father of Ḥama, who sided with Hoshaiah. On this occasion Rami b. Ḥama expressed the hope that in the learned trio would be fulfilled the. Scriptural saying, "A threefold cord is not quickly broken" (Eccl. iv. 12; B. B. 59a).

According to the tosatists (B. B. 59a, *s.v.* "Weha-Ḥut"), the Hoshaiah here cited is identical with HOSHAIAH RABBAH. Bacher ("Ag. Pal. Amor." i. 89) adopts this view, but Frankel ("Mebo," p. 85b) rightly questions its tenability. There is no doubt that Hoshaiah Rabbah's father's name was "Ḥama," but it is cited with the addition of "Father of R. Hoshaiah" (Yer. Sheb. ii. 33d; Yer. Niddah iii. 50c). Only once does the name "Ḥama b. Bisa" appear so as to leave no doubt of his being a contemporary of Judah I., and, therefore, the father of Hoshaiah Rabbah (Niddah 14b). But the patronymic is an error, and the parallel passage reads correctly: "Ḥama, the father of Hoshaiah" (Yer. Niddah ii. 49d). It is probable that Ḥama was the father of the younger Hoshaiah, and flourished contemporaneously with Rami b. Hama, the son-in-law of R. Ḥisda.

BIBLIOGRAPHY: Heilprin, *Seder ha-Dorot*, ii.

J. S. M.

ḤAMA B. ḤANINA: Palestinian amora of the third century; contemporary of R. Johanan (Shab. 147b). Like his father, Ḥanina b. Ḥama, he directed a school at Sepphoris (Yer. Sanh. x. 28a), and was well known in the circles of the halakists (comp. Shab. *l.c.*; Yer. Shab. v. 7c; Yer. Suk. ii. 52d; Yer. Meg. iii. 74b). He was distinguished as a haggadist, in which field he occupied a high position, haggadists like Levi frequently quoting him (comp. Pesiḳ. iv. 37a, vii. 67b, xvii. 132a, xxiii. 153a, b, xxxi. 195a). Who his teachers were is nowhere stated. Possibly R. Ḥiyya the Great was one of them (see Sanh. 29a: Ḥiyya's patronymic is doubtless a mistake).

In his homilies Ḥama sought to convey practical lessons. Thus, commenting on the Scriptural command, "Ye shall walk after the Lord your

God" (Deut. xiii. 5 [A. V. 4]), he asks, "How can man walk after God, of whom it is written, 'The Lord thy God is a consuming fire'?" (*ib.* iv. 23 [A. V. 24]). But, he explains, the Bible means to teach that man should follow in God's ways. "As He clothes the naked (Gen. iii. 21) so do thou clothe the naked" (Soṭah 14a). According to Ḥama death was inflicted upon Adam not so much because of his sin as to prevent wicked men in the future from proclaiming themselves immortal gods (Gen. R. ix. 5). Ḥama's ancestors were wealthy, and built many synagogues. On one occasion, while visiting, with his colleague Hoshaiah IL, the synagogues at Lydda, he proudly exclaimed, "What vast treasures have my ancestors sunk in these walls!" To this Hoshaiah responded, "How many lives have thy ancestors sunk here! Were there no needy scholars whom that treasure would have enabled to devote themselves entirely to the study of the Law?" (Yer Peah viii. 21b).

BIBLIOGRAPHY: Bacher, *Ag. Pal. Amor.* i. 447 *et seq.*; Frankel, *Mebo*, 85b; Heilprin, *Seder ha-Dorot*, ed. Maskileison, ii. 138b; Weiss, *Dor*, iii. 91.

E. C. S. M.

HAMNUNA I.: Babylonian amora of the third century; senior to Joseph b. Ḥiyya (Ket. 50b; Tosef., Ket. *s.v.* יתיב). He was a disciple of Rab (Abba Arika), from whom he received instruction not only in the Halakah (B. Ḳ. 106a), but also in ethics ('Er. 54a; comp. Ecclus. [Sirach] xiv. 11 *et seq.*). He seems to have been prominent among his fellow students, following Rab's example. What the master directed others to do or to omit, he directed his colleagues. "Charge your wives," said he, "that when standing by the dead they pluck not their hair out [for grief], lest they transgress the inhibition, 'Ye shall not make any baldness between your eyes for the dead' " (Deut. xiv. 1; Yer. Ḳid. i. 61c: comp. Yer. Ma'as. iv. 51c.; Yer. Suk. iv. 54b). He honored Rab's memory not only by citing him as an authority ('Er. 77b, *et al.*) but also by endeavoring to prevent deviations from customs once established by Rab. When a scholar came to Ḥarta de-Argaz and decided a ritualistic point contrary to the opinion of Rab, Hamnuna excommunicated him, arguing that the scholar should not have ventured to act thus at Rab's last residence (Shab. 19b). In Haggadah he is not often met with. Once he quotes a saying of Rab's ('Ab. Zarah 19b).

E. C. S. M.

HAMNUNA II.: Babylonian amora of the third and fourth centuries; in the Babylonian Talmud sometimes referred to as **Hamnuna Saba** ("the elder"), to distinguish him from a younger Hamnuna. He was a native of Harpania (Hipparenum; Neubauer, "G. T." p. 352), but paid his poll-tax at Pum-Nahara, to which place he was therefore assumed to belong (Yeb. 17a). He sat at the feet of the most prominent teachers of the latter half of the third century, among whom were Adda b. Ahabah, Judah b. Ezekiel, and 'Ula; and by most of them he was greatly respected for his talent (Giṭ. 81b; Yeb. 17a; Shebu. 34a). But he was most esteemed by his teacher Ḥisda, under whom he rapidly rose from the position of pupil to that of colleague (Shab. 97a; 'Er.. 63a; Yer. Hor. iii. 47c). Subsequently Huna became his teacher; and as long as Huna lived Hamnuna would not teach at Ḥarta de-Argaz, the place of Huna's residence ('Er. 63a). Hamnuna eventually became a recognized rabbinical authority, and the foremost scholars of his generation, like Ze'era I., applied to him for elucidations of obscure questions (Ber. 24b). The "resh galuta" (exilarch) repeatedly consulted him on scholastic points (Yer. Shab. xii. 13c; Shab. 119a). As a haggadist he strongly advocated the study of the Law, which, according to him, should precede everything, even good deeds (Ḳid. 40b). Providence decreed the destruction of Jerusalem solely because children were not schooled in the Law, as it is written, "I will pour it [fury] out upon the children abroad" (Jer. vi. 11), which is a reference to the fact that the children are abroad, and not in the schools (Shab. 119b). Therefore as soon as a child learns to talk it must be taught to say, "The Torah which Moses hath commanded us is the inheritance of the congregation of Jacob" (Deut. xxxiii. 4, Hebr.; Suk. 42a).

In the numerical value of תורה ("Torah") Hamnuna finds Scriptural support for Simlai's declaration that the Israelites received at Sinai six hundred and thirteen commandments: To the people Moses communicated תורה (400 + 6 + 200 + 5 = 611), and the first two of the Decalogue were communicated to them directly by God (Mak. 23b; comp. Ex. R. xxxiii. 7). He declared that insolence is providentially punished by absence of rain. This teaching he derives from Jer. iii. 3: "The showers have been withholden, and there hath been no latter rain"; because "thou hadst a whore's forehead, thou refusedst to be ashamed" (Ta'an. 7b). Hamnuna was a considerable liturgical author. To him are ascribed five benedictions which an Israelite should utter at the sight of different Babylonian ruins (Ber. 57b), two to be spoken on seeing large armies (Ber. 58a), and one before engaging in the study of the Torah (Ber. 11b). The last one has been universally adopted, and is still recited at the public readings of the Torah. Various other prayers are ascribed to him (Ber. 17a), one of which is incorporated in the ritual (see HAMNUNA ZUṬA). Hamnuna died at the same time as Rabbah b. Huna, and their remains were transported together for burial in Palestine.

BIBLIOGRAPHY: Bacher, *Ag. Bab. Amor.* p. 73; Frankel, *Mebo*, p. 76a; Heilprin, *Seder ha-Dorot*, ii.; Zacuto, *Yuḥasin*, ed. Filipowski, pp. 130a *et seq.*

E. C. S. M.

HAMNUNA OF BABYLONIA: Teacher of the Bible; junior of Ḥanina b. Ḥama and senior of Jeremiah b. Abba, both of whom he consulted on an exegetical question (Yer. B. B. vii. 15c; comp. Yer. Ta'an. iv. 68a; Eccl. R. vii. 7). He was the innocent cause of great provocation to Judah I., and of consequent neglect of Ḥanina. Judah lectured on Ezek. vii. 16, and misquoted it. His pupil Ḥanina publicly corrected him, and when the patriarch asked him where he had learned Bible, he replied, "From R. Hamnuna of Babylonia." As Hamnuna was Ḥanina's junior, it appeared to the patriarch that Ḥanina jested at his expense, as if implying that mere tyros knew the Bible better than he. This so angered him that he told Ḥanina, "If thou ever visit-est Babylonia, tell the people that I have appointed thee ḥakam" ("sage," a title less honorable than "rabbi "). By this Ḥanina understood that Judah would never promote him, to an academic rectorate (Yer. Ta'an. *l.c.*; Eccl. R. *l.c.*; see Ḥanina b. Ḥama).

E. C. S. M.

HAMNUNA ZUṬA: Babylonian amora of the fourth century; junior and contemporary of Hamnuna II. (hence his cognomen "Zuṭa"). Hamnuna II. had composed a penitential prayer beginning "My God! Before I was formed I was worthless". This prayer Raba adopted and recited daily, while Hamnuna Zuṭa appropriated it for recitation on the Day of Atonement (Yoma 87b; comp. Ber. 17a).

E. C. S. M.

ḤANA (HUNA) B. BIZNA: Babylonian scholar of the third and fourth centuries; judge at pumbedita (B. Ḳ. 12a). He especially cultivated the field of Haggadah, in which he became distinguished. R. Sheshet, who once attempted to criticize Ḥana's homiletic expositions, but was soon defeated, remarked, "I can not contend with Ḥana in the field of the Haggadah" (Suk. 52b). As a halakist Ḥana seems to have been an independent thinker. In spite of criticism he allowed himself to frequent pagan barber-shops in the suburbs of Nehardea ('Ab. Zarah 29a). To him belongs the credit of preserving from oblivion the name and teachings of Simon Ḥasida, a late tanna rarely mentioned by any other rabbi (Ber. 3b, 43b; Ket. 67b; Yeb. 60b; *et al.*).

E. C. S. M.

HANA B. ḤANILAI: Babylonian scholar and philanthropist of the third century; the junior of Huna I. and Ḥisda (Beẓah 21a, 40a). The Talmud relates of him that he was wont to employ scores of bakers in the preparation of bread for the poor, and that his hand was ever in his purse, ready to extend help to the needy. His house was provided with entrances on all sides, that the wayfarer might the easier find entry, and none ever left it hungry or empty-handed. He would leave food outside the house at night, that those who felt shame in soliciting might help themselves under cover of darkness. Eventually his house was destroyed. 'Ula and Ḥisda once saw the ruins; Ḥisda was much moved at the sight, and when 'Ula inquired the cause of his emotion, Ḥisda acquainted him with its former splendor and hospitality, adding, "Is not the sight of its present condition sufficient to force sighs from me?" 'Ula, however, replied, "The servant should not expect to fare better than his master: God's sanctuary was destroyed, and so was Ḥana's house; as the former, so will the latter be: God will restore it" (Ber. 58b; comp. Meg. 27a). Notwithstanding his learning and his wealth, Ḥana was extremely modest and obliging, ready even to lift physical burdens from the shoulders of the worthy. Huna once carried a shovel across the street; Ḥana met him and at once offered to relieve him. Huna, however, would not permit it. "Unless," said he, "thou art accustomed to do such things at home, I can not let thee do it here: I will not be honored through thy degradation" (Meg. 28a).

E. C. S. M.

HANAMEEL (חנמאל; R. V. **Hanamel).—Biblical Data:** Son of Shallum and cousin of Jeremiah. The latter purchased a field from him for seventeen shekels of silver in token of his belief that the Israelites would return to their land (Jer. xxxii. 7–12).

E. G. H. M. SEL.

——**In Rabbinical Literature:** Hanameel was the son of Shallum, the man who was miraculously resurrected from the dead (Pirḳe R. El. xxxiii.). His mother was the prophetess Huldah. Like his parents, he was possessed of great piety and learning; he knew the names of the angels, and could conjure them at will. Thus when the Chaldeans were besieging Jerusalem he conjured angels, who, in obedience to his summons, came down from heaven as warriors and put the enemies of Israel to flight. Thereupon God changed the names of the angels so that Hanameel's conjurations would be unavailing to prevent the destruction of Jerusalem. Hanameel, however, summoned the "Prince of the World" (שר העולם), an archangel in charge of the government of the world, who actually lifted Jerusalem up to heaven. The city could not then be destroyed until God had cast it down again, and had made it impossible for the "Prince of the World" to come to its aid (Ekah Zuṭa, ed. Buber, p. 62). A legend closely related to this haggadah is found in Lam. R. ii. 2 (ed. Buber, p. 110, end). On his father's as well as his mother's side Hanameel was a descendant of Rahab by her marriage with Joshua, being one of eight prophets that resulted from this marriage (Sifre, *l.c.*; Meg. *l.c.*; comp. Seder 'Olam R. xx.).

J. L. G.

HANAMEEL THE EGYPTIAN: High priest; flourished in the first century B.C. After assuming the government of Palestine, Herod surrounded himself with creatures of his own; from among these he chose one Hanameel to fill the office of high priest made vacant by the ignominious death of Antigonus (37 B.C.). Hanameel (Ananelus) was an Egyptian according to the Mishnah (Parah iii. 5), a Babylonian according to Josephus ("Ant." xv. 2, § 4); though of priestly descent, he was not of the family of the high priests. But Hanameel's incumbency was of short duration. Prudence compelled Herod to remove him, and to fill his place with the Hasmonean ARISTOBULUS (35 B.C.). The youthful Hasmonean, however, was too popular with the patriotic party; though he was a brother of Mariamne, Herod's beloved wife, he was treacherously drowned at Herod's instigation (35 B.C.), and Hanameel was restored to the high position. How long he continued in office historians do not state; but it could not have been for many years, since after the execution of Mariamne (29 B.C.) Herod remarried, and appointed his second father-in-law, Simon b. Boethus, to the high-priesthood, removing Joshua b. Fabi. Hanameel is credited with having prepared one of the total of seven "red heifers" (see Num. xix.) which were provided in all the centuries from Ezra's restoration to the final dispersion of the Jews (Parah *l.c.*).

BIBLIOGRAPHY: Grätz, *Gesch.* iii. 213 *et seq.*; Josephus, *Ant.* xv. 2, § 4; 3, §§ 1, 3; Jost, *Gesch. des Judenthums und Seiner Sekten*, i. 320; see also Brüll, *Mebo ha-Mishnah*, i. 55.

E. C. S. M.

HANAN (חנן): **1.** A Benjamite chief (I Chron. viii. 23). **2.** The sixth son of Azel, also a Benjarnite, of the family of Saul (*ib.* viii. 38). **3.** Son of Maachah, one of David's mighty men (*ib.* xi. 43). **4.** Progenitor of a family of the Nethinim, who returned from captivity with Zerubbabel (Ezra ii. 46; Neh. vii. 49). **5.** Son of Igdaliahu, a man of God, whose sons had a chamber in the house of the Lord (Jer. xxxv. 4). **6.** One of the Levites who assisted Ezra in the reading of the Law (Neh. viii. 7), and who sealed the covenant (*ib.* x. 10). **7.** One of the chiefs who also sealed the covenant (*ib.* x. 22). **8.** Another signatory to the covenant (*ib.* x. 26). **9.** Son of Zaccur, and one of the storekeepers of the provisions taken as tithes (*ib.* xiii. 13).

E. G. H. M. SEL.

HANAN (ḤANIN, ḤANINAN): Scholar of the third amoraic generation (third century). He was probably a Babylonian by birth and a late pupil of Rab, in whose name he reports halakot and haggadot (Yoma 41b; Suk. 15b *et seq.*; Ned. 7b); and is found associating with Anan, who lived and died in Babylonia (Ḳid. 39a). Frequently, however, he appears in Palestine, where he waged controversies with the foremost scholars of his generation: Ela, Hoshaiah II, Levi (Yer. Dem. vi. 25c; Gen. R. xxix. 4; Num. R. xiii. 8). Hanan teaches: Whoso invokes God's retribution on his neighbor suffers first. Thus, Sarah called on God to judge between her and Abraham (Gen. xvi. 5), and soon thereafter, it is written (Gen. xxiii. 2), "Sarah died... and Abraham came to mourn for Sarah, and to weep for her" (B. Ḳ. 93a). Israel's enslavement in Egypt was a divine retribution for selling Joseph. "The Holy One, blessed be He! said to the [eponyms of the] tribes, 'Joseph was sold for a servant: as ye live, ye shall annually repeat the statement, "We were servants of Pharaoh in Egypt" ' " (Midr. Teh. x 2). The last verse forms part of the Seder service. In the threefold threat conveyed in Deut. xxviii. 66, Hanan finds foreshadowed the mental anguish of him who possesses no land and is obliged to buy provisions by the year or by the week from the markets, or by the day from the shopkeeper (Yer. Shab. viii. 11a; see BEBAI I.; comp. AḤAI B. JOSIAH). Hanan married inta the patriarchal family, and for many years had no children. When at last he was blessed with a son, Hanan died. At his funeral this elegy was pronounced: "Happiness to sorrow was changed; mirth and mourning have met; joy was succeeded by wailing; at the first caress died the caresser." The child was named Hanan after its father (M. Ḳ. 25b).

BIBLIOGRAPHY: Bacher, *Ag. Pal. Amor.* iii. 86 *et seq.*; Frankel, *Mebo*, p. 86a.

E. C. S. M.

HANAN (ḤANIN), ABBA: Tanna of the second century; younger contemporary of Simon of Shezur, Josiah, and Jonathan (Mek., Mishpaṭim, 8, 12, 20; Nazir 45a). Possibly he sat at the feet of Eliezer b. Hyrcanus, in whose name he transmits many halakic midrashim (seventeen in Sifre, Num. 4 [Ḥanin], 7, 11, 23, 35, 52, 68, 72 [Ḥanin], 107 [five times], 118, 126, 133, and 137; and else where). Indeed, it may be said that Abba Hanan was simply Eliezer's mouthpiece. Only once (Sifre, Deut. 94) does he appear independent of Eliezer, and Bacher ("Ag. Tan." i. 131) represents him here as opposing his master (see Tosef., Sanh. xiv. 3); but a careful comparison of the sources proves that there is no antagonism. Eliezer's harsh verdict refers to minors who followed their elders in apostasy (שהודחו), while his junior speaks of minors who were not guilty of the crime. Occasionally Abba Hanan appears to report also in the name of Eleazar (Mek., Mishpaṭim, 20), but the version is not authentic, and Weiss ("Introduction to the Mekilta," p. xxx.) proves it to be erroneous.

E. C. S. M.

HANAN B. ABISHALOM. See HANAN THE EGYPTIAN.

HANAN THE EGYPTIAN: 1. (Hanan b. Abishalom.) One of the police judges at Jerusalem in the last decades of its independence. Several of his decisions have been preserved (Ket. xiii. 1 *et seq.*). **2.** Disciple of Akiba, quoted among "those who argued before the sages" (Sanh. 17b; comp. Yer. Ma'as. Sh. ii. 53d). Only one halakah is preserved in his name (Yoma 63b).

E. C. S. M.

HANANIAH (ḤANINA): Palestinian amora of the third and fourth centuries; junior of Ḥiyya b. Abba and Ze'era I. (Yer. Ber. vii. 11b). He was frequently described as the "comrade of the Rabbis" (חברון דרבנין). In the Babylonian Talmud he is never cited with his cognomen; and in the Jerusalem Talmud also he is frequently quoted by his prænomen alone. Thus he appears in the report of a legal controversy between him and Haggai, in which R. Ela participated (Yer. Ḳid. iii. 63d). With the latter he repeatedly had heated discussions, Ela exclaiming, "God save us from such opinions!" and Hananiah retorting, "Rather may God save us from thy opinions!" (Shab. 83b; Ket. 45b; B. Ḳ. 65b).

Hananiah was a Babylonian by birth, and was assumed to have been the brother of Rabbah b. Naḥmani ("Yuḥasin," 129a), a descendant of the priestly house of Eli (R. H. 18a; Sanh. 14b); but he and another brother, Hoshaiah ("Oshaiah" in the Babylonian Talmud), emigrated at an early age to Palestine. They settled at Tiberias, whither they ineffectually urged Rabbah to follow them (Yer. Ta'an. i. 64a; Ket. 111a). Here they plied the shoemaker's trade for a living. They established themselves on a street inhabited by prostitutes, who patronized them. Because they preserved their modesty and chastity, in spite of their evil associations, even the women learned to revere them and to swear "by the life of the saintly rabbis of Palestine" (Pes. 113b). They were also famous as workers of miracles, and when they desired to prepare some savory meal in honor of the Sabbath, legend says they were compelled to resort to transcendental means in order to produce it (Sanh. 65b). Their exemplary life as well as their scholarship prompted Johanan to ordain them as teachers, but for reasons not stated—possibly because of the associations into which their trade led them, or perhaps because of their youth—he failed to carry out his intentions. This was a source of regret to the venerable teacher, but the brothers eased his mind by pointing out that, being descendants from the house of Eli, they could not expect to be promoted to "elderships," since of that house the Bible has said: "There shall not be an old man in thine house forever" (I Sam. ii. 32; Sanh. 14a). Hananiah died on a semi-festival, and, as a mark of distinction and of general mourning, his coffin was, contrary to custom on such days, made on the public street (Yer. M. Ḳ. i. 80d).

Bibliography: Bacher, *Ag. Pal. Amor.* iii. 550; Frankel, *Mebo*, p. 88a; Zacuto, *Yuḥasin*, ed. Filipowski, p. 129a.

E. C. S. M.

HANANIAH (ḤANINA): Palestinian scholar of the fourth amoraic generation (fourth century); nephew of R. Hoshaiah, junior of Ze'era I., and contemporary of Jose II. (Yer. Ta'an. i. 64a, where his name is erroneously given as "Ḥanaiah"). Once he is represented as opposing "the rabbis of Cæsarea" in halakic controversy (Yer. Shab. i. 3a). He is also mentioned as having consulted Abba b. Zabda (Yer. Meg. iii. 74d); but the text here is so mutilated as to lose its reliability for chronological purposes (see Frankel, "Mebo," p. 88b).

E. C. S. M.

HANANIAH (ḤANINA), Nephew of R. Joshua: Tanna of the second century; contemporary of Judah b. Bathyra, Matteya b. Ḥeresh, and Jonathan (Sine, Deut. 80). Who his father was is not stated; nor is anything known of his early years. He was named after his grandfather, Hananiah, and educated by his uncle, from whom he received his cognomen. In some baraitot, however, he is cited by his prænomen alone (Suk. 20b; Ket. 79b; see Hananiah b. 'Aḳabia). In the days of Gamaliel II. he once ventured to give a decision, for which he was summoned before that patriarch; but his uncle, by reporting that he himself had given Hananiah the decision, mollified Gamaliel (Niddah 24b). It was probably about that time that Hananiah fell in with some sectaries at Capernaum. To remove him from their influence his uncle advised him to leave the country, which he did, emigrating to Babylonia, where he opened a school that eventually acquired great fame (Sanh. 32b; Eccl. R. i. 8, vii. 26). He returned to his native country with ritualistic decisions which had been communicated to him by a Babylonian scholar, and which he submitted to his uncle (Suk. 20b). But during the evil days following the Bar Kokba rebellion, seeing the noblest of his people fall before the vengeance of the Romans, he again emigrated to Babylonia, settling at Nehar-Peḳod (see Neubauer, "G. T." pp. 363 *et seq.*). The appearance of Hananiah in Babylonia threatened to produce a schism in Israel fraught with far-reaching consequences: it created a movement toward the secession of the Babylonian congregations from the central authority hitherto exercised by the Palestinian Sanhedrin.

Believing that Roman tyranny had succeeded in permanently suppressing the religious institutions which, in spite of the Jewish dispersion, had held the remnants of Israel together, Hananiah attempted to establish an authoritative body in his new home. To render the Babylonian schools independent of Palestine, he arranged a calendar fixing the Jewish festivals and bissextile years on the principles that prevailed in Palestine. In the meantime, however, Hadrian's death had brought about a favorable change in Judea. In March, 139 or 140, a message arrived from Rome announcing the repeal of the Hadrianic decrees (see Meg. Ta'an. xii.); soon thereafter the surviving rabbis, especially the disciples of Akiba. convened at Usha, and reorganized the Sanhedrin with Simon b. Gamaliel II. as president (R. H. 31b *et seq.*; see Rapoport, "'Erek Millin," pp. 233b *et seq.)*. They sought to reestablish the central authority, and naturally would not brook any rivals. Messengers were therefore despatched to Nehar-Peḳod, instructed to urge Hananiah to acknowledge the authority of the parent Sanhedrin, and to desist from disrupting the religious unity of Israel.

The messengers at first approached him in a kindly spirit, showing him great respect. This he reciprocated, and he presented them to his followers as superior personages; but when he realized their real mission he endeavored to discredit them. They, for their part, contradicted him in his lectures; what he declared pure they denounced as impure; and when at last he asked them, "Why do you always oppose me?" they plainly told him, "Because thou, contrary to law, ordainest bissextile years in foreign lands." "But did not Akiba do so before me?" asked the; to which they replied, "Certainly he did; but thou canst not compare thyself with Akiba, who left none like him in Palestine." "Neither have I left my equal in Palestine," cried Hananiah; and the messengers retorted, "The kids thou hast left behind thee have since developed into horned bucks, and these have deputed us to urge thee to retrace thy steps, and, if thou resist, to excommunicate thee." The Palestinian sources relate that the deputies, to impress upon him the enormity of secession from the parent authority, publicly parodied Scriptural passages. One of them substituted "Hananiah" for "the Lord" in "These are the feasts of the Lord" (Lev. xxiii. 4). Another recited, "Out of Babylonia shall go forth the Law, and the word of the Lord from Nehar-Peḳod," instead of "Out of Zion" and "from Jerusalem" (Isa. ii. 3). When the people corrected them by calling out the proper readings, the deputies laconically replied, גבן (="With us!" Yer. Ned. vi. 40a). They also declared that the steps taken by Hananiah and his followers were tantamount to building an altar on unholy ground and serving it with illegitimate priests. Altogether, they pointed out, his course was a renunciation of the God of Israel.

The people recognized their error, and repented; but Hananiah held out. He appealed to Judah b. Bathyra, then in Nisibis, for support; but the latter not only refused to participate in the secession movement, but prevailed on Hananiah to submit to the orders emanating from the

Judean Sanhedrin (Ber. 63a; Yer. Ned. *l.c.*). Hananiah ended his life peacefully in Babylonia (Eccl. R. i. 8).

Although Hananiah was a prominent figure in his day, rivaling for a time the patriarch in Judea, his name is connected with but few halakot, either original (Tosef., Peah, iii. 3; Ket. 79b) or transmitted ('Er. 43a; Beẓah 17b; Suk. 20b; Niddah 24b), and with still fewer halakic midrashim (Mek., Bo, 16; Sifre, Num. 49, 116; Ḥag. 10a; Shebu. 35b). As to haggadot, only two or three originated with him. One declares that where Scripture says, "King Solomon loved many strange women" (I Kings xi. 1), it does not mean to impugn his chastity; but it implies that he transgressed the Biblical inhibition, "Thou shalt not make marriages with them" (Deut. vii. 3; Yer. Sanh. ii. 20c). Another asserts that the tables of the Decalogue (Deut. iv. 13) contained after each command its scope in all its ramifications; that the Commandments were interwoven with expositions as are the billows of the sea with, smaller waves (Yer. Sheḳ. vi.49d; Cant. R. v. 14).

BIBLIOGRAPHY: Bacher, *Ag. Tan.*i. 389; Frankel, *Darke ha-Mishnah*, p. 137: Grätz, *Gesch.* iv. 202; Heilprin, *Seder ha-Dorot*, ii.; Jost, *Gesch. des Judenthums und Seiner Sekten*, ii. 109: Kobak's *Jeschurun*, vii. 14; Weiss, *Dor*, ii. 177; Zacuto, *Yuḥasin*, ed. Filipowski, pp. 35a, 66b.

S. S. S. M.

HANANIAH (ḤANINA) B. 'AḲABYA (AKIBA): Tanna of the second century; contemporary of Judah b. 'Ilai (M. Ḳ. 21a), and probably one of the younger pupils of Gamaliel II. (Ket. viii. 1). His name rarely appears in connection with haggadot; but he was firmly grounded in the Halakah. Rab expresses great admiration for Hananiah's acumen (Shab. 83b). Notwithstanding his prominence, his prænomen as well as his patronymic is uncertain: "Hananiah" and "Ḥanina" for the former, and " 'Aḳabia" and "Akiba" for the latter appearing promiscuously in connection with one and the same halakah (comp. 'Ar. i. 3; Sifra, Beḥuḳḳotai, xii. 8; 'Ar. 6b; Tosef., Parah, ix. [viii.] 9; Ḥag. 23a; Yeb. 116b). However, there is reason to believe that " 'Aḳabia" is his right patronymic, and that he was the son of 'AḲABIA B. MAHALALEEL (see "R. E. J."xli. 40, note 3). Hananiah was very fearless in the expression of his opinions and also opposed those of the leaders of academies, the "nasi" and his deputy (Tosef., Pes. viii. 7; Shab. 50a). His residence was at Tiberias, where he abrogated many restrictions which had hampered the comfort of the people ('Er. 87b, and parallel passages). Sometimes Hananiah (or Ḥanina) is cited without his patronymic (compare, for example, Yer. 'Er. viii. 25b and Shab. 83b), and one must be careful not to mistake him for an elder tanna of the same name, or vice versa (see HANANIAH [Ḥanina], nephew of R. Joshua). To avoid such mistakes one must observe the associates cited in the debate or statement. If these belong to the age of

Meïr, Jose, and Simon, Hananiah, the subject of this article, is meant; if they are of a former generation, R. Joshua's nephew is intended.

BIBLIOGRAPHY: Bacher, *Ag. Tan.* ii. 370; Brüll, *Mebo ha-Mishnah*, i. 211; Frankel, *Darke ha-Mishnah*, p. 186; Heilprin, *Seder ha-Dorot*, ii., *s.v.*

E. C. S. M.

HANANIAH B. 'AḲASHYAH: Tanna whose name became very popular by reason of a single homiletic remark, as follows: "The Holy One—blessed be He!—desired to enlarge Israel's merits; therefore He multiplied for them Torah and commandments, as it is said [Isa. xlii. 21, Hebr.], 'The Lord was pleased, in order to render him [Israel—read: צדקו] righteous, to magnify the Law and to make it great' " (Mak. iii. 16). This mishnah is usually subjoined to each chapter of the treatise Abot embodied in the rituals. One halakah also is ascribed to him (Tosef., Sheḳ. iii. 18; anonymous in Sheḳ. viii. 8). When he lived, and who his teachers were, can not be ascertained. He probably was a brother of the equally rarely cited Simon b. 'Aḳashiah.

BIBLIOGRAPHY: Bacher, *Ag. Tan.* ii. 376; Brüll, *Mebo ha-Mishnah*, i. 212; Frankel, *Darke ha-Mishnah*, p. 187.

E. C. S. M.

HANANIAH (ḤANINA) B. ḤAKINAI: Tanna of the second century; contemporary of Ben 'Azzai and Simon the Temanite (Tosef., Ber. iv. 18; see ḤALAFTA). Sometimes he is cited without his prænomen (Sifra, Emor, vii. 11; Shab. 147b). Who his early teachers were is not certainly known. From some versions of the Tosefta (*l.c.*) it appears that Ṭarfon was one of them, but that his regular teacher was Akiba. It is related that he took leave of his wife and attended Akiba twelve or thirteen years without communicating with his family, whom he recovered in a remarkable way (Ket. 62b; Lev. R. xxi. 8). He was one of the few who, though not regularly ordained, were permitted to "argue cases before the sages" (דנין לפני חכמים; Sanh. 17b; comp. Yer. Ma'as. Sh. ii. 53d). Several halakot have been preserved in his name, owing their preservation to Eleazar b. Jacob II. (Kil. iv. 8; Mak. iii. 9; Tosef., Toh. vi. 3; Ḳid. 55b); and he also left some halakic midrashim (Sifra, Meẓora', v. 16; Sifra, Emor, vii. 11, comp. Shab. 110b; Men. 62b, comp. Sifra, Emor, xiii. 8).

Hananiah also delved into the "mysteries of the Creation," concerning which he consulted Akiba (Ḥag. 14b); and he appears as the author of several homiletic remarks. According to him, God's relation to distressed Israel is expressed in Solomon's words (Prov. xvii. 17): "A brother is born for adversity"; by "brother" is understood "Israel," for it is elsewhere said (Ps. cxxii. 8): "For my brethren and companions' sakes, I will now say, Peace be within thee" (Yalḳ., Ex. 233; comp. Mek.,

Beshallaḥ, iii.). With reference to Lev. v. 21 (vi. 2) ("If a soul sin, and commit a trespass against the Lord, and lie unto his neighbor," etc.), he remarks, "No man lies [acts dishonestly] against his fellow man unless he first becomes faithless to God" (Tosef., Shebu. iii. 6). From a comparatively late date comes the statement that Hananiah b. Ḥakinai was one of the "ten martyrs" (see Zunz, "G. V." 2d ed., p. 150; see also "Masseket Aẓilut ").

BIBLIOGRAPHY: Bacher, *Ag. Tan.* i. 436; Brüll, *Mebo ha-Mishnah*, i. 148; Frankel, *Darke ha-Mishnah*, p. 136; Heilprin, *Seder ha-Dorot*, ii.; Zacuto, *Yuḥasin*, ed. Filipowski, pp. 36a, 65b.

E. C. S. M.

HANANIAH B. JUDAH: Tanna of the second century; contemporary of Akiba. His name appears only twice in rabbinic lore: once in connection with a halakic midrash, where he directs his remarks to Akiba (Sifra, Ẓaw, ii. 3), and once with a homiletic remark on the baneful effect of anger. With reference to Lev. x. 16 *et seq.*, where it is related that Moses was angry with Eleazar and Ithamar for burning the goat of the sin-offering, R. Judah (b. Hai) says: "Hananiah b. Judah was wont to say, 'Grievous is the result of passion: it caused even Moses to err.' " Judah adds: "Now that Hananiah is dead, I venture to controvert his statement, 'What provoked Moses to passion? It was his error' " (Sifra, Shemini, ii. 12).

BIBLIOGRAPHY: Bacher, *Ag. Tan.* i. 441.

E. C. S. M.

HANANIAH (ḤANINA) OF ONO: Tanna of the second century. Hananiah is remembered for a feat he accomplished in the interest of traditional law. While Akiba was in prison, awaiting his doom at the court of Tyrannus Rufus, an important marital question was debated in the academy, but without a decision being reached. Hananiah therefore ventured to approach Akiba's prison and to solicit from the master a ruling. This he obtained and brought to his colleagues (Giṭ. vi. 7; see Rashi *ad loc.)*. In connection with this question the names of Meïr and Jose are cited with that of Hananiah (Git. 67a); this places Hananiah with Akiba's younger pupils, about 139–165 C.E. He is reported to have testified before (Simon b.) Gamaliel concerning the rule governing intercalations enacted in Galilee (Tosef., Sanh. ii. 13; comp. Yer. Sanh. i. 18d *et seq.*).

E. C. S. M.

HANANIAH (ḤANINA) B. TERADION: Teacher and martyr in the third tannaitic generation (second century); contemporary of ELEAZAR, BEN PERAṬA I. and of ḤALAFTA, together with whom he established certain ritualistic rules (Ta'an. ii. 5). His residence was at Siknin, where he directed religious affairs as well as a school. The latter came to be numbered among the distinguished academies with reference to which a baraita says: "The saying [Deut. xvi, 20], 'That which is altogether just shalt thou follow,' may be construed, 'Follow the sages in their respective academies. ... Follow R. Hananiah b. Teradion in Siknin' " (Sanh. 32b). Hananiah administered the communal charity funds, and so scrupulous was he in that office that once when money of his own, designed for personal use on Purim, chanced to get mixed with the charity funds, he distributed the whole amount among the poor. Eleazar b. Jacob so admired Hananiah's honesty that he remarked, "No one ought to contribute to the charity treasury unless its administrator is like Ḥanina b. Teradion" (B. B. 10b; 'Ab. Zarah 17b). Comparatively few halakot are preserved from him (Ta'an. ii. 5, 16b; R. H. 27a; Tosef., Miḳ, vi. 3; see also Yoma 78b; Men. 54a). Hananiah ingeniously proved that the Shekinah rests on those who study the Law (Ab. iii. 2).

Hananiah's life proved that with him these were not empty words. During the Hadrianic persecutions decrees were promulgated imposing the most rigorous penalties on the observers of the Jewish Law, and especially upon those who occupied themselves with the promulgation of that Law. Nevertheless Hananiah conscientiously followed his chosen profession; he convened public assemblies and taught the Law. Once he visited Jose b. Kisma, who advised extreme caution, if not submission. The latter said: "Ḥanina, my brother, seest thou not that this Roman people is upheld by God Himself? It has destroyed His house and burned His Temple, slaughtered His faithful, and exterminated His nobles; yet it prospers! In spite of all this, I hear, thou occupiest thyself with the Torah, even calling assemblies and holding the scroll of the Law before thee." To all this Hananiah replied, "Heaven will have mercy on us." Jose became impatient on hearing this, and rejoined, "I am talking logic, and to all my arguments thou answerest, 'Heaven will have mercy on us!' I should not be surprised if they burned thee together with the scroll." Shortly thereafter Hananiah was arrested at a public assembly while teaching with a scroll before him. Asked why he disregarded the imperial edict, he frankly answered, "I do as my God commands me." For this he and his wife were condemned to death, and their daughter to degradation. His death was terrible. Wrapped in the scroll, he was placed on a pyre of green brush; fire was set to it, and wet wool was placed on his chest to prolong the agonies of death. "Wo is me," cried his daughter, "that I should see thee under such terrible circumstances!" The martyr serenely replied, "I should indeed despair were I alone burned; but since the scroll of the Torah is burning with me, the Power that will avenge the offense against the Law will also avenge the offense against me." His heart-broken disciples then asked:

"Master, what seest thou?" He answered: "I see the parchment burning while the letters of the Law soar upward." "Open then thy mouth, that the fire may enter and the sooner put an end to thy sufferings," advised his pupils; but he said, "It is best that He who hath given the soul should also take it away: no man may hasten his death." Thereupon the executioner removed the wool and fanned the flame, thus accelerating the end, and then himself plunged into the flames ('Ab. Zarah 17b *et seq.*).

It is reported that, on hearing his sentence, Hananiah quoted Deut. xxxii. 4, "He is the Rock, his work is perfect: for all his ways are judgment"; while his wife quoted the second hemistich, "A God of truth and without iniquity, just and right is he"; and his daughter cited Jer. xxxii. 19, "Great in counsel, and mighty in work: for thine eyes are open upon all the ways of the sons of men: to give every one according to his ways, and according to the fruit of his doings" (Sifre, Deut. 307; 'Ab. Zarah *l.c.*; Sem. viii.).

Of the surviving members of Hananiah's family are mentioned two daughters: the learned Beruriah, who became the wife of R. Meïr, and the one marked for degradation, whom R. Meïr succeeded in rescuing ('Ab. Zarah 18a). Hananiah had also a learned son. It is related that Simon b. Hananiah applied to this son for information on a point of ritual, and that the latter and his sister, presumably Beruriah, furnished divergent opinions. When Judah b. Baba heard of those opinions, he remarked, "Hananiah's daughter teaches better than his son" (Tosef., Kelim, B. Ḳ. iv. 17). Elsewhere it is reported of that son that he became a degenerate, associating with bandits. Subsequently he betrayed his criminal associates, wherefore they killed him and filled his mouth with sand and gravel. Having discovered his remains, the people would have eulogized him out of respect for his father, but the latter would not permit it. "I my self shall speak," said he; and he did, quoting Prov. v. 11 *et seq.* The mother quoted Prov. xvii. 25; the sister, Prov. xx. 17 (Lam. R. iii. 16; comp. Sem. xii.).

Bibliography: Bacher, *Ag. Tan.* i. 397; Brüll, *Mebo ha-Mishnah*, i. 140; Frankel, *Darke ha-Mishnah*, p. 133; Hamburger, *R. B. T.* ii. 132; Heilprin, *Seder ha-Dorot*, ii.; Zacuto, *Yuḥasin*, ed. Filipowski, p. 32a.

s. s. S. M.

ḤANINA I. See Ḥanina b. Ḥama.

ḤANINA (HANANIAH) II.: Amora of the fifth century; contemporary of the Palestinian Mani II., and of Rabina, one of the compilers of the Babylonian Talmud (Yer. Ber. iii. 6a; Niddah 66b). Ḥanina attended the schools of Palestine, his native country, and concluded his pupilage under Mani II. (Yer. Pes. i. 27d; Yer. M. Ḳ. iii. 82c). He gradually rose to his master's level and discussed with him as a "fellow student" many halakic questions (Yer. Sanh. ii. 19d; Yer. Shebu. vi. 37b). Eventually he removed to Sepphoris, where he became the religious head of the community; hence he is sometimes cited as **Ḥanina of Sepphoris** (Yer. Ned. ix. 41b). When, in consequence of Roman persecutions at Tiberias, Mani also removed to Sepphoris, Ḥanina resigned the leadership in his favor—an act of self-abnegation extolled by the Rabbis as having few parallels (Yer. Pes. vi. 33a). Ḥanina, however, did not long remain in Palestine. As the persecutions became general and intolerable, he emigrated to Babylonia, where ASHI frequently sought information from him (B. B. 25b; Ḥul. 139b). Ḥanina's family accompanied him, and were highly respected in their adopted country. There Ḥanina's daughter married the son of Rabina (Niddah 66b).

BIBLIOGRAPHY: Halévy, *Dorot ha-Rishonim*, ii. 576.

J. S. M.

ḤANINA (HANANIAH) B. ABBAHU: Palestinian amora of the fourth generation, sometimes cited as **Ḥanina of Cæsarea** (Cant. R. i. 2). The Talmud relates that his father, R. Abbahu, sent him to the academies at Tiberias to study, but that he devoted himself instead to pious deeds, such as attending the dead. Abbahu thereupon wrote to him, "Is it because there are no graves in Cæsarea that I have sent thee to Tiberias?" (see ABBAHU). In the Halakah several precedents of his father's are reported by Ḥanina (Yer. Yeb. iv. 6a; Yer Ket. iv. 29b; Yer. Ḥal. iii. 62c). He also reports a halakic midrash in the name of ABDIMA OF HAIFA (Ḳid. 33b); occasionally he endeavors to account for a predecessors opinion (Yer. Niddah iii. 50c); but nothing original from him in the domain of Halakah is preserved. In the province of the Haggadah, on the contrary, he has left some original though hyperbolic remarks. Thus, commenting on Jer. ix. 9 (A. V. 10), where the prophet declares, "Both the fowl of the heavens and the beast are fled; they are gone," Ḥanina says, "Seven hundred species of fish, eight hundred species of locust, and countless species of fowl accompanied the Israelites from Palestine into their Babylonian exile; and when the latter returned all the creatures returned with them, except the fish called 'shibbuṭa' [mullet]" (Yer. Ta'an. iv. 69b; see Jastrow, "Dict.").

In his lectures Ḥanina occasionally uses homely illustrations. Speaking on Lam. ii. 1, he says: "A king had a child: the child cried, and the king took it on his lap; it continued crying, and he raised it in his arms; still it cried, wherefore he raised it upon his shoulders. Then the child soiled him, and the king at once put it down on the floor. How different was the child's ascent from its descent! The former was gradual, the latter sudden. Thus it went with Israel. At first God took him by the arms (Hosea xi. 3), then He caused him to ride (Hosea x. 11); but when he sinned 'He cast down from heaven unto the earth the beauty of Israel' " (Lam. R. ii. 1). Ḥanina also makes use of the numerical values of letters in his endeavor to reconcile haggadic differences. One rabbi advances the opinion that the name of Israel's Messiah will be "Ẓemaḥ " (צמח = "sprout"; comp. Zech. iii. 8); another, that it will be "Menahem" (= "comforter"). Ḥanina thereupon observes, "There is no difference of opinion between them; the total value of the letters in the name suggested by the one is the same as that of the letters in the name suggested by the other" צמח (90 + 40+ 8 = 138) corresponds with מנחם (40 + 50 + 8 + 40 = 188; Yer. Ber. ii. 5a).

BIBLIOGRAPHY: Bacher, *A g. Pal. Amor.* iii. 676; Frankel, *Mebo*, p. 87b; Heilprin, *Seder ha-Dorot*, ii. 149a, 154a, Warsaw, 1897.

J. S. M.

ḤANINA (HANANIAH; ḤINENA) B. ADDA (IDDA): Babylonian scholar of the third century. He was skilled in both Halakah and Haggadah; ADDA B. AHABAH appears to have been his teacher in the former (Pes. 75a; 'Ab. Zarah 40a); in the latter he seems to have been a pupil of Tanḥum b. Ḥiyya. From Tanḥum, Ḥanina received the following illustration of the relative positions of the prophet and the elder (teacher, sage): "A king delegated two commissioners; with respect to one he wrote, 'Unless he exhibits to you my signature and my seal, credit him not'; with reference to the other he wrote, 'Even if he shows you neither my signature nor my seal, credit him.' So it is said regarding the prophet: '... and giveth thee a sign or a wonder' [Deut. xiii. 2 (A.V. 1)]; while of the sages it is said: 'According to the sentence of the law which they shall teach thee, and according to the judgment which they shall tell thee, thou shalt do' " (Deut. xvii. 11; Yer. Ber. i. 3b; Yer. Sanh. xi. 30b; Yer. 'Ab. Zarah ii. 41c; Cant. R. i. 2). In the Book of Isaiah יאמר (the future: "will say"), instead of the usual אמר ("saith"), is used eight times (i. 11, 18; xxxiii. 10; xl. 1, 25; xli. 21, twice; lxvi. 9). This peculiarity, according to Ḥanina, contains an allusion to the corresponding number of prophets that were to appear after the destruction of the (first) Temple: Joel, Amos, Zephaniah, Haggai, Zechariah, Malachi, Ezekiel, and Jeremiah (Pesiḳ. xvi. 128b; see Buber *ad loc.*). An elder namesake of Ḥanina was a tanna, contemporary of AḤAI B. JOSIAH, with whom he discussed a halakic midrash (Mek., Mlshpaṭim, v.; comp. Sifra, Ḳedoshim, ix. 6, 14).

BIBLIOGRAPHY: Bacher, *Ag. Pal. Amor.* iii. 553; idem, *Ag. Tan.* ii. 553; Frankel, *Mebo*, p. 89a; Heilprin, *Seder ha-Dorot*, ii. 143a, 148b, Warsaw, 1897.

J. S. M.

ḤANINA B. 'AGUL: Palestinian scholar of the third century; junior contemporary of Ḥiyya b. Abba and Tanḥum b. Ḥanilai. Ḥanina applied to Ḥiyya to explain why the expression "that it may go well with thee," contained in the second version of the Decalogue (Deut. v. 16), was not embodied in the first version (Ex. xx. 12). Ḥiyya thereupon gave him this remarkable answer: "Instead of asking me that, ask me whether the expression is embodied in either version: I do not even know it is there! However, apply to Tanḥum b. Ḥanilai, who has frequented the school of the expert haggadist Joshua b. Levi." Ḥanina did so, and was told that the promise was omitted from the first version because the first tablets of the Decalogue were destined to be broken (see Ex. xxxii. 19). This is explained by a later haggadist, who stated that the inclusion of the promise in the tablets that were destined to be broken would have been very discouraging to the people, who would have seen in the breaking of them a foreshadowing of the cessation of God's goodness (B. Ḳ. 54b *et seq.*). With reference to Isa. lxiv. 3 (A. V. 4: "Neither hath the eye seen, O God, beside thee, what he hath prepared for him that waiteth for him"), Ḥanina remarks: "The Jews who attended the banquet given by Ahasuerus [Esth. i.] were asked whether God would ever provide better entertainment for them; to which they replied, 'Should God furnish us the like of this we should protest, since we have had such viands at the board of Ahasuerus'" (Esth. R. i. 5, where עגול is corrupted to עטל). His name appears also in connection with a halakah which he reports as having originated with Hezekiah, probably the son of Ḥiyya (Yer. Yeb. vi. 7c).

J. S. M.

ḤANINA (HANANIAH) B. ANTIGONUS: Tanna of priestly descent; contemporary of Akiba and Ishmael (Bek. vii. 5). It is supposed that in his youth he had witnessed the service of the Temple of Jerusalem, since he knew the fluters that played before the altar (Tosef., 'Ar. i. 15; comp. 'Ar. ii. 4). If this were so, Ḥanina must have enjoyed unusual longevity, as he often appears in halakic controversy with Akiba's latest disciples. Be this as it may, he was learned in the laws relating to the priests, and many such laws are preserved in his name (Ḳid. iv. 5; Bek. vi. 3, 10, 11; vii. 2, 5; Tem. vi. 5), while precedents reported by him regarding the services and appurtenances of the Temple influenced later rabbinical opinions. On marital questions also he is often cited as an authority (Yeb. xiii. 2; Niddah vi. 13 [comp. *ib.* Gem. 52b], viii. 2), as well as on other matters (Sheb. vi. 3; 'Er. iv. 8). Some halakic midrashim also have come down from him (Bek. vii. 2, 5; Mek., Yitro, Baḥodesh, 6); but of haggadot there is only one under his name. He says: "Whosoever practises the precept concerning the fringes on the borders of [בנפי] garments (Num. xv. 38 *et seq.*) will realize the promise: 'Ten men... shall take hold of the skirt of [בכנף] him that is a Jew, saying, We will go with you: for we have heard that God is with you'" (Zech. viii. 23), "On the other hand," continues Ḥanina, "he who violates the precept concerning the skirt [כנף] is included in the verse 'take hold of the ends of [בכנפות] the earth, that the wicked might be shaken out of it' " (Job xx'xviii. 13; Sifre, Num. 115). According to him, when an aged man dies after not more than three days' sickness, his death may be termed "excision" (כרת = "cutting off"; see Jew. Encyc. iv. 484, *s.v.* DEATH), a visitation for secret violations of the Sabbath or of the dietary laws (Sem. iii. 10).

BIBLIOGRAPHY: Bacher, *Ag. Tan. i.* 378; Brüll, *Mebo ha-Mishnah*, i. 131; Frankel, *Darke ha-Mishnah*, p. 128; Weiss, *Dor*, ii. 121.

J. S. M.

ḤANINA B. DOSA: Scholar and miracle-worker of the first century; pupil of Johanan b. Zakkai (Ber. 34b). While he is reckoned among the Tannaim and is quoted in connection with a school and its disciples, no halakot and but few haggadot are preserved as from him (Baraita of R. Eliezer xxix., xxxi.; Midr. Mishle x. 2). His popularity, however, which he enjoyed throughout his life, and which rendered him immortal among the mystics, rests not on his scholarship, but on his saintliness and thaumaturgie powers. From the several maxims attributed to him it may be seen that he was a member of the Ḥasidim: "Whosoever's fear of sin precedes his learning, his learning will endure; but where learning precedes fear of sin, learning will not endure"; "Where a man's works are greater than his learning, his learning will stand; but where his learning is greater than his works, his learning will not stand"; "Whosoever earns the good-will of humanity is loved of God; but whoso is not beloved of man is not beloved of God" (Ab. iii. 9, 10; Ab. R. N. xxii. 1 [ed. Schechter, p. 35a]; for the corresponding Ḥasidean principles see Jew. Encyc. v. 225, *s.v.* ESSENES). There are, also, other teachings which betray his Ḥasidic schooling. Ḥanina, like all the ancient Ḥasidim, prayed much, and by his prayers he is said to have effected many miracles.

It is related that when the son of Johanan b. Zakkai was very sick, the father solicited the prayers of Ḥanina. Ḥanina readily complied, and the child recovered. The overjoyed father could not refrain from expressing his admiration for his wonderful pupil, stating that he himself might have prayed the whole day without doing any good. His wife, astonished at such self-abasement on the part of her famous husband, inquired, "Is Hanina greater than thou?" To this he replied, "There is. this difference between us: he is like the body-servant of a king, having at all times free access to the august presence, without even having to await permission to reach his ears; while I, like a lord before a king, must await an opportune moment" (Ber. 34b). Similarly, at the solicitation of Gamaliel II., Hanina entreated mercy for that patriarch's son, and at the conclusion of his prayers assured Gamaliel's messengers that the patient's fever had left him. This assurance created doubt in the minds of the messengers, who promptly asked, "Art thou a prophet?" To this he replied, "I am neither a prophet nor the son of a prophet; but experience has taught me that whenever my prayer flows freely it is granted; otherwise, it is rejected." The messengers thereupon noted down Hanina's declaration, and the exact time when it was made; on reaching the patriarch's residence they found that Ḥanina had spoken truly (*ib.*; comp. Ber. v. 5; Yer. Ber. v. 9d).

Ḥanina never permitted anything to turn him from his devotions. Once, while thus engaged, a lizard bit him, but he did not interrupt his prayers. To his disciples' anxious inquiries he answered that he had been so preoccupied in prayer as not even to feel the bite. When the people found the reptile, dead, they exclaimed, "Wo to the man whom a lizard bites, and wo to the lizard that bites R. Ḥanina b. Dosa!" His wonderful escape is accounted for by the assertion that the result of a lizard's bite depends upon which reaches water first, the man or the lizard; if the former, the latter dies; if the latter, the former dies. In Ḥanina's case a spring miraculously opened under his very feet (Yer. Ber. v. 9a). The Babylonian Gemara (Ber. 33a) has a different version of this miracle.

Ḥanina's prayers were efficacious in other directions also. While traveling he was caught in a shower and prayed "Master of the universe, the whole world is pleased, while Ḥanina alone is annoyed." The rain immediately ceased. Arriving home, he altered his prayer: "Master of the universe, shall all the world be grieved while Ḥanina enjoys his comfort?" Thereupon copious showers descended. With reference to his rain-governing powers it was said, "Beside Ben Dosa's prayers those of the high priest himself are of no avail" (Ta'an. 24b). When, one Sabbath eve, his daughter filled the lamp with vinegar instead of oil, and then sadly told him of her mistake, he remarked, "He who hath endowed oil with the power of burning may endow vinegar with the same power"; and the lamp burned on throughout the whole of the next day (Ta'an. 25a).

Notwithstanding his wonder-working powers, Ḥanina was very poor. Indeed, it became proverbial that, while the whole world was provided for through Hanina's great merits, he himself sustained life from one Sabbath eve to another on a basket of carob-beans. For some time the outside world had been kept in ignorance of his privations; his wife did all that was possible to maintain an appearance of comfort, and though she had no flour with which to make dough, she would put fuel into the oven every Friday and cause columns of smoke to rise, thus making her neighbors believe that, like them, she was baking the Sabbath meals. In time, however, one woman's suspicion was aroused, and she determined to surprise Ḥanina's wife and discover the truth. But a miracle prevented exposure. When the woman appeared at Ḥanina's house and looked into the smoking oven it was full of loaves. In spite of the miracle, Ḥanina's wife induced him to collect from heaven an advance portion of his future lot. Ḥanina complied with her request, and, in answer to his prayer, a golden table-leg was miraculously sent him. Husband and wife were happy; but that night the wife had a vision of heaven in which she saw the of saints feasting at three-legged tables while her husband's table had only two legs. She awoke full of regret at the importunity which had deprived his table of a leg, and insisted that he pray for the withdrawal of the treasure. This he did, and the golden leg disappeared. Of this miracle the Talmud says: "It was greater than the former, since heaven gives, but never takes" (Ta'an. 24b *et seq.*).

By a miracle Ḥanina was once prevented from partaking of untithed food. One eve of Sabbath he sat down to his frugal meal, when suddenly the table receded from him. After thinking a while he recollected that he had borrowed some spices from a neighbor and that he had not separated the required tithe. He thereupon adjusted the matter, and the table returned to him (Yer. Dem. i. 22a). It is stated that Ḥanina's donkey would not eat untithed food. Thieves had stolen the animal and confined it in their yard, furnishing it with the necessary provender; but the donkey would neither eat nor drink. As this continued for several days, the thieves concluded to free the animal, lest it starve to death and render their premises noisome. On its release it went straight home, none the worse for its long fast (Ab. R. N. viii. 8 [ed. Schechter, p. 19b]; comp. Yer. Dem. i. 21d; Shab. 112b).

Once Ḥanina was greatly grieved at not being able, with other pious people, to present something to the Temple. In his despondency he walked out of town, and, seeing a huge rock, he vowed to carry it to Jerusalem as a gift to the Holy City. He smoothed and polished it, and then looked around for help to transport it. Five laborers appeared, and offered to carry the rock to its destined place for one hundred gold pieces. Ḥanina, who did not possess half that amount, turned away in despair. Soon, however, other laborers appeared and demanded only five "sela'im," but they stipulated that Ḥanina himself should aid in the transportation. The agreement concluded, they all seized the rock, and in an instant stood before Jerusalem. When Ḥanina turned to pay the laborers they were nowhere to be found. He repaired to the Sanhedrin to inquire what disposition he should make of the uncollected wages. The Sanhedrin heard his tale and concluded that the laborers were ministering angels, not human laborers, and that Hanina was therefore at liberty to apply the money to his own use. He, however, presented it to the Temple (Cant. R. i. 1; Eccl. R. i.).

Thus was Ḥanina's life a succession of miracles (see Pes. 112b; B. Ḳ. 50a). A comparatively late mishnah remarks, "With the death of Hanina b. Dosa wonder-workers ['anshe ma'aseh'] ceased to exist" (Soṭah ix. 15). His general character was likewise extolled. A contemporary rabbi, ELEAZAR, OF MODI'IM, lecturing on Ex. xviii. 21, cited Ḥanina b. Dosa and his colleagues as illustrations of the scope of the expression "men of truth" (Mek., Yitro, Amalek, 1). Two centuries later a haggadist, commenting on Isa. iii. 3, said, "By the term 'honorable man' is meant one through whose merits Heaven respects [is favorable to] his generation; such a one was Ḥanina b. Dosa" (Ḥag. 14a). Nor was Ḥanina's wife soon forgotten; long after her death, legend relates, a party of seafarers espied a work-basket studded with diamonds and pearls. A diver attempted to seize it, but was deterred by a "bat ḳol" which said that the precious basket was designed for the wife of Ḥanina b. Dosa, who would eventually fill it with blue wool ("tekelet"; Num. xv. 38) for the saints of the future (B. B. 74a).'

Ḥanina lived at 'Arab, in Galilee, whither he was first attracted by the fame of Johanan b. Zakkai (Ber. 34b). There he served as an example of Sabbath observance (Yer. Ber. iv. 7c), and there he and his wife were buried.

BIBLIOGRAPHY: Heilprin, *Seder ha-Dorot*, ii.

S. S. M.

ḤANINA (HANANIAH) B. GAMALIEL II.: Tanna of the first and second centuries; witness, and perhaps victim, of the Roman persecutions, when, of thousands of scholars at Bethar, only his younger brother Simon b. Gamaliel II. is said to have escaped (Yer. Ta'an. iv. 69a; comp. Lam. R. ii. 2). A baraita records a halakic controversy between Ḥanina and Akiba, though the opinion of neither was adopted as law (Niddah 8a); and a mishnah cites an exegetical discussion between Ḥanina and Jose the Galilean, in which the opinion of the former was adopted by the Rabbis (Men. v. 8). His brother Simon reports as from Ḥanina a halakah opposed to his own views, but which he admits as the more reasonable (Tosef., Niddah, vii. 5); and Jose b. Ḥalafta points out that a statement made by Simeon b. Yoḥai had previously been made by Hanina (Tosef., Neg. ii. 11). Ḥanina never quotes as authorities his predecessors or contemporaries, not even his own father, and only once cites an opinion held successively by a number of his own house (Niddah 8b). It may be assumed that Tarfon was one of his teachers, for Ḥanina mentions some more or less private matters in connection with Tarfon's life, and speaks of him in reverential terms (Ned. 62b; Ḳid. 81b). At least fifteen halakot are preserved under Ḥanina's name (Weiss, "Dor," ii. 144). As a haggadist he appears inclined to adhere to the plain sense of the Scriptural texts.

The following is a specimen of Ḥanina's homiletics: "Of the Decalogue, five commandments were engraved on one tablet, and five on the other [comp. Deut. iv. 13]. The first commandment, 'I am the Lord thy God,' is therefore on a line with the sixth, 'Thou shalt not kill,' for whoso sheddeth human blood defies the Lord in whose image man was created. The second, 'Thou shalt have no other gods before me,' is in line with the seventh, 'Thou shalt not commit adultery,' for whoso serves other gods is necessarily faithless to the Lord" (comp. Ezek. xvi. 32; Hosea iii. 1); similarly with the rest of the commandments, taken in pairs (Mek., Yitro, Baḥodesh, 8). His respect for the judiciary and his sympathy with his fellow man, even when fallen, is shown in a remark on Deut. xxv., according to which the administration of legal punishment by a human tribunal exempts the sinner from deserved heavenly retribution. He further says: "Before the sinner submits to the sentence of the court he is spoken of as 'the wicked man'; but having submitted to the verdict he must again be acknowledged as 'thy brother' " (*ib.* 2–3; Mak. iii. 15; Sifre, Deut. 286). In his own house he was exceedingly strict, causing his domestics to stand in great awe of him. To avoid his displeasure they were once on the point of putting before him forbidden food in place, of some that had been lost. An amora of the third century cites this as a warning to all men not to be domineering in their homes, lest in fear of the master's displeasure the domestics commit a wrong (Giṭ. 7a).

BIBLIOGRAPHY: Bacher, *Ag. Tan.* i. 438; Brüll, *Mebo ha-Mishnah*, i. 134; Heilprin, *Seder ha-Dorot*, ii.

S. S. M.

HANINA B. ḤAMA: Palestinian halakist and haggadist; died about 250; frequently quoted in the Babylonian and the Palestinian Gemara, and in the Midrashim. He is generally cited by his prænomen alone (R. Ḥanina), but sometimes with his patronymic (Ḥanina b. Ḥama), and occasionally with the cognomen "the Great" ("ha-Gadol"; Ta'an. 27b; Pesiḳ. R. v. 15a). Whether he was a Palestinian by birth and had only visited Babylonia, or whether he was a Babylonian immigrant in Palestine, can not be clearly established. In the only passage in which he himself mentions his arrival in Palestine he refers also to his son's accompanying him (Yer. Soṭah i. 17b), and from this some argue that Babylonia was his native land. It is certain, however, that he spent most of his life in Palestine, where he attended for a time the lectures of Bar

Ḳappara and Ḥiyya the Great (Yer. Sheb. vi. 35c; Yer. Niddah ii. 50a) and eventually attached himself to the academy of Judah I. Under the last-named he acquired great stores of practical and theoretical knowledge (Yer. Niddah ii. 50b), and so developed his dialectical powers that once in the heat of debate with his senior and former teacher Ḥiyya he ventured the assertion that were some law forgotten, he could himself reestablish it by argumentation (Ket. 103b).

Judah loved him, and chose him in preference to any other of his disciples to share his privacy. Thus when Antoninus once visited Judah, he was surprised to find Ḥanina in the chamber, though the patriarch had been requested not to permit any one to attend their interview. The patriarch soothed his august visitor by the assurance that the third party was not an ordinary man (ʻAb. Zarah 10a). No doubt Hanina would have been early promoted to an honorable office had he not offended the patriarch by an ill-judged exhibition of his own superior familiarity with Scriptural phraseology (see HAMNUNA OF BABYLONIA). However, the patriarch, on his death-bed, instructed Gamaliel, his son and prospective successor, to put Ḥanina at the head of all other candidates (Yer. Taʻan. iv. 68a; comp. Ket. 103a). Ḥanina modestly declined advancement at the expense of his senior EFES, and even, resolved to permit another worthy colleague, Levi b. Sisi, to take precedence. Efes was actually principal of the academy for several years, but Sisi withdrew from the country, when Ḥanina assumed the long-delayed honors (*ib.*; Shab. 59b). He continued his residence at Sepphoris, where he became the acknowledged authority in Halakah (Yer. Sheḳ. i. 46a; Yer. Beẓah i. 60a; Yer. Giṭ. iv. 46b), and where also he practised as a physician (Yoma 49a; comp. Yer. Taʻan. i. 64a).

According to Ḥanina, 99 per cent of fatal diseases result from colds, and only 1 per cent from other troubles (Yer. Shab. xiv. 14c). He therefore would impress mankind with the necessity of warding off colds, the power to do so, he teaches, having been bestowed upon man by Providence (B. M. 107b). But neither his rabbinical learning nor his medical skill gained him popularity at Sepphoris. When a pestilence raged there, the populace blamed Ḥanina for failing to stamp it out. Ḥanina heard their murmurs and resolved to silence them. In the course of a lecture, he remarked, "Once there lived one Zimri, in consequence of whose sin twenty-four thousand Israelites lost their lives (see Num. xxv. 6–15); in our days there are many Zimris among us, and yet ye murmur!" On another occasion, when drought prevailed, the murmurs of the Sepphorites again became loud. A day was devoted to fasting and praying, but no rain came, though at another place, where Joshua b. Levi was among the suppliants, rain descended; the Sepphorites therefore made this circumstance also to reflect on the piety of their great townsman. Another fast being appointed, Ḥanina invited Joshua b. Levi to join him in prayer. Joshua did so; but no rain came. Then Ḥanina addressed the people: "Joshua b. Levi does not bring rain down for the Southerners, neither does Ḥanina keep rain away from the Sepphorites: the Southerners are soft-hearted, and when they hear the word of the Law, they humble themselves; while the Sepphorites are obdurate and never repent " (Yer. Ta'an. iii. 66c).

As a haggadist Ḥanina was prolific and resourceful—often, indeed, epigrammatic. Among his ethical aphorisms are the following: "Everything is in the power of Heaven, except the fear of Heaven." He bases this doctrine of free will on the Scriptural dictum, "And now, Israel, what doth the Lord thy God require [Hebr. שאל = "request"] of thee, but to fear the Lord thy God" (Deut. x. 12; Ber. 33b). With reference to Ps. lxxiii. 9, "They set their mouth against the heavens, and their tongue walketh through the earth," he says, "In general, man sins either against the sojourner on earth or against Heaven, but the evil-tongued sins against both" (Eccl. R. ix. 12; comp. Yer. Peah i. 16a). "Whoso avers that God is indulgent [that is, leaves sin unpunished] will find the reverse in his own life's experience; God is long-suffering, but 'his work is perfect: for all his ways are judgment' " (Deut. xxxii. 4; B. Ḳ. 50a). He predicts everlasting punishment for him who seduces a married woman, or who publicly puts his neighbor to shame, or who calls his neighbor by a nickname (B. M. 58b).

Of Ḥanina's family, one son, Shibḥat, or Shikḥat, died young (B. Ḳ. 91b); but another, Ḥama, inherited his father's talents and became prominent in his generation (see ḤAMA B. ḤANINA). One of his daughters was the wife of a scholar, Samuel b. Nadab by name ('Ar. 16b); another died during Ḥanina's lifetime, but he shed no tears at her death, and when his wife expressed astonishment at his composure he told her that he feared the effects of tears on his sight (Shab. 151b). He lived to be very old, and retained his youthful vigor to the last. He attributed his extraordinary vitality to the hot baths and the oil with which his mother had treated him in his youth (Ḥul. 24b). In his longevity he recognized a reward for the respect he had shown his learned elders (Eccl. R. vii. 7). Among his pupils were such men as JOHANAN B. NAPPAḤA and ELEAZAR II., both of whom became rabbinical authorities in their generation, and in whose distinction he lived to rejoice. One morning, while walking, leaning on the arm of an attendant, Ḥanina noticed throngs of people hurrying toward a certain place. In answer to his inquiry, he was informed that R. Johanan was to lecture at the academy of R. Benaiah. and that the people were flocking thither to hear him. Ḥanina thereupon exclaimed, "Praised be the Lord for permitting me to see the fruit of my labors before I die" (Yer. Hor. ii. 48b).

BIBLIOGRAPHY: Bacher, *Ag. Pal. Amor.* i. 1 *et seq.*; Frankel, *Mebo*, p. 86b; Grätz, *Gesch.* 2d ed., iv. 254 *et seq.*; Heilprin, *Seder ha-Dorot*, ii. 74d, Warsaw, 1897; Halévy, *Dorot ha-Rishonim*, ii. 129b *et seq.*; Weiss, *Dor*, iii. 44 *et seq.*; Zacuto, *Yuḥasin*, ed. Filipowski, pp. 141b *et.seq.*

S. S. M.

ḤANINA B. IDDI. See ḤANINA B. ADDA.

ḤANINA B. PAPA: Palestinian amora, hala-kist, and haggadist; flourished in the third and fourth centuries; a younger contemporary of Samuel b. Naḥman (Yer. Sheb. v. 36a). His name is variously written **Ḥanina, Hananiah,** and **Ḥinena** (comp. Yer. Ber. i. 4b; Yer. M. Ḳ. iii. 83c; Cant. R. i. 2; Yalḳ., Cant. i. 2). That he possessed great stores of learning is shown by the frequency with which he is cited in both Talmud and Midrash; and he enjoyed the companionship of the foremost teachers of his generation. With Simon (Shimeon) b. Pazzi he discussed exegetics, and he was associated with Abbahu and Isaac Nappaḥa on the judiciary (Giṭ. 29b; B. Ḳ. 117b). Legend has surrounded his name with supernatural incidents (see Jew. Encyc. i. 361, *s.v.* ALEXANDRI).

Ḥanina was very charitable, and distributed his gifts at night so as not to expose the recipients to shame. But as the night is assigned to the evil spirits, his procedure displeased the latter. Once the chief of the spirits met him and asked, "Do you not teach the Biblical inhibition, 'Thou shalt not remove thy neighbors landmark'? Why then do you invade my province?" Ḥanina answered, "Does not the Bible also teach, 'A gift in secret pacifieth anger'?" thus reminding the spirit that no evil could befall him. On hearing this the spirit became disheartened and fled (Deut. xix. 14; Prov. xxi. 14; Yer. Peah viii. 21b ["Hananiah"]; Yer. Sheḳ. v. 49b ["Ḥinena"]). Once Ḥanina was tempted by a matron, but at his word his body became repulsive with sores; when, by the aid of witchcraft, the temptress removed them, he ran away and hid in a haunted bath-house. There he spent the night, and escaped at daybreak (Ḳid. 39b, 81 a).

Ḥanina is reputed to have been providentially guarded against errors of judgment. On one occasion he made a mistake in connection with a mourning, and in the succeeding night was corrected by a dream in which he heard the message, "Thou hast disobeyed the mouth of the Lord" (I Kings xiii. 21; Yer. M. Ḳ. iii. 83a). In his public lectures Ḥanina frequently illustrated God's wisdom as manifested in nature (Ḥul. 60a; Niddah 31a), and expressed many eschatological thoughts. Starting with Isa. xliii. 9 ("Let all the nations be gathered together, and let the people be assembled: who among them can declare this, and show us former things? let them bring forth their witnesses, that they may be justified"), he delivered the following homily, perhaps the longest and most connected of all haggadot:

"In the future the Holy One—blessed be He I—will take a scroll of the Law, and invite all who have observed its behests to appear and receive their due reward. All nations will come promiscuously, but the Lord will say, 'Let each nation with its historians come in singly.' Edom [Rome] will then appear, when the Lord will ask, 'Wherewith have ye occupied yourselves?' Edom will answer, 'Lord of the Universe, we have erected many market-places, built many baths, amassed silver and gold: all this we did that the children of Israel might devote themselves to the practise of the Law.' Thereupon God will say, 'Consummate knaves, whatever ye have accomplished ye have done from self-interest; ye have erected market-places to people them with prostitutes; built baths to benefit yourselves: and as for the silver and the gold, that is Mine [see. Ḥag. ii. 8]. But is there one among you that can tell about this [Law]?' As soon as they hear they will depart crestfallen, and Persia will enter. To the question as to their occupation the Persians will answer that they have built bridges, conquered cities, and waged wars, all to afford Israel opportunities for keeping the Law. However, they too will be rebuked by the Lord, who will point out that whatever they have done has been prompted by selfish motives; they in turn will be asked, 'Who of you can declare this [Law]?' Persia will then retire in confusion; so it will go with every other nation except Israel.

"At last the nations will protest, 'Lord of the Universe, didst Thou ever offer us the Law, and we fail to receive it?' To which the Lord will rejoin: 'Show us former things; I have offered you seven precepts, which you accepted; did you keep them?' Whereupon they will ask, 'And did Israel.keep the Law?' Then the Lord will say, 'I Myself bear witness that Israel did.' The nations: 'May a father bear witness for a son? Thou hast said [Ex. iv. 22], "Israel is my son, even my firstborn." ' The Lord: 'Then heaven and earth will testify.' The nations: 'Heaven and earth are interested witnesses, for the Bible says [Jer. xxxiii. 25, Hebr.], "Were it not for My covenant to be kept day and night, I should not have appointed the ordinances of heaven and earth." ' The Lord: 'From among yourselves witnesses will come and testify that Israel has faithfully kepi the Law. Nimrod can testify that Abraham did not worship idols; Laban can testify that there was no ground for suspecting Jacob of misappropriation; Potiphar's wife can testify that Joseph could not be suspected of immorality; Nebuchadnezzar can testify that Hananiah, Mishael, and Azariah never bowed to an image; Darius can testify that Daniel never neglected prayer; Bildad the Shuhite, and Zophar the Naamathite, and Eliphaz the Temanite can testify that Israel has kept the Law.' Then the nations will propose: 'Give us the reward in advance, and we will keep the Law.' Thereunto the Lord will answer, 'Whoso toiled on the eve of the Sabbath [*i.e.*, stored up good deeds against the time when nothing more could be done] may feast on the Sabbath-day; but whoso did not toil on the eve of the Sabbath, whereon shall he feast during the Sabbath?' " ('Ab. Zarah 2a *et seq.*).

BIBLIOGRAPHY: Bacher, *Ag. Pal. Amor.* ii. 513 *et seq.*; Heilprin, *Seder ha-Dorot*, ii.

S. S. M.

ḤANINA (ḤANIN) B. PAZZI: Palestinian haggadist of the third and fourth centuries. His teachings are confined to the midrashic literature. It is suggested that he may have been the brother of the better-known amora Simon b. Pazzi; but if so, he never cites that brother. Among the comparatively few sayings known to be his is the following: "To the office of designer of the Tabernacle God appointed Bezaleel and Aholiab [Ex. xxxi. 2, 6]—the first being a member of Judah, the largest of the tribes; the second, of Dan, the smallest of the tribes—that people may learn not to slight the small, and that the greater should not be proud; great and small are alike before God" (Ex. R. xl, 4; Tan., Ki Tissa, 13). Speaking of the early motherhood of Hagar (Gen. xvi. 4) and of Lot's daughters (*ib.* xix. 23 *et seq.*), and comparing them with the long barrenness of Sarah, Ḥanina says, "Weeds require neither hoeing nor sowing; they spring up of themselves, and grow and thrive; while to produce wheat, how much trouble and anxiety must be endured!" (Gen. R. xlv. 4).

S. S. M.

ḤANINA OF SURA: Babylonian scholar of the fifth century; the junior of Mar Zuṭra, who reports to Ashi a halakic objection raised by Ḥanina (Niddah 52a). It is said that at one time Ḥanina's mother had such an aversion for her husband that she would not live with him. Mar Zuṭra succeeded in bringing them together again; and Ḥanina was the offspring of the reunion (Ket. 63b). In the haggadic literature he does not appear, but in halakah he is quoted as an authority (Soṭah 25b; Ḳid. 79a). He endeavors to reconcile conflicting opinions of others (Ber. 52b; Shab. 23b; see Rabbinovicz, "Diḳduḳe Soferim," *ad loc.*). According to Ḥanina, since there is no "bitter water" (see Num. v.) to prove a woman's fidelity, a man must not so readily suspect his wife of unfaithfulness, as it may lead to forced yet gratuitous separation (Soṭah 2b).

S. S. M.

ḤANINA B. TERADION. See HANANIAH B. TERADION.

ḤANINA (ḤINENA) B. TORTA: Pales tinian scholar of the third century; disciple of Johanan and contemporary of Ammi and Isaac Nappaha (Tem. 29a, 31a; Ned. 57b; comp. Yer. Ter. vii. 45a). He was born in Ṭirna, or Torta, identified by Neubauer ("G. T." p. 267; comp. p. 363) with Ṭuria in Palestine, or Be-Torta in Babylonia. If the latter identification is correct, Ḥanina was a Palestinian immigrant from Babylonia. One halakic midrash, by Jannai, is cited by him (Ned. 57b); he reports halakot in the name of Hezekiah b. Ḥiyya (Yer. Peah iii. 17d) and Hoshaiah (Yer. Ter. x. 47b); while Ḥiyya b. Abba cites Ḥanina himself as an authority (Yer. Ber. iii. 6d).

S. S. M.

ḤELBO: Amora who flourished about the end of the third century, and who is frequently mentioned in both Talmuds. It seems that Ḥelbo was at first in Babylon, where he studied under Huna, the head of the Academy of Sura, and that, like the other Babylonian amoraim, he was called "Rab" (Ned. 40a). Later he settled in Palestine, where he was ordained rabbi. He is mentioned as having spoken in the names of Abdima of Ḥaifa (Yer. Ber. iv. 4) and of Ḥama b. 'Uḳba (Yer. Meg. ii. 3). In Palestine he consulted on halakic matters R. Isaac Nappaḥa (Giṭ. 60a) and R. Samuel b. Naḥmani (B. B. 123a). Ḥelbo handed down a large number of haggadic sayings of Samuel b. Naḥmani. Ḥelbo is mentioned in the Talmud as a teacher of ethics, his sayings being delivered in the name of Huna. Among them may be quoted: "He who goes out of the synagogue must not take long steps"; "One should pay great attention to the Minḥah prayer"; "He who enjoys the banquet of a bridegroom without gladdening the latter commits a fivefold sin" (Ber. 6b); "He who sees a torn scroll of the Pentateuch must rend his garment in two places" (M. Ḳ. 26a). Ḥelbo also said, in the name of 'Ula, that he who sees the ruined cities of Judah must recite Isaiah lxiv. 9–10. In Gen. R. xliii., in the name of R. Eleazar, Ḥelbo is mentioned as a traditionist with R. Berechiah and R. Ammi. A Ḥelbo b. Ḥilfa b. Samḳaï is also mentioned (Gen. R. li.), who may be identical with the subject of this topic. Yer. Ber. vii. 1 contains a reference to a R. Ḥelbo b. Ḥanan.

BIBLIOGRAPHY: Abraham Zacuto, *Yuḥasin*, ed. Filipowski; Jehiel Heilprin, *Seder ha-Dorot*, ii.; Bacher, *Ag. Pal. Amor.* iii. 54–63.

E. C. M. SEL.

HEZEKIAH BEN PARNAK: Palestinian amora; lived at the end of the third century. The only mention of him is in Berakot 63a, in connection with the transmission of Johanan bar Nappaḥa's exegetical explanation of the fact that the section concerning the faithless wife (Num. v. 11–31) follows the section on the refusal of the priestly tithe (*ib.* v. 5–11).

BIBLIOGRAPHY: Heilprin, *Seder ha-Dorot*, ed. Warsaw, p. 128; Bacher, *Ag. Pal. Amor.* i. 219, 272.

S. M. SC.

ḤILFA. See ḤALAFTA.

HILLEL I: Doctor of the Law at Jerusalem in the time of King Herod; founder of the school called after him, and ancestor of the patriarchs who stood at the head of Palestinian Judaism till about the fifth century of the common era. Hillel was a Babylonian by birth and, according to a later tradition, belonged to the family of David (Lévi, in "R. E. J." xxxi. 202–211, xxxiii. 143). Nothing definite, however, is known concerning his origin, nor is he anywhere called by his father's name, which may perhaps have been Gamaliel. When Josephus ("Vita,"

§ 38) speaks of Hillel's great-grandson, Simeon ben Gamaliel I., as belonging to a very celebrated family (*γένους δέ σφόδρα λαμπροῦ*), he probably refers to the glory which the family owed to the activity of Hillel and Gamaliel I. Only Hillel's brother Shebna (Soṭah 21a) is mentioned; he was a merchant, whereas Hillel devoted himself to study. In Sifre, Deut. 357 the periods of Hillel's life are made parallel to those in the life of Moses. Both were 120 years old; at the age of forty Hillel went to Palestine; forty years he spent in study; and the last third of his life he passed as the spiritual head of Israel. Of this artificially constructed biographical sketch this much may be true, that Hillel went to Jerusalem in the prime of his manhood and attained a great age. His activity of forty years is perhaps historical; and since it began, according to a trustworthy tradition (Shab. 15a), one hundred years before the destruction of Jerusalem, it must have covered the period 30 B.C.–10 C.E.

According to an old tannaitic tradition founded upon Hillel's own words, Hillel went to Jerusalem with the intention of perfecting himself in the science of Biblical exposition and of tradition (Yer Pes. 33c; Tosef., Neg. i.; Sifra, Tazria', ix.). Shemaiah and Abṭalion, the "great Scripture expositors" ("darshanim"; Pes. 70b), became his teachers. The difficulties which Hillel had to overcome in order to be admitted to their school, and the hardships he suffered while pursuing his aim, are told in a touching passage (Yoma 35b), the ultimate purpose of which is to show that poverty can not be considered as an obstacle to the study of the Law. Some time after the death of Shemaiah and Abṭalion, Hillel succeeded in settling a question concerning the sacrificial ritual in a manner which showed at once his superiority over the Bene Bathyra, who were at that time the heads of the college. On that occasion, it is narrated, they voluntarily resigned their position in favor of Hillel (Tosef., Pes. iv.; Pes. 66a; Yer. Pes. 33a). According to tradition, Hillel thereupon became head of the Sanhedrin with the title of "Nasi" (prince); but this is hardly historical. All that can be said is that after the resignation of the Bene Bathyra Hillel was recognized as the highest authority among the Pharisees and the scribes of Jerusalem. He was the head of the great school, at first associated with Menahem, a scholar mentioned in no other connection, afterward with Shammai, Hillel's peer in the study of the Law (Ḥag. ii. 2; Gem. 16b; Yer. Ḥag. 77d). Hillel's only title was "Ha-Zaḳen" (the elder), a title given not to distinguish him from another of the same name, as some have held, but either to express his position among the leading scribes or to indicate his membership in the Sanhedrin.

Whatever Hillel's position, his authority was sufficient to introduce those decrees which were handed down in his name. The most famous of his enactments was the Prosbul (*προσβολή*), an institution which, in spite of the law concerning the year of jubilee (Deut. xv. 1 *et seq.*), insured the repayment of loans (Sheb. x. 3). The motive for this institution was the "amelioration of the world" ("tiḳḳun ha-'olam"), *i.e.*, of the social order (Giṭ. iv. 3), because it protected both the creditor against the loss of his property, and the needy against being refused the loan of money for fear of loss. A like tendency is found in another of Hillel's institutions, having reference to the sale of houses (Lev. xxv. 30; 'Ar. ix.). These two are the only institutions handed down in Hillel's name, although the words which introduce the prosbul (Sheb. *ib.*) show that there were others. Hillel's judicial activity may be inferred from the decision by which he confirmed the legitimacy of some Alexandrians whose origin was disputed, by interpreting the marriage document ("ketubbah") of their mother in her favor (Tosef., Ket. iv. 9; B. M. 104a). Of other official acts no mention is found in the sources.

In the memory of posterity Hillel lived, on the one hand, as the scholar who made the whole contents of the traditional law his own (Soferim xvi. 9), who, in opposition to his colleague, Shammai, generally advocated milder interpretations of the Halakah, and whose disciples as a "house," that is, as "Hillel's school," stood in like opposition to Shammai's disciples. On the other hand, he was known as the saint and the sage who in his private life and in his dealings with men practised the high virtues of morality and resignation, just as he taught them in his maxims with unexcelled brevity and earnestness. The traditions concerning Hillel's life harmonize completely with the sayings which are handed down in his name, and bear in themselves the proof of their genuineness. No wonder that the Babylonian Talmud is richer in traditions concerning Hillel than the Palestinian, since the Babylonians were especially careful to preserve the recollection of their great countryman; and in the Babylonian schools of the third century was proudly quoted the saying of the Palestinian Simeon ben Laḳish—on the whole no friend of the Babylonians—in which he placed the activity of Hillel on a level with that of Ezra, who also went up from Babylon to Jerusalem. Hillel's sayings are preserved partly in Hebrew, the language of the school, partly in Aramaic, the language of the people, or, as it is said in Ab. R. N. xii., in the language of Hillel's home ("the Babylonian language").

The saying of Hillel which introduces the collection of his maxims in the Mishnaic treatise Abot mentions Aaron as the great model to be imitated in his love of peace, in his love of man, and in his leading mankind to a knowledge of the Law (Ab. i. 12). In mentioning these characteristics, which the Haggadah then already ascribed to Moses' brother, Hillel mentions his own most prominent virtues. Love of man was considered by Hillel as the kernel of the entire Jewish teaching. When a heathen who wished to become a Jew asked him for a summary of the Jewish religion in the most concise terms, Hillel said: "What is hateful to thee, do not unto thy fellow man: this is the whole Law; the rest is mere commentary" (Shab. 31a). With these words Hillel recognized as the fundamental principle of the Jewish moral law the Biblical precept of brotherly love (Lev. xix. 18). Almost the same thing was taught by Paul, a pupil of Gamaliel, the grandson of Hillel (Gal. v. 14; comp. Rom. xiii. 8); and more broadly by Jesus when he declared the love of one's neighbor to be the second great commandment beside the love of God, the first (Matt. xxii. 39; Mark xii. 31; Luke x. 27). It may be assumed without argument that Hillel's answer to the proselyte, which is extant in a narrative in the Babylonian Talmud (comp. also Ab. R. N., recension B., cxxvi. [ed. Schechter, p. 53]), was generally known in Palestine, and that it was not without its effect on the founder of Christianity.

It has been remarked that Hillel did not, like Jesus, state the love of God to be the principal commandment of the Jewish teaching (see Delitzsch, "Jesus und Hillel," p. 17); but it must not be forgotten that Jesus gave his answer to a scribe, whereas Hillel answered the question of a prospective proselyte, to whom it was necessary first of all to show now the teachings of Judaism are to be practised by him who wishes to accept them. That the love of God had also a central position in Hillel's conception of religion needs not to be proved; this position had long been assigned to it in Judaism—since the Scripture passage in which this precept is joined immediately to the confession of the unity of God (Deut. vi. 4 *et seq.*) had been made the principal portion of the daily prayer. Moreover, the Pharisaic scribes who approved of Jesus' answer evidently belonged to Hillel's school. Hillel seems to have connected the precept of brotherly love with the Biblical teaching of man's likeness to God, on which account he calls the love of man "love of creatures" ("oheb et ha-beriyyot"); and it is worthy of note that the term "creatures" for men was then, already the common property of the language.

From the doctrine of man's likeness to God Hillel ingeniously deduced man's duty to care for his own body. In a conversation with his disciples (Lev. R. xxxiv.) he said: "As in a theater and circus the statues of the king must be kept clean by him to whom they have been entrusted, so the bathing of the body is a duty of man, who was created in the image of the almighty King of the world." In another conversation Hillel calls his soul a guest upon earth, toward which he must fulfil the duties of charity (*ib.*). Man's duty toward himself Hillel emphasized also in the first sentence of his saying (Ab. i. 14): "If I am not for myself, who is for me? and if I am only for myself, what am I? and if not now, when?" The second part of this sentence expresses the same idea as another of Hillel's teachings (Ab. ii. 4): "Separate not thyself from the congregation." The third part contains the admonition to postpone no duty—the same admonition which he gave with reference to study (Ab. ii. 4): "Say not, 'When I have time I shall study'; for you may perhaps never have any leisure."

The precept that one should not separate oneself from the community, Hillel paraphrases, with reference to Eccl. iii, 4, in the following saying (Tosef., Ber. ii., toward the end): "Appear neither naked nor clothed, neither sitting nor standing, neither laughing nor weeping." Man should not appear different from others in his outward deportment; he should always regard himself as a part of the whole, thereby showing that love of man which Hillel taught. The feeling of love for one's neighbor shows itself also in his exhortation (Ab. ii. 4): "Judge not thy neighbor till thou art in his place" (comp. Matt. vii. 1). In the following maxim is expressed also his consciousness of his own insufficiency: "Trust not thyself till the day of thy death." How far his love of man went may be seen from an example which shows that benevolence must act with regard to the needs of him who is to be helped. Thus a man of good family who had become poor Hillel provided with a riding horse, in order that he might not be deprived of his customary physical exercise, and with a slave, in order that he might be served (Tosef., Peah, iv. 10; Ket. 67b).

That the same spirit of kindness prevailed in Hillel's house is shown by a beautiful story (Derek Ereẓ v.). Hillel's wife one day gave the whole of a meal, prepared in honor of a guest, to a poor man, and at once prepared another. When she excused herself for the delay and explained its cause, Hillel praised her for her action. How firmly Hillel was persuaded that peace was ruling in his house, the following tradition teaches (Ber. 60a; Yer. Ber. 14b): When one day he came near his house and heard a noise, he expressed, in the words of Ps. cxii. 7 ("He shall not be afraid of evil tidings"), his confidence that the noise could not be in his house. His trust in God was such that whereas Shammai provided for the Sabbath already on the first day of the week, Hillel referred to Ps. lxviii. 19: "Blessed be the Lord who daily loadeth us with benefits" (Beẓah 16a).

The exhortation to love peace emanated from Hillel's most characteristic traits—from that meekness and mildness which had become proverbial, as is seen from the saying: "Let a man be always humble and patient like Hillel, and not passionate like Shammai" (Shab. 31a; Ab. R. N. xv.). Hillel's gentleness and patience are beautifully illustrated in an anecdote which relates how two men made a wager on the question whether Hillel could be made angry. Though they questioned him and made insulting allusions to his Babylonian origin, they were unsuccessful in their attempt (*ib.*). In the anecdotes about proselytes in which Hillel and Shammai are opposed to each other, Hillel's mildness and meekness appear in a most favorable light. In a paradoxical manner Hillel praised humility, in the following words (Lev. R. i. 1): "My humility is my exaltation; my exaltation is my humility" (with reference to Ps. cxiii. 5).

The many anecdotes, resting doubtless on good tradition, according to which Hillel made proselytes, correspond to the third part of his maxim: "Bring men to the Law." A later source (Ab. R. N., recension B., xxvi., toward the end) gives the following explanation of the sentence: Hillel stood in the gate of Jerusalem one day and saw the people on their way to work. "How much," he asked, "will you earn to-day?" One said: "A denarius"; the second: "Two denarii." "What will you do with the money?" he inquired. "We will provide for the necessities of life." Then said he to them: "Would you not rather come and make the Torah your possession, that you may possess both this and the future world?" This narrative has the same points as the epigrammatic group of Hillel's sayings (Ab. ii. 7) commencing: "The more flesh, the more worms," and closing with the words: "Whoever has acquired the words of the Law has acquired the life of the world to come." In an Aramaic saying Hillel sounds a warning against neglect of study or its abuse for selfish purposes: "Whoever would make a name [glory] loses the name; he who increases not [his knowledge] decreases; whoever learns not [in Ab. R. N. xii.: "who does not serve the wise and learn"] is worthy of death; whoever makes use of the crown perishes" (Ab. i. 13). Another group reads (Ab. ii. 5): "The uneducated has no aversion to sin; the ignorant is not pious; the timid can not learn, nor the passionate teach; he who is busied with trade can not become wise. In a place where there are no men, study to show thyself a man" (*ib.*). In this last sentence Hillel may have recalled how he, overcoming his modesty, manfully came forward in Jerusalem after the death of Shemaiah and Abtalion and gave a new impulse to learning, then threatened with decay. To his own activity no doubt refers the saying preserved in Aramaic (Yer. Ber. 143) and Hebrew (Tosef., Ber. vii.; Ber. 63a): "Where some gather, scatter; where they scatter, gather!" that is, "Learn where there are teachers, teach where there are learners" (another form is given in Sifre Zuṭa on Num. xxvii. 1; Yalḳ., Num. 773).

The epigrammatic and antithetic form of Hillel's sayings, as well as the almost mystic depth of his consciousness of God, may be seen from the words spoken by him at the festival of water-drawing, when, filled with a feeling of God's presence, he said: "If I am here—so says God—every one is here; if I am not here, nobody is here" (Suk. 53a; Ab. R. N. xii., without stating the occasion of the utterance). In like manner, with reference to Ex. xx. 24, and applying a proverb, Hillel makes God speak to Israel: "To the place in which I delight my feet bring me. If thou comest to mine house, I come to thine; if thou comest not to mine, I come not to thine" (Suk. *l.c.*, Tosef., Suk. iv. 3).

In an epigrammatic form Hillel expresses the moral order of the world, according to which every sin is punished (Ab. ii. 6). Seeing a skull floating on the water, he said (in Aramaic): "Because thou didst drown, thou art drowned; and in the end they that have drowned, shall be drowned." Hillel was perhaps thinking here of the misdeeds of Herod and of the retribution which he could not escape.

No indications exist of Hillel's relation to the rulers of his time; but his love of peace and his devotion to study as the most important part of his life, no doubt showed the way which his disciple Johanan ben Zakkai, under the yoke of the Romans and amidst the strife of parties which brought about the catastrophe of Jerusalem, pursued for the salvation of Judaism. A panegyric tradition concerning Hillel's pupils (Suk. 28a; B. B. 134a), which glorifies the master in the disciples, recounts that of the eighty disciples whom Hillel had (probably during the last period of his activity), thirty were worthy that the glory of God (the spirit of prophecy) should rest upon them as upon Moses; thirty, that for their sake the sun should stand still as for Joshua. It is possible that this figure, which may have had a historical basis, was a reference to the fact that among Hillel's disciples were those who, like Joshua, were ready to fight against Israel's enemy and were worthy of victory; perhaps, also, that to them belonged those distinguished and beloved teachers whom Josephus mentions ("Ant." xvii. 6, § 2), Judah ben Sarifai and Mattithiah ben Margalot, who shortly before Herod's death led a revolt directed against fixing the Roman eagle on the Temple gate. This tradition concerning Hillel's disciples mentions, moreover, two by name: Jonathan ben Uzziel and Johanan ben Zakkai (comp. also Yer. Ned. v., toward the end).

In the history of tradition Hillel's disciples are generally called "the house of Hillel" (see Bet Hillel), in opposition to Shammai's disciples, "the house of Shammai." Their controversies, which no doubt included also those of their masters, concern all branches of tradition—Midrash, Halakah, and Haggadah. Only a few decisions, belonging to these three branches, have been handed down under Hillel's name; but there can be no doubt that much of the oldest anonymous traditional literature was due directly to him or to the teachings of his masters. The fixation of the norms of the Midrash and of halakic Scripture exposition was first made by Hillel, in the "seven rules of Hillel," which, as is told in one source, he applied on the day on which he overcame the Bene Bathyra (Tosef., Sanh. vii., toward the end; Sifra, Introduction, end;

Ab. R. N. xxxvii.). On these seven rules rest the thirteen of R. Ishmael; they were epoch-making for the systematic development of the ancient Scripture exposition.

Hillel's importance as the embodiment of the religious and moral teachings of Judaism and as the restorer of Jewish Scripture exegesis is expressed in a most significant manner in the words of lamentation uttered at his death: "Wo for the meek one! Wo for the pious! Wo for the disciple of Ezra!" (Tosef., Soṭah, xiii. 3; Soṭah 48b; Yer. Soṭah, toward the end). One day while he and the sages were assembled at Jericho, a heavenly voice is said to have exclaimed: "Among those here present is one man upon whom the Holy Spirit would rest, if his time were worthy of it." All eyes were thereupon fixed on Hillel. No miracles are connected with Hillel's memory. He lived, without the glory of legend, in the memory of posterity as the great teacher who taught and practised the virtues of philanthropy, fear of God, and humility.

BIBLIOGRAPHY: Comp. the respective sections in the works of Frankel, Grätz, Geiger, Weiss, Hamburger, Renan, Derenbourg, and Schürer; Bacher, *Ag. Tan.* i. 4–14 (3d ed., 1–11); Kämpf, *Hillel der Aeltere*, in *Orient*, ix.–x; Goitein, *Das Leben und Wirken des Patriarchen Hillel*, in Berliner's *Magazin*, xi.; Franz Delitzsch, *Jesus und Hillel*, Erlangen, 1866 (3d ed., 1879); Strack, in Herzog-Hauck, *Real-Encyc.* viii. 74–76, s.v. *Hillel.*

S. S. W. B.

HILLEL II.: Patriarch (330–365); son and successor of Judah III. Only in two instances is his name quoted in connection with halakot: in one, Jose b. Abin expounds to him a law; in the other, Hillel cites a mishnah to establish a law (Yer. Ber. ii. 5a; Yer. Ter. i. 41a). Tradition ascribes to him an enactment which proved of incalculable benefit to his coreligionists of his own and of subsequent generations. To equalize the lunar with the solar year, and thereby render possible the universal celebration of the festivals on the days designated in the Bible, occasional intercalations of a day in a month and of a month in a year were required. These intercalations were determined at meetings of a special commission of the Sanhedrin. But Constantius, following the tyrannous precedents of Hadrian, prohibited the holding of such meetings as well as the vending of articles for distinctively Jewish purposes. How difficult the fixing of the annual calendar consequently became may be judged from an enigmatic letter addressed to Raba, the principal of the academy at Maḥuza, and preserved in the Talmud. It was evidently written by a friend in Palestine who wished to acquaint the Babylonian religious authorities with the condition of Judaism in its mother country, and with the resolutions of a meeting held for the purpose indicated above. It reads thus:

"A pair [of disciples], coming from Raḳḳat [Tiberias; see Meg. 6a], were apprehended by the Eagle [Romans], because in their possession they had fabrics from Luz [blue or purple yarn for fringes, the ẓiẓit]. By the grace of the All-merciful and through their own merits they escaped. Also, the burden-bearers of Naḥshon [the diviner: the commission appointed by the patriarch] desired to establish a guard [an intercalary month], but the Arameans [Romans] would not permit them. However, the commanders of the gathering [leaders of the council] convened [another time] and established a guard in the month in which Aaron the priest died" (the month of Ab; Sanh. 12a).

Almost the whole Diaspora depended for the legal observance of the feasts and fasts upon the calendar sanctioned by the Judean Sanhedrin; yet danger threatened the participants in that sanction and the messengers who communicated their decisions to distant congregations. Temporarily to relieve the foreign congregations, Huna b. Abin (doubtless with the approval, or by the order, of Hillel) once advised Raba not to wait for the official intercalation: "When thou art convinced that the winter quarter will extend beyond the sixteenth day of Nisan declare the year a leap-year, and do not hesitate" (R. H. 21a). But as the religious persecutions continued, Hillel determined to provide an authorized calendar for all time to come, though by so doing he severed the ties which united the Jews of the Diaspora to their mother country and to the patriarchate.

The emperor Julian showed himself particularly gracious to Hillel, whom he honored on many occasions. In an autograph letter to him, Julian assured him of his friendship and promised to ameliorate further the condition of the Jews. Before setting out for the war with Persia, Julian addressed to the Jewish congregations a circular letter in which he informed them that he had "committed the Jewish tax-rolls to the flames," and that, "desiring to show them still greater favors, he has advised his brother, the venerable patriarch Julos, to abolish what was called the 'send-tax.' "

BIBLIOGRAPHY: Grätz, *Gesch.* iv. 332 *et seq.*, and note 34; Halévy, *Dorot ha-Rishonim*, ii. 197; Heilprin, *Seder ha-Dorot*, ii.; Krochmal, *Yerushalayim ha-Benuyah*, Introduction, pp. 27 *et seq.*; *Maḥzor Vitry*, p. 478, Berlin, 1893.

S. S. M.

HILLEL B. BERECHIAH (JEBERECHIAH): Palestinian haggadist. He is cited only once under this name, and then as author of an interpretation which elsewhere is attributed to another (Lam. R. i. 5; comp. Sanh. 104b). He is identical with **Ila'i or Ilaa b. Berechiah,** "Hillel" being a variant of this name (comp. ELA). Under this name he appears several times (see Ta'an. 10a; Sanh. 94b; comp. Rabbinovicz, "Diḳduḳe Soferim," *ad loc.*). Among several of his homiletic interpretations, grouped together for students, there is one which declares that when two students travel together and do not discuss the Law they deserve to be consumed by fire. He deduces this from II Kings ii. 11: had Elijah and Elisha not talked of the things of the Law the fiery chariot and horses would have consumed and not merely have parted them (Soṭah 49a).

BIBLIOGRAPHY: Bacher, *Ag. Pal. Amor.* iii. 703, 764; Heilprin, *Seder ha-Dorot*, ii. 27a, Warsaw, 1897.

S. S. M.

HILLEL BEN GAMALIEL III.: Scholar of the second amoraic generation (3d cent.), son of Gamaliel III., brother of Judah II., and probably a pupil of his grandfather Judah I. (see B. B. 83b). Of his early history nothing is known. As illustrating his modesty the following incidents may be quoted: He and his brother were once at Biri, where people remonstrated against their walking on the Sabbath in shoes with golden buckles, which was not customary at that place: they resignedly removed their shoes and handed them over to their accompanying slaves. On another occasion at Kabul they were about to bathe together when the people informed them that they did not consider it moral for brothers to bathe together: Hillel and his brother thereupon desisted. In either case they could have shown the people that their acts were perfectly legal, but they preferred to comply with the local customs (Tosef., M. Ḳ. ii. 15, 16; Pes. 51a). While Hillel is not often quoted in connection with halakot, he was an able interpreter of Scripture; this accounts for Origen seeking his society and consulting him frequently on difficult Biblical passages. It was probably this Hillel that declared, "The Jews have no Messiah to expect, for they have already consumed him in the days of Hezekiah" (Sanh. 99a). He may have been prompted to this declaration by Origen's professed discovery in the Old Testament of Messianic passages referring to the founder of Christianity. Some credit Hillel, and not his better-known namesake, with the authorship of the following maxims: "Separate not thyself from the community"; "Be not confident in thyself until the day of thy death"; "Condemn not thy neighbor until thou hast been placed in his condition"; "Use no unintelligible expressions assuming that ultimately they will be understood"; "Say not 'When I have leisure I shall study': thou mayest never be at leisure" (Ab. ii. 4; see Tosef., Yom-Ṭob, *ad loc.*).

BIBLIOGRAPHY: Grätz, *Gesch.* iv. 250; Heilprin, *Seder ha-Dorot*, ii. 56a, Warsaw, 1897.

S. S. M.

ḤISDA: Babylonian amora of the third generation; died in 620 of the Seleucidan era (= 308–309; Sherira Gaon, in Neubauer, "M. J. C." i. 30; in 300, according to Abraham ibn Daud, "Sefer ha-Ḳabbalah," in

Neubauer, *l.c.* p. 58), at the age of ninety-two (M. Ḳ. 28a); descended from a priestly family (Ber. 44a). Ḥisda studied under Rab (ABBA ARIKA), who was his principal teacher; after the latter's death he attended the lectures of Huna, his companion, and of the same age as himself. He and Huna were styled "the ḥasidim of Babylon" (Ta'an. 23b); he was also one of those just ones ("ẓaddiḳim") who could bring down rain by their prayers (M. Ḳ. 28a). At first he was so poor that he abstained from vegetables because they incited the appetite (Shab. 140b), and when he walked in thorny places he raised his garments, saying: "The breaches in my legs will heal of themselves, but the breaches in my garments will not" (B. Ḳ. 91b). Later, as a brewer, he became fabulously rich (Pes. 113a; M. Ḳ. 28a). At the age of sixteen he married the daughter of Ḥanan b. Raba (Ḳid. 29b), by whom he had seven or more sons and two daughters. One of his pupils, Raba, became his son-in-law (Niddah 61b).

Ḥisda was a great casuist ('Er. 67a), and his acute mind greatly enhanced the fame of Huna's school at Sura. But his very acuteness indirectly caused a rupture between himself and Huna. The separation was brought about by a question from Ḥisda as to the obligations of a disciple toward a master to whom he is indispensable. Huna saw the point and said, "Ḥisda, I do not need thee; it is thou that needst me!" Forty years passed before they became reconciled (B. M. 33a). Ḥisda nevertheless held Huna in great esteem, and although he had established a school, built at his own expense, at Mata Meḥasya four years before Huna's death (Sherira, *l.c.*), he never published any decision during the lifetime of Huna ('Er. 62b). Huna came to recognize Ḥisda's merit later, and recommended his son Rabbah to attend his lectures (Shab. 82a).

Ḥisda presided over the Academy of Sura for ten years following the death of R. Judah (298–299; Sherira, *l.c.*), or following the death of Huna, according to Abraham ibn Daud (*l.c.*). He always preserved great respect for the memory of Rab, whom he referred to as "our great teacher, may God aid him" (Suk. 33a, *passim*). Once, holding up the gifts which are given to the priest, he declared that he would give them to the man who could cite a hitherto unknown halakah in the name of Rab (Shab. 10b). Ḥisda's halakot are frequent in the Babylonian Talmud, some being given on the authority of his pupils. His principal opponent was Sheshet. Besides deducing his halakot in a casuistic way, Ḥisda was peculiar in that he derived his halakot less from the Pentateuch than from other parts of the Bible.

Ḥisda was also an authority in Haggadah, and employed special assistants to lecture in that department ('Er. 21b). Many ethical sentences of his have been preserved (see especially Shab. 140b), mostly for students. The following two sentences may be cited: "Forbearance on the part of a father toward his child may be permitted, but not forbearance on the part of a master toward his disciple" (Ḳid. 32a); "He who opposes his master is as though he opposed the Shekinah" (Sanh. 110a). It is said that the Angel of Death, not being able to approach Ḥisda because he never ceased from studying, cleft the trunk of a cedar-tree. Terrified by the noise, Ḥisda interrupted his studies, whereupon the angel took his soul (Mak. 10a).

BIBLIOGRAPHY: Bacher, *Ag. Bab. Amor.* pp. 61 *et seq.*; Heilprin, *Seder ha-Dorot,* ii.; Weiss, *Dor,* iii. 184.

S. M. SEL.

ḤIYYA BAR ABBA (surnamed **RABBAH,** "the Great" or "the Elder," to distinguish him from an amora of the same name): Palestinian tanna; born about the middle of the second century, at Kafri, near Sura in Babylonia; pupil of Judah I., and uncle and teacher of Rab. He was a descendant of a family which claimed to trace its origin from Shimei, brother of King David (Ket. 62b). He passed the earlier part of his life in Babylonia, where he married a certain Judith. By her he had twin sons, Judah and Hezekiah (both of whom became renowned rabbis), and twin daughters, Pazi and Tavi (Yeb. 65b). Ḥiyya was unhappy in his married life, for his wife was a shrew. This was so keenly felt by Ḥiyya that when asked by his nephew for a blessing he said: "May God preserve thee from an evil that is worse than death—a contentious woman" (Yeb. 63a). Ḥiyya was especially affected by a trick she played upon him. Disguising herself, she went to him and asked whether the obligation of propagating the human race extended to women; receiving an answer in the negative, she took drugs which rendered her barren (Yeb. 65b). However, Ḥiyya's good nature was so great that he overwhelmed her with presents, meeting the astonishment of his nephew by saying that men should show themselves grateful to their wives for rearing their children and for keeping their husbands from sin (Yeb. 63a).

In the latter part of his life Ḥiyya emigrated to Tiberias, Palestine, where he established a business in silks, which he exported to Tyre (Ruth R. i. 17; Lam. R. iii. 16; Gen. R. lxix.). The high reputation acquired by him in his native country had preceded him to Palestine, and ere long he became the very center of the collegiate circle of the patriarch Judah I. Regarding him more as a colleague than as a pupil, Judah treated Ḥiyya as his guest whenever the latter chanced to be at Sepphoris, consulted him, and took him with him when he went to Cæsarea to visit Antoninus (Tan., Wayesheb). His admiration for Ḥiyya was so great that he used to say: "Ḥiyya and his sons are as meritorious as the Patriarchs" (B. M. 25b). Judah's friendship and high esteem for Ḥiyya are connected in the Ḥaggadah with a miracle. In course of a conversation with him Judah said that if the Babylonian exilarch R. Huna, who was believed to be a descendant of the family of David, came to Palestine he (Judah) would yield to him the office of patriarch. When R. Huna died and his body was brought to Palestine for burial, Ḥiyya went to Judah and said, "Huna is here," and, after pausing to notice Judah's pallor, added, "his coffin has arrived." Seriously offended, Judah banished Ḥiyya for thirty days. While the latter was away, the prophet Elijah, assuming Ḥiyya's features, presented himself to Judah and healed a toothache from which the patriarch had suffered for thirteen years. Judah was not long in discovering the truth of this wonderful cure, and his respect for Ḥiyya increased (Yer. Kil. ix.).

It was a current saying among the Palestinians that since the arrival of Ḥiyya in Palestine storms did not occur and wine did not turn sour (Ḥul. 86a). His prayers are said to have brought rain in a time of drought and to have caused a lion, which had rendered the roads unsafe, to leave Palestine (Gen. R. xxxi.). Other miracles of the same kind are credited to him. He was especially lauded by his Babylonian compatriots. Simeon ben Laḳish names him after the two other Babylonians, Ezra and Hillel, who came to Palestine to restore the study of the Torah (Suk. 20a). However exaggerated this assertion may be, Ḥiyya was certainly very active in the promotion of learning in Palestine. He founded schools for children and often acted as instructor. It is related that when Ḥanina boasted that he could reconstruct the Torah by logic should it be lost, Ḥiyya said: "To prevent such a loss I proceed in the following way: I cultivate flax, spin thread, twist ropes, and prepare traps by means of which I catch deer. The flesh of these I distribute among poor orphans, and I use the hides to make parchment, on which I write the Torah. Provided with this I go to places where there are no teachers, and instruct the children" (Ket. 103b).

Ḥiyya's activity in the field of the Halakah was very extensive. To him and his pupil Hoshea is due the redaction of the traditional halakot which had not been included by Judah in the Mishnah. These halakot are known under the various names of "Baraitot de-Rabbi Ḥiyya," "Mishnat de-Rabbi Ḥiyya," and "Mishnayot Gedolot." Some of them are introduced in the Talmud with the words "Tane Rabbi Ḥiyya," and are considered the only correct version of the halakot omitted by Judah (Ḥul. 141a). Ḥiyya was the author of original halakot also, which he derived from the Mishnah by the hermeneutic rules. Although very conservative, he opposed the issuing of new prohibitions. "Make not the fence higher than the Law itself, lest it should fall and destroy the plants" (Gen. R. xix.). Ḥiyya seems to have contributed to the Sifra the redaction of the tannaitic midrash to Leviticus, where his sayings are often quoted. From the time of Sherira Gaon, Ḥiyya was generally regarded as the author of the Tosefta; but the supposition has been rejected on very strong grounds by modern scholars. Ḥiyya's activity extended also to the Ḥaggadah. Sayings of his, and his controversies with Simeon ben Ḥalafta, Bar Ḳappara, Jonathan, and Jannai are frequently quoted in haggadic literature. The dawn is for Ḥiyya the symbol of the deliverance of Israel. "As the dawn spreads gradually, so will the deliverance of Israel come gradually" (Yer. Ber. 3b).

As a Babylonian Ḥiyya hated the Romans, whom he compared to obnoxious insects (Tan., Wayesheb, 17). "God foresaw that the Jews could not bear the yoke of the Romans, and therefore designed Babylonia for their place of residence" (Pes. 86a). Ḥiyya's views on some Biblical books are noteworthy. According to him the Book of Job is not the work of a Jew (Yer. Soṭah 15a); and Solomon wrote his works in his old age (Cant. R. 2b). Ḥiyya's haggadot are particularly rich in thoughts concerning the moral life and the relations of human beings to one another.

Ḥiyya was a physician of high repute. The Talmud quotes many of his medical utterances, among which is a description of the development of the embryo in the womb which betrays considerable medical knowledge (Nid. 25a). Ḥiyya is represented in the Talmud as having been a model of virtue and goodness; his house is said to have been always open to the poor (Shab. 151b); even his death is connected by legend with an act of charity. "The angel of death," recites a haggadah, "could not approach him. The angel therefore disguised himself as a poor man and knocked at Ḥiyya's door. Ḥiyya, as usual, gave the order to bring bread for the poor. Then the angel said: 'Thou hast compassion on the poor; why not have pity upon me? Give me thy life and spare me the trouble of coming so many times.' Then Ḥiyya gave himself up" (M. Ḳ. 28a). At his death, relates another haggadah, stones of fire fell from the skies (M. Ḳ. 25b).

Bibliography: Ibn Yaḥya, *Shalshelet ha-Ḳabbalah*, 32b; Heilprin, *Seder ha-Dorot*, ii. 128; Kirchheim, in *Orient, Lit.* ix. 611 *et seq.*; J. H. Weiss, *Dor*, ii. 198, 218; W. Bacher, *Ag. Tan.* ii. 520 *et seq.*; Baer, *Das Leben und Wirken des Tannaiten Chiyya*, in Berliner's *Magazin*, xvii. 115 *et seq.*; Mielziner, *Introduction to the Talmud*, p. 39; Halévy, *Dorot ha-Rishonim*, ii. 197.

s. I. Br.

ḤIYYA BAR ADDA: Palestinian amora of the first half of the third century; son of the sister of Bar Ḳappara; pupil of Simeon ben Laḳish. His name is connected with several halakot (Yer. Hor. iii. 5), and he handed down a number of halakic opinions in the names of Aḥa, Ḥanina, and Johanan (Yer. Ber. vi. 1; Sanh. iv.). He disputed with his uncle Bar Kappara concerning the explanation of the word הטיבו (Deut. v. 25), which he rendered "they embellished" (Lev. R. xxxii.; Cant. R. ii. 14). Ḥiyya died young, and in the funeral sermon pronounced by Simeon ben Laḳish he is compared, in allusion to the verse, "My beloved [God] is gone down into His garden, to the bed of spices, to feed in the garden, and to gather lilies" (Cant. R. vi. 2), to a lily which the gardener is desirous to gather.

BIBLIOGRAPHY: Heilprin, *Seder ha-Dorot*, ii. 132; Bacher, *Ag. Pal. Amor.* i. 341, 401.

S. I. BR.

ḤIYYA B. GAMMADA: Palestinian amora of the fourth generation (3d and 4th cent.). His principal teacher was Jose b. Saul, in whose name Ḥiyya transmitted several halakot (M. Ḳ. 22a; R. H. 24a, 30a); but he was also a pupil of Jose b. Ḥanina (Soṭah 7b) and of Assi (Meg. 31b). He transmitted halakot in the name of the council ("ḥaburah") of the last of the Tannaim (Ḥul. 30a; Shab. 3a; Pes. 64a, 73b). The following haggadic sentence Ḥiyya transmitted in the name of Jose b. Saul: "At the death of a just man the angels proclaim that one who is righteous has come, and God answers, 'Let the other ẓaddiḳim come out to meet him'" (Ket. 104a). A sentence of the same nature and ascribed to Eleazar b. Pedat (*ib.*) is attributed to R. Ḥiyya ha-Gadol in Pesiḳ. R. 2 (ed. Friedmann, p. 5, a, b). Bacher accordingly suggests that the name is to be amended into "Ḥiyya b. Gammada." Ḥiyya's love for Palestine was so great that he rolled in the dust of that country (Ket. 112b).

BIBLIOGRAPHY: Bacher, *Ag. Pal. Amor.* ii. 85; Heilprin, *Seder ha-Dorot*, ii.

S. M. SEL.

HOSHAIAH (in the Babylonian Talmud generally **Oshaya**): Palestinian amora of the third and fourth amoraic generations (died about 350 C.E.). It is supposed that his colleague Ḥanina was his brother (Sanh. 14a; see Edels, "Ḥiddushe Agadot," *ad loc.*). They were lineal descendants from Eli the priest, which circumstance they assigned as reason for Johanan's failure to ordain them. For a living they plied the shoemaker's trade (see HANANIAH [ḤANINA]). Hoshaiah and Ḥanina are mentioned in connection with a certain bath-house, the ownership of which was contested by two persons, one of whom turned over the property as "heḳdesh" (for sacred use), causing Hoshaiah, Ḥanina, and other rabbis to leave it (B. M. 6b). On the day Hoshaiah died, it is claimed, the largest date-palm in Tiberias was uprooted and fell (Yer. 'Ab. Zarah iii. 42c).

BIBLIOGRAPHY: *Yuḥasin*, ed. Filipowski, p. 118, London, 1857; Heilprin, *Seder ha-Dorot*, ii. 36, Warsaw, 1878; Frankel, *Mebo*, p. 75, Breslau, 1870; Jolles, *Bet Wa'ad*, p. 20a, Cracow, 1884; Bacher, *Ag. Pal. Amor.* iii. 565.

S. J. D. E.

HOSHAIAH RABBAH, ROBA, BERABBI or **BERIBBI:** Palestinian amora of the first amoraic generation (about 200 C.E.); compiler of baraitot explaining the Mishnah-Tosefta. He was closely associated with the successors of Rabbi, as was his father with Rabbi himself. Hoshaiah's father, Ḥama, lived in Sepphoris, the residence of Rabbi and the seat of the patriarchs (see ḤAMA B. BISA).

Hoshaiah's yeshibah, also, was for many years located at Sepphoris, where pupils crowded to hear his lectures. Johanan, one of his greatest disciples, declared that Hoshaiah in his generation was like R. Meïr in his: even his colleagues could not always grasp the profundity of his arguments ('Er. 53a). And the esteem in which Hoshaiah was held by his pupils may be gaged by the statement that, even after Johanan had himself become a great scholar and a famous teacher and no longer needed Hoshaiah's instruction, he continued visiting the master, who in the meantime had grown old and had removed his school to Cæsarea (Yer. Sanh. xi. 30b).

Hoshaiah was called the "father of the Mishnah," not so much because of his collection and edition of the mishnayot, as because of the ability with which he explained and interpreted them (see Yer. Ḳid. i. 60a; Yer. B. Ḳ. iv. 4c). Hoshaiah's most important halakic decision is directed against the standard weights and measures, held by Johanan to be traditional from the Sinaitic period. Hoshaiah's radical point of view can be traced to his theory of the development of the Mishnah. He even goes so far as to overrule both Bet Shammai and Bet Hillel with reference to offerings brought on visiting the Temple three times every year (Ḥag. i. 2). The custom of greeting mourners on the Sabbath was permitted in southern Galilee, including Cæsarea, and prohibited in other places. Hoshaiah happened to be in a certain town on the Sabbath, and, meeting mourners, greeted them, saying, "I do not know your custom, but I greet you according to our custom" (Yer. M. Ḳ. iii. 82d).

Hoshaiah's consideration for others is exemplified in his gracious apology to the blind teacher whom he had engaged for his son, and whom he did not suffer to meet visitors at dinner for fear that he might be embarrassed (Yer. Peah viii. 21b).

Hoshaiah's authority must have been very powerful in his later years, when he successfully resisted the efforts of R. Gamaliel ha-Nasi, the son of Rabbi, to introduce "demai" (the "suspicion," on buying wheat from an 'am ha-areẓ, that he had not separated the tithes) into Syria (Yer. Ḥal. iv. 60a). It is also indicated by his remarkable interposition in regard to the mishnah which declares that "a Gentile's testimony in the case of an 'agunah is allowed only if stated as a matter of fact and without any intention to testify "(Yer. Yeb. xvi. 5; Yeb. 121b).

The haggadic utterances of Hoshaiah are numerous, scattered principally in Midrash Rabbah, which some have erroneously attributed to him because of the opening words "R. Hoshaiah Rabbah." In Genesis Rabbah, Hoshaiah's text with reference to the Creation is the verse "Then I was by him, as one brought up [= אמון] with him" (Prov. viii. 30). He transposes the letters to read אומן ("an architect"), and explains that "wisdom" (the Torah) was used as an instrument by God to create the universe. He illustrates this by the example of an earthly king who, in building a palace, needs an architect with plans and specifications. Freudenthal points out the analogy between Philo's ideas and those of Hoshaiah, and Bacher expresses his opinion that if Hoshaiah had not himself read the philosopher's works, he at least had heard of them from Origen, the most important champion of Philo ("J. Q. R." iii. 357). In a dialogue with Hoshaiah regarding circumcision, a "philosopher" (identified as Origen by Bacher) asked: "If the rite possesses such virtue, why did not God create the first man circumcised?" Hoshaiah replied that man, with all things created on the first six days, needs improving and perfecting, and that circumcision conduces to perfection (Gen. R. xi. 6). Bacher quotes a pasage in which Hoshaiah refuted the incarnation dogma: "When God created Adam the angels mistook him for a deity and wished to sing the hymn 'Holy! Holy! Holy!' But when God put Adam to sleep they knew him to be mortal, as the prophet said: 'Cease ye from man, whose breath is in his nostrils: for wherein is he to be accounted of?'" (Isa. ii. 22; Gen. R. viii. 10).

There are more examples in the Talmud to justify the assertion that Hoshaiah as the representative of Judaism was in constant touch with the early Christians at Cæsarea, and particularly with Origen, who was ordained presbyter at Cæsarea in 228, and who in 231 opened a philosophical and theological school which was attended by persons from all parts, anxious to hear his interpretation of the Scriptures. Origen died in 254 at Tyre, so that his last twenty-five years were spent in the region in which most of the Amoraim lived. The "philosopher" whom the latter mention as controverting Hoshaiah's Biblical interpretations was doubtless Origen himself or one of his students. The influence brought to bear by Hoshaiah and others probably induced Origen to formulate the doctrine of the different degrees of dignity in the Trinity, for which Origen was accused as a heretic.

Hoshaiah was very strict in requiring from a proselyte both circumcision and immersion (baptism) in the presence of three rabbis (Yeb.

46b); this was very likely directed against the free conversion of the Gentiles by the Christian Jews. In a case of partition by heirs or partners the Mishnah says: "They can not divide the Scriptures between them, even when all parties are satisfied." Hoshaiah adds: "even if they wish to divide by volumes, one to take the Psalms and another the Chronicles" (Yer. B. B. i. 13a). It is explained that such an exchange would be considered as unequal and as giving the impression that one Biblical book is holier than another. This is more easily understood in view of the exaltation by the Judæo-Christians of the Psalms in comparison with the other books of the Old Testament, especially with the Chronicles, as against the contrary view of Judaism, which recognizes no preference between the various books.

BIBLIOGRAPHY: *Yuḥasin*, ed. Filipowski, p. 118; *Seder ha-Dorot*, ii. 36; Frankel, *Mebo*, p. 74; Jolles, *Bet Wa'ad*, p. 20a; Bacher, *Ag. Pal. Amor.* i. 89–108; *J. Q. R.* iii. 357.

E. C. J. D. E.

HOSHAIAH ZE'ERA DE-MIN ḤABRAYA: Palestinian amora of the third amoraic period (died about 350 C.E.). In the Tosafot it is claimed that "Ḥabraya" was the name of his birth-place, but according to Rashi the word means a "society of colleagues," and the surname "Ze'era" (minor, junior) is used to distinguish him from Hoshaiah the Elder (Ḥul. 12b). He belonged to the rabbis "of the south" (southern Galilee), and may be identified with Hoshaiah, the brother of Ḥanina, who was also a "ḥaber." Only one halakah is mentioned in the name of Hoshaiah Ze'era (Niddah 26a).

BIBLIOGRAPHY: Heilprin, *Seder ha-Dorot*, ii. 36; *Aruch Completum*, p. 316.

E. C. J. D. E.

HUNA (called also **Huna the Babylonian**): Babylonian amora of the second generation and head of the Academy of Sura; born about 216 (212 according to Grätz); died in 296–297 (608 of the Seleucidan era; Sherira Gaon, in Neubauer, "M. J. C." i. 30) or in 290 according to Abraham ibn Daud ("Sefer ha-Ḳabbalah," in Neubauer, *l.c.* p. 58). He lived in a town called דרוקרת (Ta'an. 21b), identified by Wiesener ("Scholien zum Babylonischen Talmud," ii. 193) with Tekrit, but read by Grätz דיוקרת (= "Diokart"). He was the principal pupil of Rab (Abba Arika), under whom he acquired so much learning that one of Raba's three wishes was to possess Huna's wisdom (M. Ḳ. 28a). He was also styled "one of the Babylonian ḥasidim," on account of his great piety (Ta'an. 23b); and the esteem in which he was held was so great that, though not of a priestly family, he read from the Torah on Sabbaths and holy days the first passage, which is usually read by a priest. Ammi and Assi, honored Palestinian priests, considered Huna as their superior (Meg. 22a; Giṭ. 59b). Although Huna was related to the family of the exilarch (Sherira Gaon, *l.c.*) he was so poor at the beginning of his career that in order to buy wine to consecrate the Sabbath he had to pawn his girdle (Meg. 27b). But Rab blessed him with riches, and Huna displayed great wealth at the wedding of his son Rabbah (*ib.*). He owned numerous flocks of sheep, which were under the special care of his wife, Ḥobah (B. Ḳ. 80a), and he traveled in a gilded litter (Ta'an. 20b). Huna was very generous. When the houses of the poor people were thrown down by storms he rebuilt them; at meal-times the doors of his house would be left open, while his servants cried, "He who is hungry, let him come and eat" (*ib.*).

After Rab's death Huna lectured in his stead in the Academy of Sura, but he was not appointed head till after the death of Rab's companion, Samuel (*c.* 256). It was under Huna that the Academy of Sura, till then called "sidra," acquired the designation of "metibta" (Hebr. "yeshibah"), Huna being the first "resh metibta" (Hebr. "rosh yeshibah"; comp. Zacuto "Yuḥasin,"p. 118b, Königsberg, 1857; and see ACADEMIES IN BABYLONIA). Under Huna the academy increased considerably in importance, and students flocked to it from all directions; during his presidency their number reached 800, all supported by himself (Ket. 106a). Thirteen assistant lecturers ("amora'e") were occupied in teaching them. When his pupils, after the lesson, shook their garments they raised so great a cloud of dust that when the Palestinian sky was overcast it was said, "Huna's pupils in Babylon have risen from their lesson" (*ib.*). Under Huna, Palestine lost its ascendency over Babylonia; and on certain occasions he declared the schools of the two countries to be equal (Giṭ. 6a; B. Ḳ. 80a). In Babylonia, during his lifetime, the Sura academy held the supremacy. He presided over it for forty years, when he died suddenly, more than eighty years of age (M. Ḳ. 28a). His remains were brought to Palestine and buried by the side of Ḥiyya Rabbah (*ib.* 25a).

Huna's principal pupil was Rab Ḥisda, who had previously been his fellow pupil under Rab. Other pupils of his whose names are given were: Abba b. Zabda, Rab Giddel, R. Ḥelbo, R. Sheshet, and Huna's own son, Rabbah (Yeb. 64b).

He transmitted many of Rab's halakot, sometimes without mentioning Rab's name (Shab. 24a *et al.*). His own halakot are numerous in the Babylonian Talmud, and although some of his decisions were contrary to Rab's (Shab. 21a, b, 128a), he declared Rab to be the supreme authority in religious law (Niddah 24b). Huna's deductions were sometimes casuistical; he interpreted the text verbatim even where the context seems to prohibit such an interpretation (Shab. 20a; Men. 36a; *et al.*). According to Huna, the halakah transmitted in the Mishnah and Baraita is not always to be taken as decisive (Ber. 24b, 59b). He had some knowledge of medicine and natural history, and used his knowledge in many of his halakic decisions (Shab. 20a, 54b; Yeb. 75b). He also interpreted many of the difficult words met with in the Mishnah and Baraita (Shab. 53b, 54b, *et al.*).

Huna was equally distinguished as a haggadist, and his haggadot were known in Palestine, whither they were carried by some of his pupils, Ze'ira among them. His interpretation of Prov. xiv. 23, transmitted by Ze'ira, is styled "the pearl" (Pesiḳ. ii. 13b; comp. Yer. Shab. vii. 2, where also many halakot of his are preserved, transmitted by Ze'ira). Many of his haggadot, showing his skill in Biblical exegesis, are found in the Babylonian Talmud, some in the name of Rab, some in his own. He took special pains to reconcile apparently conflicting passages, as, for instance, II Sam. vii. 10 and I Chron. xvii. 10 (Ber. 7b). He endeavored to solve the problem presented by the sufferings of the righteous, inferring from Isa. liii. 10 that God chasteneth those whom He loves (Ber. 5a). The following of Huna's utterances may be given: "He who occupies himself with the study of the Law alone is as one who has no God" (inferred from II Chron. xv. 3; 'Ab. Zarah 17b). "When leaving the synagogue, one must not take long steps" (Ber. 6b). "He who recites his prayer behind the synagogue is called 'impious'" = "rasha'" (inferred from Ps. xii. 9 [A. V. 8]; *ib.*). "He who is accustomed to honor the Sabbath with light will have children who are scholars; he who observes the injunction as to the mezuzah will have a beautiful house; he who observes the rule as to the ẓiẓit will have fine clothes; he who consecrates the Sabbath and the holy days as commanded will have many skins filled with wine" (Shab. 23b). Huna was very tolerant, and on several occasions he recommended mild treatment of Gentiles (B. Ḳ. 113a; B. M. 70a). He was also very modest; he was not ashamed, before he was rich, to cultivate his field himself, nor to return home in the evening, with his spade on his shoulder (Meg. 28a). When two contending parties requested him to judge between them, he said to them: "Give me a man to cultivate my field and I will be your judge" (Ket. 105a). He patiently bore Rab's hard words, because the latter was his teacher ('Er. 15a; Yer. 'Er. i. 3), but he showed on several occasions that a scholar must not humiliate himself in presence of an inferior (Ket. 69a; B. M. 33a).

BIBLIOGRAPHY: Bacher, *Ag. Bab. Amor.* pp. 52–60; Grätz, *Gesch.* 3d ed., iv. 291 *et seq.*; Halévy, *Dorot ha-Rishonim*, ii. 411 *et seq.*; Heilprin, *Seder ha-Dorot*, ii.; Lichtmann, in *Keneset Yisrael*, iii. 297–303; Weiss, *Dor*, iii. 182 *et seq.*

S. M. SEL.

HUNA, ABBA HA-KOHEN. See HUNA BAR ABBIN.

HUNA BAR ABBIN HA-KOHEN (called also **Neḥunya, Ḥuna, and Ḥunya):** Palestinian amora of the first half of the fourth century; pupil of R. Jeremiah, in whose name he reports some halakic and haggadic sayings (Yer. Dem. 21d; Pes. 36d; and frequently). That the name "Neḥunya," from which are derived "Ḥuna" and "Ḥunya," designates Huna is shown by the fact that a saying which is quoted in the Pesiḳta (xviii. 174) in the name of Huna is given by his pupil Tanḥuma in the Midrash Tehillim (to Ps. xiv. 6) in the name of Neḥunya. Huna occupied a prominent position in the school of Tiberias, directed by Jose, with whom he had halakic controversies (Yer. Sheḳ. 48b). Huna sojourned some time in Babylonia (Yer. R. H. ii. 2) and was well acquainted with the halakot of the Babylonian amoraim, often quoted by him in the Yerushalmi. It was probably during his residence there that he made the acquaintance of Raba, head of the school of Maḥoza, to whom he made an important communication concerning intercalary months (Yer. R. H. 21a). With regard to certain calendary calculations, Huna relates that in consequence of the Roman persecutions (under Gallus) the rabbis of Tiberias, who had sought refuge in a grotto, deliberated on the advisability of intercalating an additional month. In the grotto they distinguished day from night by lamps, which were dim in the daytime and bright at night (Gen. R. xxxi.). Huna seems to have had some medical knowledge; he speaks of the effects of *Rubia tinctorum* (madder = פואה) and asafetida (חלתית), in which latter article he traded (Yer. Shab. 8b, 17c). Although of a priestly family Huna refused to take tithes (Yer. Ma'as. Sh. ii. 2).

Huna was an able haggadist, and his sayings are frequently quoted in midrashic literature. His haggadot bear the stamp of ardent patriotism. He appears as a bitter enemy of the Romans, to whom, according to him, the Psalmist applied the epithet נבל (Ps. xiv. 1), because they filled Palestine with Jewish corpses (Midr. Teh. to Ps. *ad loc.*). "In three things," he declared, "the Greeks are superior to the Romans: in legislation, in painting, and in literature" (Gen. R. xvi. 4). Huna held the study of the Law in such high estimation that he declared it could atone for a deadly sin (Lev. R. xxv.). Huna considered envy the greatest sin. Israel was exiled only because it transgressed the tenth commandment (Pes. R. 24).

BIBLIOGRAPHY: Heilprin, *Seder ha-Dorot*, ii. 125; Z. Frankel, *Mebo*, p. 83b; Bacher, *Ag. Pal. Amor.* iii. 272 *et seq.*

S. I. BR.

HUNA B. ḤANINA (ḤINENA): Babylonian amora of the fifth generation (4th cent.). His principal teachers were Abaye (in whose school R. Safra and Abba b. Huna were his fellow pupils; B. B. 167b) and Raba; R. Papa, his senior, was a fellow pupil under Raba (Sanh.

87a). On one occasion Huna and Huna b. Naḥman contested Raba's decision ('Ab. Zarah 57b). Huna has transmitted a halakah in the name of Ḥiyya b. Rab (Ber. 30a).

BIBLIOGRAPHY: Heilprin, *Seder ha-Dorot,* ii.

S. M. SEL.

HUNA B. JOSHUA: Babylonian amora of the fifth generation; died in 410 (Samson of Chinon, "Sefer Keritut," p. 26a, Cremona, 1558). He was the pupil of Raba (Ḳid. 32b), who seems to have been his principal teacher, and who sometimes praised him (Hor. 10b), but occasionally blamed him (Ket. 85a; Giṭ. 73a). He appears to have been the pupil of Abaye also (R. H. 24b). His principal companion was R. Papa, from whom he was inseparable, both in and out of school ('Er. 12a; Ber. 58b; *et al.*). When R. Papa became head of the school of Naresh (נרש), Huna was appointed president of the general assembly ("resh kallah") in the same school (Ber. 57a). As senior pupils, Huna and R. Papa took part in the halakic deliberations of their teachers. Their halakot are often mentioned in the Babylonian Talmud, and, according to Moses of Coucy ("Sefer Miẓwot Gadol," i., No. 67), Isaac Alfasi decided with them against R. Huna I., head of the Academy of Sura.

Huna was wealthy (Hor. 10b); he never walked more than four cubits bareheaded (Shab. 118b); he ate very slowly, so that R. Papa consumed in the same time four times as much and Rabina eight times as much (Pes. 89b). Huna lived to a great age, outliving Raba by fifty-seven years. Once in the lifetime of R. Papa, Huna fell desperately ill, but his life was spared to him because he was forbearing (R. H. 17a).

BIBLIOGRAPHY: Halévy, *Dorot ha-Rishonim,* ii. 505 *et seq.*; Heilprin, *Seder ha-Dorot,* ii.; Weiss, *Dor,* iii. 205.

S. M. SEL.

HUNA B. NATHAN: Babylonian scholar of the fourth and fifth centuries. He was the pupil of Amemar II. and a senior and companion of ASHI, to whom he repeated several of Amemar's sayings and halakot (Giṭ. 19b; B. B. 55a, 74b). He was wealthy; but though "in him learning and dignity met," he was nevertheless subject to Ashi (Giṭ. 59a). He had access to the royal court of Persia, and the esteem in which he was held by King Yezdegerd is instanced by the fact that on one occasion at court (as told by Huna to Ashi) the king himself adjusted Huna's belt (Zeb. 19a). According to Sherira (Neubauer, "M. J. C." i. 32), Huna was exilarch in the time of Ashi. Another Huna b. Nathan was a companion of Raba (Ned. 12a) and, apparently, a pupil of Naḥman (Ket. 7a).

BIBLIOGRAPHY: Halévy, *Dorot ha-Rishonim,* ii. 517; Heilprin, *Seder ha-Dorot,* ii.; Lazarus, in Brüll's *Jahrb.* x. 110, 111.

S. M. SEL.

I

IDI: Name of several Babylonian amoraim who flourished from the middle of the second to the middle of the fifth century. In the Talmud "Idi" is sometimes interchanged with "Ada" (אדא = אידי), according to the variation of pronunciation between eastern and western Syriac, as in the case of "Abba" = "Iba," "Ami" = "Imi," "Asi" = "Isi," "Ḥasda" = "Ḥisda."

S.S. J. D. E.

IDI B. ABIN NAGGARA: Babylonian amora of the fourth period (about 350). His father, whose name ("Naggara"="carpenter") probably indicates his occupation, came from Nerash or Nerus (נרשאה), in Babylonia. The son, Idi (or Ada), gave an explanation in the presence of R. Joseph (Shab. 60a), had discussions with Abaye on various occasions (B. M. 35b), and likewise gave explanations in the presence of Rabbah ('Er. 56b; Ḳid. 40a). He also had occasion to appear in the court of Ḥisda (B. B. 33a). Idi was the brother of Ḥiyya. Passing the door of their father's house one Friday evening, Huna (b. Ḥiyya of Pumbedita) noticed that the house was illuminated with candles; whereupon Huna predicted that two shining lights would issue from that house. The prophecy was verified in the birth of Idi and Ḥiyya (Shab. 23b). Idi married the daughter of a priest, who bore him two sons—Sheshet and Joshua (Pes. 49a). Idi took advantage of his wife's position as a kohen to accept "the shoulder, and the two cheeks, and the maw" as the share due to a priest (Deut. xviii. 3), a custom which prevailed even during the Exile (Ḥul. x. 1). Idi was considered the main authority in Nerash, where he introduced a certain ordinance (Ned. 67b). Idi seems to have moved at a later period to Shekanzib, where he had occasion to receive Papa and Huna, whom he treated in a somewhat slighting manner (Yeb. 85a).

S. S. J. D. E.

IDI OF CÆSAREA. See IDI B. JACOB II.

IDI OF ḤUṬRA. See IDI B. JACOB II.

IDI B. JACOB II: Babylonian amora of the second period (about 250). Idi was a disciple of Johanan. The journey from Idi's home in Babylonia to the yeshibah of Johanan at Tiberias occupied about three months, and two journeys there and back in the year left him but one day each six months to attend the yeshibah. This caused his comrades to call him "the one-day scholar." Idi answered by quoting Job xii. 4. Johanan, however, begged Idi not to call down the punishment of Heaven, and delivered a lecture in the yeshibah on the text "They seek me daily" (יום יום; Isa. lviii. 2), concluding with the statement that to devote a single day to learning the laws of God is as meritorious as devoting a whole year to study. On the other hand, one day spent in doing evil is equivalent to one year of iniquity; which explains the imposition of forty years of punishment for forty days of evil (Num. xiv. 34; Ḥag. 5b). Idi was likewise known as Idi of Ḥuṭra (Yer. Shab. v., end; M. Ḳ. v. 2), and is probably identical with Idi of Cæsarea (IDIT).

S. S. J. D. E.

IMMA SHALOM: Wife of ELIEZER BEN HYRCANUS and sister of GAMALIEL II. Of her early life but little is known. She was probably brought up under the care of her brother, and is therefore sometimes cited as his daughter (ברתיה דר"ג, Sanh. 39a; see Rabbinovicz, "Diḳduḳe Soferim," *ad loc.* and 90b *et seq.*); and she received an education befitting the sister of a nasi and a daughter of the family of Hillel the Great. That she put her accomplishments to use is seen from the anecdotes preserved in rabbinic lore. On one occasion she heard a skeptic taunting her brother: "Your God is not strictly honest, or He would not have stolen a rib from sleeping Adam" (Gen. ii. 21). "Leave him to me," said Imma Shalom; "I will answer him." Turning to the skeptic, she requested him to summon a constable. The skeptic inquired: "What need hast thou for a constable?" "We were robbed last night," she answered, "of a silver cruet, and the thief left in its place a golden one." "If that is all," exclaimed the skeptic, "I wish that thief would visit me every day!" "And yet," retorted Imma, "thou objectest to the removal of the rib from sleeping Adam! Did he not receive in exchange a woman to wait on him?"

Imma Shalom's marriage with Eliezer ben Hyrcanus was blessed with extraordinarily handsome children (Ned. 20a). In spite of Eliezer's avowed antagonism to the education of women, he thoroughly appreciated his wife's intellectual gifts. He not only passed on to her some traditions ('Er. 63a), but even obeyed her in matters ritualistic. After the rupture between her brother Gamaliel and her husband she feared that the complaints of so great and wronged a man as Eliezer would be answered by Heaven, and that the wrong done him would be visited on her brother; she therefore requested her husband not "to fall on his face," that is, not to offer a prayer (such as Ps. vi. 10 or xxv. 19) for deliverance from enemies. Eliezer complied with her request, of which she reminded him at the proper time each day. One morning, however, she did not do so, and found him in the midst of the prayer; she sorrowfully exclaimed, "Cease, thou hast killed my brother!" Not long after Gamaliel's death occurred. Asked by Eliezer what had led her to expect such dire consequences, she stated that there was a tradition in her family that while all other gates of prayer are sometimes closed the gates for the cry of oppression are never closed (B. M. 59b).

Imma Shalom survived both her husband and her brother. She dutifully tended the former in his last moments, although his disposition had become soured (Sanh. 68a). A story is told of a mock suit between Imma Shalom and her brother, in which the pretensions of a certain judge were exposed. The judge (the Talmud calls him "philosophos") appears to have been a Jewish Christian who boasted of his honesty and impartiality. Imma Shalom presented him with a golden lamp, and then brought a suit against her brother for a share in their father's estate. The judge favored her claim. Gamaliel protested on the ground of the provision "in our Law"—"Where there is a son, a daughter inherits nothing" (see Num. xxvii. 8 *et seq.*); but the judge replied, "Since your people have come under foreign government the law of Moses has been superseded by other writings, which rule that son and daughter inherit alike." Gamaliel then presented him with a Libyan ass and renewed his protest. Then the judge reversed his previous decision, saying, "I have read further in those writings, arid there it is written, 'I came neither to take away from the law of Moses nor to add to the law of Moses' [comp. Matt. v. 17], and in that law it is written that where there is a son a daughter inherits not." Imma Shalom thereupon exclaimed, "Let thy light shine as a lamp" (comp. Matt. v. 16), in allusion to her gift. But Gamaliel said, "An ass came and upset the lamp" (Shab. 116a *et seq.*).

BIBLIOGRAPHY: Zirndorf, *Some Jewish Women*, pp. 139 *et seq.*

S. S. M.

ISHMAEL B. ELISHA: Tanna of the first and second centuries (third tannaitic generation). He was a descendant of a wealthy priestly family in Upper Galilee (Tosef., Ḥal. i. 10; B. Ḳ. 80a; comp. Rabbinovicz, "Diḳduḳe Soferim," *ad loc.*; Ḥul. 49a), and presumably the grandson of the high priest of the same name. As a youth he was carried away by the Romans, but Joshua b. Hananiah, succeeding in purchasing his liberty, restored him to Palestine, where he rapidly developed into an accomplished scholar (Tosef., Hor. ii. 5; Giṭ. 58a). Of his teachers, only Nehunya ben ha-Ḳanah is expressly mentioned (Sheb. 26a), but he doubtless learned much from his benefactor, between whom and himself grew up a close friendship; Joshua called him "brother" ('Ab. Zarah ii. 5; Tosef., Parah, x. [ix.] 3), a term by which he was afterward known to his colleagues (Yad. iv. 3; Sanh. 51b).

Ishmael's teachings were calculated to promote peace and goodwill among all. "Be indulgent with the hoary head," he would say, "and be kind to the black-haired [the young]; and meet every man with a friendly mien" (Ab. iii. 12). What he taught he practised. Even toward strangers he acted considerately. When a heathen greeted him, he answered kindly, "Thy reward has been predicted"; when another abused him, he repeated coolly, "Thy reward has been predicted." This apparent inconsistency he explained to his puzzled disciples by quoting Gen. xxvii. 29: "Cursed be every one that curseth thee, and blessed be he that blesseth thee" (Ter. Ber. viii. 12a; Gen. R. lxvi. 6). He was fatherly to the indigent, particularly to poor and plain maidens, whom he clothed attractively and provided with means, so that they might obtain husbands (Ned. ix. 10; 66a). One Friday night, while absorbed in the study of the Bible, he inadvertently turned the wick of a lamp; and he vowed that when the Temple was rebuilt he would offer there an expiatory sacrifice (Shab. 12b).

He manifested the same spirit of hope in declining to countenance the refusal of the ultra-patriotic to beget children under the Roman sway (Tosef., Soṭah, xv. 10 [comp. ed. Zuckermandel]; B. B. 60b). Even under the conditions then existing he recommended early marriage. He said, "The Scripture tells us, 'Thou shalt teach them [the things thou hast seen at Horeb] to thy sons and to thy sons' sons; and how may one live to teach his sons' sons unless one marries early?"(Deut. iv. 9, Hebr; Yer. Ḳid. i. 29b; Ḳid. 61a; see Samuel Edels *ad loc.*).

Ishmael was one of the prominent members of the Sanhedrin at Jabneh ('Eduy. ii. 4), and when that august body was forced by circumstances to move to Usha, Ishmael attended its sessions there (B. B. 28b), though his residence was at Kefar 'Aziz, on the borders of Idumæa, where Joshua b. Hananiah once visited him (Kil. vi. 4; Ket. v. 8). He gradually developed a system of halakic exegesis which, while running parallel with that of Akiba, is admitted to be the more logical. Indeed, he established the principles of the logical method by which laws may be deduced from laws and important decisions founded on the plain phraseology of the Scriptures. Like Akiba, he opened up a wide field for halakic induction, but, unlike Akiba, he required more than a mere jot or a letter as a basis for making important rulings (comp. Sanh. 51b). He was of opinion that the Torah was conveyed in the language of man (see Yer. Yeb. viii. 8d; Yer. Ned. i. 36c), and that therefore a seemingly pleonastic word or syllable can not be taken as a basis for new deductions. In discussing a supposititious case with Akiba, he once exclaimed, "Wilt thou indeed decree death by fire on the strength of a single letter?" (Sanh. 51b). The plain sense of the

Scriptural text, irrespective of its verbal figures, was by him considered the only safe guide.

To consistently carry out his views in this direction Ishmael drew up a set of thirteen hermeneutic rules by which he interpreted Scripture. As a basis for these rules he took the seven rules of Hillel, and on them built up his own system, which he elaborated and strengthened by illustrating them with examples taken from the Scriptures (comp. Gen. R. xcii. 7). Even these rules he would not permit to apply to important questions, such as capital cases in which no express Scriptural warrant for punishment existed; he would not consent to attach a sentence of death, or even a fine, to a crime or misdemeanor on the strength of a mere inference, however logical, where no such punishment is clearly stated in Scripture (Yer. 'Ab. Zarah v. 45b), or to draw a rule from a law itself based on an inference (Yer. Ḳid. i. 59a). His rules were universally adopted by his successors, tannaim as well as amoraim, although occasionally he himself was forced to deviate from them (see Sifre, Num. 32).

Thus his name became permanently associated with the Halakah; but in the province of the Haggadah also it occupies a prominent place (M. Ḳ. 28b). In answer to the question whether future punishment will be limited to the spirit or to the body, or whether in equity any punishment at all should be inflicted on either, seeing that neither can sin when separated from the other, Ishmael draws this parallel: A king owning a beautiful orchard of luscious fruit, and not knowing whom to trust in it, appointed two invalids—one lame and the other blind. The lame one, however, tempted by the precious fruit, suggested to his blind companion that he ascend a tree and pluck some; but the latter pointed to his sightless eyes. At last the blind man raised his lame companion on his shoulders, and thus enabled him to pluck some of the fruit. When the king came, noticing that some fruit had disappeared, he inquired of them which was the thief. Vehemently asserting his innocence, each pointed to the defect which made it impossible for him to have committed the theft. But the king guessed the truth, and, placing the lame man on the shoulders of the other, punished them together as if the two formed one complete body. Thus, added Ishmael, will it be hereafter: soul and body will be reunited and punished together (Lev. R. iv. 5; comp. Sanh. 91a *et seq.*).

Ishmael laid the foundation for the halakic midrash on Exodus, the MEKILTA; and a considerable portion of the similar midrash, the SIFRE on Numbers, appears also to have originated with him or in his school, known as "Debe R. Ishmael." Some suppose that he was among the martyrs of Bethar (comp. Ab. R. N. xxxviii. [ed. Schechter, p. 56b]); the more generally received opinion, however, is that one of the martyrs, a high priest, was a namesake (Ned. ix. 10).

BIBLIOGRAPHY: Bacher, *Ag. Tan.* i. 240 *et seq.*; Brüll, *Mebo ha-Mishnah,* i. 103 *et seq.*; Frankel, *Darke ha-Mishnah,* pp. 105 *et seq.*; Grätz, *Gesch.* i v. 60; Hamburger, *R. B. T.* ii. 526 *et seq.*; Heilprin, *Seder ha-Dorot,* ii.; Hoffmann, *Einleitung in die Halachischen Midraschim,* pp. 5 *et seq.*; Weiss, *Dor,* ii. 101 *et seq.*; idem, introduction to his edition of *Mekilta,* x. *et seq.*; Zacuto, *Yuḥasin,* ed. Filipowski, p. 25.

S. S. M.

ISHMAEL B. JOHANAN B. BAROḲA: Tanna of the second century (fourth tannaitic generation); contemporary of Simon b. Gamaliel II. These two rabbis are often quoted together, either as opposing, or as agreeing with, each other (Tosef., 'Er. iv. [v.] 2; *ib.* Yeb. xiii. 5). Joshua b. Ḳarḥah also appears to have been of their circle, and the trio joined in opinions on marital questions (Tosef., Yeb. *l.c.*, Tosef., Ket. ix. 2; comp. Yeb. 42b, 75a; see SANHEDRIN). Once Ishmael is cited as opposing his father, JOHANAN B. BAROḲA, on a question of civil law (B. Ḳ. x. 2, *ib.* p. 114b; comp. Alfasi and Rosh *ad loc.*). While his name is connected with about forty halakot, on dietary laws, sacrifices, and Levitical cleanness, as well as on civil law, he is but little known in the province of the Haggadah. He says, "Whoso learns in order to teach is aided by Heaven to learn and to teach; but whoso learns in order the more fully to discharge his duties, him Heaven enables to learn and teach and practise" (Ab. iv. 5). Elsewhere he points out that the pious man must not live in the neighborhood of the wicked, for when punishment providentially falls upon the latter the former suffers also (Ab. R. N. ix. [ed. Schechter, p. 20a; comp. p. 34b]).

BIBLIOGRAPHY: Bacher, *Ag. Tan.* ii. 369; Brüll, *Mebo ha-Mishnah,* i. 209; Frankel, *Darke ha-Mishnah,* p. 185; Weiss, *Dor,* ii. 167.

S. S. M.

ISHMAEL B. JOSE B. ḤALAFTA: Tanna of the end of the second century. Ishmael served as a Roman official together with Eliezer b. Simon, and was instrumental in suppressing the hordes of Jewish freebooters that had collected during the war between Severus and Rescennius Niger (193). His activity in this direction was greatly resented by the Jews, who never forgave him for handing over fellow Jews to the Roman authorities for execution (Meg. 84a). In halakic literature he is known by his citations of his father's sayings which he transmitted to Judah I., with whom he read Lamentations and the Psalms (Lam. Rab. ii. 420; Midr. Teh. iii. 1). He had a wide knowledge of the Scriptures, and could write down from memory the whole of the Bible (Yer. Meg. 74d).

Ishmael b. Jose was not on good terms with the Samaritans. On one occasion, when he was passing through Neopolis on a pilgrimage to Jerusalem, the Samaritans jeeringly invited him to pray on Mount Gerizim instead of on "those ruins [Jerusalem]"; Ishmael retorted that the object of their veneration was the idols hidden there by Jacob (Gen. R. lxxxi.; comp. Gen. xxxv. 4). Sanh. 38b would indicate that he also had occasional passages with Christians.

As a judge, Ishmael was noted for absolute integrity (Mak. 24a). His modest bearing called forth high praise from his master. The treasures of Tyre shall be "for them that dwell before the Lord" (Isa. xxiii. 18) refers, said R. Judah, to Ishmael b. Jose and to others who, like him, consider themselves as of little account, but for whom some day a greater glory waits (Eccl. R. i. 7). The following gives an instance of his timely wit: Compelled to say something agreeable about a very ugly woman, he in vain sought ground for a compliment, until he learned that her name was "Liḥluḥit" (the dirty one). "Ah!" said he, "there is something beautiful about her—her name, which suits her uncommonly well." His haggadic interpretation of למנצח מזמור (Ps. iii.) may be given as an example of his method of exegesis. He explains it to mean "a psalm to Him who causes man to conquer himself." "Sing a psalm to Him who feels a great joy in being conquered. Come and behold! God's way is not man's way. One who is defeated is depressed, but God rejoices in being conquered, as seen in Psalm cvi. 23, where the joy of the Lord is expressed at the fact that Moses, His chosen one, was victorious in his mediation for Israel" (Pes. 119a; see Rashi *ad loc.*).

BIBLIOGRAPHY: Weiss, *Dor*, 286; Bacher, *Ag. Tan.* ii. 407–411; Graetz, *Hist.* ii. 467–469.

S. S. S. LEV.

ISHMAEL BEN ḲIMḤIT (ḲAMḤIT [קמחית]): High priest under Agrippa I.; probably identical with Simon, son of Κάμιθος (or Κάμη), mentioned by Josephus ("Ant." xx. 1, §§ 3 *et seq.*). He is known as having had a hand so large that it could contain four cabs of flour (Yoma 47a). Once, while talking with an Arab (or with the Arabian king), the latter's saliva fell on Ishmael's garment and made him unclean, so that his brother officiated in his stead (*ib.*; Tosef., Yoma, iv. [iii.] 20). In Yer. Yoma i. 1, Lev. R. xx. 7, and Tan., Aḥare Mot, 9, this story is related of Simeon ben Ḳimḥit. According to the Talmudic sources mentioned above, "Ḳimḥit" was the name of the mother of Ishmael, or Simeon; she had seven sons, all of whom became high priests.

BIBLIOGRAPHY: Derenbourg, *Hist.* p. 197, Paris, 1867; Grätz, *Gesch.* 4th ed., iii., note 19 (pp. 738–739); *idem*, in *Monatsschrift*, xxx. 53 *et seq.*

S. M. SEL.

ISHMAEL BEN PHABI (FIABI) II.: High priest under Agrippa II.; not to be identified (as by Grätz and Schürer) with the high priest of the same name who was appointed by Valerius Gratus and who officiated during 15–16 of the common era. Ishmael was a worthy successor of the high priest Phinehas. He was appointed to the office by Agrippa in the year 59, and enjoyed the sympathy of the people. He was very rich; his mother made him, for the Day of Atonement, a priestly robe which cost 100 minæ. Ishmael at first followed the Sadducean method of burning the sacrificial red heifer, but finally authorized the procedure according to the Pharisaic teaching. Being one of the foremost ten citizens of Jerusalem sent on an embassy to Emperor Nero, he was detained by the empress at Rome as a hostage. He was beheaded in Cyrene after the destruction of Jerusalem, and is glorified by the Mìshnah teachers (Parah iii. 5; Soṭah ix. 15; Pes. 57a; Yoma 35b).

BIBLIOGRAPHY: Josephus, *Ant.* xx. 8, §§ 8, 11; idem, *B. J.* vi. 2, § 2; Schürer, *Gesch.* ii. 219; Ad. Büchler, *Das Synedrion in Jerusalem*, pp. 67, 96, Vienna, 1902.

G. M. K.

ISSI (ISI, ISSA). See JOSE.

J

JACOB B. ABBA: 1. Babylonian scholar of the third century; junior to Rab (B. M. 41a). He was an expert dialectician, and prevailed in argument even against his famous senior (Yer. Sanh. vii. 25c).

2. Amora of the fourth century; contemporary of Abaye and Raba (b. Joseph). His patronymic is variously given as "Abba," "Abaye," "Abina," "Abu-ha," "Abun," and "Aibu" (comp. Yer. Sanh. x. 28b; Gen. R. xlii. 3; Ruth R., proem, 7; Tan., Aḥare Mot, 7; *ib.*, ed. Buber, 9; Num. R. ii. 26). As regards his nativity, he appears in the company of Palestinian scholars (Pesiḳ. viii. 71a; Lev. R. xxviii. 6), but also, before the leaders of the fourth amoraic generation, in Babylonia ('Er. 12a; Ḳid. 31b). The fact, however, that he was a favorite in Babylonia would make it seem more probable that he was a Babylonian by birth. Whenever Jacob returned from school his father and mother would vie with each other in waiting on him; but this Jacob did not consider consonant with the respect due from child to parent; he therefore appealed to Abaye, who told him: "Thy mother's services thou mayest receive, but not those of thy father, who is himself a scholar" (Ḳid. 31a). He doubtless visited Palestine, since he is mentioned in the company of Palestinians; but as an old man he is found in Babylonia (Zeb; 70b).

BIBLIOGRAPHY: Heilprin, *Seder ha-Dorot*, ii.

S. S. S. M.

JACOB BAR ABINA (ABIN; BUN): Palestinian amora of the fourth century. He is known as having transmitted the haggadot of Samuel b. Naḥman, Abbahu, and Abba b. Kahana (Eccl. R. i. 5). Jacob is reported to have had a heated controversy with R. Jeremiah on the question of the payment of taxes to the Roman government (Yer. M. Ḳ. iii. 1).

BIBLIOGRAPHY: Bacher, *Ag. Pal. Amor.* iii. 712–713 *et passim*; Heilprin, *Seder ha-Dorot*, ii.

S. S. M. SEL.

JACOB BAR AḤA: 1. Palestinian amora of the third generation (latter part of the third century); contemporary of R. Ze'era. He rarely gives opinions of his own, but repeats halakot and homiletic remarks in the names of earlier authorities. In Yer. Ber. 11a he communicates in the name of Rabbi Johanan a halakah relating to grace at meals. In the name of R. Eleazar (probably ben Pedat) he reports that in the words "Hide not thyself from thine own flesh" (Isa. lviii. 7) the prophet refers to a divorced wife, whom her former husband has to support (Lev. R. xxxiv. 14).

Jacob bar Aḥa associated with Assi (Yer. Meg. 74b); and it is also recorded that he once took a meal together with Ze'era, Ḥiyya bar Abba, and Ḥanina, and was invited to say grace (Yer. Ber. 11a).

2. Palestinian amora of the fourth generation; a contemporary of Hezekiah, with whom he associated (Yer. Ber. ii. 5a, iii. 6a; Ket. v. 30a).

BIBLIOGRAPHY: Zacuto, *Yuḥasin*, ed. Königsberg, 95a; Frankel, *Mebo ha-Yerushalmi*, 104b, 105a; Bacher, AG. *Pal. Amor.* ii. 178 and Index; Heilprin, *Seder ha-Dorot*, i. 236.

S. S. I. BR.

JACOB B. ELEAZAR: Spanish grammarian of the first third of the thirteenth century. The assumption that he lived in the first third of the twelfth century (Geiger's "Jüd. Zeit." xi. 235; Grätz, "Gesch." 3d ed., vi. 110; Winter and Wünsche, "Jüdische Litteratur,".ii. 183) is erroneous. He was probably a native of Toledo, where he had access to the famous Bible Codex Hilleli (David Ḳimḥi, "Miklol," ed. Fürst, p. 78b); subsequently he went to southern France, where he wrote "Gan Te'udot" (see below) at the request of Samuel and Ezra, the sons of Judah, who, according to Steinschneider (in "Z. D. M. G." xxvii. 558), are identical with Judah b. Nathanael's sons of the same names, mentioned by Al-Ḥarizi.

Jacob ben Eleazar's chief work, the "Kitab al-Kamil" (Hebr. "Sefer ha-Shalem"), written in Arabic, has long since been lost. Tanḥum Yerushalmi, who quotes it in his lexicon (see Bacher, "Aus dem Wörterbuche Tanchum Jerushalmi's," 1903, p. 42), says in the introduction to his Bible commentary that the book was in reality, and not merely metaphorically, complete, as its name indicated ("R. E. J." xl. 141). Tanḥum's contemporary Abraham Maimonides also cites the work in his Pentateuch commentary ("Zeit. für Hebr. Bibl." ii. 155).

The "Kitab al-Kamil," which probably included a grammar and a lexicon, is cited frequently by David Ḳimḥi; in about twenty articles of his "Sefer ha-Shorashim" he quotes opinions of Jacob's, some of which are most original and remarkable (see ed. Lebrecht and Biesenthal, p. xxviii.). Many citations are found also in an anonymous Hebrew-Arabic lexicon (Steinschneider, "Die Arabische Literatur der Juden," p. 290). As late as the fourteenth century the work was freely quoted by Isaac Israeli of Toledo in his commentary on Job (Neubauer, "Cat. Bodl. Hebr. MSS." No. 383; "Oẓar Neḥmad," iii. 151). A Hebrew author of Damascus (date unknown) says that complete copies of the "Kitab al-Kamil" had been found in Egypt ("Zeit. für Hebr. Bibl." ii. 154). It may be assumed that, the work being very large, only a limited number of copies existed. If Israelson's assumption (really originating with Poznanski in "Zeit. für Hebr. Bibl." ii. 156) is justified, long portions of the grammatical part of the "Kitab al-Kamil" are still extant; namely, the fragments found in a St. Petersburg manuscript and elsewhere, which have been ascribed to the earlier grammarian Isaac ibn Yashush. This fragmentary grammatical work also quotes the Codex Hilleli.

Certain Hebrew works bearing the name of Jacob b. Eleazar have been assigned, and probably correctly, to the author of the "Kitab al-Kamil"; and they are probably among the twelve works by him dealing with different subjects which Tanḥum Yerushalmi mentions (see "R. E. J." xl. 141, note 5).

The following three works of Jacob b. Eleazar are still extant: (1) "Gan Te'udot," a parenetic work on the human soul, written in mosaic style (formerly Halberstam MS., now in the Montefiore collection at Ramsgate; see "R. E. J." xv. 158). Copies of this work, under a different title, seem to be also in the libraries of the Vatican and the Escurial (see Steinschneider in "Z. D. M. G." xxvii. 555 *et seq.*). (2) "Meshalim," parables in "maḳamah" form, written in 1233 at the instance of friends, in order to show that Hebrew was as good a language as Arabic (Munich MS. No. 207). (3) "Sefer Kalilah wa-Dimnah," a Hebrew version of the famous book of fables, in rimed prose, written for a certain Benveniste. Only the beginning of this translation bas been preserved (Neubauer, "Cat. Bodl. Hebr. MSS." No. 384); this has been edited by Joseph Derenbourg ("Deux Versions Hébraïques du Livre de Kalilah et Dimnah," pp. 311–388, Paris, 1881). Two liturgical poems by Jacob b. Eleazar are enumerated in Zunz, "Literaturgesch." p. 201.

BIBLIOGRAPHY: Steinschneider, *Die Arabische Literatur der Juden*, pp. 158 *et seq.*; idem, *Hebr. Uebers.* p. 878; Geiger's *Jud. Zeit.* xi. 232 *et seq.*; idem, *Oẓar Neḥmad*, ii. 159 *et seq.*

T. W. B.

JACOB OF KEFAR HANAN (ḤANIN): Palestinian amora of the third generation (3d and 4th cent.). Jacob is especially known as a haggadist (Pesiḳ. iv. 30b; Gen. R. xxxii. 5; Yer. Ber. v. 2; Yer. Ta'an. i. 1), but most of his haggadic sayings have been transmitted only by his pupils and successors. Once (Pesiḳ. R 33 [ed. Friedmann, p. 153b]) his name occurs as "Jacob of Kefar Hananiah."

BIBLIOGRAPHY: Bacher, *Agada der Palästinensischen Amoräer*, iii. 569–571.

S. S. M. SEL.

JACOB OF KEFAR ḤIṬṬAYA (חיטייא): Palestinian scholar of the second century; contemporary of Judah I. Jacob is said to have been in the habit of visiting his teacher every day (Ḥag. 5b). Heilprin ("Seder ha-Dorot," ii.) concluded that he was a pupil of Akiba and teacher of Judah I.; this, however, is not certain.

S. S. M. SEL.

JACOB OF KEFAR, NEBURAYA: Judæo-Christian of the fourth century. Neburaya is probably identical with Nabratain, a place to the north of Safed, where, according to Schwarz ("Tebu'at ha-Areẓ," p. 103a), is the tomb of Jacob as well as that of Eleazar of Modi'im. Jacob was well known as a haggadist before he embraced Christianity; and in two instances his haggadot met with the approval of the Rabbis. One of these may be quoted: in the school of Cæsarea he interpreted Hab. ii. 19 as being a rebuke of simony. On the same occasion he indicated Isaac b. Eleazar as a worthy candidate for the rabbinate (Yer. Bik. iii. 3; Midr. Shemu'el vii.).

Jacob was also consulted at Tyre on halakic matters; but his decisions were not accepted. He decided (1) that the rules of sheḥiṭah should be applied, to fish, and (2) that a son born of a Gentile woman may be circumcised on the Sabbath. On account of these decisions Jacob incurred reprimands from R. Haggai, who ordered him to be flogged. Jacob, after presenting some arguments against this punishment, finally acknowledged that he deserved it (Pesiḳ. R. 14 [ed. Friedmann, p. 61a]; Pesiḳ. iv. 35b–36a; Yer. Yeb. ii. 6 and parallels). His heresy was not generally known.

Only Jacob's contemporary Isi of Cæsarea counts him among the Judæo-Christians, applying to him the Biblical word "sinner" (Eccl. R. vii. 47). The appellation "Jacob Mina'ah" (= "Jacob the Heretic"), met with in the Midrashim, may refer to the subject of this article.

BIBLIOGRAPHY: Bacher, *Ag. Pal. Amor.* iii. 709–711 *et passim*; Heilprin, *Seder ha-Dorot*, ii.; Levy, in *Ha-Maggid*, xiv. 245; Neubauer, *G. T.* p. 270.

S. S. M. SEL.

JACOB OF KEFAR SEKANYA (SIMAÏ): Judæo-Christian of the first century; mentioned on two occasions, in both Talmuds and in the Midrash. Meeting R. Eliezer in the upper market-place of Sepphoris, he asked him for an opinion on a curious ritualistic question bearing upon Deut. xxiii. 18. As R. Eliezer declined to give an opinion, Jacob acquainted him with the interpretation of Jesus derived from Micah i. 7. R. Eliezer was pleased with the interpretation and was consequently suspected of Christian leanings by the governor ('Ab. Zarah 17a; Eccl. R. i. 24; Tosef., Ḥul. ii. 24). On another occasion R. Eleazar ben Dama, nephew of R. Ishmael, having been bitten by a serpent, Jacob went to heal him in the name of Jesus. R. Ishmael objecting, Jacob proved from the Torah that one may seek healing from any source whatever. But in the meantime R. Eleazar died, and R. Ishmael rejoiced that his nephew had not been defiled by the treatment of a Christian (Yer. Shab. iv., end, where "Kefar Simaï" is given; 'Ab. Zarah 23b; Eccl. R. *l.c.*).

BIBLIOGRAPHY: Bacher, *Ag. Tan.* i. 113; Grätz, *Gesch.* 3d ed., iv. 44; Neubauer, *G. T.* p. 234.

G. M. SEL.

JACOB BEN ZABDA: Palestinian amora of the fourth generation (4th cent.); junior contemporary, and probably pupil, of Abbahu, in whose name he repeats several halakic decisions and homiletic remarks (Yer. Dem. 23c; Pes. 29d; Pesiḳ. 75b; Sheb. iv. 35a; Niddah ii. 6a). He also repeats halakot in the names of Jeremiah and Jose II. (Kelim i. 1).

Jacob was a firm believer in the powers of magic. Bread or other eatables found on the road must not be touched, according to him, because such food may have been laid there for magical purposes (Lev. R. xxxvii.). From the words "And the people spake against God, and against Moses" (Num. xxi. 5) Jacob infers that he who speaks against his teacher is as though he insulted the majesty of God (Midr. Teh. xxx.).

BIBLIOGRAPHY: Zacuto, *Yuḥasin*, ed. Königsberg, 64b; Heilprin, *Seder ha-Dorot*, i. 236; Bacher, *Ag. Pal. Amor*, ii., passim; Frankel, *Mebo ha-Yerushalmi*, p. 105.

S. S. I. BR.

JADDUA: High priest at the time of the Second Temple. According to Neh. xii. 11, his father's name was Jonathan, but according to verse 22 of the same chapter, it was Johanan. If both of these names are correct, and if Johanan was the son of Jonathan, or vice versa, Jaddua belonged to the sixth generation after Jeshua, the first high priest who returned from the Exile; but if "Jonathan" and "Johanan" refer to one person, then Jaddua was of the fifth generation. A certain Jaddus, son of Joannes, whose brother Manasseh married Sanballat's daughter, officiated at the time of Alexander the Great (Josephus, "Ant." xi. 7, § 2); and between this date and the return from the Exile there are six, rather than five, generations. Indeed, even six seem to be too few. The hypothesis that Johanan and Jonathan were father and son is therefore the more probable, since the Jaddua mentioned by Nehemiah seems to be identical with the Jaddus mentioned by Josephus; but it must be noted that the Septuagint has once Ἰωδαέ and once Ἰδούα, which do not correspond well with Ἰαδδοῦς, found in Josephus. The high priest whom Alexander the Great greeted respectfully before the gates of Jerusalem was Jaddus, according to Josephus ("Ant." xi. 8, § 4); while in Talmudic accounts the same story is told of Simon the Just. But as Jaddua's son was the same Onias ("Ant." xi. 8, § 7) who was, according to another source (I Macc. xii. 7, 8, 20), a contemporary of King Areus of Sparta (309–265 B.C.), and as the often-mentioned Simon the Just was Onias' son ("Ant." xii. 2, § 5), there is an insolvable discrepancy between Josephus and the Talmud. Josephus must be given the preference here, as it is well known that the Talmud was inclined to group all the legends of that period around the person of Simon; and the act of Alexander the Great seems to be merely a legend.

The Christian chroniclers, as Eusebius, the "Chronicon Paschale," and Syncellus, of course follow Josephus; while the Jewish chroniclers of the Middle Ages tried to solve the difference in a naive way which excited the ridicule of Azariah dei Rossi ("Me'or 'Enayim," § 37). The Jewish sources write the name in the form עדו or עדוא; *e.g.*, Simon Duran in "Magen Abot," p. 4d (Leipsic, 1855). A more detailed account of the person of Jaddua would have to deal with the question how the lists of high priests in Nehemiah and in Joseplms are to be interpreted.

BIBLIOGRAPHY: Herzfeld, *Gesch. des Volkes Israel*, ii. 368; Grätz, *Gesch.* 2d ed., ii. 221; Schürer, *Gesch.* 3d ed., i. 182; Skreinka, *Beiträge zur Entwickelungsgesch. der Jüdischen Dogmen*, pp. 140–153, Vienna, 1861; Krauss, in *J. Q. R.* x. 361.

G. S. KR.

JANNAI. See YANNAI.

JEHUDA. See JUDAH.

JEREMIAH: Palestinian scholar of the fourth century; always quoted by the single name "Jeremiah," though sometimes that name is used for Jeremiah b. Abba. A Babylonian by birth, he passed his youth in his native land without giving much promise of gaining celebrity as a scholar (Ket. 75a), He emigrated to Cæsarea, in Palestine, where he made rapid progress in his studies. Among his teachers were Abbahu (B. M. 16b); Samuel b. Isaac, whose homilies he very frequently reports (Yer. Peah i. 16b; Yer. Meg. i. 70d; Yer. Hag. i. 76c); and Assi II. (Giṭ. 44a; Ḥul. 21a); but his principal teacher was his countryman Ze'era. Both Ze'era and Abbahu loved the young scholar as a son (M. Ḳ. 4a; B. M. 16b). Ammi employed Jeremiah as tutor to his son (Yer. Beẓah v. 63a). Once while Ze'era and his pupil were engaged in some halakic investigation the hour of prayer arrived, and Jeremiah began to betray impatience at being detained. Ze'era, noticing it, reproved him with the words, "He that turneth away his ear from hearing the law, even his prayer shall be abomination" (Prov. xxviii. 9; Shab. 10a).

Jeremiah developed such industrious habits as to evoke from his teacher the remark that since the death of Ben 'Azzai and Ben Zoma, with whom industry ended, there had not been so zealous a student as Jeremiah (Yer. Ned. viii. 40d; comp. Soṭah ix. 15). But in his anxiety to acquire knowledge and accuracy he developed extreme captiousness. He frequently provoked the laughter of the college, except of his teacher (Niddah 23a); and ultimately his ultra-subtleties became insufferable. His considerate preceptor time and again warned him against pursuing his arguments beyond the bounds of the Halakah (R. H. 13a; Soṭah 16b), but it proved of no avail. At last his colleagues gave vent to their displeasure. The college was seriously discussing a point of law, when Jeremiah broke in with what appeared to be a ridiculous objection, whereupon he was ordered out of the academy (B. B. 23b). It happened that after the death of the great teachers a legal problem vexed the minds of the scholars, and there was none to solve it. It was submitted to Jeremiah, who returned it with the solution, which he prefaced with the humble words: "Although I am not worthy [to be consulted by you], your pupil's opinion inclines this way." On receipt of this, which was taken as an apology for the past, his colleagues reinstated him (B. B. 165b).

Thenceforth Jeremiah was the undisputed head of the scholastic circle at Tiberias (Yer. Shab. i. 3d, iii. 6c; comp. *ib.* vi. 8a), and questions were addressed to him from different parts of Palestine. Nor was his fame limited by the boundaries of his adopted country. In Babylonia also his opinions carried great weight, and when a contemporary or later Babylonian scholar introduced a statement by the phrase "It is said in the West," it was generally assumed that that statement emanated from Jeremiah (Sanh. 17b). The reverence in which he was held by his former countrymen appears from the following colloquy between his younger contemporaries Abaye and Raba: Said the former: "One Palestinian scholar is worth two of ours"; where-upon the other remarked: "And yet when one of ours emigrates to Palestine he is worth two of the natives. Take, for example, Jeremiah; although while he was here he could not comprehend our teachers, since emigrating to Palestine he has risen to such eminence as to look upon us as 'stupid Babylonians'" (Ket. 75a). Indeed, not only did Jeremiah repeatedly apply this epithet to Babylonian scholars, but he spoke disdainfully of his native land as well. Whenever an opinion by a Babylonian scholar met with his disapprobation, he would say: "Those Babylonian simpletons! they dwell in a land of darkness and advance opinions of darkness" (Pes. 84b; Yoma 57a; Bek. 25b).

With the leadership of the scholastic circle the management of public affairs was entrusted to him. He considered this occupation as paramount to engaging in the study of the Law (Yer. Ber. v. 8d); but it sometimes occasioned him unpleasantness. On one occasion some serious trouble threatened the Jews of Tiberias, and much treasure was required to avert it. Jeremiah was called upon to assess the people, and in discharging this duty he displeased his older colleague Jacob b. Bun. Jeremiah had called on Jacob for a considerable contribution, whereupon he remarked, "Jeremiah, is still at his tricks: he deserves excommunication." The feeling between them became so bitter that they excommunicated each other, though they soon revoked their decrees and became reconciled (Yer. M. Ḳ. iii. 81d).

Jeremiah had many pupils, among them JONAH and Hezekiah II., who stood in the front rank of the scholars of the next generation. His name is frequently found in the departments of the Halakah and the Haggadah, in the Babylonian as well as in the Palestinian Gemara, and in the Midrashim. He left the following directions for his interment: "Clothe me in white garments with sleeves, put stockings and shoes on my feet, place a staff in my hand, and lay me down on my side. Thus equipped, when the Messiah comes I shall be ready to follow him" (Yer. Kil. ix. 32b; Yer. Ket. xii. 35a).

BIBLIOGRAPHY: Bacher, *Ag. Pal. Amor.* iii. 95; Frankel. *Mebo*, p. 107b; Halevy, *Dorot ha-Rishonim,ii.* 356; Weiss, *Dor*, iii. 107.

S. S. S. M.

JEREMIAH B. ABBA (**b. Wa** in the Palestinian Talmud): Babylonian amora of the third century; disciple and fellow of Rab (Ber. 27b). In Yerushalmi his patronymic is often omitted (comp. 'Er. 21a with Yer. 'Er. ii. 20a: see also *ib.* 19d and ABINA). Jeremiah devoted himself to the study of the Halakah; but he is also cited in connection with haggadot. Most of the latter are embodied in the Babylonian version of the treatise Sanhedrin (pp. 91a, 92b, 93b, 103a). A specimen of these follows. The Jewish Bible canon not recognizing a separation of the Book of Nehemiah from that of Ezra, the Talmud raises the question, "Since what is contained in the Book of Ezra has been told by Nehemiah b. Hachaliah why is there no Biblical book bearing the name of Nehemiah?" To this Jeremiah answers, "Because Nehemiah claimed credit for what he had done, saying, ' Remember [A. V. "Think upon"] me, O my God, for good, according to all that I have done for this people'" (Neh. v. 19; Sank. 93b). He proves from Scriptural texts that the following four classes of persons will never be admitted into the Divine presence: (1) scorners; as it is said (Hosea vii. 5), "He stretched out his hand with [Hebr. משך = "withdraweth from"] scorners"; (2) liars; as it is said (Ps. ci. 7), "He that telleth lies shall not tarry in my sight"; (3) deceivers; as it is said (Job xiii. 16), "A hypocrite shall not come before him"; and (4) slanderers; as it is said (Ps. v. 5, Hebr.), "Evil shall not dwell with Thee" (Sanh. 103a).

BIBLIOGRAPHY: Bacher, *Ag. Pal. Amor.* iii. 582; Heilprin, *Seder ha-Dorot*, ii., *s.v.*

S. S. S. M.

JEREMIAH OF DIFTA: Babylonian amora of the fourth century; contemporary of Papi (B. B. 52a; 'Ab. Zarah 40a). Babbina, who eventually assisted in the compilation of the Babylonian Gemara, was his pupil. Once, while they were studying, a certain man passed them without covering his head (out of respect to the scholars). Rabbina thereupon remarked, "How bold this fellow is!" But Jeremiah rejoined, "Possibly he comes from Mata Meḥasya, where scholars are not rare and people pay no special attention to them" (Ḳid. 32b).

S. S. S. M.

JEREMIAH BEN ELEAZAR: 1. Palestinian scholar of the second century; contemporary of Simeon b. Gamaliel, the father of Judah I. He is known through one haggadah, transmitted by his pupil Bar Ḳappara, and giving various reasons for the death of the two sons of Aaron, Nadab and Abihu (Pesiḳ. xxvii. 112b; Lev. R. xx. 8; Tan., Aḥare Mot, 7). Ephraem Syrus ("Opera," i. 240) adopted an explanation by Jeremiah without mentioning his name (comp. Graetz in "Monatsschrift," iii. 319). Jeremiah's son **Eleazar** is mentioned in Pesiḳ, R. 23 (ed. Friedmann, p. 117b) and Soṭah 4a.

2. Haggadist of the third amoraic generation (second half of the third century). Bacher places him among the Palestinian haggadists, although several of his haggadot are found in the Babylonian Talmud, while only one is recorded in Yerushalmi (Shab. vi. 10).

Jeremiah's haggadot are numerous; and a whole group of them is found in 'Er. (18a–19a). He inferred from Ps. cxxxix. 5 that Adam was created with two faces, one of a man and one of a woman, and that God afterward cleft them asunder ('Er. 18a). In Gen. R. viii. 1 this opinion is ascribed to Samuel b. Naḥman, while Jeremiah's opinion is stated to have been that Adam was created a hermaphrodite. From Gen. v. 3 Jeremiah concluded that all the time that Adam lived under the curse (that is, till the age of 130) he begot demons and spirits ('Er. 18b). According to Jeremiah, the builders of the Tower of Babel were divided into three different groups, which respectively had the intention of dwelling there, of establishing there the cult of idolatry, and of waging war against God. The first group was dispersed; the second was punished by a confusion of language; and the third was transformed into one of apes, demons, and spirits (Sanh. 109a). Jeremiah also indicated the crow as a bird of prophecy (Lev. R. xxxii. 2).

BIBLIOGRAPHY: Bacher, *Ag. Pal. Amor.* iii. 583–587.

S. S. M. SEL.

JESUS B. PHABI: High priest (*c.* 30 B.C.). He was deposed by Herod the Great, his office being given to Simon, the son of Boethus, the king's father-in-law (Josephus, "Ant." xv. 9, § 3). Jesus' father's name in this passage of Josephus (ed. Niese) has the form *Φοαβι*; the same name was borne by the high priests Ishmael b. Phabi I. (*c.* 15 C.E.) and II. (*c.* 60 C.E.), and is found in rabbinical works (also פואבי, פיאבי פאבי).

The name is probably Egyptian (see Parthey, "Aegyptische Personennamen," *s.v.* *Φαβίς*); hence the many variants in Greek as well as in Hebrew texts. It follows from this that Jesus b. Phabi was a native of Egypt, like his predecessor Hananeel (Parah iii. 5) and his successor Simon, who was of the family of the Boethusians.

BIBLIOGRAPHY: Grätz, *Gesch.* 4th ed., iii. 223; Schürer, *Gesch.* 3d ed., ii. 216; Krauss, *Lehnwörter*, ii. 419; Wilcken, *Griechische Ostraha aus Aegypten und Nubien*, Index, s.v. *Φαμῖν* and *Φᾶφις*, Leipsic and Berlin, 1899.

G. S. KR.

JOHANAN B. BAROḲA: Teacher of the second century (second and third tannaitic periods); disciple of Joshua b. Hananiah and colleague of Eleazar b. Ḥiṣma (Tosef., Soṭah, vii. 9; Ḥag. 3a). He maintained a scholarly intercourse with Johanan b. Nuri. Quite a considerable number of halakot has been handed down in his name, and many of them, particularly those concerning marital and civil affairs, were adopted as law ('Er. viii. 2; B. Ḳ. x. 2; B. B. viii. 5; Kelim, xvii. 11). He is also cited in the Haggadah. According to him, the saying (Gen. i. 28), "Be fruitful, and multiply, and replenish the earth," implies that the duty of racial propagation devolves upon woman as well as upon man (Yeb. vi. 6). He taught that whoever profanes the name of God, even secretly, is punished publicly, whether the deed is committed intentionally or unintentionally (Ab. iv. 4; Ab. R. K, ed. Schechter, p. 35a).

BIBLIOGRAPHY: Bacher, *Ag. Tan.* i. 448, Brüll. *Mebo ha-Mishnah*, i. 137; Frankel. *Darke ha-Mishnah*, p. 131; Weiss, *Dor*, ii. 122.

S.S. S. M.

JOHANAN GADI (Greek, Γαδδις): Eldest of the five sons of Mattathias the Maccabee (I Macc. ii. 2; Josephus, "Ant." xii. 6, § 1), though the least important. When JONATHAN took the leadership and was being hard pressed in the country east of the Jordan, he sent Johanan with the baggage to the friendly Nabatæans; but another tribe, the sons of Jambri, seized it and killed Johanan. His death was avenged by his brothers Jonathan and Simeon (I Macc. ix. 35–42; Josephus, "Ant" xiii. 1, §§ 2–3; "B. J." i. 1, § 6). This tragic end is in strong contrast to the surname "Gadi" (גדי, meaning probably "the Lucky"). The rabbinical sources ascribe more importance to Johanan. but these accounts are confused (see "R. E. J." xxx. 215).

G. S. KR.

JOHANAN B. GUDGADA: Scholar and chief gatekeeper at the Temple in the last years of its existence (Tosef., Sheḳ. ii. 14); senior of Joshua b. Hananiah. He survived the destruction of Jerusalem, and was present at the memorable sessions of the Jabneli (Jamnia) Sanhedrin that laid the foundation of the Talmudic treatise 'EDUYOT, and before which he gave certain "evidences" (Yeb. xiv. 2; Giṭ. v. 5; comp. 'Eduy. vii. 9). One rabbinical source makes of him a disciple of Gamaliel II. and an expert mathematician (Hor. 10a); but this evidently rests on an error, דיב'נ (= R. JOHANAN B. NURI) having been mistaken for ריב"ג (= R. Johanan b. Gudgada). As it reads, the story is anachronistic, since Johanan was older than Joshua, who was the senior of Gamaliel. Of Johanan's life and work nothing more is known than that he gave the above-mentioned evidences (see also Ḥul. 55b), and that he was a ḤABER (Ḥag. ii. 7).

Two of Johanan's grandsons, or nephews, are said to have lived in the days of Rabbi. They were deaf-mutes, but regularly attended Rabbi's lectures, and by the motions of their heads and lips appeared to follow and understand him (Ḥag. 3a). Now, as Johanan had reached the age of manhood prior to the destruction of the Temple (70 C.E.), it is chronologically incredible that his nephews, or even his grandsons, should have attended Rabbi's lectures in the last decades of the second century. It might therefore be assumed that here also ריב"נ was misread

ריב"ג, were it not that another, more reliable source precludes that assumption. There it is said: "The sons of Johanan b. Gudgada were deaf-mutes; still they were entrusted with the direction of ritualistic matters in Jerusalem" (Tosef., Ter. i. 1; Yer. Ter. i. 40b). They were therefore contemporaries of Joshua; and accordingly it may be conjectured that in the Babylonian version the initial sign in ר"י (= R Joshua) was converted into the letter ב; hence the erroneous name רבי ("Rabbi").

BIBLIOGRAPHY: Brüll, *Mebo ha-Mishnah*, i. 93; Frankel, *Darke ha-Mìshnah*, p. 99; Heilprin, *Seder ha-Dorot*, ii., *s.v.*; Weiss, *Dor*, ii. 122.

S. S. S. M.

JOHANAN BEN HA-ḤORANIT: Palestinian tanna of the first generation; disciple of Hillel (according to Frankel, "Darke ha-Mishnah," p. 53, note 8, a disciple of Shammai) and teacher of Eleazar b. Zadok. Once, during a famine, his pupil Eleazar found him eating dry bread with salt and told his father thereof, whereupon the latter, a disciple of Shammai, sent Johanan some olives. But Johanan, noticing that the olives were wet, and therefore, according to Hillel, liable to be unclean, refused to eat them (Tosef., Suk. ii. 3; Yeb. 15b). It is also recorded that a visit was paid to him, on the Feast of Tabernacles, by the elders of both Hillel's and Shammai's schools (Suk. 28a; 'Er. 13b).

BIBLIOGRAPHY: Heilprin, *Seder ha-Dorot*, ii.; Weiss, *Dor*, i. 177.

S. S. M. SEL.

JOHANAN BEN MERIYA: Palestinian amora of the fifth or sixth generation (4th and 5th cent.). Johanan is frequently mentioned in the Talmud of Jerusalem in connection with both halakic and haggadic subjects, instances of the latter, however, predominating. In a controversy between R. Mana and R. Hananiah as to whether any high place may temporarily be used by a prophet as an altar, Johanan used Josh. viii. 30 and I Sam. vii. 9 to support the affirmative opinion of Hananiah (Yer. Meg. i. 14; Lev. R. xxii. 6; Midr. Teh. to Ps. xxvii. 6, where the name "Jacob" occurs). He also transmitted a haggadah of Johanan b. Nappaha (Yer. Peah i. 1).

BIBLIOGRAPHY: Bacher, *AG. Pal. Amor.* iii. 722; Frankel, *Mebo ha-Yerushalmi*, p. 97b.

S. S. M. SEL.

JOHANAN B. NAPPAḤA (HA-NAPPAḤ): Palestinian scholar; born at Sepphoris in the last quarter of the second century; died at Tiberias 279. He is generally cited as "Johanan," but sometimes by his cognomen only (Yer. R. H. ii. 58b; Sanh. 96a), which he himself uses once (Mak. 5b); but he is never cited by both together. He traced his descent from the tribe of Joseph (Ber. 20a), but he knew neither of his parents, his father having died before, and his mother at, his birth;

he was brought up by his grandfather. His first teachers were the last Tannaites or semi-Tannaites Yannai, Ḥanina b. Ḥama, and Hoshaiah Rabbah. For a short time he also attended the lectures of Judah I. (Rabbi); but, as he himself said, his acquaintance with Rabbi was only slight (see Yer. Beẓah v. 63a.) He mentions again his pupil-age under Rabbi in a reference to an occasion when he sat seventeen rows behind Rab (Abba Arika), and could not comprehend the discussions (Pes. 3b; Ḥul. 137b). But in the short time he sat under him he is said to have manifested such aptness as to convince Rabbi that great things might reasonably be expected of him (Yoma 82b). By Hanina he was instructed in the homiletic interpretation of the Bible—except the books of Proverbs and Ecclesiastes (Yer. Hor. iii. 48b)—and probably in medicine, in which he became skilled ('Ab. Zarah 28a).

Johanan had an agreeable presence and a pleasing disposition; he was kind and considerate to the stranger as well as to his brethren; to the non-observant as to the pious; to the 'am ha-areẓ as to the ḥaber; wherefore he was beloved by his teachers and honored by all (B. M. 84a; Yer. 'Ab. Zarah iii. 42c; Meg. 10b, 16a; 'Ab. Zarah 26b; Yer. Dem. ii. 23a; Bek. 31a). For a time he subsisted on the proceeds of some arable land, a vineyard, and an olive-orchard, which he had inherited, and which he sold one after another in order to obtain an education. As he expressed it, he exchanged the things that God created in six days for the things the delivery of which required forty days (Ex. xx. 11, xxxiv. 28; Deut. ix. 10; Cant. R. viii. 7). But all his resources having been at last exhausted, he was compelled to follow some bread-winning occupation. After a short time, however, he felt impelled to return to his school, where he earned, not without a struggle, the encomiums of his masters (Ta'an. 21a; Yeb. 57a; Yer. Yeb. viii. 9b; Yer. R. H. ii. 58a *et seq.*; Shab. 112b; 'Er. 24a). At last, owing to the universal homage paid to the young master, the patriarch accorded him a pension, and soon a lecturer's place was found for him.

Johanan began teaching at his native place, Sepphoris, and quickly became very popular there. One day his former teacher Ḥanina noticed unusually large crowds hurrying toward one place. Inquiring the reason of his attendant, he was told that Johanan was to lecture at the college lately presided over by R. Banna'ah, and that the people were flocking to hear him. Ḥanina thereupon thanked God for permitting him to see his life's work bearing such blessed fruit (see HANINA B. ḤAMA). How long Johanan continued to act as teacher at Sepphoris can not be ascertained; but he removed some time before Ḥanina's death. They had disagreed on two points of ritual, and Johanan, not wishing to oppose his master at his home, removed to Tiberias (Yer. Beẓah i. 60a; Yer. Sheb. ix. 38c, where the text is mutilated). It is doubtful whether the two ever met again. With his other teachers he maintained intimate relations to the end of their days. This was particularly the case with Hoshaiah. He, too, removed from Sepphoris and settled at Cæsarea, where he opened a college and whither Johanan often went from Tiberias to consult him on difficult problems (Yer. Ter. x. 47a; Yer. Ḥal. i. 58b). These visits to his aged teacher Johanan continued during the last thirteen years of Hoshaiah's life, but they were merely social visits, Johanan no longer needing Hoshaiah's help: "He that pays his respects to his teacher is considered as one waiting on the Divine Presence" (Yer. Sanh. xi. 30b).

At Tiberias Johanan opened an academy, which soon drew large numbers of gifted students, native and foreign, among whom were the great scholars Abbahu, Ammi, Assi II., Eleazar ben Pedath, Ḥiyya ben Abba, Jose ben Ḥanina, and Simon ben Abba; as many scores of his disciples accepted and taught his decisions, and as he himself did not confine his labors to the precincts of the college, but visited and lectured at other places (Yeb. 64b; Ket. 7a), his fame spread far and wide, and his name more than that of any other teacher was on the lips of scholars. In the Diaspora, whither his teachings were carried by his disciples, his authority was almost as great as in his native land, and few contemporary scholars in Babylonia opposed him. As for Johanan himself, he recognized no foreign authority except that of Rab (ABBA ARIKA), his senior schoolmate under Judah I. With Rab, Johanan kept up a correspondence, and addressed him as "our master in Babylonia." After Rab's death Johanan wrote to Rab's colleague SAMUEL, but addressed him as "our colleague in Babylonia." Samuel sent him a complete calendar covering the intercalations for a period of sixty years; Johanan, however, admitted merely that Samuel was a good mathematician. But when Samuel transmitted to him a mass of disquisitions on the dietary laws, Johanan exclaimed, "I still have a master in Babylonia!" He even resolved to pay him a visit, but rumor made him believe that Samuel had in the meantime died (Ḥul. 95b).

Johanan pursued a strictly analytical method in his studies of the Halakah. Penetrating deeply into the sense of the Mishnah, and subjecting every part to a thorough examination and careful comparison with more or less related laws, he soon perceived that Rabbi's compilation contained contradictory decisions, based in many cases on the opinions of individuals. These he endeavored to reconcile; but as that could not always be done, he perforce rejected many halakot adopted in the Mishnah, preferring the authority of baraitas taught by his former masters Ḥiyya and Hoshaiah. To carry out his line of thought systematically and consistently he laid down certain rules for the final decision of cases where two or more tannaim were found to have entertained opposite opinions, or where halakot are ascribed to recognized authorities, but are in conflict with anonymous opinions given elsewhere. Some rules of this kind had been devised before his, but had proved insufficient. Johanan therefore elaborated and supplemented them (see Yer. Ter. in. 42a; Shab. 39b; 'Er. 46a *et seq.*; Yeb. 42b; Giṭ. 75a), and most of his rules are to this day authoritative for the student of Talmud. All of them were collected in the geonic period and embodied in the so-called "Order of the Tannaim and Amoraim" (סדר תנאים ואמודאים; abridged, סתו"א), which, is ascribed to Naashon b. Zadok of the ninth century (see Grätz, "Einleitung in den Talmud von Ibn-Aknin," p. vii.). Later Talmudists, seeing that Johanan was so prolific an amora that his name is more frequently mentioned in the Gemara than any other, ascribed to him the compilation of the Palestinian Gemara (see Maimonides, "Haḳdamah," ed. Hamburger, p. 58, Berlin, 1902). Modern scholars for obvious reasons deny this, but admit that he projected the compilation, which, however, was not completed till over a century after him. The Midrash to the Book of Psalms also has been erroneously ascribed to Johanan (see Buber, "Midrash Tehillim," Introduction, p. 2a). He was one of the most prolific haggadists.

In his religious decisions Johanan was comparatively liberal. He aided Judah II. in the repeal of the prohibition against using oil made by pagans ('Ab. Zarah 36a); he permitted Greek to be studied by men, because it enabled them to defend themselves against, informers, and by women because familiarity with that language is an attractive accomplishment in their sex (Yer. Peah i. 15c); he allowed the painting of decorative figures on the walls (Yer. 'Ab, Zarah iii. 42d). Under certain circumstances he permitted emigration from Palestine: "If thou art mentioned [nominated by the Romans] for office make the Jordan thy boundary friend [escape over the Jordan], even on a semiholiday" (Yer. M. Ḳ. ii. 81b).

Johanan is the subject of many legends (Ber. 5b; Yer. Ber. v. 9a; Ḥag. 15b; B. Ḳ. 117a *et seq.*; B. M. 84a; B. B. 75a), in which some further traits of his are preserved. His servants he treated with great kindness: "Did not he that made me in the womb make him?" (Job xxxi. 15; Yer. B. Ḳ. viii. 6c). He was blessed with many children, but lost ten sons. The last one is said to have died by falling into a caldron of boiling water. The bereft father preserved a joint of the victim's little finger, which he exhibited to mourners in order to inspire resignation. "This is a bone from the body of my tenth son," he would say (Ber. 5b; see Ḥiddushe Geonim *ad loc.*). However, he himself was not resigned at the death of his brother-in-law Resh Laḳish, his fellow amora, whom he affectionately called "my counterpart" (שכנגדי—Ket. 54b, 84b). He mourned for him long and deeply, weeping often and crying, "Bar Laḳish, where art thou? O Bar Laḳish!" At last he became melancholy, and for three years and a half could not attend his college; but it seems that he finally recovered his health and resumed his labors (Yer. Meg. i. 72b; B. M. 84a). On his death-bed he ordered that he should be dressed neither in white nor in black, but in scarlet, so that on awaking after death he would not feel out of place in the company either of the pious or of the wicked (Yer. Ket. xii. 35a; Gen. R. xcvi. 5).

BIBLIOGRAPHY: Bacher, *Ag. Pal. Amor.* i. 205–339; Frankel, *Mebo*, pp. 95b–97b; Grätz, *Gesch.* 2d ed., iv. 257 *et seq.*; Halevy, *Dorot ha-Rishonim*, ii. 149b *et seq.*; Hamburger, *R. B. T.*; Heilprin, *Seder ha-Dorot*, ii.; Jost, *Gesch. des Judenthums und Seiner Sekten*, ii. 149, *passim*; Weiss, Dor, iii. 69 *et seq.*

S. S. S. M.

JOHANAN B. HA-NAZUF: Friend of Gamaliel II. (first and second centuries). It is related that ḤALAFTA once went to Tiberias and found Gamaliel at the house of Johanan b. ha-Nazuf (= "the excommunicated"), reading a targum of the Book of Job. Ḥalafta informed the patriarch that he had been present at Jerusalem when a targum of the same book was laid before his grandfather Gamaliel I., and that that patriarch had ordered it entombed in a wall. Thereupon the second Gamaliel also ordered that the targum be suppressed (Tosef., Shab. xiii. [xiv.] 2; Shab. 115a). This Johanan has been identified by Levy ("Wörterbuch," i. 470) and Berliner ("Onkelos," ii. 90) with Johanan Sofer, scribe or secretary to Gamaliel II. J. Derenbourg, however, thinks that he was the sou of Eliezer b. Hyrcanus, and, consequently, the nephew of Gamaliel II. ("Magyar Zsidó-Széemle," iii. [1885] 434; comp. Sanh. 68a).

BIBLIOGRAPHY: Grätz, *Gesch.* 3d ed., iii. 373; Frankel, *Darke ha-Mishnah*, p. 57; Joel Müller, *Briefe und Responsen in der Vorqaonäischen Literatur*, pp. 7, 21, Note 29.

S. S. S. M.

JOHANAN B. NURI: Tanna of the first and second centuries; junior of Gamaliel II. and senior of Akiba (Sifra, Ḳedoshim, iv. 9; 'Ar. 16b; comp. Sifre, Deut. 1). A great halakist, always provided with satisfactory answers to all questions, he was familiarly called "pedler's basket" or "bundle of halakot" (Ab. R. N. xviii.; Giṭ. 67a); the number and diversity of halakot cited under his name in the Mishnah alone, about forty, justify those appellations. Besides exhaustive rabbinical knowledge, he acquired familiarity with the general science of his time, especially geometry. It was said of him, as of his colleague Eleazar b. Ḥisma, that he could approximately state the number of drops contained in the sea; like Eleazar, also, he was very poor. Through the influence of Joshua b. Hananiah both were appointed by Gamaliel to remunerative offices (see ELEAZAR B. ḤISMA; comp. Sifre, Deut. 16).

Johanan showed himself grateful to Gamaliel. When, after that patriarch's death, Joshua proposed a change in a rule established by Gamaliel, Johanan opposed him: "I have observed that the head is always followed by the trunk; as long as Gamaliel lived we observed the rule laid down by him, and now you propose to veto his directions. Joshua, we shall not harken to thee" ('Er. 41a). Between him and Ḥalafta also intimate scholarly relations existed (comp. Tosef., B. B. ii. 10 with B. B. 56b and parallels).

In his discussions of halakot Johanan considered expediency and economy as well as law and authority. When Ṭarfon declared that only olive-oil was appropriate for the Sabbath-lamp, Johanan became impatient: "And what shall the Babylonians do where none but sesame-oil is to be had; and what shall the Medians do, who have nothing but nut-oil; and the Alexandrians, who have nothing but radish-oil; or the Cappadocians, who have only naphtha?" (Shab. 26a). On another occasion, when Akiba suggested that a married woman who has become the common talk of the "spinsters by the moon" ought to be divorced, Johanan remarked," In that case there is no chance for a daughter of Judah to live with a husband! Only where infidelity is fully established by legal evidence may a divorce be imposed" (Giṭ. 89a: see Deut. xix. 15, xxiv. 1). In the Haggadah he is not often cited. He was very pious, and therefore later rabbis said that when one dreams of Johanan b. Nuri one may hope to develop a wholesome fear of sin (Ab. R. N. xl. [ed. Schechter, p. 64b]).

BIBLIOGRAPHY: Bacher, *Ag. Tan.* i. 372; Brüll, *Mebo ha-Mishnah*, i. 122; Frankel. *Darke ha-Mishnah*, p. 123; Hamburger, *R. B. T.*; Weiss, *Dor*, ii. 118.

S. S. S. M.

JOHANAN HA-SANDALAR ("the sandal-maker"): Tanna of the second century; one of Akiba's disciples that survived the Hadrianic persecutions and transmitted the traditional law (Gen. R. lxi. 3; Eccl. R. xi. 6; comp. Yeb. 62b). With several colleagues he repaired to the Valley of Rimmon to institute a leap-year, and in the course of the discussions that ensued he betrayed considerable passion. Meïr had just cited an opinion which he ascribed to Akiba, but the authenticity of which Johanan denied, adding, "I have waited on R. Akiba standing [by his side as an advanced student] longer than thou didst sitting [as a mere hearer]." The learned company took umbrage at this derogatory remark, and murmured, "Johanan ha-Sandalar is a true Alexandrian [given to gasconade]." The incident, however, ended in reconciliation, and the disputants did not leave the session without kissing each other (Yer. Ḥag. iii. 78d; see Rapoport, "'Erek Millin," p. 102a). Because he is called here "a true Alexandrian," it is assumed that he was a native of Alexandria.

As a halakist he is sometimes cited in the Mishnah (Yeb. xii. 5; Ket. v. 4; Kelim v. 5), and Simon b. Gamaliel II. reports two halakot from him (Tosef., Kelim, B. Ḳ. iv. 2, 5). To obtain an authoritative decision in a doubtful case he once exposed himself to great danger; it was during the Hadrianic persecutions, when many rabbis had been put to death for teaching Judaism, and Akiba was imprisoned and awaiting his doom at the command of Rufus. A marital question agitated the collegians, and Johanan undertook to procure the closely guarded master's advice upon it. Disguised as a pedler, he offered some trifle for sale near the prison: "Who wants, needles? Who wants hooks? How about private Ḥaliẓah?" Akiba, looking out through an aperture, said in reply, "Hast thou spindles? Hast thou kasher?" (= "valid!"—Yer. Yeb. xii. 12d). At one time during the persecutions, Johanan and Eleazar I. (b. Shammua) left Palestine, intending to betake themselves to Judah b. Bathyra in Nisibis; but they did not carry out their intention. By the time they arrived at Sidon they felt too homesick to proceed any farther, and returned (Sifre, Deut. 80).

In the Haggadah Johanan is not mentioned, except as author of the following maxim: "An assembly that aims to glorify the name of the Omnipresent will have permanence, but one that does not so aim will not endure" (Ab. iv. 11; comp. Ab. R. N. xl. [ed. Schechter, pp. 64b, 65a]).

Bibliography: Bacher, *Ag. Tan.* ii. 265; Brüll. *Mebo ha-Mishnah*, i. 198; Frankel, *Darke ha-Mishnah*, p. 175; Grätz, *Gesch.* 2d ed., iv. 177, 186; Weiss, Dor, ii. 166; Zacuto, *Yuḥasin*, p. 47a.

S. S. S. M.

JOHANAN B. TORTA: Scholar of the first and second centuries; contemporary of Akiba. When Akiba hailed Bar Kokba as the Messiah, the latter exclaimed, "Akiba, grass will have grown out of thy jaws ere the Son of David appears" (Yer. Ta'an. viii. 68d; Lam. R. ii. 2). To a legend of a cow that refused to work on a Sabbath, and thereby caused the conversion of Johanan, who had been a pagan, is referred Johanan's by-name "ben Torta" (son of a cow; Pesiḳ. R. xiv. 56b *et seq.*). No halakot are ascribed to him, and only one haggadah bears his name: "Shiloh was destroyed because there sacred things were treated contemptuously" (see I Sam. ii. 17); "the first Jerusalem Temple was destroyed because at the time people perpetrated the sins of idolatry, incest, and bloodshed. But we know that in the age of the later Temple people studied the Law and carefully tithed their produce: why then were they exiled? Because they loved Mammon and hated one another! From this we may learn that to hate man is grievous in the eyes of the Omnipresent, and that it is paramount to idolatry, incest, and bloodshed" (Tosef., Men. xiii. 22; comp. Yoma 9a *et seq.*).

BIBLIOGRAPHY: Bacher, *Ag. Tan.* ii. 557; Grätz, *Gesch.* 2d ed., iv. 150; Heilprin, *Seder ha-Dorot*, ii. (see *ib.* s.v. *Ḥanina b. Torta*).

S. S. S. M.

JOHANAN B. ZAKKAI: The most important tanna in the last decade of the Second Temple, and, after the destruction of Jerusalem, the founder and first president of the academy at Jabneh. According to the theory formulated in the Mishnah (Ab. ii. 8), that traditions were handed down through an unbroken chain of scholars, Johanan, in receiving the teachings of Hillel and Shammai, formed the last link in that chain. But it is rather as a pupil of Hillel than of Shammai that he is known (Suk. 28a). Before his death Hillel is said to have prophetically designated Johanan, his youngest pupil, as "the father of wisdom" and "the father of coming generations" (Yer. Ned. v., end, 39b). Like that of Hillel, Johanan's life was divided into periods of forty years each. In the first of these he followed a mercantile pursuit; in the second he studied; and in the third he taught (R. H. 30b). Another version has it (Sifre, Deut. 357) that in the last forty years of his life he was a leader of Israel. If the last statement be accepted as approximately correct, and it is assumed that Johanan lived at the latest one decade after the destruction of Jerusalem, his public activity as the recognized leader of the pharisaic scribes must have begun between the years 30 and 40 of the common era.

Some data have been preserved concerning Johanan's public activity in Jerusalem before the destruction of the Temple. Together with Simon b. Gamaliel I. he sent orders to the different districts of Palestine concerning the delivery of the tithe (statement of his pupil Joshua b. Neḥunya in the Mekilta of Simeon b. Yoḥai; Midr. ha-Gadol to Deut. xxvi. 13). He refuted the objections of the Sadducees to the Pharisees (Yad. iv. 5), and opposed the halakah of the Sadducees (Men. 65a; B. B. 115b). He prevented a Sadducean high priest from following the Sadducean regulations at the burning of the red heifer (Tosef., Parah, iii. 8; comp. Parah iii. 7, 8). It was Johanan's activity as a teacher in Jerusalem which, was especially extolled by tradition. His school was called the "great house," after the expression in II Kings xxv. 9 (Yer. Meg. 73d). It was the scene of many incidents that formed the subjects of anecdote and legend (Lam. R. i. 12, *passim*; Gen. R iv.). The oft-repeated story concerning Johanan's most important pupil, Eliezer b. Hyrcanus, shows Johanan's bet ha-midrash (academy) as the scene of a pathetic meeting between son and father (Tan., ed. Buber, to Gen. xiv. 1). An old tradition (Pes. 26a) relates that Johanan sat in the shadow of the Temple and lectured the whole day; but that of course was not the permanent place for his teaching. The statements regarding five of his pupils, his verdict concerning them, and the question he put to them as to the best road for a person to pursue through life (Ab. ii. 8) are reminiscences of the period before the destruction. Johanan's residence in 'Arab, a place in Galilee, which was perhaps his home, belongs to this period. Two questions of a legal nature (regarding the observance of the Sabbath) which he answered while there (Shab. xvi. 7, xxii. 3) gave rise to the statement that he lived there for eighteen years (probably a round number) and that he was moved by the religious indifference of the inhabitants to exclaim: "O Galilee, Galilee, thou hatest the Torah; hence wilt thou fall into the hands of robbers!" Another prophetical exclamation of a similar nature is ascribed to Johanan. The gates of the Temple had ominously opened of themselves, whereupon he apostrophized the sanctuary: "O Temple, Temple, why dost thou frighten thyself? I know of thee that thou shalt be destroyed;. Zechariah the son of Iddo [Zech. xi. 1] has already prophesied concerning thee: 'Open thy doors, O Lebanon, that the fire may devour thy cedars '" (Yoma 39b; comp. Ab. R. N., Recension B, vii., ed. Schechter, p. 21).

Johanan's part in the last struggle of Jerusalem against Rome has been immortalized in the legends concerning the destruction of that city, which, however, have a historical kernel (Giṭ. 56b; Lam. R. i. 5; Ab. R. N. iv.). He counseled peace; and when the strife of parties in the besieged city became unbearable he had himself carried to the Roman camp in a coffin. Like Josephus, Johanan prophesied imperial honors for the general Vespasian, quoting the words of the prophet Isaiah: "Lebanon [that is, the sanctuary] shall fall by a mighty one" (Isa. x. 34). He sought and obtained permission to settle in Jabneh (Jamnia) and to exercise his profession of teacher there. In Jabneh, surrounded by his pupils, Johanan received the terrible news that the Temple was burned to ashes. They tore their garments, wept, and made lamentation as for the dead (Ab. R. N. iv.). But the aged master in the catastrophe which had befallen the Jewish people kept his vigor unimpaired. He converted the school at Jabneh into a center for Judaism in Palestine. The college, of which he was president, exercised the functions of the great law court (Sanhedrin) of Jerusalem, and by this institution of an authorized board the continuity of spiritual leadership was maintained uninterrupted. Johanan saw to it that Jabneh took the place of Jerusalem as the Jewish religious center. He ordained that certain privileges peculiar to Jerusalem and the sanctuary should be transferred to Jabneh (R. H. iv. 1, 3). Other regulations of his dealt with the determination of the exact time when the new month begins—a matter then very important—and with the acceptance of the testimony on which such determination is based (*ib.* iv. 41; Baraita, R. H. 21b). His order that, as had been customary in the Temple, the trumpets should sound in Jabneh on New-Year's Day even when it fell on the Sabbath, was opposed, but unsuccessfully, by some of the members of the council (Baraita, R. H. 29b).

It is not known how long Johanan remained at the head of the bet ha-midrash and of the legal council. It may be accepted as certain that Johanan was succeeded by Gamaliel II. while the former was still living, inasmuch as he did not die in Jabneh; for it is related (Eccl. R. vii. 7; comp. Ab. R. N. xiv.) that his pupils went to Jabneh after his death. And furthermore, since a place, Berur Ḥayil, is mentioned as the seat of a legal council over which Johanan presided (Sanh. 32b; Sifre, Deut. 144), and at another time it is related that Joshua b. Hananiah visited his teacher in Berur Ḥayil (Tosef., Ma'aser al-Rishon, i. 1), it may be concluded that Johanan spent the last years of his life and died at this place, which was near Jabneh (concerning the name comp. Krauss's conjecture in Berliner's "Magazin," xx. 119; Derenbourg, in "Monatsschrift," xxxvii. 304). His pupils were present at his death. The solemn conversation between the dying master and his disciples (Ber. 28b) begins with a question from the latter: "Light of Israel, pillar of the sanctuary, strong hammer, why dost thou weep?" These remarkable epithets characterize the work of Johanan and his importance for his period. The blessing which just before his death he pronounced upon his pupils at their desire consisted of the prayer: "May it be God's will that the fear of heaven be as strong in you as the fear of flesh and blood" (*ib.*). His last words were: "Put the vessels out of the house, that they may not become unclean, and prepare a throne for Hezekiah, the King of Judah, who is coming" (*ib.*). By this puzzling reference to Hezekiah, Johanan plainly meant the coming of the Messiah, of which he was thinking in his last moments. A son of Johanan died before him (Ab. R. N. xiv., end). In one anecdote (B. B. 10b) his sister's sons are mentioned. One of these nephews, Ben Baṭiaḥ, is named as one of the Zealot leaders (Lam. R. to i. 4; JEW. ENCYC. ii. 673).

Johanan ben Zakkai's motto was, "If thou hast learned much of the Torah, do not take credit for it; for this was the purpose of thy creation" (Ab. ii. 8). He found his real calling in the study of the Law. The following description of him was handed down by tradition (Suk. 28a): "He never spoke an idle word; he did not go four yards without reflecting on the Torah and without the phylacteries; no one ever preceded him in entering the bet ha-midrash; he never slept in the bet ha-midrash, and was always the last to leave it; no one ever found him engaged in anything but study." His knowledge was spoken of as though it included the whole of Jewish learning (Ab. R. N. xiv., end; Suk. 28a; B. B. 134a; Masseket Soferim xvi. 8). He advises a priestly family in Jerusalem, the members of which died young, to occupy itself with the study of the Torah so as to ward off the curse of dying in the prime of life, which is laid upon the descendants of Eli (from whom they may have descended) in I Sam. ii. 23 (R. H. 18a). He, however, warned against a one-sided devotion to study, as in his verdict concerning scholars and those free of sin: "Whoever possesses both these characteristics at the same time is like an artist who has his tools in his hands" (Ab. R. N. xxii.).

In the halakic tradition Johanan is but seldom referred to as an originator of maxims. His halakah is doubtless to be found in that of Hillel's school and in the sayings of his pupils, especially of Eliezer and Joshua. The haggadic tradition, on the other hand, connects numerous and varied sayings with his name. Mention may first be made of conversations between him and his pupils, or between him and unbelievers who were versed in the Bible, in which questions of textual interpretation were discussed. At one time he asked his pupils what the words in Prov. xiv. 34 meant (Pesiḳ., ed. Buber, 12b; comp. B. B. 10b, where the accounts of two conversations have been confused). He himself interpreted them as follows: "Benevolence [ḥesed] on the part of a nation has the atoning power of a sin-offering" (B. B. *l.c.*). In the same sense he interpreted the words of the prophet (Hosea vi. 6), "I desired mercy [ḥesed], and not sacrifice," with which he comforted his pupils for the destruction of the Temple and the discontinuance of the sacrifice of atonement (Ab. R. N. iv.). He answered several questions of a polemical tendency put by a Roman commander (*ἡγεμών*), who can not be identified owing to the different ways in which his name is written. These questions referred to the contradiction between the figures in Num. iii. 22, 28, 34 and the total sum in verse 39 of the same chapter (Bek. 5b), between Ex. xxxviii. 26 and 27 (*ib.*), and between Gen. i. 20 and ii. 19 (Ḥul. 27b); also to the legal regulation in Ex. xxi. 29 (Yer. Sanh. 19b), and to the law concerning the red heifer (Pesiḳ. 40a). In connection with the last-mentioned question Johanan refers the Gentile to a Gentile analogy: Just as the evil spirit is driven out of a person possessed through burning certain roots and by other means, so the process of purification drives out the "unclean spirit" (Zech. xiii. 2). To his pupils, however, who were not satisfied with this answer, he said: "By your lives, death does not make impure, nor water clean; but it [the law concerning the red heifer] is a decree of the All Holy, whose reasons we must not question" (comp. Lazarus, "Die Ethik des Judentums," i. 189, 246).

A special group of Johanan's haggadic text interpretations is given the name "ḥomer," which term is related to the designation "doreshe ḥamurot," applied to the ancient expositors of the Bible. In this group the interpretations are symbolic, seeking to penetrate into the spirit of the Bible text.

One source (Tosef., B. Ḳ. vii. 3 *et seq.*) puts five such explanations of Johanan together. They answer the following questions: "Why is the ear of a Hebrew slave bored who voluntarily refuses to be made free?" (Ex. xxi. 6; comp. Ḳid. 22b). "Why is iron excluded from the building: material of the altar?" (Ex. xx. 25; Deut. xxvii. 5; comp. Mek., Yitro, Baḥodesh, 11). "What does the remarkable word 'asher ' in Lev. iv. 22 mean?" (comp. Hor. 10b). "Why was Israel exiled specially to Babylon?" (comp. Pes. 87b). "Why were only the first tables of the testimony, and not the second, considered to be the work of God?" (Ex. xxxii. 16).

Besides the explanations to these questions, Johanan gave others of a similar character. He explained why a thief is punished more severely than a robber (B. Ḳ. 79b), and by explaining the Biblical numbers symbolically he answered the question: "Why does the Scripture [Ex. xxii. 1] ordain fivefold restitution for an ox and only, fourfold for a sheep?" (*ib.*). The forty days of rain during the Flood which destroyed sinful man (Gen. vii. 12) corresponded, he said, to the forty days of the formation of the human embryo (Gen. R. xxxii.). The ten gerah (= a half-shekel) of the atonement money (Ex. xxx. 13) corresponded to the Ten Commandments, for the transgression for which atonement is to be made (Pesiḳ. 19b).

Among other things Johanan explained the following:

The exhortation to those who are freed from military service to return home (Deut. xx. 5–7):—this, he said, was given in order that the cities of Israel might not become depopulated in times of war (Sifre, Deut. 192). The passage Gen. ii. 19:—he does not find that the account of the creation of the animals is here repeated but that their subjection to man is described (Gen. R. xvii). The words "And the eyes of them both were opened" (Gen. iii. 7):—this means that God opened their eyes to the evil they had brought upon future generations (Gen. R. xix.). Abraham's rision of the future (Gen. xv. 18):—this showed Abraham the present world only, not the future one (Gen. R. xliv.).

Johanan's views on piety (comp. his motto given above) correspond to his teaching that Job's piety was not based on the love of God, but on the fear of Him (Job i. 1; Soṭah v. 5, reported by Joshua b. Hananiah). He explains the exhortation in Eccl. ix. 8 allegorically: "White garments and costly oils are not meant here," he says (Eccl. R. ix. 6), "for the Gentile peoples have these in plenty: it is rather an exhortation to fulfil the Law, to do good deeds, and to study the Scriptures."

In a tradition concerning the knowledge of esoteric doctrines ("Ma'aseh Bereshit" and "Ma'aseh Merkabah"), related by Jose b. Judah, a tanna of the second half of the second century, it is said that Joshua b. Hananiah, the pupil of Johanan, under the eye of his master occupied himself with esoteric doctrines and that Akiba learned them from him (Ḥag. 14b). According to another tradition (*ib.*), it was Eleazar b. 'Arak with whom Johanan studied the mystic doctrines. A remarkable saying of Johanan's has been preserved, which is in accord with his study of mystic doctrines (Ḥag. 13a; comp. Pes. 94b). In this saying man is advised to bring the infinity of God, the Creator of the world, nearer to his own conception by imagining the space of the cosmos extended to unthinkable distances.

In conclusion may be mentioned the historical meaning which Johanan, on a certain sad occurrence, gave to a verse, of the Song of Solomon (Yitro, Baḥodesh, 1). In Ma'on, a town of southern Judea, Johanan saw, probably not long after the destruction of Jerusalem, a young Jewess picking out grains of barley from the ordure of an Arab's horse, in order to still her hunger. Johanan said to his pupils who were with him: "My whole life long I have tried to understand that sentence in the Song of Solomon [i. 8]: 'If thou know not, O thou fairest, among women,' etc. Now for the first time I catch its meaning: 'You did not wish'—so goes the word reproving Israel—'to submit to God; hence you are made subject to foreign peoples. You did not wish to pay God a half-shekel for each person; now you pay 15 shekels to the government of your enemies. You did not wish to repair the roads and streets for the holiday pilgrims; you must now repair the road-houses and watch-towers for your oppressors. And in you is fulfilled the prophecy [Deut. xviii. 47–48, R. V.]: Because thou servedst not the Lord thy God with joyfulness, and with gladness of heart, by reason of the abundance of all things, therefore shalt thou serve thine enemies, which the Lord shall send against thee, in hunger and in thirst, and in nakedness, and in want of all things.'"

Johanan felt the fall of his people more deeply than any one else, but—and in this lies his historical importance—be did more than any one else to prepare the way for Israel to rise again.

Bibliography: Frankel, *Mebo*; Grätz, *Gesch.* iii.; Weiss, *Dor*, i.; Brüll, *Einleitung*; Derenbourg, *Histoire*; Bacher, *Ag. Pal. Tannaiten*, 2d ed., i. 22–42; W. Landau, in *Monatsschrift*, i. 163; Joseph Spitz, *R. Jochanan b. Zakkai*, 1883; Schlatter, *Jochanan b. Zakkai, der Zeitgenosse der Apostel*, 1899.

S. S. W. B.

JONAH: Palestinian amora of the fourth century; leading rabbinical authority in the fourth amoraic generation. With Jose II., his early school-mate and lifelong colleague and business partner, he studied under Ze'era I. and Ela (Bek. 30a; Yer. Ter. ii. 41d); and when, as young men, they called on Abbahu to express their sympathy with him in his bereavement, he treated them as prominent scholars (Yer. Sanh. vi. 23d). But Jonah's special master was Jeremiah (Yer. Ḥal. i. 57c, ii. 58b). From these masters and others the youths acquired a thorough familiarity with the traditions, and gradually rose from pupils to fellows. Thus, it is said, "Haggai opened the discourse and Jonah and Jose closed it" (Yer. R. H. ii. 58b). Finally they succeeded to the rectorate of the academy at Tiberias. In his office Jonah was distinguished by his paternal care for his pupils, to whom he gave both advice and material support (Yer. Beẓah i. 60c). According to the Biblical and rabbinical requirement he gave away the tithe of his income, but to those who studied the Law, not to priests or Levites, deriving his authority from II Chron. xxxi. 4 (Yer. Ma'as. Sh. v. 56b). When he discovered a worthy man who was poor, he would aid him in such a way as not to hurt his self-respect. "I understand," he would say to him, "that you have fallen heir to an estate" or "that your debtors will soon pay you; borrow some money of me, which you may repay when you come into possession of your fortune." As soon as the proffered loan had been accepted he would relieve the borrower from his promise by telling him, "This money is thine as a gift." This procedure he regarded as suggested by the Psalmist: "Blessed is he that considereth [Hebr. משכיל = "dealeth prudently with"] the poor" (Ps. xli. 2 [A. V. 1]; Yer. Peah viii. 21b; Midr. Teh. to passage).

Jonah also enjoyed a certain respect among the Romans (Yer. Ber. v. 9a; Ta'an. 23b). He was included among those styled תקיפי דארעא דישראל ("the mighty ones of the land of Israel"), because, the Rabbis explained, of the efficacy of his prayers in times of drought. The following miracle is related of him: Once, on a Sabbath, fire broke out on his premises. A Nabatæan whose property adjoined Jonah's attempted to extinguish it, but Jonah would not permit him thus to profane the Sabbath. "Dost thou rely on thy good luck?" mockingly asked the Nabatæan; to which Jonah replied, "Yes"; whereupon the fire was quenched (Yer. Yoma viii. 45b). As rectors of the academy at Tiberias, Jonah and Jose had many disciples, some of whom became leaders in the next generation, and spread and perpetuated their master's doctrines. Jonah left a worthy son and successor in the person of Mani II.

BIBLIOGRAPHY: Bacher, *Ag. Pal. Amor.* iii. 220–231; Frankel, *Mebo*, p. 98a; Halevy, *Dorot ha-Rishonim*, ii. 183b; Weiss, *Dor*, iii. 110.

S. S. S. M.

JONATHAN (NATHAN) OF BET GUBRIN (= Eleutheropolis; Rapoport, "'Erek Millin," pp. 53 *et seq.*): Palestinian scholar of the third century; junior of Joshua b. Levi and senior of Simon b. Pazzi (Cant. R. i. 1). He confined his labors to the Haggadah, and contributed to the Midrash several homilies, some of which, however, are given under different names in other compilations. One of his sayings was: "Four great languages have been given to the world: Greek for song, Aramaic for dirges, Hebrew for conversation, Latin for war" (Yer. Meg. i. 71b; comp. Esth. R. iv. 6; Midr. Teh. xxxi. 21).

BIBLIOGRAPHY: Bacher, *Ag. Pal. Amor.* iii. 592.

S. S. S. M.

JONATHAN BEN HORḲINAS (ARCHINAS): Palestinian scholar of the first century; contemporary of Eleazar b. Azariah and a disciple of the school of Shammai. He was reputed for his acuteness, in recognition of which he was styled "bekor saṭan" (= "first-born as adversary," *i.e.*, a fierce disputant; Yer. Yeb. i. 6; Yeb. 16a; comp. Rashi *ad loc.*, and rabbinic dictionaries, *s.v.* "Bekor"). R. Zemaḥ, however, amends the reading to "bekor shoṭeh" (lit. "foolish first-born son"; applied to a son first-born to the mother—but not to the father; Zacuto, "Yuḥasin," ed. Filipowski, p. 11). Although the school of Hillel was the standard authority in halakic matters, Jonathan prevailed upon some of the Rabbis to permit, in accordance with the school of Shammai, marriage between a man and his brother's widow, where she was the co-wife of his daughter. The Jerusalem Talmud (Yeb. *l.c.*) relates concerning this the following incident: The disciples of Hillel, having heard that a son of Horḳinas had granted this permission, credited it to Dosa b. Horḳinas, Jonathan's older brother, of the school of Hillel, and consequently went to Dosa for an explanation. Dosa referred them to his brother Jonathan, who, he said, had three hundred arguments in favor of such a marriage. The Rabbis then went to Jonathan, whom Dosa had warned by letter to prepare for a visit from the wise men of Israel. Jonathan, accordingly, explained to the Rabbis his arguments, but they could not understand them. Becoming impatient, he cast clods of earth at them and drove them out through three different doors. Then he wrote to his brother: "Thou hast informed me of the visit of the wise men of Israel, but those that came to me are in need of learning." Meeting Akiba, Jonathan said to him: "Thou art lucky to have acquired such renown while them hast not yet acquired the knowledge of a cowherd" (Yeb. *l.c.*).

BIBLIOGRAPHY: Grätz, *Gesch.* 3d ed., iv. 20; Heilprin, *Seder ha-Dorot*, ii.

J. M. SEL.

JOSE (Joseph), ABBA, BEN DOSITAI (Dosai; Derosai; Dosa): Palestinian tanna of the second century; mentioned as both halakist and haggadist. He transmitted a halakah of R. Jose the Galilean (Tosel, Ta'an. ii. 6). His haggadot consist chiefly of reconciliations between contradictory Biblical passages, almost all of them being transmitted by Rabbi (Judah I.). A series of them is in the Sifre to Num. 42; they are reproduced in Num. R. xi. 19, and single haggadot occur in Sanh. 52a, Yoma 22a, Zeb. 116b, and elsewhere. Lev. R. xxiv. 3 and Tan., Ḳedoshim, 9, preserve a demon-story the hero of which is called Jose of Ẓitor; while according to Midr. Teh. to Ps. xx. 7, where the same story occurs, the hero is Abba Jose b. Dositai.

BIBLIOGRAPHY: Bacher, *Ag. Tan.* ii. 388; idem, *Ag. Pal. Amor.* ii. 450; Heilprin, *Seder ha-Dorot*, ii.

S. S. M. SEL.

JOSE, ABBA, BEN ḤANIN: Palestinian tanna of the last decades before the destruction of the Temple; contemporary of ELIEZER B. JACOB and of ḤANINA B. ANTIGONUS, with both of whom he is mentioned in a halakic discussion (Tosef., Suk. iv. 15). His name occurs also as "Abba Jose b. Hanan," or "b. Johanan" (which is erroneously followed by "ish Yerushalayim"), "Abba Joseph," and "Abba Issi." Jose's halakot are also mentioned in Sifre, Num. 8, Mid. ii. 6, and Soṭah 20b. He transmitted a haggadah of Abba Cohen Bardela.(Sifre, Deut. 2) and one of Samuel ha-Ḳaṭon (Derek Ereẓ Zuṭa ix.). A sentence of Jose's, rebuking the priestly families that acted violently toward the people, transmitted by Abba Saul b. Boṭnit, reads as follows: "Wo unto me for the house of Baithus and its rods; wo unto me for the house of Ḥanin and its calumnious whispering; wo unto me for the house of Ḳatros and its pens; wo unto me for the house of ISHMAEL B. PHABI and its fists" (Pes. 57a, where he is called "Abba Joseph").

In Yeb. 53b an "Abba Jose b. Johanan" ("b. Hanan" in Rashi) is mentioned as having transmitted a halakah of R. Meïr, who lived a century later. Bacher ("Ag Tan." i. 46, note 2) therefore supposes that the author of the sentence quoted above was Abba Saul b. Boṭnit, and that it was transmitted by the Abba Jose of Yebamot (comp. Büchler, "Die Priester und der Cultus," p. 30).

BIBLIOGRAPHY: Bacher, in *R. E. J.* xxxvii. 299; Heilprin, *Seder ha-Dorot,* ii.

S. S. M. SEL.

JOSE, ABBA, OF MAḤUZA: Scholar of the third (?) century; mentioned once only (Mek., Beshallaḥ, Wayeḥi, 3), a haggadah of his being transmitted by R. Nathan. In Mek., Bo, 17, there is mentioned an Abba Jose together with R. Jonathan; and as the above-mentioned haggadah of Abba Jose is ascribed in Men. (37a) to R. Jose ha-Ḥorem, Weiss (introduction to his edition of the Mekilta, p. xxix.) conjectures that "ha-Ḥorem" may be amended to "ha-Maḥuzi."

S. M. SEL.

JOSE B. ABIN (called also **Jose b. Abun** and **Jose b. R. Bun):** Palestinian amora of the fifth generation (4th cent.); son of R. Abin I. (Bacher, "Ag. Pal. Amor." iii. 724) and the teacher of R. Abin II. (Yer. Ned. 3b). He was at first the pupil of R. Jose of Yodḳart, but the latter's indifference to his own family caused Jose to leave him and follow R. Assi or Jose II. (Ta'an. 23b; Weiss, "Dor," iii. 117). Jose was the most important among the last halakists of the Palestinian amoraim. He had a thorough knowledge not only of the Palestinian customs and halakot, but of the Babylonian, a fact that has led some scholars to maintain that Jose must have resided at some time in Babylonia. It is probable, however, that he derived his knowledge of Babylonian teaching from his father, who had traveled in Babylonia.

Jose's chief work in the field of the Halakah was the expounding of the Mishnah and the halakot of the Amoraim, though some halakot are credited to him. In Haggadah he excelled in the transmission and elucidation of the sayings of his predecessors, especially those of R. Ḥiyya, Joshua b. Levi, R. Johanan, and R. Simeon b. Laḳish.

His chief halakic opponents were R. Mana and Jose b. Zebida.

Bibliography: Bacher, *Ag. Pal. Amor.* iii. 724 *et seq.*; Weiss, Dor, iii. 117 *et seq.*; Heilprin, *Seder ha-Dorot*, ii. 224; Frankel, *Mebo*, 102a; Halevy, *Dorot ha-Rishonim*, iii. 122 *et seq.*

S. S. A. S. W.

JOSE (ISI, ISSI) BEN AḲABYA (AKIBA): Tanna of the beginning of the third century. The name "Issi" or "Assa" is derived from "Jose," and was borne by many tannaim and amoraim; hence the confusion that prevails in the Talmud concerning the identity of each of them, the same halakic or haggadic saying being attributed sometimes to one and sometimes to another of that name. Thus the prohibition against riding on a mule is reported in the Yerushalmi (Kil. 31c) in the name of Issi ben Aḳabya, while in the Tosefta (Kil. v. 6) it is attributed to Issi ha-Babli, who is undoubtedly identical with Issi ben Judah. Bacher supposes that Issi ben Aḳabya was the brother of Hananiah ben Aḳabya, the interpreter ("meturgeman") of R. Judah. Issi was a diligent student of the Bible, and some of his interpretations have been preserved in the midrashic literature. From I Kings viii. 64 he infers that the expression מזבח אדמה (Ex. xx. 24) means an altar of copper filled with earth (Mekilta to Ex. xx. 24). In reference to Ex. xxi. 14 he says that though the murderer of a heathen can not be convicted by a Jewish tribunal, he must answer for his crime to God (Mekilta, *ad loc.* 80b). The permission expressed in Deut. xxiii. 25 is, according to Issi, extended to everybody and not only to the workers in the field; but the permission applies only to the harvest time (Yer. Ma'as. 50a).

Bibliography: Heilprin, *Seder ha-Dorot*, ii. 225; Bacher, *Ag. Tan.* ii. 371.

S. S. I. Be.

JOSE THE GALILEAN: Tanna; lived in the first and second centuries of the common era. Jose was a contemporary and colleague of R. Akiba, R. Ṭarfon, and R. Eleazar b. Azariah. Neither the name of his father nor the circumstances of his youth are known, though his name ("ha-Gelili") indicates that he was a native of Galilee. He suffered from the prejudice commonly held against the Galileans by the Judeans; on one occasion a woman whom he had met on the street and had requested to direct him to Lydda called him a "stupid Galilean" ("Gelili shote"; 'Er. 53b). When he entered the academy at Jabneh, he was entirely unknown. It is also noted that he was extremely modest and addressed R. Ṭarfon as "my master" ("rabbi"; Zeb. 57a). He was, nevertheless, a thorough scholar even then, and his arguments nonplused both R. Ṭarfon and R. Akiba. His first appearance at Jabneh thus obtained for him general recognition, and the two rabbis considered him not as a pupil, but as a colleague. Akiba was obliged to endure more than one sharp criticism from Jose, who once said to him: "Though thou expound the whole day I shall not listen to thee" (Zeb. 82a). R. Ṭarfon expressed his high esteem of Jose by interpreting Dan. viii. 4–7 as though it contained an allusion to him: "I saw the ram, that is, R. Akiba, and saw that no beast might stand before him; and I beheld the hegoat, that is, Jose the Galilean, come, and cast him down to the ground" (Tosef., Miḳ. vii. 11; Sifre, Num. [ed. Friedmann, p. 44a]). As a matter of fact, Jose was the only one who opposed Akiba successfully, and the latter frequently abandoned his own interpretation in favor of his opponent's (Ḥag. 14a; Pes. 36b).

Jose frequently showed a tendency to revert to the older Halakah, explaining the text according to its literal meaniag (Mek., Bo [ed. Weiss, pp. 4b, 9b]; Mek., Beshallaḥ [ed.Weiss, p. 44a]; Sifre, Deut. [ed. Friedmann, p. 97b]; 'Ab. Zarah 45a; *et al.*). But generally his halakic exegesis differed little from that of Akiba, and both often employed the same rules of interpretation (comp. Ket. 44a; Ḳid. 32b; Pes. 23a, 36a; Beẓah 21a, b). Only two of his halakot need be cited here. He taught that poultry may be cooked in milk and eaten (Ḥul. 113a), as was done in his own native town (*ib.* 116a); also that at the Passover one may enjoy anything that is leavened, except as food (Pes. 28b). Of his haggadic opinions the two following may be mentioned: The command of the Torah that the "face of the old man" shall be honored (Lev. xix. 32) includes, by implication, the young man who has acquired wisdom (Ḳid. 32b). The words "He shall rule over thee" (Gen. iii. 16) do not refer to power of every description (Gen. R. xx.).

Jose's married life was unhappy. His wife was malicious and quarrelsome, and frequently insulted him in the presence of his pupils and friends; on the advice of the latter he divorced her. When she married again and was in straitened circumstances, he was magnanimous enough to support her and her husband (Gen. R. xvii.).

Jose was famed, moreover, for his piety. An amora of the third century says: "When, for their sins, there is drought in Israel, and such a one as Jose the Galilean prays for rain, the rain cometh straightway" (Yer. Ber. 9b). The popular invocation, "O Jose ha-Gelili, heal me!" survived even to the tenth century. This invocation is justly condemned by the Karaite Sahal b. Maẓliaḥ (comp. Pinsker, "Liḳḳuṭe Ḳadmoniyyot," p. 32).

BIBLIOGRAPHY: Frankel, *Hodegetica in Mischnam*, pp. 125–127, Leipsic, 1859; Brüll, *Einleitung in die Mischna*, pp. 125–130, Frankfort-on-the-Main, 1876; Bacher, *Ag. Tan.* i. 252–265; Weiss, *Dor*, ii. 119–120.

S. J. Z. L.

JOSE BEN ḤALAFTA (called also simply **Jose**): Palestinian tanna of the fourth generation (2d cent.). Of his life only the following few details are known: He was born at Sepphoris; but his family was of Babylonian origin (Yoma 66b). According to a genealogical chart found at Jerusalem, he was a descendant of Jonadab b. Rechab (Yer. Ta'an. iv. 2; Gen. R. xcviii. 13). He was one of Akiba's five principal pupils, called "the restorers of the Law" (Yeb. 63b), who were afterward ordained by Judah b. Baba (Sanh. 14a). He was, besides, a pupil of Johanan b. Nuri, whose halakot he transmitted (Tosef., Kelim, B. Ḳ. lxxxii. 7; B. B. lxxxvii.), and of Eutolemus ('Er. 35a; R. H. 15a). It is very likely that he studied much under his father, Ḥalafta, whose authority he invokes in several instances (B. Ḳ. 70a; Me'i. 17b). But his principal teacher was Akiba, whose system he followed in his interpretation of the Law (Pes. 18a; Yeb. 62b). After having been ordained in violation of a Roman edict (Sanh. *l.c.*), Jose fled to Asia Minor (B. M. 84b), where he stayed till the edict was abrogated. Later he settled at Usha, then the seat of the Sanhedrin. As he remained silent when his fellow pupil Simeon b. Yoḥai once attacked the Roman government in his presence, he was forced by the Romans to return to Sepphoris (Shab. 33b), which he found in a decaying state (B. B. 75b). He established there a flourishing school; and it seems that be died there (Sanh. 109a; comp. Yer. 'Ab. Zarah iii. 1). Jose's great learning attracted so many pupils that the words "that which is altogether just shalt thou follow" (Deut. xvi. 20) were interpreted to mean in part "follow Jose to Sepphoris" (Sanh. 32b). He was highly extolled after his death. His pupil Judah ha-Nasi I. said: "The difference between Jose's generation and ours is like the difference between the Holy of Holies and the most profane" (Yer. Giṭ. vi. 9).

His halakot are mentioned throughout the greater part of the Mishnah, as well as in the Baraita and Sifra. His teaching was very systematic. He was opposed to controversy, declaring that the antagonism between the schools of Shammai and Hillel made it seem as if there were two Torahs (Sanh. 88b). For the most part, Jose adopted a compromise between two contending halakists (comp. Ter. x. 3; 'Er. viii. 5 [= 86a]; Yoma iv. 3 [= 43b]). Like his master Akiba, Jose occupied himself with the dots which sometimes accompany the words in the Bible, occasionally basing his halakot on such dots (Pes. ix. 2 [= 93b]; Men. 87b). He was generally liberal in his halakic decisions, especially in interpreting the laws concerning fasts (Ta'an. 22b) and vows (Ned. 21b, 23a). In those cases where there was a difference of opinion between Jose and his contemporaries, it was Jose's decision that was adopted as the norm for the practise (Yer. Ter. iii. 1; 'Er. 51a).

Jose was also a prominent haggadist; and the conversation which he had with a Roman matron, resulting in her conviction of the superiority of the Jewish religion (Gen. R. lxviii. 4), shows his great skill in interpreting Biblical verses. Jose is considered to be the author of the Seder 'Olam Rabbah, a chronicle from the Creation to the time of Hadrian, for which reason it is called also "Baraita de R Jose b. Ḥalafta" (Yeb. 82b; Niddah 46b; comp. Shab. 88a). This work, though incomplete and too concise, shows Jose's system of arranging material in chronological order.

Jose is known for his ethical dicta, which are characteristic, and in which he laid special stress on the study of the Torah (comp. Ab. iv. 6). He exemplified Abtalion's dictum, "Love the handicrafts" (*ib.* i. 9); for he was a tanner by trade (Shab. 49a), and followed a craft then commonly held in contempt (Pes. 65a). A series of Jose's ethical sayings in Shab. 118b shows his tendency toward Essenism. As has been said above, Jose was opposed to disputation. When his companion Judah desired to exclude Meïr's disciples from his school, Jose dissuaded him (Ḳid. 52a; Nazir 50a). One of his characteristic sayings is, "He who indicates the coming of the Messiah [הנותן את הקץ], he who hates scholars and their disciples, and the false prophet and the slanderer, will have no part in the future world" (Derek Ereẓ R. xi.). According to Bacher, in "Monatsschrift," xlii. 505–507, this was directed against the Hebrew Christians.

Owing to Jose's fame as a saint, legend describes him as having met Elijah (Ber. 3a; Sanh. 113b). Jose, complying with the Law, married the wife of his brother who had died childless; she bore him five sons: Ishmael, Eleazar, Menahem, Ḥalafta (who died in his lifetime), and Eudemus (Yer. Yeb. i. 1).

BIBLIOGRAPHY: Bacher, *Ag. Tan.* ii. 150–190; idem, *Ag. Pal. Amor.* ii. 158 *et passim*; Brüll, *Mebo ha-Mishnah*, pp. 156–160, 178–185, Frankfort-on-the-Main, 1876; Frankel. *Darke ha-Mishnah*, pp. 164–168; idem, in *Monatsschrift*, iv. 206–209; Joël. *ib.* vi. 81–91; Weiss, *Dor*, ii. 161–164.

S. S. M. SEL.

JOSE B. JACOB B. IDI: Palestinian amora of the fourth generation (4th cent.). He was the colleague of R. Judan of Magdala (Yer. Ta'an. i. 3), and one of the expounders of the haggadot of R. Aha the Lydian. He has also some original sayings, in one of which he makes the statement—based on I Kings xii; 27, and with reference to Deut. xxxi. 11—that Jeroboam was elected king in the Sabbatical year, when the head of the nation was required to read publicly in the Temple at Jerusalem the prescribed portion of the Law; and that, in order to avoid celebrating the festival in the Holy City, where he would have had the mortification of seeing the King of Judea read the Law, he (Jeroboam) set up another place of worship with the golden calves (Yer. 'Ab. Zarah 39b). Only one halakah of Jose's has been preserved (Yer. Yeb. 10d).

BIBLIOGRAPHY: Bacher, *Ag. Pal. Amor.* iii. 739; Frankel. *Mebo*, p. 95a.

S. S. A. S. W.

JOSE BEN JOEZER OF ZEREDAH: Rabbi of the early Maccabean period; possibly a disciple of Antigonus of Soko, though this is not certain. He belonged to a priestly family. With him and Jose ben Johanan of Jerusalem, his colleague, begins the period known in Jewish history as that of the "zugot" (duumvirate), which ends with Hillel and Shammai. According to an old tradition, the member of the "zugot" mentioned first occupied the office of president of the Sanhedrin, while the one mentioned second served in the capacity of vice-president. Jose belonged to the party of the Ḥasidim, and was a decided adversary of Hellenism. To prevent Jews from settling beyond Palestine he declared all heathen countries "unclean" (Shab. 46a). He declared also glass utensils "unclean," probably because they were manufactured in heathen countries. In other respects, however, he was very liberal, and received the surname "Sharaya" ("one who permits") for having rendered three liberal decisions on certain ritual questions ('Eduy. viii. 4; Pes. 15a).

The first halakic controversy known in the Talmud was that between Jose ben Joezer and his colleague Jose ben Johanan. It arose over the question whether the laying of hands on the heads of the sacrifices is permitted on feast-days (Ḥag. ii. 2). Jose ben Joezer was distinguished for his piety, and is called "the pious of the priesthood" ("ḥasid shebi-kehunnah"; Ḥag. ii. 7). He professed great veneration for scholars, one of his sayings being: "Let thy house be a meeting-place for the wise; powder thyself in the dust of their feet, and drink their words with eagerness" (Abot iv. 4). Jose was probably among the sixty pious men who, at the instigation of the high priest Alcimus, the son of his sister, were crucified by the Syrian, general Bacchides (I Macc. vii. 16).

The Midrash reports the following dialogue between Alcimus and Jose ben Joezer while the latter was on the way to execution:

> Alcimus: "See the profit and honors that have fallen to my lot in consequence of what I have done, whilst thou, for thy obstinacy, hast the misfortune to die as a criminal." Jose, quietly: "If such is the lot of those who anger God, what shall be the lot of those who accomplish His will?" Alcimus: "Is there any one who accomplished His will more than thou?" Jose: "If this is the end of those who accomplish His will, what awaits those who anger Him?"

On this Alcimus was seized with remorse and committed suicide (Gen. R. *i.* 65). Jose ben Joezer left a son whom he had disinherited for bad conduct (B. B. 133b).

BIBLIOGRAPHY: *Yuḥasin*, p. 60a, ed. Königsberg; Heilprin, *Seder ha-Dorot*, p. 211, ed. Warsaw; Weiss, Dor, i. 98; Braunschweiger, *Die Lehrer der Mishnah*, p. 165, Frankfort-on-the-Main, 1903; Z. Frankel. *Darke ha-Mishnah*, pp. 31, 32; Grätz, *Gesch.* 3d ed., iii. 3; Schürer, *Gesch.* ii. 202, 352, 357, 407.

S. S. I. BR.

JOSE (JOSEPH) BEN JOHANAN: President of the Sanhedrin in the second century B.C.; a native of Jerusalem. He and Jose b. Joezer were the successors and, it is said, the disciples of Antigonus of Soko (Ab. i. 4–5), and the two together formed the first of a series of duumvirates that transmitted the traditional law; in each pair one, according to tradition, was prince-president ("nasi"), and the other vice-president, of the Sanhedrin ("ab bet din"; Ḥag. ii. 2 [16a]). One of Jose's sayings was: "Let thy house be opened wide; and let the needy be thy household; and prolong not converse with woman" (Abot i. 5). A disagreement between the two colleagues in regard to halakic decisions gave rise to the formation of two different schools (see JOSE B. JOEZER). Both men were opposed to Hellenism, and both belonged to the Ḥasidim. Jose b. Joezer and Jose b. Johanan were the last of the "eshkolot" (derived by some from σχολή; Rapoport, "'Erek Millin," p. 237) (Soṭah ix. 9 [47a]; comp. Tosef., B. Ḳ. viii. 13; Yer. Soṭah ix. 10).

BIBLIOGRAPHY: Frankel. *Darke ha-Mishnah*, pp. 29 *et seq.*; Grätz, *Gesch.* 3d ed., ii. 274, iii. 3; *idem*, in *Monatsschrift*, xviii. 30 *et seq.*; Heilprin. *Seder ha-Dorot*, ii.; Schürer, *Gesch.* 3d ed., ii. 202, 352, 357; Weiss, *Dor*, i. 103 *et seq.*

S. S. M. SEL.

JOSE BEN JOSE: The earliest payyetan known by name; flourished, at the latest, about the end of the sixth century in Palestine. He is called "ha-yatom" (the orphan), probably because, bearing his father's name, it was assumed that the latter died either before his son's birth or before his circumcision. Earlier sources state that Jose was a priest, even a high priest, but this assertion is not supported. As a poet Jose deserves the recognition and appreciation which have been accorded him. His style is raised above the level of mere prose by his use of new though not difficult words and paraphrases, and by frequent archaic expressions. He employs no rime, nor is he conversant with the other self-imposed restrictions of payyeṭanic poetry. The use of acrostics constitutes the only external ornamentation of his compositions, which are distinguished by depth of thought, conciseness of expression, imagination, and tenderness. The parallelism characteristic of his verse lends it additional charm. In one of his poems (No. 2, below) he employs the refrain.

The following poems of his are known: (1) אהללה אלהי אשירה עזו, an intercalation in the Musaf prayer for New-Year's Day designated by the term "teḳi'ata," a term which is found already in the Talmud. The "teḳi'ata" is recited on the second day of the New-Year in the Polish and German rituals. (2) אמנם אשמינו עצמו, a sort of confession of sins ("widdui") for the evening of the Day of Atonement (Kol Nidre), with quadruple alphabet and two alternating refrains, included in the Polish and German rituals, although in most communities only a part of it is recited. (3) אזכיר גבורות אלוה, an "'abodah" for the Day of Atonement, including the alphabet ten times in acrostics, while the letter ת occurs eighteen times. Saadia has included the poem in his Siddur (Oxford MSS.), and Rosenberg has reprinted it in "Kobeẓ Ma'ase Yede Ge'onim Kad" (Berlin, 1856). (4) אתה כוננת עולם ברב־חסד, another abodah that has been assigned to Jose. Zunz quotes many passages to show that it frequently corresponds in phraseology with the "Azkir." The initial letters of its verses form a quadruple alphabet, which is followed by a second quadruple alphabet. It was formerly recited in Burgundy and France, and is still used in the communities of Asti, Fossano, and Moncalvo, in Piedmont. Luzzatto has printed it in Rosenberg's "Kobeẓ" (pp. 111 *et seq.*], and as an appendix to the Italian Maḥzor (ed. Leghorn, 1861, ii. 212 *et seq.*); it is also printed in the separate edition of Luzzatto's "Mebo." The introduction אתן תהלה (reprinted in Zunz's "Literaturgesch." p. 646) by an unknown author—said to be the apostle Peter—belongs to this 'abodah. The 'abodah אתה כוננת עולם מראש, included in Spanish rituals, was written before Jose's time, and has been ascribed to him only through being confounded with his poem dealing with the same subject and beginning in the same way. (5) A piyyuṭ, of which only one verse has been preserved. אור עולם has also been ascribed to him, though its authorship is doubtful. It is a short fragment of the earliest known "Yoẓer," which originally contained probably the entire alphabet quadrupled in acrostics. In the Polish and German rituals it precedes the "Yoẓer" on feast-days; in the Roman ritual it precedes the Sabbath prayers also.

BIBLIOGRAPHY: Rapoport, *Bikkure ha-'Ittim*, 1829, p. 116; Sachs, in Rosenberg's *Kobeẓ*, ii. 85; Luzzatto, *ib.* p. 107; idem, *Mebo*, pp. 9, 13; Landsbuth, *'Ammude ha-'Abodah*, p. 85; Zunz, in Geiger's *Jüd. Zeit.* ii. 306; idem, *Literaturgesch.* pp. 26, 643; Harkavy, *Studien und Mittheilungen*, v. 105.

H. B.

G.

JOSE B. JUDAH: Tanna of the end of the second century. He is principally known through his controversies with R. Judah I. As specimens of his exegeses, the following may be given here. On the expression הין צדק (Lev. xix. 36) he comments, "Let thy yea be yea and thy nay nay" (Sifre to the verse; B. M. 49a; comp. Matt. v. 37). Deut. viii. 5

he explains thus: "Dear to God are the afflictions destined for man, for on whomsoever they come, the glory of God reposes, as it is said, 'It is the Lord thy God who chastiseth thee'" (Sifre, Deut. vi. 5). As characteristic of his poetical mind, the following may be cited as his view on the repose and peacefulness of the Sabbath: "Two angels, a good and a bad one, accompany man on the Sabbath eve from the synagogue into his house. When the man finds the lamp lit, the table laid, and the bed made, the good angel prays, 'May it be Thy will, O Lord, that it be the same next Sabbath!' to which the evil angel, against his will, responds 'Amen!' If, however, the man finds his house in disorder, the wicked angel says, 'May it be the same next Sabbath!' to which the good angel is forced to respond 'Amen!'" (Shab. 119b).

Of a controversial nature is probably the saying in which Jose insists that the proselyte must show his readiness to accept even the precepts of the sages in their capacity as interpreters of the Law (see Tosef., Demai, ii. 5; Sifra, Lev. xix. 34). Jose, like his father, Judah b. 'Ilai, and through the teachings of his father, was the depositary of many old traditions, which appear in his name.

BIBLIOGRAPHY: Weiss, *Dor*; Bacher, *Ag. Tan.* ii. 417–421.

S. S. S. LEV.

JOSE B. ḲAẒRATA (Ḳuẓira; Ḳaẓra): Palestinian amora of the first amoraic generation; son-in-law of R. Jose. Kohut is of the opinion that the surname is derived from "Ḳaẓẓara" (washer); but in Tan., Wayeḥi, the name "Ḳaẓra" is found. Two other amoraim with this patronymic are mentioned in the Talmud—R. Johanan b. Ḳaẓrata and R. Isaac b. Ḳaẓrata; but as both of them cite R. Jona, an amora of the third generation, they can not have been Jose's brothers. Jose b. Ḳaẓrata taught that the Creator chose the finest earth with which to make the first man (Gen. R. xiv.). In Yer. B. B. x. 17 Jose discusses a halakah concerning marriage in which he maintains the interests of woman.

BIBLIOGRAPHY: Heilprin, *Seder ha-Dorot*, s.v.; Frankel, *Mebo*; Kohut, *Aruch Completum*; Bacher, *Ag. Pal. Amor.* iii. 596.

S. S. A. H. R.

JOSE HA-KOHEN ("the Pious"): Tanna of the second generation; flourished in the first and second centuries; pupil of Johanan ben Zakkai. It is said of him that he never allowed any writing of his to remain in the hands of a heathen, lest he should carry it on Sabbath (Tosef., Shab. xvii. 13; Shab. 19a). Jose valued friendship above all worldly goods. "The good a man should cleave to is a good friend, and the evil a man should shun is an evil neighbor" (Ab. ii. 12). His maxim was: "Let the property of thy friend be precious unto thee as thine own; set thyself to learn the Torah, for it is not an heirloom unto thee, and let all thy actions be taken in the name of Heaven" (*ib*). Jose's name is associated in the Halakah with that of Zechariah ha-Ḳaẓẓab (Ket. 27a). The Haggadah has preserved two sayings of Jose. One is connected with the death of the son of Johanan ben Zakkai. Jose endeavored to console the father by reminding him that the high priest Aaron lost two sons in one day and yet he continued his services in the Tabernacle without interruption (Ab. R. N. xiv.). The other was in answer to a question addressed by a female proselyte to the patriarch concerning the seeming contradiction between Deut. x. 17 and Num. vi. 26. Illustrating his answer by a parable, Jose said that Deut. x. 17 refers to offenses against man that can not be forgiven, while Num. vi. 26 refers to offenses against God that are always forgiven (R. H. 17b). Jose is said to have been devoted to mystical studies (Yer. Hag. ii.).

BIBLIOGRAPHY: Heilprin, *Seder ha-Dorot*, ii. 211; Weiss, *Dor*, i. 192, ii. 73; Bacher, *Ag. Tan.* i. 67 *et seq.*

S. S. I. BR.

JOSE OF MALLAḤAYA: Palestinian amora of the fourth generation. According to his explanation of Ps. lvii. 5 the disasters that overtook the Jews were caused by their inclination to slander, common among them even in the time of David (Lev. R. xxvi.). There are two halakot emanating from him, one referring to the transfer of land (Yer. Ḳid. 60c), the other prescribing the rules governing the purification of utensils that have been used by Gentiles (Yer. 'Ab. Zarah 41c).

BIBLIOGRAPHY: Bacher, *Ag. Pal. Amor.* iii. 724; Heilprin, *Seder ha-Dorot*; Kohut, *Aruch Completum*.

S. S. A. H. R.

JOSE OF MAON: Popular preacher of the beginning of the third century; delivered his addresses in a synagogue at Tiberias which bore the name of the locality—"Maon" (מעונאה), whence probably his surname מעונאה (—"of Maon"). He is said to have been aggressive in his speeches and to have been no respecter of persons; he attacked even the house of the patriarch (Yer. Sanh. ii.; Gen. R. lxxx, 1). See JUDAH II.

BIBLIOGRAPHY: Heilprin, *Seder ha-Dorot*, ii. 221; Frankel. *Mebo*, p. 101b; Bacher, *Ag. Pal. Amor.* ii. 114, note 5; iii. 595 *et seq.*

S. S. I. BR.

JOSE B. NEHORAI: Palestinian amora of the first generation; halakot are transmitted in his name by Johanan (Rashi, B. M. 41a). Of his haggadic explanations the following may be cited: With reference to Eccl. iii. 15 he explains the word נרדף to mean "the persecuted," "the hunted," and gives the passage the meaning that God will always assist the persecuted, and that even when a righteous man persecutes a wicked man God will assist the latter. Jose gives various Scriptural instances in support of this view (Lev. R. xxvii. 5). As to the religious rites which children are required to perform R. Jose thought that they have an educational purpose, but are not obligatory (Yer. Ber. iii. 6b). He taught also that, except in the case of taxes for maintaining schools, the tax-collectors must not be harsh in their dealings (Lev. R. xxx. 1).

Bibliography: Bacher, *Ag. Pal. Amor.* iii. 597; Heilprin, *Seder ha-Dorot*: Frankel. *Mebo.*

S. S. A. H. R

JOSE B. SAUL: Palestinian amora of the first generation (3d cent.). He is known chiefly as a transmitter of the sayings and traditions of the patriarch Judah I., whose disciple he was. These as well as his own sayings are further transmitted by R. Joshua b. Levi and by Ḥiyya ben Gamda. In one place the following order is given: Simon b. Pazzi says in the name of R. Joshua b. Levi in the name of R. Jose b. Saul in the name of R. Judah ha-Nasi in the name of the holy assembly of Jerusalem (Bezah 14b, 27a; Tamid 27b). The Palestinian Talmud has preserved only one anecdote of his in the Aramaic ('Ab. Zarah ii. 3). His brothers were Johanan and Ḥalafta, with the former of whom he used to hold halakic controversies (Shab. 125b).

Bibliography: Bacher, *Ag. Pal. Amor.* iii. 598; Heilprin, *Seder ha-Dorot*, ii. 221, Warsaw, 1882.

S. S. A. S. W.

JOSEPH (JOSE) B. ḲISMA: Tanna of the first and second centuries; contemporary and senior of Hananiah b. Teradion. He is never cited in connection with halakot, but some ethical and esckatological sayings of his are preserved in the Talmud. He prized association with scholars more than gold; and when a rich man once offered him great wealth as an inducement to follow him to a place where no sages lived, he declined it: "If all the precious metals of the world were offered me, I would not live but in the atmosphere of the Torah; as David has said, 'The Law of Thy mouth is better unto me than thousands of gold and silver'" (Ps. cxix. 72). Nevertheless, when, in disregard of the Roman prohibition against teaching the Law, Hananiah b. Teradion held public assemblies and taught, Jose endeavored to dissuade him from pursuing that dangerous course (see Hananiah b. Teradion). This came to the ears of the Romans, and when Jose died the foremost among them attended his funeral ('Ab. Zarah 18a). On one occasion at the bet ha-midrash of Tiberias, he witnessed a warm controversy between Jose b. Ḥalafta and Eleazar b. Shammua, in which the debaters became so excited that they rent a scroll between them; thereupon he severely reprimanded them, and predicted that the bet ha-midrash eventually would be converted into a pagan temple. It is said that his prediction was fulfilled (Yer. Sheḳ. ii. 47a). Asked by his pupils "When will the Messiah come?" he exacted from them a promise not to call for signs to satisfy them of the accuracy of his prediction before he answered their question; and when they had promised, he replied: "When this gate shall have twice fallen and been restored, and fallen again, then, before it shall be restored the third time, the Messiah will come." Before his death he ordered that his coffin be placed deep in the ground; for, said he, "a time will come when to every palm in Babylonia a Persian horse will be tethered, and out of every coffin in Palestine Median horses will feed" (Sanh. 98a *et seq.*).

The word "Ḳismaḥ" is a locative noun, probably identical with "Ḳesam," by which Targ. Yer. (Num. xxxiv. 4) renders "Azmon." Neubauer ("G. T." p. 280) suggests its identity with "Ḳasmeya," name of a place in Upper Galilee.

BIBLIOGRAPHY: Bacher, *Ag. Tan.* i. 401; Grätz, *Gesch.* 2d.ed., iv. 174.

S. S. S. M.

JOSHUA B. ABIN: Palestinian amora of the fourth century whose name is associated chiefly with haggadot. He transmitted a haggadah of Levi and a halakah of 'Anani b. Sason. There are also extant some of his own haggadic sayings, and some paraphrases by him of Biblical verses (Bacher, "Ag. Pal. Amor." in. 731; Heilprin, "Seder ha-Dorot," ii. 195).

S. S. A. S. W.

JOSHUA (Jesus) BEN DAMNAI: High priest about 62–63 C.E. He was appointed by King Agrippa II., after Anan, son of Anan, had been deposed (Josephus, "Ant." xx. 9, § 1). Joshua also was soon deposed by the king, and in his place Jesus (Joshua) b. Gamaliel (Gamla) received the high-priestly dignity. A strife ensued between the deposed and the new high priest; they insulted each other in the public streets and even threw stones at each other (*ib.* § 4), but Jesus b. Gamaliel remained the victor.

BIBLIOGRAPHY: Schürer, *Gesch. des Jüdischen Volkes*, 3d ed., i. 584, ii. 220.

G. S. KR.

JOSHUA (JESUS) BEN GAMLA: A high priest who officiated about 64 C.E. He married the rich widow Martha of the high-priestly family Boethos (Yeb. vi. 4), and she by bribing Agrippa II. (not Jannai, as Talmudic sources say) secured for him the office of high priest (Yeb: 61a; Yoma 18a; comp. "Ant." xx. 9, § 4). Although Joshua himself was not a scholar, he was solicitous for the instruction of the young, and provided schools in every town for children over five years of age, earning thereby the praises of posterity (B. B. 21a). The two lots used on the Day of Atonement, hitherto of boxwood, he made of gold (Yoma iii. 9).

Joshua did not remain long in office, being forced, after a year, to give way to Matthias ben Theophil ("Ant." xx. 9, § 7). Together with the former high priest Anan and other men of rank, he opposed, but without success, the election of Phinehas b. Samuel (68) as high priest ("B. J." iv. 3, § 9). He attempted peaceably to prevent the fanatic and pugnacious Idumeans from entering Jerusalem, then torn by internal dissensions. After they had come into possession of the city, these fanatics took bloody vengeance on him, by executing him, as well as Anan, as traitors to their country (68) ("B. J." iv. 5, § 2).

Bibliography: In addition to the authorities mentioned above, Derenbourg, *Histoire de la Palestine*, p. 248: Grätz, in *Monatsschrift*, xxx. 59; Strassburger, *Gesch. der Erziehung bei den Israeliten*, p. 20; Schürer, *Gesch. der Juden*, i. 584, 618; ii. 221, 424.

G. S. Kr.

JOSHUA B. HANANIAH: A leading tanna of the first half-century following the destruction of the Temple. He was of Levitical descent (Ma'as. Sh. v. 9), and served in the sanctuary as a member of the class of singers ('Ar. 11b). His mother intended him for a life of study, and, as an older contemporary, Dosa b. Harkinas, relates (Yer. Yeb. 3a), she carried the child in his cradle into the synagogue, so that his ears might become accustomed to the sounds of the words of the Torah. It was probably with reference to his pious mother that Johanan b. Zakkai thus expressed himself concerning Joshua ben Hananiah: "Hail to thee who gave him birth" (A b. ii. 8). According to another tradition (Ab. R. N. xiv.) Johanan b. Zakkai praised him in the words from Eccl. iv. 12: "And a threefold cord is not quickly broken." Perhaps he meant that in Joshua the three branches of traditional learning, Midrash, Halakah, and Haggadah, were united in a firm whole; or possibly he used the passage in the sense in which it was employed later (Eccl. R. iv. 14; B. B. 59a), to show that Joshua belonged to a family of scholars even to the third generation.

Joshua ben Hananiah was one of the five who formed the inner circle of Johanan's pupils (Ab. ii. 8). In enumerating them tradition places him at the head together with Eliezer b. Hyrcanus. Tradition also frequently mentions these two together as upholders of opposite views. They were both present at the celebration of the circumcision of Elisha b. Abuyah (Aḥer), in Jerusalem, and diverted themselves by connecting passages in the Pentateuch with others in the Prophets and the Hagiographa (Yer. Ḥag. 77b). It was also Eliezer and Joshua who rescued Johanan ben Zakkai from the besieged city and brought him into the camp of Vespasian.

After the destruction of the Temple Joshua opposed the exaggerated asceticism with which many wished to show their grief, *e.g.*, in going without meat and wine because the altar on which they had sacrificed animals and poured libations of wine had been destroyed. He represented to them that to be consistent they ought to eat no figs or grapes, since no more first-fruits were offered, and that they ought even to refrain from bread and water, since the festival of drawing water (Joshua describes this festival in Yer. Suk. 55b) had been discontinued, and the showbread as well as the two loaves of the feast of first-fruits could no longer be sacrificed (Tosef., Soṭah, end; B. B. 60b). With such arguments Joshua supported the efforts of his teacher to make the grief at the loss of the Temple, which until then had been the center of religious life, less bitter. His opposition to asceticism, however, was due also to his mild and temperate nature, which caused him to say in regard to the severe regulations which had been adopted by the school of Shammai shortly before the destruction of the sanctuary: "On that day they overstepped the boundary." As he declared in a dispute on this subject with his colleague Eliezer, "they have poured water into a vessel full of oil, thus causing the costly oil to run to waste" (Yer. Shab. 3c; comp. Shab. 153b).

Joshua saw the greatest danger to the community in the sickly offshoots of piety. The following he calls "enemies of general prosperity": the foolishly pious (pious at the wrong time); sly sinners; the woman who shows an overpious bearing; and the "plague of the Pharisees," the hypocrites who pretend to be saints (Soṭah iii. 4, 21b; Yer. Soṭah 21b). In his motto of life (Ab. ii. 11) he recommends temperance and the love of mankind as a security for individual happiness. An evil eye (grudging), evil inclination (passion), and hatred of mankind, he says, bring people out of the world. In the same spirit he answers the question put by Johanan ben Zakkai to his pupils as to the best standard of conduct. He declares that one should seek association with a good companion and avoid a bad one (Ab. ii. 11). Various anecdotes illustrate the opposition between Joshua, who represented the teachings of Hillel, and his colleague Eliezer, who represented the teachings of Shammai, much in the same way as the opposition between Hillel and Shammai is depicted elsewhere (Gen. R. lxx., beginning; Eccl. R. i. 8; Ḳid. 31a).

Joshua's permanent residence was in Beki'in, a place between Jabneh and Lydda (Sanh. 32b), where he followed the trade of a needier (Yer. Ber. 7d). This occupation did not in any degree diminish the respect paid to him as one of the influential members of the academy at Jabneh. After the death of Johanan b. Zakkai, he was the heartiest supporter of Gamaliel's efforts to bring about the predominance of the views of Hillel's followers over those of Shammai's, and thus to end the discord which had so long existed between the schools. But he was the very one whom Gamaliel humiliated on a certain occasion when the authority of the president was in question (R. H. 25a; Yer. R. H. 58b). Joshua's pliant disposition did not shield him from humiliation by Gamaliel a second time; and the wrong done to this highly esteemed scholar was the cause of Gamaliel's removal from office. He soon obtained Joshua's forgiveness, and this opened the way for his reinstatement; but he was now obliged to share his office with Eleazar b. Azariah, who had originally been appointed his successor (Ber. 28a).

Joshua esteemed Eleazar very highly, and on one occasion called out in his emphatic manner: "Hail to thee, Father Abraham, for Eleazar b. Azariah came forth from thy loins!" (Tosef., Soṭah, vii.; Ḥag. 3a; Yer. Ḥag., beginning). When it became necessary to present the case of the Palestinian Jews at Rome, the two presidents, Gamaliel and Eleazar, went as their representatives, and Joshua b. Hananiah and Akiba accompanied them. This journey of the "elders" to Rome, and their stay in the Imperial City, furnished material for many narratives. In one of these the Romans call on Joshua b. Hananiah to give proofs from the Bible of the resurrection of the dead and of the foreknowledge of God (Sanh. 90b). In another, Joshua comes to the aid of Gamaliel when the latter is unable to answer the question of a "philosopher" (Gen. R. xx.). In one anecdote, concerning a sea voyage undertaken by Gamaliel and Joshua, the astronomical knowledge of the latter is put to use. He is said to have calculated that a comet would appear in the course of the voyage (Hor. 10a).

After Gamaliel's death (comp. M. Ḳ. 27a; Yer. M. Ḳ. 83a), the first place among the scholars fell to Joshua, since Eliezer b. Hyrcanus was under a ban. Joshua wished to do away with a regulation of Gamaliel's, but met with opposition on the part of the council ('Er. 41a). Joshua stood by the deathbed of his colleague Eliezer b. Hyrcanus and called to him: "O master, thou art of more value to Israel than God's gift of the rain; since the rain gives life in this world only, whereas thou givest life both in this world and in the world to come" (Mek., Yitro, Baḥodesh, 10; Sifre, Deut. 32; comp. Sanh. 101a). When, after Eliezer's death, the other law scholars, Eleazar b. Azariah, Ṭarfon, and Akiba, contested some of his opinions, Joshua said to them: "One should not oppose a lion after he is dead" (Giṭ. 83a; Yer. Giṭ. 50a). Eleazar, also, seems to have died some time before Joshua.

In the beginning of Hadrian's rule Joshua appears as a leader of the Jewish people. When the permission to rebuild the Temple was again refused, he turned the excited people from thoughts of revolt against

Rome by a speech in which he skilfully made use of a fable of Æsop's concerning the lion and the crane (Gen. R. lxiv., end). About the same time Joshua by his eloquence prevented the whole area of the Temple from being pronounced unclean because one human bone had been found in it (Tosef., 'Eduy. iii. 13; Zeb. 113a). Joshua lived to witness Hadrian's visit to Palestine; and he followed the emperor to Alexandria (130). The conversations between Joshua and Hadrian, as they have been preserved in the Babylonian Talmud and the Palestinian Midrash, have been greatly modified and exaggerated by tradition; but they nevertheless present in general a just picture of the intercourse between the witty Jewish scholar and the active, inquisitive emperor, the "curiositatum omnium explorator," as Tertullian calls him. In Palestinian sources Joshua answers various questions of the emperor: how God created the world (Gen. R. x.); concerning the angels (*ib.* lxxviii., beginning; Lam. R. iii. 21); as to the resurrection of the body (Gen. R. xxviii.; Eccl. R. xii. 5); and with reference to the Decalogue (Pesiḳ. R. 21). In the Babylonian Talmud three conversations are related, which resemble that on the Decalogue, in that Joshua silences the emperor's mockery of the Jewish conception of God by proving to him God's incomparable greatness and majesty (Ḥul. 59b, 60aj. Joshua also rebukes the emperor's daughter when she mocks at the God of the Jews (*ib.* 60a); in another place she is made to repent for having mocked Joshua's appearance (Ta'an. on Ned. 50b). The emperor's question concerning the odor of Sabbath food is a mocking one (Shab. 119a). Once Joshua told the emperor that he would dream of the Parthians (Ber. 56a). At another time he excused his own non-appearance at a meeting by cleverly describing the infirmities of his old age (Shab. 152a). In one conversation, preserved by a later authority (Jellinek, "B. H." v. 132), Joshua defended the justice of God, which was doubted by the emperor. Once a dispute in pantomime took place in the emperor's palace between Joshua and a Judæo-Christian ("Min"), in which Joshua maintained that God's protective hand was still stretched over Israel (Ḥag. 5b). In another conversation Joshua defended the honor of Israel against a heretic, who had attacked it, by quoting from Micah vii. 4 ('Er. 101a).

Some of the questions addressed to Joshua by the Athenian wise men, found in a long story in the Babylonian Talmud (Bek. 8b *et seq.*), contain polemical expressions concerning Christianity (Güdemann, "Religionsgeschichtliche Studien," pp. 89, 136 *et seq.*). The historical basis for this remarkable tradition is found in Hadrian's association with Joshua b. Hananiah, in Joshua's visit to Athens, and in his intercourse with Athenian scholars and philosophers. Its conclusion is an echo of the myth of the Danaides; and it is supposed to demonstrate the superiority of the "wise men of the Jews" over the "elders of Athens." Embodied in this tradition are the stories in which the wit of Athens is conquered by the cleverness of the men of Jerusalem (Lam. R. i. 1, *s.v.* "Rabbati"). In one of these the pupils of Johanan b. Zakkai make sport of an Athenian. That the tradition contains in parts polemics against Christianity is explained by the fact that Joshua b. Hananiah fought the heresy of the Judæo-Christians. The same spirit is manifested in the story concerning his nephew Hananiah (Eccl. R. i. 25). It is related that when Joshua ben Hananiah was about to die, the scholars standing round his bed mourned, saying: "How shall we maintain ourselves against the unbelievers?" Joshua comforted them with words from Jer. xlix. 7: "If counsel has been taken away from the children [of God, *i.e.*, Israel], the wisdom of these [the enemy] has also perished" (Ḥag. 5b).

After his death Joshua's importance was extolled in the words: "Since Rabbi Joshua died, good counsel has ceased in Israel" (Baraita, Soṭah, end). Not long after Joshua's death the thinkers were superseded by the men of action; and Bar Kokba, enthusiastically greeted by Joshua's most influential pupil, Akiba b. Joseph, raised the flag of rebellion against Rome. That this step had not been taken earlier was due to Joshua's influence.

In the haggadic tradition Joshua b. Hananiah's exegetical controversies with two of his most prominent contemporaries occupy an important place. These two are his colleague Eliezer ben Hyrcanus, who is frequently mentioned in the Halakah also as holding an opposite opinion, and Eleazar of Modi'im, who belonged to the school of Jabneh and was especially known as the author of haggadic expositions of the Bible. The controversies between Eliezer and Joshua refer to cosmology; to eschatology, comprising views on the Messianic period as well as on the future world and the resurrection; and to the interpretation of various Biblical passages. The controversies between Joshua b. Hananiah and Eleazar of Modi'im are found in the tannaitic midrash to Exodus; and they form at the same time a continuous double commentary on the sections concerning the stay of the Israelites at Marah (Ex. xv. 22–27), the miracle of the manna (*ib.* xvi.), the fight with Amalek (*ib.* xvii.), and the visit of Jethro (*ib.* xviii.). In these controversies Joshua, as a rule, stands for the literal meaning of the words and the historical interpretation of the contents, putting emphasis on the meaning demanded by the context. The Alexandrian Jews addressed twelve questions to Joshua (Niddah 69b). They fall into four groups: (1) three halakic, (2) three haggadic, (3) three foolishly ignorant questions (a sort of parody on the questions of halakic casuistry), and (4) three questions taken from practical life. Eleven questions also were addressed to him concerning the special position of woman in physical, spiritual, social, and religious matters (Gen. R. xvii., end). Some of these with his answers are: "Why is a man easy, a woman difficult, to persuade?" "Man was created out of earth, which easily dissolves in water; woman was created from bone, which is not affected by water."—"Why does a man have his head uncovered while a woman has hers covered?" "Whoever has committed a sin is ashamed before people; thus woman is ashamed on account of Eve's sin, and consequently covers her head."—"Why do women take precedence in funeral processions?" "Because they have brought death into the world."

Joshua ben Hananiah was regarded by posterity as a man always ready with an answer, and as the victorious representative of Jewish wit and wisdom. This is shown in the accounts of his conversations with heathens and in other narratives. He himself tells of three encounters in which he had to yield the palm to the wit of a woman and a child. He introduces the story in these words: "No one ever overcame me except a woman, a boy, and a maid" ('Er. 53b; comp. Lam. R. i. 1, section "Rabbati," end). Joshua explains the end of verse 18 of Ps. ix. to mean that there are even among the Gentiles pious people who will have a share in the life everlasting (Tosef., Sanh. xiii. 2; comp. Sanh. 105a). "The Psalms," he also said, "do not refer to the personal affairs of David, but to the affairs of all Israel" (Pes. 117b). If a man learns a halakic sentence in the morning and two sentences in the evening, and he is busy the whole day at his trade, it will be accounted to him as though he had fulfilled the whole Torah (Mek., Beshallaḥ, Wayassa', 2). Holidays are intended to be employed one-half for worldly enjoyment, one-half for study (Pes. 68b; Beẓah 15b). From Ruth ii. 19 it may be concluded that the poor person who receives does more for the giver than the giver does for the recipient (Lev. R. xxxiv.; Ruth R. *ad loc.*).

BIBLIOGRAPHY: Frankel, *Darke*; Graetz; Weiss, *Dor*; Brüll, *Einleitung*; Derenbourg, *Histoire*; Bacher, *Agada der Tann.* 2d ed., 123–187, 196–210; A. Lewysohn, *Toledot R. Yehoshua' b. Ḥananiah*, in Keller's *Bikkurim*, i. 26–35.

S. S. W. B.

JOSHUA B. ḲARḤA: Tanna of the second century; contemporary of the patriarch Simeon b. Gamaliel II. Some regard him as the son of Akiba who was named "Kereaḥ" = "bald" (Rashi on Bek. 58a; Rashbam on Pes. 112a). This is incorrect (comp. Tosef., Pes. 112a), for he never mentions Akiba, and would have done so had Akiba been his father. Only a few halakot of his have been preserved, his utterances having been mostly haggadic.

Joshua was bald; and once in a dispute with a heretic who taunted him on this score, he refuted his opponent with remarkable readiness of wit (Shab. 152a). His affection for his people is shown by the indignation with which he rebuked Eleazar b. Simeon, who had delivered the Jewish freebooters over to the Romans, upbraiding him with the words: "Thou vinegar son of wine [= "Degenerate scion of a noble father"], how long wilt thou give the people of our God unto death?" (B. M. 83b).

He lived to a great age; and when he blessed Judah ha-Nasi he added the wish that the latter might live half as long as himself (Meg. 28b).

BIBLIOGRAPHY: Frankel. *Hodegetica in Mischnam*, p. 178, Leipsic, 1859; Brüll, *Einleitungin die Mischna*, p. 202, Frankfort-on-the-Main; Bacher, *Ag. Tan.* ii. 308–321; Heilprin, *Seder ha-Dorot*, pp. 189–190.

S. J. Z. L.

JOSHUA B. LEVI: Palestinian amora of the first half of the third century. He was the head of the school of Lydda in southern Palestine, and an elder contemporary of Johanan bar Nappaḥa and Simeon b. Laḳish, who presided over the school in Tiberias (Gen. R. xciv.). With the former, Joshua often engaged in haggadic discussions (B. B. 116a; Meg. 27a; Shebu. 18b). It is doubtful whether the words "ben Levi" mean the son of Levi, whom some identify with Levi ben Sisi, or a descendant of the tribe of Levi (Grätz, "Gesch." iv. 263; Frankel, "Mebo," p. 91b; Weiss, "Dor," iii. 60; Bacher, "Ag. Pal. Amor." i. 124).

Joshua b. Levi was a pupil of Bar Ḳappara, whom he often quotes; but he considers his greatest indebtedness as being due to R. Judah b. Pedaiah, from whom he learned a great number of halakot (Ex. R. vi.; Eccl. R. vii. 7; Gen. R. *l.c.*). Another of his teachers was R. Phinehas ben Jair, whose piety and sincerity must have exerted a powerful influence upon the character of Joshua. Joshua himself was of a very gentle disposition. He was known for his modesty and piety; and whenever he instituted public fasting and prayer, it was said that his appeals were answered (Yer. Ta'an. 66c).

His love of peace likewise prevented him from making any attacks against the "Christian heresy" ("minut") that was then gaining ground. He was tolerant even to the Jewish Christians, though they often annoyed him; and he forbore cursing one of them, pronouncing rather Ps. cxlv. 9, "God's mercies extend over all His creatures" (Ber. 7a; 'Ab. Zarah 4b). His love of justice and his fear lest the innocent should suffer on account of the guilty (Yoma 19b) led him to pronounce against the custom then prevailing of removing from office a reader who, by omitting certain benedictions, had aroused the suspicion of heresy (Yer. Ber. 9c).

Joshua was a public-spirited man and devoted a considerable portion of his time to furthering the public welfare (Eccl. R. vii. 7). His wealth, and the additional circumstance of his being allied to the patriarchal family through the marriage of his son Joseph (Ḳid. 33b), must have added to his authority. He was recognized as a representative of Palestinian Jewry, for he is found in company with his friend R. Ḥanina interceding on behalf of his people before the proconsul in Cæsarea, who accorded Joshua and his colleague much honor and respect (Yer. Ber. 9a). On another occasion, when the city of Lydda was besieged because a political fugitive had found refuge there, Joshua saved the city and its inhabitants by surrendering the refugee (Yer. Ter. 46b; Gen. R. *l.c.*). He also made a journey to Rome, but on what mission is not known (Gen. R. xxxiii.).

Although R Joshua b. Levi was connected through family ties with the patriarchal house, and always manifested his high esteem for its members (Ḳid. 33b), yet it is largely due to him that the friendship between the southern yeshibot and the patriarchal house diminished (that such friendship existed see 'Er. 65b; Yer. Pes. 32a). For Joshua was the first to ordain fully his own pupils in all cases where ordination was requisite (Ned. 42b), thus assuming a power that hitherto had lain in the hands of the nasi alone.

In the field of Halakah Joshua was of considerable importance, his decisions being generally declared valid even when disputed by his contemporaries R. Johanan and Simeon ben Laḳish. He was lenient, especially in cases where cleanliness and the preservation of health were involved (Shab. 121b; Yer. Yoma 44d). Joshua devoted himself to the elucidation of the Mishnah; and his own halakot resemble in their form and brevity the mishnayot of the Tannaim.

In the Haggadah, however, he is even of greater importance. Of that study he entertained a high opinion, and he explained Ps. xxviii. 5, "the works of God," as referring to the Haggadah (Midr. Teh. xxviii. 5). Similarly in Prov. xxi. 21 he identifies "glory" ("kabod") with Haggadah (B. B. 9b). There is also a reference to a book ("pinkes") by Joshua ben Levi which is presumed by some to have presented haggadic themes (Weiss, "Dor," p. 60); but this can not be well reconciled with the fact that Joshua disparaged greatly the writing down of haggadpt (Yer. Shab. 15c; Midr. Teh. xxii. 4; Bacher, *l.c.* p. 129, against Weiss, *l.c.*, who assumes that the "pinḳes" was the work of another rabbi of the same name).

It is beyond doubt, however, that the Haggadah occupied a very important place in the teaching of Joshua b. Levi; this is evident from the many haggadot quoted in his name directly or given in his name by his disciples and contemporaries.

As an exegete Joshua b. Levi is of some importance, his interpretations often enabling him to deduce halakot. Some of his explanations have been accepted by later commentators (*e.g.*, Ibn Ezra and others on Ex. xv. 1; see Ex. R. xxiii.).

Joshua b. Levi was an earnest student, and his emphasis of study is seen when he speaks of God as saying to David (Ps. lxxxiv. 11) that "better" in His sight is "one day" of study in the Law "than a thousand" sacrifices (Mak. 10a; Midr. Teh. cxxii. 2). Though learning is of paramount importance (Meg. 27a), still he also insists on piety. He who attends morning and evening the synagogue service will have his days prolonged (Ber. 8a), and he who moves his lips in prayer will surely be heard (Lev. R. xvi., end; Yer. Ber. 9d). He instituted a number of rules regulating the reading of the Law in the synagogue on week-days (Ber. 8a) and other matters relating to the service, many of which are to this day in force in the synagogue (Soṭah 39b).

Some of Joshua's philosophical and theological opinions are recorded. Speaking of the attributes of God, he represents Him (Yoma 69b; Yer. Ber. 11c; Yer. Meg. 74c) as "great, mighty, and aweinspiring" (Deut. x. 17). He conceives the relation between Israel and God as most intimate, and he expresses it in the words, "Not even a wall of iron could separate Israel from his Father in heaven" (Pes. 85b; Soṭah 38b). In his doctrine of future reward and punishment, paradise receives those that have performed the will of God, while the nether world becomes the habitation of the wicked ('Er. 19a). In Ps. lxxxiv. 5 he finds Biblical authority for the resurrection of the dead (Sanh. 91b), and in Gen. R. xxvi. he expresses the liberal view that immortality is the portion not only of Israel, but of all other nations as well. In a legend (Sanh. 98a) Joshua is represented as inquiring of the Messiah the time of his advent, which Elijah answers will be the time when Israel shall harken unto God's voice (Ps. xcv. 7). In another connection he speaks of the futility of estimating the time of the coming of the Messiah (Midr. Teh. ix. 1; Lev. R. xix.).

In legend, Joshua b. Levi is a favorite hero. He is often made to be the companion of Elijah the prophet in the latter's wanderings on earth (Pesiḳ. 86a); he likewise has dealings with the Angel of Death (Ber. 51a). While yet alive, he is permitted to visit paradise and the nether world; and he sends thence a description of what he sees to R. Gamaliel through the submissive Angel of Death (Derek Ereẓ Zuṭa i., end). Many of these interesting legends relating to Joshua have been collected in separate small works entitled "Ma'aseh de-Rabbi Yehoshua' ben Lewi" and "Masseket Gan 'Eden we-Gehinnom."

BIBLIOGRAPHY: Bacher, *Ag. Pal. Amor.* i. 124–194; Frankel, *Mebo*, p. 91b; Grätz, *Gesch.* iv. 263; Hamburger, *R. B. T.* ii. 520; Weiss, Dor, iii. 59; Steinschneider, *Cat. Bodl.* col. 610–612.

S.S H. AB.

JOSHUA (HA-KOHEN) BEN NEHEMIAH: Palestinian amora of the fourth century. He seems to have devoted himself almost entirely to the Haggadah, for no halakic opinion of his is known. in the Talmud he is mentioned in one passage only (Sheḳ. ii. 4), but his name occurs frequently in midrashic literature. Many of his haggadic sayings have been preserved. Joshua frequently made use of parables. "A king was angry with his queen. The king nevertheless went to a goldsmith and purchased for her an ornament. He did thus after she had angered him; what would he have done had she not angered him! In like manner God wrought miracles for Israel, even though he (Israel) bad angered Him by saying, ' Is the Lord among us, or not?' [Ex. xvii. 7, 12–16]. How much more would God have blessed him had he done according to His will!" (Pesiḳ. R. No. 12 [ed. Friedmann, p. 50b]). Some of Joshua's haggadic interpretations are based on the symbolism of numbers (see Tan., Yitro, 19). In addition to his own haggadot he transmitted those of others, especially Eleazar II., Samuel b. Isaac, Ḥanina b. Isaac, and Aḥa.

BIBLIOGRAPHY: Bacher, *Ag. Pal. Amor.* iii. 303–309.

S. J. Z. L.

JOSHUA B. PERAḤYAH: President ("nasi") of the Sanhedrin in the latter half of the second century B.C. He and his colleague Nittai of Arbela were the second of the five pairs of scholars who received and transmitted the tradition (Ab. i. 6; Ḥag. 16a; see ZUGOT). At the time of the persecution of the Pharisees by John Hyrcanus, Joshua was deposed—a disgrace to which his words in Men. 109b apparently allude. To escape Hyrcanus, he fled to Alexandria; but he was recalled to Jerusalem when the persecutions ceased and the Pharisees again triumphed over the Sadducees (Soṭah 47a, Talmud ed., Amsterdam and Berlin, 1865). The same passage refers to a pupil of Joshua's who according to many may have been Jesus (comp. Krauss, "Das Leben Jesu," p. 182, Berlin, 1902). Only a single halakah of Joshua's has been preserved (Tosef., Maksh. iii. 4), besides the following ethical maxim which shows his gentle judgment of his fellow men and his eagerness to spread knowledge among the people: "Get thee a teacher; win thee a friend; and in judging incline toward the side of innocence" (Ab. i. 6).

BIBLIOGRAPHY: Weiss, Dor, i. 125–128; Grätz, *Gesch. der Juden*, iii. 73, 87, 113, Leipsic, 1888.

S. J. Z. L.

JOSHUA PHABI. See JESUS BEN PHABI.

JOSHUA OF SHIKNIN: Amora of the third century; known especially as a transmitter of Levi's Haggadah. He also quotes a haggadic sentence by Aḥa (Lev. R. xxxi. 5). Of his own work only a haggadic sentence, quoted by Yusta b. Shunam, is known: "The death of sinners excludes them from heaven and earth, whilst the death of the righteous establishes them in both" (Tan., Wayeẓe, 6 [ed. Buber, i. 148]).

BIBLIOGRAPHY: Bacher, *Ag. Pal. Amor.* iii. 730.

S. S. S. KR.

JOSIAH: Tanna of the second century; the most distinguished pupil of R. Ishmael. He is not mentioned in the Mishnah, perhaps because he lived in the south (Sanh. 88b), and his teachings were consequently unknown to the compiler of the Mishnah, Judah ha-Nasi, who lived at Tiberias and Beth-she'arim in northern Palestine. This is the explanation proposed by Frankel and Brüll; but the fact may have been that the Mishnah of Meïr, which served as the basis of Rabbi's Mishnah, did not accept the development of the teachings of Ishmael as formulated by Josiah and R. Jonathan, and they were consequently omitted by Rabbi from his Mishnah (Hoffmann, in Berliner's "Magazin," 1884, pp. 20 *et seq.*). Josiah is frequently mentioned in the Mekilta together with Jonathan. All their differences concerned only interpretations of Biblical passages, never halakot. During Hadrian's persecution Josiah seems to have fled from Palestine; for he was at Nisibis, where he delivered precepts in the college of Judah b. Bathyra (Sifre, Num. 123; *ib.* Deut. 218).

BIBLIOGRAPHY: Weiss, Dor, ii. 114: Frankel. *Hodegetica in Mischnam*, pp. 146–149, Leipsic, 1859; Bacher, *Ag. Tan.* ii. 351–364.

S. J. Z. L.

JUDAH I.: Patriarch; redactor of the Mishnah; born about 135; died about 220. He was the first of Hillel's successors to whose name the title of hereditary dignity, "ha-Nasi" (= "the prince"), was added as a permanent epithet; and accordingly in traditional literature he is usually called "Rabbi Judah ha-Nasi." In a large portion of such literature, however, and always in the Mishnah, he is simply called "Rabbi," the master par excellence. He is occasionally called "Rabbenu" (= "our master"; see Yeb. 45a; Men. 32b; comp. Abbahu's sentence, Yer. Sanh. 30a). The epithet "ha-Ḳadosh" (= "the holy") was occasionally added to "Rabbenu." Two of Judah's prominent pupils, Rab and Levi, in speaking of him (Pes. 37b; Shab. 156a), add to the term "Rabbi" the explanatory sentence, "Who is this?" "Rabbenu ha-Ḳadosh" (Frankel, "Darke ha-Mishnah," p. 191, erroneously considers this as a later gloss). The epithet "holy" is justified by Judah's singularly moral life (Shab. 118b; Yer. Meg. 74a; Sanh. 29c). It may have been borrowed from the terminology which was used by the inhabitants of the city of Sepphoris; for Jose b. Ḥalafta also praises his colleague Meïr as a holy and moral man (Yer. Ber. 5, below; comp. Gen. R. c., where the second term is missing). The epithet "holy" is by no means analogous to the epithet "divus," used to designate the Roman emperors ("He-Ḥaluẓ," ii. 93). It is likewise incorrect to interpret (as Levy, "Neuhebr. Wörterb." iv. 255) the sentence of Ḥiyya, a pupil of the patriarch, in Ket. 103b to mean that the title "holy" was not used after Rabbi's death, for Ḥiyya intends what is repeated elsewhere in different words (Soṭah, end), namely: "At Rabbi's death 'humility and the fear of sin ' ceased." The three virtues holiness, humility, and the fear of sin occur in this sequence in the series of virtues enumerated by Phinehas b. Jair (Soṭah ix., end, and parallel passages).

According to a statement handed down in Palestine (by Abba b. Kahana, Gen. R. lviii.; Eccl. R. i. 10) and in Babylonia (Ḳid. 72b), Judah I. was born on the same day on which Akiba died a martyr's death. The place of his birth is not known; nor is it recorded where his father, Simon b. Gamaliel II., sought refuge with his family during the persecutions under Hadrian. On the restoration of order in Palestine, Usha became the seat of the academy and of its director; and here Judah spent his youth. It may be assumed that his father gave him about the same education that he himself had received, and that his studies included Greek (Soṭah 49b; comp. Bacher, "Ag. Tan." ii. 325); indeed, his knowledge of Greek fitted him for intercourse with the Roman authorities. He had a predilection for this language, saying that the Jews of Palestine who did not speak Hebrew should consider Greek as the language of the country, while Syriac (Aramaic) had no claim to that distinction (Soṭah *ib.*). In Judah's house pure Hebrew seems to have been spoken; and the choice speech of the "maids of the house of Rabbi" became famous (Meg. 18a; R. H. 26b; Naz. 3a; 'Er. 53a).

Judah devoted himself chiefly to the study of the traditional and of the written law. In his youth he had close relations with most of the great pupils of Akiba; and as their pupil and in converse with other prominent men who gathered about his father at Usha and later at Shefar'am, he laid the foundations of that wide scholarship which enabled him to undertake his life-work, the redaction of the Mishnah. His teacher at Usha was Judah b. 'Ilai, who was officially employed in the house of the patriarch as judge in religious and legal questions (Men. 104a; Sheb. 13a). In later years Judah was wont to tell how when a mere boy he read the roll of Esther at Usha in the presence of Judah b. 'Ilai (Meg. 20a; Tosef., Meg. ii. 8).

Judah felt especial reverence for Jose b. Ḥalafta, that one of Akiba's pupils who had the most confidential relations with Simon b. Gamaliel. When, in later years, Judah raised objections to Jose's opinions, he would say: "We poor ones undertake to attack Jose, though our time compares with his as the profane with the holy!" (Yer. Giṭ. 48b). Judah hands down a halakah by Jose in Men. 14a. At Meron, in Galilee (called also "Teḳoa'"; see Bacher, *l.c.* ii. 76), Judah was a pupil of Simeon b. Yoḥai ("when we studied the Torah with Simeon b. Yoḥai at Teḳoa'"; Tosef., 'Er. viii. 6; Shab. 147b; comp. Yer. Shab. 12c). Judah also speaks of the time when he studied the Torah with Eleazar b. Shammua' ('Er. 53a; Yeb. 84a; comp. Men. 18a). Judah did not study with Meïr, evidently in consequence of the conflicts which had separated this famous pupil of Akiba from the house of the patriarch. He regarded it as great good fortune, however, to have beheld even Meïr's back, though he was not allowed to look him in the face, as one should regard one's teacher according to Isa. xxx. 20 ('Er. 13b; Yer. Beẓah 63a, where an anachronistic anecdote is connected with this saying of Judah's). Nathan the Babylonian, who also took a part in the conflict between Meïr and the patriarch, was another of Judah's teachers; and Judah confessed that once, in a fit of youthful ardor, he had failed to treat Nathan with due reverence (B. B. 131a; in different version Yer. Ket. 29a; B. B. 16a). In halakic as well as in haggadic tradition Judah's opinion is often opposed to Nathan's. In the tradition of the Palestinian schools (Yer. Shab. 12c; Yer. Pes. 37b) Judah b. Ḳorshai, the halakic specialist mentioned as assistant to Simon b. Gamaliel (Hor. 13b), is designated as Judah's real teacher. Jacob b. Ḥanina is also mentioned as one of Judah's teachers, and is said to have asked him to repeat halakic sentences (Sifre, Deut. 306). The R. Jacob whose patronymic is not given and in whose name Judah quotes halakic sentences is identical with one of these two tannaim (Giṭ. 14b; comp. Tosef., 'Ab. Zarah, v. 4). In an enumeration of Judah's teachers his father, Simon b. Gamaliel, must not be omitted (B. M. 85b). In the halakic tradition the view of the son is often opposed to that of the father, the latter generally advocating the less rigorous application (see Frankel, *l.c.* p. 184). Judah himself says ('Er. 32a): "My opinion seems to me more correct than that of my father"; and he then proceeds to give his reasons. Humility was a virtue ascribed to Judah, and he admired it greatly in his father, who openly recognized Simeon b. Yoḥai's superiority, thus displaying the same modesty as the Bene Bathyra when they gave way to Hillel, and as Jonathan when he voluntarily gave precedence to his friend David (B. M. 84b, 85a).

Nothing is known regarding the time when Judah succeeded his father as leader of the Palestinian Jews. According to a tradition (Mishnah Soṭah, end), the country at the time of Simon b. Gamaliel's death not only was devastated by a plague of locusts, but suffered many other hardships. It was for this reason, it may be assumed, that Judah, on beginning his public activity, transferred the seat of the patriarchate and of the academy to another place in Galilee, namely, Bet She'arim. Here he officiated for a long time. During the last seventeen years of his life he lived at Sepphoris, which place ill health had induced him to select on account of its high altitude and pure air (Yer. Kil. 32b; Gen. R. xcvi.; Ket, 103b). But it is with Bet She'arim that the memory of his activity as director of the academy and chief judge is principally associated: "To Bet She'arim must one go in order to obtain Rabbi's decision in legal matters," says a tradition concerning the various seats of the directors of the academies (Sanh. 32b). The chronology of Judah's activity is based entirely on assumption. The year of his death is deduced from the statement that his pupil Rab left Palestine for good not long before Judah's death, in 530 of the Seleucidan era (hence 219; see "R. E. J." xliv. 45–61). He assumed the office of patriarch during the reign of Marcus Aurelius and Lucius Verus (*c.* 165). Hence Judah, having been born about 135, became patriarch at the age of thirty, and died at the age of about eighty-five.

It is difficult to harmonize the many anecdotes, found in Talmudic and midrashic literature, relating to Judah's intercourse with an emperor named Antoninus (see JEW. ENCYC. i. 656) with the accounts of the various bearers of that name; and they therefore can not be used in a historic account of Judah's life and activity. However, as Marcus Aurelius visited Palestine in 175, and Septimius Severus in 200, there is a historical basis for the statement that Judah came into personal relations with some one of the Antonines; the statement being supported by the anecdotes, although they may report more fiction than truth. In many of these narratives references to the emperor apply really to the imperial representatives in Palestine. The assumption that not Judah I., but his grandson, Judah II., is the patriarch of the Antonine anecdotes (so Graetz) seems untenable in view of the general impression made by the personality of the patriarch; the tradition doubtless refers to Judah I. The splendor surrounding Judah's position, a splendor such as no other incumbent of the same office enjoyed, was evidently due to the favor of the Roman rulers. Although the Palestinian Jews had to contend with serious difficulties, and were persecuted during the patriarch's tenure of office, covering more than fifty years, yet it was on the whole a period of peace and one favorable to the activity of the academy. Judah I., who united in himself all the qualifications for internal and external authority, was naturally the chief personage of this period, which was destined, in virtue of its importance, to close the epoch of the Tannaim, and to inaugurate definitely with Judah I.'s life-work the epoch of the Amoraim. Judah's importance, which gave its distinctive impress to this period, was characterized at an early date by the saying that since the time of Moses the Torah and greatness, *i.e.*, knowledge and rank, were united in no one to the same extent as in Judah I. (Giṭ. 59a; Sanh. 36a).

It is a curious fact, explainable by the nature of the sources, that only scattered data concerning Judah's official activity are to be found. These data refer to: the ordination of his pupils (Sanh. 5a, b); the recommendation of pupils for communal offices (Yeb. 105a; Yer. Yeb. 13a); orders relating to the announcement of the new moon (Yer. R. H. 58a, above); amelioration of the law relating to the Sabbatical year (Sheb. vi. 4; Yer. Sheb. 37a; comp. Ḥul. 7a, b), and to decrees relating to tithes in the pagan frontier districts of Palestine (Yer. Dem. 22c; Ḥul. 6b). The last-named he was obliged to defend against the opposition of the members of the patriarchal family (Ḥul. *l.c.*). The ameliorations he intended for the fast of the Ninth of Ab were prevented by the college (Meg. 5b; Yer. Meg. 70c). Many religious and legal decisions are recorded as having been rendered by Judah together with his court, the college of scholars (Giṭ. v. 6; Oh. xviii. 9; Tosef., Shab. iv. 16; see also Yeb. 79b, above; Ḳid. 71a).

The authority of Judah's office was enhanced by his wealth, which is referred to in various traditions. In Babylon the hyperbolical statement was subsequently made that Rabbi's equerry was more wealthy than King Sapor. The patriarch's household was compared to that of the emperor (Ber. 43a, 57b). In connection with a sentence by Simeon b. Yoḥai, Simeon b. Menasya praised Judah I. by saying that he and his sons united in themselves beauty, power, wealth, wisdom, age, honor, and the blessings of children (Tosef., Sanh. xi. 8; Baraita Ab. vi. 8). During a famine Judah opened his granaries and distributed corn among the needy (B. B. 8a). But he denied himself the pleasures procurable by wealth, saying: "Whoever chooses the delights of this world will be deprived of the delights of the next world; whoever renounces the former will receive the latter" (Ab. R. N. xxviii.).

No definite statements regarding the redaction of the Mishnah, in virtue of which Judah became one of the most important personages of Jewish history, are to be found either in the Mishnah itself or in the remaining voluminous traditional literature. The Mishnah contains many of Judah's own sentences, which are introduced by the words, "Rabbi says." The work was completed, however, only after Judah's death, sentences by his son and successor, Gamaliel III., being included also (Ab. ii. 2–4). But no proofs are required to show that the Mishnah, aside from this final revision, is Judah's work. Both the Talmuds assume as a matter of course that Judah is the originator of the Mishnah—"our Mishnah," as it was called in Babylon—and the author of the explanations and discussions relating to its sentences. However, the Mishnah, like all the other literary documents of Jewish tradition, can not be ascribed to any one author in the general acceptance of that term; hence Judah is correctly called its redactor, and not its author.

The Halakah, the most important branch of ancient Jewish traditional science, found its authoritative conclusion in Judah's Mishnah, which is based ou the systematic division of the halakic material as formulated by Akiba; Judah following in his work the arrangement of the halakot as taught by Meïr, Akiba's foremost pupil (Sanh. 86a). Judah's work in the Mishnah appears both in what he included and in what he rejected. The mass of tannaitic Halakah sentences still found in the Tosefta and in the baraitot of both Talmudim shows that Judah had no small task in selecting the material that he included in his work. Also the formulating of halakic maxims on controverted points required both his unusual technical knowledge and his undisputed authority; and the fact that he did not invariably lay down the rule, but always admitted divergent opinions and traditions both of the pre-Hadrianic time and, more especially, of Akiba's eminent pupils, evidences his circumspection and his consciousness of the limits imposed upon his authority by tradition and by its recognized representatives. For questions relating to the Mishnah, including the one whether Judah edited it orally or in writing, see MISHNAH.

Among Judah's contemporaries in the early years of his activity were Eleazar b. Simeon, Ishmael b. Jose, Jose b. Judah, and Simeon b. Eleazar, the sons respectively of Simeon b. Yoḥai, Jose b. Ḥalafta, Judah b. 'Ilai, and Eleazar b. Shammua'; their relations to Judah are discussed in the articles under their respective names. The following among his better-known contemporaries and pupils may be mentioned: Simon b. Manasseh, Phinehas b. Jair; Eleazar ha-Ḳappara and his son Bar Ḳappara, the Babylonian Ḥiyya, Simon b. Ḥalafta, and Levi b. Sissi. Among his pupils who taught as the first generation of Amoraim after his death are: Ḥanina b. Ḥama and Hoshaiah in Palestine, Hab and Samuel in Babylon.

Judah's motto (Ab. ii. 1) is divided into three parts. In the first he answers the question, what course a man should follow in life, with the words: "Let him so act that his deeds will be for his own glory [*i.e.*, approved by his conscience] and praised by men" (another answer by Judah to the same question is recorded in Baraita Tamid 28a). In the second part he remarks that the least commandment should be as rigorously observed as the greatest. In the third he says that the most effective preventive of sin is the consciousness "that there is above us an eye that sees, an ear that bears, and a book in which all the deeds of men are recorded." His deep religious feeling appears in his explanation of certain passages of Scripture—I Sam. xxviii. 15; Amos iv. 13, v. 15; Zeph. ii. 3; Lam. iii. 29; Eccl. xii. 14—which reminded him of the divine judgment and of the uncertainty of acquittal, and made him weep (Yer. Ḥag. 77a; Lev. R. xxvi.; Midr. Shemuel xxiv.).

Judah was, indeed, easily moved to tears. He exclaimed, sobbing, in reference to three different stories of martyrs whose deaths made them worthy of future life: "One man earns his world in an hour, while another requires many years" ('Ab. Zarah 10b, 17a, 18a; for a sentence by Judah on the ranking of the pious in the future world see Sifre, Deut. 47). He began to weep when Elisha b. Abuya's (Aḥer's) daughters, who were soliciting alms, reminded him of their father's learning (Yer. Ḥag. 77c; comp. Ḥag. 15b). And in a legend relating to his meeting with Phinehas b. Jair (Ḥul. 7b) he is represented as tearfully admiring the pious Phinehas' unswerving steadfastness, protected by a higher power. He was frequently interrupted by tears when explaining Lam. ii. 2 and illustrating the passage by stories of the destruction of Jerusalem and of the Temple (Lam. R. ii. 2; comp Yer. Ta'an. 68d). Ḥiyya found him weeping during his last illness because death was about to deprive him of the opportunity of studying the Torah and of fulfilling the commandments (Ket. 103b). The following story shows his delicacy of feeling. He said to a calf, which, while being led to the slaughtering-block, looked at him with tearful eyes, as if seeking protection: "Go; for thou hast been created for this purpose!" To this unkind attitude toward the suffering animal he ascribed his years of illness, which he bore with great resignation. Once, when his daughter was about to kill a small animal which was in her way, he said to her: "Let it live, child; for it is written (Ps. cxlv. 9): 'His [the Lord's] tender mercies are over all'" (B. M. 85a; Gen. R. xxxiii.). His appreciation of animal life appears also in the prayer which he said when eating meat or eggs (Yer. Ber. 10b): "Blessed be the Lord who has created many souls, in order to support by them the soul of every living being." When wine seventy years old cured him of a protracted illness, he prayed: "Blessed be the Lord, who has given His world into the hands of guardians" ('Ab. Zarah 40b). He privately recited daily the following supplication on finishing the obligatory prayers (Ber. 6b; comp. Shab. 30b): "May it be Thy will, my God and the God of my fathers, to protect me against the impudent and against impudence, from bad men and bad companions, from severe sentences and severe plaintiffs, whether a son of the covenant or not." In regard to the inclination to sin ("yeẓer ha-ra'") he said: "It is like a person facing punishment on account of robbery who accuses his traveling companion as an accomplice, since he himself can no longer escape. This bad inclination reasons in the same way: 'Since I am destined to destruction in the future world, I will cause man to be destroyed also'" (Ab. R. N. xvi.). It is not unlikely that Judah was the author of the parable of the blind and the lame with which he is said to have illustrated in a conversation with Antoninus the judgment of the body and the soul after death (Mek., Beshallaḥ, Shirah, 2; Sanh. 91a, b;

see a similar parable by him in Eccl. R. v. 10). The impulse to sin is the topic of another conversation between Judah and Antoninus (Gen. R. xxxiv.; Sanh. 91b). Judah's sentence, "Let thy secret be known only to thyself; and do not tell thy neighbor anything which thou perceivest may not fitly be listened to" (Ab. R. N. xxviii.), exhorts to self-knowledge and circumspection. On one occasion when at a meal his pupils expressed their preference for soft tongue, he made this an opportunity to say, "May your tongues be soft in your mutual intercourse" (*i.e.*, "Speak gently without disputing"; Lev. R. xxxiii., beginning). The following sentence shows a deep insight into the social order: "The world needs both the perfumer and the tanner: but happy he who engages in the fragrant trade; and wo to him who engages in the vile-smelling trade! The world needs both the male and the female: but happy he who 1ms male children; and wo to him who has female children" (Pes. 65a; Ḳid. 82b; comp. Gen. R. xxvi.). He praises the value of work by saying that it protects both from gossip and from need (Ab. R. N., Recension B, xxi.). The administration of justice has taken its place beside the Decalogue (Ex. xx., xxi.); the order of the world depends on justice (A. V. "judgment," Prov. xxix. 4); Zion is delivered by justice (Isa. i. 27); the pious are praised for their justice (Ps. cvi. 3).

Judah sums up the experiences of a long life spent in learning and in teaching in the confession, which also throws light upon his character, "I have learned much from my masters, more from my colleagues than from my masters, and more from my pupils than from all the others" (Mak. 10a; Tan., Ta'an. 7a). Judah indicates that one can also learn from a young teacher: "Do not look to the jug, but to its contents: many a new jug is full of old wine; and many an old jug does not even contain new wine" (Ab. iv. 20). He forbade his pupils to study on the public highway (probably in order to put a stop to abuses), basing his prohibition on his interpretation of Cant. vii. 2 (M. Ḳ. 16a, b); and he deduced from Prov. i. 20 the doctrine, "Whoever studies the Torah in secret will find public renown through his scholarship" (*ib.*). He connected with Deut. xi. 12 the question: "Why is it written, ' for whom the Eternal, thy God, cares '? Does not God care for all countries? The answer is: 'Scripture means to say that although God seems to care only for the land of Israel, yet for its sake He also cares for all other countries. God is similarly called the protector of Israel (Ps. cxxi. 6), although He protects all men (according to Job xii. 10), but only for the sake of Israel' " (Sifre, Deut. 38). According to Joshua b. Levi, Judah interpreted Jer. xlix. 20 to mean that the Romans, the destroyers of the Temple, will in time be destroyed by the Persians (Yoma 10a).

In Judah's Bible exegesis those portions may be noted in which he undertakes to harmonize conflicting Biblical statements. Thus he harmonizes (Mek., Bo, 14) the contradictions between Gen. xv. 13 ("400 years") and verse 16 of the same chapter ("the fourth generation"); Ex. xx. 16 and Deut. v. 18 (*ib.* Yitro, Baḥodesh, 8); Num. ix. 23, x. 35 and *ib.* (Sifre, Num. 84); Deut. xiv. 18 and Lev. xi. 14 (Ḥul, 63b). The contradiction between Gen. i. 25 and verse 24 of that chapter, in the latter of which passages among the creatures created on the sixth day is included as a fourth category the "living souls"—a category not included in verse 25—Judah explains by saying that this expression designates the demons, for whom God did not create bodies because the Sabbath had come (Gen. R. vii., end).

Noteworthy among the other numerous Scriptural interpretations which have been handed down in Judah's name are those in which he cleverly introduces etymological explanations, as of the following: Ex. xix. 8–9 (Shab. 87a); Lev. xxiii. 40 (Suk. 35a); Num. xv. 38 (Sifre, Num. 115); II Sam. xvii. 27 (Midr. Teh. to Ps. iii. 1); Joel i. 17 (Yer. Peah 20b); Ps. lxviii. 7 (Mek., Bo, 16).

David did not really commit sin with Bath-sheba, but only intended to do so, according to Judah's interpretation of the words "to do the evil" (II Sam. xii. 9). Rab, Judah's pupil, ascribes this apology for King David to Judah's desire to justify his ancestor (Shab. 56a). A sentence praising King Hezekiah (Ḥul. 6b) and an extenuating opinion of King Ahaz (Lev. R. xxxvi.) have also been handed down in Judah's name. Characteristic of Judah's appreciation of the Haggadah is his interpretation of the word "wa-yagged" (Ex. xix. 9) to the effect that the words of Moses attracted the hearts of his hearers, like the Haggadah (Shab. 87a). The anecdote related in Cant. R. i. 16 (comp. Mek., Beshallaḥ, Shirah, 9) indicates Judah's methods of attracting his hearers' attention in his discourses.

Judah was especially fond of the Book of Psalms (see 'Ab. Zarah 19a; Midr. Teh. to Ps. iii. 1) He paraphrased the wish expressed by David in Ps. xix. 14, "Let the words of my mouth... be acceptable in thy sight," thus: "May the Psalms have been composed for the coming generations; may they be written down for them; and may those that read them be rewarded like those that study halakic sentences" (Midr. Teh. to Ps. i. 1). In reference to the Book of Job he said that it was important if only because it presented the sin and punishment of the generations of the Flood (Gen. R. xxvi., end). He proves from Ex. xvi. 35 that in the arrangement of the sections of the Torah there is no chronological order (Sifre, Num. 64). Referring to the prophetic books, he says: "All the Prophets begin with denunciations and end with comfortings" (Midr. Teh. to Ps. iv. 8). Even the genealogical portions of the Book of Chronicles must be interpreted (Ruth R. ii., beginning). It appears from a note in Pesiḳ. R. xlvi. (ed. Friedmann, p. 187a) that there was a haggadic collection containing Judah's answers to exegetical questions. Among these questions may have been the one which Judah's son Simeon addressed to him (according to Midr. Teh. to Ps. cxvii. 1).

Judah's death is recorded in a touching account (Yer. Kil. 32b; Ket. 104a; Yer. Ket. 35a; Eccl. R. vii. 11, ix. 10). No one had the heart to announce the patriarch's demise to the anxious people of Sepphoris, until the clever Bar Ḳappara broke the news in a parable, saying: "The heavenly host and earth-born men held the tables of the covenant; then the heavenly host was victorious and seized the tables." Judah's testamentary wishes, which referred to his successor and to his family as well as to his interment, have likewise been handed down (*ib.*). In accordance with his express desire he was buried at Bet She'arim, where he had lived at one time and where he had long since prepared his tomb (Ket. 103b, below); but, according to the work "Gelilot Ereẓ Yisrael," his tomb was shown at Sepphoris.

BIBLIOGRAPHY: Hamburger, *R. B. T.* ii. 440–450; Bacher, *Ag. Tan.* ii. 454–486; Büchler, *R. Jehuda I.L und die Städte Palästina's*, in *J. Q. R.* xiii. 683–740; Moses Kunitz, *Bet Rabbi*, Vienna, 1805; and the bibliography to the article *Antoninus*.

S. S. W. B.

JUDAH II.: Patriarch; son of Gamaliel III. and grandson of Judah I.; lived at Tiberias in the middle of the third century. In the sources he is called "Judah," "Judah Nesi'ah" (="ha-Nasi"), and occasionally "Rabbi" like his grandfather; as Judah III. is also designated as "Judah Nesi'ah," it is often difficult, sometimes impossible, to determine which one of these patriarchs is referred to. In halakic tradition Judah II. was especially known by three ordinances decreed by him and his academy; one of these ordinances referred to a reform of the divorce laws (Yer. Giṭ. 48d; Giṭ. 46b). Especially famous was the decree permitting the use of oil prepared by pagans, incorporated in the Mishnah with the same formula used in connection with decrees of Judah I.—"Rabbi and his court permitted" ('Ab. Zarah ii. 9; comp. Tosef., 'Ab. Zarah iv. 11). This ordinance, which abrogated an old law, was recognized as authoritative in Babylonia by Samuel and, subsequently, by Rab, who at first hesitated to accept it (see Yer. 'Ab. Zarah 41d; 'Ab. Zarah 37a). Simlai, the famous haggadist, endeavored to induce the patriarch to abrogate also the prohibition against using bread prepared by pagans. Judah, however, refused to do so, alleging that he did not wish his academy to be called the "loosing court" ('Ab. Zarah 37a). Judah could not carry out his intention of omitting the fast-day of the Ninth of Ab when it fell on the Sabbath (Yer. Meg. 70b; Meg. 2b). The patriarch was by no means regarded by his great contemporaries as their equal in scholarship, as appears from a curious meeting between Yannai and Judah II. (see B. B.

111a, b; another version occurs in Yer. Sanh. 16a, where Johanan accompanies Yannai).

Hoshaiah was in especially friendly relations with Judah (see Yer. Yeb. 9b; Yer. Beẓah 60d, bottom; B. Ḳ. 19b; in another version Yer. B. Ḳ. 2d; Yer. Meg. 70d; Meg. 7a, b; in Pes. 87b, where Hoshaiah refutes an inimical opinion on heretics at the request of the patriarch, Judah I. is probably meant; see Bacher, "Ag. Pal. Amor." i. 96). Together with Joshua b. Levi, Judah assisted at Laodicea at the reception of a female proselyte into Judaism (Yer. Yeb. 8d). Jonathan b. Eleazar was his companion at the baths of Gadara (Yer. Ḳid. 64d). The relations between the patriarch and Johanan, the leader of the Academy of Tiberias, seem to have been friendly (Ta'an. 24a); Johanan accepted the regular material support offered to him by the patriarch (Soṭah 21a). He also induced the patriarch to visit Simeon ben Laḳish, who had fled from Tiberias in consequence of having made offensive remarks in regard to the dignity of the patriarchate, and invite him to return (Yer. Sanh. 19d; Yer. Hor. 47a; Midr. to Sam. vii.).

On another occasion it was Simeon ben Laḳish who succeeded in softening Judah's indignation toward a daring preacher, Jose of Maon, who had denounced the rapacity of the patriarchal house (Yer. Sanh. 20d; Gen. R. lxxx.). Simeon ben Laḳish, moreover, seems to have exhorted the patriarch to unselfishness. "Take nothing," said he, "so that you will have to give nothing [to the Roman authorities]" (Gen. R. lxx.). Simeon ben Laḳish also reminded the patriarch of the need of providing for elementary education in the various cities, referring to the saying, "A city in which there are no schools for children is doomed to destruction" (Shab. 119b; see Bacher, *l.c.* i. 347). Judah was not so unimportant in the field of the Halakah as might appear from some of the details mentioned above, since Simeon ben Laḳish, who was not his pupil, hands down a whole series of halakic sentences in the name of "Judah Nesi'ah" (*i.e.*, Judah II.; see "Seder ha-Dorot," ed. Maskileison, ii. 177; Halevy, "Dorot ha-Rishonim," ii. 30 *et seq.*). Simeon ben Laḳish doubtless survived Judah and repeated his traditions. Simeon handed down also some of Judah's haggadic sentences (see Shab. 119b; Yer. M. Ḳ. 82c). The passage (Nazir 20c) referring to Simeon ben Laḳish as "sitting before Judah" and explaining a midrash does not refer to him as a pupil, but as a member of the college. This view is supported by 'Ab. Zarah 6b, which speaks of Simeon as "sitting before Judah Nesi'ah"; here the patriarch asks Simeon what to do in a certain case, and Simeon clearly appears as the better halakist, not as the patriarch's pupil.

Judah's relations to the scholars of his time in general appear from the following controversy in reference to Ps. xxiv. 6: "One of them says: 'The time is adapted to the leader ["parnas"]'; another says: 'The leader is adapted to the time'" ('Ar. 17a). It was probably the patriarch who expressed the opinion that the leader is adapted to the time in which he is called to leadership, and that he must not be blamed for his own incapacity. In the above-mentioned meeting between Judah and the daring preacher Jose of Maon (Gen. R. lxxx.; Yer. Sanh. 20d) it is the latter who utters the maxim, "As the time, so the prince." On another occasion Judah openly confessed his incapacity. Once during a drought he had ordered a fast and prayed in vain for rain. Thereupon he said, "What a difference between Samuel of Ramah [referring to I Sam. xii. 18] and Judah, the son of Gamaliel! Wo to the time which has such a tent-peg, and wo to me that I have come at such a time!" Rain soon fell in consequence of this self-abasement (Ta'an. 24a).

Various stories of Judah's youth, referring to him and his brother Hillel, have been preserved. "Judah and Hillel, the sons of R. Gamaliel [Gamaliel III.], on their trip to Kabul, in Galilee, and to Biri" (Tosef., Mo'ed, ii., end; Yer. Pes. 30d; Pes. 51a) "offend against the customs of both places. In Kabul they meet with a solemn reception" (Sem. viii.). Grätz identifies this Hillel, Judah's brother, with the "patriarch Joullos" (Ἰοῦλλος πατριάρχης), with whom Origen conversed at Cæsarea on Biblical subjects (Origen on Psalms, i. 414; see Grätz, "Gesch." 2d ed., iv. 250, 483; "Monatsschrift," 1881, pp. 443 *et seq.*); but as Hillel himself was not a patriarch, it may be assumed that it was Judah who conversed with Origen. Origen probably misread ΙΟΥΛΟΣ for ΙΟΥΔΑΣ. This assumption agrees with the above-mentioned statement about Hoshaiah's close relations with the patriarch, for it may be assumed as a fact that Hoshaiah had intercourse with Origen at Cæsarea ("Monatsschrift," *l.c.*; "J. Q. R" in. 357–360; Bacher, "Ag. Pal. Amor." i. 92).

BIBLIOGRAPHY: Grätz, *Gesch.* 2d ed., iv. 241 *et seq.*; Frankel, *Mebo*, pp. 92a *et seq.*; Weiss, Dor, iii. 65 *et seq.*; Halevy, *Dorot ha-Rishonim*, ii. 36 *et seq.* and *passim*; Bacher, *Ag. Pal. Amor.* iii. 581.

S. S. W. B.

JUDAH III.: Patriarch; son of Gamaliel IV. and grandson of Judah II. The sources do not distinguish between Judah II. and Judah III, and, since the title "Nesi'ah" was borne by both, which of the two in any citation is meant by "Judah Nesi'ah" can be gathered only from internal evidence, especially from the names of the scholars mentioned in the context. Judah III. held the office of patriarch probably during the close of the third and the beginning of the fourth century. He was a pupil of Johanan (d. 279); in a question regarding the time of the new moon, which he sent to Ammi, he introduces a sentence taught to him by Johanan with the words: "Know that R. Johanan has taught us thus all his life long" (R. H. 20a). In a conversation with the famous haggadist Samuel b. Naḥman, he refers to a haggadic sentence by Eleazar b. Pedat (Yer. Ḥag. 77a; Gen. R. xii.). Judah III. commissioned Johanan's pupils Ammi and Assi, who directed the Academy of Tiberias after Eleazar's death, to organize the schools for children in the Palestinian cities (Yer. Ḥag. 76c; Pesiḳ. 120b); Ammi especially appears as his councilor in haggadic questions (Beẓah 27a; M. Ḳ. 12b, 17a; 'Ab. Zarah 33b). Once he questioned Ammi regarding the meaning of Isa. xxvi. 4 (Men. 29a); he also visited the baths of Gadara with Ammi (Yer. 'Ab. Zarah 42a, 45b).

Ammi protested against the number of fast-days which Judah set in times of trouble, saying that the community should not be overburdened (Ta'an. 14a, b). Once Ḥelbo, a pupil of the above-mentioned Samuel b. Naḥman, requested Judah, who had absented himself from a fast-day service held in the public square of the city, to take part in the service, which would thereby become more efficacious (Yer. Ta'an. 65a). The prominent amora Jeremiah is said (Yer. Meg. 74) to have reproached Judah in a letter for hating his friends and loving his enemies (comp. II Sam. xix. 6). Germanus, Judah's Roman slave, is mentioned several times (Yer. Shab. 8c; Yer. Yoma 45b; Yer. 'Ab. Zarah 42a). The most important event of Judah III.'s patriarchate is the visit of the emperor Diocletian to Palestine (see JEW. ENCYC. iv. 606, where "Judah III." should be read instead of "Judah II."). One Friday the patriarch was called upon hurriedly to visit Diocletian at Cæsarea Philippi, and his extraordinarily quick journey thither from Tiberias gave rise to a legend (Yer. Ter. viii., end; Gen. R. lxiii.) in which the aged Samuel b. Naḥman appears. (On the Church father Epiphanius' reference to the patriarch see Grätz, "Gesch." 2d ed., iv. 483.) When Judah III. died (*c.* 320) Ḥiyya bar Abba compelled his colleague Ze'era, who was of priestly descent, to ignore, in honor of the dead patriarch, the prescriptions to be observed by the Aaronides (Yer. Ber. 6b; Nazir 5b, c). This scene took place in the "synagogue of the vine" at Sepphoris; hence it is to be assumed that Judah III. was buried at Sepphoris. He was succeeded by his son Hillel II.

BIBLIOGRAPHY: Grätz, *Gesch.* 2d ed., iv. 301 *et seq.*; Halevy, *Dorot ha-Rishonim*, ii.

S. S. W. B.

JUDAH IV.: Patriarch; son of Gamaliel V. and grandson of Hillel II. Beyond his name and the fact that he officiated during the last two decades of the fourth century, nothing is known of him. He is probably identical with the "Judah Nesi'ah" who addressed a question on Ruth iii. 7 to the haggadist Phinehas b. Ḥama (Ruth R. v.; Bacher, "Ag. Pal.

Amor." iii. 312). With his son Gamaliel VI. the patriarchate of Hillel's descendants ceased in Palestine.

BIBLIOGRAPHY: Grätz, *Gesch.* 2d ed., iv. 384, 484.

S. S. W. B.

JUDAH B. AMMI: Palestinian amora of the third generation (4th cent.); the son, perhaps, of the celebrated R. Ammi (Bacher, "Ag. Pal. Amor." iii. 715). His house was a rendezvous for scholars, and R. Ze'era, when exhausted by study, would sit at the threshold of Judah's house, so that as the rabbis came and went he could rise in their honor ('Er. 28b). Judah b. Ammi transmitted a number of halakic decisions in the name of Simeon b. Laḳish (Yer. Ter. ii. 3).

BIBLIOGRAPHY: Heilprin, *Seder ha-Dorot*, ii. 182; *Ag. Pal. Amor.* iii. 715.

E.C. A. S. W.

JUDAH B. BABA: Tanna of the second century; martyred (at the age of seventy) during the persecutions under Hadrian. At that time the government forbade, among other things, the ordination of rabbis, an infraction of the law being punished by the death of both ordainer and ordained and by the destruction of the city in which the ordination took place. Judah b. Baba nevertheless called together five—according to others, seven—disciples qualified for ordination, took them to a defile between Usha and Shefara'm, and duly ordained them. They were detected, and while his disciples, at his urging, fled, he, too old and feeble to flee, was slain by the Roman soldiery, who hurled 300 javelins at his body (Sanh. 14a). So great was the fear of the Romans that people did not dare even to praise him publicly.

In the Haggadah he not only appears as an authority, but is the subject of many sayings and legends. He was known as "the Ḥasid," and it is said that wherever the Talmud speaks of "the Ḥasid," either he or Judah b. Ilai is meant; he was considered by his contemporaries as perfectly stainless (B. Ḳ. 103b). From eight (or eighteen) years of age until his death he enjoyed little sleep; he fasted for twenty-six years in succession; and he defied the Emperor of Rome in his presence (Jellinek, "B. H." ii. 69; vi. 25 *et seq.*, 35).

In the Halakah, he was the author of some decisions; he also transmitted a number of important halakot ('Eduy. vi.), the most remarkable being that one witness to the death of the husband is sufficient to justify permitting the wife to marry again (Hamburger, "R. B. T." ii. 451). Akiba was his most powerful opponent in halakic disputes (Bacher, "Ag. Tan." i. 404).

BIBLIOGRAPHY: Grätz, *Gesch.* iv. 59, 164; Bacher, *Ag. Tan.* i. 403 *et seq.*; Heilprin, *Seder ha-Dorot*, ii. 165; Frankel. *Darke ha-Mishnah*, p. 129; Brüll. *Mebo ha-Mishnah*, i. 133; Weiss, Dor, ii. 119.

S. S. A. S. W.

JUDAH B. EZEKIEL: Babylonian amora of the second generation; born in 220; died at Pumbedita in 299. He was the most prominent disciple of Rab (Abba Arika), in whose house he often stayed, and whose son Ḥiyya was his pupil (ʻEr. 2b). After Rab's death Judah went to R. Samuel, who esteemed him highly and called him "Shinena" (="sharpwitted"; Ber. 36a; Ḳid. 32a). He remained with Samuel until he founded a school of his own at Pumbedita. Judah possessed such great zeal for learning and such tireless energy that he even omitted daily prayer in order to secure more time for study, and prayed but once in thirty days (R. H. 35a). This diligence, together with a remarkably retentive memory, made it possible for him to collect and transmit the greater part of Rab's, as well as many of Samuel's, sayings; the Talmud contains about four hundred haggadic and halakic sayings by the former, and many by the latter, all recorded by Judah b. Ezekiel; while a number of other sayings of Rab's that occur in the Talmud without the name of the transmitter likewise were handed down by Judah (Rashi to Ḥul. 44a).

In recording the words of his teachers, Judah used extreme care, and frequently stated explicitly that his authority for a given saying was uncertain, and that his informant did not know positively whether it was Rab's or Samuel's (Ḥul. 18b). His own memory, however, never failed him, and the traditions recorded by him are reliable. When his brother Rami says, in one place, that a certain sentence of Rab's, quoted by Judah, should be disregarded (Ḥul. 44a), he does not question the accuracy of Judah's citation, but implies that Rab had afterward abandoned the opinion quoted by Judah, and had, in a statement which the latter had not heard, adopted an opposite view.

Judah b. Ezekiel introduced a new and original method of instruction in the school which he built up at Pumbedita; by emphasizing the need of an exact differentiation between, and a critical examination of, the subjects treated, he became the founder of Talmudic dialectics (Sanh. 17b; Ḥul. 110b; B. M. 38b). His method of instruction, however, did not please some of his older pupils, and they left him; among these was Zeʻera, who went to Palestine despite Judah's declaration that no man should leave Babylonia for that country (Ket. 111a). But the new method was acceptable to most of his disciples, and was especially attractive to the young, so that the school at Pumbedita steadily increased in importance and popularity. After the death of Huna, head of the Academy of Sura, most of his pupils went to Pumbedita, which, until the death of Judah, remained the only seat of Talmudic learning. Although Judah devoted himself chiefly to dialectics, he did not fail to interpret the mishnayot, to explain peculiar words in them (Pes. 2a;

M. Ḳ. 6b), or to determine the correct reading where several were given (Beẓah 35b; Suk. 50b).

Judah gave little attention to Haggadah, and what work he did in that field was almost entirely lexicographical (Ned. 62b; Ḥul. 63a; Ta'an. 9b; Giṭ. 31b). In his daily conversation he took pains to acquire the habit of exact and appropriate expression, for which his contemporary Naḥman b. Jacob praised him (Ḳid. 70a, b). A lover of nature, Judah was a close observer of the animal and plant life around him. "When in the springtime thou seest Nature in her beauty thou shalt thank God that He hath formed such beautiful creatures and plants for the good of mankind" (R. H. 11a). Several of his explanations of natural phenomena have been preserved (Ta'an. 3b, 9b), as well as etymologies of the names of animals and descriptions of their characteristics (Ḥul. 63a; M. Ḳ. 6b; Shab. 77b).

Judah was celebrated for his piety, and it is related that whenever he ordained a fast in time of drought rain fell (Ta'an. 24a). According to him, piety consists chiefly in fulfilling one's obligations to one's fellow creatures and in observing the laws of "meum et tuum" (B. Ḳ. 30a). It was probably for this reason that he applied himself chiefly to the Mishnaic treatise Neziḳin (Ber. 20a).

BIBLIOGRAPHY: Bacher, *Ag. Bab. Amor.* pp. 47–52; Weiss, Dor, iii., 186–189.

J. J. Z. L.

JUDAH B. ḤIYYA: Palestinian amora of the first generation (3d cent.); son of the famous R. Ḥiyya. In Midr. Shemuel xi., and in Yer. Sanh. 29b, he is called also **Judah be-Rabbi.** He was the twin brother of Hezekiah (Yeb. 65b) and son-in-law of Yannai, who outlived him (Ket. 62b). Judah b. Ḥiyya is sometimes called "Rabbi" (Sanh. 37b), although it would seem that he was never ordained, since he is more frequently mentioned without this title. He and his brother Hezekiah are often termed simply the "sons of Ḥiyya" (Yoma 5b, *et al.*) or "the young people" (Ḥul. 20a), although both were celebrated for their learning and piety. Simeon ben Laḳish states that they left Babylonia with their father and went to Palestine, and spread learning there (Suk. 20a). Their piety is extolled in Ḥul. 86a and B. M. 85b.

Judah was extremely diligent, and would spend the entire week in the seminary away from his family, going home only for the Sabbath (Ket. 62b). Besides the discussions which Judah and Hezekiah held with Johanan ('Ab. Zarah 46a) and Joshua b. Levi (Zeb. 116a), and the sayings that are ascribed to both brothers, many maxims bave been preserved that belong to Judah alone. The following sentence of his may be mentioned: "Cain did not know where life leaves the body, and consequently inflicted many blows upon Abel before he finally wounded him in the neck and killed him" (Sanh. 37b).

BIBLIOGRAPHY: Bacher, *Ag. Pal. Amor.* i. 48–52; Frankel, *Mebo*, pp. 91a, 123b.

J. J. Z. L.

JUDAH BEN ILAI: One of the most important tannaim of the second century; born at Usha, a city of Galilee (Cant. R. ii.). His teachers were his father (himself a pupil of Eliezer b. Hyrcanus), Akiba, and Ṭarfon. He studied under the last-named in early youth (Meg. 20a), and was so closely associated with him that he even performed menial services for him (Tosef., Neg. viii. 1). Judah b. Baba ordained him as teacher at a time when the Roman government forbade such a ceremony. Almost at the beginning of Hadrian's persecution Judah ben Ilai was forced to flee from Usha and conceal himself; and he often related episodes of the "times of peril" (Tosef., 'Er. viii. 6; Suk. i. 7). When, after the revocation of Hadrian's edicts of persecution, the pupils of Akiba held their reunions and councils in Usha, Judah received the right to express his opinion before all others, thus being "Rosh ha-Medabbebrim" (leader among the speakers), on the ground that he was the best authority on the traditions (for other grounds see Cant. R. ii., 4; Ber. 68b; Shab. 33a). He was intimately associated with the patriarch Simon b. Gamaliel II., in whose house he is said to have been entrusted with the decision in matters pertaining to the religious law (Men. 104a). He was also able to win the confidence of the Romans by his praise of their civilizing tendencies as shown in their construction of bridges, highways, and market-places (Shab. 33a).

Judah's personal piety was most rigid; and he observed many of the practises of the Ḥasidim and the Essenes. He drank no wine except on the days when the Law required, and preferred to eat only vegetable food (Ned. 49b). On Friday, after he had bathed and clad himself in white to prepare for the Sabbath, he seemed to his pupils an angel. According to a later rule of interpretation, Judah b. Ilai is meant in all passages reading, "It once happened to a pious man" (B. Ḳ. 104a). He was naturally passionate and irascible (Ḳid. 52b); but such was his self-control that be seemed the reverse. Thus he once showed exceptional mildness when he had an opportunity to reconcile a married pair (Ned. 66b). The study of the Law was his chief and dearest occupation; and he lamented the fact that such a devotion was no longer wide-spread as in former times. Yet his interest in the joys and sorrows of his fellow men was keener still. Whenever a funeral or a wedding-procession passed, be interrupted his study to join it (Ket. 17a).

Judah lived in the utmost poverty. His wife made with her own hands a cloak which served them both in turn: the wife as she went to the market; the husband on his way to the college. Nevertheless, he declined all assistance, since he had accustomed himself to the simplest mode of life, and on principle desired to have no delight in this world (Ned. 40b). His high conception of the calling and the responsibility of a teacher of the Law, as well as his mild judgment of the multitude, was expressed in his interpretation of Isa. lviii. 1: "Show my people their transgression"—that is, the teachers of the Law, from whose errors wickedness arises—"and the house of Jacob their sins"—that is, the ignorant, whose wickedness is only error (B. M. 33b).

Judah often teaches the Mishnah of Eliezer, which he had received from his father (Men. 18a), and frequently explains the traditional halakot by particularizations introduced by the phrases "Ematai?" (= "When does this statement apply?") and "Bameh debarim amurim?" (= "In what connection was this said?" Ḥul. v. 3; Ber. ii. 4). His most frequent teachings, however, are the doctrines of his master Akiba. His own halakot he sets forth in the form of midrashim; for, in his view, mishnah and midrash are identical (Ḳid. 49a). Those who devote themselves only to the Mishnah, that is, to the stereotyped Halakah without its Scriptural basis, he terms "enemies" (B. M. 33b); but those who direct their attention to the Scriptures are "brothers." Yet it is only they who interpret or expound the Bible who receive this latter name; for he who makes a literal translation of a verse of Scripture is a "liar," and he who adds to it a "blasphemer" (Tosef., Meg., end).

In his interpretation of the Scriptures and in the deduction of legal requirements from it Judah adheres strictly to the method of his teacher Akiba, whose rules of exegesis he adopts. It is thus that he explains a word apparently superfluous (Bek. 43b; Pes. 42a), and employs the rules of "al tiḳri" ('Ar. 13b) and "noṭariḳon" (Men. 29b). Nevertheless, he interprets also according to the older Halakah in cases where he deduces a definition from the literal wording of a passage, and bases his explanation strictly on its obvious meaning, "debarim ki-ketaban" (Pes. 21b, 91a; Zeb. 59b). The greater portion of the Sifra, or halakic midrash on Leviticus which originated in the school of Akiba, is to be attributed to Judah, nearly all the anonymous statements in it being his, "Setam Sifra R. Yehudah" ('Er. 96b). Of his exegetical principles only one need be noted: "In the Holy Scriptures certain phrases which border on blasphemy have been altered" (Mek., ed. Weiss, 46a).

Many haggadic utterances and traditions of Judah's have been preserved. His traditions regarding the Temple at Jerusalem are very numerous; and special interest attaches to his accounts of the origin of the Temple of Onias (Men. 109b) and of the Septuagint (Meg. 9), as well as to his description of the synagogue at Alexandria (Suk. 51b) and of the conditions and institutions of antiquity (Tosef., Ter. i. 1; Shab. v. 2; and many other passages).

Many of Judah's maxims and proverbs have likewise been preserved; a few are cited here: "Great is beneficence: it quickeneth salvation" (B. B. 10a). "Great is toil: it honoreth the toiler" (Ned. 49b). "Who teacheth his son no trade, guideth him to robbery" (Ḳid. 29a). "The best path lies midway" (Ab. R. N. xxviii.).

Judah attained a very great age, surviving his teachers and all of his colleagues. Among his disciples who paid him the last honors was Judah ha-Nasi. His grave was shown at Ensetim beside the tomb of his father ("Seder ha-Dorot," p. 169).

BIBLIOGRAPHY: Frankel, *Hodegetica in Mischnam*, pp. 158–164, Leipsic, 1859; Brüll, *Einleitung in die Mischna*, pp. 169–178, Frankfort-on-the-Main; Hamburger, *R. B. T.* ii. 452–460; Bacher, *Ag. Tan.* ii. 191–234; Hoffmann, *Einleitung in die Halachischen Midraschim*, p. 26.

S. J. Z. L.

JUDAH BEN LAḲISH: Tanna of the second century. His name occurs only in the Tosefta and the Mekilta. He is the author of the halakah to the effect that a corpse may be carried on the Sabbath to save it from a fire (Shab. 43b). Besides this halakah, which is transmitted by him alone, there is. another (Tosef., Sach. i. 7) which prescribes that after a judge has heard both sides, and has formed an opinion, he may not say: "I will not judge between you."

A few of Judah's haggadic utterances also have; been preserved; *e.g.*: "The children of Israel had two Arks of the Covenant. In one were the broken tables of stone; in the other, the Book of the Torah" (Tosef., Soṭah, vii. 18). "The Ark of the Covenant was not carried to Babylon, but was hidden in the Temple itself" (Yoma 53a). "When a scholar neglects learning, Prov. xxvii. 8 may be applied to him" (Ḥag. 9b).

BIBLIOGRAPHY: Brüll, *Einleitung in die Mischna*, p. 249, Frankfort-on-the-Main; Bacher, *Ag. Tan.* ii. 494–495.

S. J. Z. L.

JUDAH B. PEDAYA (known also as **Bar Padah**): Palestinian amora of the first generation (3d cent.); nephew of Bar Ḳappara. Among his numerous pupils the most important was the haggadist Joshua b. Levi, who claimed to have received numerous halakot from Judah (Ex. R. vi.; Eccl. R. vii. 7). According to another statement of Joshua b. Levi (Gen. R. xciv.), Judah was the most important of the haggadists of the South, and discussed Talmudic questions with the patriarch Judah I. His halakic and haggadic sayings are numerous in both Talmuds (Weiss, "Dor," iii. 63). In his haggadic interpretations he often departs from the traditional vocalization. Thus, in Gen. R. (to Gen. xix. 12), he reads "pe" instead of "po," and supposes that the angels forbade Lot to entreat forgiveness for the people of Sodom after they had manifested their shameful desires (Gen. R. xxvi.).

BIBLIOGRAPHY: Heilprin, *Seder ha-Dorot*, ii. 311; Bacher, *Ag. Pal. Amor.* iii. 579; Frankel, *Mebo*, p. 70b.

E. C. A. S. W.

JUDAH BEN SIMEON BEN PAZZI (called also **Judah b. Pazzi** and **Judah b. Simon**): Palestinian amora and haggadist of the beginning of the fourth century. He frequently transmits halakic and haggadic aphorisms under the name of his father and of R Joshua b. Levi, R. Johanan, and Simeon b. Laḳish. In his own haggadic maxims Judah frequently employs parables, of which one may be cited: "A wolf broke into the fold and seized a kid. Then came a strange dog which barked at the wolf and fought with him for the kid. Thereupon the wolf said: 'Why dost thou bark at me? Have I taken aught that was thine?' Such a dog was Balak, who opposed the Israelites because they had overcome Sihon and Og" (Yelammedenu, in Yalḳ., Num. xxii.).

BIBLIOGRAPHY: Bacher, *Ag. Pal. Amor.* iii. 160–220.

S. J. Z. L.

JUDAH B. ZIPPORI: Instigator of an uprising against Herod the Great. Shortly before the latter's death two prominent scribes of Jerusalem, one of whom was Judah b. Zippori (Josephus, "Ant." xvii. 6, § 2, has *Σαριφαῖος*; "B. J." i. 33, § 2, has *Σεπφεραῖος*; ed. Niese), thought it a good opportunity to tear down the golden eagle that Herod had placed above the gate of the Temple. They incited the young men of Jerusalem, some of whom were their own pupils, and these, on a false report of Herod's death, cut down the eagle. Thereupon a party of soldiers seized forty of them and took them before the king. They did not deny their deed; and the angry king had the ringleaders, among them the two scribes, burned alive; the remainder he delivered for punishment to his servants, who killed them.

G. S. KR.

K

KAHANA B. TAḤLIFA: Babylonian amora of the third century. He is mentioned only twice in the Babylonian Talmud; viz., in Men. 66b, where he refutes R. Kahana, and in 'Er. 8b, where he quotes a sentence of R. Kahana b. Minyomi, who seems to have been his teacher.

Kahana b. Taḥlifa apparently emigrated to Palestine, perhaps in company with R. Zera; for Yer. 'Ab. Zarah ii. 9 mentions him together with Zera and with Hanan b. Bo. This is not certain, however; for the passage reads: "R. Zera, Kahana b. Tahlifa, and Hanan b. Bo," which may be rendered also "R. Zera Kahana" ("the priest"), since Zera was a priest (Yer. Ber. iii. 5). On this assumption Bar Taḥlifa can not be identical with Kahana b. Taḥlifa.

S. S. J. Z. L.

ḲAMẒA and BAR ḲAMẒA: Two persons who, according to a Talmudic legend (Git. 55b–56a), were the cause of the destruction of Jerusalem. A certain man, having prepared a banquet, sent an invitation by his servant to his friend Ḳamẓa. The servant, by a mistake, delivered the invitation to his enemy Bar Ḳamẓa, who came and was expelled by the master of the house. Bar Ḳamẓa sought revenge for the outrage by denouncing the Jews of Jerusalem as having revolted against the Roman emperor, declaring, in support of his allegation, that if the emperor were to send an offering to the Temple, the priests would refuse to accept it. The emperor therefore sent him with a calf which he ordered to be sacrificed on the altar, but Bar Ḳamẓa made a blemish in the calf which caused it to become unfit for the altar. The result was the siege of Jerusalem by the Romans.

The identification of Ḳamẓa and Bar Ḳamẓa with Hanania and Eliezer ben Hanania by Zipser was shown by J. Derenbourg to be improbable. The latter recognizes in it the name of *Κομφός*, who, according to Josephus ("Vita," § 9), was one of the notables of Tiberias and a strong adherent of the Romans.

Bibliography; J. Derenbourg, *Essai sur l'Histoire et la Géographie de la Palestine*, Paris, 1867.

S. S. M. Sel.

ḲAṬṬINA: Babylonian amora of the second generation (3d cent.); known both as halakist and as haggadist. He was a pupil of Rab (Abba Arika); and his lialakot are frequently mentioned in the Babylonian Talmud, as transmitted either by himself (Ta'an. 7b; Yoma 54a; *et al.*) or in his name by Ḥisda (Bek. 35a; Ar. 32a) and Rabbah b. Huna (Bek. 44b). It was Ḳaṭṭina who inferred from Isa. xii. 11 that the existence of the world is divided into periods of 6,000 years each, with intervals of 1,000 years of chaos (R. H. 31a; Sanh. 97a).

Bibliography: Bacher, *Ag. Bab. Amor.* p. 71; Heilprin, *Seder ha-Dorot*, ii.

S. S. M. Sel.

L

LEVI I. See Levi b. Sisi.

LEVI II.: Palestinian scholar of the third century (third amoraic generation); contemporary of Ze'era I. and Abba b. Kahana (Yer. Ma'as.

iii. 51a). In a few instances he is quoted as Levi b. Laḥma (Ḥama; comp. Yer. R. H. iv. 59a with R. H. 29b; Yer. Ta'an. ii. 65a with Ta'an. 16a; see Rabbinovicz, "Diḳduḳe Soferim," to Ber. 5a, Ta'an. *l.c.*, Zeb. 53b). In later midrashim the title "Berabbi" is sometimes added to his name (Pesiḳ. R. xxxii. 147b; Num. R. xv. 10; Tan., Beha'aloteka, 6; comp. Pesiḳ. xviii. 135a; Tan., *l.c.* ed. Buber, p. 11; see LEVI BAR SISI). He quotes halakic and homiletic utterances by many of his predecessors and contemporaries; but as he quotes most frequently those of Ḥama b. Ḥanina, it may be conjectured that he was the latter's pupil, though probably he received instruction at Johanan's academy also. In this academy he and Judah b. Naḥman were alternately engaged to keep the congregation together until Johanan's arrival, and each was paid for his services two "selas" a week. On one occasion Levi advanced the theory that the prophet Jonah was a descendant of the tribe of Zebulun, deducing proof from Scripture. Soon after Johanan lectured on the same subject, but argued that Jonah was of the tribe of Asher. The next week being Judah's turn to lecture, Levi took his place and reverted to the question of Jonah's descent, proving that both Johanan and himself were right: on his father's side Jonah was descended from Zebulun; on his mother's, from Asher. This skilful balancing of their opposing opinions so pleased Johanan that he declared Levi capable of filling an independent lectureship, and for twenty-two years thereafter Levi successfully filled such an office (Gen. R. xcviii. 11; Yer. Suk. v. 55a). This incident seems to indicate that Levi's earlier years were spent in poverty; later, however, he seems to have been better circumstanced, for he became involved in litigations about some houses and consulted Johanan on the case (Yer. Sanh. iii. 21d).

Levi's name but rarely appears in halakic literature, and then mostly in connection with some Scriptural phrase supporting the dicta of others (see Yer. Ber. i. 2c, 3d *et seq.*; Yer. Ter. iv. 42d [where his patronymic is erroneously given as "Ḥina"]). In the Haggadah, on the contrary, he is one of the most frequently cited. In this province he became so famous that halakists like Ze'era I., who had no special admiration for the haggadist (Yer. Ma'as. iii. 51a), urged their disciples to frequent Levi's lectures and to listen to them attentively, for "it was impossible that he would ever close a lecture without saying something instructive" (Yer. R. H. iv. 59b; Yer. Sanh. ii. 20b). In these lectures he would frequently advance different interpretations of one and the same text, addressing one to scholars and the other to the masses (Gen. R. xliv. 4; Eccl. R. ii. 2). Sometimes he would discuss one subject for months in succession. It is reported that for six months he lectured on I Kings xxi. 25—"There was none like unto Ahab, which did sell himself to work wickedness in the sight of the Lord." Then he dreamed that Ahab appeared to him and remonstrated with him: "Wherein have I sinned against thee and how have I offended thee that thou shouldst continually dwell on that part of the verse which refers to my wickedness and disregard the last part, which sets forth the mitigating circumstance—'whom Jezebel his wife stirred up'?" (הסתה = "instigated," "incited"). During the six months following, therefore, Levi spoke as Ahab's defender, lecturing from the same verse, but omitting the middle clause (Yer. Sanh. x. 28b).

Levi divided all haggadists into two classes: those who can string pearls (*i.e.*, cite apposite texts) but can not perforate them (*i.e.*, penetrate the depths of Scripture), and those who can perforate but can not string them. Of himself, he said that he was skilled in both arts (Cant. R. i. 10). Once, however, he so provoked Abba b. Kahana by what was a palpable misinterpretation that the latter called him "liar" and "fabricator." But it is authoritatively added that this happened once only (Gen. R. xlvii. 9). He and Abba were lifelong friends, and the latter manifested his admiration for his colleague's exegesis by publicly kissing him (Yer. Hor. iii. 48c).

To render Scriptural terms more intelligible Levi frequently used parallels from cognate dialects, especially from Arabic (Gen. R. lxxxvii. 1; Ex. R. xlii. 4; Cant. R. iv. 1); and to elucidate his subject he would cite popular proverbs and compose fables and parables. Thus, commenting on Ps. vii. 15 (A. V. 14), "He... hath conceived mischief, and brought forth falsehood," he says: "The Holy One having ordered Noah to admit into the ark pairs of every species of living beings, Falsehood applied, but Noah refused to admit him unless he brought with him his mate. Falsehood then retired to search for a mate. Meeting Avarice, he inquired, 'Whence comest thou? ' and on being told that he too had been refused admission into the ark because he had no mate, Falsehood proposed that they present themselves as mates. But Avarice would not agree to this without assurance of material gain; whereupon Falsehood promised him all his earnings, and Avarice repeated the condition agreed upon. After leaving the ark Avarice appropriated all of Falsehood's acquisitions, and when the latter demanded some share of his own, Avarice replied, 'Have we not agreed that all thy earnings shall be mine? ' This is the lesson: Falsehood begets falsehood" (Midr. Teh. to Ps. vii. 15; Hamburger ["R. B. T." *s.v.* "Fabel"] erroneously ascribes this fable and several others to Levi bar Sisi). Levi became known among his contemporaries as מדא דשמעתא (= "master of traditional exegesis"; Gen. R. lxii. 5).

BIBLIOGRAPHY: Bacher, *Ag. Pal. Amor.* ii. 296–436; Frankel, *Mebo*, p. 111a; Heilprin, *Seder ha-Dorot*, ii., s.v. *Levi b. Sisi*, with whom he erroneously identifies Levi II.; Weiss, *Dor*, iii. 135.

S. S. S. M.

LEVI B. SISI (SISYI; SUSYI): Palestinian scholar; disciple of the patriarch Judah I. and school associate of his son Simeon ('Ab. Zarah 19a); one of the semi-tannaim of the last decades of the second century and of the early decades of the third. He assisted Judah in the compilation of the Mishnah and contributed baraitot (Yoma 24a). Many of Levi's baraitot were eventually embodied in a compilation known as "Ḳiddushin de-Be Lewi" (Ḳid. 76b; B. B. 52b). In the Babylonian Gemara Levi is seldom quoted with his patronymic, and neither in that nor in the Jerusalem Gemara nor in the Midrashim is he quoted with the title of "Rabbi." Keeping this in mind, the student of rabbinics will easily determine whether passages written under the name "Levi" without a patronymic must be credited to Levi bar Sisi or to a younger namesake who is almost always cited as "R. Levi" (see LEVI II). But although Levi bar Sisi is not given the title "Rab," he was highly esteemed among the learned, and in many instances where an anonymous passage is introduced with the statement למדין לפני חכמים (= "it was argued before the sages") it is to be understood that the argument referred to was advanced by Levi before Judah I. (Sanh. 17b; comp. Men. 80b; Me'i. 9b; see Rashi and Tos. *ad loc.*).

Judah I. later spoke of Levi bar Sisi as of an equal. But the latter did not always succeed in impressing the public. At the request of a congregation at Simonias to send it a man who could act at once as lecturer, judge, superintendent of the synagogue, public scribe, and teacher, and attend to the general congregational affairs, Judah I. sent Levi. When, however, Levi entered on office he signally failed to satisfy the first requirement. Questions of law and of exegesis were addressed to him, and he left them unanswered. The Simonias congregation charged the patriarch with having sent it an unfit man, but the patriarch assured it that he had selected for it a man as able as himself. He summoned Levi and propounded to him the questions originally propounded by the congregation; Levi answered every one correctly. Judah thereupon inquired why he did not do so when the congregation submitted those questions; Levi answered that his courage had failed him (Yer. Yeb. xii. 13a; comp. Yeb. 105a; Gen. R. lxxxi. 2). A late midrash speaks of him as a Biblical scholar and good lecturer (Pesiḳ. xxv. 165b).

After Judah's death Levi retired with Ḥanina b. Ḥama from the academy, and when Ḥanina received his long-delayed promotion Levi removed to Babylonia, whither his fame had preceded him (Shab. 59b; see ḤANINA B. ḤAMA). He died in Babylonia, and was greatly mourned by scholars. In the course of a eulogy on him delivered by Abba bar Abba it was said that Levi alone was worth as much as the whole of humanity (Yer. Ber. ii. 5c).

BIBLIOGRAPHY: Bacher, *Ag. Tan.* ii. 536; Frankel, *Mebo*, p. 110b; Halevy, *Dorot ha-Rishonim*, ii. 60a; Heilprin, *Seder ha-Dorot*, ii.; Weiss, *Dor*, ii. 192.

S. S. S. M.

M

MENAHEM BEN JAIR: Leader of the SICARII. He was a grandson of Judas of Galilee, the founder of the Zealot party, of which the Sicarii were a branch. Menahem checked the lawlessness of the Sicarii, who, under his leadership, in 66 C.E., stormed the fortress of Masada and slew the Roman garrison. Later they entered the fortress of Antonia, after its garrison had been forced to retreat by the Zealots under Eleazar ben Ananias, and ruthlessly murdered the maimed and helpless left behind by the Romans. Exulting in his successes, Menahem now demanded the leadership of the Zealots, sought recognition as the Messiah, and led his men into still more cruel acts of violence. Eleazar ben Ananias, realizing that the Sicarii were a menace, turned the Zealots against Menahem, who lied to Ophla, but was captured and executed. He was succeeded by his brother Eleazar.

BIBLIOGRAPHY: Grätz, *Gesch.* 4th ed., iii. 432, 457 *et seq.*; Josephus, *B. J.* ii. 17, §§ 8–10.

D. S. J. L.

MISHNAH (construct state, **Mishnat**): A noun formed from the verb “shanah,” which has the same meaning as the Aramaic “matnita,” derived from “teni” or “tena.” The verb “shanah,” which originally meant “to repeat,” acquired in post-Biblical Hebrew the special force of “to teach” and “to learn” that which was not transmitted in writing but only orally; the development of connotation being due to the fact that the retention of teachings handed down by word of mouth was possible only by frequent recitation.

“Mishnah,” the derivative of the verb “shanah,” means therefore: (1) “instruction,” the teaching and learning of the tradition, the word being used in this sense in Ab. iii. 7, 8; and (2) in a concrete sense, the content of that instruction, the traditional doctrine as it was developed down to the beginning of the third century of the common era. “Mishnah” is frequently used, therefore, to designate the law which was transmitted orally, in contrast to “Miḳra,” the law which is written and read (*e.g.*, B. M. 33a; Ber. 5a; Ḥag. 14a; ‘Er. 54b; Ḳid. 30a; Yer. Hor. iii. 48c; Pes. iv. 130d; Num. R. xiii.; and many other passages); and the term includes also the halakic midrashim, as well as the TOSEFTA or explanatory additions to the Mishnah (Ḳid. 49b). In this wider sense the word was known to the Church Fathers, who, however, regarded it as the feminine form of "mishneh," analogous to "miḳneh" and "miḳnah," and supposed that it signified "second teaching" (comp. " 'Aruk," *s.v.* לתורה שהיא שנייה), translating it by *δευτέρωσις* (see the passages in Schürer, "Gesch." 3d ed., i. 113).

The term "mishnah" connotes also (3) the sum and substance of the teachings of a single tanna (*e.g.*, Giṭ. 67a; Yeb. 49b, 50a: "mishnat R. Eliezer b. Ya'aḳob" = "the teachings of R. Eliezer b. Jacob"; comp. Rashi *ad loc.*); or it may mean (4) the view of a tanna in regard to some one matter (*e.g.*, Men. 18a: "mishnat R. Eliezer" = "the view of R. Eliezer," and the expressions "mishnah rishonah" = "the earlier view," and "mishnah aḥaronah" = "the later view," Ḥag. 2a; Ket. v. 29d; M. Ḳ. iii. 83b). It may furthermore denote (5) a single tenet (*e.g.*, B. M. 33b; Hor. 13h; B. Ḳ. 94b; Shab. 123b), being in this sense parallel to the expression HALAKAH (on the difference between the two see Frankel, "Hodegetica in Mischnam," p. 8). It is used also for (6) any collection of such tenets, being thus applied to the great Mishnaic collections ("Mishnayot Gedolot") of R. Akiba, R. Ḥiyya, R. Hoshaiah, and Bar Ḳappara, in Lam. R., Introduction, and in Cant. R. viii. 2 (comp. Yer. Hor. iii. 48c; Eccl. R. ii.).

Finally the name "Mishnah" is applied particularly to (7) the collection of halakot made by R. Judah ha-Nasi I. (generally called "Rabbi"), which constitutes the basis of the Talmud, and which, with many additions and changes, has been transmitted to the present time. In Palestine this collection was called also "Halakot," as in Yer. Hor. iii. 48c; Ber. i. 53c; Lev. R. iii. (comp. Frankel, *l.c.* p. 8). The designation "Talmud" is likewise applied to R. Judah ha-Nasi's Mishnah (Yer. Shab. v. 1, 7b; Beẓah ii. 1, 61b; Yeb. viii. 9a; comp. also Frankel, *l.c.* p. 285; O. H. Schorr in "He-Ḥaluz," 1866, p. 42; A. Krochmal in the introduction to "Yerushalayim ha-Benuyah," p. 6; Oppenheim, "Zur Gesch. der Mischna," p. 244).

The "Mishnah of R. Judah," however, is not to be regarded as a literary product of the third century, nor R. Judah as its author. It is, on the contrary, a collection which includes almost the entire material of the oral doctrine as developed from the period of the earliest halakic exegesis down to that of the fixed and crystallized halakot of the early third century. Judah ha-Nasi, who was the redactor of this work, included in his compilation the largest and most important portion of the earlier collections that he had at hand, and fortunately preserved, for the most part without change, the traditional teachings which he took from older sources and collections; so that it is still possible to distinguish the earlier from the later portions by their form and mode of expression.

In order to obtain a correct conception of the Mishnah, as well as of its value and importance, it is necessary to consider its relation to preceding collections of similar content as well as the general development of the oral doctrine from the earliest midrash of the Soferim down to the time when the Halakah received its final form.

According to a reliable tradition, contained in the Letter of Sherira Gaon (Neubauer, "M. J. C." p. 15) and confirmed by other sources (Hoffmann, "Die Erste Mischna," pp. 6–12), the earliest form of discussion of halakic regulations was the Midrash; and vestiges of such halakot may still be found in the Mishnah.

In addition to this form of the Midrash, which connects the halakic interpretation with the Scriptural passage on which it is based, the independent, definitive Halakah, apart from Scripture, was used in very early times in certain cases, and collections of such halakot were compiled (comp. Hoffmann, *l.c.* p. 11, note 2). As early as the time of the Second Temple the definitive Halakah was used more frequently than the midrashic form, the change having begun, according to geonic accounts, as early as the time of Hillel and Shammai (comp. Hoffmann, *l.c.* pp. 12–14). Although it can not be assumed that a collection of halakot, arranged in six orders, was undertaken when this change was made, or that Hillel himself edited a Mishnah, as Lerner has attempted to show (Berliner's "Magazin," 1886, pp. 1–20), it is probable that the material of the Mishnah first began to be collected at the time of the "Ziḳne Bet Shammai" and "Ziḳne Bet Hillel," the elder pupils of Shammai and Hillel. The beginnings of the present Mishnah may be found in this first mishnah collection, which in the completed text is termed "Mishnah Rishonah" (Sanh. iii. 4; 'Eduy. vii. 2; Giṭ. v. 6; Nazir vi. 1). A large portion of this first Mishnah is still preserved in its original form, notwithstanding the many changes to which it was subjected by the Tannaim; for many portions can be proved to have been redacted, in the form which they now bear, at the time of the schools of Shammai and Hillel, while the Temple was still standing (comp. Hoffmann, *l.c.* pp. 15–20; *idem*, "Bemerkungen zur Kritik der Mischna," in Berliner's "Magazin," 1881, pp. 170 *et seq.*).

This first collection of the Mishnah and its separation from the Midrash were intended, on the one hand, to reduce the traditional Halakah to a shorter form, and, on the other, to fix the disputed halakot as such; of these disputed halakot there were then but few. The isolation of the Halakah from the Midrash not only resulted in a shorter and more definite form, but also removed many differences then existing. Indeed in many cases the divergency had been merely one of form, the proof and the derivation from Scripture being differently stated for the same halakah by different teachers. This earliest Mishnah was intended to afford the teachers both a norm for their decisions and a text-book for their classes and discourses, and thus to preserve the uniformity of teaching. It did not accomplish this purpose entirely, however; for when the political disorders and the fall of the Jewish state diverted attention from careful doctrinal studies, many halakot of the Mishnah were forgotten, and their wording became a subject of controversy. Since, moreover, in addition to these differences each tanna taught the first Mishnah according to his own conception of it, the one Mishnah and the one doctrine developed into many mishnayot and many doctrines (Sanh. 88b; Soṭah 47b). This multiplication occurred during the period of the later "Bet Hillel" and "Bet Shammai" (comp. Letter of Sherira Gaon, *l.c.* pp. 4, 9; Hoffmann, *l.c.* p. 49).

To avert the danger which threatened the uniformity of doctrine, the synod of Jabneh was convened (Tosef., 'Eduy. i. 1; comp. Letter of Sherira Gaon, *l.c.* p. 5; Dünner, "Einiges über Ursprung und Bedeutung desTraktates Eduyot," in "Monatsschrift," 1871, pp. 37 *et seq.*), and under the presidency of Gamaliel II. and Eleazar b. Azariah it undertook to collect the ancient halakot, to examine and determine their wording, and to discuss and decide their differences; thus there arose the collection 'EDUYOT (Ber. 28a). This compilation, that in its original form was much larger than the treatise that now bears its name, included all the halakot which were then known, whether controverted or not, and was in a certain sense a revision of the first Mishnah. Even in the present form of the treatise there are many " 'eduyot" which are expressly said to have modified the earlier Mishnah; and there are many others, not so characterized, which must likewise be regarded as modifications of the Mishnah as redacted for the first time. But neither the first Mishnah nor its revision, the 'Eduyot collection, was arranged topically or systematically. It is true, a geonic responsum, which was printed in "Sha'are Teshubah," No. 187 (Leipsic, 1858) and erroneously ascribed to Sherira (comp. Harkavy, "Einleitung zu den Teschubot Hageonim," pp. x. *et seq.*), refers to six orders of the Mishnah said to date from the time of Hillel and Shammai, as does also the "Seder Tanna'im we-Amora'im" (ed. Luzzatto, p. 7), but this statement, which is probably based on Ḥag. 14a, is untrustworthy.

The earliest Mishnah, however, must have been divided in some way, possibly into treatises, although such a division, if it existed, was certainly arranged formally and not topically like the present tractates and orders. The several halakot were grouped together by a common introductory phrase, which served as the connecting-link, as may be inferred from various traces of this old method of grouping still to be seen in the Mishnah, especially in the last treatises of the order Mo'ed.

These phrases (comp. Oppenheim, *l.c.* p. 270) referred for the most part to the similarity or the contrast between two or more halakot. Moreover, the name of the author or of the transmitter was often used as the connecting-link for the various halakot, as is evident from the treatise 'Eduyot in its present form (Dünner, *l.c.* pp. 62–63; A. Krochmal, in "He-Ḥaluẓ," ii. 81–82).

The 'Eduyot collection, which now became the basis for the discourses delivered in the schools, was the means of preserving the uniformity of teaching; but, as the mass incorporated in it was difficult to handle, there was a growing need for a methodical arrangement. R. Akiba, therefore, undertook a sifting of this traditional material, and made a mishnaic collection which he edited systematically by arranging the different subjects in different treatises, and perhaps also by combining the various treatises into orders. In the present Mishnah this collection is often mentioned in contradistinction to the first Mishnah (Sanh. iii. 4, and elsewhere; comp. Frankel, *l.c.* p. 210; Hoffmann, *l.c.* p. 38).

The passage Ab. R. N. xviii. 1 indicates that Akiba arranged his Mishnah according to topics (comp. Oppenheim, *l.c.* pp. 237 *et seq.*); and a like inference is to be drawn from the expression "tiḳḳen" (Yer. Sheḳ. v. 1), which does not mean "to correct," as A. Krochmal supposed ("Yerushalayim ha-Benuyah," pp. 34b–35a), but "to arrange," "to redact," the same word being applied to the work of Judah ha-Nasi in the redaction of his Mishnah (Yeb. 64b). Similarly the term "sidder," meaning "to arrange," is applied both to Akiba's work (Tosef., Zab. i. 5) and to that of R. Judah ha-Nasi (Yer. Pes. iv. 30d), thus justifying the conclusion that Akiba's method of division and arrangement of the Mishnah was the same as that followed by Judah ha-Nasi. Two treatises are definitely known to have been included in their present form in Akiba's Mishnah, in which they even bore their present names. E. Meïr mentions the treatise 'Uḳẓin by name in Hor. 13b; and R. Jose in like manner names the treatise Kelim (Kelim, end): both of these tannaim, who antedated Judah ha-Nasi, undoubtedly designated by these names the treatises Kelim and 'Uḳẓin as included in the Mishnah of their teacher Akiba.

R. Akiba's treatment of the old Mishnah in editing his own Mishnah collection was entirely arbitrary. He excluded many of the halakot contained in the original text; and those which he accepted he endeavored to found upon some text, explaining their phraseology, and tracing their origin, but striving most of all to present the Halakah in short, clear, and explicit form (comp. Tosef., Zab. i. 5). Many halakic sentences which he included called for more detailed explanation. For the sake of brevity, however, and to aid his pupils in memorizing the

Mishnah, he omitted the required explanations and made an additional collection containing the comments to the Mishnah, thus laying the foundation for the Tosefta (comp. Letter of Sherira Gaon, *l.c.* p. 16; Frankel, *l.c.* p. 306; Oppenheim, *l.c.* p. 270).

Akiba's method, which reduced the halakic collections to an orderly system, soon found imitators; and nearly every tannaitic head of a school, who, in virtue of his position, had a mishnaic collection, sooner or later adopted Akiba's method of dividing and arranging the material. R. Meïr especially followed this system, availing himself of it when the increasing number of new halakot, discovered and established by Akiba's pupils, rendered a new mishnaic collection necessary. In this compilation he included the larger portion of Akiba's Mishnah, but also drew upon other existing collections, such as that of Abba Saul (comp. Lewy, "Ueber Einige Fragmente aus der Mischna des Abba Saul," Berlin, 1876). He likewise incorporated many old halakot known in the schools but excluded by Akiba. He frequently cited the opinions of Akiba, without naming him, as "setam" and therefore authoritative for halakic decisions; but sometimes, when the opinion of the majority was opposed to Akiba's view, he designated the former as "setam" and binding for the Halakah (comp. Oppenheim, *l.c.* p. 315).

R. Meïr's collection had a wide circulation, although it was not able to displace the other compilations. As every tanna at the head of a school, however, had, as stated above, his own mishnaic collection in which the halakot of preceding teachers as well as their controversies were differently expounded, the uniformity in teaching which the redactors of the Mishnah had desired and which had almost been attained was again lost; for there were as many different teachings as there were Mishnah collections. There was good ground, therefore, for the complaint that the religious world was thrown into disorder by the teachers who gave halakic decisions according to their own mishnaic collections (Soṭah 22a), since a clear and reliable Halakah could not be found in any individual compilation (Shab. 138b, 139a).

To remedy this evil and to restore uniformity of teaching, Judah ha-Nasi undertook his collection, arrangement, and redaction of the Mishnah, which work has survived to the present time. He followed his own method so far as the selection and presentation of the material were concerned, but adopted the systems of Akiba and Meïr in regard to the division and arrangement. This Mishnah was intended to serve practical purposes and to be an authority in deciding religious and legal questions. Judah often gives, therefore, the opinion of a single teacher, where he regards it as the correct one, in the name of "the sages" ("ḥakamim") (Ḥul. 85a); and in order that the opinion of a single scholar may prevail as final, he ignores the fact that this view was controverted by many others. At times he, without mentioning his name, quotes his own opinion as "setam," to record it as authoritative (comp. Oppenheim, *l.c.* p. 347, No. 16). Frequently, too, he explains or limits the earlier Halakah (see Yer. Hor. i. 46a), and endeavors to find a compromise in the case of disputed halakot, or he himself decides the cases in which the halakah is to follow one opinion and in which the other (comp. Frankel, *l.c.* pp. 195 *et seq.*).

In addition to the practical purpose of restoring and preserving uniformity of halakic doctrine and of providing for teachers an authority for their decisions, Judah ha-Nasi had another purely theoretical object in view; namely, the preservation of the teachings of the ancients, except those which he regarded as relatively unimportant or which he considered to have been preserved in some other place in his collection. This fact explains many peculiarities of the Mishnah, which were regarded as shortcomings by those who considered it a legal code. The following are some of these peculiarities: Judah ha-Nasi quotes the opinion of a single authority even when invalidated, and he quotes the original view of a scholar even after such scholar had himself retracted it (Ḥul. 32b; comp. Oppenheim, *l.c.* p. 344). He quotes also a given halakah in one passage as being controverted ("maḥloket") and in another passage as authoritative ("setam"), or vice versa; and he cites contradictory teachings in different places. All these peculiarities are due to the fact that Judah wished to preserve the ancient teachings; and to attain this object more completely he included in his Mishnah, in addition to the collections of Akiba and Meïr, which formed his chief sources, the major portion of all the other mishnayot (Yer. Shab. xvi. 15c); according to a later account, he used in all thirteen collections (Ned. 41a). He dealt independently with his material; for while he frequently made no changes in the wording or form of the old Mishnah, and even included old halakot which had long since been refuted, he altered various others (comp. Hoffmann, "Bemerkungen zur Kritik der Mischna," in Berliner's "Magazin," 1881, pp. 127 *et seq.*). He expounded many of the old halakot ('Ar. iv. 2; Sanh. ix. 3; Yer. Sanh. 27a; comp. Oppenheim, *l.c.* p. 347), following certain rules (Yer. Ter. i. 2, 40c), and endeavoring to determine the text of the old Mishnah (Yer. Ma'as. Sh. v. 1, 55d; comp. Letter of Sherira Gaon, *l.c.* pp. 9–10; Frankel, *l.c.* p. 214). The less-known halakot, as well as those which the pupils of Akiba had propounded, were interpreted by Judah ha-Nasi according to his conception of them. In this way he impressed upon his Mishnah the stamp of uniformity, and gave it the appearance of a work thoroughly revised, if not new; and his compilation displaced its predecessors by its inclusion of the major portion of their contents with the exception of those halakot which appeared to him untenable, or to which he had alluded in some other passage of his Mishnah.

Because of his personal prominence and his dignity as patriarch (comp. J. S. Bloch, "Einblicke," etc., pp. 59 *et seq.*), his Mishnah soon became the only one used in the schools, and was known to teachers and students alike, Judah thereby attaining his object of restoring uniform teachings. Whereas the exposition of the various halakot given by the Tannaim and called "[Tannaitic] Talmud," had been used hitherto in preference to the dry mishnaic collections (comp. Letter of Sherira Gaon, *l.c.* pp. 18–19), most of the teachers now resorted to R. Judah's Mishnah, which included both the halakot themselves and the expository tannaitic Talmud (this fact explains the application of the name "Talmud" to his Mishnah; B. M. 33a; Yer. Shab. xvi. 15c). Interest in this work was so highly esteemed that a haggadist said: "The study of the Mishnah is equal to sacrifice" (Lev. R. vii.). Every pupil was supposed, as a matter of course, to be familiar with the Mishnah of R. Judah ha-Nasi; and when any one propounded a sentence which was to be found in it, his hearers exclaimed, "What! do we not learn that ourselves from the Mishnah?" According to R. Joshua b. Levi, "The Mishnah is a firm iron pillar"; and none may stray from it (*ib.* xxi.). "The passage, Num. xv. 31, 'He hath despised the word of the Lord,' denotes him who does not consider the Mishnah " (baraita quoted by Isaac Alfasi in his compendium to Sanh. x.). It was considered the only authority for legal decisions. R. Johanan said, "The correct halakic decision is always the one which is declared in the Mishnah to be incontrovertible" ("Halakah ki-setam Mishna"; Yeb. 42b, and parallel passages); and the most conclusive refutation of a sentence was to prove that it was contradicted by the Mishnah. If a decision was accidentally made contrary to the Mishnah, the decision at once became invalid (Sanh. 6a, 33a; Ket. 84a, 100a). The Amoraim regarded the Mishnah as the Tannaim did the Scripture; and many of them interpreted and expounded it (comp. Bacher "Ag. Bab. Amor." p. 33, note 207 on Rab). Even subsequently, when the collections which were made by the pupils of Judah ha-Nasi were widely used, his Mishnah remained the sole authority. In cases where the Mishnah conflicted with the Baraita, the former was considered decisive (Suk. 19b; B. Ḳ. 96b), while there is but a single example to show that the Gemara preferred the Baraita in such a disputed case (see JEW. ENCYC. ii. 516a, *s.v.* BARAITA). Some amoraim, such as Ilfa and Simeon b. Laḳish, even regarded the later collections as unnecessary and useless, since their entire contents were included by implication in the Mishnah, and all questions could be explained from it without the aid of the subsequent compilations (Yer. Kil. i. 6, 27a; Yer. B. Ḳ. v. 5a; Yer. Ḳid. iii. 64b; Ta'an. 22a; comp. Oppenheim, *l.c.* pp. 344–345).

Another sentence, likewise derogatory to these later collections, says: "If Rabbi has not taught it, how does R. Ḥiyya [the collector of the baraitot] know it?"

This Mishnah, however, has not been preserved in the form in which Rabbi redacted it; for, as stated above, it was subjected to many changes, and received numerous additions before it reached its definitive form. Notwithstanding the superiority of Rabbi's Mishnah to its predecessors, it had many defects, some of which may still be seen in the present Mishnah. Though Rabbi himself subsequently renounced many of his Mishnaic opinions, as his views changed in the course of time, he retained such discarded opinions in his Mishnah as he had held them in his younger days (B. M. 44a; 'Ab. Zarah 52b; Yer. 'Ab. Zarah iv. 44a). Occasionally he recorded one decision as authoritative in one passage of his Mishnah, considering it the correct view, and, deciding later in favor of an opposite opinion, he in another place gave this also as authoritative without retracting or suppressing his former view (Sheb. 4a). These shortcomings would not have been serious, since Rabbi did not intend to furnish a mere halakic code, if he had not failed to include in his collection many halakot which were taught in his school and which were, therefore, highly important, not only for halakic decision, but also for a knowledge of tradition in general. He furthermore excluded his own halakot and the points of divergence between him and his contemporaries. These omissions were the most serious defects in his Mishnah for his pupils, since, being a compendium of the entire traditional instruction, it must have seemed incomplete inasmuch as it did not include the teachings of the last tannaim, whose legal decisions should certainly have been incorporated in it if it was to serve as an authoritative code. Rabbi's pupils R. Ḥiyya, R. Hoshaiah, Levi, and Bar Ḳappara began, therefore, even during Rabbi's lifetime and with his knowledge, to make additions and emendations to his Mishnah. Rabbi, who was aware of the deficiencies of his work, probably approved many of these corrections (comp. Oppenheim, *l.c.* pp. 344 *et seq.*), and added some himself (Yer. Ket. iv. 29a, b). Most of the changes, however, were such as were contrary to his views, and were consequently concealed from him by his pupils (comp. Weiss, "Dor," ii. 191).

Thus arose new collections by R. Ḥiyya, R. Hoshaiah, and Bar Ḳappara, which were called "Mishnayot Gedolot," since they were more voluminous than Rabbi's collection. As these new compilations imperiled the uniformity of teaching, which was possible only through the existence of a Mishnah familiar to all teachers, the "Debe Rabbi" (the scholars of Rabbi's school) undertook a revision of his Mishnah, probably long after his death. They made various changes and a large number of additions in agreement with current demands; and in this form the Mishnah has been transmitted to the present time. The majority of the additions made by the Debe Rabbi betray their later origin, although some of them are known to be supplementary only by statements in the Gemara. For instance, the discussion between R. Hezekiah and R. Johanan, in Men. 104b, indicates that the passage in the present Mishnah (Men. xiii. 2), beginning "Rabbi omer," is a later addition of which Hezekiah and Johanan did not know. The same is true of Mishnah Sanh. ix. 2, since the R. Simeon there mentioned is Rabbi's son, as is shown by Yerushalmi (*ad loc.* 27a, b). Mishnah 'Ab. Zarah ii. 6, where a decision of Judah ha-Nasi is quoted, also comes in this category, since it refers to Judah II., grandson of Judah ha-Nasi I., the original redactor of the Mishnah (comp. Tos. 'Ab. Zarah 36a, *s.v.* "Asher"). In general, all the passages in which something concerning Rabbi is related, or something which he did either alone (Sheb. vi. 4) or together with his colleague (Oh. xviii. 19), must be regarded as later accretions (comp. Frankel, *l.c.* pp. 215 *et seq.*); and the same statement holds good of all the passages in which Rabbi's opinion is quoted after that of other tannaim. On the other hand, there are passages concluding with "dibre Rabbi" (the words of Rabbi), which are not necessarily additions; for Rabbi may in such instances have quoted his own opinion anonymously as setam, as he frequently did, and the words "dibre Rabbi" may have been added by later editors. Various sentences of the Tosefta also found their way into the Mishnah (comp. Hoffmann, *l.c.* pp. 156 *et seq.*). Many of these are haggadic in nature, such as those at the end of the treatises Makkot, 'Uḳẓin, Ḳinnim, Ḳiddushin, and Soṭah, as well as many sentences in the treatise Abot, which must be regarded as accretions. The later origin of many of these sentences is at once indicated by the name of the author, as in the cases of R. Joshua b. Levi, who belonged to the first generation of Amoraim ('Uḳẓin, end); Simon, son of Judah ha-Nasi (Ab. ii. 2); and Hillel, grandson of Judah ha-Nasi (*ib.* ii. 4 *et seq.*; comp. Lipmann Heller in Tos. Yom-Ṭob, *ad loc.*). Aside from these additions, the Debe Rabbi emended the phraseology and single words of the Mishnah (comp. Yer. Ḳid. iii. 64c), even as Rabbi himself had done (comp. B. M. iv. 1.; 'Ab. Zarah iv. 4, and the Babylonian and Palestinian Gemaras, *ad loc.*).

Many of Rabbi's own emendations have been preserved in the different readings of Yerushalmi and Babli, although the differences between these two versions are not all due to his changes, as Rapoport assumes ("Kerem Ḥemed," vii. 157–167); for most of the differences not due to philological causes must be ascribed to the different mishnaic schools. In addition to the Debe Rabbi, later amoraim also emended the Mishnah if the received reading seemed untenable. These emendations were then incorporated into the Mishnah; those made by the Babylonian amoraim into the Mishnah which was taught in the Babylonian schools; and those made by the Palestinian amoraim into the Mishnah as taught in the Palestinian schools. Thus, in 'Ab. Zarah i., the Mishnah in the Palestinian Talmud was corrected according to the Gemara (Yer. 'Ab. Zarah i. 39d), while the Mishnah in the Babylonian Talmud retained its original reading. Sometimes—curiously enough—the Mishnah of the Palestinian Talmud was corrected to harmonize with the results of the discussion in the Babylonian Talmud, and vice versa (comp. O. H. Schorr in "He-Ḥaluẓ," vi. 32–47; Frankel, "Mebo," pp. 19a–22a), although only a few of these emendations, of which there are many in the Talmud—introduced by the phrases "sami mi-kan" = "omit from here," or "hasuri miḥasra" = "something missing," or "teni kak" = "teach thus"—found their way into the Mishnah itself. Many of the amoraim objected to corrections in the Mishnah, holding that the phraseology chosen by the ancients in their mishnaic collections should be retained unchanged (Yer. Nazir i. 51a).

The Mishnah is written in a peculiar kind of Hebrew, which is far more different from the Hebrew of the earlier books of the Old Testament than from that of some of the later ones and which is, therefore, correctly designated as "Neo-Hebraic." This language was spoken by the people of Palestine as late as the second century of the common era, but was cultivated especially by the scholars; so that it was called "leshon ḥakamim" = "the speech of the wise." It contains many old Hebraic terms which were preserved in popular speech, although they are not found in the Bible, as well as numerous foreign elements, especially from Aramaic, Greek, and Latin; the scholars being forced to adopt these loan-words as terms for objects and concepts which were formerly unknown and for which there were no designations in the Hebrew vocabulary. Foreign words were especially used to designate implements borrowed from foreign peoples (comp. Weiss, "Mishpaṭ Leshon ha-Mishnah," pp. 1–7; A. Geiger, "Lehrbuch zur Sprache der Mischna," pp. 1–3); and these borrowed terms were so Hebraized as to be taken by many for native words.

From the first there were various opposing opinions regarding the problems when and by whom the Mishnah was reduced to writing. According to the Letter of Sherira Gaon (*l.c.* pp. 2, 9, 12), Judah ha-Nasi himself performed this task; and this view is supported by Rabbenu Nissim b. Jacob (in the preface to his "Sefer ha-Mafteaḥ," ed. J. Goldenthal, p. 3a, Vienna, 1847), Samuel Nagid (in his "Mebo ha-Talmud"), Maimonides (in the introduction to his commentary on the Mishnah and in the preface to the Yad ha-Ḥazaḳah), Meïri (in his "Bet ha-Beḥirah"), and a commentary on Pirḳe Abot (pp. 6a, 8b, 9a, Vienna, 1854);

and many other medieval authors, as well as some modern scholars (comp. Strack, "Einleitung in den Talmud," p. 54), hold the same opinion. Rashi, on the other hand (see his commentary on Shab. 13b; 'Er. 62b; B. M. 33a; Suk. 28b; Ket. 19b), with some tosafists and other medieval and modern authors (comp. Strack, *l.c.* p. 55), held not only that the Mishnah was not reduced to writing by Rabbi himself, but that even the later amoraim did not have it in written form. He maintained that it, together with the Gemara, was written by the Saboraim. This view is based principally on the passage Giṭ. 60b, which declares that it was forbidden to record halakot, as well as on certain other statements of the Amoraim (comp. *e.g.*, Tan., Ki Tissa, ed. Buber, pp. 59b *et seq.*), which draw a distinction between the Bible as being a written doctrine and the Mishnah as a system of teaching which is not and may not be reduced to writing. It is, however, extremely unlikely that such a systematized collection, dealing with problems so numerous and so diverse, could have been transmitted orally from generation to generation; and this improbability is increased by the fact that in the Talmud remarks concerning "resha" and "sefa" (the "first" and the "last" cases provided for in a single paragraph) are frequently added to Mishnah quotations, a fact explicable only on the assumption that the text of the Mishnah was definitely fixed in writing.

It must be assumed, therefore, that Rabbi himself reduced the Mishnah to writing in his old age, transgressing in a way the interdiction against recording halakot, since he deemed this prohibition liable to endanger the preservation of the doctrine. He did not abrogate this interdiction entirely, however; for the oral method of instruction continued, the teacher using the written Mishnah merely as a guide, while the pupils repeated the lesson orally. Thus the distinction between "miḳra" (the law to be read) and "mishnah" (the oral teaching) was retained (comp. "Paḥad Yiẓḥaḳ," *s.v.* "Mishnah," pp. 219 *et seq.*; Frankel, "Hodegetica in Mischnam," pp. 217–218; Brüll, "Einleitung," ii. 10–13; Weiss, "Dor," p. 216).

The Mishnah has been transmitted in four recensions: (1) the manuscripts and editions of the mishnayot; (2) the Babylonian Talmud, in which the several mishnayot are separated by the Gemara in those treatises which have it, while in the treatises which have no Gemara they follow in sequence; (3) the Palestinian Talmud, in which the Gemara follows each entire chapter of the Mishnah, the initial words of the mishnaic sentences to be expounded being repeated (of this version only the first four orders and chapters i.–iv. of the treatise Niddah of the sixth order are extant); (4) "the Mishnah on which the Palestinian Talmud rests," published by W. H. Lowe in 1883 after the Mishnah manuscript (Add. 470, 1) in the library of the University of Cambridge.

On the relation of the first three editions to one another see above (comp. A. Krochmal, "Yerushalayim ha-Benuyah," Introduction, pp. 10–14; Frankel, *l.c.* pp. 219–223; Weiss, *l.c.* ii. 313). The relation of the fourth version to the preceding three has not yet been thoroughly investigated.

The Mishnah is divided into six main parts, called orders (Aramaic, "sedarim," plural of "seder"; Hebr. " 'arakin," plural of " 'erek"), the ששה סדרי משנה (as in B. M. 85b) or the שש ערכי משנה (Pesiḳ., ed. Buber, 7a; Cant. R. vi. 4) being therefore frequently mentioned. The abbreviated name ש"ס ("shas") was formed from the initial letters of ששה סדרים (Ḥag. 3a, 10a; M. Ḳ. 10b). Each order contains a number of treatises, "masseḳtot" (Mishnah, ed. Lowe, fol. 32a; Midr. Teh. to Ps. civ.) or "massekot" (Mishnah, ed. Lowe, fol. 69a), plural of "masseket," or "massektiyyot" (Cant. R. vi. 9), the singular of which is "massekta." Each treatise is divided into chapters, "peraḳim" (singular, "pereḳ") (Ned. 8a; Ḥag. 9a; Men. 99b), and each chapter into paragraphs or sentences, "mishnayot," or "halakot" in the Palestinian Talmud (see above).

The six orders are first mentioned by R. Ḥiyya (B. M. 85b), and represent the original division. A division into five orders is nowhere mentioned, although Geiger ("Einiges über Plan," etc., p. 487), misinterpreting the Midrash passage Num. R. xiii., considers only five orders to be enumerated there. Ulla (Meg. 28b), when he alludes to those who teach and learn only four orders, does not imply that the Mishnah was divided into four orders, but refers merely to those who study only four. This conclusion is confirmed by a conversation in which Simeon b. Laḳish communicates to a man who has studied only the first four orders a sentence belonging to the sixth order (Meg. 28b). The geonic tradition ("Sha'are Teshubah," No. 143) which refers to seven orders of the Mishnah seems to include the "Small Treatises" ("Massektot Ḳeṭannot"; Hoffmann, *l.c.* pp. 98–99). The names of the orders are old, and are mentioned by Simeon b. Laḳish (Shab. 31a), who enumerates them, according to his interpretation of Isa. xxxiii. 6, in the following sequence: Zera'im, Mo'ed, Nashim, Neziḳin, Ḳodashim, Ṭohorot. This is the original order, which is found also in Num. R. xiii. There are other enumerations with different sequences. R. Tanḥuma has the following in Yalḳ., Ps. xix.: Nashim, Zera'im, Ṭohorot, Mo'ed, Ḳodashim, Nezikin. He gives another series in 'Num. R. xiii.: Nashim, Zera'ìm, Mo'ed, Ḳodashim, Ṭohorot, Neziḳin. As R. Tanḥuma evidently does not intend to give the actual sequence but only to explain the verses as referring to the orders of the Mishnah, he adapts his enumeration of the orders to the sequence of the verses. That Simeon b. Laḳish's sequence is the correct one maybe proved also from other sources. For example, Ta'an.

24b has: "In the days of Rab Judas they went in their studies only as far as the order Neziḳin; but we study all six orders." The parallel passage reads: "We have proceeded in our studies as far as 'Uḳẓin" (the end of the sixth order Ṭohorot). It is clear from Meg. 28b that formerly only four orders were studied, of which Neziḳin formed the conclusion (according to Ta'an. 24a, where the shorter course of study in former times is mentioned in another form of expression). That the treatise 'Uḳẓin of the order Ṭohorot was the end of the sixth order is shown by Ber. 20a. It is seen, therefore, that the order Neziḳin is always mentioned as the fourth, and the order Ṭohorot as the sixth and last, thus conforming to the sequence of Simeon b. Laḳish (comp. Brüll, *l.c.* ii. 15; Weiss, *l.c.* iii. 186). Isaac ibn Gabbai, author of the mishnaic commentary "Kaf Naḥat," has, consequently, no grounds for his reversal of the arrangement of the orders (comp. Lipmann Heller, *l.c.* Preface); nor is there any foundation for the attempt of Tobias Cohn to reverse the sequence ("Aufeinanderfolge der Mischna Ordnungen," in Geiger's "Jüd. Zeit." iv. 126 *et seq.*). For a justificatiou of the accepted sequence see the introduction of Maimonides to his commentary on the Mishnah; Frankel, *l.c.* p. 254; Brüll, *l.c.* ii. 15–16. It can not be ascertained whether Rabbi himself originated this sequence, or whether the orders were thus discussed in the academies. Isaac Alfasi and Asher b. Jehiel apply the Talmudic passage "En seder le-Mishnah" (= "Rabbi observed no definite sequence in the Mishnah") to the orders as well, and infer that this arrangement did not originate with Rabbi himself. Other authorities, however, assert that the passage "En seder le-Mishnah" refers only to the treatises, and not to the orders; for here Rabbi himself observed a definite series (comp. Lipmann Heller, *l.c.*; *idem*, commentary on Soṭah ix. 1). This view seems to be the correct one, since Simeon b. Laḳish, who was in his youth a pupil of Rabbi (Yer. Beẓah v. 2, 63a), refers to this sequence of the orders as being well known. The names of the several orders, which are frequently mentioned in the Talmud (Suk. 4b; Shab. 54b; Meg. 7a; Nid. 8a; Bek. 30b), were selected according to the subject of most of the treatises belonging to them.

The division of the Mishnah into treatises is a very old device, the collections upon which Rabbi drew being also arranged in this same way. II Esd. xiv. 44–46 mentions, in addition to the twenty-four written books of the Old Testament, seventy other books which may not be written down, having been given by God to Moses for oral communication to the elders of the people. According to an assumption of Ginsberg's, which is supported by a comparison of the passage in Esdras with its parallel in the Tan., Ki Tissa (ed. Buber, pp. 58b–59a), these seventy books are the seventy treatises of the oral teachings, and hence of the Mishnah. The number seventy may be obtained by counting either the seven small treatises (comp. R. Kirchheim, Preface to his edition of them, Frankfort-on-the-Main, 1851), or, as Ginsberg obtains it, the halakic midrashim Sifra and Sifre, the first of which was divided into nine parts. In any case, it is evident that the division into treatises is a very old one, and that Rabbi arranged his Mishnah in conformity with it, although, as has been said, the present division is not the original one which he adopted, but has been subjected to many changes.

Sixty-three treatises are now extant, although the traditional number is only sixty, as Cant. R. vi. 9 says, "Sixty queens, these are the sixty treatises of the halakot." The three "babot," or gates, at the beginning of the order Neziḳin formed originally only a single treatise, which also was called "Neziḳin" (B. Ḳ. 102a; B. M. 10a, b; Lev. R. xix.), and which was divided into three treatises on account of its size. Makkot was originally a dependent treatise combined with Sanhedrin, of which it formed the end (comp. Maimonides' introduction to his commentary on the Mishnah). The names of the treatises, which were derived mostly from the contents, but occasionally from the initial letter, are old, being known to the Amoraim, and in part even to the Tannaim.

The following treatises are mentioned by name in the Talmud: Baba Ḳamma and Baba Meẓi'a (B. Ḳ. 102a); Bekorot (Beẓah 20a); Berakot (B. Ḳ. 30a); 'Eduyot under the name "Beḥirta" (Ber. 27a) as well as under its own name (Ber. 28a); Kelim (Mishnah Kelim, end); Keritot (Sanh. 65a); Ketubot (Soṭah 2a); Ḳiddushin (Ḳid. 76b); Ḳodashim (B. M. 109b); Makkot (Sheb. 2b); Menaḥot (Men. 7a); Middot (Yoma 16a); Nazir and Nedarim (Soṭah 2a); Oholot under the name "Ahilot" ('Er. 79a); Rosh ha-Shanah (Ta'an. 2a); Shebu'ot (Sheb. 2b); Tamid (Yoma 14b); Terumot (Pes. 34a); 'Uḳẓin (Hor. 13b); Yoma (Yoma 14b); and Zebaḥim under the name "Sheḥitat Ḳodashim" (B. M. 109b). The names of the treatises have, however, been subjected to various changes, and have, in some cases, been replaced by later terms. Thus the earlier name "Mashḳin" gave way to the later "Mo'ed Ḳaṭan"; "Zebaḥim" was substituted for "Sheḥiṭat Ḳodashim"; and "Sheḥiṭat Ḥullin" was abbreviated to "Ḥullin" (on the names comp. A. Berliner in "Ha-Misderonah," i. 20 *et seq.*, 40 *et seq.*; see also Frankel, *l.c.* p. 255; Brüll, *l.c.* ii. 18–20). The treatises belonging to each order deal with similar subjects, or have some other bond of relationship which causes them to be placed in a given order. Although there are some tractates, such as Nazir (comp. Naz. 2a) and Berakot, which apparently do not belong to the order in which they are included, a closer examination reveals the reason for their inclusion (comp. Maimonides' introduction to his commentary on the Mishnah; Brüll, *l.c.* ii. 17–18; Weiss, *l.c.* ii. 207; Geiger, *l.c.* p. 486).

It is a harder task to define the principle on which the treatises are arranged within the various orders; and this difficulty is increased by the existence of many different sequences, especially since it is uncertain which of these is the oldest. According to the Letter of Sherira Gaon (*l.c.* pp. 12–13), Rabbi observed no definite sequence, but discoursed on each massekta singly without reference to the other treatises, changing their arrangement at will. This statement is supported by ʻAb. Zarah 7a, which states that for two treatises there was no definite order in the Mishnah—an assertion which is all the more trust, worthy since it is recognized as a principle in making halakic decisions as well. It appears, on the other hand, from various passages in the Talmud (*e.g.*, Sheb. 2b; Soṭah 2a; Taʻan. 2a), that even at an early period a certain arrangement of the several treatises within their respective orders was followed, and it is necessary, therefore, to adopt Hoffmann's view (in Berliner's "Magazin," 1890, pp. 322–323) that a definite sequence was gradually developed and observed in the course of instruction in the Palestinian and Babylonian academies. The teachers of these schools arranged their material on pedagogic lines, and in interpreting an order of the Mishnah they selected the longest treatise for the beginning of the lesson, when the minds of their pupils were still fresh, and then passed on to the smaller tractates. Likewise in Maimonides' sequence, which was the one generally adopted, the treatises from the second to the sixth order are arranged according to length, as Geiger has remarked ("Einiges über Plan," etc., in Geigers "Wiss. Zeit. Jüd. Theol." ii. 480 *et seq.*); and this principle is evident in the first order likewise (Hoffmann, *l.c.* p. 323; Geiger, *l.c.* p. 402). Maimonides' sequence seems, therefore, to have been the same as that adopted in the Palestinian and Babylonian academies, and hence was the original one (for other reasons for this sequence see Maimonides' introduction to his commentary on the Mishnah; Frankel, *l.c.* pp. 255–264; Brüll, *l.c.* ii. 20–27).

The division of the several treatises into chapters as well as the sequence of these chapters was the work of Rabbi himself (Letter of Sherira Gaon, *l.c.* p. 13). The portion discussed each day constituted an independent pereḳ; and this term was, therefore, applied elsewhere to a single discourse also (Ber. 11b; ʻEr. 36b; on a statement in the "Seder Tanna'im we-Amora'im," to the effect that the Saboraim divided the treatises into chapters, see M. Lerner, "Die Aeltesten Mischna-Compositionen," in Berliner's "Magazin," 1886, p. 3, note 1). Generally speaking, the original division and sequence of the chapters have been preserved, as appears from various passages of the Talmud (R. H. 31b; Suk. 22b; Yeb. 9a; Ket. 15a; Niddah 68b; Zeb. 15a). The names of the chapters taken from the initial letters are likewise old, and some of them are mentioned even in the Talmud (B. M. 35b; Niddah 48a). In the course of time, however, various changes were made in the division, sequence, and names of the chapters; thus, for example, the division of Tamid into seven chapters is not the original one. On other variations in sequence see Frankel, *l.c.* pp. 264–265, and on the changes in the names see Berliner in "Ha-Misderonah," i. 40b.

There are altogether 523 chapters in the Mishnah, divided as follows: Zera'im 74 (Bikkurim 3), Mo'ed Ḳaṭan 88, Nashim 71, Neziḳin 73 (Abot 5), Ḳodashim 91, Ṭohorot 126. Some authorities reckon 524 chapters by adding a sixth chapter to Abot, while others count 525 by adding a sixth chapter to Abot and a fourth chapter to Bikkurim.

The division of the chapters into paragraphs, which is likewise very old, has not been preserved in its original form, the different recensions of the present Mishnah having a different division (comp. Frankel, *l.c.* p. 265). The several paragraphs are mostly cast in the form of the fixed Halakah without a Scripture passage, although Weiss (*l.c.* ii. 211, notes 1–6) has enumerated 217 passages in which the Halakah is given together with the Scriptural text on which it is based, hence assuming the form of the Midrash. Some of these midrashic sentences in the Mishnah have the form of the earliest exegesis of the Soferim (comp. Frankel, *l.c.* p. 5), and there are also many passages modeled on the tannaitic Talmud (comp. Weiss, *l.c.* ii. 209–210).

The following is the list of the mishnaic orders with their treatises, according to Maimonides, the deviations in both Talmudim being given at the end of each order (for details see separate articles under the names of the respective orders and treatises; and on variations in certain editions of the Mishnah comp. Strack, *l.c.* pp. 9–12):

I. The order **Zera'im** ("Seeds") contains the following eleven treatises: (1) Berakot ("Blessings"), divided into nine chapters; deals with the rules for the daily prayer, and other prayers and blessings. (2) Pe'ah ("Corner"); eight chapters; deals with the regulations concerning the corners of the field (Lev. xix. 9, 10; xxiii. 22; Deut. xxiv. 19–22), and with the rights of the poor in general. (3) Demai ("Doubtful"); seven chapters; deals chiefly with various cases in which it is not certain whether the offering of the fruit has been given to the priests. (4) Kilayim ("Of Two Sorts"; "Heterogeneous"); nine chapters; deals chiefly with rules regarding forbidden mixtures (Lev. xix. 19; Deut. xxii. 9–11). (5) Shebi'it ("Sabbatical Year"); ten chapters; deals with the regulations concerning the seventh year (Ex. xxiii. 11; Lev. xxv. 1–8; Deut. xv. 1 *et seq.*). (6) Terumot ("Offerings"); eleven chapters; deals with the laws regarding the offering to be given to the priest (Num. xviii. 8 *et seq.*; Deut. xviii. 4). (7) Ma'aserot or Ma'aser Rishon ("Tithes" or "First Tithes"); five chapters; deals with the prescription regarding the tithe to be given to the Levites (Num. xviii. 21–24). (8) Ma'aser Sheni ("Second Tithe"); five chapters; deals with the rules concerning the tithe or its equivalent which was to be eaten at Jerusalem (Deut. xiv. 22–26). (9) Ḥallah ("Cake"); four chapters; deals with the laws regarding the heave-offering of dough to he given to the priests (Num. xv. 18–21). (10) 'Orlah ("Foreskin of the Trees"); three chapters; deals chiefly with the regulations of Lev. xix. 23–25. (11) Bikkurim ("First-Fruits"); three chapters; deals with the laws in Ex. xxiii. 19; Deut. xxvi. 1 *et seq.*

In many editions of the Mishnah, even early ones like those of Naples 1492, and of Riva 1559, as well as in most of the editions of the Babylonian Talmud, a fourth chapter to the eleventh treatise, which does not belong to the Mishnah, has been added (comp. the gloss in the Wilna edition of the Talmud, p. 87b). The sequence of the treatises of this first order in both the Talmudim corresponds with that of Maimonides.

II. Mo'ed ("Festivals") includes the following twelve treatises: (1) Shabbat ("Sabbath"); twenty-four chapters; deals with the laws regarding the seventh day as a day of rest (Ex. xvi. 23 *et seq.*, xx. 8–11, xxiii. 12, xxxiv. 21, xxxv. 2–3; Deut. v. 12–15). (2) 'Erubin ("Mingling"); ten chapters; deals with the means by which inconvenient regulations regarding the Sabbath may be legally obviated. (3) Pe-saḥim ("Passover Festivals"); ten chapters; deals with the prescriptions regarding the Passover and the paschal sacrifice (Ex. xii., xiii. 6–8, xxiii. 15, xxxiv. 15 *et seq.*; Lev. xxiii. 5 *et seq.*; Num. ix. 2–14, xxviii. 16 *et seq.*). (4) Sheḳalim ("Shek-els"); eight chapters; treats chiefly of the poll-tax of a half-shekel for each male, prescribed in Ex. xxx. 12–16, and which was devoted to defraying the expenses of the services of the Temple. (5) Yoma ("Day"), called also "Kippurim" or "Yom ha-Kippurim" (= "Day of Atonement"); eight chapters; deals with the prescrip-tions regarding worship and fasting on the Day of Atonement (Lev. xvi., xxiii. 26–32). (6) Sukkah or Sukkot ("Booth"); five chapters; deals with the regulations concerning the Feast of Tabernacles, the Tabernacle, and the garland on it (Lev. xxiii. 34–36; Num. xxix. 12 *et seq.*; Deut. xvi. 13–16). (7) Beẓah ("Egg"; so called from the first word, but originally termed, according to its subject, "Yom-Ṭob" = "Feast-Day"); five chapters; deals chiefly with the rules to be observed on the feast-days. (8) Rosh ha-Shanah ("New-Year Feast"); four chapters; deals chiefly with the regulation of the calendar by the new moon, and with the services on the New-Year. (9) Ta'anit ("Fasting"); four chapters; deals chiefly with the special fast-days in times of drought or other untoward occurrences. (10) Megillah ("Esther Scroll"): four chapters; contains chiefly regulations and prescriptions regarding the reading of the scroll of Esther at Purim, and the reading of other passages in the synagogue. (11) Mo'ed Ḳaṭan ("Half-Feasts"; originally called "Mashḳin," after its initial word); three chapters; deals with the regulations concerning the intermediate feast-days, or the days between the first two and the last two days of Pesaḥ and Sukkah. (12) Ḥagigah ("Feasting"); three chapters; deals among other things with the manner of observance of the three principal feasts.

In the Babylonian Talmud the treatises of the order Mo'ed are arranged as fol-lows: Shabbat, 'Erubin, Pesaḥim, Beẓah, Ḥagigah, Mo'ed Ḳaṭan, Rosh ha-Shanah, Ta'anit, Yoma, Sukkah, Sheḳalim, and Megillah; while the sequence in the Pal-estinian Talmud is Shabbat, 'Erubin, Pesaḥim, Yoma, Sheḳalim, Sukkah, Rosh ha-Shanah, Beẓah, Ta'anit, Megillah, Ḥagigah, and Mo'ed Ḳaṭan.

III. Nashim ("Women") contains the following seven treatises: (1) Yebamot ("Widows Obliged to Contract a Levirate Marriage"); sixteen chapters; deals chiefly with the rules for the levirate marriage and of the ḤALIẒAH, whereby the widow is enabled to contract another marriage (Deut. xxi. 5–10). (2) Ketubot ("Marriage Contracts); thirteen chapters; deals chiefly with the mutual duties and rights of husband and wife. (3) Nedarim ("Vows"); eleven chapters; deals with the regulations concerning vows (Num. xxx. 2–17). (4) Nazir ("Nazarite"; called also "Nezirut" = "Nazariteship"); nine chapters; deals chiefly with the prescriptions regarding the Nazarite vows (Num. vi. 1–21). (5) Giṭṭin ("Documents"; "Bills of Divorce"); nine chapters; deals chiefly with the laws for the dissolution of marriage (Deut. xxiv. 1–4). (6) Soṭah ("Woman Suspected of Adultery"); nine chapters; deals chiefly with rules concerning a woman suspected of infidelity (Num. v. 11–31). (7) Ḳiddushin ("Betrothal"); four chapters; discusses the question how, by what means, and under what conditions a legal marriage may be contracted.

In the Babylonian Talmud the sequence of the treatises in this order is as follows: Yebamot, Ketubot, Ḳiddushin, Giṭṭin, Nedarim, Nazir, and Soṭah. In the Palestinian Talmud the sequence is: Yebamot, Soṭah, Ketubot, Nedarim, Giṭṭin, Nazir, and Ḳiddushin.

IV. Neziḳin ("Injuries"; called also "Yeshu'ot"="Deeds of Help," as in Num. R. xiii.) contains the following ten treatises: (1) Baba Ḳamma ("First Gate"); ten chapters; deals chiefly with injuries and compensation for damages. (2) Baba Meẓi'a ("Middle Gate"); ten chapters; deals chiefly with the laws relating to sales, leases, objects found, and usury, (3) Baba Batra ("Last Gate"); ten chapters; deals chiefly with the rights of sale, the ownership of real estate, and the rights of succession. (4) Sanhedrin ("Court of Law"); eleven chapters; deals chiefly with judicial procedure and criminal law. (5) Makkot ("Blows," "Punishments"); three chapters; deals chiefly with the regulations concerning the number of stripes imposed as punishment by law (Deut. xxv. 1–3). (6) Shebu'ot ("Oaths"); eight chapters; deals chiefly with the rules regarding different oaths (Lev. v. 4 *et seq.*). (7) 'Eduyot, or 'Ediyyot ("Evidences"); eight chapters; contains the testimony of later teachers regarding statements of earlier authorities, a large part of this material being contained in other portions of the Mishnah as well. (8) 'Abodah Zarah ("Idolatrous Worship"); five chapters; deals chiefly with the regulations concerning the attitude of the Jews toward idolatry and idolaters. (9) Abot, or Pirḳe Abot ("Sayings of the Fathers"); five chapters; contains maxims and aphorisms. A sixth chapter called "Pereḳ Ḳinyan ha-Torah" (="Acquisition of the Law") was subsequently added to this treatise, but it does not belong to the Mishnah. (10) Horayot, or Hora'ot ("Decisions"); three chapters; deals chiefly with such religious and legal decisions as had been made through error.

The sequence of these treatises is as follows in the Babylonian Talmud: Baba Ḳamma, Baba Mezi'a, Baba Batra, 'Abodah Zarah, Sanhedrin, Makkot, Shebu'ot, Horayot, 'Eduyot, and Abot. The usual sequence is observed in the Mishnah of the Palestinian Talmud.

V. Ḳodashim ("Holy Things") contains the following eleven treatises: (1) Zebaḥim ("Sacrifice"; originally called "Sheḥiṭat Ḳodashim" = "Slaughtering of the Holy Animals"; B. M.'109b)'; fourteen chapters; deals chiefly with the laws regarding sacrifices (Lev. i. *et seq.*). (2) Menaḥot ("Meat-Offering"); thirteen chapters; deals chiefly with the rules concerning meat-offerings (Lev. ii.; v. 11–13; vi. 7–16; vii. 9–10; xiv. 10–20; xxiii. 13, 16; Num. v. 11 *et seq.*, *vi.* 13–20, xv. 24, xxviii., xxix.). (3) Ḥullin ("Profane": called also "Sheḥiṭat Ḥullin"—"Slaughtering of Non-Consecrated Animals"); twelve chapters; deals chiefly with the laws for slaughtering and with other rules relating to the eating of meat. (4) Bekorot ("First-Born"); nine chapters; deals chiefly with the regulations concerning the various firstlings (Ex. xiii. 2, 12 *et seq.*; Lev. xxvii. 26 *et seq.*; Num. viii. 16–18, xviii. 15–17; Deut. xv. 19 *et seq.*). (5) 'Arakin ("Estimations"); nine chapters; deals chiefly with the prescriptions regarding the ransom of those who have been dedicated to God (Lev. xxvii. 2 *et seq.*). (6) Temurah ("Exchange"); seven chapters; deals chiefly with the laws regarding the exchange of a dedicated animal (Lev. xxvii. 10, 33). (7) Keritot ("Extirpations"); six chapters; deals among other subjects with the punishment by excommunication ("karet"), which is frequently mentioned in the Old Testament. (8) Me'ilah ("Trespass"); six chapters; deals with the rules concerning trespass in the case of a dedicated object (Num. v. 6–8). (9) Tamid ("The Daily Morning and Evening Burnt Offering"); deals among other subjects with the regulations for the daily sacrifice (Ex. xxix. 38–42; Num. xxviii. 2–8). In the editions of the Mishnah, Tamid is divided into seven chapters, excepting in Löwe's edition, where it has but six; while Levi b. Gershon (RaLBaG) enumerates only five chapters for Tamid in the introduction to his commentary on the Pentateuch. (10) Middot ("Measures"); five chapters; describes the apartments and furniture of the Temple. (11) Ḳinnim ("Birds' Nests"); three chapters; deals with the prescriptions regarding the offering of doves (Lev. i. 14–17, v. 1 *et seq.*, xii. 8).

In the Babylonian Talmud the sequence of the treatises of this order, is as follows: Zebaḥim, Menaḥot, Bekorot, Ḥullin, 'Arakin, Temurah, Keritot, Meli'ah, Ḳinnim, Tamid, and Middot.

VI. Ṭohorot ("Purifications") contains the following twelve treatises: (1) Kelim ("Utensils"); thirty chapters; deals chiefly with the regulations concerning the different kinds of uncleanness of vessels (Lev. xi. 32 *et seq.*; Num. xix. 14 *et seq.*, xxxi. 20 *et seq.*). (2) Oholot, or Ahilot ("Tents"); eighteen chapters; deals chiefly with the laws regarding the defilement occasioned by a corpse (Num. xix. 14–20). (3) Nega'im ("Leprosy"); fourteen chapters; deals with the rules concerning the various kinds of leprosy (Lev. xiii., xiv.) (4) Parah ("Red Heifer"); twelve chapters; deals with the regulations concerning the red heifer and the purificative ashes obtained from it (Num. xix.). (5) Ṭohorot ("Purities"; euphemistic for "Impurities"); ten chapters; deals with minor defilements. (6) Miḳwa'ot, or Miḳwot ("Ritual Baths"); ten chapters; deals with the regulations concerning the bathing of the defiled (Lev. xiv. 8, xv. 5 *et seq.*). (7) Niddah ("Menstruous Woman"); ten chapters; deals with the laws concerning the defilement caused by menstruation (Lev. xii., xv. 19 *et seq.*). (S) Makshirin ("Predisposings"; called also "Mashḳin" = "Liquids"); six chapters; deals with the rule which declares that an object is defiled by contact with anything unclean only in case it was wet beforehand (Lev. xi. 34, 37, 38). (9) Zabim ("Sufferers from Discharges"); five chapters; deals with the rules in Lev. xv. (10) Ṭebul Yom ("He Who Has Taken a Ritual Bath on That Same Day"); four chapters; deals chiefly with the effect produced upon an entire object which has come in contact with a "ṭebul yom," who, according to Lev. xv. 5, is unclean until sundown, even though this contact has been only partial. (11) Yadayim ("Hands"); four chapters; deals chiefly with the defilement and cleansing of the hands. (12) 'Uḳẓin ("Stems"); three chapters; deals chiefly with the relation of the fruit to the stems, skins, and seeds, with reference to defilement, uncleanness of the fruit affecting the stems, skins, and seeds, and vice versa.

In the Babylonian Talmud the sequence of the treatises in Ṭohorot is as follows: Niddah, Kelim, Oholot, Nega'im, Parah, Ṭohorot, Miḳwa'ot, Makshirin, Zabim, Ṭebul Yom, Yadayim, and 'Uḳẓin.

The Mishnah is extant in many editions, although only the earlier ones can be mentioned here: first edition, Naples, 1492, fol., with the Hebrew commentary of Maimonides; Venice, Justiniani, 1546–50, fol.; Venice, 1549, 4to, with the commentary of Obadiah Bertinoro; Riva di Trento, 1559, fol., with the commentaries of Maimonides and Obadiah; Sabbionetta and Mantua, 1559–63, 4to; Venice, 1606, fol., with the same two commentaries.

Many commentaries on the Mishnah have been written. Maimonides wrote one in Arabic with a general introduction on the history, origin, and arrangement of the Mishnah. This commentary, which was translated into Hebrew several times, is printed in many editions of the text. The Arabic original of several treatises has recently been published, in addition to that of the entire sixth order, edited by Derenbourg (comp. the enumeration in Strack, *l.c.* p. 113 and Appendix); the Hebrew translation, which is faulty in many passages, being corrected to agree with it.

Asher b. Jehiel of Germany (d. Toledo 1327) wrote a commentary on the first and sixth orders, which was first printed in the Amsterdam edition of the Talmud, 1714–16, and in the Frankfort-on-the-Main edition, 1720–21. R. Samson of Sens also wrote a commentary on the same orders, which is printed in most of the editions of the Talmud. R. Obadiah Bertinoro (end of 15th cent.) wrote a commentary on the entire Mishnah, which is printed in most editions. The commentaries "Tosefot Yom-Ṭob" by Yom-Ṭob Lipmann Heller (1579–1654) and "Tif'eret Yisrael" by Israel Lipschütz are likewise printed in many editions of the Mishnah. The following commentaries may also be mentioned: "Kaf Naḥat," by Isaac ibn Gabbai, printed in the Venice edition of the Mishnah, 1609, and in some other editions; "'Eẓ ha-Ḥayyim" (Leghorn, 1653 *et seq.*), by Jacob Ḥagiz; "Ḳab we-Naḳi," by Elisha b. Abraham, in ed. Amsterdam, 1697, 1698, etc.; "Zera' Yiẓḥaḳ," by Isaac b. Jacob Ḥayyut, Frankfort-on-the-Oder, 1739; "Sefer Bet Dawid," Amsterdam, 1739; "Melo Kaf Naḥat," by Senior Phoebus b. Jacob, in ed. Offenbach, 1737; Berlin, 1832–34; "Sefer Mishnat Rabbi Natan," on Zera'im (Frankfort-on-the-Main, 1862), by Nathan Adler; and "Liḳḳuṭe ha-Mishnah" (Breslau, 1873), by Shraga Phoebus Frenkel.

Of the translations of the Mishnah the following may be mentioned: (1) "Mischna sive Totius Hebræorum Juris, Rituum, Antiquitatum ac Legum Oralium Systema cum Clarissimorum Rabbinorum Maimonidis et Bartenoræ Commentariis Integris; Quibus Accedunt Variorum Auctorum Notæ ac Versiones in Eos Quos Ediderunt Codices; Latinitate Dona vit ac Notis Illustravit Guilielmus Surenhusius," Amsterdam, 1698–1703,

6 vols., fol.; the text in Hebrew and Latin, with the commentaries of Maimonides and Obadiah Bertinoro in a Latin translation. (2) "Mishnayot," Berlin, 1832–34, 6 parts, 4to. (3) Vocalized Hebrew text of the Mishnah, with German translation in Hebrew letters. (4) The commentary "Melo Kaf Naḥat," and (5) a brief German introduction with notes, published by the Gesellschaft von Freunden des Gesetzes und der Erkenntniss, generally known as "Jost's translation." (6) Johann Jacob Rabe, "Mischnah, oder der Text des Talmuds Uebersetzt und Erläutert," 6 parts, 4to, Onolzbach, 1760–1763. A new edition of the vocalized Hebrew text with a German translation has been undertaken by D. Hoffmann and E. Baneth, of which several parts have appeared. An Italian translation by Vittorio Castiglione is likewise in course of publication (1904).

BIBLIOGRAPHY: *Letter of Sherira Gaon*, ed. Neubauer, in *M. J. C.* pp. 3–41, Oxford, 1887; Maimonides, introduction to his commentary on the Mishnah, printed in many editions of the Talmud after the treatise *Berakot*; Z. Frankel, *Hodegetica in Mischnam*, Leipsic, 1859; J. Brüll, *Mebo ha-Mishnah*, part i., Frankfort-on-the-Main, 1876; part ii., *ib.* 1885; S. J. Rapoport, in *Kerem Ḥemed*, vii. 157–167; A. Krochmal, *Toledot R. Yehudah ha-Nasi*, in *He-Ḥaluẓ*, ii. 75–83; idem, *ib.* iii. 118–124; *idem*, preface to his *Yerushalayim ha-Benuyah*, Lemberg, 1867; O. H. Schorr, in *He-Ḥaluz*, 1866, pp. 41–44; vi. 32–47; Z. Frankel, *Introductio in Talmud Hierosolymitanum*, pp. 19a–22a, Breslau, 1870; Joachim Oppenheim, *Zur Gesch. der Mischna*, in *Bet Talmud*, ii. 143–151, 172–179, 237–245, 269–273, 304–315, 343–355 (also reprinted separately, Presburg, 1882); A. Geiger, *Einiges über Plan und Anordnung der Mischna*, in Geiger's *Wiss. Zeit. Jüd. Theol.* 1836, ii. 474–492; idem, *Lehrbuch zur Sprache der Mischna*, Breslau, 1845; Isaac Lampronti, *Paḥad Yiẓḥaḳ*, s.v. *Mishnah*; W. Landsberg, *Plan und System in der Aufeinanderfolge der Einzelnen Mischnas*, in *Monatsschrift*, 1873, pp. 208–215; Tobias Cohn, *Aufeinanderfolge der Mischnaordnungen*, in Geiger's *Jüd. Zeit.* 1866, iv. 126–140; Dünner, *Veranlassung, Zweck und Entwicklung der Halakischen und Halakischexegetischen Sammlungen Während der Tannaimperiode im Umriss Dargestellt*, in *Monatsschrift*, 1871, pp. 137 *et seq.*, 158 *et seq.*, 313 *et seq.*, 363 *et seq.*, 416 *et seq.*, 449 *et seq.*, idem, *R. Jehuda Hanasi's Anteil an Unserer Mischna*, ib. 1872, pp. 161 *et seq.*, 218 *et seq.*; idem, *Einiges über Ursprung und Bedeutung des Traktates Edoyot*, ib. 1871, pp. 33–42, 59–77; D. Hoffmann, *Die Erste Mischna und die Controversen der Tannaim*, Berlin, 1882; idem, *Bemerkungen zur Kritik der Mischna*, in Berliner's *Magazin*, 1881, pp. 121–130,169–177; 1882, pp. 96–105, 152–163; 1884, pp. 17–30, 88–92, 126–127; M. Lerner, *Die Aeltesten Mischna-Compositionen*, ib. 1886, pp. 1–20; J. Derenbourg, *Les Sections et les Traités de la Mischna*, in *R. E. J.* 1881, iii. 205–210; A. Berliner, in *Ha-Misderonah*, i. 20 *et seq.*, 40 *et seq.*; J. S. Bloch, *Einblicke in die Gesch. der Entstehung der Talmudischen Literatur*, Vienna, 1884; I. H. Weiss, *Dor*, ii. 182–184, 207–217; idem, *Mishpat Leshon ha-Mishnah*, ib. 1867; L. A. Rosenthal, *Ueber den Zusammenhang der Mischna; Ein Beitrag zu Ihrer Entstehungsgesch.* Strasburg, 1891–92; idem, *Die Mischna, Aufbau und Quellenscheidung*, ib. 1903.

E. C. J. Z. L.

N

NAḤMAN BAR ISAAC: Babylonian amora of the fifth generation; died in 356; like Raba, a pupil of R. Naḥman b. Jacob. While he was still young his halakic knowledge was known and esteemed; and he was chosen resh kallah (see JEW. ENCYC. i. 146b, *s.v.* ACADEMIES IN BABYLONIA). He went to Sura, where R. Naḥman b. Ḥisda drew particular attention to him and frequently repeated his responsa in the bet ha-midrash (Ḥul. 88b; Shebu. 12b; Ta'an. 21b).

At Raba's death Naḥman bar Isaac became his successor as head of the school which was transferred from Maḥuza to Pumbedita. This position he held for four years. He contributed to the Halakah chiefly by collecting, arranging, and transmitting the teachings and decisions of his predecessors, which were thus saved from oblivion. He also employed mnemonic sentences to facilitate the memorization of the halakot which he had arranged, thus beginning the redaction of the Talmud. He recognized distinctly his position as regards the Halakah, saying of himself "I am neither a sage nor a seer, nor even a scholar as contrasted with the majority. I am a transmitter and a codifier, and the bet ha-midrash follows me in its decisions" (Pes. 105b). He is frequently mentioned in the Haggadah as one who arranges and explains the words of other authorities, and he frequently cites Biblical passages in support of their teachings ('Ar. 33a). When the interpretations of others deviate from the Masoretic vocalization, Naḥman endeavors to show that reference to the consonantal basis of the word in question allows such varying explanations (Yoma 38b, 75b). He often interprets rare or ambiguous terms in the Mishnah by citing analogous passages (Beẓah 35b; Yoma 32b).

On the other hand, Naḥman has also many independent maxims of his own, of which the following may serve as examples: "Why is wisdom likened to a tree? (Prov. iii. 18). Because as a tiny piece of wood kindles a large one, so the small promotes the great in the study of the Law" (Ta'an. 7a). "Conceit is altogether reprehensible" (Soṭah 5a). So is anger (Ned. 22b). "Pride is expressly forbidden in the Torah" (Soṭah 19a; comp. Deut. viii. 14).

Naḥman affected a witty mode of expression; and he often played on the names of the scholars who brought baraitot before him (Ber. 39b, 53b; Giṭ. 41a). He also frequently employed proverbs (Yoma 86a; Shab. 54a; Soṭah 22a).

BIBLIOGRAPHY: Hamburger, *R. B. T.* ii. 83 *et seq.*; Bacher, *Ag. Bab. Amor.* pp. 133–134.

W. B. J. Z. L.

NAḤMAN BAR JACOB (generally called simply **R. Naḥman**): Babylonian amora of the third generation; died 320; pupil of Mar Samuel. He was chief justice of the Jews who were subject to the exilarch, and was also head of the school of Nehardea. On the destruction of that town, he transferred his pupils to Shekanẓib. His marriage with the daughter of the wealthy resh galuta enabled him to live in luxury and to entertain scholars and strangers lavishly. Thus R. Isaac of Palestine, who visited Babylon, stayed at Naḥman's house and enjoyed his hospitality. When the guest on leaving was asked by his host to bless him, the former answered with the beautiful parable of the tree which sheltered the weary traveler beneath its shade and fed him with its fruit, so that the grateful wanderer blessed it with the words, "May thy scions be like unto thee." "And I," added R. Isaac, "can bless thee, who art blessed with material and spiritual wealth, only with the prayer that thy scions too may be like unto thee" (Ta'an. 5b–6a). R. Naḥman had such a sense of his own worth that he said: "If some one now living were to become the Messiah, he must resemble me" (Sanh. 98b). He also permitted himself, in his capacity of justice, to decide civil cases without consulting his colleagues (*ib.* 5a). He was likewise the author of the important ruling that a defendant who absolutely denies his guilt must take the so-called rabbinical oath "shebu'at hesset" (Shebu. 40b). As a haggadist, Naḥman was less important, although he is said to have used many collections of haggadot (Ber. 23b). He was fond of collecting in one passage a number of Aramaic aphorisms (see Yoma 28b–29a), and used sturdy popular expressions in his speech (Ḥul. 12a, 172a; Ta'an. 24a). His haggadic remarks relating to Biblical personages were likewise made in this style, as the following specimens will show: "It is not seemly for women to be conceited; the two prophetesses Deborah and Huldah had hateful names, namely, 'bee' and 'weasel'" (Meg. 14b). "Shamelessness avails even in the face of Heaven; for God allowed Balaam to make the journey to Balak after He had forbidden it" (Sanh. 105a).

BIBLIOGRAPHY: Hamburger, *R. B. T.* ii. 819 *et seq.*; Bacher, *Ag. Bab. Amor.* pp. 79–83; *Seder ha-Dorot*, pp. 283 *et seq.*

W. B. J. Z. L.

NAHUM OF GIMZO: Tanna of the second generation (first century). In the Talmud (Ta'an. 21a; Yer. Sheḳ. v. 15) he is called "ish gam zu" (the man of "gam zu"); and this name is explained as referring to Nahum's motto. It is said that on every occasion, no matter how unpleasant the circumstance, he exclaimed "Gam zu le-ṭobah" (This, too, will be for the best). The correct reading in the passages in question, however, is "ish Gimzo" (the man of Gimzo), the error being due to a confusion of the place-name with the motto. In another Talmudic passage (Pes. 22b; comp. Ḳid. 57a), owing to a confusion of ג and ע, he is called "Nehemiah the 'Imsoni" (= "Gimsoni"; comp. Grätz in "Monatsschrift," 1870, p. 527).

Nahum was the teacher of Akiba, and taught him the exegetical principles of inclusion and exclusion ("ribbui u-mi'uṭ"). Only one halakah of his has been preserved (Ber. 22a); but it is known that he interpreted the whole Torah according to the rule of "ribbui u-mi'uṭ" (Shebu. 26a). He used to explain the accusative particle את by saying that it implied the inclusion in the object of something besides that which is explicitly mentioned. In the sentence "Thou shalt fear the Lord thy God" (Deut. x. 20), however, he did not explain the word את before יהוה (= "the Lord"), since he did not wish to cause any one to share in the reverence due to God; and he justified his inconsistency with the explanation that the omission in this passage was as virtuous as was the interpretation in all the other passages (Pes. 22b).

It is related that in later years Nahum's hands and feet became paralyzed, and he was afflicted with other bodily ailments. He bore his troubles patiently, however, and even rejoiced over them. In answer to a question of his pupils as to why, since he was such a perfectly just man, he had to endure so many ills, he declared that he had brought them on himself because once when he was on the way to his father-in-law's and was carrying many things to eat and drink, he met a poor man who asked him for food. As he was about to open the bundle the man died before his eyes. In deepest grief, and reproaching himself with having perhaps caused by his delay the man's death, he cursed himself and wished himself all the troubles to which his pupils referred (Ta'an. 21a). Various other stories are told of miracles that happened to him (*ib.*).

BIBLIOGRAPHY: J. Brüll, *Einleitung in die Mischna*, i. 94–95; Bacher, *Ag. Tan.* i. 61–64.

W. B. J. Z. L.

NAHUM THE MEDE: Tanna of the first generation (first century); lived in Jerusalem. According to R. Nathan, he was one of the three most renowned "dayyane gezelot" (criminal judges) in Jerusalem (Ket. 105a; Yer. Ket. xiii. 1; Frankel, "Darke ha-Mishnah," p. 63). He was one of the seven great contemporaries of Johanan b. Zakkai who had survived the destruction of Jerusalem by the Romans (Grätz, "Gesch." iv. 20) and who probably became members of the Sanhedrin at Jabneh.

Only six halakot of Nahum's have been preserved in the Talmud, three of which were said not to have been recognized ("nishtaḳa' ha-dabor"; 'Ab. Zarah 7). Some, however, attribute to him four other and anonymous halakot (Weiss, "Dor," i. 182).

The opposition to the decisions of Nahum, according to the view of a later amora, seems to have been due to the dislike of the Palestinians to scholars of other countries.

BIBLIOGRAPHY: Grätz, *Gesch*, iv. 22; Frankel, *Darke ha-Mishna*, p. 63, Leipsic, 1859.

E. C. A. S. W.

NATHAN: Palestinian tanna of the third generation (2d cent.); son of a Babylonian exilarch. For some unknown reason he left Babylonia and his bright prospects there for Palestine, where he was made chief of the school at Usha (Hor. 13b; Grätz, "Gesch." iv. 185). Later he was entrusted by the patriarch R. Simon b. Gamaliel III. to secure a reconciliation with R. Hananiah of Babylon, who had declared himself independent of the Sanhedrin of Judea and had established one in Babylon—a mission which Nathan, in company with R. Isaac, successfully executed (Grätz, *l.c.* pp. 188 *et seq.*). According to Halevy (in "Dorot ha-Rishonim," p. 185), however, both Nathan and Isaac were still residents of Babylon.

Soon afterward dissensions occurred between Nathan and R. Meïr, on the one side, and the president, R. Simon, on the other, owing to an attempt by the latter to abolish the equality hitherto existing among all members of the school, by restricting the tokens of esteem shown by the community to other members of the school lower in distinction than the president. Nathan and Meïr conspired to depose Simon and to usurp his authority themselves; but the plot came to his knowledge, and he caused the conspirators to be expelled from the school. The two knew, however, how to make their absence felt. They sent in slips on which were written puzzling halakic questions; so that a member of the school once exclaimed: "We are inside, and the learning is outside!" Both Nathan and Meïr were ultimately readmitted on condition that the name of neither should thenceforth be mentioned in connection with his halakic decisions, but that a pseudonym should be used instead. In the case of Nathan this pseudonym was "some say"; in that of Meïr, "others say" (Hor. 13b).

Nathan was a high Talmudic authority. Numerous halakic decisions and haggadic sayings of his are recorded. To him is attributed also the authorship of the treatise entitled "Abot de-Rabbi Natan," a kind of tosefta to the Pirḳe Abot. He is said also to have been the author of the baraita "Mem Ṭet Middot," no longer extant, on Haggadah and mathematics (Frankel, "Darke ha-Mishnah," p. 191, Leipsic, 1859).

Nathan's chief opponent in halakic decisions was the patriarch R. Judah I., whom, however, he is said to have assisted in the collaboration of the Mishnah (B. M. 86a, and Rashi *ad loc.*) and who held him in high esteem (B. B. 131a).

BIBLIOGRAPHY: Grätz, *Gesch.* ed. Leipsic, 1893, iv. 173, 185, 187; Heilprin, *Seder ha-Dorot*, ii. 290, Warsaw, 1882; Halevy, *Dorot ha-Rishonim*, ii. 97, 185, Frankfort-on-the-Main, 1901; *Abot de-Rabbi Natan*, ed. Schechter, Vienna, 1887; the article ABOT DE-RABBI NATAN and the bibliography there given.

W. B. A. S. W.

NEHARDEA (NEARDA): City of Babylonia, situated at or near the junction of the Euphrates with the Nahr Malka; one of the earliest centers of Babylonian Judaism. As the seat of the exilarch it traced its origin back to King Jehoiachin. According to Sherira Gaon (Letter of Sherira Gaon, in Neubauer, "M. J. C." i. 26), Jehoiachin and his co-exilarchs built a synagogue at Nehardea, for the foundation of which they used earth and stones which they had brought, in accordance with the words of Ps. cii. 17 (A. V. 16), from Jerusalem (comp. a similar statement in regard to the founding of the Jewish city of Ispahan, in "Monatsschrift," 1873, pp. 129, 181). This was the synagogue called "Shaf we-Yatib," to which there are several references dating from the third and fourth centuries (R. H. 24b; 'Ab. Zarah 43b; Niddah 13a), and which Abaye asserts (Meg. 29a) was the seat of the Shekinah in Babylonia. The Aaronic portion of the Jewish population of Nehardea was said to be descended from the slaves of Pashur ben Immer, the contemporary of King Jehoiachin (Ḳid. 70b).

There are also other allusions in the Talmud (*ib.*) casting doubt upon the purity of blood of the Nehardean Jews. The fact that Hyrcanus, the high priest, lived for a time in that city as a captive of the Parthians (Josephus, "Ant." xv. 1, § 2) may explain the circumstance that as late as the third century certain of its inhabitants traced their descent back to the Hasmoneans. The importance of the city during the last century of the existence of the Second Temple appears from the following statement made by Josephus (*ib.* xviii. 9, § 1): "The city of Nehardea is thickly populated, and among other advantages possesses an extensive and fertile territory. Moreover, it is impregnable, as it is surrounded by the Euphrates and is strongly fortified." Reference to the extent of the territory of Nehardea is made in the Talmud also (Ket. 54a). In addition to the Euphrates, the "King's Canal" (Nehar [Nahr] Malka) formed one of the natural defenses of the city (Ḳid. 70b; Shab. 108b); the ferry over the river (or perhaps over the canal) is likewise mentioned (Ḳid. 70b; Ḥul. 50b). "Nehardea and Nisibis," says Josephus further (*ib.*), "were the treasuries of the Eastern Jews; for the Temple taxes were kept there until the stated days for forwarding them to Jerusalem." Nehardea was the native city of the two brothers ANILAI and ASINAI, who in the first third of the first century C.E. founded a robber-state on the Euphrates, and caused much trouble to the Babylonian Jews. After the destruction of Jerusalem, Nehardea is first mentioned in connection with R. Akiba's sojourn there (Yeb., end). From the post-Hadrianic tannaitic period there is the anecdote referring to the debt which AḤAI B. JOSIAH had to collect at Nehardea (Giṭ. 14b; Bacher, "Ag. Tan." ii. 385).

Nehardea emerges clearly into the light of history at the end of the tannaitic period. Shela's school was then prominent, and served to pave the way for the activity of the Babylonian academies. Samuel, whose father, Abba b. Abba, was an authority in Nehardea, established the reputation of its academy, while Rab, who likewise taught there for a time, made Sura, situated on the Euphrates about twenty parasangs from Nehardea, the seat of an academy destined to achieve a still greater reputation. The history of Nehardea is summed up in that of Samuel's activity (see SAMUEL B. ABBA). Soon after his death (254) it was destroyed by Papa b. Neser (Odenathus), in 259; and its place as seat of the second academy was taken by Pumbedita.

Nehardea, however, soon regained its importance; for the eminent Naḥman b. Jacob dwelt there. There are several references to his activity (see Ḳid. 70a; B. B. 153a; Ket. 97a; Meg. 27b). Raba tells of a walk which he took with Naḥman through the "Shoemaker street," or, according to another version, through the "Scholars' street" (Ḥul. 48b). Certain gates of Nehardea, which even in the time of Samuel were so far covered with earth that they could not be closed, were uncovered by Naḥman ('Er. 6b). Two sentences in which Naḥman designates Nehardea as "Babel" have been handed down (B. Ḳ. 83a; B. B. 145a). Sheshet also dwelt there temporarily (Ned. 78a). According to a statement dating from the fourth century, an amora heard in Nehardea certain tannaitic sentences which had until then been unknown to scholars (Shab. 145b; Niddah 21a). Nehardea always remained the residence of a certain number of learned men, some of whom belonged to the school of Maḥuza, which was of considerable prominence at that time, and some to that of Pumbedita. About the middle of the fourth century the famous scholar Ḥama was living at Nehardea; the maxim "By the 'amoraim of Nehardea' Ḥama is meant" (Sanh. 17a) became a canon in the Babylonian schools.

Toward the end of the fourth and at the beginning of the fifth century Nehardea again became a center of Babylonian Judaism through Amemar's activity, though this was overshadowed by that of Ashi, the director of the Academy of Sura. It was Ashi who had the seat of the exilarchate, which belonged as an ancient privilege to Nehardea, transferred to Sura (Letter of Sherira Gaon, *l.c.* i. 32). Amemar attempted in Nehardea to introduce the recitation of the Decalogue into the daily prayer ritual, but was dissuaded from doing so by Ashi. Another of Amemar's liturgical innovations is mentioned in Suk. 55a (on the relation of Ashi to Amemar see Halevy, "Dorot ha-Rishonim," ii. 515 *et seq.*, iii. 68 *et seq.*). Other scholars of the fourth and fifth centuries who are mentioned in the Talmud as natives of Nehardea are Dimi (Ḥul. 113a), who subsequently presided at Pumbedita as second successor to Ḥama (Letter of Sherira Gaon, *l.c.*); Zebid (M. Ḳ. 37b), Naḥman (Ḥul. 95b), Ḥanan (Ḳid. 81b; Niddah 66b), Simai (Sheb. 12b; Mak. 16a). Adda b. Minyomi was called the "judge of Nehardea" (Sanh. 17b). Aḥa of Be-Ḥatim from the vicinity of Nehardea is mentioned by Sherira Gaon (Halevy, *l.c.* i. 25) as one of the saboraic authorities of the sixth century. Mar R. Ḥanina is mentioned, among the earliest geonim of Pumbedita, as residing at Nehardea at the time of Mohammed. This is the last reference in Jewish history to Nehardea. Benjamin of Tudela, however, mentions the ruins of the synagogue Shaf-Yatib, two days' journey from Sura, and one and one-half from Pumbedita ("Itinerary," ed. Grünhut, p. 64).

A few scattered data concerning Nehardea may be added. It was an ancient liturgical custom there to read pericopes from the Hagiographa on Sabbath afternoons (Shab. 116b). The surrounding country was said to be unsafe because of Bedouin robbers (B. B. 36a). An ancient rule of procedure of the court of Nehardea is mentioned in Ket. 87a. Lydda in Palestine, and Nehardea are mentioned in the third century as cities whose inhabitants were proud and ignorant (Yer. Pes. 32a; comp. Bab. Pes. 62b; see Bacher, "Ag. Pal. Amor." i. 60). Nehardea is famous in the history of the Masorah because of an ancient tradition relating to the number of verses in the Bible; it is here said that Hamnuna (Bacher, *l.c.* i. 2) brought this tradition from Nehardea, where he had received it from Naḳḳai (see "M. J. C." i. 174; Strack, "Diḳduḳ Ṭe'amim," p. 56). Certain readings of the Biblical text are characterized by tradition—especially by the Masorah to the Pentateuch Targum (Onḳelos)—as being those of Sura, and certain others as of Nehardea (see Berliner, "Die Massorah zum Targum Onkelos," pp. xiii. *et seq.*, 61–70, Leipsic, 1877).

BIBLIOGRAPHY: Neubauer, *G. T.* pp. 230, 350; Hirschensohn, *Sheba' Ḥokmot*, p. 164, Lemberg, 1885.

G. W. B.

NEHEMIAH OF BETH-HORON: Amora of the first generation; lived in the third century at Beth-horon, a small town northwest of Jerusalem. In the different sources he has various names, being called either "Neḥunya [his correct name; Suk. 44a] from the Valley of Beth-horon" (*i.e.*, from lower Beth-horon, there being an upper town of this name), "Ḥunya of Horon" (Yer. Sheb. 38c), or "Ḥanina of Beth-horon" (Yer. 'Ab. Zarah 42c). He seems to have been highly respected, both as a scholar and as a pious man. His advice was frequently sought in the regulation of the calendar at Jerusalem; and it was said that whenever he went to the city for that purpose, the waters divided before him (*ib.*). Only a few of his halakic sentences have been preserved. R. Johanan transmits in his name some halakot said to be based on a very ancient tradition (Suk. 44a). Some haggadic sentences by him have also been preserved, *e.g.*, Gen. R. lxxiii. and Yer. Ma'as. Sh. 55d, although this latter interpretation is ascribed in the Babylonian Talmud (M. Ḳ. 5a) to R. Abbahu.

Nehemiah had a learned son named **Uzziel,** who is mentioned in Yer. Ma'as. Sh. (*l.c.*). It appears, from a comparison of this passage in Yerushalmi with that in the Babylonian Gemara (M. Ḳ. 5a), that this son was named after his grandfather, who was apparently a prominent man, being called "Uzziel Rabba" = "Uzziel the Great" (M. Ḳ. *l.c.*).

BIBLIOGRAPHY: Heilprin, *Seder ha-Dorot*, p. 127.

W. B. J. Z. L.

NEḤUNYA OF BETH-HORON. See NEHEMIAH OF BETH-HORON.

NEḤUNYA BEN HA-ḲANAH (called also **Neḥunya ha-Gadol** = "the Great"): Tanna of the first and second centuries. It appears from B. B. 10b that Neḥunya was a contemporary, but not a pupil, of Johanan b. Zakkai. He was the teacher of Ishmael b. Elisha. Neḥunya was rich and had a large retinue of servants; but he was distinguished for his meekness and forgiving nature, to which he attributed his attainment of great age (Meg. 28a); two short prayers composed by him exhibit the same qualities (Ber. iv. 2; Yer. Ber. iv. 2).

According to the statement of R. Johanan (Shebu. 26a), Neḥunya interpreted the entire Torah by the hermeneutic rule known as the "general and particular" ("kelal u-feraṭ"), which rule has also been adopted by his pupil Ishmael in eight of his thirteen hermeneutic rules. Neḥunya is frequently mentioned in the Talmud; in Ḥul. 129b he is referred to as the antagonist of Eliezer and Joshua in regard to a halakah (comp., however, 'Eduy. vi. 2). He said that the Pharaoh of the Exodus was rescued from the Red Sea, that he repented, that he afterward reigned in Nineveh, and that it was he who in the time of Jonah exhorted the inhabitants of Nineveh to repentance (Pirḳe R. El. xliii.). Neḥunya is known also for his ethical saying: "Whoso receives upon him the yoke of the Torah, from him is removed the yoke of royalty and that of worldly care; and whoso throws off the yoke of the Torah, upon him is laid the yoke of royalty and that of worldly care" (Ab. iii. 6; Ab. R. N. recension B, xxxii. [ed. Schechter, p. 68]).

As Ishmael b. Elisha, Neḥunya's disciple, is regarded by the cabalists as their chief representative, Neḥunya is considered to have been Ishmael's teacher in mysticism also. He is generally supposed to have been the author of the daily prayer beginning אנא בכח, the initials of which form the forty-two-lettered name of God. He is also supposed by some to have been the author of the BAHIR and of the "Sefer ha-Peli'ah".

BIBLIOGRAPHY: Bacher, *Ag. Tan.* i. 54–56; Frankel, *Darke ha-Mishnah*, p. 99: Heilprin, *Seder ha-Dorot*, ii.; Steinschneider, *Cat. Bodl.* cols. 2056 *et seq.*

W. B. M. SEL.

NICANOR: Son of Patroclus, and general and friend of Antiochus Epiphanes, who in 165 B.C. sent him and GORGIAS with an army against the Jews (I Macc. iii. 38; II Macc. viii. 9). In anticipation of an easy victory, he had brought 1,000 slave-dealers into the camp, to whom he intended to sell the captive Jews; but when Gorgias was defeated by Judas Maccabeus, Nicanor was obliged to flee in disguise to Antioch (II Macc. viii. 34–36). He is identical with the Nicanor whom Josephus ("Ant." xii. 5, § 5) calls governor of Samaria. He may also be the Nicanor who was master of the elephants (II Macc. xiv. 12) and who was sent four years later by King Demetrius I. against the Jews, whom he is said to have hated (I Macc. vii. 26).

The battles of this Nicanor are related differently in the three sources, I and II Maccabees and Josephus. Although there is complete agreement in the statement that Nicanor approached Judas in a friendly way, he, according to I Macc. vii. 27, sought thereby to vanquish his opponent by treachery, whereas, according to II Macc. xiv. 28, he marched against Judas unwillingly and only at the king's command. The latter passage gives a detailed account of his threat to destroy Jerusalem and to turn the sanctuary into a temple of Dionysus unless Judas were delivered to him by the priests, who declared under oath, however, that they were ignorant of his hiding-place (comp. I. Macc. vii. 33–38). According to II Macc. xiv. 17, Nicanor also joined battle with Simon, the brother of Judas, but this whole narrative (*ib.* xiv. 12–30) seems unhistorical except for the statement that he was defeated at Capharsalama by Judas (I Macc. vii. 32). The contrary assertion of Josephus ("Ant." xii. 10, § 4), that Judas was defeated at Capharsalama and fled to the castle at Jerusalem, is shown to be incorrect by the mere fact that the citadel was then in possession of the Syrians, and could not, therefore, have served as a refuge for the Jews.

With new reenforcements from Syria, Nicanor advanced from Jerusalem upon Beth-horon, while Judas encamped opposite him at Adasa. There a decisive battle was fought on the 13th of Adar, 161, in which Nicanor was totally defeated; he himself was slain and every man in his army was killed. In celebration of this complete victory the Jews instituted the 13th of Adar as a holiday (I Mace, vii. 39–50; II Macc. xv.

1–36; Josephus, *l.c.* xii. 10, § 5). With this important event the author of II Maccabees closes his book.

"Nicanor Day" is also mentioned in the rabbinical sources (Meg. Ta'an. xii.; Ta'an. 18b; Yer. Ta'an. ii. 13 *et seq.*, 66a), which give an amplified and highly colored account of the mutilation of Nicanor's body; this is likewise mentioned in both books of the Maccabees, but not in Josephus. According to II Macc. xv. 36, Nicanor Day is one day before Mordecai Day, or Purim. Since this day was the fast-day of Esther, and therefore the direct opposite of a feast-day, the Palestinian teachers effected a compromise by placing the fast-day of Esther after Purim, while Nicanor Day was celebrated as appointed (Soferim 17). There is no trace of its celebration later than the seventh century.

Later rabbinical sources are very confused in regard to Nicanor. According to the "Megillat Antiochus" (in Jellinek, "B. H." v.), he was slain by Johanan, the son of Mattathias. The Hebrew "Yosippon" (ch. xxiv.) confuses the general Nicanor with the alabarch Nicanor, after whom a gate of Jerusalem was named.

BIBLIOGRAPHY: Derenbourg, *Hist.* p. 63; Grätz, *Gesch.* 4th ed., iii. 564; Schürer, *Gesch.* 3d ed., i. 218.

G. S. KR.

NICODEMUS (NAḲDIMON) BEN GORION: Lived at Jerusalem in the first century C.E.; the wealthiest and most respected member of the peace party during the revolution in the reign of Vespasian. Ta'anit 19b relates that during a pilgrimage he engaged twelve cisterns for the people and promised their owner twelve hundred talents of silver for them. It is supposed that his original name was Buna and that his name of Nicodemus was the result of a pun (*ib.* 21a). In the war against Titus he, like his two friends Kalba Sabbua' and Ben Ẓiẓit, took the part of the Romans and influenced Bar Giora against the Zealots, who therefore burned the immense quantities of provisions which the three friends had accumulated (see Giṭ. 56a).

BIBLIOGRAPHY: *Lamentations Rabbah* i. 5; *Ecclesiastes Rabbah* vii. 11; Josephus, *B. J.* ii. 17, § 10; v. 1, § 4; Grätz, *Gesch.* 2d ed., iii. 527–528, and note 4.

E. G. H. S. O.

NITTAI OF ARBELA: Vice-president of the Sanhedrin under the nasi Joshua b. Peraḥyah at the time of John Hyrcanus. In Yer. Ḥag. ii. 76d he is called **Mattai of Arbela.** Arbela was a city of Galilee not far from Tiberias. No halakot of his are extant, but some of his apothegms have been preserved which afford a glimpse of his character. They are as follows: "Withdraw thyself from an evil neighbor; join not thyself unto the wicked; and renounce not the hope of retribution" (Ab. i. 7).

These bitter utterances contrast sharply with the gentle maxims of his colleague Joshua b. Peraḥyah. Nittai seems to have spoken thus after John Hyrcanus had deserted the party of the Pharisees and joined the Sadducees, persecuting his former friends. The phrase "renounce not the hope of retribution" was intended to comfort the Pharisees with the thought that Hyrcanus himself would not escape punishment, while the other two injunctions were designed to keep them from joining the Sadducees.

BIBLIOGRAPHY: Weiss, *Dor*, i. 132; Z. Frankel, in *Monatsschrift*, 1852, pp. 410–413; idem, *Hodegetica in Mischnam*, pp. 33–34, Leipsic, 1859.

S. J. Z. L.

P

PAPA: Babylonian amora of the fifth generation; born about 300; died 375; pupil of Raba and Abaye. After the death of his teachers he founded a school at Neres, a city near Sura, in which he officiated as "resh metibta," his friend and associate, R. Huna b. Joshua, acting as "resh kallah" (356–375). Papa's father seems to have been wealthy and to have enabled his son to devote himself to study (Yeb. 106a; Rashi *ad loc.*). Papa inherited some property from his father; and he also amassed great wealth by brewing beer, an occupation in which he was an expert (Pes. 113a; B. M. 65a). He likewise engaged in extensive and successful business undertakings (Pes. 111b), and his teacher Raba once said of him: "Happy is the righteous man who is as prosperous on earth as only the wicked usually are!" (Hor. 10b).

But Papa and his partner Huna were not always overscrupulous in their business, and their teacher said to them at times: "Ye would take the coats from people's backs" (Giṭ. 73a; Ket. 85a). Papa sold his beer at a higher price than ordinary because he gave the buyer credit, although this practise was regarded as a kind of usury (B. M. 65a). He was avaricious in other ways, and frequently refused to aid the poor (B. B. 9a, 10a). As his second wife he had married the daughter of Abba Sura'ah (of Sura), with whom he does not seem to have lived happily (comp. Sanh. 14b); for she prided herself on the nobility of her ancestry as contrasted with his own. He therefore said, referring to his own experience: "Be circumspect and not hasty in marrying, and take a wife from a class of society lower than thine own" (Yeb. 63a).

Papa was not a great scholar; and he lacked independence of judgment. In the case of two conflicting opinions he tried to accept both (Ber. 11b,

59b; Meg. 21b; Ḥul. 17b, 46a, 76b; Shab. 20a). He was, consequently, not greatly respected as a scholar; and R. Idi b. Abin termed him and Huna b. Joshua "dardeki" (children; Pes. 35a; Yeb. 85a). R. Huna b. Manoah, Samuel b. Judah, and R. Ḥiyya of Vestania, pupils of Raba, came, after their teacher's death, to attend Papa's lectures, which they found obscure and vague. They communicated their opinions to one another by signs, to the great chagrin of Papa, who noticed them, and said: "Let the scholars ["rabbanan"] go in peace" (Ta'an. 9a, b). R. Simai b. Ashi (father of R. Ashi), who also attended Papa's lectures, often embarrassed him by questions; so that Papa once fell on his knees and prayed that God might protect him from being humiliated by Simai. Simai, who was a silent witness of this scene, thereupon resolved to desist; and he asked no further questions at any time. Papa was extremely anxious to obtain a reputation as scholar, but he also endeavored to do honor to all other scholars. He never excommunicated one (M. Ḳ. 17a), and whenever, during his business journeys, he came to a place in which a scholar lived he visited him (Niddah 33b). Once when an unseemly reference to scholars escaped him, he fasted in atonement (Sanh. 100a), although he disliked fasting and it did not agree with him (Ta'an. 24b; R. H. 18b).

He made journeys in connection with his business (Ber. 42; Meg. 21; Niddah 33b), and thus gained much knowledge of the world. He was especially interested in the collection of popular proverbs which he considered as authoritative, using them even to refute the words of a sage (Ber. 59a). The aphorisms quoted by him include the following: "If no grain is in the house, quarrels knock at the door and enter" (B. M. 59a); "Sow corn for thy use that thou mayest not be obliged to purchase it; and strive to acquire a piece of property" (Yeb. 63a).

BIBLIOGRAPHY: Abraham Mordecai Piyorka, *Toledot R. Papa*, in *Oẓar ha-Sifrut*, 1896, v. 213–218; Weiss, *Dor*, iv. 204–206; Heilprin, *Seder ha-Dorot*, pp. 315–317, Warsaw, 1882; Grätz, *Gesch.* 3d ed., iv. 338, where he is erroneously called "Papa b. Hanan"; Bacher, *Ag. Pal. Amor.* pp. 141–143.

W. B. J. Z. L.

PEDAT B. ELEAZAR: Palestinian amora of the fourth generation (first half of the fourth century). He was his father's pupil (Ber. 77b; M. Ḳ. 20a) and the assistant lecturer ("amora") of R. Assi. If the latter asked him to repeat any of his father's sentences, if he himself had heard them from the lips of his father, he introduced them with the words: "So says my teacher in the name of my father"; but in other cases he said: "So says my teacher in the name of R. Eleazar." He transmitted also sentences in the name of his father (Yer. Yoma 39d) and of R. Hoshaiah (Oshaya) (Yer. Suk. 54d).

Pedat was an intimate friend of Zera and JEREMIAH BEN ELEAZAR, who transmitted halakic sentences of his (Yer. Ned. 38a). Several of his haggadic interpretations have been preserved, including the following: "Deut. i. 17 does not indicate presumption on the part of Moses. On the contrary, he means to say: 'Bring difficult questions to me: I will decide them, if I can; if I can not, I will hear them and lay them before God for his decision'" (Midr. Shemuel, xiv.). He remarks, in connection with Gen. i. 2: "It is a law of nature that the air moves on the surface of the water, even when the sun is shining with its greatest heat" (Gen. R. ii.).

BIBLIOGRAPHY: Bacher, *Ag. Pal. Amor.* iii. 617; Frankel, *Mebo*, p. 121, Breslau, 1870; Heilprin, *Seder ha-Dorot*, p. 312, Warsaw, 1882.

W. B. J. Z. L.

PERUSHIM. See PHARISEES.

PHABI: High-priestly family which flourished about the period of the fall of the Second Temple.

The name, with which may be compared *Φαβέας* (variant, *Φαμέας*), that of a Carthaginian general (Suidas, *s.v.* Ἀμίλκας), was borne by the high priests Jesus ben Phabi, Ishmael ben Phabi I., and Ishmael ben Phabi II. All three of these are mentioned in Josephus, while the name of Ishmael occurs also in the Mishnah (Parah iii. 5) and frequently in the Talmud. The orthography of the name, which is apparently Egyptian in origin, has in Josephus the forms *Φοαβι*, *Φαβι*, *Φαβη* (comp. also Zonaras, "Annales," v. 16), while in his "Hypomnesticon" (see "Byzantinische Zeitschrift," xi. 129) is found the form *Φαυβη* (*ὁ του*). In the rabbinical sources the name is spelled either פאבי, פיאבי, or פואבי, which present the same uncertainties as the Greek form.

G. S. KR.

PHARISEES (*Φαρισαῖοι*; Aramaic, "Perishaya"; Hebr. "Perushim"): Party representing the religious views, practises, and hopes of the kernel of the Jewish people in the time of the Second Temple and in opposition to the priestly Sadducees. They were accordingly scrupulous observers of the Law as interpreted by the Soferim, or Scribes, in accordance with tradition. No true estimate of the character of the Pharisees can be obtained from the New Testament writings, which take a polemical attitude toward them, nor from Jose-phus, who, writing for Roman readers and in view of the Messianic expectations of the Pharisees, represents the latter as a philosophical sect. "Perisha" (the singular of "Perishaya") denotes "one who separates himself," or keeps away from persons or things impure, in order to attain the degree of holiness and righteousness required in those who would commune with God (comp., for "Perishut" and "Perisha," Tan., Wayeẓe, ed. Buber, p. 21; Abot iii. 13; Soṭah ix. 15; Midr. Teh. xv. 1; Num. R. x. 23; Targ. Gen. xlix. 26).

The Pharisees formed a league or brotherhood of their own ("ḥaburah"), admitting only those who, in the presence of three members, pledged themselves to the strict observance of Levitical purity, to the avoidance of closer association with the 'AM HA-AREẒ (the ignorant and careless boor), to the scrupulous payment of tithes and other imposts due to the priest, the Levite, and the poor, and to a conscientious regard for vows and for other people's property (Dem. ii. 3; Tosef., Dem. ii. 1). They called their members "ḥaberim" (brothers), while they passed under the name of "Perishaya," or "Perushim." Though originally identical with the ḤASIDIM, they reserved the title of "ḥasid" for former generations ("ḥasidim ha-rishonim"), retaining, however, the name "Perishut" (= Ἀμιξία = "separation," in contradistinction to Ἐπιμιξία = "intermingling") as their watchword from the time of the Maccabean contest (see II Macc. xiv. 37; comp. verse 8). Yet, while the more rigorous ones withdrew from political life after the death of Judas Maccabeus, refused to recognize the Hasmonean high priests and kings as legitimate rulers of the Temple and of the state, and, as Essenes, formed a brotherhood of their own, the majority took a less antagonistic attitude toward the Maccabean dynasty, who, like Phinehas, their "father," had obtained their title by zeal for God (I Macc. ii. 54); and they finally succeeded in infusing their own views and principles into the political and religious life of the people.

It was, however, only after a long and protracted struggle with the Sadducees that they won their lasting triumph in the interpretation and execution of the Law. The Sadducees, jealously guarding the privileges and prerogatives established since the days of Solomon, when Zadok, their ancestor, officiated as priest, insisted upon the literal observance of the Law; the Pharisees, on the other hand, claimed prophetic or Mosaic authority for their interpretation (Ber. 48b; Shab. 14b; Yoma 80a; Yeb. 16a; Nazir 53a; Ḥul. 137b; *et al.*), at the same time asserting the principles of religious democracy and progress. With reference to Ex. xix. 6, they maintained that "God gave all the people the heritage, the kingdom, the priesthood, and the holiness" (II Macc. ii. 17, Greek). As a matter of fact, the idea of the priestly sanctity of the whole people of Israel in many directions found its expression in the Mosaic law; as, for instance, when the precepts concerning unclean meat, intended originally for the priests only (Ezek. xliv. 31; comp. verse 14 and Judges xiii. 4), were extended to the whole people (Lev. xi.; Deut. xiv. 3–21); or when the prohibition of cutting the flesh in mourning for the dead was extended to all the people as "a holy nation" (Deut. xiv. 1–2; Lev. xix. 28; comp. Lev. xxi. 5); or when the Law itself was transferred from the sphere of the priesthood to every man in Israel (Ex. xix. 22–24; Deut. vi. 7, xi. 19; comp. xxxi. 9; Jer. ii. 8, xviii. 18).

The very institution of the synagogue for common worship and instruction was a Pharisaic declaration of the principle that the Torah is "the inheritance of the congregation of Jacob" (Deut. xxxiii. 3, Hebr.). In establishing schools and synagogues everywhere and enjoining each father to see that his son was instructed in the Law (Yer. Ket. vii. 32c; Ḳid. 29a; Sifre, Deut. 46), the Pharisees made the Torah a power for the education of the Jewish people all over the world, a power whose influence, in fact, was felt even outside of the Jewish race (see R. Meïr in Sifra, Aḥare Mot, 13; Matt, xxiii. 15; comp. Gen. R. xxviii.; Jellinek, "B. H." vi., p. xlvi.). The same sanctity that the priests in the Temple claimed for their meals, at which they gathered with the recitation of benedictions (I Sam. ix. 13) and after ablutions, the Pharisees established for their meals, which were partaken of in holy assemblies after purifications and amidst benedictions (Geiger, "Urschrift," pp. 121–124). Especially were the Sabbath and holy days made the means of sanctification, and, as at the sacrifices, wine was used in honor of the day. A true Pharisee observed the same degree of purity in his daily meals as did the priest in the Temple (Tosef., Dem. ii. 2; so did Abraham; according to B. M. 87a), wherefore it was necessary that he should avoid contact with the 'am ha-areẓ (Ḥag. ii. 7).

From Temple practise were adopted the mode of slaughtering (Sifre, Deut. 75; Ḥul. 28a) and the rules concerning "ta'arubot" (the mingling of different kinds of food; comp. Hag. ii. 12; Zeb. viii.; Ḥul. viii. 1) and the "shi'urim" (the quantities constituting a prohibition of the Law; Yoma 80a). Though derived from Deut. vi. 7 (comp. Josephus, "Ant." iv. 8, § 3), the daily recital of the "Shema'," as well as the other parts of the divine service, is a Pharisaic institution, the Pharisees having established their ḥaburah, or league, in each city to conduct the service (Ber. iv. 7; comp. "Ant." xviii. 2, § 3; Geiger, "Urschrift," p. 379). The tefillin, or PHYLACTERIES, as a symbolical consecration of head and arm, appear to be a counterpart of the high priest's diadem and breastplate; so with the MEZUZAH as a symbolical consecration of the home, though both were derived from Scripture (Deut. vi. 8–9, xi. 18–19; Sanh. x. [xi.] 3), the original talismanic character having been forgotten (comp. Ex. xii. 13; Isa. lvii. 8).

In the Temple itself the Pharisees obtained a hold at an early date, when they introduced the regular daily prayers besides the sacrifice (Tamid v. 1) and the institution of the "Ma'amadot" (the representatives of the people during the sacrifices). Moreover, they declared that the priests were but deputies of the people. On the great Day of Atonement the high priest was told by the elders that he was but a messenger of the Sanhedrin and must officiate, therefore, in conformity with their (the Pharisees') rulings (Yoma i. 5; comp. Josephus, "Ant." xviii. 1, § 4). While the Sadducean priesthood regarded the Temple as its domain and took it to be the privilege of the high priest to offer the daily burnt offering from his own treasury, the Pharisees demanded that it be furnished from the Temple treasury, which contained the contributions of the people (Sifra, Ẓaw, 17; Emor, 18). Similarly, the Pharisees insisted that the meal-offering which accompanied the meat-offering should be brought to the altar, while the Sadducees claimed it for themselves (Meg. Ta'an. viii.). Trivial as these differences appear, they are survivals of great issues. Thus the high priests, who, as may be learned from the words of Simon the Just (Lev. R. xxi., close; comp. Ber. 7a; Yoma v. 1, 19b), claimed to see an apparition of the Shekinah when entering the Holy of Holies, kindled the incense in their censers outside and thus were enveloped in the cloud when entering, in order that God might appear in the cloud upon the mercy-seat (Lev. xvi. 2). The Pharisees, discountenancing such claims, insisted that the incense must be kindled by the high priest within the Holy of Holies (Sifra, Ahare Mot, 3; Tosef., Yoma i. 8; Yoma 19b; Yer. Yoma i. 39a).

On the other hand, the Pharisees introduced rites in the Temple which originated in popular custom and were without foundation in the Law. Such was the water-procession of the people, on the night of Sukkot, from the Pool of Siloam, ending with the libation of water in the morning and the final beating of the willow-trees upon the altar at the close of the feast. The rite was a symbolic prayer for the year's rain (comp. Zach. xiv. 16–18; Isa. xiii. 3, xxx. 29; Tosef., Suk. iii. 18); and while the Ḥasidim took a prominent part in the outbursts of popular rejoicing to which it gave rise, the Sadducean priesthood was all the more averse to it (Suk. iv. 9–v. 4; 43b, 48b; Tosef., Suk. iii.). In all these practises the Pharisees obtained the ascendency over the Sadducees, claiming to be in possession of the tradition of the fathers ("Ant." xiii. 10, § 6; 16, § 2; xviii. 1, §§ 3–4; Yoma 19b).

Yet the Pharisees represented also the principle of progress; they were less rigid in the execution of justice ("Ant." xiii. 10, § 6), and the day when the stern Sadducean code was abolished was made a festival (Meg. Ta'an. iv.). While the Sadducees in adhering to the letter of the law required "an eye for an eye and a tooth for a tooth," the Pharisees, with the exception of Eliezer b. Hyrcanus, the Shammaite, interpreted this maxim to mean due compensation with money (Mek., Mishpaṭim, 8; B. Ḳ. 84b; comp. Matt. v. 38). The principle of retaliation, however, was applied consistently by the Sadducees in regard to false witnesses in cases involving capital punishment; but the Pharisees were less fair. The former referred the law "Thou shalt do unto him as he had intended unto his brother" (Deut. xix. 19, Hebr.) only to a case in which the one falsely accused had been actually executed; whereas the Pharisees desired the death penalty inflicted upon the false witness for the intention to secure the death of the accused by means of false testimony (Sifre, Deut. 190; Mark i. 6; Tosef., Sanh. vi. 6; against the absurd theory, in Mak. 5b, that in case the accused has been executed the false witness is exempt from the death penalty, see Geiger, *l.c.* p. 140). But in general the Pharisees surrounded the penal laws, especially the death penalty, with so many qualifications that they were rarely executed (see Sanh. iv. 1, vi. 1; Mak. i. 10).

The laws concerning virginity and the levirate (Deut. xxii. 17, xxv. 9) also were interpreted by the Pharisees in accordance with the dictates of decency and common sense, while the Sadducees adhered strictly to the letter (Sifre, Deut. 237, 291; Yeb. 106b; instead of "Eliezer b. Jacob" [as siding with the Sadducees] probably "Eliezer ben Hyrcanus" should be read). The difference concerning the right of inheritance by the daughter as against the son's daughter, which the Sadducees granted and the Pharisees denied (Yad. iv. 7; Meg. Ta'an. v.; Tosef., Yad. ii. 20; Yer. B. B. vii. 16a), seems to rest on differing practises among the various classes of people; the same is true with regard to the difference as to the master's responsibility for damage done by a slave or a beast (Yad. iv. 7; B. Ḳ. viii. 4; but see Geiger, *l.c.* pp. 143–144).

Of decisive influence, however, were the great changes wrought by the Pharisees in the Sabbath and holy days, inasmuch as they succeeded in lending to these days a note of cheerfulness and domestic joy, while the Sadducees viewed them more or less as Temple festivals, and as imposing a tone of austerity upon the common people and the home. To begin with the Day of Atonement, the Pharisees wrested the power of atoning for the sins of the people from the high priest (see Lev. xvi. 30) and transferred it to the day itself, so that atonement was effected even without sacrifice and priest, provided there was genuine repentance (Yoma viii. 9; Sifra, Aḥare Mot, 8). So, too, the New Moon of the seventh month was transformed by them from a day of trumpet-blowing into a New-Year's Day devoted to the grand ideas of divine government and judgment. On the eve of Passover the lessons of the Exodus story, recited over the wine and the maẓẓah, are given greater prominence than the paschal lamb (Pes. x.). The Biblical command enjoining a pilgrimage to the Temple in the festival season is fulfilled by going to greet the teacher and listen to his instruction on a festal day, as in former days people went to see the prophet (Suk. 27b, after II Kings iv. 23; Beẓah 15; Shab. 152a; Sifra to Lev. xxiii. 44).

But the most significant change was that which the Feast of Weeks underwent in its transformation from a Feast of Firstlings into a Feast of the Giving of the Law (Mek., Yitro, Baḥodesh, 3; Ex. R. xxxi.), The Boethusians, as the heirs of the Sadducees, still retained a trace of the agricultural character of the feast in adhering to the letter of the law which places the offering of the ʻomer (sheaf of the wave-offering) on the morrow after the Sabbath and the Shabuʻot feast on the morrow after the seventh Sabbath following (Lev. xxiii. 15–16); whereas the Pharisees, in order to connect the Shabuʻot feast with Passover and lend it an independent historical character, boldly interpreted the words "the morrow after Sabbath" as signifying "the day following the first Passover day," so that Shabuʻot always falls upon the close of the first week of Siwan (Meg. Taʻan. i.; Men. 65a, b; Shab. 88a).

Especially significant are the Pharisaic innovations in connection with the Sabbath. One of them is the special duty imposed upon the mistress of the home to have the light kindled before Sabbath (Shab. ii. 7), whereas the Samaritans and Karaites, who were in many ways followers of Sadducean teachings, saw in the prohibition against kindling fire on Sabbath (Ex. xxxv. 3) a prohibition also against light in the home on Sabbath eve. The Samaritans and Karaites likewise observed literally the prohibition against leaving one place on Sabbath (Ex. xvi. 29), while the Pharisees included the whole width of the Israelitish camp—that is, 2,000 ells, or a radius of one mile—in the term "place," and made allowance besides for carrying things (which is otherwise forbidden; see Jer. xvii. 21–24) and for extending the Sabbath limit by means of an artificial union of spheres of settlement. Their object was to render the Sabbath "a delight" (Isa. lviii. 13), a day of social and spiritual joy and elevation rather than a day of gloom. The old Ḥasidim, who probably lived together in large settlements, could easily treat these as one large house (see Geiger, "Jüd. Zeit." ii. 24–27). Yet while they excluded the women from their festal gatherings, the Pharisees, their successors, transformed the Sabbath and festivals into seasons of domestic joy, bringing into increasing recognition the importance and dignity of woman as the builder and guardian of the home (comp. Niddah 38a, b; and Book of Jubilees, i. 8, with Ezra's injunction; B. Ḳ. 82a).

In regard to the laws of Levitical purity, which, in common with primitive custom, excluded woman periodically, and for weeks and months after childbirth, from the household (Lev. xii. 4–7, xv. 19–24), to which laws the ancient Ḥasidim adhered with austere rigor (Shab. 64b; Horowitz, "Uralte Toseftas," iv.–v.; "Pitḥe Niddah," pp. 54–56; Geiger, *l.c.* ii. 27–28), the Pharisees took the common-sense course of encouraging the wife, despite the letter of the Law, to take her usual place in the home and appear in her wonted dignity before her husband and children (Ket. 61a; Shab. 64b). So, too, it was with the Pharisaic leader Simeon b. Shetaḥ, who, in the reign of Queen Salome Alexandra, introduced the marriage document in order to protect the wife against the caprice of the husband; and while the Shammaites would not allow the wife to be divorced unless she gave cause for suspicion of adultery (Sifre, 269; Giṭ. ix. 10, 90b; comp. Matt. v. 32), the Hillelites, and especially Akiba, in being more lenient in matters of divorce, had in view the welfare and peace of the home, which should be based upon affection (see Friedmann, "Pseudo-Seder Eliyahu Zuṭa," xv. 3). Many measures were taken by the Pharisees to prevent arbitrary acts on the part of the husband (Giṭ. iv. 2–3 *et al.*). Possibly in order to accentuate the legal character of the divorce they insisted, against Sadducean custom, on inserting in the document the words "according to the law of Moses and of Israel" (Yad. iv. 8; but comp. Meg. Ta'an. vii.).

It was on account of such consideration for the welfare of the home that they stood in high favor with the Jewish women ("Ant." xvii. 2, § 4). They discountenanced also the Sadducean custom of special purifications for the officiating priest (Parah iii. 7; Tosef., ii. 1), and laid more stress upon the purification of the Temple vessels and upon the holiness of the Scripture scrolls, which, according to them, transmitted their holiness to the hands which touched them so as to make them "defile" (*i.e.*, make "taboo") the things touched by them (Yad. iv. 6; Tosef., ii. 20; Tosef., Ḥag. iii. 35; see Geiger, "Urschrift," pp. 134–136).

Most of these controversies, recorded from the time previous to the destruction of the Temple, are but faint echoes of the greater issues between the Pharisaic and Sadducean parties, the latter representing the interests of the Temple, while the former were concerned that the spiritual life of the people should be centered in the Torah and the Synagogue. While the Sadducean priesthood prided itself upon its aristocracy of blood (Sanh. iv. 2; Mid. v. 4; Ket. 25a; Josephus, "Contra Ap." i., § 7), the Pharisees created an aristocracy of learning instead, declaring a bastard who is a student of the Law to be higher in rank than an ignorant high priest (Hor. 13a), and glorying in the fact that their most prominent leaders were descendants of proselytes (Yoma 71b; Sanh. 96b). For the decision of their Scribes, or "Soferim" (Josephus, *σοφισταί*; N. T., *γραμματεῖς*), consisting originally of Aaronites, Levites, and common Israelites, they claimed the same authority as for the Biblical law, even in case of error (Sifre, Deut. 153–154); they endowed them with the power to abrogate the Law at times, and they went so far as to say that he who transgressed their words deserved death (Ber. 4a). By dint of this authority, claimed to be divine (R. H. 25a), they put the entire calendric system upon a new basis, independent of the priesthood. They took many burdens from the people by claiming for the sage, or scribe, the power of dissolving vows (Ḥag. i. 8; Tosef., i.).

On the whole, however, they added new restrictions to the Biblical law in order to keep the people at a safe distance from forbidden ground; as they termed it, "they made a fence around the Law" (Ab. i. 1; Ab. R. N. i.–xi.), interpreting the words "Ye shall watch my watch" (Lev. xviii. 30, Hebr.) to mean "Ye shall place a guard around my guard" (Yeb. 21a). Thus they forbade the people to drink wine or eat with the heathen, in order to prevent associations which might lead either to intermarriage or to idolatry (Shab. 17b). To the forbidden marriages of the Mosaic law relating to incest (Lev. xviii.–xx.) they added a number of others (Yeb. ii. 4). After they had determined the kinds of work prohibited on the Sabbath they forbade the use of many things on the Sabbath on the ground that their use might lead to some prohibited labor. It was here that the foundation was laid of that system of rabbinic law which piled statute upon statute until often the real purpose of the Law was lost sight of. But such restrictions are not confined to ritual laws. Also in regard to moral laws there are such additional prohibitions, as, for instance, the prohibition against what is called "the dust of slanderous speech" (Yer. Peah i. 16a) or "the dust of usury" (B. M. 61b), or against unfair dealings, such as gambling, or keeping animals that feed on property of the neighbors (Tosef., B. Ḳ. vii. 8; Tosef., Sanh. v. 2, 5; Sanh. 25b, 26b).

The aim and object of the Law, according to Pharisaic principles, are the training of man to a full realization of his responsibility to God and to the consecration of life by the performance of its manifold duties: the one is called "'ol malkut shamayim" (the yoke of God's Kingship) and the other "'ol hamiẓwot" (the yoke of His commandments). Every morning and evening the Jew takes both upon himself when reciting the "Shema'" (Ber. ii. 2). "The Torah preaches: Take upon yourselves the yoke of God's Kingdom; let the fear of God be your judge and arbiter, and deal with one another according to the dictates of love" (Sifre, Deut. 323). So says Josephus: "For the Jewish lawgiver all virtues are parts of religion" ("Contra Ap." ii., §§ 17, 19; comp. Philo, "De Opificio Mundi," §§ 52, 55). Cain and the generation of the Flood sinned in that they denied that there are a Judgment and a Judge and a future of retribution (Targ. Yer. to Gen. iv. 8; Gen. R. xxvi.). The acceptance of God's Kingship implies acceptance of His commandments also, both such as are dictated by reason and the human conscience and such as are special decrees of God as Ruler (Sifra, Aḥare Mot, 13). It means a perfect heart that fears the very thought of sin (Sifra, Ḳedoshim, 2); the avoidance of sin from love of God (*ib.* 11); the fulfilment of His commandments without expectation of reward ('Ab. Zarah 19a); the avoidance of any impure thought or any act that may lead to sin (*ib.* 20b, with reference to Deut. xxiii. 10). The acceptance of God's Kingship implies also recognition of His just dealing with man, and a thankful attitude, even in misfortune (Sifre, Deut. 32, 53; Sifra, Shemini, 1; Mek., Yitro, 10; Ber. ix. 5, 60b). God's Kingship, first proclaimed by Abraham (Sifre, Deut. 313) and accepted by Israel (Mek., Yitro, Baḥodesh, 2–3), shall be universally recognized in the future.

This is the Messianic hope of the Pharisees, voiced in all parts of the synagogal liturgy; but it meant also the cessation of the kingdom of the worldly powers identified with idolatry and injustice (Mek., 'Amalek). In fact, for the ancient Ḥasidim, God's Kingship excluded that of any other ("Ant." xviii. 1, § 6). The Pharisees, who yielded to the temporary powers and enjoined the people to pray for the government (Abot iii. 2), waited nevertheless for the KINGDOM OF GOD, consoling themselves in the meantime with the spiritual freedom granted by the study of the Law (Abot vi. 2), "He who takes upon himself the yoke of the Torah, the yoke of the worldly kingdom and of worldly care, will be removed from him" (Abot iii. 5). Josephus ("B. J." ii. 8, § 14; "Ant." xiii. 5, § 9; xviii. 1, § 3) carefully avoids mentioning the most essential doctrine of the Pharisees, the Messianic hope, which the Sadducees did not share with them; while for the Essenes time and conditions were predicted in their apocalyptic writings. Instead, Josephus merely says that "they ascribe everything to fate without depriving man of his freedom of action." This idea is expressed by Akiba: "Everything is foreseen [that is, predestined]; but at the same time freedom is given" (Abot iii. 15). Akiba, however, declares, "The world is judged by grace [not by blind fate nor by the Pauline law], and everything is determined by man's actions [not by blind acceptance of certain creeds]." Similar to Josephus' remark is the rabbinical saying, "All is decreed by God except fear of God" (Ber. 33b). "Man may act either virtuously or viciously, and his rewards or punishments in the future shall be accordingly" ("Ant." xviii. 1, § 3). This corresponds with the "two ways of the Jewish teaching" (Ab. R. N. xxv.). But it was not the immortality of the soul which the Pharisees believed in, as Josephus puts it, but the resurrection of the body as expressed in the liturgy, and this formed part of their Messianic hope.

In contradistinction to the Sadducees, who were satisfied with the political life committed to their own power as the ruling dynasty, the Pharisees represented the views and hopes of the people. The same was the case with regard to the belief in angels and demons. As Ecclesiastes and Ecclesiasticus indicate, the upper classes adhered for a long time to the Biblical view concerning the soul and the hereafter, caring little for the ANGELOLOGY and DEMONOLOGY of the Pharisees. These used them, with the help of the MA'ASEH BERESHIT and MA'ASEH MERKABAH, not only to amplify the Biblical account, but to remove from the Bible anthropomorphisms and similarly obnoxious verbiage concerning the Deity by referring them to angelic and intermediary powers (for instance, Gen. i. 26), and thereby to gradually sublimate and spiritualize the conception of God.

The Pharisees are furthermore described by Josephus as extremely virtuous and sober, and as despising luxuries; and Ab. R. N. v. affirms that they led a life of privation. The ethics of the Pharisees is based upon the principle "Be holy, as the Lord your God is holy" (Lev. xix. 2, Hebr.); that is, strive to imitate God (Sifra and Tan., Ḳedoshim, 1; Mek., Shirah, 3; Sifre, Deut. 49; comp. Matt. v. 48: "Be ye therefore perfect, even as your Father which is in heaven is perfect"). So "Love thy neighbor as thyself" is declared by them to he the principal law (Shab. 30a; Ab. R. N., text B, xxvi. [ed. Schechter, p. 53]; Sifra, Ḳedoshim, 4) and, in order to demonstrate its universality, to be based on the verse declaring man to be made in the image of God (Gen. v. 1). "As He makes the sun shine alike upon the good and the evil," so does He extend His fatherly love to all (Shir ha-Shirim Zuṭa, i.; Sifre, Num. 134, Deut. 81, 40). Heathenism is hated on account of the moral depravity to which it leads (Sifre, Num. 157), but the idolater who becomes an observer of the Law ranks with the high priest (Sifra, Aḥare Mot, 13). It is a slanderous misrepresentation of the Pharisees to state that they "divorced morality and religion," when everywhere virtue, probity, and benevolence are declared by them to be the essence of the Law (Mak. 23b–24a; Tosef., Peah, iv. 19; *et al.*).

Nothing could have been more loathsome to the genuine Pharisee than HYPOCRISY. "Whatever good a man does he should do it for the glory of God" (Ab. ii. 13; Ber. 17a). Nicodemus is blamed for having given of his wealth to the poor in an ostentatious manner (Ket. 66b). An evil action may be justified where the motive is a good one (Ber. 63a). Still, the very air of sanctity surrounding the life of the Pharisees often led to abuses. Alexander Jannæus warned his wife not against the Pharisees, his declared enemies, but against "the chameleon- or hyena- ["ẓebo'im"-] like hypocrites who act like Zimri and claim the reward of Phinehas" (Soṭah 22b). An ancient baraita enumerates seven classes of Pharisees, of which five consist of either eccentric fools or hypocrites: (1) "the shoulder Pharisee," who wears, as it were, his good actions ostentatiously upon his shoulder; (2) "the wait-a-little Pharisee," who ever says, "Wait a little, until I have performed the good act awaiting me"; (3) "the bruised Pharisee," who in order to avoid looking at a woman runs against the wall so as to bruise himself and bleed; (4) "the pestle Pharisee," who walks with head down like the pestle in the mortar; (5) "the ever-reckoning Pharisee," who says, "Let me know what good I may do to counteract my neglect"; (6) "the God-fearing Pharisee," after the manner of Job; (7) "the God-loving Pharisee," after the manner of Abraham (Yer. Ber. ix. 14b; Soṭah 22b; Ab. R. N., text A, xxxvii.; text B, xlv. [ed. Schechter, pp. 55, 62]; the explanations in both Talmuds vary greatly; see Chwolson, "Das Letzte Passahmahl," p. 116). R. Joshua b. Hananiah, at the beginning of the second century, calls eccentric Pharisees "destroyers of the world" (Soṭah iii. 4): and the term "Pharisaic plagues" is frequently used by the leaders of the time (Yer. Soṭah iii. 19a).

It is such types of Pharisees that Jesus had in view when hurling his scathing words of condemnation against the Pharisees, whom he denounced as "hypocrites," calling them "offspring of vipers" ("hyenas"); "whited sepulchers which outwardly appear beautiful, but inwardly are full of dead men's bones"; "blind guides," "which strain out the gnat and swallow the camel" (Matt. vi. 2–5, 16; xii. 34; xv. 14; xxiii. 24, 27, Greek). He himself tells his disciples to do as the Scribes and "Pharisees who sit on Moses' seat bid them do"; but he blames them for not acting in the right spirit, for wearing large phylacteries and ẓiẓit, and for pretentiousness in many other things (*ib.* xxiii. 2–7). Exactly so are hypocrites censured in the Midrash (Pes. R. xxii. [ed. Friedmann, p. 111]); wearing tefillin and ẓiẓit, they harbor evil intentions in their breasts. Otherwise the Pharisees appear as friends of Jesus (Luke vii. 37, xiii. 31) and of the early Christians (Acts v. 38, xxiii. 9; "Ant." xx. 9, § 1).

Only in regard to intercourse with the unclean and "unwashed" multitude, with the 'am ha-areẓ, the publican, and the sinner, did Jesus differ widely from the Pharisees (Mark ii. 16; Luke v. 30. vii. 39, xi. 38, xv. 2, xix. 7). In regard to the main doctrine he fully agreed with them, as the old version (Mark xii. 28–34) still has it. Owing, however, to the hostile attitude taken toward the Pharisaic schools by Pauline Christianity, especially in the time of the emperor Hadrian, "Pharisees" was inserted in the Gospels wherever the high priests and Sadducees or Herodians were originally mentioned as the persecutors of Jesus, and a false impression, which still prevails in Christian circles and among all Christian writers, was created concerning the Pharisees.

It is difficult to state at what time the Pharisees, as a party, arose. Josephus first mentions them in connection with Jonathan, the successor of Judas Maccabeus ("Ant." xiii. 5, § 9). Under John Hyrcanus (135–105) they appear as a powerful party opposing the Sadducean proclivities of the king, who had formerly been a disciple of theirs, though the story as told by Josephus is unhistorical ("Ant." xiii. 10, § 5). The Hasmonean dynasty, with its worldly ambitions and aspirations, met with little support from the Pharisees, whose aim was the maintenance of a religious spirit in accordance with their interpretation of the Law. Under Alexander Jannæus (104–78) the conflict between the people, siding with the Pharisees, and the king became bitter and ended in cruel carnage ("Ant." xiii. 13, § 5; xiv. 1, § 2). Under his widow, Salome Alexandra (78–69), the Pharisees, led by Simeon ben Sheṭaḥ, came to power; they obtained seats in the Sanhedrin, and that time was afterward regarded as the golden age, full of the blessing of heaven (Sifra, Beḥuḳḳotai, i.; Ta'an. 23a). But the bloody vengeance they took upon the Sadducees led to a terrible reaction, and under Aristobulus (69–63) the Sadducees regained their power ("Ant." xiii. 16, § 2–xiv. 1, § 2).

Amidst the bitter struggle which ensued, the Pharisees appeared before Pompey asking him to interfere and restore the old priesthood while abolishing the royalty of the Hasmoneans altogether ("Ant." xiv. 3, § 2). The defilement of the Temple by Pompey was regarded by the Pharisees as a divine punishment of Sadducean misrule (Psalms of Solomon, i., ii., viii. 12–19). After the national independence had been lost, the Pharisees gained in influence while the star of the Sadducees waned. Herod found his chief opponents among the latter, and so he put the leaders of the Sanhedrin to death while endeavoring by a milder treatment to win the favor of the leaders of the Pharisees, who, though they refused to take the oath of allegiance, were otherwise friendly to him ("Ant." xiv. 9, § 4; xv. 1, § 1; 10, §4; 11, §§ 5–6). Only when he provoked their indignation by his heathen proclivities did the Pharisees become his enemies and fall victims (4 B.C.) to his bloodthirstiness ("Ant." xvii. 2, § 4; 6, §§ 2–4). But the family of Boethus, whom Herod had raised to the high-priesthood, revived the spirit of the Sadducees, and thenceforth the Pharisees again had them as antagonists; still, they no longer possessed their former power, as the people always sided with the Pharisees ("Ant." xviii. 1, § 4). In King Agrippa (41–44) the Pharisees had a supporter and friend, and with the destruction of the Temple the Sadducees disappeared altogether, leaving the regulation of all Jewish affairs in the hands of the Pharisees.

Henceforth Jewish life was regulated by the teachings of the Pharisees; the whole history of Judaism was reconstructed from the Pharisaic point of view, and a new aspect was given to the Sanhedrin of the past. A new chain of tradition supplanted the older, priestly tradition (Abot i. 1). Pharisaism shaped the character of Judaism and the life and thought of the Jew for all the future. True, it gave the Jewish religion a legalistic tendency and made "separatism" its chief characteristic; yet only thus were the pure monotheistic faith, the ethical ideal, and the intellectual and spiritual character of the Jew preserved in the midst of the downfall of the old world and the deluge of barbarism which swept over the medieval world.

BIBLIOGRAPHY: J. Elbogen, *Die Religionsanschauung der Pharisäer*, Berlin, 1904; Geiger, *Urschrift*, Breslau, 1857; idem, *Sadducäer und Pharisäer*, in *Jüd. Zeit.* 1863; Schürer, *Gesch.* 3d ed., ii. 380–419 (where list of the whole literature is given); Wellhausen, *Die Pharisäer und Sadducäer*, Göttingen, 1874.

K.

PHASAEL: Elder brother of Herod the Great. Both Phasael and Herod began their careers under their father, ANTIPATER, who appointed the former to be governor of Jerusalem, and Herod governor of Galilee (Josephus, "Ant." xiv. 9, § 2; "B. J." i. 10, § 4). While Antony was in Bithynia about 41 B.C., accusations were brought before him against the two brothers, who were objects of hatred to the Jewish party, but the shrewd Herod succeeded in obtaining the dismissal of the charges ("Ant." xiv. 12, § 2; "B. J." i. 12, § 4). It was impossible, however, for the elders of the Jews to rest content with the administrations of Herod and Phasael; and charges were again brought against them before Antony at Antioch. Once more the accusations proved to be fruitless, for Antony was indebted to Antipater, while even the weak Hyrcanus II. pleaded for them; so that Antony appointed them tetrarchs ("Ant." xiv. 13, § 1; "B. J." i. 12, § 5). Meanwhile the Hasmonean ANTIGONUS endeavored to seize the Jewish throne; and in Jerusalem there were frequent conflicts between his retainers and those of the two brothers, which were especially perilous on the Jewish Feast of Pentecost. Phasael defended the walls, and Herod the palace, thus routing their antagonists, whereupon Antigonus invoked the aid of the Parthians. In spite of Herod's warning, Phasael allowed himself to be inveigled with Hyrcanus to the camp of the Parthian leader Barzapharnes, where both were imprisoned ("Ant." xiv. 13, §§ 5–6; "B. J." i. 13, §§ 4–5). They were then handed over to Antigonus, who caused Hyrcanus to be mutilated, a disgrace which Phasael escaped by dashing out his own brains, having the joy of knowing before he died that his brother Herod had escaped from Jerusalem and was safe ("Ant." xiv. 13, g§ 6–9; "B. J." i. 13, §§ 6–8).

Josephus speaks of Phasael as a brave and noble man. His son, who likewise bore the name Phasael, and seems to have been posthumous, married Herod's daughter Salampsio, by whom he had five children ("Ant." xviii. 5, § 4; according to "B. J." i. 28, § 6, the elder Phasael was the husband of this Salampsio). The son of Herod by Pallas was called Phasael by Herod, who likewise honored his brother's memory by naming a city northeast of Jericho "Phasaelis," and a tower of his palace at Jerusalem "Phasaelus."

G. S. KR.

PHINEHAS B. ḤAMA (generally called **R. Phinehas,** and occasionally **Phinehas ha-Kohen**): Palestinian amora of the fourth century; born probably in the town of Siknin, where he was living when his brother Samuel died (Midr. Shemuel ix.). He was a pupil of R. Jeremiah, of whose ritual practises he gives various details (*e.g.*, in Yer. Kil. 29b; Yer. Ḥag. 80b; Yer. Ket. 41a), and of R. Hilkiah. He seems also to have lived for a time in Babylonia, since a R. Phinehas who once went from that country to Palestine is mentioned in Yer. 'Er. 22d as conversing with R. Judah b. Shalom. This passage apparently refers to Phinehas b. Ḥama, as a conversation between him and Judah b. Shalom is also related elsewhere (*e.g.*, Ex. R. xii.); and it likewise explains the fact that R. Phinehas transmitted a halakah by Ḥisda (Yer. Sanh. 25c). His haggadic aphorisms, mentioned in B. B. 116a, were, therefore, probably propounded by him during his residence in Babylonia, and were not derived from Palestine, as Bacher assumes ("Ag. Pal. Amor." p. 311, note 5).

When the purity of the descent of the Jewish families in Babylonia was doubted in Palestine, Phinehas publicly proclaimed in the academy that in this respect Palestine outranked all countries excepting Babylonia (Ḳid. 71a). Many halakic sentences by Phinehas have been preserved, most of which occur in citations by Hananiah (*e.g.*, Yer. Demai 23b; Yer. Ma'as. 50c; Bik. 65d; Yer. Pes. 30d; and elsewhere). Phinehas himself occasionally transmitted earlier halakic maxims (*e.g.*, Yer. Pes. 29c), and is frequently the authority for haggadic aphorisms by such scholars as R. Hoshaiah (Lam. R. proem xxii.; Cant. R. v. 8, end), Reuben (Tan., Ḳedoshim, beginning), Abbahu (Gen. R. lxviii. 1), and many others (comp. Bacher, *l.c.* p. 314, note 4).

Phinehas' own haggadah is very extensive, and includes many maxims and aphorisms, as well as homiletic and exegetic interpretations. The following citations may serve as examples of his style: "Poverty in the house of man is more bitter than fifty plagues" (B. B. 116a). "A chaste woman in the house protecteth and reconcileth like an altar" (Tan., Wayishlaḥ, on Gen. xxxiv. 1). "While other laws decree that one must renounce his parents on pledging his allegiance as a follower and soldier of the king [the reference may be to Matt. x. 35–37], the Decalogue saith: 'Honor thy father and thy mother'" (Num. R. viii. 4). "Ps. xxvi. 10 refers to dice-players, who reckon with the left hand and sum up with the right, and thus rob one another" (Midr. Teh. *ad loc.*). "The name that a man wins for himself is worth more than that which is given him by his father and mother" (Eccl. R. vii. 4).

Bibliography: Bacher, *Ag. Pal. Amor.* iii. 310–344.

E. C. J. Z. L.

PHINEHAS BEN JAIR: Tanna of the fourth generation; lived, probably at Lydda, in the second half of the second century; son-in-law of Simeon ben Yoḥai and a fellow disciple of Judah I. He was more celebrated for piety than for learning, although his discussions with his father-in-law (Shab. 33b) evince great sagacity and a profound knowledge of tradition. A haggadah gives the following illustration of Phinehas' scrupulous honesty: Once two men deposited with him two seahs of wheat. After a prolonged absence of the depositors Phinehas sowed the wheat and preserved the harvest. This he did for seven consecutive years, and when at last the men came to claim their deposit he returned them all the accumulated grain (Deut. R. iii.).

Phinehas is said never to have accepted an invitation to a meal and, after he had attained his majority, to have refused to eat at the table of his father. The reason given by him for this course of conduct was that there are two kinds of people: (1) those who are willing to be hospitable, but can not afford to be so, and (2) those who have the means but are not willing to extend hospitality to others (Ḥul. 7b). Judah I. once invited him to a meal, and exceptionally he decided to accept the invitation; but on arriving at the house of the patriarch he noticed in the yard mules of a certain kind the use of which was forbidden by local custom on account of the danger in handling them. Thereupon he retraced his steps and did not return (Ḥul. *l.c.*).

Special weight was laid by Phinehas upon the prescriptions relating to the tithe. This feature of Phinehas' piety is described hyperbolically in the Haggadah. The latter relates a story of a mule belonging to Phinehas which, having been stolen, was released after a couple of days on account of its refusal to eat food from which the tithe had not been taken (Gen. R. xlvi.; comp. Ab. R. N. viii., end). To Phinehas is attributed the abandonment by Judah I. of his project to abolish the year of release (Yer. Demai i. 3; Ta'an. iii. 1).

Phinehas draws a gloomy picture of his time. "Since the destruction of the Temple," he says, "the members and freemen are put to shame, those who conform to the Law are held in contempt, the violent and the informer have the upper hand, and no one cares for the people or asks pity for them. We have no hope but in God" (Soṭah 49a). Elsewhere he says: "Why is it that in our time the prayers of the Jews are not heard? Because they do not know the holy name of God" (Pesiḳ. R. xxii., end;

Midr. Teh. to Ps. xci. 15). Phinehas, however, believes in man's perfectibility, and enumerates the virtues which render man worthy to receive the Holy Spirit. The Law, he says, leads to carefulness; carefulness, to diligence; diligence, to cleanliness; cleanliness, to retirement; retirement, to purity; purity, to piety; piety, to humility; humility, to fear of sin; fear of sin, to holiness; holiness, to the reception of the Holy Spirit; and the Holy Spirit, to resurrection ('Ab. Zarah. 20b; with some slight variants, Soṭah ix. 15).

The Haggadah records many miracles performed by Phinehas. Among these is that of having passed on dry ground through the River Ginai, which he had to cross on his way to ransom prisoners (Yer. Demai i. 3). According to another version, Phinehas performed this miracle while he was going to the school to deliver a lecture. His pupils, who had followed him, asked if they might without danger cross the river by the same way, whereupon Phinehas answered: "Only those who have never offended any one may do so" (Ḥul. 7a). To Phinehas is attributed the authorship of a later midrash entitled "Tadshe" or "Baraita de-Rabbi Pineḥas ben Ya'ir." The only reasons for this ascription are the facts (1) that the midrash begins with Phinehas' explanation of Gen. i. 11, from which the work derives its name, and (2) that its seventh chapter commences with a saying of his on the tree of knowledge (see JEW. ENCYC. viii. 578, *s.v.* MIDRASH TADSHE). Phinehas was buried in Kefar Biram.

BIBLIOGRAPHY: Heilprin, *Seder ha-Dorot*, ii.; Jellinek, *B. H.* iii. 164 *et seq.*, vi. 29; *Ben Chananja*, iv. 374; Bacher, *Ag. Tan.* ii. 495 *et seq.*; Isaac Halevy, *Dorot ha-Rishonim*, ii. 48; Braunschweiger, *Die Lehrer der Mischna*, p. 241, Frankfort-on-the-Main, 1903; Epstein, *Beiträge zur Jüdischen Alterthumskunde*, i., p. x.

W. B. I. BR.

R

RAB ASHI. See ASHI.

RABA (properly, **R. Aba**) **B. 'ULLA:** Babylonian amora of the third generation. The exact time at which he lived is uncertain, although he was a friend of 'Ulla, the pupil of R. Johanan (Yeb. 77a; Ḥag. 25b). His comments are mentioned before those of Raba b. Joseph b. Ḥama ('Er. 21b; see the variants in the edition of Rabbinowitz) and R. Papa (Ḥul. 91a). Raba was also a haggadist, and some of his maxims have been preserved (Shab. 31b, 62b), one of which is as follows: "When the Bible says, 'Be not over much wicked' [Eccl. vii. 17], it does not imply that one may sin a little; but it is rather an exhortation to him who has once committed evil not to repeat his iniquity, but to repent" (Shab. 31b, according to the correct reading in Yalḳ., Eccl.; see the variants in Rabbinowitz's "Variæ Lectiones" *ad loc.*).

This Raba b. ʿUlla must not be confounded with the later Rabbah b. ʿUlla, who was a pupil of Bibe b. Abaye (ʿEr. 8a), although confusion frequently occurs in the writing of their names.

Bibliography: Heilprin, *Seder ha-Dorot*, ii. 337, Warsaw, 1882; Bacher, *Ag. Bab. Amor.* pp. 139–140.

W. B. J. Z. L.

RABA (B. JOSEPH B. ḤAMA): Babylonian amora of the fourth generation; born about 280 C.E. at Maḥoza (where his father was a wealthy and distinguished scholar); died there in 352 (Sherira, in Neubauer, "M. J. C." i. 32). In his youth Raba went to Sura, where he attended the lectures of R. Ḥisda and associated with Rami b. Ḥama. About ten years after the latter's death Raba married his widow, the daughter of R. Ḥisda (Yeb. 34b).

The teachers of Raba were R. Joseph, Rabbah, and, chiefly, R. Naḥman b. Jacob (who lived in Maḥoza). The chief companion of his studies was Abaye, who was about the same age, and both of them developed the dialectic method which R. Judah and their teacher Rabbah had established in their discussions of tradition; their debates became known as the "Hawayot de Abaye we-Raba" (Suk. 28a). Raba surpassed Abaye in dialectics; his conclusions and deductions were as logical as they were keen, whereas those of Abaye, although very ingenious, were not always sound.

When, after the death of R. Joseph, Abaye was chosen head of the Academy of Pumbedita (Hor. 14a), Raba founded a school of his own in Maḥoza, and many pupils, preferring his lectures to those of Abaye, followed him thither (B. B. 22a). After Abaye's death Raba was elected head of the school, and the academy was transferred from Pumbedita to Maḥoza, which, during the lifetime of Raba, was the only seat of Jewish learning in Babylonia.

Raba occupied a prominent position among the transmitters of the Halakah, and established many new decisions and rulings, especially in ceremonial law (*e.g.*, Ḥul. 42b, 43b, 46b, 47a, b; Pes. 30a). He strove to spread the knowledge of the Halakah by discoursing upon it in lectures, to which the public were admitted, and many of his halakic decisions expressly state that they were taken from such discourses (ʿEr. 104a; Shab. 143a; Pes. 42a; B. B. 127a). He was a master of halakic exegesis, not infrequently resorting to it to demonstrate the Biblical authority underlying legal regulations. He adopted certain hermeneutic principles which were in part modifications of older rules and in part his own (comp. Bacher, "Ag. Bab. Amor." pp. 131–132). He was regarded as a greater authority than Abaye, and in cases where there was a difference of opinion between them Raba was generally followed; there are only six instances in which Abaye's decision was preferred (Ḳid. 52a).

Raba was as preeminent in Haggadah as in Halakah. In addition to the lectures to his pupils, he used to hold public discourses, most of them haggadic in character, and many of his interpretations of the Haggadah are expressly said to have been delivered in public (*e.g.*, Sanh. 107a, 108b, 109a; Ḥag. 3a, 15b; 'Er. 21b; *et al.*). Even more numerous are the interpretations which, although not expressly stated to have been delivered in public, seem to have been presented before a general audience, since they do not differ from the others in form. The greater part of these expositions, which frequently contain popular maxims and proverbs (comp. Bacher, *l.c.* pp. 124 *et seq.*), refer to the first books of the Hagiographa—Psalms, Proverbs, Job, Song of Songs, and Ecclesiastes.

Bacher justly infers from this that the haggadic lectures of Raba were delivered in connection with the Sabbath afternoon service, at which, according to a custom observed in Nehardea and later, probably, in Maḥoza also, parashiyyot were read from the Hagiographa (Shab. 116b; Rapoport, "'Erek Millin," pp. 170 *et seq.*). Raba therefore appended his haggadic discourse to the section which had been read.

The study of the Law is a frequent topic of Raba's Haggadah. In the reckoning in the future world each one will be obliged to state whether he devoted certain times to study, and whether he diligently pursued the knowledge of the Law, striving to deduce the meaning of one passage from another (Shab. 31a). The Torah, in his view, is a medicine, life-giving to those who devote themselves to it with right intent, but a deadly poison for those who do not properly avail themselves of it (Yoma 72b). "A true disciple of wisdom must be upright; and his interior must harmonize with his exterior" (*ib.*). Raba frequently emphasizes the respect due to teachers of the Law (*e.g.*, Sanh. 99b; Shab. 23b), the proper methods of study ('Ab. Zarah 19a), and the rules applicable to the instruction of the young (B. B. 21a). In his Haggadah, furthermore, he repeatedly discusses the characters of Biblical history (Sanh. 108b; B. B. 123a; Soṭah 34b; etc.).

Raba was secretly initiated, probably by his teacher R. Joseph, into haggadic esoterism (Bacher, *l.c.* p. 130); he is the author of a number of aphorisms which are tinged with mysticism (see especially Sanh. 65b). On one occasion he wished to lecture in the academy upon the Tetragrammaton, but an old man prevented him, reminding him that such knowledge must be kept secret (Pes. 50a). Raba enjoyed the special protection of the mother of Shapur II., the reigning King of Persia (Ta'an. 24b), and for this reason, and in consideration of large sums which he secretly contributed to the court (Ḥag. 5b), he succeeded in making less severe Shapur's oppressions of the Jews in Babylonia.

BIBLIOGRAPHY: Heilprin, *Seder ha-Dorot,* ii. 323–327; Grätz, *Gesch.* iv. 331–337; A. I. Jaffe, in Berlinert *Magazin,* 1885, pp. 217–224; Bacher, *Ag. Bab. Amor.* pp. 108 *et seq.*, 414–433; Weiss, *Dor,* iii. 200–209; Halevy, *Dorot ha-Rishonim,* ii. 473–480.

W. B. J. Z. L.

RABA B. ADA: Babylonian amora of the third generation; pupil of R. Judah b. Ezekiel at Pumbedita (Beẓah 33b). He quoted sayings by Rab which he had heard from his (Raba's) father or from R. Judah (Men. 39a; Yoma 53b; comp. Ta'an. 24b), and aphorisms by R. Isaac (Tem. 29a; Mak. 18b), but none of his own sayings has been preserved.

BIBLIOGRAPHY: Heilprin, *Seder ha-Dorot,* ii. 337.

W. B. J. Z. L.

RABBAH B. ABUHA: Babylonian amora of the second generation; teacher and father-in-law of R. Naḥman b. Jacob. He was related to the house of the exilarchs (Letter of Sherira Gaon, in Neubauer, "M. J. C." i. 23; Halevy, "Dorot ha-Rishonim," ii. 412), and is even said to have been an exilarch himself (Weiss, "Dor," iii. 176; Bacher, "Ag. Bab. Amor." p. 46). He lived at Nehardea; and after the destruction of that city in 259 he went with his son-in-law to Maḥoza, where they both settled (Letter of Sherira; *l.c.* p. 29). There are allusions to a number of decisions and rulings made by him while at the latter city (Yeb. 115b; Shab. 59b; 'Er. 26a). He was a pupil of Rab (Abba Arika), whom he frequently cited as an authority (Sanh. 63a; Shab. 129b, 130b; 'Er. 75b, 85a, 86a; Giṭ. 62b; and many other passages).

Rabbah was not a prominent teacher; and he himself admitted that he was not thoroughly versed even in the four orders of the Mishnah, which were generally studied in the schools (B. M. 114b). Some of his interpretations of various mishnaic passages have been preserved (*e.g.*, Ber. 53b; Shab. 57a; Sheb. 49b), as well as confirmations of earlier halakot (*e.g.*, B. Ḳ. 46b; Shab. 149a), and halakic decisions of his own (*e.g.*, Ber. 21b; Shab. 76b; B. M. 91b). The following haggadic maxim by him may be cited here: "The commandment to love one's neighbor [Lev. xix. 18] must be observed even in the execution of a criminal, since he should be granted as easy a death as possible" (Ket. 37b). According to a legend, Rabbah was a friend of the prophet Elijah (Meg. 15b; B. M. 114a, b), who gave him leaves from paradise, so that he became rich (B. M. *l.c.*).

BIBLIOGRAPHY: Heilprin, *Seder ha-Dorot,* ii. 335–336. Warsaw, 1882; Weiss, *Dor,* iii. 176–177; Bacher, *Aq. Bab. Amor.* pp. 46, 81; Halevy, *Dorot ha-Rishonim,* ii. 206a–207b.

W. B. J. Z. L.

RABBAH B. ḤANA (B. ABBA B. ḤANA OF KAFRI): Babylonian amora of the first generation; nephew of R. Ḥiyya and cousin of Abba Arika (Rab; Sanh. 5a). Like Rab, he went to Palestine, where he was one of the prominent pupils of Judah ha-Nasi I. When he was about to return to Babylonia he was empowered by the latter, at the instance of R. Ḥiyya, to decide all forms of religious questions and to officiate as dayyan (*ib.*). After his return Rabbah was frequently associated with his cousin Rab (Ḳid. 59a; B. B. 52a). He transmitted a saying of his uncle R. Ḥiyya (Yer. B. K. x. 7b); and some of his own halakic sayings have been preserved (Ḥul. 100a, where "Rabbah b. Ḥana" should be read instead of "Rabbah bar bar Ḥana"; Yer. Beẓah iv. 62d; Yer. Shab. iv. 7a; Yer. Giṭ. i. 43b, quoted by Ze'era).

BIBLIOGRAPHY: Heilprin, *Seder ha-Dorot,* ii. 331; Frankel, *Mebo,* p. 57a, b; Grätz, *Gesch.* iv. 197, 257.

W. B. J. Z. L.

RABBAH BAR BAR ḤANA: Babylonian amora of the second generation; grandson of Ḥana, the brother of Ḥiyya. He went to Palestine and became a pupil of R. Johanan, whose sayings he transmitted. Rabbah bar bar Ḥana (Rabbah bar Rabbah bar Ḥana) does not seem to have enjoyed high regard in his adopted country, for it was taken as a matter of course that R. Simeon b. Laḳish should not do him the honor of addressing him in public (Yoma 9b). After a somewhat prolonged sojourn in Palestine he returned to Babylonia, residing both at Pumbedita and at Sura. In the former city he at first refused to attend the lectures of R. Judah b. Ezekiel (Shab. 148a), but he soon became his friend, and was consulted by him in difficult cases (M. Ḳ. 17a). Judah and his pupil Rabbah b. Naḥmani once visited Rabbah, who was ill, and submitted a halakic question to him. While they were there a Zoroastrian priest ("geber") suddenly appeared and extinguished the lamp, the day being a festival of Ormuzd, on which Jews were forbidden to have fire in their houses (Grätz, "Gesch." 2d ed., iv. 292). Rabbah thereupon sorrowfully exclaimed: "O God, let us live either under Thy protection, or at least under the protection of the children of Esau" (the Romans; Giṭ. 16b–17a).

The persecutions of the Babylonian Jews by the Sassanids caused Rabbah to resolve to return to Palestine (Pes. 51a), although it is nowhere said that he carried out that intention. During his residence at Sura he wished to introduce the recitation of the Decalogue into the daily prayer, but was dissuaded by R. Ḥisda (Ber. 12a). Later he visited Maḥoza, and he tells of the wonderful feats he saw performed. there by a juggler (B. B. 73a, b; comp. Bacher, "Ag. Bab. Amor." p. 88, note 7, with Neubauer, "G. T." p. 398).

Some haggadic sayings by Rabbah bar bar Ḥana have been preserved. He compares the Law to fire (Jer. xxiii. 29), in that as fire does not start of itself neither does the Law endure in solitary study (Ta'an. 7a). His interpretations of Prov. ix. 3, 14 and Isa. xxviii. 26 (see Sanh. 38a, 105a) also are noteworthy; his saying that "the soul of one pious man is worth the whole world" (Sanh. 103b) is especially memorable.

Rabbah bar bar Ḥana's stories of his marvelous experiences during his voyages and his journeys through the desert have become famous. These accounts may be divided into two classes. In the first he records his observations, generally beginning with the words "I have seen." Among these are his remarks regarding the identity of the most fertile part of Palestine—"the land flowing with milk and honey" (Ket. 111b–112a); the distance between Jericho and Jerusalem (Yoma 39b); the area of the district in the plains of Moab mentioned in Num. xxxiii. 49 as the camp of the children of Israel (Yoma 75b); the castor-oil plant cultivated in Palestine, or the gourd of Jonah (Shab. 21a). Here also belong his accounts of his relations with the Arabs, one of whom once used a term which explained to him the word יהבך in Ps. lv. 23 (Ket. 72b, 75a; Yeb. 120b; R. H. 26b).

The other group of the narratives of Rabbah bar bar Ḥana includes his fantastic adventures on the sea and in the desert. In these stories one of the most conspicuous figures is the Arab who was the guide of Rabbah and his companions on their journey through the desert. This Arab knew the route so well that he could tell from the odor of the sand when a spring was near (B. B. 73b). The travelers passed through the desert in which the children of Israel wandered for forty years, and the Arab showed Mount Sinai to Rabbah, who heard the voice of God speaking from the mountain and regretting Israel's exile. The Arab likewise pointed out the place where Korah and his followers had been swallowed by the earth, and from the smoking abyss Rabbah heard the words, "Moses is truth and his teachings are truth, but we are liars" (B. B. 74a). He was shown the gigantic bodies of the Israelites who had died in the desert, lying face upward, and the place where heaven and earth almost touched, so that he could watch the rotation of the heavenly spheres around the earth in twenty-four hours (*ib.*).

Rabbah's stories of his adventures on the sea resemble tales of other navigators concerning the immense size of various marine animals. As an example the following one may be cited: "Once, while on a ship, we came to a gigantic fish at rest, which we supposed to be an island, since there was sand on its back, in which grass was growing. We therefore landed, made a fire, and cooked our meal. But when the fish felt the heat he rolled over, and we would have drowned had not the ship been near" (B. B. 73b). Here the resemblance to the later voyage of Sindbad is obvious. Rabbah himself tells how his tales were received. In regard to two of them his colleagues remarked, "All Rabbahs are asses and all Bar bar Ḥanas fools" (B. B. 74a). Rabbah's stories have called forth an entire literature; in addition to the numerous commentaries on the haggadic portions of the Talmud which dwell by preference on these accounts, more than twenty essays interpreting and annotating them have appeared in various periodicals.

BIBLIOGRAPHY: Heilprin, *Seder ha-Dorot*, ii. 331: Bacher, *Ag. Bab. Amor.* pp. 87–93.

W. B. J. Z. L.

RABBAH B. ḤANAN: Babylonian amora of the fourth generation; pupil of Rabbah bar Naḥmani and a colleague of Abaye, who was of the same age and had been his fellow student (Ber. 48a, according to the correct reading; comp. Rabbinowitz, "Variæ Lectiones"). Rabbah bar Naḥmani declared that both his pupils would eulogize their teacher after his death (Shab. 153a). Rabbah ben Ḥanan frequently conversed with Abaye; addressing questions to him ('Er. 14b, 38b, 45a, 68a, 75b; Shab. 148b; Men. 14b; Bek. 54a), and he once called Abaye "tarda" (heedless one; Ker. 18b). He associated much with Raba also, expounding problems for him (Zeb. 55a) or addressing questions to him (Men. 40a; Beẓah 12b). He resided at Artebana, a small town near Pumbedita, which he could easily reach on the Sabbath ('Er. 51b), and he was evidently wealthy (*ib.*; comp. Rashi *ad loc.*).

BIBLIOGRAPHY: Heilprin, *Seder ha-Dorot*, p. 335, Warsaw, 1883.

W. B. J. Z. L.

RABBAH B. ḤIYYA OF CTESIPHON: Babylonian amora of the second generation. He is said to have performed the ceremony of ḥaliẓah in a manner which was considered allowable only by one tanna, the majority disapproving. For this he was censured by R. Samuel (Yeb. 704a).

BIBLIOGRAPHY: Heilprin, *Seder ha-Dorot*, p. 337.

W. B. J. Z. L.

RABBAH B. HUNA: Babylonian amora of the third generation; died in 322; son of R. Huna, the head of the Academy of Sura (Heilprin, "Seder ha-Dorot," ii. 167b). He was a man of true piety (Shab. 31a, b) and genuine modesty (M. Ḳ. 28a; comp. Giṭ. 43a), and was urged by his father to attend R. Ḥisda's lectures diligently and to profit by his acumen. At first, however, Rabbah held aloof because matters were discussed which did not appeal to his earnest nature (Shab. 82a); but later he became closely associated with R. Ḥisda, and was appointed judge under him (*ib.* 10a); subsequently the two treated of haggadic subjects together (Pes. 110a, 117a; Soṭah 39a). After the death of R. Ḥisda, Rabbah became the head of the Academy of Sura, though he apparently held this position without the approval of the exilarch. His general relations with the exilarchate were by no means friendly, and he declared himself independent of its authority (Sanh. 5a).

A number of halakic and a few haggadic sentences of Rabbah b. Huna have been preserved: "He who is insolent must be considered a transgressor" (Ta'an. 7b). "When one falls into a rage he loses the respect of God" (Ned. 22b). "He who possesses learning [in the Torah], but is without the fear of God, is like unto a steward to whom have been given the keys of the inner storehouses but not the outer keys; he can not gain access to the storehouses" (Shab. 31a, b).

BIBLIOGRAPHY: Heilprin, *Seder ha-Dorot*, pp. 167b, 168a, Warsaw, 1882; Weiss, Dor, iii. 195; Bacher, *Ag. Bab. Amor.* pp. 62–63.

W. B. J. Z. L.

RABBAH B. LIWAI: Babylonian amora of the fourth generation; contemporary of Raba b. Joseph b. Ḥama, two of whose decisions he proved to be wrong, thus compelling their annulment (Pes. 40b; 'Ab. Zarah 65b). A saying of his has been preserved (Nid. 46b). Raba was extremely vexed with him, and once, when a misfortune befell Rabbah, Raba said that it was a punishment for having confuted him during a public discourse (Pes. 110a).

BIBLIOGRAPHY: Heilprin, *Seder ha-Dorot*, ii. 335, Warsaw, 1882.

W. B. J. Z. L.

RABBAH B. MARI: Babylonian amora of the fourth generation, who resided for a time in Palestine and then returned to his home (Yoma 78a), where he transmitted aphorisms of R. Johanan (B. Ḳ. 92a) and especially of R. Joshua b. Levi (Ber. 42b, 44a). He also delivered haggadic lectures ('Er. 86), of which some passages were known even in Palestine (Yoma 86b; B. B. 16b), although his name is mentioned neither in the Palestinian Talmud nor in midrashic literature.

He was a frequent visitor at the house of Raba (Ber. 42b), on whose haggadah he exercised great influence. Raba asked for the Biblical bases of the ideas expressed in many aphorisms current among scholars (B. Ḳ. 92a; Yeb. 62b), and the answers given satisfied him. Raba also showed Rabbah thirteen popular proverbs, for which the latter gave references to the Bible (B. Ḳ. *l.c.*); and it is noteworthy in this connection that Rabbah cited a passage from Ben Sira (Ecclus. [Sirach] xiii. 15) and that he regarded the latter as one of the hagiographic "ketubim." In reply to Raba's inquiries, Rabbah b. Mari also interpreted the passages in Jer. xxxiv. 5 and II Kings xxii. 20 as being in entire harmony with Jer. xxxix. 7 and II Chron. xxxv. 23 (M. Ḳ. 28b).

BIBLIOGRAPHY: Heilprin, *Seder ha-Dorot*, ii. 169a, Warsaw, 1882; Bacher, *Ag. Bab. Amor.* pp. 124–127.

W. B. J. Z. L.

RABBAH B. MATNA: Babylonian amora of the fourth generation; contemporary and colleague of R. Zera II. Rabbah was slow and careful in his methods, and his conclusions were generally correct and were accepted as authoritative in practical matters (Hor. 14a). Rabbah is mentioned in two other passages in the Talmud; one being Shab. 21a, where he transmits a baraita, and the other Pes. 34a, where he comments on a difficult mishnaic passage.

BIBLIOGRAPHY: Heilprin, *Seder ha-Dorot*, ii. 338, Warsaw, 1882; Halevy, *Dorot ha-Rishonim*, ii. 460–461.

W. B. J. Z. L.

RABBAH B. NAḤMAN B. JACOB: Babylonian amora of the third generation; contemporary of Rabbah b. Huna, with whom he was closely associated. The latter visited him at his home (Shab. 119a), and once sent him a question, addressing him with the words, "May our teacher teach us" (Yeb. 25a). These friendly relations, however, were subsequently disturbed, for Rabbah b. Naḥman once had some of Rabbah b. Huna's trees cut down because they stood on the banks of a river and interfered with the river traffic. When Rabbah b. Huna heard of this he cursed Rabbah b. Naḥman: "May the offspring of him who caused these trees to be cut down be uprooted." It is related that Rabbah b. Naḥman's children died in consequence of this malediction (B. M. 108a).

BIBLIOGRAPHY: Heilprin, *Seder ha-Dorot*, ii. 336, Warsaw, 1882.

W. B. J. Z. L.

RABBAH B. NAḤMANI: Babylonian amora of the third generation; born about 270; died about 330; a descendant of a priestly family of Judea which traced its lineage to the prophet Eli (R. H. 18a). He was a pupil of R. Huna at Sura and of R. Judah b. Ezekiel at Pumbedita, and so distinguished himself as a student that R. Huna seldom decided a question of importance without consulting him (comp. Giṭ. 27a; B. M. 18b; B. B. 172b; Yeb. 61b). His brethren in Palestine were little pleased with his residence ia Babylonia, and wrote to him to come to the Holy Land, where he would find a teacher in R. Johanan, since it would be far better for him, wise though he was, to have a guide than to rely on himself in his studies (Ket. 111a). Rabbah, however, seems not to have answered this urgent request, and apparently never left Babylonia, all supposed evidence to the contrary being refuted by Bacher ("Ag. Bab. Amor." pp. 97 *et seq.*). In Shebu. 10b and Ned. 57a, where Rabbah is asked by R. Ḥisda, "Who will listen to thee and thy teacher R. Johanah?" the latter is only figuratively called Rabbah's teacher. There is no foundation for the theory which attributes to Rabbah the authorship of the haggadic compilation Bereshit Rabbah and of the other midrashic works bearing the designation of "Rabbah" (Abraham ibn Daud, "Sefer ha-Ḳabbalah," in Neubauer, "M. J. C." p. 58).

Rabbah was not a prolific haggadist and was, therefore, scarcely fitted to project such a collection of haggadot. While most of his halakic aphorisms have been preserved, only about ten of his haggadic sayings are known (Sanh. 21b, 26b; Shab. 64a; Pes. 68b; Meg. 15b; Ḥag. 5b; 'Ar. 8b; 'Er. 22a; Giṭ. 31b); evidently he had little interest in haggadic exegesis. His main attention was devoted to the Halakah, which he endeavored to elucidate by interpreting the mishnaic decisions and the baraitot, and by determining the fundamental reasons for the various Pentateuchal and rabbinical laws and explaining the apparent contradictions contained in them. He often asks: "Why did the Torah command this?" "Why did the sages forbid this?" His keen dialectics won him the name of "'Oḳer Harim" (uprooter of mountains; Ber. 64a), since he deduced new conclusions by separating individual passages from their normal context. He did not confine his interest to the practical ordinances of the Mishnah, however, like his teacher R. Judah, but studied the entire six mishnaic orders (Ta'an. 24a, b), and even in the remoter subject of the Levitical regulations on cleanness and uncleanness he was the leading authority (B. M. 86a).

On the death of R. Judah, Rabbah was elected "resh metibta" of the Academy of Pumbedita, which office he held until his death, twenty-two years later (Ber. 64a; Letter of Sherira Gaon, in Neubauer, "M. J. C." pp. 30–31). He greatly increased the prestige of the academy and attracted a host of auditors, so that during the "kallah" months his audience is said to have numbered twelve thousand (B. M. 86a). He was wont to begin his lectures with witty aphorisms and interesting anecdotes which put his audience in a cheerful mood and made it receptive of serious thoughts (Shab. 30b).

Rabbah frequently tested the judgment of his audience, and quickened its attention by captious questions and paradoxical halakot (Ber. 33b). With all his critical ability, however, he was unable to free himself from certain views on demonology which he shared with his colleagues (Ḥul. 105; comp. Bacher, *l.c.* p. 101, note). Rabbah was highly esteemed by scholars, but was hated by the people of Pumbedita because of his severe and frequent denunciation of their fraudulent proclivities (Shab. 153a; Rashi *ad loc.*).

Rabbah and his family lived in great poverty, and seem to have suffered various calamities; even his death was a wretched one. The charge was brought against him that during the kallah months his twelve thousand auditors took advantage of his lectures to escape their poll-tax. Bailiffs were sent to seize him; but, being warned, he fled, and wandered about in the vicinity of Pumbedita. His body, which had been concealed by the birds (B. M. 86a), was found in a thicket where he had hidden from his pursuers. Many legends exist concerning his death (*ib.*).

BIBLIOGRAPHY: Heilprin, *Seder ha-Dorot*, ii. 332–334, Warsaw, 1882; Weiss, *Dor*, iii. 190–191; Halevy, *Dorot ha-Rishonim*, ii. 218a–220a; Grätz, *Gesch.* iv. 322–327; Bacher, *Ag. Bab. Amor.* pp. 97–101.

W. B. J. Z. L.

RABBAH OF PARZIḲI: Babylonian amora of the sixth generation; contemporary of R. Ashi, with whom he often had discussions (Soṭah 26b; Pes. 76b; B. Ḳ. 36a). His learned son Huna also was a pupil of R. Ashi.

BIBLIOGRAPHY: Heilprin, *Seder ha-Dorot*, ii. 338.

W. B. J. Z. L.

RABBAH B. SAMUEL (called also **Abba b. Samuel**): Babylonian amora of the second half of the third century; son of Mar Samuel of Nehardea. He was an associate of R. Ḥiyya bar Abba, to whom he addressed a question (Zeb. 105a, where he is called Abba), of R. Ḥisda (B. Ḳ. 98b), and of R. Sheshet ('Er. 11b, 39b; Sheb. 45b). To the two last named he communicated a number of baraitot previously unknown to them. Rabbah b. Samuel was evidently well versed in these traditions, since he appears in Hag. 17b and R. H. 20a as expounding them. In Ber. 29a he raises an objection to a tradition of his lather as cited by R. Naḥman, and in Ber. 40a he transmits others of R. Ḥiyya. A number of his own apothegms, both halakic (Shab. 12b; Yer. Sanh. 21c) and haggadic (Yeb. 63b; B. B. 15b; Meg. 14a, b), have been preserved.

BIBLIOGRAPHY: Heilprin, *Seder ha-Dorot*, ii. 336, Warsaw, 1882; Bacher, *Ag. Pal. Amor.* iii. 532–533.

W. B. J. Z. L.

RABBAH B. SHELA: Babylonian amora of the fourth generation; contemporary of Raba, and a judge (Ket. 104b), probably at Pumbedita. His strict honesty is shown by a judicial maxim of his which states that a judge may not borrow anything from those who are under his jurisdiction, unless he is in a position to lend something in return, since otherwise he may be bribed by the kindness which has been done to him in the making of the loan in question (Ket. 105b). Rabbah was probably a pupil of R. Ḥisda, to whom he once addressed a halakic question (Shab. 81a, b); he also quotes some of Ḥisda's halakic and haggadic passages (Shab. 7a, 33a). He likewise transmitted maxims in the name of R. Naḥman (B. B. 155b) and of R. Matna (Ḥag. 23a). Several of his interpretations of Biblical passages have been preserved, some being his independent opinions (Yoma 54a, b; Men. 87a; Ned. 41a), while others were derived from his predecessors (Ta'an. 2a; Soṭah 35b; B. B. 123b).

According to a legend, Rabbah had a conversation with Elijah in which he asked what was the occupation of God, receiving the answer that He was promulgating halakic maxims in the name of the sages, although there were no citations from R. Meïr, because he had studied under Aḥer (Elisha b. Abuyah). Rabbah replied: "Why is this? R. Meïr has studied only the Torah under Aḥer, and has disregarded his other teachings, like one who finds a pomegranate and eats the fruit, but throws away the rind." Thereupon Elijah said: "Because of thine argument God has just quoted an aphorism by R. Meïr" (Ḥag. 15b).

BIBLIOGRAPHY: Heilprin, *Seder ha-Dorot*, ii. 336–337, Warsaw, 1882; Bacher, *Ag. Bab. Amor.* ii. 140–141.

W. B. J. Z. L.

RABBAH TUSFA'AH (TOSEFA'AH): Babylonian amora of the seventh generation. He was a pupil of Rabina I. (Suk. 32a; comp. Halevy, "Dorot ha-Rishonim," iii. 96) and a contemporary of Rabina II., with whom, sometimes, he is mentioned in the Talmud (Shab. 95a; M. Ḳ. 4a). A few independent decisions of Rabbah have been preserved (Ber. 50a; Yeb. 80b). One of them (Yeb. 80b) assumes that the pregnancy of a woman may extend from nine to twelve months. The chief work of Rabbah was to complete, by additions and amplifications, the compilation of the Talmud begun by R. Ashi. These additions consisted for the most part of short, explanatory remarks, indispensable for an understanding of Talmudic themes or for deciding between the conflicting opinions of older authorities (Halevy, *l.c.* p. 20). From these additions and amplifications (tosafot) to the Talmud he is said to have derived his name of Tosefa'ah (= "the completer"; Halevy, *l.c.* iii. 19; Brüll's "Jahrb." ii. 19). It is more probable, however, that he was so named after his birthplace—Tusfah = Thospia (Brüll, *l.c.*). Rabbah Tosefa'ah is seldom mentioned by name in the Talmud—only in nine places. However, all sayings in the Babylonian Talmud introduced by "Yesh omerim" (some say) are ascribed to him (Heilprin, "Seder ha-Dorot," iii. 337; Brüll, *l.c.* ii. 13). Rabbah Tosefa'ah succeeded Mar b. R. Ashi (Tabyomi) as head of the Academy of Sura, which position he held for six years. He died in 494 (Sherira, in Neubauer, "M. J. C. M. 34; Abraham ibn Daud, "Sefer ha-Ḳabbalah," *ib.* i. 59).

BIBLIOGRAPHY: Heilprin, *Seder ha-Dorot,* ii. 337; Weiss, Dor, iii. 314–315; Brüll, *Jahrb.* ii. 12–13, Frankfort-on-the-Main, 1876; Grätz, *Gesch.* iv. 374; Halevy, *Dorot ha-Rishonim,* iii. 95–98.

W. B. J. Z. L.

RABIN B. ADDA: Babylonian amora of the third generation; brother of Rabbah b. Adda and pupil of Judah b. Ezekiel of Pumbedita (Beẓah 33b). He transmitted traditions by R. Isaac (Ber. 6a; Pes. 8b, where he is called **Abin**) and a decision of Rabbi's, but none of his own has been preserved.

W. B. J. Z. L.

RABINA I.: Babylonian amora of the fifth generation; died about 420. He was a pupil of Raba b. Joseph b. Ḥama, and his extreme youthfulness at that time is shown by the fact that his teacher designated him and Ḥama b. Bisa as "dardeḳi" (children; B. B. 16b). He frequently addressed questions to Raba (Mak. 8a; Men. 67a), whose sayings he cites (Shab. 136a, b). At an early age Rabina was recognized as a teacher, leaving the academy at Maḥoza while Raba was still living ('Er. 63a; Halevy, "Dorot ha-Rishonim," ii. 543–544). Wherever he lived he was recognized as a teacher and judge, and was called upon to render independent decisions ('Er. 40a; Giṭ. 73a). Rabina was on friendly terms with Naḥman b. Isaac (Giṭ. 32b; Hor. 9a), and was a colleague of R. Aḥa (b. Raba), with whom he had many disputations on legal questions, Rabina being inclined to liberal interpretations while R. Aḥa upheld those more rigorous. Rabina's decisions always prevailed, with the exception of three cases in which, contrary to his custom, he advocated stern measures (Ḥul. 93b). When R. Ashi became director of the Academy of Sura (or Matah Meḥasya), Rabina became a student there, although he was at least as old as Ashi—perhaps even a few years older; however, he was rather the associate of Ashi ("talmid ḥaber") than his pupil ('Er. 63a). Next to Ashi, Rabina had the greatest share in the redaction of the Talmud undertaken by Ashi and his colleagues. Rabina died seven years before Ashi.

BIBLIOGRAPHY: Heilprin, *Seder ha-Dorot,* ii. 339; Halevy, *Dorot ha-Rishonim,* ii. 536–550, iii. 74–85.

W. B. J. Z. L.

RABINA II. (B. HUNA): Babylonian amora of the seventh generation. He did not remember his father, R. Huna, who died while Rabina was still a child, but the Talmud states several times that his mother communicated to him the opinions held by his father (Ber. 39b; Men. 68b). After his fathers death, his maternal uncle, Rabina I., became his guardian (Ket. 100b). Rabina II. officiated as judge at Sura shortly after Ashi's death (Ket. 69a), and was a colleague of Mar

b. Ashi (Men. 37b; Ber. 36a), although he was not so prominent. After Rabbah Tosefa'a's death Rabina became, for a year (474), director of the Academy of Sura (Abraham ibn Daud, "Sefer ha-Ḳabbalah," in Neubauer, "M. J. C." i. 61). According to Sherira Gaon (Neubauer, *Le.* i. 34), Rabina, "the last of the Hora'ah" (B. M. 86a), died in 500. His death marks the close of the amoraic period and of the completion of the Talmud redaction.

BIBLIOGRAPHY: Grätz, *Gesch.* iv. 377; Halevy, *Dorot ha-Rishonim*, iii. 5–14.

W. B. J. Z. L.

RABINA III. OF UMZA: Sabora of the first generation; died Adar, 508. Nothing further about him is known (Sherira Gaon, in Neubauer, "M. J. C." i. 34; Grätz, "Gesch." iv. 377).

W. B. J. Z. L.

RAFRAM I. (BEN PAPA): Babylonian amora of the fourth century. In his youth he was a pupil of R. Ḥisda. (Shab. 82a), in whose name he transmits various halakic and haggadic sayings (Ber. 26b; Shab. 81a; 'Er. 83a; Ta'an. 13a; Ḳid. 81b; Ber. 8a, 59a). He succeeded Rab Dimi as head of the school in Pumbedita. He died, according to Abraham ibn Daud, in 387; according to Sherira Gaon, in 395.

BIBLIOGRAPHY: Abraham ibn Daud, *Sefer ha-Ḳabbalah*, in Neubauer, *M. J. C.* i. 59; Sherira Gaon, *ib.* i. 32; Heilprin, *Seder ha-Dorot*, ii. 314; Weiss, Dor, iii. 207; Halevy, *Dorot ha-Rishonim*, iii. 85–89.

W. B. J. Z. L.

RAFRAM II.: Babylonian amora of the seventh generation; he was a pupil of R. Ashi, to whom he frequently addressed questions (Ket. 95b; Giṭ. 42a), and a colleague of Rabina II. (Yoma 78a). He succeeded R. Gebiha as head of the Academy of Pumbedita, and held that position from 433 until his death in 443 (Sherira, in Neubauer, "M. J. C." i. 34; Abraham ibn Daud, *ib.* i. 61).

BIBLIOGRAPHY: Halevy, *Dorot ha-Rishonim*, iii. 85–89.

W. B. J. Z. L.

RAMI B. EZEKIEL: Babylonian amora of the third generation; younger brother of Judah b. Ezekiel, the founder of the Academy of Pumbedita. He studied under his father, Ezekiel (Sanh. 80b). Disregarding the opinion of his brother Judah that it was a sin to leave Babylon for Palestine, Rami went to Bene-Berak (a city southeast of Joppa), where Akiba's academy had once stood, and there he became convinced that Palestine was indeed a land flowing with milk and honey (Ket. 111b). He subsequently returned to Babylonia, however, and corrected many of the sayings which his brother Judah had cited in the names of Rab and Samuel: "Harken not to the sayings quoted by my brother in the name of Rab [or Samuel], for Rab [or Samuel] spake thus" (Ket. 21a, 60a, 76b; Ḥul. 44a). Rami occasionally quotes a baraita (Shab. 138a; 'Er. 14b, 58b). He had friendly relations with Rab Huna (Shab. 138b).

BIBLIOGRAPHY: Heilprin, *Seder ha-Dorot*, ii. 343; Grätz, *Gesch.* iv. 297.

W. B. J. Z. L.

RAMI B. ḤAMA: Babylonian amora of the third generation; a pupil of K. Ḥisda, and a fellow student of Raba, who was somewhat his junior (B. B. 12b; Suk. 29a; comp. Rabbinowitz, "Variæ Lectiones"). He frequently addressed questions to R. Ḥisda (Ket. 86b; Yoma 58a; Pes. 27b; 'Er. 8b, 73a). R. Ḥisda once asked him a question to which Rami found an answer in a mishnah; R. Ḥisda thereupon rewarded him by rendering him a personal service (B. Ḳ. 20a, b). He was also associated with R. Naḥman, whom he often endeavored to refute ('Er. 34b; B. M. 65a; Ḥul. 35a). Rami married the daughter of his teacher Ḥisda; when he died, at an early age, his colleague Raba married his widow. Raba declared that his premature death was a punishment for having affronted Manasseh b. Taḥlifa, a student of the Law, by treating him as an ignoramus (Ber. 47b). Rami b. Ḥama was possessed of rare mental acuteness, but Raba asserted that his unusual acumen led him to reach his conclusions too hastily. He attempted to decide questions independently, and would not always search for a mishnah or baraita to support an opinion. His pupil Isaac b. Judah left him, therefore, to study under R. Sheshet, saying that although a decision might apparently be based on correct reasoning, it must be ignored if a mishnah or a baraita could be found that contradicted it; but a decision rendered in agreement with a mishnah or a baraita does not become invalid, even where another mishnah or baraita can be cited in opposition to it (Zeb. 96b). Rami b. Ḥama's daughter married R. Ashi (Beẓah 29b).

BIBLIOGRAPHY: Heilprin, *Seder ha-Dorot*, ii. 343.

W. B. J. Z. L.

RAMI B. TAMRE: Babylonian amora of the third generation; a native of Pumbedita, and probably a pupil of R. Judah. He once went to Sura on the eve of the Day of Atonement, and attracted attention by conduct which was not regarded as permissible there. According to Ḥul. 110a, b, he justified his behavior, when brought before R. Ḥisda, by citing a saying of R. Judah's, thereby proving himself an acute scholar. In the same passage he is identified with Rami b. Diḳuli, who transmits a saying of Samuel in Yeb. 80a. In another passage he is designated as the father-in-law of Rami b. Diḳuli (Men. 29b).

BIBLIOGRAPHY: Heilprin, *Seder ha-Dorot, ii.* 344.

W. B. J. Z. L.

REḤUMAI (I.), RAB: Babylonian amora of the fifth generation; pupil of Raba b. Joseph b. Ḥama. He addressed some questions to Abaye (Pes. 39a; Nazir 13a). He died on the eve of a Day of Atonement, and the manner of his death is told as follows: He was wont to return home on the eve of every Day of Atonement, but on the last occasion he was so engrossed in his studies that the time for departure passed and left him still at Maḥoza. His wife waited for him in vain, and at last gave expression to her disappointment in tears. As a punishment for his neglect, so runs the legend, it was decreed in heaven that he should die. Accordingly, the roof on which he was sitting fell in and he was killed (Ket. 62b).

BIBLIOGRAPHY: Heilprin, *Seder ha-Dorot*, ii. 342; Halevy, *Dorot ha-Rishonim*, iii. 12.

W. B. J. Z. L.

REḤUMAI II.: Babylonian amora of the seventh generation; pupil of Rabina I., for whom he expounded a saying of Huna b. Taḥlifa (Zeb. 77a). After Rafram II., Reḥumai II. was the head of the Academy of Pumbedita from 443 to 456, dying during the persecutions of the Jews under Yezdegerd II (Sherira, in Neubauer, "M. J. C." i. 34, where it is said that he was frequently called Naḥumai; Grätz, "Gesch." iv. 371; Halevy, "Dorot ha-Rishonim," iii. 12–13).

W. B. J. Z. L.

REḤUMAI III.: One of the early saboraim; died in 505, in the month of Nisan. In 'Er. 11a he is mentioned with his contemporary R. Jose; each of them gives a different explanation of an expression used by an earlier authority (Sherira, in Neubauer, "M. J. C." i. 34, 45; Halevy, "Dorot ha-Rishonim," iii. 13; Grätz, "Gesch." iv. 377).

W. B. J. Z. L.

RESH LAḲISH. See SIMEON BEN LAḲISH.

S

SADDUCEES (Hebrew, צדוקים; Greek, Σαδδουκαῖοι): Name given to the party representing views and practises of the Law and interests of Temple and priesthood directly opposite to those of the PHARISEES. The singular form, "Ẓadduḳi" (Greek, Σαδδουκαῖος), is an adjective denoting "an adherent of the Bene Ẓadok," the descendants of Zadok, the high priests who, tracing their pedigree back to Zadok, the chief of the priesthood in the days of David and Solomon (I Kings i. 84, ii. 35; I Chron. xxix. 22), formed the Temple hierarchy all through the time of the First and Second Temples down to the days of Ben Sira (II Chron. xxxi. 10; Ezek. xl. 46, xliv. 15, xlviii. 11; Ecclus. [Sirach] li. 12 [9], Hebr.), but who degenerated under the influence of Hellenism, especially during the rule of the Seleucidæ, when to be a follower of the priestly aristocracy was tantamount to being a worldly-minded Epicurean. The name, probably coined by the Ḥasidim as opponents of the Hellenists, became in the course of time a party name applied to all the aristocratic circles connected with the high priests by marriage and other social relations, as only the highest patrician families intermarried with the priests officiating at the Temple in Jerusalem (Ḳid. iv. 5; Sanh. iv. 2; comp. Josephus, "B. J." ii. 8, § 14). "Haughty men these priests are, saying which woman is fit to be married by us, since our father is high priest, our uncles princes and rulers, and we presiding officers at the Temple"—these words, put into the mouth of Nadab and Abihu (Tan., Aḥare Mot, ed. Buber, 7; Pesiḳ. 172b; Midr. Teh. to Ps. lxxviii. 18), reflect exactly the opinion prevailing among the Pharisees concerning the Sadducean priesthood (comp. a similar remark about the "haughty" aristocracy of Jerusalem in Shab. 62b). The Sadducees, says Josephus, have none but the rich on their side ("Ant." xiii. 10, § 6). The party name was retained long after the Zadokite high priests had made way for the Hasmonean house and the very origin of the name had been forgotten. Nor is anything definite known about the political and religious views of the Sadducees except what is recorded by their opponents in the works of Josephus, in the Talmudic literature, and in the New Testament writings.

Josephus relates nothing concerning the origin of what he chooses to call the sect or philosophical school of the Sadducees; he knows only that the three "sects"—the Pharisees, Essenes, and Sadducees—dated back to "very ancient times" (*ib.* xviii. 1, § 2), which words, written from the point of view of King Herod's days, necessarily point to a time prior to John Hyrcanus (*ib.* xiii. 8, § 6) or the Maccabean war (*ib.* xiii. 5, § 9). Among the Rabbis the following legend circulated: Antigonus of Soko, successor of Simon the Just, the last of the "Men of the Great Synagogue," and consequently living at the time of the influx of Hellenistic ideas, taught the maxim, "Be not like servants who serve their master for the sake of wages [lit. "a morsel"], but be rather like those who serve without thought of receiving wages" (Ab. i. 3); whereupon two of his disciples, Zadok and Boethus, mistaking the high ethical purport of the maxim, arrived at the conclusion that there was no future retribution, saying, "What servant would work all day without obtaining his due reward in the evening?" Instantly they broke away from the Law and lived in great luxury, using many silver and gold vessels at their banquets; and they established schools which declared the enjoyment of this life to be the goal of man, at the same time pitying the Pharisees for their bitter privation in this world with no hope of another world to compensate them. These two schools were called, after their founders, Sadducees and Boethusians (Ab. R. N. v.).

The unhistorical character of this legend is shown by the simple fact, learned from Josephus, that the Boethusians represent the family of high priests created by King Herod after his marriage to the daughter of Simon, the son of Boethus ("Ant." xv. 9, § 3; xix. 6, § 2). Obviously neither the character of the Sadducees nor that of the Boethusians was any longer known at the time the story was told in the rabbinical schools. Nor does the attempt to connect the name "Sadducees" with the term "ẓedeḳ" or "ẓedaḳah" (= "righteousness"; Epiphanius, "Panarium," i. 14; Derenbourg, "Histoire de la Palestine," p. 454) deserve any more consideration than the creation by Grätz ("Gesch." 3d ed., iii. 88, 697) and others, for the purpose of accounting for the name, of a heretic leader called Zadok. Geiger's ingenious explanation ("Urschrift," pp. 20 *et seq.*), as given above, indorsed by Wellhausen ("Die Pharisäer und die Sadducäer," p. 45), is very generally approved to-day (see Schürer, "Gesch." 3d ed., ii. 408); and it has received striking confirmation from the special blessing for "the Sons of Zadok whom God has chosen for the priesthood" in the Hebrew Ben Sira discovered by Schechter (see Schechter and Taylor, "Wisdom of Ben Sira," 1899, p. 35). In the New Testament the high priests and their party are identified with the Sadducees (Acts v. 17; comp. *ib.* xxiii. 6 with *ib.* xxii. 30, and John vii. 30, xi. 47, xviii. 3 with the Synoptic Gospels; see also "Ant." xx. 9, § 1).

The views and principles of the Sadducees may be summarized as follows: (1) Representing the nobility, power, and wealth ("Ant." xviii. 1, § 4), they had centered their interests in political life, of which they were the chief rulers. Instead of sharing the Messianic hopes of the Pharisees, who committed the future into the hand of God, they took the peopled destiny into their own hands, fighting or negotiating with the heathen nations just as they thought best, while having as their aim their own temporary welfare and worldly success. This is the meaning of what Josephus chooses to term their disbelief in fate and divine providence ("B. J." ii. 8, § 14; "Ant." xiii. 5, § 9).

(2) As the logical consequence of the preceding view, they would not accept the Pharisaic doctrine of the resurrection (Sanh. 90b; Mark xii. 12; Ber. ix. 5, "Minim"), which was a national rather than an individual hope. As to the immortality of the soul, they seem to have denied this as well (see Hippolytus, "Refutatio," ix. 29; "Ant." x. 11, § 7).

(3) According to Josephus (*ib.* xiii. 10, § 6), they regarded only those observances as obligatory which are contained in the written word, and

did not recognize those not written in the law of Moses and declared by the Pharisees to be derived from the traditions of the fathers. Instead of accepting the authority of the teachers, they considered it a virtue to dispute it by arguments.

(4) According to Acts xxiii. 8, they denied also the existence of angels and demons. This probably means that they did not believe in the Essene practise of incantation and conjuration in cases of disease, and were therefore not concerned with the ANGELOLOGY and DEMONOLOGY derived from Babylonia and Persia.

(5) In regard to criminal jurisdiction they were so rigorous that the day on which their code was abolished by the Pharisaic Sanhedrin under Simeon b. Shetaḥ's leadership, during the reign of Salome Alexandra, was celebrated as a festival (Meg. Ta'an. iv.; comp. Ket. 105a). They insisted on the literal execution of the law of retaliation: "Eye for eye, tooth for tooth" (Ex. xxi. 24; Meg. Ta'an. iv.; B. Ḳ. 84a; comp. Matt. v. 38). On the other hand, they would not inflict the death penalty on false witnesses in a case where capital punishment had been wrongfully carried out, unless the accused had been executed solely in consequence of the testimony of such witnesses (Mak. i. 8; Tosef., Sanh. vi. 6, where "Boethusians" stands for "Sadducees").

(6) They held the owner of a slave fully as responsible for the damage done by the latter as for that done by the owner's ox or ass; whereas the Pharisees discriminated between reasonable and unreasonable beings (Yad. iv. 7).

(7) They also insisted, according to Meg. Ta'an. iv., upon a literal interpretation of Deut. xxii. 17 (comp. Sifre, Deut. 237; Ket. 46; see also the description of the custom still obtaining at weddings among the Jews of Salonica, in Braun-Wiesbaden's "Eine Türkische Reise," 1876, p. 235), while most of the Pharisaic teachers took the words figuratively. The same holds true in regard to Deut. xxv. 9: "Then shall his brother's wife... spit in his [her deceased husband's brother's] face," which the Pharisees explained as "before him" (Yeb. xii. 6; see Weiss, "Dor," i 117, note).

(8) They followed a traditional practise of their own in granting the daughter the same right of inheritance as the son's daughter in case the son was dead (Meg. Ta'an. v.; Tos. Yad. ii. 20; B. B. viii. 1, 115b).

(9) They contended that the seven weeks from the first barley-sheaf-offering ("'omer") to Pentecost should, according to Lev. xxiii. 15–16, be counted from "the day after Sabbath," and, consequently, that Pentecost should always be celebrated on the first day of the week (Meg. Ta'an. i.; Men. 65a). In this they obviously followed the old Biblical view which regards the festival of the firstlings as having no connection whatsoever with the Passover feast; whereas the Pharisees, con-

necting the festival of the Exodus with the festival of the giving of the Law, interpreted the "morrow after the Sabbath" to signify the second day of Passover.

(10) Especially in regard to the Temple practise did they hold older views, based upon claims of greater sanctity for the priesthood and of its sole dominion over the sanctuary. Thus they insisted that the daily burnt offerings were, with reference to the singular used in Num. xxviii. 4, to be offered by the high priest at his own expense; whereas the Pharisees contended that they were to be furnished as a national sacrifice at the cost of the Temple treasury into which the "sheḳalim" collected from the whole people were paid (Meg. Ta'an. i. 1; Men. 65b; Sheḳ. iii. 1, 3; Grätz, *l.c.* p. 694).

(11) They claimed that the meal-offering belonged to the priest's portion; whereas the Pharisees claimed it for the altar (Meg. Ta'an. viii.; Men. vi. 2).

(12) They insisted on an especially high degree of purity in those who officiated at the preparation of the ashes of the Red Heifer. The Pharisees, on the contrary, demonstratively opposed such strictness (Parah iii. 7; Tos. Parah iii. 1–8).

(13) They declared that the kindling of the incense in the vessel with which the high priest entered the Holy of Holies on the Day of Atonement was to take place outside, so that he might be wrapped in smoke while meeting the Shekinah within, according to Lev. xvi. 2; whereas the Pharisees, denying the high priest the claim of such supernatural vision, insisted that the incense be kindled within (Sifra, Aḥare Mot, 3; Yoma 19b, 53a, b; Yer. Yoma i. 39a, b; comp. Lev. R. xxi. 11).

(14) They extended the power of contamination to indirect as well as to direct contact (Yad. iv. 7).

(15) They opposed the popular festivity of the water libation and the procession preceding the same on each night of the Sukkot feast, as well as the closing festivity, on which the Pharisees laid much stress, of the beating of the willow-trees (Suk. 43b, 48b; Tos. Suk. iii. 16; comp. "Ant." xiii. 13, § 5).

(16) They opposed the Pharisaic assertion that the scrolls of the Holy Scriptures have, like any holy vessel, the power to render unclean (taboo) the hands that touch them (Yad. iv. 6).

(17) They opposed the Pharisaic idea of the 'ERUB, the merging of several private precincts into one in order to admit of the carrying of food and vessels from one house to another on the Sabbath ('Er. vi. 2).

(18) In dating all civil documents they used the phrase "after the high priest of the Most High," and they opposed the formula introduced by the Pharisees in divorce documents, "According to the law of Moses and Israel" (Meg. Ta'an. vii.; Yad. iv. 8; see Geiger, *l.c.* p. 34).

Whether the Sadducees were less strict in regard to the state of impurity of woman in her periods (Niddah iv. 2), and what object they had in opposing the determination by the Pharisees of the appearance of the new moon (R. H. ii. 1, 22b; Tos. R. H. i. 15), are not clear. Certain it is that in the time of the Tannaim the real issues between them and the Pharisees were forgotten, only scholastic controversies being recorded. In the latter the Sadducees are replaced by the late Boethusians, who had, only for the sake of opposition, maintained certain Sadducean traditions without a proper understanding of the historical principles upon which they were based. In fact, as Josephus ("Ant." xviii. 1, § 3) states in common with the Talmudical sources (Yoma 19b; Niddah 33b), the ruling members of the priesthood of later days were forced by public opinion to yield to the Pharisaic doctors of the Law, who stood so much higher in the people's esteem. In the course of time the Sadducees themselves adopted without contradiction Pharisaic practises; it is stated (Shab. 108a) that they did so in regard to the tefillin, and many other observances appear to have been accepted by them (Hor. 4a; Sanh. 33b).

With the destruction of the Temple and the state the Sadducees as a party no longer had an object for which to live. They disappear from history, though their views are partly maintained and echoed by the Samaritans, with whom they are frequently identified (see Hippolytus, "Refutatio Hæresium," ix. 29; Epiphanius, *l.c.* xiv.; and other Church Fathers, who ascribe to the Sadducees the rejection of the Prophets and the Hagiographa; comp. also Sanh. 90b, where "Ẓaddukim" stands for "Kutim" [Samaritans]; Sifre, Num. 112; Geiger, *l.c.* pp. 128–129), and by the Karaites (see Maimonides, commentary on Ab. i. 3; Geiger, "Gesammelte Schriften," iii. 283–321).

The Book of Ecclesiastes in its original form, that is, before its Epicurean spirit had been toned down by interpolations, was probably written by a Sadducee in antagonism to the Ḥasidim (Eccl. vii. 16, ix. 2; see P. Haupt, "Koheleth," 1905; Grätz, "Koheleth," 1871, p. 30). The Wisdom of Ben Sira, which, like Ecclesiastes and older Biblical writings, has no reference whatsoever to the belief in resurrection or immortality, is, according to Geiger, a product of Sadducean circles ("Z. D. M. G." xii. 536). This view is partly confirmed by the above-cited blessing of "the Sons of Zadok" (Hebrew Ben Sira, li. 129; see also C. Taylor, "Sayings of the Fathers," 1897, p. 115). Also the first Book of Maccabees is, according to Geiger (*l.c.* pp. 217 *et seq.*), the work of a Sadducee. Allusion to the Sadducees as "sinners" is found in the Psalms of Solomon (i. 1, iv. 1–10); they are "severe in judgment" (comp. "Ant." xiii. 10, § 6; xx. 9, § 1), "yet themselves full of sin, of lust, and hypocrisy"; "men pleasers," "yet full of evil desires" (*ib.* viii. 8; see H. E. Ryle and M. R. James, "Psalms of the Pharisees Commonly Called 'Psalms of Solomon,'" 1891, xlvi–xlviii. and elsewhere; Kautzsch, "Apokryphen," pp. 128 *et seq.*). Still more distinctly are the Sadducees described in the Book of Enoch (xciv. 5–9, xcvii.–xcviii., xcix. 2, civ. 10) as: "the men of unrighteousness who trust in their riches"; "sinners who transgress and pervert the eternal law." Sadducees, if not in name, at least in their Epicurean views as opposed to the saints, are depicted also in the Book of Wisdom (i. 16–ii. 22), where the Hellenistic nobility, which occupied high positions likewise in Alexandria, is addressed.

In the New Testament the Sadducees are mentioned in Matt. iii. 7 and xvi. 1, 6, 11, where they are identical with the HERODIANS (Mark xii. 13), that is, the Boethusians (Matt. xxii. 23, 34; Mark xii. 18; Acts iv. 1, v. 17, xxiii. 6–8). In John's Gospel they simply figure as "the chief priests" (vii. 23, 45; xi. 47, 57; xviii. 3).

In rabbinical literature careful discrimination must be made between the tannaitic period and that of the Amoraim. The Mishnah and Baraita in the passages quoted above indicate at least a fair knowledge of the character and doctrines of the Sadducees (see, for instance, R. Akiba in Yoma 40b), even though the names "Boethusians" and "Sadducees" occur promiscuously (see Grätz, "Gesch." iii. 693). In the amoraic period the name "Ẓadduḳi" signifies simply "heretic," exactly like the term "min" = "gnostic"; in fact, copyists sometimes replaced, it may be intentionally, the word "min" by "Ẓadduḳi," especially when Christian gnostics were referred to. However, in many cases in which "Ẓadduḳim" stands for "minim" in the later Talmud editions the change was due to censorship laws, as is shown by the fact that the manuscripts and older editions actually have the word "minim." Thus the Ẓadduḳi who troubled R. Joshua b. Levi with Biblical arguments (Ber. 7a; Sanh. 105b), the one who argued with R. Abbahu and Beruriah (Ber. 10a), the one who bothered R. Ishmael with his dreams (*ib.* 56b), and the one who argued with R. Ḥanina concerning the Holy Land in the Messianic time (Giṭ. 57a; Ket. 112a) and regarding Jesus ("Balaam," Sanh. 106b), were Christian gnostics; so were also the two Ẓadduḳim in the company of R. Abbahu (Suk. 48b). But the Ẓadduḳim who argue in favor of dualism (Sanh. 37a [the original version of the Mishnah had "apikoresin" or "minim"], 38b–39a; Ḥul. 87a) are gnostics or Jewish heretics, as are also those spoken of as "a vile people" (Yeb. 63b). "Birkat ha-minim," the benediction against Christian informers and gnostics, is called also "Birkat ha-Ẓadduḳim" (Ber. 28b, 29a). "The writings of the Ẓadduḳim" (Shab. 116a) are gnostic writings, the same as "Sefarim Ḥiẓonim" (Sanh. x. 1; "Sifre ha-Minim," Tos. Shab. xiii. 5). So it is said of Adam that he was a Ẓadduḳi, that is, a gnostic who did not believe in God as the Giver of the Law (Sanh. 38b). "The Ẓadduḳim and informers"

(Derek Ereẓ Rabbah ii.; Derek Ereẓ Zuṭa i) are Christian gnostics. In Hor. 11a a Ẓadduḳi is declared to be a transgressor of the dietary and other Mosaic laws, nay, an idolater. On the other hand, the Ẓadduḳim who conversed with Rab Sheshet (Ber. 58a), with Raba (Shab. 88a), and with R. Judah (Ned. 49b) seem to have been Manicheans. See PHARISEES.

BIBLIOGRAPHY: See that given under PHARISEES.

K.

SAMA B. RABBA: Babylonian amora; last head of the Pumbedita Academy. He was the successor of Raḥumai II., and officiated for about twenty years (456–476). He was a contemporary of Mar b. Ashi and of Rabba Tusfa'ah. Tradition relates that, in consequence of the prayers of the two school-leaders Mar b. Ashi and Sama b. Rabba, Yezdegerd II. was devoured in his bed by a dragon with the result that the persecution of the Jews ceased. Sama is mentioned three times in the Talmud (B. M. 42b; Zeb. 16a; Ḥul. 47b). Nothing else is known concerning him.

BIBLIOGRAPHY: Letter of Sherira Gaon, in Neubauer, *M. J. C.* i. 34; Heilprin, *Seder ha-Dorot*, ii. 96; Grätz, *Gesch.* iv. 373.

W. B. J. Z. L.

SAMA B. RAḲTA: Babylonian amora of the sixth generation. He was a contemporary of Rabina I., with whom he disputed concerning a halakah (Ḳid. 9a), and to whom he communicated a saying of Rab Awia (B. M. 10b, the correct reading in Rabbinowitz). He is probably identical with the R. Sama who with Rabina sat before R. Ashi (Men. 42a).

BIBLIOGRAPHY: Heilprin, *Seder ha-Dorot*, ii. 297.

W. B. J. Z. L.

SAMUEL BEN ABBA: Palestinian amora of the latter half of the third century. Although a pupil of Johanan, he did not receive ordination (Yer. Bik. 65c). He declined to permit Hela and Jacob to do him honor by rising before him (*ib.*). He appears to have been a pupil also of R. Assi and Ze'era, to whom he addressed several halakic question (Kid. 59b; Yer. M. Ḳ. 82d; Yer. Ḥag. 76a; Yer. Yeb. 2c; Yer. Naz. 52c; 'Er. 9a; Yoma 47a). He is sometimes confounded with the great Samuel (Tan., Bo, 10; Midr. Teh. to Ps. xix. 4).

BIBLIOGRAPHY: Frankel. *Mebo*, p. 125b; Bacher, *Ag. Pal. Amor.* p. 619.

W. B. S. O.

SAMUEL BEN ABBAHU: Babylonian amora of the fourth century. He engaged in a ritual controversy with R. Aḥai in regard to the use of the Circassian goat as food. Samuel was disposed to permit it to be eaten, but R. Aḥai opposed him. Finally it became necessary to refer the question to Palestine for adjudication; the answer was in favor of Samuel ben Abbahu (Ḥul. 59b).

W. B. S. O.

SAMUEL BEN AMMI: Palestinian amora of the beginning of the fourth century. He is known through his controversies with other scholars. He contended, for instance, that II Chron. xiii. 17 should be interpreted as meaning that King Abijah of Judea allowed the bodies of the fallen Israelites to remain exposed until the faces had become unrecognizable, in order that their widows might be prevented from remarrying (Yer. Yeb. 15c; Gen. R. lxv., lxxiii.; Ruth R. vii.).

Bibliography: Bacher, *Ag. Pal. Amor.* ii. 163, 501.

W. B. S. O.

SAMUEL BEN JOSE BEN BUN (ABUN): Palestinian amora of the fourth century, in whose time the Jerusalem Talmud is said to have been arranged and completed by his father, Jose. Some of his sayings have been preserved in Yer. R. H. i. 5; Ber. i. 6; Soṭah ix. 5; and Ḳid. iv. 8.

Bibliography: Frankel, *Mebo*, p. 125b; Weiss, *Dor*, iii. 118–119; Bacher, *Ag. Pal. Amor.* iii. 749.

W. B. S. O.

SAMUEL HA-ḲAṬON: Tanna of the second generation; lived in the early part of the second century of the common era. His surname "ha-Ḳaṭon" (= "the younger") is explained by some as an epithet given him on account of his extreme modesty, while others regard it as an allusion to the fact that he was only slightly inferior to the prophet Samuel (Yer. Soṭah 24b). It is also possible, however, that the name was first applied to him posthumously, since he died at an early age.

Samuel was so humble that when, during a conference on the intercalation of a month to make a leap-year, the nasi asked an outsider to withdraw, Samuel, not wishing the intruder to feel humiliated, arose and said that he was the one who had come without invitation (Sanh. 11c). He was, moreover, held in such esteem by his contemporaries that when, in an assembly of sages, a voice was heard proclaiming that one of those present was worthy of the Holy Spirit ("Ruaḥ ha-Ḳodesh"), the entire company considered that Samuel was intended (Yer. Soṭah, *l.c.*).

None of his halakot has been preserved; but some of his haggadic aphorisms are still extant, including the following: When asked to explain Eccl. vii. 15 he said: "The Creator of the world knows and understands that the pious may waver; wherefore God says, 'I will take him away in his righteousness' [this being the meaning of "be-ẓidḳo"], that he may not falter" (Eccl. R. *ad loc.*). The words "and all the upright in heart shall follow it" (Ps. xciv. 15) are interpreted as meaning that the holy may expect their reward only in the future world (Midr. Teh. *ad loc.*).

Samuel was exceedingly pious, and once, when he ordered a fast on account of drought, rain fell on the very morning of the day designated by him for the fast (Ta'an. 25b). According to Brüll, he originated the use of the in vocation "Ribbono shel 'Olam" = "Lord of the World," that he might avoid pronouncing the name of God (comp. Shab. 33a, where he employs this periphrasis of the divine name). Samuel is known especially for the anathema against Judæo-Christians, Minæans, and informers ("birkat ha-minim") which he composed at the request of the patriarch Gamaliel II., and which was incorporated into the daily "Shemoneh 'Esreh" prayer (Ber. 28b–29a). He is known also for the sinister prophecy uttered by him on his death-bed: "Simeon and Ishmael are doomed to destruction; their companions, to death; the people, to pillage; and bitter persecutions shall come upon them" (Soṭah 48b). This prophecy, which many of those present did not understand, was fulfilled in its entirety (comp. Krochmal, "Moreh Nebuke ha-Zeman," p. 62). His favorite maxim, Prov. xxiv. 17, shows his pious and humane character, although some deny that this was his motto (Ab. iv. 19; comp. Rahmer's Jüdisches Lit.-Blatt," 1892, p. 195), while others ascribe to him the apothegm on the ages of life (Ab. v. 21; Taylor, "Sayings of the Jewish Fathers," p. 23).

BIBLIOGRAPHY: Brüll, *Einleitung in die Mischna*, i. 98–99, Frankfort-on-the-Main, 1876; Bacher, *Ag. Tan.* i. 370–372; Grätz, *Gesch.* iv. 59.

W. B. J. Z. L.

SAMUEL MAR. See SAMUEL YARḤINA'AH.

SAMUEL BEN NAḤMAN (NAḤMANI): Palestinian amora; born at the beginning of the third and died at the beginning of the fourth century. He was a pupil of R. Jonathan ben Eleazar (Pes. 24a) and one of the most famous haggadists of his time (Yer. Ber. 12d; Midr. Teh. to Ps. ix. 2). He was a native of Palestine and may have known the patriarch Judah I. (Gen. R. ix.). It appears that he went to Babylon in his youth but soon returned to Palestine (Sanh. 98b). He seems, however, to have gone to Babylon a second time in an official capacity in order to determine the intercalation of the year, which, for political reasons, could not be done in Palestine (Yer. Ber. 2d; Pes. 54b). As an old man he went to the court of Empress Zenobia (267–273) to petition her to pardon an orphaned youth who had committed a grave political crime (Yer. Ter. 46b). In the days of Judah II., Samuel ben Naḥman appears among the most intimate associates of the patriarch, with whom he went (286) to Tiberias at Dioeletian's order; later he joined the emperor at Paneas (Yer. Ter. ix., end; Gen. R. lxiii.). In the school Samuel held a position of authority; to him is ascribed the rule that during the heat of the day instruction should be suspended (Lam. R. i. 3, end; Midr. Teh. to Ps. xci. 6). On account of his fame as a haggadist questions were addressed to him by such authorities as the patriarch Judah II. (Gen. R. xii., end), Simeon ben Jehozadak (Gen. R. iii., beginning; Lev. R. xxxi.; Pes. 145b; Midr. Teh. to Ps. civ.; Tan. to Wayaḳhel, beginning; Ex. R. 1., beginning), Ammi (Lev. R. xxxi., beginning; Lam. R. i. 13), Ḥanina ben Pappa (Pes. 157a; Midr. Teh. to Ps. lxv.; Lam. R. iii. 45; Yer. Sheb. 35b), and Ḥelbo (B. B. 123a, b).

Among the transmitters of Samuel's sayings were Ḥelbo, the haggadist Levi, Abbahu (Lev. R. xxxv., end; Yer. Ta'an. iii.), and Eleazar ben Pedaṭ (Pes. 159b). Of Samuel's sons two are known by name—Naḥman and Hillel; sayings of both have been preserved (Gen. R. x., xxxii.; Midr. Teh. to Ps. lii.; Yer. Sheb. 36b; Yer. Ḳid. 61c; Eccl. R. i. 4; Midr. Shemu'el xv., on Neh. viii. 17). Samuel ben Naḥman's decisions and sayings concern the study of dogma (Yer. Peah 17a; Meg. 74d; Ḥag. 76d), prayer (Pes. 157a, b; Deut. R. ii.; Yer. Ber. 7a; Gen. R. lxviii.), and Sabbath regulations (Gen. R. xi., end; Pesiḳ. R. 23; Yer. Shab. 15a); the history of Israel and the nations and empires (Pes. 15b, 151b; Lev. R. ii., beginning, xxiv., end, xxix.; Num. R. ii., end; Yer. Sheb. 35b; Yer. 'Ab. Zarah 44b); the ordinances regarding proselytes (Cant. R. vi. 2; Yer. Ber. 5b, c); Scripture ('Ab. Zarah 25a; B. B. 15a; Gen. R. vi., end; Cant. R. i. 1, end), halakic exegesis (Yer. Sheḳ. 45d; Yer. Shab. 9b; Yer. Ḥal. 57b), and Biblical characters and narratives (B. B. 123a; 'Ab. Zarah 25a; Yer. Yeb. 9c; Yer. Ber. 4b; Tosef., Shab. vii., 25; Gen. R. xlii., xlix., lxii., xcviii.; Ex. R. xliii.; Lev. R. xi.; Pes. vi.; Eccl. R. vii. 1; Midr. Shemu'el xxiii.).

Especially noteworthy is Samuel b. Naḥman's description of the grief of the patriarchs Abraham, Isaac, Jacob, and of Rachel, over the destruction of the Temple (Lam. R., Pref. 24, end). It is written in beautiful Hebrew prose, and is accompanied by dramatic dirges in Aramaic. Then follow the dirges of all the Patriarchs, which they intone when Moses for the second time has communicated to them the sad tidings. Finally, Moses himself chants a lament, addressed partly to the sun and partly to the enemy.

Other utterances of Samuel b. Naḥman's refer to homiletics (Gen. R. xiv., xx., xliii.; B. B. 123b; Ḥul. 91d; Shab. 113b), to God and the world (Gen. R. xxxiii.; Pes. 139a; 'Er. 22a; B. Ḳ. 5a, b), and to eschatology (Gen. R. viii.; Midr. Teh. to Ps. lxxiii., end; Pes. 156b; Midr. Shemu'el xix.; Eccl. R. i. 8).

BIBLIOGRAPHY: Bacher, *Ag. Pal. Amor.* i. 477–551, ii., and iii.; Frankel, *Mebo*, pp. 146 *et seq.*: Weiss, *Dor.* iii. 66; Jellinek, *B. H.* vi. 104.

W. B. S. O.

SAMUEL YARḤINA'AH (generally known as **MAR SAMUEL**): Babylonian amora of the first generation; son of Abba b. Abba; teacher of the Law, judge, physician, and astronomer; born about 165 at Nehardea, in Babylonia; died there about 257. As in the case of many other great men, a number of legendary stories are connected with his birth (comp. "Halakot Gedolot," Giṭṭin, end; Tos. Ḳid. *s.v.* מאי). His father, who subsequently was known only by the designation Abuh di-Shemu'el ("father of Samuel"), was a silk-merchant. R. Judah b. Bathyra ordered a silken garment from him, but refused to take it after Abba had procured it, and when the latter asked him the reason of his refusal, R. Judah answered, "The commission was only a spoken word, and was not sufficient to make the transaction binding." Abba thereupon said, "Is the word of a sage not a better guaranty than his money? " "You are right," said R. Judah; "and because you lay so much stress upon a given word you shall have the good fortune of having a son who shall be like the prophet Samuel, and whose word all Israel will recognize as true." Soon afterward a son was born to Abba, whom he named Samuel (Midr. Shemu'el, x. [ed. Buber, p. 39a]).

Even as a boy Samuel displayed rare ability (Yer. Ket. v. 30a; Yer. Peah viii. 21b). His first teacher was an otherwise unknown, insignificant man, and Samuel, who knew more about a certain legal question than did his teacher, would not submit to ill treatment by him (Ḥul. 107b). Then Samuel's father, who was himself a prominent teacher of the Law, recognized as such even by Rab (Abba Arika; Ket. 51b), undertook to instruct the boy. As he seems to have been unequal to this task he sent him to Nisibis to attend the school of the rabbi who had predicted the boy's birth, that he might there acquire a knowledge of the Law ("Tanya," Hilkot "Abel," ed. Horowitz, p. 137, quoted from Yer.; comp. also Mordecai on M. Ḳ. 889). Samuel seems to have remained only a short time at Nisibis. On his return to Nehardea he studied under Levi b. Sisi, who was in Babylon before the death of Judah ha-Nasi I. (see A. Krochmal in "He-Ḥaluẓ," i. 69), and who exerted a great influence on Samuel's development. Samuel made such rapid progress and became so proficient in his studies that he soon associated as an equal with his teacher (Hoffmann, "Mar Samuel," p. 70).

Apart from the Bible and the traditional Law, which were usually the only subjects of study of the Jewish youth of that time, Samuel was instructed, probably in his early youth, in other sciences. It is likely that he accompanied his father on the latter's journey to Palestine (Yer. B. M. iv. 9c; Yer. Pes. v. 32a); for after his teacher Levi b. Sisi had gone to Palestine there was no one in Babylon with whom he could have studied. According to an account in the Talmud (B. M. 85b), which Rapoport declares to be a later addition (" 'Erek Millin," pp. 10, 222), but which may have some basis in fact, Samuel is said to have cured R. Judah ha-Nasi I. of an affection of the eyes. Although Samuel was at that time too young to study directly under R. Judah, he studied under the pupils of the patriarch, especially with Ḥama b. Ḥanina (comp. Hoffmann, *l.c.* pp. 71–73; Fesslier, "Mar Samuel, der Bedeutendste Amora," p. 14, note 1).

After having acquired a great store of knowledge in Palestine, his studies there including the Mishnah edited by R. Judah ha-Nasi as well as the other collections of traditional lore, Samuel left the Holy Land, probably with his father, and returned to his native city. His reputation as a teacher of the Law having preceded him, many pupils gathered about him. As he was especially well versed in civil law, the exilarch Mar 'Uḳba, who was his pupil, appointed him judge of the court at Nehardea, where he was associated with his friend the learned and clever Ḳarna. This court was regarded at that time as the foremost institution of its kind. In Palestine, as well as in Babylon, Samuel and Ḳarna were called the "judges of the Diaspora" (dayyane Golah; Sanh. 17b). Upon the death of R. Shila, the director of the Academy ("resh sidra") of Nehardea, Mar Samuel was appointed to the office, after it had been refused by Rab, who would not accept any post of honor at Nehardea, Samuel's home (Letter of Sherira Gaon, in Neubauer, "M. J. C." p. 28). The Academy of Nehardea entered upon a brilliant phase of its existence under Samuel' s directorate, and, with the academy founded by Rab at Sura, enjoyed a high general reputation.

Rab at Sura and Mar Samuel at Nehardea established the intellectual independence of Babylon. Young men taking up the study of the Law there were no longer obliged to go to Palestine, since they had the foremost teachers at home. Babylon now came to be regarded, in a sense, as a second Holy Land. Samuel taught, "As it is forbidden to migrate from Palestine to Babylon, so is it forbidden to migrate from Babylon to other countries" (Ket. 111a). After Rab's death no new director was elected, and Rab's greatest pupil, R. Huna, who became president of the court of Sura, subordinated himself to Mar Samuel in every respect, asking his decision in etery difficult religio-legal question (Giṭ. 66b, 89b; comp. Sanh. 17b; Tos. *ib.*, *s.v.* אלא, the phrase "be Rab" referring to R. Huna).

The Academy of Nehardea was now the only one in Babylon, and its director, Samuel, who survived Rab about ten years, was regarded as the highest authority by the Babylonian Jews. Even R. Johanan, the most prominent teacher in Palestine, and who at first looked upon Samuel merely as a colleague, became so convinced of his greatness, after Samuel had sent him a large number of responsa on important ritual laws, that he exclaimed, "I have a teacher in Babylon" (Ḥul. 95b).

As a man, Mar Samuel was distinguished for his modesty, gentleness, and unselfishness, being always ready to subordinate his own interests to those of the community. He said: "A man may never exclude himself from the community, but must seek his welfare in that of society" (Ber. 49b). He demanded seemly behavior from every one, saying that any improper conduct was punishable by law (Ḥag. 5a). One should help one's fellow man at the first signs of approaching difficulties, so as to prevent them, and not wait until he is in actual distress (*ib.*). In his solicitude for helpless orphans he imposed upon every court the task of acting as father to them (Yeb. 67b; Giṭ. 37a, 52b); and he declared that a loan taken from an orphan was not canceled in the Sabbatical year, even if no prosbul had been made out for it (Giṭ. 36b–37a). He stored his grain until prices had risen, in order to sell it to the poor at the low prices of the harvest-time (B. B. 90b). In order to save the people from being cheated he ordered the merchants never to take a profit of more than one-sixth of the cost price (B. M. 40b), and he was ready even to temporarily modify the Law in order to prevent them from selling at a high price goods necessary for the fulfilment of a religious duty (Pes. 30a; Sukkah 34b). In a certain case also he permitted the infraction of a religious prescription in order to keep people from harm (Shab. 42a).

Mar Samuel was very modest in his associations with others, openly honoring any one from whom he had gained any knowledge (B. M. 33a). He never obstinately insisted on his own opinion, but yielded as soon as he was convinced of being in error ('Er. 90a, b; Ḥul. 76b; Ber. 36a). He was friendly to all men, and declared: "It is forbidden to deceive any man, be he Jew or pagan" (Ḥul. 94a). "Before the throne of the Creator there is no difference between Jews and pagans, since there are many noble and virtuous among the latter" (Yer. R. H. i. 57a). He taught that the dignity of manhood should be respected even in the slave: the slave is given to the master only as a servant, and the master has no right to treat him with condescension or to insult him (Niddah 17a, 47a). Once, when a female slave had been taken away from Samuel and he had unexpectedly recovered her by paying a ransom, he felt obliged to liberate her because he had given up hope of recovering, her (Giṭ. 38a).

Mar Samuel seems to have possessed a thorough knowledge of the science of medicine as it was known in his day; this is evident from many of his medical maxims and dietetic rules scattered through the Talmud. He energetically opposed the view then current, even in intelligent circles, that most diseases were due to the evil eye, declaring that the source of all disease must be sought in the noxious influence exercised by the air and the climate upon the human organism (B. M.

107b). He traced many diseases to lack of cleanliness (Shab. 133b), and others to disturbances of the regular mode of living (B. B. 146a). He claimed to possess cures for most diseases (B. M. 113b), and was especially skilful in treating the eye (B. M. 85b); he discovered an eye-salve which was known as the "ḳillurin [κολλύριον] of Mar Samuel," although he himself said that bathing the eyes with cold water in the morning and bathing hands and feet with warm water in the evening were better than all the eye-salves in the world (Shab. 7Sa, 108b). Samuel discovered also a number of the diseases of animals (Ḥul. 42b). He sometimes drew the figure of a palm-branch as his signature (Yer. Giṭ. ix. 50d), although this was, perhaps, used by physicians generally at that time as a sign of their profession (Rapoport, " 'Erek Millin," p. 17).

From the scattered references in the Talmud it is impossible to determine exactly Mar Samuel's proficiency in astronomy; but he knew how to solve many mathematical problems and how to explain many phenomena. He says himself: "Although I am as familiar with the courses of the stars as with the streets of Nehardea, I can not explain the nature or the movements of the comets" (Ber. 58b). Samuel devoted himself especially to that branch of applied astronomy that deals with calendric science, which he taught to his colleagues and pupils. His astronomical studies of the revolutions of the moon enabled him to predict the beginning of the month ("rosh ḥodesh") as it was determined in Palestine, and he claimed to be able to remove the necessity of celebrating double holy days in the Diaspora (R. H. 20b; comp. Rashi *ad loc.*). He also computed a calendar for sixty years, which he subsequently sent to R. Johanan, the head of the Palestinian teachers, as a proof of his knowledge (Ḥul. 95b). He was called "Yarḥina'ah ("yeraḥ"—"month") because of this familiarity with calendric science and this ability to determine independently the beginning of the month (B. M. 85b). According to Krochmal "He-Ḥaluẓ," i. 76), "Shoḳed," another name given to Samuel, means "astronomer" (Yer. Ket. iv. 28b); but Hoffmann's view that "Shoḳed" (for which Babli has "Shaḳud"; Ket. 43b) means "the watchful, diligent one," is more likely correct. This name is said to have been given to Samuel because, despite his medical and astronomic studies, he devoted himself to the study of the Law.

Following the example of his teacher Levi b. Sisi, Mar Samuel collected the traditions handed down to him; his collection of baraitot, called "Tanna debe Shemu'el" in the Talmud (Shab. 54a; 'Er. 70b, 86a, 89b; Pes. 3a, 39a, b; Beẓah 29a; R. H. 29b; Yoma 70a; Meg. 30a; Zeb. 22a), was noted for its correctness and trustworthiness, although it was not held in such high esteem as were the collections of R. Ḥiyya and R. Hoshaiah (Letter of Sherira Gaon, *l.c.* p. 18). Samuel did much to elucidate the Mishnah, both by his textual explanations (Shab. 104b; Pes. 119b; Giṭ. 67b; B. M. 23b; 'Ab. Zarah 8b, 32a; R. H. 18a; Ḳid. 76b) and by his precise paraphrasing of ambiguous expressions and his references to other traditions. He is chiefly important, however, because of his promulgation of new theories and his independent decisions both in ritual and in civil law. However, in the field of ritual law he was not considered as great an authority as his colleague Rab, and practical questions were always decided according to Rab's views as against those of Samuel (Niddah 24b; Bek. 49b). In civil law his authority was the highest in Babylon, and his decisions became law even when contrary to Rab's (*ib.*).

Mar Samuel amplified and expanded earlier legal theories and originated many new legal maxims. He formulated the important principle that the law of the country in which the Jews are living is binding upon them (B. Ḳ. 113b). This principle, which was recognized as valid from a halakic point of view, made it a religious duty for the Jews to obey the laws of the country. Thus, although the Jews had their own civil courts, Mar Samuel thought that the Persian law should be taken into account and that various Jewish regulations should be modified according to it (B. M. 108a; B. B. 55a). On account of his loyalty to the government and his friendship with the Persian king, Shabur I., Samuel was called **Shabur Malka** (B. B. 115b). Fürst ("Orient, Lit." 1847, No. 3, p. 39) and Rapoport (*ib.* p. 196) refer, each differently, the name of **Aryok,** given to Samuel (comp. Shab. 53a; Ḳid. 39a; Men. 38b; Ḥul. 76b), to his close relations with the Neo-Persians and their king. Older commentators explain this name without reference to such relations (Tos. Shab. 53a; Rashi *ad loc.*; comp. Fessler, *l.c.* p. 9, note 1).

It was due to Mar Samuel's influence with the Persian king that the Jews were granted many privileges. On one occasion Samuel even made his love for his own people subsidiary to his loyalty to the Persian king and to his strict view of the duties of a citizen; for when the news came that the Persians, ou capturing Mazaca (Cæsarea), in Cappadocia, had killed 12,000 Jews who had obstinately opposed them, Samuel refrained from displaying any sorrow (M. Ḳ. 26a). But he had a great love for his people, and he loyally cherished the memory of the former kingdom of Judah. Once, when one of his contemporaries adorned himself with a crown of olive, Samuel sent him the following message: "The head of a Jew that now wears a crown while Jerusalem lies desolate, deserves to be separated from its trunk" (Yer. Soṭah ix. 24b, c). Samuel expected the restoration of the Jewish state in Palestine to come about in a natural way, through permission given to the Jews by the various governments to return to Palestine and establish an independent state there (Ber. 34b).

Mar Samuel was unfortunate in his family life. He had no sons, and his two daughters were captured by soldiers during the war with the Romans. They were taken to Sepphoris, in Palestine, where they were ransomed by coreligionists, but both died at an early age after having been married successively to a relative (Ket. 23a; Yer. Ket. ii. 26c). The esteem in which Mar Samuel was held appears from the fact that no one thought of attributing his misfortune to any sin committed by him; it was explained rather as being in consequence of some offense committed in Babylon by R. Ḥananya, the nephew of R. Joshua (Yer. Ket. ii. 8; comp. Ket. 23a). After his death Samuel was glorified in legend.

BIBLIOGRAPHY: Heilprin, *Seder ha-Dorot*, ii. 350–852, Warsaw, 1878; Weiss, *Dor*, iii. 161–176; *Ha-Asif*, 1885, ii. 262–274; 1886, iii. 287–291, 333: Halevy, *Dorot ha-Rishonim*, ii. 400–410; Grätz, *Gesch*. 3d ed., iv. 263 *et seq*., 270–272: D. Hoffmann, *Mar Samuel*, Leipsic, 1873; Siegmund Fessier, *Mar Samuel der Bedeutendste Amora*, Halle, 1879; Felix Kanter, *Beiträge zur Kenntniss des Rechtssystems und der Ethik Mar Samuels*, Bern, 1895; Bacher, *Ag. Bab Amor*., pp. 37–45.

W. R. J. Z. L.

SANHEDRIN (סנהדרין): Hebrew-Aramaic term originally designating only the assembly at Jerusalem that constituted the highest political magistracy of the country. It was derived from the Greek *συνέδριον*. Josephus uses *συνέδριον* for the first time in connection with the decree of the Roman governor of Syria, Gabinius (57 B.C.), who abolished the constitution and the then existing form of government of Palestine and divided the country into five provinces, at the head of each of which a sanhedrin was placed ("Ant." xiv. 5, § 4). Jerusalem was the seat of one of these. It is improbable, however, that the term "synhedrion" as a designation for the chief magistracy was used for the first time in connection with this decree of Gabinius; indeed, from the use made of it in the Greek translation of the Proverbs, Bacher concludes that it must have been current in the middle of the second century B.C.

In the Talmudic sources the "Great" Sanhedrin at Jerusalem is so called in contradistinction to other bodies designated by that name; and it was generally assumed that this Great Sanhedrin was identical with the Sanhedrin at Jerusalem which is mentioned in the non-Talimidic sources, in the Gospels, and in Josephus. The accounts in the two different sets of sources referring to the Sanhedrin, however, differ materially in their main characteristics. The Great Sanhedrin is designated in the Talmudic sources as "Sanhedrin Gedolah ha-yoshebet be-lishkat ha-gazit" = "the Great Sanhedrin which sits in the hall of hewn stone" (Sifra, Wayiḳra, ed. Weiss, 19a). The mention of "Sanhedrin" without the epithet "gedolah" (Yer. Sanh. i. 19c) seems to presuppose another body than the Great Sanhedrin that met in the hall of hewn stone. For neither Josephus nor the Gospels in speaking of the Sanhedrin report any of its decisions or discussions referring to the priests or to the Temple service, or touching in any way upon the religious law, but they refer to the Sanhedrin exclusively in matters connected with legal procedure, verdicts, and decrees of a political nature; whereas the Sanhedrin in the hall of hewn stone dealt, according to the Talmudic sources, with questions relating to the Temple, the priesthood, the sacrifices, and matters of a kindred nature. Adolf Büchler assumes indeed that there were in Jerusalem two magistracies which were entirely different in character and functions and which officiated side by side at the same time. That to which the Gospels and Josephus refer was the highest political authority, and at the same time the supreme court; this alone was empowered to deal with criminal cases and to impose the sentence of capital punishment. The other, sitting in the hall of hewn stone, was the highest court dealing with the religious law, being in charge also of the religious instruction of the people (Sanh. xi. 2–4).

I. The Political Sanhedrin: This body was undoubtedly much older than the term "sanhedrin." Accounts referring to the history of the pre-Maccabean time represent a magistracy at the head of the people, which body was designated GERUSIA. In 203 Antioclms the Great wrote a letter to the Jews in which he expressed his satisfaction that they had given him a friendly reception at Jerusalem, and had even come to meet him with the senate (*γερουσία*; "Ant." xii. 3, § 3). Antiochus V. also greeted the gerusia in a letter to the Jewish people. This gerusia, which stood at the head of the people, was the body that was subsequently called "sanhedrin." The date and the manner of its origin can not now be determined. Josephus calls it either *συνέδριον* or *βουλή*, and its members *πρεσβύτεροι* (= "elders," *i.e.*, זקנים) or *βουλευταί* (="councilors"), whose number was probably the same as that of the members of the Sanhedrin in the hall of hewn stone, namely, seventy or seventy-one. There are no references to indicate whence the Sanhedrin derived its authority or by whom it was elected, unless it be assumed that the convocation of that body by the high priest and at times by the Jewish king, as mentioned in the sources, refers to the manner of its election. This Sanhedrin, which was entirely aristocratic in character, probably assumed its own authority, since it was composed of members of the most influential families of the nobility and priesthood (comp. Sanh. iv. 2, where there is an allusion to the composition of this body). The Pharisees had no great influence in this assembly, although some of its members may have been friendly to them at various times. Though there are no definite references to gradations in rank among the several members, there seems to have been a committee of ten members, *οἱ δέκα πρῶτοι*, who ranked above their colleagues (comp. Schürer, "Gesch." 3d ed., ii. 201–202).

The meetings took place in one of the chambers of the Temple in order that the discussions and decrees might thereby be invested with greater religious authority. According to a passage in the Mekilta (Mishpaṭim, 4 [ed. Weiss, p. 87a]), the Sanhedrin, which was empowered to pass the sentence of capital punishment, sat "in the vicinity of the altar," *i.e.*, in one of the chambers of the inner court of the Temple. It was called "the hall of the *βουλευταί*" because the latter sat there. Subsequently it was called "lishkat parhedrin" = "the hall of the *πρόεδροι*" (Yoma 8b). In this hall there was also a private room for the high priest (Yoma 10a; Tosef., Yoma, i. 2). The *βουλευταί* or the *πρόεδροι*, assembled in this private room (comp. Matt. xxvi. 57; Mark xiv. 63) before they met in the hall.

The Sanhedrin did not, however, always retain this place of meeting; for, according to Josephus, the *βουλή* was in the vicinity of the xystus ("B. J." v. 4, § 2), hence beyond the Temple mount, or, according to Schürer (*l.c.* ii. 211), on it, though not within the inner court. In the last years of the Jewish state, therefore, to which the account in Josephus must be referred, the Sanhedrin left its original seat, being compelled to do so perhaps by the Pharisees, who, on gaining the upper hand, would not permit the secular Sanhedrin to sit in the sanctuary. Indeed, while the Sanhedrin still sat in the Temple, it was decreed that a mezuzah was to be placed in the hall of the *πρόεδροι*. This was not required in any of the other apartments of the Temple; and R. Judah b. Ila'i, who was otherwise thoroughly informed as to the earlier institutions of the Temple, was unable to assign a reason for the decree (Yoma 10a). It may be explained only on the assumption that it was intended to secularize the sittings of this Sanhedrin. It may have been for the same reason that the body was subsequently excluded entirely from the Temple, inasmuch as the latter and its apartments were intended for the cult and matters connected with it, while the discussions and decrees of this Sanhedrin were political and secular in nature.

The extant references to the Sanhedrin are not sufficient to give an exact and detailed idea of its functions and of the position which it occupied. It is certain, however, that the extent of its power varied at different times, and that the sphere of its functions was restricted in various ways by the Roman government. One of these restrictions was Gabinius' above-mentioned division of the Jewish territory into five provinces, each with a sanhedrin of its own, whereby the authority and the functions of the Sanhedrin of Jerusalem were materially diminished. Its power was insignificant under Herod and Archelaus. After the death of these rulers its authority again increased, the internal government of the country being largely in its hands. It administered the criminal law, and had independent powers of police, and hence the right to make arrests through its own officers of justice. It was also empowered to judge cases that did not involve the death penalty, only capital cases requiring the confirmation of the procurator.

The high priest, who from the time of Simeon was also the head of the state, officiated as president of the Sanhedrin. He bore the title "nasi" (prince), because the reins of government were actually held by him. Subsequently, when they were transferred to other hands, the high priest retained the title of nasi as president of the Sanhedrin. The powers of the latter official were restricted under the procurators, without whose permission the body could not be convened ("Ant." xx. 9, § 1). This Sanhedrin, since it was a political authority, ceased to exist when the Jewish state perished with the destruction of Jerusalem (70 C.E.).

II. The Religious Sanhedrin: This body, which met in the hall of hewn stone and was called also "the Great Bet Din" or simply "the Bet Din in the hall of hewn stone" (Tosef., Hor. i. 3; Tosef., Soṭah, ix. 1; Yer. Sanh. i. 19c), was invested with the highest religious authority. According to Talmudic tradition it originated in the Mosaic period, the seventy elders who were associated with Moses in the government of Israel at his request (Num. xi. 4–31) forming together with him the first Sanhedrin (Sanh. i. 6). The institution is said to have existed without interruption from that time onward (comp. Yer. Sanh. i. 18b, where, in a comment on Jer. lii. 24 *et seq.* and II Kings xxv. 18 *et seq.*, it is said that Nebuzar-adan brought the Great Sanhedrin to Riblah before Nebuchadnezzar); but the fact that no passage whatever in the pre-exilic books of the Bible refers to this institution seems to indicate that it was not introduced before the time of the Second Temple. Originally it was probably not a regularly constituted authority, but merely a synod which convened on special occasions for the purpose of deliberating on important questions or of issuing regulations referring to religious life. The first assembly of this nature was that held under Ezra and Nehemiah (Neh. viii.–x.), which was called "the Great Synagogue" ("Keneset ha-Gedolah") in Jewish scholastic tradition. Subsequently, at a date which can not be definitely determined, this occasional assembly was replaced by a standing body. The latter, which was called "Sanhedrin" or "Bet Din," was regarded as the continuation of the synods which had previously been convened only occasionally.

It further appears from Ab. i. 2–4 that the Great Bet Din was regarded as a continuation of the Keneset ha-Gedolah; for the so-called "zugot" who were at the head of the Great Bet Din are named after the men of the Great Synagogue, which was regarded as the precursor of the Great Bet Din. This explains why the latter is sometimes called also "synagogue" (כנישתא; Meg. Ta'an., in Neubauer, "M. J. C." ii. 16). Originally the members of this bet din also were priests belonging to prominent families, probably under the presidency of the high priest. The Pharisees, however, held at various times more or less prominent positions in this body, according as they were the victors or the vanquished in their conflict with the Sadducees. When John Hyrcanus toward the end of his reign turned from the Pharisees ("Ant." xvi. 11, § 1), he seems to have effected their dismissal from the Sanhedrin or bet din and to have formed a Sadducean bet din (Sanh. 52b), or a Sadducean Sanhedrin, as it is called in another passage (Meg. Ta'an. *l.c.* p. 17). Under Alexander Jannæus, Simeon b. Sheṭah succeeded in ousting the Sadducean members from the bet din and in reorganizing it so that it was composed only of Pharisees. But the latter lost their prestige in the subsequent quarrel with Alexander, gaining the upper hand again only under his successor, Salome Alexandra, from which time the Great Bet Din was composed exclusively of Pharisees. According to the Mishnah (Sanh. i. 5; Sheb. ii. 2), the bet din, at least during the last years of its existence at Jabneh, where it had been reorganized, consisted of seventy or seventy-one members, according as the president was included in or omitted from the list. Simeon b. 'Azzai (first half of the 2d cent.) says that seventy-two elders ("zeḳenim," *i.e.*, members of the Sanhedrin) were present when R. Eleazar b. Azariah was elected president together with Rabban Gamaliel II. (Zeb. i. 3; Yad. iii. 5, iv. 2); this was one more than the usual number, and included probably, besides the seventy other members, the two presidents, Gamaliel and Eleazar b. Azariah. According to R. Jose b. Ḥalafta, the members of the Great Bet Din were required to possess the following qualifications: scholarship, modesty, and popularity among their fellow men (Tosef., Ḥag. ii. 9; Sanh. 88b). According to an interpretation in Sifre, Num. 92 (ed. Friedmann, p. 25b), they had also to be strong and courageous. Only such were eligible, moreover, as had filled three offices of gradually increasing dignity, namely, those of local judge, and member successively of two magistracies at Jerusalem (Jose b. Ḥalafta, *l.c.*). R. Johanan, a Palestinian amora of the third century, enumerates the qualifications of the members of the Sanhedrin as follows: they must be tall, of imposing appearance, and of advanced age; and they must be learned and must understand foreign languages as well as some of the arts of the necromancer (Sanh. 19a).

The hall of hewn stone ("lishkat ha-gazit") in which the bet din sat was situated on the southern side of the inner court of the Temple (Mid. v. 4). It was used for ritual purposes also, the priests drawing lots there for the daily service of the sacrifices, and also reciting the "Shema'" there (Tamid ii., end, to iii., beginning; iv., end, to v., beginning). The larger part of the hall was on the site of the court of laymen. There were two entrances: one from the court of the priests, which was used by the latter; the other in the Water gate, used by the laity. The Great Bet Din sat daily, except on the Sabbath and on feast-days, between the morning and evening sacrifices (Tosef., Sanh. vii. 1). On the Sabbath and on feast-days, on which there were no meetings in the hall of hewn stone, the members of the bet din assembled in the schoolhouse on the Temple mount (*ib.*). According to the accounts given in the Talmudic sources, the Great Bet Din had the following functions, which it exercised in part as a body and in part through committees of its members: It had supervision over the Temple service, which was required to be conducted in conformity with the Law and according to Pharisaic interpretation. It decided which priests should perform the Temple service (Mid., end). It supervised especially important ritual acts, as the service on the Day of Atonement (Yoma i. 3). It had in charge the burning of the Red Heifer and the preparation of the water of purification (Tosef., Sanh. iii. 4). When the body of a murdered person was found, members of the Great Bet Din had to take the necessary measurements in order to determine which city, as being the nearest to the place of the murder, was to bring the sacrifice of atonement (Soṭah ix. 1; Tosef., Sanh. iii. 4; comp. Soṭah 44b–45a). It had also to decide as to the harvest tithes (Peah ii. 6). It sat in judgment on women suspected of adultery, and sentenced them to drink the bitter water (Sotah i. 4). It arranged the calendar (R. H. ii. 5 *et seq.*], and provided correct copies of the Torah roll for the king, and probably for the Temple also (Tosef., Sanh. iv. 4; Yer. Sanh. ii. 20c). In general it decided all doubtful questions relating to the religious law (Sanh. 88b) and rendered the final decision in regard to the sentence of the teacher who promulgated opinions contradicting the traditional interpretation of the Law "zaḳen mamreh"; Sanh. xi. 2–4).

Two persons were at the head of the bet din: one, the actual president with the title "nasi"; the other, the second president or vice-president, who bore the title "ab bet din" (father of the court). The existence of these two offices is well authenticated from the time following the Hadrianic persecution. R. Johanan (3d cent.) says that in the college which was regarded as the continuation of the Great Bet Din in the hall of hewn stone R. Nathan officiated as second president "ab bet din") side by side with R. Simeon b. Gamaliel II., who was president ("nasi"; Hor. 13b). In a mishnah (Ḥag. ii. 2) five pairs of scholars are enumerated who were at the head of the Great Bet Din at the time of the Second Temple; and it is stated that one of each pair was nasi and the other ab bet din. These five pairs of scholars, who collectively are also designated "zugot" (Peah ii. 6), were at the same time the most prominent representatives of the tradition (Ab. i. 1 *et sec.*) and at the head of the Pharisaic school. There is therefore no reason to doubt the statement that from the time the bet din came under Pharisaic influence these Pharisaic teachers stood at its head. The fact that the high priest had formerly been the president of this bet din explains why there were two presidents. Since the high priest was probably frequently prevented from presiding at the meetings, or was perhaps not competent to do so, another officer had to be chosen who should be the actual director of the body. The double office was retained when, with the growing influence of the Pharisees, the nasi of the bet din was a scribe and no longer the high priest. The title "nasi," which the president of the bet din bore, may have originated at the time when the high priest—the real prince and the head of the state—acted as president. The following reason also may have determined the retention of the title, even after the high priest no longer officiated as president: The bet din, which, as shown above, was called also כנישתא (corresponding to the Hebrew עדה), was identified with the Biblical "'edah" (comp. Sifre, Deut. 41 [ed. Friedmann, p. 59b]; Sifra, Wayiḳra, ed. Weiss, 19a, where it is expressly stated that the Great Bet Din in the hall of hewn stone is the 'edah); and, since only a director of the 'edah is called "nasi" in Ex. xvi. 22 and Num. iv. 34, it may have seemed desirable to retain the title "nasi" for the president of the bet din.

Business at the meetings of the bet din was transacted according to a certain order. Reliable traditions describing the procedure and the balloting have been preserved in the Mishnah; but it is impossible to distinguish between the regulations obtaining in the bet din at the time of the Second Temple and those obtaining in the school of Jabneh, which was regarded as a continuation of the Sanhedrin. The following are some of these regulations: The members of the bet din sat in a semicircle in order that they might see one another (Sanh. iv. 2; Tosef., Sanh. viii. 1). The president sat in the center (Tosef., *l.c.*). Two secretaries recorded the various opinions expressed by the members; according to one tradition there were three secretaries (Sanh. *l.c.*). When a question was raised and a member of the college declared that he was in possession of a tradition according to which the question might be decided, such tradition was decisive. When no member knew of any tradition relating to the question at issue, discussion followed and a ballot was taken (Tosef., Sanh. vii. 1). Three rows of scholars sat in front of the bet din, and filled vacancies in the latter when necessary (Sanh. iv. 4; Tosef., Sanh. viii. 2). This regulation, however, refers only to the school of Jamnia and not to the bet din of the time of the Second

Temple; for only such men were appointed to membership in the latter as had previously sat in less important bodies.

After the destruction of the Temple at Jerusalem and the downwall of the Jewish state, the Academy of Jabneh was organized as the supreme religious authority, being therefore regarded as the continuation of the Great Bet Din in the hall of hewn stone. The later Jewish academies under the presidency of the patriarchs of the family of Hillel—hence, down to the end of the fourth century—were also regarded as the continuation of that institution (this is the meaning of the sentence "The bet din of the hall of hewn stone went on ten journeys until it finally settled at Tiberias"; R. H. 31a, b); they accordingly retained its organization, and the president bore the title of nasi, the second president officiating side by side with him as ab bet din.

BIBLIOGRAPHY: Schürer, *Gesch.* ii. 188–189, where the literature on the subject is given; Jacob Reifmainn, *Sanhedrin*, Berdychev, 1888; Bacher, art. *Sanhedrin*, in Hastings, *Dict. Bible*; Adolf Büchler, *Das Synhedrium in Jerusalem und das Grosse Bet Din in der Quaderkammer des Jerusalemisehen Tempels*, Vienna, 1902, the chief source for the view given above.

W. B. J. Z. L.

SANHEDRIN ("Court"): Name of a treatise of the Mishnah, Tosefta, and both Talmudim. It stands fourth in the order Neziḳin in most editions, and is divided into eleven chapters containing seventy-one paragraphs in all. It treats chiefly of courts and their powers, of qualifications for the office of judge, and of legal procedure and criminal law.

Ch. i.: Cases which are brought before a court of three judges (§§ 1–3), before a small sanhedrin of twenty-three members (§ 4), or before the Great Sanhedrin at Jerusalem consisting of seventy-one, or, according to R. Judah, of seventy members (§ 5); origin of the requirement that there should be seventy (or seventy-one) members in the Great Sanhedrin, and twenty-three in the smaller body; minimum number of inhabitants entitling a city to a Sanhedrin (§ 6).

Ch. ii.: Rights of the high priest (§ 1); rights and duties of the king, who may neither judge nor be judged, and may declare war only with the consent of the Great Sanhedrin; his share of the booty; he may not accumulate treasure for himself; he must have a copy of the Torah made for himself; the reverence due him (§§ 2–5).

Ch. iii.: Suits involving money which are decided by arbitrators; cases in which one party may reject the judge selected or the witness cited by the other party; persons debarred from acting either as judges or as witnesses (§§ 1–5); examination of witnesses, each of whom is questioned separately, with a subsequent comparison of their testimony (§ 6); announcement of the verdict by the president of the board; no judge may say to either party: "I wished to acquit thee, but I was overruled by the majority of my colleagues" (§ 7); if he who loses the case later produces written testimony or a witness in his favor, the sentence is reversed (§ 8).

Ch. iv.: Difference in the proceedings and in the number of judges between trials in which money is involved and criminal cases in which the life of the defendant is in jeopardy, the former being conducted before three judges and the latter before a sanhedrin of twenty-three members (§§ 1–2); the sanhedrin sat in a semicircle, so that all the members might see one another, while the clerks recorded the reasons which the judges gave either for acquittal or for condemnation (§ 3); three rows of scholars versed in the Law sat in front of the sanhedrin, one or more of them being called upon at need to fill the bench, in case a quorum of judges was not present (§ 4); address to the witnesses in criminal cases, reminding them of the value of a human life; in this connection it is said that Adam is called the ancestor of the whole human race, in order that no one might superciliously say to his fellow man: "My great grandfather was more important than thine" (§ 5).

Ch. v.: Examination of the witnesses regarding the time, place, and circumstances of the case, and the coherency of the testimony given; consultation and mode of procedure on the part of the judges (§§ 1–5);

Ch. vi.: How the condemned man is led to the place of execution; proclamation of the verdict, so that a reversal may be possible at the last moment if proofs of innocence are produced (§ 1); the condemned man is exhorted to confess his sins that he may atone for them by his death (§ 2); method of stoning to death, and cases in which those who are stoned are hanged after death, and the manner of hanging (§§3–4); burial-place of those who have been executed, and the demeanor of their relatives (§§ 5–6).

Ch. vii.: The four methods of capital punishment—stoning, burning, beheading, and strangling—and the manner of each (§§ 1–3); crimes punishable by stoning (§§ 4–11).

Ch. viii.: The circumstances in which a stubborn and rebellious son (comp. Deut. xxi. 18 *et seq.*) is regarded and sentenced as such (§§ 1–4); the stubborn son, like the burglar (comp. Ex. xxii. 1), is treated with severity in order that he may be prevented from committing greater crimes; in this connection the cases are given in which one about to commit a crime may be killed to prevent its commission (§§ 5–7).

Ch. ix.: Criminals who are burned and those who are beheaded; cases in which homicide is not regarded as murder (§§ 1–2); cases in which a mistake is made as to the identity of criminals condemned to death so that it is impossible to tell what punishment each one has deserved (§ 3); cases in which one has committed two different crimes, and so deserves two different forms of capital punishment (§ 4); criminals who are placed in solitary confinement ("kipah"; § 5); cases in which a criminal taken in the act may be killed by any one without being brought before a court (§ 6).

Ch. x.: Those who have no part in the future world; the problem whether the Ten Tribes will return at some future time from the place of their exile (§§ 1–3); the idolatrous city (comp. Deut. xiii. 13 *et seq.*; §§ 4–6).

Ch. xi.: Criminals who are strangled (§ 1); the dissenting teacher ("zaḳen mamreh") and the proceedings against him (§§ 2–4); the false prophet and the one who makes predictions in the name of idols (§§ 5–6). In the Mishnah of the Babylonian Talmud the order of the tenth and eleventh chapters is inverted.

The Tosefta to Sanhedrin is divided into fourteen chapters, and contains many interesting haggadic interpretations and sayings besides the additions and supplements to the Mishnah. Especially noteworthy is the attempt in iv. 5 to explain how the people sinned in asking for a king (I Sam. viii.), and thus to remove the discrepancy between I Sam. xii. 17 and Deut. xvii 14–20; there is likewise an interesting discussion of the problem whether the script in which the Torah was originally given to the people was changed, and, if so, when the alteration was made (v. 7–8). Other remarkable passages (xi. 6, xiv. 1) state that the laws set forth in Deut. xiii. 13–18 and xxi. 18–21 are valid in theory only, since they never have been and never will be enforced in practise.

The Gemara of both the Talmudim contains a mass of interesting maxims, legends, myths, stories, and haggadic sayings and interpretations in addition to its elucidations of the passages of the Mishnah, the number of haggadot on the tenth (or eleventh) chapter being especially large. Among the interesting passages of the Babylonian Gemara may be noted the disputations with the heretics (38b–39a); the attempts to find the belief in the resurrection of the dead outlined in the Bible, and the polemics against heretics who deny the resurrection (90b–91a, 91b, 92a); the discussion whether the resurrection of the dead described in Ezek. xxxvii. is to be interpreted merely as a figurative prophetic vision or whether it was a real event (92b); and the discussions and computations of the time at which the Messiah will appear, with the events which will attend his coming (97b–99a).

Especially noteworthy in the Palestinian Gemara are the legend of the angel who assumed the form of Solomon and deprived him of his throne (20c); the story of the execution of the eighty sorceresses of Ashkelon on one day by Simeon b. Sheṭaḥ (23d); and the account of the unfortunate and undeserved death of Simeon b. Sheṭaḥ's son (23b).

W. B. J. Z. L.

SAUL, ABBA: Tanna of the third generation. In Ab. R. N. xxix. mention is made of an Abba Saul b. Nanos whom Lewy ("Ueber Einige Fragmente aus der Mischnah des Abba Saul," in "Berichte über die Hochschule für die Wissenschaft des Judenthums in Berlin," 1876) regards as identical with the Abba Saul of this article. The Abba Saul bar Nash mentioned in Niddah 25b is probably likewise identical with him. As Abba Saul explicitly refers, in Tosef., Sanh. xii., to an opinion of R. Akiba's, and, in Tosef., Kil. iv. and Oh. vi., to disagreements between the latter and Ben 'Azzai, as well as between Akiba and the ḥakamim, it may be concluded that he was a pupil of R. Akiba and that he lived in the middle of the second century C.E. The reference to "bet Rabbi" in Pes. 34a, where Abba Saul is said to have prepared the bread according to Levitical rules of purity in "Rabbi's " house, must be construed as referring to the house of the patriarch R. Simeon b. Gamaliel II., not to that of R. Judah ha-Nasi I. (comp. Lewy, *l.c.* p. 21, and note 42).

The "Abba" in "Abba Saul" is titular only, and is not a part of this tanna's name. Nor does he appear to have held the title of rabbi. Abba Saul was tall of stature, and his business is said to have been that of burying the dead (Niddah 24b). Some of the haggadic sayings of Abba Saul that have been preserved throw light on his inner life and his lofty character. He explains the word אנוהו in Ex. xv. 2 as though it were composed of אני and והוא, and interprets it as meaning that man must endeavor to imitate God and, like Him, show charity and benevolence (Mek., Beshallaḥ, Shirah, ii. [ed. Weiss, p. 44a]). To Lev. xix. 2 ("Ye shall be holy: for I the Lord your God am holy") he cites the parallel, "The king's companions must do according to the king's will" (Sifra, Ḳedoshim, i. [ed. Weiss, p. 86c]). "Discord in the school causes general corruption" (Derek Ereẓ Zuṭa ix.), and "Morality is greater than learning" (Sem. xi.) are others of his sayings.

Abba Saul devoted himself assiduously to the study of the mode of worship in the Temple (comp. Z. Frankel, "Darke ha-Mishnah," pp. 177 *et seq.*; Pes. 13b, 86b; Beẓah 29b; Yoma 19b; Niddah 61a, 71b). He also made a collection of mishnayot which in many respects differed from others; this collection has partly been preserved in the present Mishnah, whose redactor, Judah ha-Nasi, occasionally made use of some passages in it which were at variance with other mishnaic compilations.

BIBLIOGRAPHY: J. Brüll, *Einleitung in die Mischnah*, i. 200–201.

W. B. J. Z. L.

SAUL, ABBA, B. BAṬNIT: Tannaof the second and first centuries B.C. According to Derenbourg, his mother was a Batanian proselyte, whence he derived his name "ben Baṭnit"; it appears from

Ned. 23a, however, that "Baṭnit" is a masculine proper name. Abba Saul was engaged in commerce with R. Eleazar b. Zadok, together with whom he issued a regulation referring to the Sabbath law (Shab. xxiv. 5). It is said of him that he filled his liquid measures with wine on the eve of the feast-days in order to be able to give it to the children on those days (Beẓah iii. 8). He is the transmitter, or perhaps the author (comp. Bacher, "Ag. Tan." i. 46, note 2), of a sentence referring to the outrages and misdemeanors committed by some of the priestly families (Pes. 57a).

BIBLIOGRAPHY: Derenbourg, *Hist.* p. 233; Bacher, *Ag. Tan.* i. 46, 50, 371.

W. B. J. Z. L.

SHAMMAI (called also **Shammai ha-Zaḳen** [= "the Elder"]): Scholar of the first century B.C. He was the most eminent contemporary and the halakic opponent of HILLEL, and is almost invariably mentioned along with him. After Menahem the Essene had resigned the office of vice-president ("ab bet din") of the Sanhedrin, Shammai was elected to it, Hillel being at the time president ("nasi"; Ḥag. ii. 2). Shammai was undoubtedly a Palestinian, and hence took an active part in all the political and religious complications of his native land. Of an irascible temperament and easily excited, he lacked the gentleness and tireless patience which so distinguished Hillel. Once, when a heathen came to him and asked to be converted to Judaism upon conditions which Shammai held to be impossible, he drove the applicant away; whereas Hillel, by his gentle manner, succeeded in converting him (Shab. 31a).

Nevertheless Shammai was in no wise a misanthrope. He himself appears to have realized the disadvantages of his violent temper; hence he recommended a friendly attitude toward all. His motto was: "Make the study of the Law thy chief occupation; speak little, but accomplish much; and receive every man with a friendly countenance" (Ab. i. 15). He was modest even toward his pupils (B. B. 134b; comp. Weiss, "Dor," i. 163, note 1).

In his religions views Shammai was strict in the extreme. He wished to make his son, while still a child, conform to the law regarding fasting on the Day of Atonement; and he was dissuaded from his purpose only through the insistence of his friends (Yoma 77b). Once, when his daughter-in-law gave birth to a boy on the Feast of Tabernacles, he broke through the roof of the chamber in which she lay in order to make a sukkah of it, so that his new-born grandchild might fulfil the religious obligation of the festival (Suk. 28a). Some of his sayings also indicate his strictness in the fulfilment of religious duties (comp. Beẓah 16a).

In Sifre, Deut. § 203 (ed. Friedmann, 111b) it is said that Shammai commented exegetically upon three passages of Scripture. These three examples of his exegesis are: (1) the interpretation of Deut. xx. 20 (Tosef., 'Er. iii. 7); (2) that of II Sam. xii. 9 (Ḳid. 43a); and (3) either the interpretation of Lev. xi. 34, which is given anonymously in Sifra on the passage, but which is the basis for Shammai's halakah transmitted in 'Orlah ii. 5, or else the interpretation of Ex. xx. 8 ("Remember the Sabbath"), which is given in the Mekilta, Yitro, 7 (ed. Weiss, p. 76b) in the name of Eleazar b. Hananiah, but which must have originated with Shammai, with whose custom of preparing for the Sabbath (Beẓah *l.c.*) it accords.

Shammai founded a school of his own, which differed fundamentally from that of Hillel (see BET HILLEL AND BET SHAMMAI); and many of Shammai's sayings are probably embodied in those handed down in the name of his school.

BIBLIOGRAPHY: Grätz, *Gesch.* iii. 213–214; Weiss, *Dor*, i 163–164, 170–174; Bacher, *Ag. Tan.* i. 11–12; Frankel, *Hodegetica in Mischnam*, pp. 39–40, Leipsic, 1859.

W. B. J. Z. L.

SIMEON I.: Son of Hillel and father of Gamaliel I. Nothing is known of him except his name and the fact that he was the successor of Hillel as president of the Sanhedrin (Shab. 15a).

W. B. J. Z. L.

SIMEON II. (BEN GAMALIEL I.): President of the Great Sanhedrin at Jerusalem in the last two decades before the destruction of the Temple. Not merely'a scholar, but a man of resolution and courage also, he was one of the leaders in the revolt against the Romans. Although he was the chief of the Pharisees during the revolt, he did not hesitate to make common cause with the Sadducean former high priest Anan. Even his adversary Josephus praises him, saying that Simeon was a circumspect and energetic man, who would have carried the revolt to a successful conclusion if his counsel had been consistently followed (Josephus, "Vita," § 38). Simeon b. Gamaliel died before the outbreak was quelled; he is said to have been executed by the Romans (Sem. viii.), though this statement lacks historical support.

Little is known of his activity as a teacher of the Law, though it may be assumed that he followed the liberal interpretations of his grandfather Hillel. He held that no rules and regulations should be imposed upon the people which they were unable to follow (Tosef., Sanh. ii. 13). Once, when poultry was very dear at Jerusalem, so that the women obliged to bring their offering of doves were hardly able to bear the great expense, Simeon issued a decree permitting a woman who ordinarily would be obliged to offer five pairs of doves to offer only one pair; in consequence of this decree the price declined to one-fourth (Ker. i. 7). No other halakot by him have been preserved, although probably many of his halakic sentences are included in those of the "Bet Hillel." His rule of life was: "All my days I have grown up among sages, and I have found that there is nothing better than silence, and that he who talks much gives rise to sin. Not interpretation and study but work is the most virtuous thing" (Abot i. 17).

BIBLIOGRAPHY: Frankel, *Hodegetica in Mischnam*, pp. 63–64; Brüll, *Einleitung in die Mischna*, i. 55–57; Weiss, *Dor*, i. 190–191; Grätz, *Gesch.* iii. 470.

W. B. J. Z. L.

SIMEON (BEN GAMALIEL II.): Tanna of the third generation, and president of the Great Sanhedrin. Simeon was a youth in Bethar when the Bar Kokba war broke out, but when that fortress was taken by the Romans he managed to escape the massacre (Giṭ. 58a; Soṭah 49b; B. Ḳ. 83a). On the restoration of the college at Usha, Simeon was elected its president, this dignity being bestowed upon him not only because he was a descendant of the house of Hillel, but in recognition of his personal worth and influence. There were many children in his family, one-half of whom were instructed in the Torah, and the other half in Greek philosophy (*ib.*). Simeon himself seems to have been trained in Greek philosophy; this probably accounts for his declaring later that the Scriptures might be written only in the original text and in Greek (Meg. 9b; i. 8; Yer. Meg. 71c). Simeon appears to have studied natural science as well, for some of his sayings betray a scientific knowledge of the nature of plants and animals, while others concern the anatomy of the human body and the means of avoiding or of curing disease (Ber. 25a, 40a; Shab. 78a, 128b; Yeb. 80b; Ket. 59b, 110b). It is not known who were his teachers in the Halakah; he transmits sayings of R. Judah b. Ilai (Tosef., Kelim, B. Ḳ. v. 4), of R. Meïr (Tosef., B. M. iv. 15; Ket. vi. 10), and of R. Jose b. Ḥalafta (Tosef., Dem. iii. 12; Tos. Ṭoh. xi. 16). The last-named was honored as a teacher by Simeon, who addressed questions to him, and put many of his decisions into practise (Suk. 26a; Tosef., Dem. iii. 14).

During Simeon's patriarchate the Jews were harried by daily persecutions and oppressions. In regard to these Simeon observes: "Our forefathers knew suffering only from a distance, but we have been surrounded by it for so many days, years, and cycles that we are more justified than they in becoming impatient" (Cant. R. iii. 3). "Were we, as of yore, to inscribe upon a memorial scroll our sufferings and our occasional deliverances therefrom, we should not find room for all" (Shab. 13b).

Jewish internal affairs were more firmly organized by Simeon b. Gamaliel, and the patriarchate attained under him a degree of honor previously unknown. While formerly only two persons, the nasi and the ab bet din, presided over the college, Simeon established the additional office of ḥakam, with authority equal to that of the others, appointing R. Meïr to the new office. In order, however, to distinguish between the dignity of the patriarchal office and that attaching to the offices of the ab bet din and the ḥakam, Simeon issued an order to the effect that the honors formerly bestowed alike upon the nasi and the ab bet din were henceforth to be reserved for the patriarch (nasi), while minor honors were to be accorded the ab bet din and the ḥakam. By this ruling Simeon incurred the enmity of R. Meïr, the ḥakam, and of R. Nathan, the ab bet din (Hor. 13b), Simeon had made this arrangement, not from personal motives, but in order to increase the authority of the college over which the nasi presided, and to promote due respect for learning. His personal humility is evidenced by his sayings to his son Judah, as well as by the latter's sayings (B. M. 84b, 85a).

In halakic matters Simeon inclined toward lenient interpretation of the laws, and he avoided adding to the difficulties attending their observance. In many instances in which an act, in itself not forbidden by Biblical law, had later been prohibited merely out of fear that it might lead to transgressions, Simeon declared it permissible, saying that "fear should not be admitted as a factor in a decision" (Shab. 13a, 40b, 147b; Yoma 77b; B. M. 69b; Bek. 24a; Pes. 10b). Of his halakic opinions about thirty relating to the Sabbath regulations and fifteen referring to the seventh year ("shebi'it") have been preserved, in nearly all of which the liberality of views is evident. He always took into consideration the common usage, and he often maintained that the ultimate decision must follow common tradition (Ket. vi. 4; B. M. vii. 1; B. B. x. 1). The habits of the individual must also be considered (Ta'an. 30a). In his regulations regarding the legal relations of man and wife he made it an invariable rule to protect the rights and the dignity of the latter in preference to those of the former (Ket. v. 5, vii. 9, xiii. 10). He endeavored to protect the slaves and secure to them certain rights (Giṭ. 12b, 37b, 40b). The weal of the community is more important than the interests and rights of the individual, and the latter must be sacrificed to the former (Ket. 52b; Giṭ. 37b). He especially strove to maintain the authority of the magistrates; according to his opinion the decisions of a court of law must be upheld, even though a slight error has been made; otherwise its dignity would suffer (Ket. xi. 5).

Simeon's decisions are mostly founded on sound common sense and an intimate acquaintance with the subjects treated, and, with three exceptions (B. B. 173b; Giṭ. 74b; Sanh. 31a), his views, as set forth in the Mishnah, have been accepted as valid (Giṭ. 75a). He often cites the conditions of the past, which he learned probably from the traditions of his house, and which are highly important for the knowledge of older customs and habits. He speaks of the earlier festive celebrations in Jerusalem on the Fifteenth of Ab and on the Day of Atonement (Ta'an. iv. 8); of the customs followed there at meals when guests were present (Tosef.. Ber. iv. 9 *et seq.*); of the work on the pools of Siloah ('Ar. 1b); of the nature of the marriage contract (Tosef., Sanh. vii. 1) and the bill of divorce (Tosef., Giṭ. ix. 13).

Several of Simeon's haggadic sayings and decisions also have been preserved. "The moral and social constitution of the world rests on three principles—truth, justice, and peace" (Abot i. 18). "Great is peace, for Aaron the priest became famous only because he sought peace" ("pereḳ ha-shalom"; comp. Mal. ii. 6). "Justice must be accorded to non-Jews as to Jews; the former should have the option of seeking judgment before either a Jewish or a pagan court" (Sifre, Deut. 16 [ed. Friedmann, p. 68b]). Simeon praised the Samaritans for observing more strictly than did the Israelites such commandments of the Torah as they recognized (Ḳid. 76a). The Scripture is in many places to be understood figuratively and not literally (Sifre, Deut. 25 [ed. Friedmann, p. 70a]). "It is unnecessary to erect monuments to the pious; their sayings will preserve their memories" (Yer. Sheḳ. 47a;. Gen. R. lxxxii. 11).

BIBLIOGRAPHY: Heilprin, *Seder ha-Dorot*, ii. 368–370; Frankel, *Hodegetica in Mischnam*, pp. 178–185; Weiss, *Dor*, ii. 171–177; Brüll, *Einleitung in die Mischna*, i. 203–209; Ph. Bloch, in *Monatsschrift*, 1864, pp. 81–97, 121–133; Grätz, *Gesch.* iv. 173, 187–189; Bacher, *Ag. Tan.* ii. 322–334.

W. B. J. Z. L.

SIMEON B. ABBA: Palestinian amora of the third generation; pupil of Ḥanina b. Ḥama, who esteemed him highly, and of Johanan, who would have been glad to ordain him (Sanh. 14a). Simeon's family came originally from Babylonia; Simeon himself lived in Palestine in such great poverty that his teacher Johanan applied to him the saying of Eccl. ix. 11, "Bread is not to the wise" (Hebr.; Yer. Bik. 65d). On the advice of his teacher Ḥanina he married, successively, the two daughters of Mar Samuel, the head of the school of Nehardea, who had been taken to Palestine as prisoners (Ket. 23a). Both of them, however, died a short time after their marriage (Yer. Ket. ii. 26a). When Simeon desired to travel abroad, and requested his teacher Ḥanina to give him a letter of recommendation, the latter dissuaded him from his project, declaring, "To-morrow I shall go to thy father's, where they will reproach me, saying, 'We had a worthy scion in the land of Israel, and thou hast allowed him to go to another country'" (Yer. M. Ḳ. 81c).

After the death of Ḥanina, and while Johanan was still living, Simeon left Palestine and settled in Damascus. But after Johanan's death, Abbahu wrote to Simeon at Damascus and persuaded him to return to Palestine (Yer. Bik. 68d). According to one tradition, Simeon was a grave-digger in Sepphoris. In this occupation, which involved the collecting of bones from old graves, he evolved the peculiar idea that he could tell by the appearance of a bone what the person to whom it had belonged had been accustomed to drink: black bones belonged to persons who had been accustomed to drink cold water, red bones to wine-drinkers, while white bones showed that their owners had drunk warm water (Gen. R. lxxxix. 2).

Simeon transmitted sayings of his teachers Ḥanina and Johanan, also of Joshua b. Levi and Simeon b. Laḳish. Many of his own haggadic sayings have been preserved. One of them runs: "There are two kinds of acts of love, that of participation in a wedding ceremony, and that of participation in a funeral. When two occur together, and thou hast an opportunity to attend one, but not both, and dost not know which to choose, be taught by the words of Solomon, who said, 'It is better to go to the house of mourning than to go to the house of feasting'" (Eccl. vii. 2; Tan., Wayishlaḥ, 23 [ed. Buber, p. 88a]).

Bibliography: Bacher, *Ag. Pal. Amor.* ii. 201–204.

W. B. J. Z. L.

SIMEON B. ABSALOM: Amora the period of whose activity is not known. Only two haggadic sentences by him have been preserved. One, on Judges iv. 5, declares that Deborah sat under a palm-tree instead of in her house, in order to escape any possible suspicion (Meg. 14a). The other explains why David, when fleeing from Absalom, composed a "mizmor" or psalm (Ps. iii.) and not a "ḳinah" or lament (Ber. 7b).

Bibliography: Bacher, *Ag. Pal. Amor.* iii. 775.

W. B. J. Z. L.

SIMEON B. 'AḲASHYAH: Tanna of the second generation. Only one of his haggadic sentences has been preserved, namely, that explaining Job xii. 12, 20, in which he declares that coarse and uneducated persons lose in intelligence as they grow old, while scholars become more intelligent with advancing years (Ḳin. iii. 6).

Bibliography: Heilprin, *Seder ha-Dorot*, ii. 364.

W. B. J. Z. L.

SIMEON B. BOETHUS: The first high priest of the family of Boethus in the Temple of Jerusalem. He was a native of Alexandria. He owed his appointment as high priest to his daughter Mariamne, who captivated Herod by her beauty, the king advancing her father in office in order to give Mariamne a certain rank when he made her his wife. When Herod subsequently put away this second Mariamne, Simeon was deposed from the high-priesthood.

BIBLIOGRAPHY: Grätz, *Gesch.* iii. 223–235.

W. B. J. Z. L.

SIMEON B. ELEAZAR: Tanna of the fourth generation; probably a son of R. Eleazar b. Shammua'. He was a pupil of R. Meïr, whose sentences, both halakic and haggadic, he transmitted (Ḥul. 6a; Shab. 134a; 'Er. 29a). The following anecdote, related of him, shows how he strove for perfection, a characteristic which is evidenced in his ethical sentences also: Once, on returning in a very joyful mood from the academy to his native city, he met an exceedingly ugly man who saluted him. Simeon did not return the greeting, and even mocked the man on account of his ugliness. When, however, the man said to him, "Go and tell the Master, who created me, how ugly His handiwork is," Simeon, perceiving that he had sinned, fell on his knees and begged the man's pardon. As the latter would not forgive him, Simeon followed him until they came near to the tanna's native city, when the inhabitants came out to meet him, greeting him respectfully as rabbi. The man thereupon said to them, "If this is a rabbi may there be few like him in Israel," and told them what had occurred; he, however, forgave Simeon when the people begged him to do so. Simeon went the same day to the school and preached a sermon, exhorting all the people to be pliable like a reed and not unbending like a cedar (Ta'an. 20a, b, where the preferable reading has "Simon b. Eleazar"; see Rabbinowitz, "Variæ Lectiones," *ad loc.*; Ab. R. N. xli.).

Simeon, like his teacher R. Meïr, engaged in polemic discussions with the Samaritans, who denied the resurrection, proving to them that it was taught by the Bible, namely, by Num. xv. 31 (Sifre, Num. 112 [ed. Friedmann, p. 33b]). In the Halakah, Simeon appears most frequently as the opponent of R. Judah ha-Nasi I. Simeon formulated an exegetic rule for the interpretation of those passages in the Bible in which points are placed over certain letters or entire words, in conformity with a tradition which was even then sanctioned: If the letters without points exceed in number those punctuated the exposition must be based on the former; but if the reverse be true, the letters with points must be interpreted (Gen. R. xlviii. 17).

Many haggadic sentences by Simeon have been preserved, including the following: "He who is prompted by love to perform ethical and religious acts is greater than he who is prompted to them by fear" (Soṭah 31a). "When the old people say, 'Tear down,' and the young people say, 'Build,' listen to the old and not to the young; for the tearing down of the old people is building, and the building of the young people is tearing down, as the story of Rehoboam, the son of Solomon, teaches" (Meg. 31b). "There are two kinds of friends: one that reproves you, and the other that praises you. Love him who reproves you, and hate him who praises you; for the former leads you to the future life, while the latter leads you out of the world" (Ab. R. N. xxix.). "The sentence 'Thou shalt love thy neighbor as thyself: I am the Lord' [Lev. xix. 18] was uttered with a great oath; meaning 'I, the Eternal One, have created him. If thou lovest him, I will surely reward thee for it; and if thou lovest him not, then I am the judge ready to punish" (Ab. R. N. xvi.). "Three things the left hand shall ward off, while the right hand draws them on, namely, desire, a child, and a wife" (Soṭah 47a). "Have you ever seen an animal that is obliged to follow a trade or that must painfully support itself? Yet animals were created for the purpose of serving man, while man was created to serve his Creator. Should not, therefore, man, rather than the animals, be able to support himself without toil? Man, however, has deteriorated in his works, and therefore in his nature, and has been deprived of his nourishment" (Ḳid. iv. 13).

Some fine parables by Simeon have also been preserved (Ab. R. N. i., vi.; Mek., Yitro, Baḥodesh, 5 [ed. Weiss, p. 74a]).

Bibliography: Frankel, *Hodegetica in Mischnam*, p. 200; Brüll, *Mebo ha-Mishnah*, i. 236–238; Heilprin, *Seder ha-Dorot*, ii. 370; Bacher, *Ag. Tan.* ii. 422–436.

W. B. J. Z. L.

SIMEON BAR GIORA. See Bar Giora, Simon.

SIMEON B. ḤALAFTA: One of the teachers of the transition period between the Tannaim and the Amoraim. He was a friend of Ḥiyya, and is mentioned several times as differing with him in regard to haggadic sentences (Lam. R. i. 2; Pesiḳ. xi. [ed. Buber, p. 98b], xxv. [p. 164a]). He lived at 'En-Tina, a locality near Sepphoris, and occasionally visited the patriarch R. Judah I. at the latter place. He was a pupil of R. Judah, and lived in such indigence that the patriarch often relieved him (Ruth R. v. 7), His advancing age obliged him to discontinue his visits to Judah; and when the latter inquired into the cause of his absence he gave as a reason his debility (Shab. 152a). He was highly respected. Once when he took leave of Judah the patriarch ordered his son to ask Simeon for a blessing, and Simeon responded with the words: "God grant that you will neither cause shame to others nor be shamed by others." As the patriarch's son took this blessing to be a mere empty phrase, his father reminded him that God had once blessed Israel with these same words (M. Ḳ. 9b, according to the correct reading of Rabbinowitz in "Diḳduḳe Soferim"). The honor in which Simeon b. Ḥalafta was held also appears from Ḥanina's remark that he (Ḥanina) merited a hale old age in view of his visits to the aged Simeon b. Ḥalafta; on his journeys from Tiberias to Sepphoris Ḥanina had been wont to make a detour to 'En-Tina in order to visit Simeon (Yer. Ta'an. 68a).

Various legends are connected with the person of Simeon b. Ḥalafta. Once, on returning from Sepphoris to 'En-Tina he met the angel of death, who said to him in the course of conversation that he had no power over persons who were like Simeon, since on account of their good deeds God often prolongs their span of life (Deut. R. ix. 1). On another occasion, when in danger of being torn by lions, Simeon was miraculously saved (Sanh. 59b). Once a precious stone is said to have been sent to him from heaven in a miraculous way (Ruth R. iii. 4; comp. Perles in "Monatsschrift," 1873, pp. 27 *et seq.*). Many stories are told of his observations and experiments in zoology, and he was designated by the epithet "'asḳan" = "the busy one" or "the experimenter." He is said to have saved the life of a hen by attaching a reed to her dislocated hip-bone; and he made new feathers grow on another hen which had lost her feathers (Ḥul. 57b). Still other experiments by him are recounted (*ib.*; Lev. R. xxii.).

Simeon b. Ḥalafta is rarely mentioned in the halakic tradition, but very frequently in the Haggadah, in which he is especially noted for the parables which he employed in his Scriptural exegesis. Some of these may be mentioned here. He explains the regulation (Ex. xii. 43 *et seq.*) that circumcision should precede participation in the Feast of Pesaḥ by the following parable: "A king gave a banquet, commanding that only those guests who wore his badge should be admitted. So God instituted a banquet in celebration of the deliverance from Egyptian bondage, commanding that only those should partake of it who bore on their bodies the seal of Abraham" (Ex. R. xix. 6). The following is a parable on the relation between God and Israel: "A king took to wife a matron who brought two precious stones as her marriage portion; and he gave her in addition two other gems. When the woman lost the stones she had brought, he took away those which he had given to her; but when she found her own again, the king gave back those of his gift, and had all the gems made into a crown for her. Similarly Israel brought the precious stones 'justice' and 'right,' which it had received from Abraham [Gen. xviii. 19 (A. V. "justice and judgment")], into the covenant which it made with God. God gave in addition two other precious stones, 'mercy' [Deut. vii. 12] and 'compassion' [Deut. xiii. 18]. When Israel lost justice and right [Amos vi. 12] God took away mercy and compassion [Yer. xvi. 5]. When Israel again produces what it has lost [Isa. i. 27] God will also restore what He has taken away [Isa. liv. 10], the four precious stones together becoming a crown for Israel" (comp. Hos. ii. 21; Deut. R. iii. 1). Other Scriptural explanations by Simeon are not expressed in parables. For instance, he applies Prov. xviii. 7, "A fool's mouth is his destruction," to the words of the builders of the Tower of Babel (Gen. xi. 4; Gen. R. xxxviii. 11). The ladder which Jacob beheld in his vision (Gen. xxviii. 12), and which stood on earth and reached to heaven, indicated to him those of his descendants who would be engulfed in the earth, namely, Korah and his followers (Num. xvi. 32), and also Moses, who was to ascend to heaven (Ex. xxiv. 1; Tan., Wayyeẓe, ed. Buber, p.75a). The following sentences by Simeon may be mentioned here: "Since the fist of hypocrisy has become all-powerful, judgment has become perverted; the good deeds of the individual are destroyed; and no man may say to another, 'My merits are greater than thine'" (Soṭah 41b). "All the future bliss, the blessings, and the comfortings which the Prophets have beheld, apply to the penitent, while the sentence [Isa. lxiv. 3, Hebr.] 'neither hath the eye seen, O God, besides thee, what he hath prepared for him that waiteth for him' applies to the person who has never tasted sin" (Eccl. R. i. 8). His sentence in praise of peace was included in the Mishnah ('Uḳẓin iii. 12): "God has found no better vessel than peace to hold the blessing to be given to Israel, as it is written (Ps. xxix. 11): 'The Lord giveth strength unto his people; the Lord will bless his people with peace.'"

BIBLIOGRAPHY: Heilprin, *Seder ha-Dorot*, ii. 364–365, Warsaw, 1882; Frankel, *Mebo*, p. 128b, Breslau, 1870; Bacher, *Ag. Tan.* ii. 530–536.

W. B. J. Z. L.

SIMEON HE-ḤASID (= "the Pious"): Tanna; period of activity unknown. He is not mentioned in the Mishuah; and only one haggadic sentence of his has been preserved, in a baraita. It refers to Job xxii., and states that the 974 generations which should have been added to the 26 which were created before the revelation of the Law on Mount Sinai were distributed among the generations created subsequently, and that they constitute the insolent who are found in every age (Ḥag. 13b, 14a).

W. B. J. Z. L.

SIMEON B. JAKIM: Palestinian amora of the third generation; pupil of R. Johanan, to whom he often addressed scholarly questions (Yer. 'Orlah i. 60d; Yer. B. B. 16b), and contemporary of R. Eliezer. He was a prominent teacher and was considered an important authority (Yer. Sanh. 21d). Together with R. Eliezer he is mentioned in the Babylonian Talmud also, although under the name Simeon b. Eliakim (Ket. 50b).

BIBLIOGRAPHY: Frankel, *Mebo ha-Yerushalmi*, p. 129a.

W. B. J. Z. L.

SIMEON B. JEHOZADAK: Palestinian amora of the first generation; probably the teacher of Johanan, who has transmitted several halakic sayings of his (R. H. 34b; Yoma 43b; ʻAb. Zarah 47a; Ned. 45a; Niddah 10b; Taʻan. 28b). Simeon lived to be very old, and when he died Yannai and Johanan followed his remains to the grave (Yer. Naz. 56a). Simeon b. Jehozadak was a haggadist also, and several of his haggadic sayings have been preserved, handed down almost without exception by Johanan. "A scholar who does not avenge insults, but who harbors resentment like Nahash, King of the Ammonites, is no true scholar" (Yoma 22b; comp. Bacher, "Ag. Pal. Amor." i. 121). "One against whose ancestry no reproach can be brought should not be given charge of a congregation, because it is well to be able to say to one entrusted with such a charge, if he becomes proud, 'Look behind thee, and see whence them comest'" (Yoma *l.c.*). "Better that a letter of the Torah should be put aside than that God's name should be publicly profaned" (Yeb. 79a). A few examples of Simeon's method of halakic exegesis occur in Sukkah (27a) and Baba Meẓiʻa (22b).

BIBLIOGRAPHY: Bacher, *Ag. Pal. Amor.* i. 119–123; Heilprin, *Seder ha-Dorot*, ii. 373–374.

W. B. J. Z. L.

SIMEON B. JOSE B. LEḲONYA: Tanna of the fourth generation; contemporary of R. Judah ha-Nasi I. He was the brother-in-law of Eleazar b. Simeon, whose son he educated and instructed in the Torah (B. M. 85a). Only a few of his halakic sentences have been preserved (Bek. 38b; Yer. Pes. 33b). He gave as a reason for the thirty-nine kinds of work forbidden on the Sabbath that the word "melakah" (work) occurs thirty-nine times in the Torah (Shab. 49b); but this enumeration is inexact, since the word occurs oftener—indeed, Simeon seems to have disregarded purposely some passages in making his list. Among his haggadic sentences the following is especially interesting, as indicating the indestructibility of Judaism: "In this world Israel is compared to the rock [Num. xxiii. 9; Isa. li. 1] and to the stones [Gen. xlix. 24; Ps. cxviii. 22], while the nations of the earth are compared to the potsherds [Isa. xxx. 14]. The proverb says: 'If the stone fall upon the pot, wo to the pot; and if the pot falls upon the stone, wo to the pot.' Thus, whoever seeks to trouble Israel will not be allowed to go unpunished" (Esth. R. vii. on iii. 6).

BIBLIOGRAPHY: Heilprin, *Seder ha-Dorot*, ii. 372–373, Warsaw, 1882: Bacher, *Ag. Tan.* ii. 488–489.

W. B. J. Z. L.

SIMEON B. JUDAH: Tanna of the fourth generation; a native of Kefar 'Ikos (comp. on this name H. Hildesheimer, "Beiträge zur Geographie Palästinas," pp. 12, 81, Berlin, 1886). He is mentioned almost exclusively as a transmitter of the sentences of Simeon b. Yoḥai. Two of his own exegetic sentences also have been handed down. To Ex. xiv. 15, "Wherefore criest thou unto me?" he says that the cry of the Israelites for aid had preceded that of Moses (Mek., Beshallaḥ, iii. [ed. Weiss, p. 35b]). In Deut. xxxii. 6 ויכננך is to be derived from כן (= "foundation," "basis," or "means"): "He placed thee upon thy foundation" (Sifre, Deut. 309 [ed. Friedmann, p. 134a]). In another sentence of his that has been preserved mention is made of a certain place in Galilee in which were said to be leprous stones, *i.e.*, stones from a house infected with leprosy (Tosef., Neg. vi. 1).

BIBLIOGRAPHY: Heilprin, *Seder ha-Dorot,* ii. 371, Warsaw, 1882; Frankel, *Hodegetica in Mischnam,* p. 199; Brüll, *Einleitung in die Mischna,* xi. 232 *et seq.*; Bacher, *Ag. Tan.* ii. 392.

W. B. J. Z. L.

SIMEON BEN JUDAH HA-NASI I.: One of the teachers during the transition period between the Tannaim and the Amoraim. He was the younger son of Judah, and although far more learned than his brother Gamaliel, his father had intended that he should become ḥakam only, while Gamaliel was to be Judah's successor as "nasi" (Ket. 103b). Simeon was particularly friendly with R. Ḥiyya, with whom he once undertook a journey (Gen. R. lxxix. 8), and with Bar Ḳappara, who was one of his fellow students (M. Ḳ. 16a; Ber. 13b). He surpassed both of these in halakic as well as in haggadic exegesis. R. Ḥiyya learned from him the exposition of a part of the Psalms; Bar Ḳappara, a part of the halakic midrash to Leviticus. It therefore annoyed Simeon that both refused to do him honor (Ḳid. 33a). His father called him "the light of Israel" ('Ar. 10a; Men. 88b), and he was very kind-hearted (B. B. 8a) and candid (*ib.* 164b). He did not approve his grandfather's and his father's habit of citing the sayings of R. Meïr without mentioning the latter's name.

Simeon introduced many emendations into the text of the Mishnah, according to readings which he had heard from his father, as, for example, B. M. iii. 1, and 'Ab. Zarah iv. 1, where, in the Mishnah to the Palestinian Talmud, his readings have been preserved (comp. B. M. 44a; 'Ab. Zarah 52b). One of Simeon's sayings, also, has been preserved in the Mishnah (Mak. iii. 15); in it he contends that if man is rewarded for abstaining from the drinking of blood, for which he has no natural craving, his reward ought to be much greater for abstaining from robbery and fornication, to which he has an inborn inclination.

BIBLIOGRAPHY: Heilprin, *Seder ha-Dorot,* ii. 372, Warsaw, 1882.

W. B. J. Z. L.

SIMEON THE JUST (שמעון הצדיק): High priest. He is identical either with Simeon I. (310–291 or 300–270 B.C.), son of Onias I., and grandson of Jaddua, or with Simeon II. (219–199 B.C.), son of Onias II. Many statements concerning him are variously ascribed by scholars to four different persons who bore the same surname; *e.g.*, to Simeon I. by Fränkel and Grätz; to Simeon II. by Krochmal and Brüll; to Simon Maccabeus by Löw; and to Simeon the son of Gamaliel by Weiss.

About no other high priest does such a mixture of fact and fiction center, the Talmud, Josephus, and the Second Book of Maccabees all containing accounts of him. He was termed "the Just" either because of the piety of his life and his benevolence toward his compatriots (Josephus, "Ant." xii. 2, § 5), or because he took thought for his people (Ecclus. [Sirach] l. 4). He was deeply interested both in the spiritual and in the material' development of the nation. Thus, according to Ecclus. (Sirach) l. 1–14, he rebuilt the walls of Jerusalem, which had been torn down by Ptolemy Soter, and repaired the damage done to the Temple, raising the foundation-walls of its court and enlarging the cistern therein so that, it was like a pool (that these statements can apply only to Simeon I. is shown by Grätz, and they agree, moreover, with the Talmudic accounts of Simeon's undertakings).

When Alexander the Great marched through Palestine in the year 333, Simeon the Just, according to the legend, dressed in his eight priestly robes went to Kefar Saba (Antipatris) to meet him (Yoma 69a), although Josephus (*l.c.* xi. 8, § 4) states that Alexander himself came to Jerusalem (but see JEW. ENCYC. i, 341b, vii. 51b). The legend further declares that as soon as the Macedonian saw the high priest, he descended from his chariot and bowed respectfully before him. When Alexander's courtiers criticized his act, he replied that it had been intentional, since he had had a vision in which he had seen the high priest, who had predicted his victory. Alexander demanded that a statue of himself be placed in the Temple; but the high priest explained to him that this was impossible, promising him instead that all the sons born of priests in that year should be named Alexander and that the Seleucidan era should "be introduced (Lev. R. xiii., end; Pesiḳ. R, section "Parah"). This story appears to be identical with III Macc. ii., where Seleucus (Kasgalgas) is mentioned (Soṭah 33a; Yer. Soṭah ix. 3; Cant. R. 38c; Tosef., Soṭah, xiii.). During the administration of Simeon the Just the RED HEIFER is said to have been burned twice, and he therefore built two wooden bridges from the Temple mount to the Mount of Olives (Parah iii. 6; Yer. Sheḳ. iv. 2).

Simeon occupied a position intermediate between the Hasmoneans and the Hellenists, while, as he himself boasted, he was an opponent of the Nazarites and ate of the sacrifice offered by one of that sect only on a single occasion. Once a youth with flowing hair came to him and wished to have his head shorn. When asked his motive, the youth replied that he had seen his own face reflected in a spring and it had pleased him so that he feared lest his beauty might become an idol to him. He therefore wished to offer up his hair to God, and Simeon then partook of the sin-offering which he brought (Naz. 4b; Ned. 9b; Yer. Ned. 36d; Tosef. Naz. iv.; Yer. Naz. i. 7).

During Simeon's administration seven miracles are said to have taken place. A blessing rested (1) on the offering of the first-fruits, (2) on the two sacrificial loaves, and (3) on the loaves of show-bread, in that, although each priest received a portion no larger than an olive, he ate and was satiated without even consuming the whole of it; (4) the lot cast for God (see Lev. xvi. 8) always came into the right hand; (5) the red thread around the neck of the ram invariably became white on the Day of Atonement; (6) the light in the Temple never failed; and (7) the fire on the altar required but little wood to keep it burning (Yoma 39b; Men. 109b; Yer. Yoma vi. 3). Simeon is said to have held office for forty years (Yoma 9a; Yer. Yoma i. 1, v. 2; Lev. R. xxi.). On a certain Day of Atonement he came from the Holy of Holies in a melancholy mood, and when asked the reason, he replied that on every Day of Atonement a figure clothed in white had ushered him into the Holy of Holies and then had escorted him out. This time, however, the apparition had been clothed in black and had conducted him in, but had not led him out—a sign that that year was to be his last. He is said to have died seven days later (Yoma 39b; Tosef., Soṭah, xv.; Yer. Yoma v. 1).

Simeon the Just is called one of the last members of the Great Synagogue, but it is no longer possible to determine which of the four who bore this name was really the last.

The personality of Simeon the Just, whose chief maxim was "The world exists through three things: the Law, worship, and beneficence" (Ab. i. 2), and the high esteem in which he was held, are shown by a poem in Ecclus. (Sirach) l., which compares him, at the moment of his exit from the Holy of Holies, to the sun, moon, and stars, and to the most magnificent plants. This poem appeared with certain changes in the ritual of the evening service for the Day of Atonement, where it begins with the words אמת מה נהדר; a translation of it is given in Grätz, "Gesch." ii. 239, and in Hamburger, "R. B. T." ii. 111. After Simeon's death men ceased to utter the TETRAGRAMMATON aloud (Yoma 30b; Tosef. Soṭah, xiii.).

BIBLIOGRAPHY: Zunz, *G. V.* 1st ed., p. 36; Gedaliah ibn Yaḥya, *Shalshelet ha-Kabbhalah*, ed. Amsterdam, p. 83a; Dei Rossi. *Me'or 'Enayim*, iii., ch. xxii., p. 90; Krochmal, *Moreh Nebuke ha-Zeman*, p. 109, Lemberg, 1851; *Orient, Lit.* 1845, pp. 33 *et seq.*, *Ben Chananja*, i. 253; Herzfeld, *Gesch. des Volkes*

Jisrael, i. 189, 194, 196, 200, 201, 374–378, 408; ii. 147, 148, 245, 557; Ewald, *Gesch.* iii., part ii., note 310; *He-Ḥaluẓ*, viii. 2; Frankel, in *Monatsschrift*, i. 208 *et seq.*, 410 *et seq.*; idem, *Hodegetica in Mischnam*, pp. 29, 30, Leipsic, 1859; Geiger, *Urschrift*, p. 476; Weiss, *Zur Gesch. der Jüdischen Tradition*, i. 82–87, Vienna, 1871; Derenbourg, *Histoire de la Palestine*, pp. 46–47; Löw, *Gesammelte Schriften*, 1889, i. 399–449; Hamburger, *R. B. T.* pp. 1115–1119; Heilprin, *Seder ha-Dorot*, pp. 137a-138b, Warsaw, 1889; Brüll, *Mebo ha-Mishnah*, pp. 11–14, Frankfort-on-the-Main, 1876; Grätz, *Gesch.* ii. 221, 235, *et passim*; *Monatsschrift*, 1857, pp. 45–56; Schürer, *Gesch.* i. 182; ii. 352, 355 *et seq.*; iii. 159.

W. B. S. O.

SIMEON BAR ḲAPPARA. See Bar Ḳappara.

SIMEON OF ḲIṬRON: Tanna of whom only one haggadic saying has been preserved. This is to the effect that it was on account of the bones of Joseph, which the Israelites brought with them out of Egypt, that the sea opened before them (Mek., Beshallaḥ, 3 [ed. Weiss, p. 35b]).

Bibliography: Heilprin, *Seder ha-Dorot*, ii. 378; Bacher, *Ag. Tan.* ii. 560.

W. B. J. Z. L.

SIMEON B. LAḲISH (called also **Resh Laḳish**): One of the two most prominent Palestinian amoraim of the second generation (the other being his brother-in-law and halakic opponent R. Johanan); born *c.* 200; died *c.* 275. Nothing is known of his ancestry except his father's name. According to Grätz ("Gesch." v. 240), his birthplace was Bostra, east of the Jordan; yet even from early youth he appears to have lived in Sepphoris, where he studied with R. Johanan. Like the latter, he ascribed his knowledge of the Torah to his good fortune in having been privileged to see the patriarch Judah ha-Nasi (Yer. Ber. 63a). According to Halevy ("Dorot ha-Rishonim"), he was a pupil of R. Judah Nesiah (grandson of Rabbi), in whose name he transmits many sayings. Bacher supposes that he was a pupil of Bar Ḳappara, since he often hands down sayings in his name ("Ag. Pal. Amor." i. 340). He appears also to have attended the seminary of R. Hoshaiah, whom he cites (Ḳid. 80a; Me'i. 7b; Bek. 13a), questions (Yeb. 57a), and calls the "father of the Mishnah" (Yer. B. Ḳ. 4c).

Many stories are told of Simeon's gigantic strength and of his corpulence. He was accustomed to lie on the hard ground, saying, "My fat is my cushion" (Giṭ. 47a). Under the stress of unfavorable circumstances he gave up the study of the Torah and sought to support himself by a worldly calling. He sold himself to the managers of a circus ("ludii," "ludiarii"), where he could make use of his great bodily strength, but where also he was compelled to risk his life continually in combats with wild beasts (*ib.*). From this low estate he was brought back to his studies by R. Johanan. It is said that the latter saw him bathing in the Jordan, and was so overcome by his beauty that at one bound he was beside him in the water. "Thy strength would be more appropriate for studying the Law," said R. Johanan; "And thy beauty for women," answered Resh Laḳish. Thereupon R. Johanan said, "If thou wilt turn again to thy studies I will give thee to wife my sister, who is still more beautiful." Resh Laḳish agreed, and R. Johanan led him back to a life of study (B. M. 84a). R. Johanan might be called a teacher of R. Simeon b. Laḳish (Ḥul. 139a; Ber. 31a); but the latter, through his extraordinary talent and his exhaustless diligence, soon attained so complete a knowledge of the Law that he stood on an equal footing with R. Johanan. They are designated as "the two great authorities" (Yer. Ber. 12c). While R. Johanan was still in Sepphoris, teaching at the same time as Ḥanina, Simeon b. Laḳish stood on an equality with him and enjoyed equal rights as a member of the school and council (Yer. Sanh. 18c; Yer. Niddah ii. 50b).

When R. Johanan went to Tiberias and founded an academy there, Simeon accompanied him and took the second position in the school (comp. B. Ḳ. 117a). He exceeded even R. Johanan in acuteness, and the latter himself admitted that his right hand was missing when R. Simeon was not present (Yer. Sanh. ii. 19d, 20a). "When he discussed halakic questions it was as if he were uprooting mountains and rubbing them together," says 'Ula of him (Sanh. 24a). R. Johanan was often compelled by Simeon's logic to surrender his own opinion and accept that of Simeon (Yer. Yoma 38a), and even to act in accordance with the latter's views (Yer. 'Er. 18c). Yet it is said in praise of R. Simeon that all his objections to R. Johanan's conclusions were founded on the Mishnah, and that with him it was not a question of showing himself to be in the right, but of securing a clear and well-established decision, and that when he could find no support for his opioion he was not ashamed to abandon it (Yer. Giṭ. iii. 44d). He had a strong love of truth and an unusually courageous way of saying what he thought. He even declared to the patriarch Judah Nesiah that fear of the latter would never induce him to keep back God's word or any opinion derived from it (Yer. Sanh. 20a); and once he ventured to convey a veiled rebuke to the patriarch for avarice (Gen. R. lxxviii. 16). Neither did he hesitate to revoke decisions of his colleagues, including R. Johanan, even when action had already been taken in accordance with those decisions (Yer. Ket. 32d, 37a; B. B. 16b; Ket. 54b, 84b). On one occasion, when R. Johanan presented a halakic demonstration before R. Yannai, and the latter praised him for it, Simeon boldly declared, "In spite of K. Yannai's great praise, R. Johanan's opinion is not correct" (Yer. Soṭah ii. 18b). He would defend his views fearlessly before the whole faculty

(Ḳid. 44a), and sometimes he ventured to give a decision that conflicted with the Mishnah (Yer. Ter. vii. 44c; Yer. Ḥag. iii. 79c). Nevertheless, his opinions, when they differed from those of R. Johanan, were not recognized as valid, except in three cases mentioned in the Babylonian Talmud (Yeb. 36a).

No one equaled Simeon ben Laḳish in diligence and eagerness to learn. It was his custom regularly to repeat a section from the Mishnah forty times (Ta'an. 8a); he boasted that even R. Ḥiyya, who was renowned for his diligence, was no more diligent than he (Yer. Ket. xii. 3). In order to urge his pupils to continual industry, he often quoted a proverb which he ascribed to the Torah: "If thou leavest me one day, I shall leave thee for two" (Yer. Ber. ix. 14d). His conscientiousness and delicately balanced sense of honor are also celebrated. He avoided association with people of whose probity he was not fully convinced; hence the testimony of any one allowed to associate with Simeon b. Laḳish was accredited even in the absence of witnesses (Yoma 9a). Simeon ben Laḳish was faithful to his friends, and was ever ready to render them active assistance. This is shown by the way in which, at the risk of his own life, he rescued R. Assi, who had been imprisoned and was regarded as practically dead by his colleagues (Yer. Ter. 46b). Once his vigorous interference saved R. Johanan's property from injury (*ib.*).

The independence which Simeon ben Laḳish manifested in the discussion of halakic questions was equally pronounced in his treatment of haggadic matters. In haggadah, also, he held a prominent position, and advanced many original and independent views which struck his contemporaries with amazement and which did not win respect until later. His haggadot include exegetical and homiletical interpretations of the Scriptures; observations concerning Biblical characters and stories; sayings concerning the Commandments, prayer, the study of the Law, God, the angels, Creation, Israel, and Rome, Messianic and eschatological subjects, as well as other dicta and proverbs. Some of his haggadic sentences are as follows: "Should the sons of Israel find rest with the people among whom they are scattered, they would lose their desire to return to Palestine, the land of their fathers" (Lam. R. i. 3). "Israel is dear to God, and He takes no pleasure in any one that utters calumnies against Israel" (Cant. R. i. 6). "The proselyte, however, is dearer to God than was Israel when it was gathered together at Sinai, because Israel would not have received the Law of God without the miracles of its revelation, whereas the proselyte, without seeing a single miracle, has consecrated himself to God and accepted the kingdom of heaven" (Tan., Lek Leka, ed. Buber, p. 32a). "The world exists only by virtue of the breath which comes from the mouths of school-children. The instruction of the young should not be interrupted, even by the building of a sanctuary" (Shab. 119b). "The words of the Torah can be remembered only by one who sacrifices himself for the sake of studying them" (Ber. 63b; Shab. 83b). "Israel took the names of the angels from the Babylonians during the period of the Exile, because Isaiah [vi. 6] speaks only of 'one of the seraphim,' without calling him by name; whereas Daniel names the angels Michael and Gabriel" (Yer. R. H. 56d). "Job never actually existed; he is only the imaginary hero of the poem, the invention of the poet" (Yer. Soṭah 20d).

Simeon ben Laḳish's haggadah is especially rich in maxims and proverbs: "No man commits a sin," says Simeon, "unless struck by momentary insanity" (Soṭah 3a). "Adorn [*i.e.*, instruct] thyself first; afterwards adorn others" (B. M. 107b). "Greater is he that lends than he that gives alms; but he that aids by taking part in a business undertaking is greater than either" (Shab. 63a). "Do not live in the neighborhood of an ignorant man who is pious" (*ib.*). "Who commits the sin of adultery only with the eyes is an adulterer" (Lev. R. xxiii. 12; comp. a similar statement in Matt. v. 28).

In his haggadot Simeon frequently makes use of similes, some of which recall the days when he won a livelihood in the circus. In general, he spoke unreservedly of that time; yet an allusion to his earlier calling made by his colleague and brother-in-law R. Johanan wounded him so deeply that he became ill and died. This happened as follows: On one occasion there was a dispute as to the time when the different kinds of knives and weapons might be considered to have been first perfected. The opinion of Simeon ben Laḳish differed from that of R. Johanan, whereupon the latter remarked, "A robber knows his own tools" (B. M. 84a). R. Johanan alluded to Simeon's life as a gladiator, in which a knowledge of sharp weapons was a matter of course. This speech of R. Johanan's not only caused the illness and death of Simeon b. Laḳish, but it had also a disastrous influence on his reputation. The saying, which was certainly used figurtively, was taken literally by many later scholars, and the opinion became current that Simeon had been a robber, or even a robber chief, in his younger days, an opinion which found expression in Pirḳe Rabbi Eli'ezer (xliii.). Yet nowhere is there the slightest authority for such a statement (comp. Weiss, "Dor," iii. 84, and Bacher, *l.c.* i. 344, note 5). R. Johanan was in despair at the death of Simeon, and it is said that he kept calling, "Where is Bar Leḳisha, where is Bar Leḳisha?" He soon followed Simeon to the grave (B. M. 84a).

BIBLIOGRAPHY: Bacher, *Ag. Pal. Amor.* i. 340–418; Frankel, *Mebo*, pp. 129b-130a; Grätz, *Gesch.* 3d ed., iv. 240–242; Halevy, *Dorot ha-Rishonim*, ii. 159a-164a; Heilprin, *Seder ha-Dorot*, ii. 374–376, Warsaw, 1882; Weiss, *Dor*, iii. 80–85.

W. B. J. Z. L.

SIMEON B. MENASYA: Tanna of the fourth generation, and contemporary of R. Judah ha-Nasi I., with whom he engaged in a halakic discussion (Beẓah 21a). He and Jose b. Meshullam formed a society called "Ḳehala Ḳaddisha" (the Holy Community), because its members devoted one-third of the day to the study of the Torah, one-third to prayer, and the remaining third to work (Yer. Ma'as. Sheni 53d; Eccl. R. ix. 9). Simeon b. Menasya is not mentioned in the Mishnah, his sentence in Ḥag. ii. 7 being a later addition; but some halakic sentences by him have been preserved elsewhere (Tosef., Kelim, B. B. iv. 10; Zeb. 94a, 97).

A larger number of his haggadic sentences have come down, including the following: Referring to Ps. xliv. 23, he says, "It is not possible for one to be killed every day; but God reckons the life of the pious as though they died a martyr's death daily" (Sifre, Deut. 32 [ed. Friedmann, p. 73a]). Prov. xvii. 14, he says, contains a rule for a judge desirous of effecting a compromise between two contending parties. Before the judge has heard the statements of both parties, or before he has made up his mind as to the nature of his decision, he may set aside the Law and call upon the parties to settle the matter amicably. Afterward, however, he may not do so, but must decide according to the Law (Sanh. 6b). "Canticles was inspired by the Holy Ghost, while Ecclesiastes expresses merely the wisdom of Solomon" (Tosef., Yad. ii. 14). Especially noteworthy is Simeon's interpretation of Ex. xxxi. 14, "Ye shall keep the Sabbath therefore; for it is holy unto you." "The words 'unto you,'" he says, "imply that the Sabbath is given to you, and that you are not given to the Sabbath" (Mek., Ki Tissa [ed. Weiss, p. 109b]; comp. Mark ii. 27, where Jesus says, "The Sabbath was made for man, and not man for the Sabbath").

BIBLIOGRAPHY: Heilprin, *Seder ha-Dorot*, ii. 271–272: Frankel, *Hodegetica in Mischnam*, p. 202; Brüll, *Einleitung in die Mischna*, i. 239–340; Bacher, *Ag. Tan.* ii. 489–494.

W. B. J. Z. L.

SIMEON OF MIZPAH: Tanna of the first generation; contemporary of R. Gamaliel I., together with whom he went to the bet din in the hall of hewn stone in order to learn a decision regarding the corner of the field ("pe'ah"; Pe'ah ii. 6). He is said to have made a collection of halakot referring to the services in the Temple on the Day of Atonement ("Seder Yoma"; Yoma 14b).

W. B. J. Z. L.

SIMEON BEN NANOS: Tanna of the second generation; contemporary of R. Ishmael and R. Akiba, with whom he often engaged in halakic discussions. He is often mentioned merely by the name

"Ben Nanos." He acquired a high reputation on account of his intimate knowledge of Jewish civil jurisprudence; and R. Ishmael said that whoever wished to occupy himself with the study of this branch of the Law ought to learn from Simeon b. Nanos (B. B. x. 8). Several of Simeon's sayings bearing on civil law have been preserved (B. B. vii. 3, x. 8; Sheb. vii. 5), as well as some of his opinions on other halakic subjects (Bik. iii. 9; Shab. xvi. 5; 'Er. x. 15; Giṭ. viii. 10; Men. iv. 3). Neither the names of his teachers nor those of his pupils are known.

BIBLIOGRAPHY: Frankel, *Hodegetica in Mischnam*, p. 129; Brüll, *Einleitung in die Mischna*, i. 132–133; Weiss, *Dor*, ii. 123; Heilprin, *Seder ha-Dorot*, ii. 363.

W. B. J. Z. L.

SIMEON B. NETHANEEL: Tanna of the first generation; pupil of R. Johanan b. Zakkai (Ab. ii. 8), and son-in-law of R. Gamaliel I. (Tosef., 'Ab. Zarah, iii. 10). He belonged to a noble priestly family; and his teacher, R. Johanan b. Zakkai, praised him for his piety and his fear of sinning (Ab. *l.c.*). Simeon held that the most important habit to be acquired by man is that of carefully considering the consequences of each one of his deeds; while the worst practise, which a person should be careful to shun, is that of not paying one's debts (Ab. ii. 9). No halakot by Simeon have been preserved; but the following sentence, indicating his great piety, has been handed down: "Never neglect to recite the 'Shema'' and the daily prayer; and when thou prayest beg mercy of God and be careful to commit no deed of which thine own conscience may accuse thee" (Ab. ii. 13).

BIBLIOGRAPHY: Heilprin, *Seder ha-Dorot*, ii. 361; Frankel, *Hodegetica in Mischnam*, pp. 90–91; Brüll, *Einleitung in die Mischna*, i. 87.

W. B. J. Z. L.

SIMEON HA-PAḲOLI (הפקולי): Tanna of the second generation; contemporary of R. Gamaliel II. at Jabneh. He arranged the eighteen benedictions of the daily prayer (SHEMONEH 'Esreh) in the sequence in which they have been handed, down (Ber. 28a). The name "Paḳoli" is said to have been derived from Simeon's occupation, which was that of a dealer in flax and wool (Rashi on Ber. 18a). Nothing further is known concerning him.

BIBLIOGRAPHY: Heilprin, *Seder ha-Dorot*, ii. 361; Brüll, *Einleitung in die Mischna*, pp. 97–98.

W. B. J. Z. L.

SIMEON B. PAZZI: Palestinian amora of the third generation. In Palestine he was called merely "Simon," this being the Greek form of his Hebrew name "Shim'on," but in Babylon he was generally called by his full name, Shim'on b. Pazzi. According to the tosafot (B. B. 149a, *s.v.*

רב מרי), "Pazzi" was his mother's name; but according to "Yuḥasin," *s.v.* פזי, and Frankel ("Mebo," 121a), it was a masculine proper name, and, therefore, designated Simeon's father. According to Bacher, "Pazzi" was a family name which several other Palestinian amoraim bore. The Pazzi family, which lived at Tiberias, the seat of the patriarch, was highly respected; and Simeon, so far as is known, was its most important member; Later he lived in the south (Yer. Beẓah 60c), and was the pupil of Joshua b. Levi; but he held friendly intercourse with the authorities of the school of Tiberias, *e.g.*, Eleazar b. Pedat, Abbahu, and Ammi. Simeon lived for a time at Babylon, also, in the house of the exilarch. Here Ze'era requested him not to allow the abuses committed by the exilarchate to pass unreprehended, even though his reproof should prove ineffective (Shab. 55a). In Babylon he delivered haggadic lectures, some sentences of which have been preserved in Babli (Pes. 56a; Soṭah 41b; 'Ab. Zarah 18a).

Simeon was considered a halakic authority also. Rabbah b. Naḥmani was informed by his brothers in Palestine of a halakic decision in which Isaac, Simeon, and Oshaya concurred, this Simeon being, taken to be Simeon b. Pazzi (Ket. 111b). Certain instructions which Simeon gave to the computers of the calendar have been preserved. He enjoined them to observe that as a rule neither the feast of the blowing of the shofar (New-Year) nor that of the willow (the seventh day of the Feast of Tabernacles) should fall on the Sabbath, but when necessary that one or the other should be set upon that day, the former rather than the latter should be chosen (Yer. Suk. 54b).

Simeon occupies an important position among his contemporaries, chiefly in the field of the Haggadah, both independent and transmitted. He handed down an unusually large number of sentences by his teacher Joshua b. Levi, of whose haggadot he is the principal transmitter. But he handed down also halakic sentences by Joshua (Ḥul. 45a). He furthermore transmitted halakot of Johanan, Simeon b. Laḳish, Ḥanina, Jose b. Ḥanina, Samuel b. Naḥman, Simeon b. Abba, and Bar Ḳappara (comp. Bacher, "Ag. Tan." ii. 438, note 6). His own haggadot contain exegetic and homiletic interpretations and comments, including parables, sentences, and maxims on God, the world, prayer, the study of the Law, Israel, and Rome.

The following are examples of Simeon's haggadot: "When God was about to create the first man He consulted with His attendant angels, of whom some were for and some against the proposed creation: 'Mercy and truth are opposed to each other; benevolence and peace have taken up arms against each other' [Ps. lxxxv. 11, Hebr.]. Mercy said, 'Man shall be created; for he will perform works of mercy.' Truth said, 'He shall not be created; for he is full of deceit.' Benevolence said, 'He shall be created; for he will do good works.' Peace said, 'He shall not be created; for he is filled with dissension.' Then Gad took Truth and threw her to the ground [Dan. viii. 12]. But the angels said, 'Why, O Lord of the world, dost thou thus dishonor Truth? Cause her to spring out of the earth'" (Ps. lxxxv. 12; Gen. R. viii. 5). Simeon explains the word וייצר, employed in Gen. ii. 7 in narrating the creation of man, as if it were composed of the two words "wai" and "yeẓer" or "yoẓer." "It, therefore, implies," he says, "the complaint of man wavering between the sensual and the divine: 'Wo to me because of my impulses ["yeẓer"]; wo to me because of my Creator ["yoẓer"]'" (Ber. 61a; 'Er. 18a). The sentence "but Abraham stood yet before the Lord" (Gen. xviii. 22) is, according to Simeon, an emendation of the scribes, the original having read, "The Eternal stood yet before Abraham" (Gen. R. xlix. 12). The prophecies of Beeri, Hosea's father, consisted of two verses only; and since these were not sufficient to form a separate book, they were included in the Book of Isaiah, being the verses Isa. viii. 19–20 (Lev. R. vi. 6). "When the patriarch Jacob was about to reveal the Messianic time to his children [Gen. xlix. 1], the presence of God departed from him, whereupon he said: 'Has an unworthy child sprung from me, as Ishmael sprang from my grandfather Abraham, and as Esau from my father Jacob?' In answer his sons exclaimed, '"Hear, O Israel: the Lord our God is one Lord" [Deut. vi. 5]; as only one God is in thy heart, so only one God is in ours.' Jacob then said, 'Praised be the name of the glory of His kingdom for ever and ever'" (Pes. 56a, according to the reading in Rabbinowitz, "Variæ Lectiones," *ad loc.*). "Phinehas is called in Judges ii. 1 the angel of the Lord because his face shone like a torch when the Holy Ghost was resting upon him" (Lev. R. i. 1). "The Dardanoi [Romans] are designated by the term 'Dodanim' [Gen. x. 4] or 'Rodanim' [I Chron. i. 7, Hebr.]. The first of these terms connotes the people as the cousins of Israel; the second, as its oppressors" (Gen. R. xxxvii. 1). "Wherever a story in Scripture begins with the words 'After the death of... it came to pass,' it refers to a retrogression, to a discontinuance of something that the deceased had brought about; *e.g.*, after Moses' death [Josh. i. 1] the manifestations of mercy [the well, the manna, and the protecting clouds] ceased; after the death of Joshua [Judges i. 1] Israel was again attacked by the remnant of the native population; and after Saul's death [II Sam. i. 1] the Philistines again entered the country" (Gen. R. lxii. 7).

Bibliography: Heilprin, *Seder ha-Dorot,* ii. 377; Bacher, *Ag. Pal. Amor.* ii. 437–474.

W. B. J. Z. L.

SIMEON THE PIOUS. See Simeon he-Ḥasid.

SIMEON BEN HA-SEGAN (called also simply **Ha-Segan**): Tannai of the second generation. Some halakic sayings of his have been preserved in the Mishnah, all of which have been transmitted by Simeon ben Gamaliel (Sheḳ. viii. 5; Ket. ii. 8; Men. xi. 9). He is perhaps identical with Simeon ben Kahana, in whose name Simeon ben Gamaliel also transmits halakic sayings (Tosef., Parah, xi. 6).

BIBLIOGRAPHY: Heilprin, *Seder ha-Dorot,* ii. 362; Frankel. *Hodegetica in Mischnam,* p. 100; Brüll. *Einleitung in die Mischna,* i. 95–96; Bacher, *Ag. Tan.* ii. 324, note 4.

W. B. J. Z. L.

SIMEON BEN SHEṬAḤ: Teacher of the Law and president of the Sanhedrin during the reigns of Alexander Jannæus and his successor, Queen Alexandra (Salome). Simeon was a brother of the queen (Ber. 48a), and on this account was closely connected with the court, enjoying the favor of Alexander. During the reign of this ruler the Sanhedrin consisted almost entirely of Sadducees, Simeon being the only Pharisee; nevertheless he succeeded in ousting the Sadducean members and in replacing them with Pharisees (Meg. Ta'an. x.). Having accomplished this, Simeon recalled from Alexandria the Pharisees who had been compelled to seek refuge there during the reign of John Hyrcanus, among these fugitives being Joshua b. Peraḥyah, the former president of the college (Soṭah 47a, ed. Amsterdam; comp. also Yer. Sanh. 23c and Ḥag. 41d). Joshua was elected president anew, and Simeon assumed the office of vice-president ("ab bet din"; see Weiss, "Dor," i. 135, note 1). Upon the death of Joshua, Simeon became president and Judah ben Ṭabbai vice-president.

The attitude of Alexander Jannæus toward the Pharisees, however, soon underwent a change; and they were again compelled to flee, even Simeon himself being obliged to go into hiding (Ber. 48a; a different reason for Simeon's flight is, however, given in Yer. Naz. 54b). About this time certain Parthian envoys came to Alexander's court and were invited to the king's table, where they noticed the absence of Simeon, by whose wisdom they had profited at previous visits. Upon the king's assurance that he would do the fugitive no harm, the queen caused her brother to return to the court. Upon his reappearance Simeon took his place between the royal couple with a show of self-consciousness which surprised the king; whereupon Simeon remarked, "The wisdom which I serve grants me equal rank with kings" (Yer. Naz. 54b; Ber. 48a).

After his return Simeon enjoyed the king's favor, and when, upon the latter's death, Queen Alexandra succeeded to the rulership, Simeon and his party, the Pharisees, obtained great influence. Together with his colleague, Judah ben Ṭabbai, Simeon began to supersede the Sadducean teachings and to reestablish the authority of the Pharisaic interpretation of the Law. He is therefore justly called "the restorer of the Law," who "has given back to the crown of learning its former brightness" (Ḳid. 66a). Simeon discarded the penal code which the Sadducees had introduced as a supplement to the Biblical code (Meg. Ta'an. iv.); and almost all the teachings and principles introduced by him are aimed against the Sadducean interpretation of the Law. Of Simeon's enactments two were of especial importance. One consisted in the restriction of divorces, which were then of frequent occurrence. Simeon arranged that the husband might use the prescribed marriage gift ("ketubah") in his business, but that his entire fortune should be held liable for it (Yer. Ket. viii. 32c). Inasmuch as a husband of small means could ill afford to withdraw a sum of money from his business, Simeon's ruling tended to check hasty divorces. The other important act referred to the instruction of the young. Up to Simeon's time there were no schools in Judea, and the instruction of children was, according to Biblical precepts, left to their fathers. Simeon ordered that schools be established in the larger cities in which the young might receive instruction in the Holy Scriptures as well as in the traditional knowledge of the Law (Yer. Ket. *l.c.*).

Simeon was exceedingly strict in legal matters. Upon one occasion he sentenced to death eighty women in Ashkelon who had been convicted of sorcery. The relatives of these women, filled with a desire for revenge, brought false witnesses against Simeon's son, whom they accused of a crime which involved capital punishment; and as a result of this charge he was sentenced to death. On the way to the place of execution the son protested his innocence in so pathetic a manner that even the witnesses were moved to admit the falsity of their testimony. When the judges were about to liberate the condemned man he called their attention to the fact that, according to the Law, a witness must not be believed when he withdraws a former statement, and he said to his father, "If you desire that the welfare of Israel shall be strengthened by thy hand, then consider me as a beam on which you may tread without regret" (Yer. Sanh. 23b). The execution then proceeded. This sad event was probably the reason why Simeon issued a warning that witnesses should always be carefully cross-questioned (Ab. i. 9).

Simeon's fairness toward non-Jews is illustrated by the following narrative: Simeon lived in humble circumstances, supporting himself and his family by conducting a small business in linen goods. Once his pupils presented him with an ass which they had purchased from an Arab. On the neck of the animal they found a costly jewel, whereupon they joyously told their master that he might now cease toiling since the proceeds from the jewel would make him wealthy. Simeon, however, replied that the Arab had sold them the ass only, and not the jewel; and he returned the gem to the Arab, who exclaimed, "Praised be the God of Simeon ben Sheṭaḥ!" (Yer. B. M. ii. 8c; Deut. *R.* iii. 5).

BIBLIOGRAPHY: Landau, in *Monatsschrift*, 1853, pp. 107–122, 177–180; Weiss, *Dor*, i. 134 *et seq.*; Heilprin, *Seder ha-Dorot*, ii. 360; Grätz, *Gesch.* iii., Index.

W. B. J. Z. L.

SIMEON SHEZURI: Tanna of the second generation and pupil of R. Ṭarfon (Men. 31a; Tosef., Demai, v. 22). He was called "Shezuri" after his native place, Shizur, which is probably identical with Saijur, west of Kafr 'Anan (comp. Neubauer, "G. T." p. 278). Simeon's tomb is said to be in the vicinity of this place (Schwarz, "Tebu'at ha-Areẓ," p. 101). A few halakic sentences by him have been preserved in the Mishnah (Demai iv. 1; Sheb. ii. 8; Giṭ. vi. 5; Ḥul. iv. 5; Ker. iv. 3; Kelim xviii. 1; Ṭoh. iii. 2; Ṭebul Yom iv. 5); and the halakic practise follows his opinion (Men. 30b; Ḥul. 75b). Another noteworthy sentence by him also has been preserved (Naz. 45b).

BIBLIOGRAPHY: Heilprin, *Seder ha-Dorot*, ii. 365, Warsaw, 1882; Frankel, *Hodegetica in Mischnam*, pp. 131–132; Brüll, *Einleitung in die Mischna*, i. 138.

W. B. J. Z. L.

SIMEON OF SHIḲMONA: Tanna of the second generation and pupil of Akiba. He was a native of Shiḳmona, a locality in the vicinity of Mt. Carmel (see Neubauer, "G. T." p. 197). Only three sentences of his, exegetic ones, have been preserved. They were transmitted by his fellow pupil R. Ḥidḳa; and all of them express the principle that good and evil are brought about through the respective agencies of good and of evil persons. Thus the Sabbath-breaker mentioned in Num. xv. 32 was the cause of the law relating to the punishment for desecrating the Sabbath (Sifre, Num. 114. [ed. Friedmann, p. 34a]); the pious questioners described in Num. ix. 7 were the cause of the law concerning the Pesaḥ Sheni (Sifre, Num. 68 [ed. Friedmann, p. 17b]); and the demand of the daughters of Zelophehad led to the enunciation of the law relating to the inheritance of property (Sifre, Num. 133 [ed. Friedmann, p. 49b]).

BIBLIOGRAPHY: Heilprin, *Seder ha-Dorot*, p. 364; Bacher, *Ag. Tan.* i. 445–446.

W. B. J. Z. L.

SIMEON B. ṬARFON: Tanna of the second generation. Four exegetic sentences by him have been preserved: (1) "Ex. xxii. 11, 'Then shall an oath of the Lord be between them,' means that the person taking the oath and the one who causes him to do so are alike responsible if perjury is proved." (2) "Ex. xx. 10 should be read 'tan'if' = 'to contribute to the commission of adultery'; and the interdiction applies also to the furnishing of opportunity for adultery." (3) "In Deut. i. 27 [Hebr.] the word 'wa-teragenu,' which should be explained as NOṬARIḲON, means: 'You spied out and desecrated God's dwelling among you.'" (4) "In Deut. i. 7 the Euphrates is called 'the great river' [although it is not really such] because it is the boundary river of Palestine, according to the proverb, 'Approach the anointed, and you yourself will smell of ointment'" (Sheb. 47b).

BIBLIOGRAPHY: Frankel, *Hodegetica in Mischnam*, p. 137; Bacher, *Ag. Tan.* i. 447–448.

W. B. J. Z. L.

SIMEON OF TEMAN: Tanna of the second generation. He disputed with R. Akiba on a halakic sentence deduced from Ex. xxi. 18 (Tosef., Sanh. xii. 3; B. Ḳ. 90b). He was in collegial relations with R. Judah b. Baba (Beẓah 21a; Tosef., Beẓah, ii. 6). Some of his halakic sentences are included in the Mishnah (Yeb. iv. 13; Ta'an. iii. 7; Yad. i. 3); and a haggadic sentence by him also has been preserved, to the effect that God's intervention in dividing the sea at the time of the Exodus was deserved by Israel because of the covenant of the circumcision (Mek., Beshallaḥ, iii. [ed. Weiss, p. 35b]).

BIBLIOGRAPHY: Heilprin, *Seder ha-Dorot*, ii. 362–363, Warsaw, 1882; Frankel. *Hodegetica in Mischnam*, p. 137; Brüll. *Einleitung in die Mischna*, i. 149; Bacher, *Ag. Tan.* i. 444–445.

W. B. J. Z. L.

SIMEON B. YANNAI: Palestinian amora of the third century. He transmits a halakic saying of his father's which he had received from his sister, who had heard it uttered (Yer. Shab. 14b, 15d). Some of Simeon's haggadic explanations of Scriptural passages are extant, of which the following may be mentioned: On the passage in Ps. xii. 5, "now will I arise," he remarks: "As long as Jerusalem remains enveloped in ashes the might of God will not arise; but when the day arrives on which Jerusalem shall shake off the dust [Isa. lii. 2], then God will be 'raised up out of His holy habitation'" (Zech. ii, 17 [A. V. 13]; Gen. R. lxxv. 1). On Ps. cvi. 16 *et seq.* he says: "The people had decided to elect as their leaders Dathan and Abiram instead of Moses and Aaron [Num. xiv. 4], with the result that the earth opened and swallowed up Dathan and covered the company of Abiram" (Midr. Teh. to Ps. cvi. 5 [ed. Buber, p. 228a]).

BIBLIOGRAPHY: Franke, *Mebo*, p. 129a; Bacher, *Ag. Pal. Amor.* iii. 623–624.

W. B. J. Z. L.

SIMEON BEN YOḤAI: Tanna of the second century; supposed author of the Zohar; born in Galilee; died, according to tradition, at Meron, on the 18th of Iyyar (= Lag be-'Omer). In the Baraita, Midrash, and Gemara his name occurs either as Simeon or as Simeon ben Yoḥai, but in the Mishnah, with the exception of Ḥag. i. 7, he is always quoted as R. Simeon. He was one of the principal pupils of Akiba, under whom he studied thirteen years at Bene-Beraḳ (Lev. R. xxi. 7 *et al.*). It would seem, from Ber. 28a, that Simeon had previously studied at Jabneh, under Gamaliel II. and Joshua b. Hananiah, and that he was the cause of the quarrel that broke out between these two chiefs. But considering that about forty-five years later, when Akiba was thrown into prison, Simeon's father was still alive (see below), and that Simeon insisted upon Akiba's teaching him even in prison, Frankel ("Darke ha-Mishnah," p. 168) thinks Ber. 28a is spurious. Simeon's acuteness was tested and recognized by Akiba when he first came to him; of all his pupils Akiba ordained only Meïr and Simeon. Conscious of his own merit, Simeon felt hurt at being ranked after Meïr, and Akiba was compelled to soothe him with soft words (Yer. Ter. 46b: Yer. Sanh. i. 19a). During Akiba's lifetime Simeon was found occasionally at Sidon, where he seems to have shown great independence in his halakic decisions.

The following incident of Simeon's stay at Sidon, illustrating both his wit and his piety, may be mentioned: A man and his wife, who, though they had been married ten years, had no children, appeared before Simeon at Sidon to secure a divorce. Observing that they loved each other, and not being able to refuse a request which was in agreement with rabbinical law, Simeon told them that as their wedding was marked by a feast they should mark their separation in the same way. The result was that both changed their minds, and, owing to Simeon's prayer, God granted them a child (Pesiḳ. xxii. 147a; Cant. R. i.. 4). Simeon often returned to Akiba, and once he conveyed a message to him from his fellow pupil Ḥanina ben Ḥakinai (Niddah 52b; Tosef., Niddah, vi. 6).

Simeon's love for his great teacher was profound. When Akiba was thrown into prison by Hadrian, Simeon, probably through the influence of his father, who was in favor at the court of Rome, found a way to enter the prison. He still insisted upon Akiba's teaching him, and when the latter refused, Simeon jestingly threatened to tell his father, Yoḥai, who would cause Akiba to be punished more severely (Pes. 112a). After Akiba's death Simeon was again ordained, with four other pupils of Akiba's, by Judah b. Baba (Sanh. 14a).

The persecution of the Jews under Hadrian inspired Simeon with a different opinion of the Romans than that held by his father. On more than one occasion Simeon manifested his anti-Roman feeling. When, at a meeting between Simeon and his former fellow pupils at Usha, probably about a year and a half after Akiba's death (*c.* 126), Judah ben Ila'i spoke in praise of the Roman government, Simeon replied that the institutions which seemed so praiseworthy to Judah were for the benefit of the Romans only, to facilitate the carrying out of their wicked designs. Simeon's words were carried by Judah b. Gerim, one of his own pupils, to the Roman governor, who sentenced Simeon to death (according to Grätz, this governor was Varus, who ruled under Antoninus Pius, and the event took place about 161). Simeon was compelled to seek refuge in a cavern, where he remained thirteen years, till the emperor, possibly Hadrian, died (Yer. Sheb. ix. 38d; Shab. 33b; Pesiḳ. 88b; Gen. R. lxxix. 6; Eccl. R. x. 8; Esth. R. i. 9). Two different accounts of Simeon's stay in the cavern and of his movements after leaving it are given in Shabbat (*l.c.*) and in the five other sources just mentioned. The latter, of which Yer. Sheb. ix. 38d seems to be the most authentic, relate, with some variations, that Simeon, accompanied by his son Eleazar (in Yer. Sheb. Simeon alone), hid himself in a cavern near Gadara, where they stayed thirteen years, living on dates and the fruit of the carob-tree, their whole bodies thus becoming covered with eruptions. One day, seeing that a bird had repeatedly escaped the net set for it by a hunter, Simeon and his son were encouraged to leave the cavern, taking the escape of the bird as an omen that God would not forsake them. When outside the cavern, they heard a "bat ḳol" say, "Ye are [singular in Yer. Sheb.] free"; they accordingly went their way. Simeon then bathed in the warm springs of Tiberias, which rid him of the disease contracted in the cavern, and he showed his gratitude to the town in the following manner:

Tiberias had been built by Herod Antipas on a site where there were many tombs (Josephus, "Ant." xviii. 2, § 3), the exact locations of which had been lost. The town therefore had been regarded as unclean. Resolving to remove the cause of the uncleanness, Simeon planted lupines in all suspected places; wherever they did not take root he knew that a tomb was underneath. The bodies were then exhumed and removed, and the town pronounced clean. To annoy and discredit Simeon, a certain Samaritan secretly replaced one of the bodies. But Simeon learned through the power of the Holy Spirit what the Samaritan had done, and said, "Let what is above go down, and what is below come up." The Samaritan was entombed; and a schoolmaster of Magdala (but comp. Buber, note 180, to Pesiḳ. x. 90a), who mocked Simeon for his declaration, was turned into a heap of bones.

According to the version, in Shab. *l.c.*, Simeon and Eleazar hid in a cavern, whereupon a carob-tree and a spring miraculously appeared there. In order to spare their garments they sat naked in the sand, in consequence of which their skin became covered with scabs. At the end of twelve years the prophet Elijah announced to them the death of the emperor, and the consequent annulment of the sentence of death against them. When they came forth Simeon observed people occupied with agricultural pursuits to the neglect of the Torah, and, being angered thereby, smote them by his glances. A bat ḳol then ordered him to return to the cavern, where he and Eleazar remained twelve months longer, at the end of which time they were ordered by a bat ḳol to come forth. When they did so, Simeon was met by his son-in-law Phinehas b. Jair (comp., however, Zacuto, "Yuḥasin," ed. Filipowski, p. 46), who wept at seeing him in such a miserable state. But Simeon told him that he ought to rejoice, for during the thirteen years' stay in the cavern his knowledge of the Torah had been much increased. Simeon then, in gratitude for the miracle that had been wrought for him, undertook the purification of Tiberias. He threw some lupines into the ground, whereupon the bodies came to the surface at various places, which were then marked as tombs. Not only was the man who mocked at Simeon's announcement of the purification of Tiberias turned into a heap of bones, but also Simeon's pupil and delator, Judah b. Gerim.

It appears that Simeon settled afterward at Meron, the valley in front of which place was filled, at Simeon's command, with gold dinars (Tan., Peḳude, 7; Ex. R. lii. 3; comp. Yer. Ber. ix. 13d; Pesiḳ. x. 87b; Gen. R. xxxv. 2). On the other hand, it is said that Simeon established a flourishing school at Tekoa, among the pupils of which was Judah I. (Tosef., 'Er. viii. [v.] 6; Shab. 147b). It has been shown by Grätz that this Tekoa evidently was in Galilee, and hence must not be identified with the Biblical Tekoa, which was in the territory of Judah (II Chron. xi. 6). Bacher ("Ag. Tan." ii. 76) endeavors to show that Tekoa and Meron were one arid the same place.

As the last important event in Simeon's life it is recorded that, accompanied by Eleazar b. Jose, he was sent to Rome with a petition to the emperor for the abolition of the decree against the three main observances of the Jewish religion, and that his mission was successful (Me'i. 17b). The reason Simeon was chosen for this mission is stated (*ib.*) to have been that he was known as a man in whose favor miracles often were wrought. At Rome, too, Simeon's success was due to a miracle, for while on the way he was met by the demon Ben Temalion, who offered his assistance. According to agreement, the demon entered into the emperor's daughter, and Simeon exorcised it when he arrived at the Roman court. The emperor then took Simeon into his treasure-house, leaving him to choose his own reward. Simeon found there the vexatious decree, which he took away and tore into pieces (comp. "Tefillot R. Shim'on b. Yoḥai" in Jellinek, "B. H." iv. 117 *et seq.*, where, instead of "Ben Temalion," "Asmodeus" occurs). This legend, the origin of which apparently is non-Jewish, has been the subject of discussion by modern scholars. Israel Lévi (in "R. E. J." viii. 200 *et seq.*) thinks it is a variation of the legend, found in the "Acta

Apostolorum Apocrypha" (ed. Tischendorf, pp. 246 *et seq.*), of the apostle Bartholomew exorcising a demon that had taken possession of the daughter of Polymnius, the King of India. Israel Lévi's opinion was approved by Joseph Halévy (in "R. E. J." x. 60 *et seq.*). Bacher (*ib.* xxxv. 285 *et seq.*) thinks there is another Christian legend which corresponds more closely to the Talmudic narrative, namely, that narrated by Simeon Metaphrastes in "Acta Sanctorum" (vol. ix., Oct. 22, 1896), according to which Abercius exorcised a demon from Lucilla, the daughter of Marcus Aurelius.

Simeon is stated to have said that whatever might be the number of persons deserving to enter heaven he and his son were certainly of that number, so that if there were only two, these were himself and his son (Suk. 45b; Sanh. 97b; comp. Shab. 33b). He is also credited with saying that, united with his son and Jotham, King of Judah, he would be able to free the world from judgment (Suk. *l.c.*; comp. Yer. Ber. ix. 13d and Gen. R. xxxv. 3 [where Simeon mentions Abraham and the prophet Ahijah of Shiloh, instead of his son and Jotham]). Thus, on account of his exceptional piety and continual study of the Law, Simeon was considered as one of those whose merit preserves the world, and therefore during his life the rainbow was never seen, that promise of God's forbearance not being needed (Yer. Ber. *l.c.*).

Simeon's halakot are very numerous; they are met with in all the treatises of the Talmud except Berakot, Ḥallah, Ta'anit, Nedarim, Tamid, and Middot. He greatly valued the teaching of his master Akiba, and he is reported to have recommended his pupils to follow his own system of interpretation ("middot") because it was derived from that of Akiba (Giṭ. 67a). But this itself shows that Simeon did not follow his teacher in every point; indeed, as is shown below, he often differed from Akiba, declaring his own interpretations to be the better (Sifre, Deut. 31; R. H. 18b). He was independent in his halakic decisions, and did not refrain from criticizing the tannaim of the preceding generations (comp. Tosef., Oh. iii. 8, xv. 11). He and Jose b. Ḥalafta were generally of the same opinion; but sometimes Simeon sided with Meïr (Kelim iii. 5; Me'i. 11a). Like the other pupils of Akiba, who, wishing to perpetuate the latter's teaching, systematized it in the foundation of the Mishnah (R. Meïr), Tosefta (R. Nehemiah), and Sifra (R. Judah), Simeon is credited with the authorship of the SIFRE, (Sanh. 86a) and of the MEKILTA DE-RABBI SHIM'ON, the former work being a halakic midrash to Numbers and Deuteronomy, the latter a similar midrash to Exodus.

The particular characteristic of Simeon's teaching was that whether in a halakah or in a haggadic interpretation of a Biblical command, he endeavored to find the underlying reason therefor (B. M. 115a *et al.*).

This often resulted in a material modification of the command in question. From many instances the following may be taken: In the prohibition against taking a widow's raiment in pledge (Deut. xxiv. 17) it was Judah b. Ila'i's opinion that no difference is to be made between a rich and a poor widow. But Simeon gives the reason for such a prohibition, which was that if such a pledge were taken it would be necessary to return it every evening (comp. Ex. xxii. 25–26), and going to the widow's home every morning and evening might compromise her reputation; consequently, he declares, the prohibition applies only in the case of a poor widow, since one who is rich would not need to have the garment returned in the evening (B. M. *l.c.*).

Simeon's name was widely identified with this halakic principle of interpretation, and his teacher Akiba approved of it; therefore his contemporaries often applied to him when they wished to know the reason for certain halakot (Tosef., Zeb. i. 8). Simeon also divided the oral law into numbered groups, of which fifteen are preserved in the Talmud. He especially favored the system of giving general rules, of which there are a great number (Bik. iii. 10; Zeb. 119b *et al.*). All this shows that he was systematic, and that he had the power of expressing himself clearly (Sheb. ii. 3; 'Er. 104b). He was dogmatic in his halakic decisions, but where there was a doubt as to which of two courses should be followed, and the Rabbis adopted a compromise, he admitted the legality of either course (Yeb. iii. 9). He differed from Akiba in that he did not think that particles like "et," "gam," and others contain in themselves indications of halakot (Men. 11b); but in many instances he showed that he was opposed to R. Ishmael's opinion that the Torah speaks as men do and that seemingly pleonastic words can never serve as the basis for deducing new laws (Sifre, Re'eh, 119; R. H. 8b; Zeb. 108b *et al.*).

Simeon is very prominent also in the Haggadah, and his utterances are numerous in both Talmuds. Many of his sayings bear on the study of the Torah, which, according to him, should be the main object of man's life. Notwithstanding the stress he laid on the importance of prayer, and particularly on the reading of the "Shema'," he declared that one must not, for the sake of either, interrupt the study of the Torah (Yer. Ḥag. ii. 77a.). "There are three crowns," he says, "the first being that of the Torah" (Ab. iv. 13); he completes his sentence with the words, "But the crown of a good name mounts above them all," showing that, in addition to studying the Law, one must execute the commands by which he can acquire a good name. The Torah, also, is one of the three good gifts which God gave to Israel and which can not be preserved without suffering (Mek., Yitro, Baḥodesh, 10; Sifre, Deut. 32; Ber. 5a). But recognizing the difficulty of occupying oneself with the study of the

Torah and of providing a livelihood at the same time, Simeon said that the Torah was given only for those who ate the manna or the priestly meals (Mek., Beshallaḥ, Wayeḥi, 1, Wayassa', 2). He declared also that had he been on Mount Sinai when God delivered the Torah to Israel, he would have requested two mouths for man, one to be used exclusively as a means for repeating and thus learning the Torah. But then he added, "How great also would be the evil done by delators ["moserim"] with two mouths!" (Yer. Shab. i. 3a, b; Yer. Ber. i. 3b).

Among Simeon's many other utterances may be mentioned those with regard to repentance, and some of his ethical sayings. "So great is the power of repentance that a man who has been during his lifetime very wicked ["rasha' gamur"], if he repent toward the end, is considered a perfectly righteous man" (Tosef., Ḳid. i. 14; Ḳid. 40b; Cant. R. v. 16). He was particularly severe against haughtiness, which, he declared, is like idolatry (Soṭah 4b), and against publicly shaming one's neighbor: "One should rather throw himself into a burning furnace than shame a neighbor in public" (Ber. 43b). He denounced the crimes of usury, deceitful dealing, and disturbing domestic peace (Yer. B. M. 10d; B. M. 58b; Lev. R. ix.). His animosity toward the Gentiles generally and toward feminine superstition is expressed in the following utterance: "The best of the heathen merits death; the best of serpents should have its head crushed; and the most pious of women is prone to sorcery" (Yer. Ḳid. iv. 66c; Massek. Soferim xv. 10; comp. Mek., Beshallaḥ, Wayeḥi, 1, and Tan., Wayera, 20). His hostility to the Romans, mentioned above, is expressed also in his maxims; thus, alluding probably to the Parthian war which broke out in the time of Antoninus Pius, he said: "If thou hast seen a Persian [Parthian] horse tied in Palestine, then hope for the arrival of the Messiah" (Cant. R. viii. 10; Lam. R. i. 13).

R. Simeon combined with his rationalism in halakah a strange mysticism in his haggadic teachings, as well as in his practise. He spoke of a magic sword, on which the Name was inscribed, being given by God to Moses on Sinai (Midr. Teh. to Ps. xc. 2; comp. *ib.* to Ps. xxxvi. 8; Gen. R. xxxv.); and he ascribed all kinds of miraculous powers to Moses (Me'i. 17b; Sanh. 97b). After his death he appeared to the saints in their visions (B. M. 84b; Ket. 77b; Sanh. 98a). Thus his name became connected with mystic lore, and he became a chief authority for the cabalists; for this reason the Zohar first appeared under the name of Midrash de-Rabbi Shim'on ben Yoḥai. There exist, besides, two apocryphal midrashim ascribed to this tanna (published by Jellinek, "B. H." iii.78 *et seq.*, iv. 117 *et seq.*). The first is entitled "Nistarot de R. Shim'on b. Yoḥai"; the second, "Tefillat R. Shim'on b.Yoḥai"; both of them bear on the Messianic time, but the second is more complete. The main point of these midrashim is that while Simeon was hidden in the cavern, he fasted forty days and prayed to God to rescue Israel from such persecutions. Then Meṭaṭron revealed to him the future, announcing the various Mohammedan rulers, the last one of whom would perish at the hands of the Messiah. As in similar Messianic apocrypha, the chief characters are Armilus and the three Messiahs—Messiah b. Joseph, Messiah b. Ephraim, and Messiah b. David.

As to the festival called "Hillula de-Rabbi Shim'on ben Yoḥai," which is celebrated on Simeon's supposed tomb at Meron, on the 18th of Iyyar.

BIBLIOGRAPHY: Bacher, *Ag. Tan.* ii. 70 *et seq.*; Brüll, *Mebo ha-Mishnah*, pp. 185 *et seq.*; Frankel, *Darke ha-Mishnah*, pp. 168 *et seq.*; Grätz, *Gesch.* 3d ed., iv. 180 *et seq.*, note 20; Grünhut, in *Magyar Zsidó Szemle*, xvii. 63; Heilprin, *Seder ha-Dorot*, ii.; Joël, in *Monatsschrift*, v. 365 *et seq.*, 401 *et seq.*; Kaminka, in *Ha-Meliẓ*, xxix., Nos. 75, 77; Paucher, in *Ha-Asif*, iv. 120; Weiss, *Dor*, ii. 157 *et seq.*; Moses Konitz, *Ben Joḥai*, Budapest, 1815; Louis Lewin, *Rabbi Simon ben Jochai*, Frankfort-on-the-Main, 1893.

K. M. SEL.

T

TALMID ḤAKAM (plural, **Talmide Ḥakamim**): Honorific title given to one well versed in the Law. Prizing knowledge, especially that of the Torah, above all worldly goods, the talmide ḥakamim formed in Jewish society a kind of aristocracy having many privileges and prerogatives as well as duties. To the Jews, birth, riches, and other advantages are as nothing in comparison with learning. The Mishnah says: "A scholarly bastard takes precedence over an ignorant high priest" (Hor. 13a). In the Middle Ages the talmid ḥakam enjoyed the full confidence of his coreligionists, who consulted him not only in spiritual matters, but also in worldly affairs. Even when he held no official position in the community, he supervised the cult, determined the time and form of prayers, verified weights and measures, etc. To enable him to devote himself entirely to study, Jewish legislation exempted him from the payment of taxes and from performing any specific duties (Shulḥan 'Aruk, Yoreh De'ah, 243).

Although modesty is one of the cardinal virtues of the talmid ḥakam, he is enjoined to uphold his rank and not to compromise his dignity. As in the case of a king, he is riot permitted to allow any one to omit the performance of any public act of reverence due to him, inasmuch as in him the Law is honored or slighted (Maimonides, "Yad," Teshubah, iii.). There are, according to the Talmud, six acts which a talmid ḥakam ought to avoid: to go abroad in perfumed garments; to walk alone at night; to wear shabby shoes; to converse with a woman in the street, even if she be his wife; to sit in the society of an ignoramus; and to be the last to enter the bet ha-midrash (Ber. 43b). With regard to association with an ignoramus, the Talmud says: "The talmid ḥakam is first likened by the ignoramus to a vase of gold; if he converses with him, he is looked upon as a vase of silver; and if he accepts a service from him, he is regarded as a vase of earth" (Sanh. 52b). Among the privileges of the talmid ḥakam is the right of declining to present himself as a witness in suits concerning money transactions before a judge who is his inferior in knowledge (Shulhan 'Aruk, Ḥoshen Mishpaṭ, 28).

The talmid ḥakam was expected to be familiar with all branches of human learning. "He who understands astronomy," says R. Johanan, "and does not pursue the study of it, of that man it is written: 'But they regard not the work of the Lord, neither consider the operation of his hands'" (Isa. v. 12). R. Johanan says also that only he who is able to answer all halakic questions, even those which deal only with the insignificant treatise Kallah, is a talmid ḥakam worthy to be appointed leader of a community (Shab. 114a). In accordance with this view of the standard of learning required in one who aspires to the title of talmid ḥakam, some later rabbinical authorities assert that in modern times no one deserves to be called by that epithet ("Keneset ha-Gedolah" on Yoreh De'ah, § 18).

The principles in accordance with which the talmid ḥakam must live are enumerated in the first chapter of Derek Ereẓ Zuṭa, opening with the following sentence: "The way of the wise is to be modest, humble, alert, and intelligent; to endure injustice; to make himself beloved of men; to be gracious in his intercourse even with subordinates; to avoid wrong-doing; to judge each man according to his deeds; to act according to the motto 'I take no pleasure in the good things of this world, seeing that life here below is not my portion.' Wrapped in his mantle, he sits at the feet of the wise; no one can detect any thing unseemly in him; he puts pertinent questions, and gives suitable answers."

E. C. I. BR.

TANḤUM BAR ḤANILAI (or **ILAI**): Palestinian amora of the third century, although his father's name suggests a Babylonian origin. He transmitted the sayings of Joshua ben Levi, Johanan, and Bar Ḳappara. In the Babylonian Talmud he appears as the author of decisions which in the Jerusalem Talmud are attributed to older authorities. Thus, in Sanh. 93a he is said to be the author of a decision which in Pesiḳ. xi. (ed. Buber, p. 99a) is ascribed to Eleazar b. Pedat. On the other hand, halakic sentences of his have been preserved in the Jerusalem Talmud (Ma'as. 48b; Hag. 76a; Ter. 41c; Shab. 5d; Ta'an. 65a). Among those who transmitted sayings of his were Abbahu (Cant. R. ii. 7) and Tanḥuma (Pesiḳ. R. 112).

It appears from Yer. Ta'an. 65a, b that Tanḥum bar Ḥanilai was active as a preacher, and that he once preached with Abba bar Zabdai and Josefa. He died during a Ḥanukkah festival (Yer. M. Ḳ., end). His sayings were of a high ethical and moral character: "God speaks thus to Israel: 'My daughter [*i.e.*, the Torah] is in thy hands; thy daughter [soul] is in My hands. If thou protect Mine, then will I protect thine'" (Tan., Ki Tissa, end). With regard to the prohibition against certain kinds of food, he said: "A physician once visited two sick people; the one who had no hope of recovery was permitted to eat everything, while the one who had every prospect of recovery was allowed only certain foods. So God treats the Jews; because they have hope of a future life, He gives them certain dietary laws; while the heathen, who have no part in the life to come, are permitted to eat of all things" (Lev. R. xiii. 2).

Tanḥum bar Ḥanilai's haggadah is especially characteristic because of his system of connecting the last words of one Bible paragraph with the opening words of the next, as Lev. i. 16 with ii. 1 (Lev. R. iii. 4), Lev. xii. 2 *et seq.* with xiii. 2 *et seq.* (Lev. R. xv. 5), Ps. xciv. 1 with xciii. 5 (Midr. Teh. *ad loc.*), and Num. v. 12 *et seq.* with v. 2 *et seq.* (Num. R. ix. 4). Haggadic sayings of his are quoted in the following places: Sanh. 7a, 100a; 'Ab. Zarah 18b, 19b; B. M. 86b; Shab. 22a; Ḥag. 7a; Ber. 8b, 13b; Meg. 15b; Mak. 10a; Yer. Ta'an. 68c; Gen. R. iv. 6, xci., beginning; Pesiḳ. R. 21, end; Ex. R. xlii., end; and Lev. R. xxvi. The Midrash Mishle begins with a prooemium by Tanḥum bar Hahilai, although his name is not mentioned in any other part of the book. He is mentioned twice in the Pirḳe Rabbi Eli'ezer (xxxix., xlix.) by the name of Tanḥum.

BIBLIOGRAPHY: Heilprin, *Seder ha-Dorot*, ii. 283a; Bacher, *Ag. Pal. Amor.* iii. 627–636 and Index: Frankel. *Mebo*, p. 131a.

W. B. S.O.

TANḤUM B. ḤIYYA: Palestinian amora of the third century; a pupil of Simeon b. Pazzi, whose sayings he transmits. In the Babylonian Talmud he is constantly referred to as R. Tanḥum b. Ḥiyya of Kefar 'Akko (M. Ḳ. 25b; Yeb. 45a), of which place he was a native; he resided, however, in Tiberias, where on one occasion, with the aid of Aha, the lord of the castle, he ransomed some Jewish women who probably had been taken there by Roman troops (Yeb. 45a). He was a member of the commission which determined the intercalations of the calendar (Yer. Sanh. 6c). He was on terms of friendship with Assi, who visited him (Yer. Shab. 6c), and he maintained friendly relations with Hananiah b. Papa (Yer. M. Ḳ. 83c). Tanḥum was wealthy and philanthropic. It is recorded that when his mother purchased meat for the household a similar quantity was always purchased for distribution among the poor (Lev. R. xxxiv. 1).

Only three halakic sayings by him have been preserved (Bek. 57b; Yer. Meg. 75a, twice); but several of his haggadic utterances are extant. The following may be mentioned: "When one who has learned, taught, and observed the Law fails to prevent the evil which it is in his power to prevent, or to confirm the good which it is in his power to confirm, then shall smite him the curse pronounced [Deut. xxvii. 26] over those who fail to confirm 'all the words of this law'" (Yer. Soṭah 21d). He interpreted Prov. vi. 32 ("Whoso committeth adultery with a woman lacketh understanding") as referring to those who seek office for the sake of gain (Pesiḳ. R. 22 [ed. Friedmann, p. 111a]). Tanḥum was the author also of a prayer to be read by any one who has had an ominous dream (Yer. Ber. 9a). It was told in Babylon that when Tanḥum died all the statues in Tiberias moved from their places (M. Ḳ. 25b, according to the correct reading in Rabbinovicz's "Variæ Lectiones," *ad loc.*).

BIBLIOGRAPHY: Frankel. *Mebo*, pp. 130b, 131a; Bacher, *Ag. Pal. Amor.* iii. 636–639.

W. B. J. Z. L.

TANḤUM BAR JEREMIAH: Palestinian amora of the fourth century; pupil of R. Manis the Elder. In the town of Hefer in Galilee he once rendered a legal decision on a religious question, whereupon his attention was called to the fact that his action was unwarranted, since his teacher resided within twelve miles of that place. Only one halakic decision of his—regarding the liturgy—is extant (Yer. Ber. 7b). He was the author of several haggadic sentences (Midr. Teh. to Ps. xxxi.; Gen. R. iv. 8; Lam. R. ii. 1; and Pesiḳ. 163b).

BIBLIOGRAPHY: Bacher, *Ag. Pal. Amor.* iii. 751–752; Frankel. *Mebo*, p. 131 a; Heilprin, *Seder ha-Dorot*, ii. 192b.

E. C. S. O.

TANḤUMA B. ABBA: Palestinian amora of the fifth generation; one of the foremost haggadists of his time. He was a pupil of Ḥuna b. Abin (Num. R. iii.; Geru. R. xli.), from whom he transmits halakic (Yer. Ḥal. 57d; Shab. 10c) as well as haggadic sayings (Yer. Pe'ah 15b; Shab. 11d; 'Ab. Zarah 43a). He received instruction also from Judah b. Shalom (Midr. Teh. to Ps. cxix. 2) and R. Phinehas (Yer. Sheḳ. 49d). According to Bacher, he resided in Nave, a town in Peræa (comp. Neubauer, "G. T." p. 23).

Of Tanḥuma's life the Babylonian Talmud relates the following incident, probably based on an actual occurrence. The emperor—a

Christian ruler no doubt being meant—said to Tanḥuma, "Let us all become one people." To this the latter replied, "Yes; but since we are circumcised we can not become like you; whereas you, by having yourself circumcised, may become like us." The emperor thereupon said, "You have answered me correctly; but he who worsts the king must be thrown to wild beasts." This was done, but the animals did Tanḥuma no harm. An unbeliever who stood by remarked that perhaps they were not hungry, whereupon he himself was thrown after Tanḥuma and was instantly torn to pieces (Sanh. 39a).

With regard to Tanḥuma's public activity, the only fact known is that he ordered a fast on account of a drought. Two fasts were held, but no rain came, whereupon Tanḥuma ordered a third fast, saying in his sermon: "My children, be charitable unto each other, and God will be merciful unto you." On this occasion one man gave money to his divorced wife, who was in need; Tanḥuma thereupon lifted his face toward the heavens and prayed: "Lord of the Universe, this hard-hearted man took pity on his wife when he saw that she was in need, and helped her, although not obliged to do so; how much more shouldest Thou, the Gracious and Merciful, be filled with pity when Thou seest Thy beloved children, the sons of Abraham, Isaac, and Jacob, in need." As soon as he had ceased praying, rain came, and the world was relieved of its distress (Gen. R. xxxiii.; Lev. R. xxxiv.).

Tanḥuma is not often mentioned as a halakist: a few remarks on and explanations of halakic teachings are ascribed to him in the Palestinian Talmud (Yer. 'Er. 26c; Pes. 37b, d; Yoma 44d; Sheḳ. 47c; Ta'an. 67a), while the Babylonian Talmud mentions an objection raised by him against a halakic thesis advanced by the Palestinian schools (Ḥul. 55b). As a haggadist, on the other hand, he is frequently mentioned, and the numerous haggadic sentences of his which are still preserved touch every province of the Haggadah. He often points out the Scriptural bases for the sayings of older authors, always using the characteristic formula of introduction: "I give the reason"; that is, "I cite the Biblical authority" (Yer. Ber. 12c; Gen. R. iv. 3; Lev. R. xxi.). He also explains and annotates older sayings (Gen. R. xxiv.), adjusts differing traditions (Lev. R. xxiv. 5), and varies the text of old haggadic sentences (Gen. R. xliii. 3). His own haggadic teachings differ but little from those of his contemporaries, although some of his interpretations approach the simple exegetic method. An example of this is furnished by his interpretation of Eccl. iii. 11, where he explains the word "ha-kol" as meaning "the universe" (Gen. R. ix. 2).

Tanḥuma often made use of symbolism to illustrate his thought. Some of his haggadic utterances may be quoted: "Just as the spice-box contains all kinds of fragrant spices, so must the wise youth be filled with all kinds of Biblical, mishnaic, halakic, and haggadic knowledge" (Cant. R. v. 13). On Isa. xlv. 3 Tanḥuma said: "Nebuchadnezzar grudged his son and successor Evil-merodach his treasures, wherefore he filled iron ships with gold and sunk them in the Euphrates. When Cyrus conquered Babylonia and decided to rebuild the Temple in Jerusalem, he diverted the river into another channel, and 'the treasures of darkness, and hidden riches of secret places' were given to him" (Esth. R. iii. 1).

Tanḥuma often held religious disputations with non-Jewish, especially Christian, scholars; and he himself tells of one which took place in Antioch (Gen. R. xix. 4). He was asked concerning Gen. iii. 5, where the word "Ke-Elohim [yode'e ṭob wa-ra']" seems to point to a plurality of gods. Tanḥuma replied that such a construction was refuted by the immediately preceding words, "yodea' [singular] Elohim." His frequent intercourse with non-Jews led him to formulate the following rule: "When a non-Jew greets you with a blessing, answer him with an 'Amen'" (Yer. Ber. 12c; Suk. 54a). The Pesiḳta Rabbati contains about eighty proems said to have originated with Tanḥuma, and beginning with the phrase "Thus said R. Tanḥuma." A great number of proems bearing his name are found also in the Midrash Tanḥuma. In addition to these proems several lengthy sections of the Pesiḳta Rabbati as well as of the Midrash Tanḥuma are followed by the note "Thus explained [or "preached"] R. Tanḥuma.".

BIBLIOGRAPHY: Weiss, *Dor*, iii. 142–144; Frankel, *Mebo*, p, 131a, b; Buber, *Einleitung zum Midrash Tanḥuma*, pp. 3a, 4a; Bacher, *Ag. Pal. Amor.* iii. 465–514.

W. B. J. Z. L.

TANḤUMA B. YUDAN: Palestinian amora of the fourth century, some of whose haggadic utterances have been preserved. The words ואחר כבוד in Ps. lxxiii. 24 are interpreted by him as implying that on account of the honor in which Esau held his father, Isaac, the recognition of Jacob's merit in this world was delayed (Pesiḳ. R. xxiii. 124a). On account of the different meanings of the two names of God he declared (Yer. Ber. 14b), with reference to Ps. lvi. 2, that he praised the name of God regardless of whether it indicated severe justice ("middat ha-din") or mild grace ("middat ha-raḥamim"). From the fact that in Judges vi. 24 (see margin) God is given the name of "Peace" he deduces that it is forbidden to use the word "peace" as a terra of greeting in an unclean place (Lev. R. ix., end). Two other sayings of Tanḥuma b. Yudan are really transmitted baraita sentences (Yer. Ber. 11d [comp. Frankel, "Mebo," p. 24b]; Yer. Yoma 38b; in the latter passage it is noted that the saying is contained in a baraita).

BIBLIOGRAPHY: Frankel, *Mebo*, p. 131 a; Bacher, *Ag. Pal. Amor.* iii. 752–753; Heilprin, *Seder ha-Dorot*, ii. 192a.

W. B. J. Z. L.

TANNAIM AND AMORAIM: The name "tanna" is derived from the Aramaic "teni" or "tena" (="to teach"), and designates in general a teacher of the oral law, and in particular one of the sages of the Mishnah, those teachers of the oral law whose teachings are contained in the Mishnah and in the Baraita. The term was first used in the Gemara to indicate a teacher mentioned in the Mishnah or in a baraita, in contradistinction to the later authorities, the Amoraim. Not all the teachers of the oral law who are mentioned in the Mishnah are called tannaim, however, but only those belonging to the period beginning with the disciples of Shammai and Hillel and ending with the contemporaries of Judah ha-Nasi I. The authorities preceding that period are called "zeḳenim ha-rishonim" (the former elders). In the time of the Amoraim the name "tanna" was given also to one well versed in the Mishnah and the other tannaitic traditions.

The period of the Tannaim, which lasted about 210 years (10–220 C.E.), is generally divided by Jewish scholars into five or six sections or generations, the purpose of such division being to show which teachers developed their principal activity contemporaneously. Some of the tannaim, however, were active in more than one generation. The following is an enumeration of the six generations and of the more prominent tannaim respectively belonging to them:

First Generation (10–80 C.E.): Principal tannaim: the Shammaites (Bet Shammai) and the Hillelites (Bet Hillel), 'Aḳabya b. Mahalaleel, Rabban Gamaliel the Elder, Ḥanina, chief of the priests ("segan ha-kohanim"), Simeon b. Gamaliel, and Johanan b. Zakkai.

Second Generation (80–120): Principal tannaim: Rabban Gamaliel II. (of Jabneh), Zadok, Dosa b. Harkinas, Eliezer b. Jacob, Eliezer b. Hyrcanus, Joshua b. Hananiah, Eleazar b. Azariah, Judah b. Bathyra.

Third Generation (120–140): Principal tannaim: Ṭarfon, Ishmael, Akiba, Johanan b. Nuri, Jose ha-Gelili, Simeon b. Nanos, Judah b. Baba, and Johanan b. Baroḳa. Several of these flourished in the preceding period.

Fourth Generation: This generation extended from the death of Akiba (*c.* 140) to that of the patriarch Simeon b. Gamaliel (*c.* 165). The teachers belonging to this generation were: Meïr, Judah b. Ilai, Jose b. Ḥalafta, Simeon b. Yoḥai, Eleazar b. Shammua, Johanan ha-Sandalar, Eleazar b. Jacob, Nehemiah, Joshua b. Ḳarḥa, and the above-mentioned Simeon b. Gamaliel.

Fifth Generation (165–200): Principal tannaim: Nathan ha-Babli, Symmachus, Judah ha-Nasi I., Jose b. Judah, Eleazar b. Simeon, Simeon b. Eleazar.

Sixth Generation (200–220): To this generation belong the contemporaries and disciples of Judah ha-Nasi. They are mentioned in the Tosefta and the Baraita but not in the Mishnah. Their names are: Polemo, Issi b. Judah, Eleazar b. Jose, Ishmael b. Jose, Judah b. Laḳish, Ḥiyya, Aha, Abba (Arika). These teachers are termed "semitannaim"; and therefore some scholars count only five generations of tannaim. Christian scholars, moreover, count only four generations, reckoning the second and third as one (Strack, "Einleitung in den Talmud," pp. 77 *et seq.*).

For the term "amora" and a list of the generations of amoraim, see Amora.

W. B. J. Z. L.

The following list enumerates all the zeḳenim ha-rishonim, tannaim, and amoraim mentioned in the Talmudic-Midrashic literature, those who are well known and frequently mentioned as well as those whose names occur once only in the Mishnah and Tosefta or in the Talmud and Midrash. To this pretannaitic period belong the so-called "pairs" ("zugot") of teachers: Simeon the Just and Antigonus of Soko; Jose ben Joezer and Jose ben Johanan; Joshua ben Perahyah and Nittai of Arbela; Judah ben Tabbai and Simeon ben Sheṭaḥ; Shemaiah and Abtalion; Hillel and Shammai.

Stars indicate that separate articles appear under the names so marked.

List of Tannaim.

Abba Benjamin
*Abba Doresh
Abba Eleazar b. Dula'i
Abba Eleazar b. Gamaliel
*Abba Gorion of Sidon
*Abba Ḥanin
*Abba Jose b. Dosetai
*Abba Jose b. Ḥanin
*Abba Jose of Maḥoza
Abba Jose Torti
Abba Joseph the Horonite
Abba Kohen of Bardala
*Abba Saul
*Abba Saul b. Baṭnit
Abba Yudan of Sidon
*Absalom the Elder
*Abtalion
Abtolemus
Abtolos
Admon
*Aḥa I.
Aḥai b. Josiah
'Aḳabya b. Mahalaleel
*Akiba b. Joseph
*Antigonus of Soko
Antoninus
Azariah
*Baba ben Buṭa
Baitos b. Zonin
*Bar Ḳappara
*Ben Bag-Bag
Ben Buḳri
Ben Paṭuri
Benaiah

*Benjamin (an Egyptian proselyte)
Dosa
Dosa b. Harkinas
*Dosetai
*Dosetai b. Judah
*Dosetai of Kefar Yatma
*Dosetai b. Yannai
*Eleazar ben Aḥwai
*Eleazar ben 'Arak
*Eleazar b. Azariah
*Eleazar ben Dama
Eleazar ben Hananiah ben Hezekiah
Eleazar b. Ḥarsom
*Eleazar b. Ḥisma
*Eleazar b. Jacob
*Eleazar b. Jose
*Eleazar b. Judah of Bartota
Eleazar b. Judah of Kefar Obelim
*Eleazar ha-Ḳappar
*Eleazar b. Mattai
*Eleazar of Modi'im
*Eleazar ben Peraṭa I.
*Eleazar ben Peraṭa II.
Eleazar b. Phinehas
Eleazar b. Pilai (or Piabi)
*Eleazar b. Shammua
*Eleazar b. Simeon
Eleazar b. Yannai
*Eliezer ben Hyrcanus
*Eliezer b. Isaac
*Eliezer b. Jacob (1st cent.)
*Eliezer b. Jose ha-Gelili
Eliezer b. Judah (contemporary of Judah I.)
*Eliezer b. Taddai
*Eliezer b. Zadok, I.
*Eliezer b. Zadok, II.
*Elisha ben Abuyah
*Ephraim Maḳsha'ah
*Eurydemus ben Jose
*Gamaliel I.
*Gamaliel II. (of Jabneh)
*Gamaliel III. (b. Judah I.)
*Ḥalafta
Ḥalafta b. Ḥagra
Ḥalafta b. Jose
*Ḥalafta b. Karuya
*Ḥalafta of Kefar Hananiah
*Hanan, Abba
*Hanan the Egyptian
Hanan b. Menahem
*Hananiah (nephew of R. Joshua)
Hananiah b. 'Adai
*Hananiah b. 'Aḳabya
*Hananiah b. 'Aḳashyah
*Hananiah b. Ḥakinai
Hananiah b. Hezekiah b. Garon
Hananiah b. Jose ha-Gelili
*Hananiah b. Judah
*Hananiah of Ono
*Hananiah (Ḥanina) b. Teradion
Hananiah of Ṭibe'im
*Ḥanina
*Ḥanina b. Adda
*Ḥanina b. Antigonus
*Hanina b. Dosa
*Ḥanina b. Gamaliel II.
Ḥanina Segan ha-Kohanim
Hezekiah Abi 'Iḳḳesh
*Ḥidḳa
*Hillel
*Ḥiyya bar Abba (Rabbah)
Ḥiyya b. Eleazar ha-Ḳappar
Ḥiyya b. Naḥmani
Huzpit the Meturgeman
Ilai
Isaac
Ishmael b. Eleazar b. Azariah
*Ishmael b. Elisha
*Ishmael b. Johanan b. Baroka
*Ishmael b. Jose b. Ḥalafta
*Jacob of Kefar Ḥiṭṭaya
*Jacob b. Ḳorshai (R. Jacob)
Jaddua (Babylonian pupil of R. Meïr)
*Jeremiah
Jeshebab
*Johanan b. Baroḳa
Johanan b. Dahabai
*Johanan b. Gudgada
*Johanan ben ha-Ḥoranit
Johanan b. Joseph
Johanan ben Joshua
Johanan b. Josiah
Johanan b. Matthias

*Johanan b. Nuri
*Johanan ha-Sandalar
*Johanan b. Torta
*Johanan ben Zakkai
Jonathan b. Abtolemus
Jonathan b. Bathyra
Jonathan b. Joseph
Jonathan b. Meshullam
*Jonathan ben Uzziel
Jose (son of the Damascene)
*Jose b. 'Aḳabya
Jose b. Assi
Jose b. Eleazar
Jose b. Eliakim
Jose b. Elisha
*Jose ha-Gelili
Jose b. Gilai
Jose b. Gurya
*Jose b. Ḥalafta
Jose b. Ḥanina
Jose ha-Ḥoram
*Jose ben Joezer
*Jose ben Johanan
Jose ben Josiah
*Jose (Ise) ben Judah
Jose b. Ḳaẓrata
Jose b. Kippor
Jose b. Ḳisma
*Jose ha-Kohen
Jose b. Menahem
Jose b. Meshullam
Jose of Modi'im
Jose b. Petros
Jose b. Shammai
Jose b. Yasyan
Jose b. Zimra
Joshua b. Akiba
Joshua b. Bathyra
Joshua ha-Garsi
*Joshua b. Hananiah
Joshua b. Hyrcanus
Joshua b. Jonathan
Joshua b. Kaposai
*Joshua b. Ḳarḥa
Joshua b. Mamal
Joshua b. Matthias
*Joshua b. Peraḥyah
Joshua b. Ziruz
*Josiah
*Judah I. (ha-Nasi)
Judah b. Agra
*Judah b. Baba
*Judah b. Bathyra
Judah b. Dama
Judah b. Doroteus
Judah b. Gadish
Judah b. Gamaliel
Judah b. Gerim
Judah b. Hananiah
*Judah ben Ilai
Judah b. Jair
Judah b. Johanan b. Zakkai
Judah b. Jose
Judah ha-Kohen
*Judah ben Laḳish
Judah b. Naḳosa
Judah b. Nehemiah
Judah b. Ro'eẓ
Judah b. Shammua
Judah b. Simeon
Judah b. Ṭabbai
Judah b. Temah
Levi ha-Saddar
*Levi b. Sisi
Levitas of Jabneh
*Mattithiah b. Ḥeresh
Mattithiah b. Samuel
*Me'asha
*Meïr
Menahem of Galya
Menahem b. Jose
Menahem b. Nappaḥa
Menahem b. Sagnai
Mona
Monobaz
*Nahum of Gimzo
Nahum ha-Lablar
*Nahum the Mede
*Nathan
Nehemiah
Nehemiah of Bet Deli
Nehorai
Neḥunya b. Elinathan
Neḥunya b. Gudgada

*Neḥunya ben ha-Ḳanah
*Nittai of Arbela
*Onias ha-Me'aggel
*Onḳelos
Pappias
*Pappos b. Judah
Perida
Phinehas ben Jair
Polemo
*Reuben ben Strobilus
Samuel the Younger
Shammai
Shela
Shemaiah
Simai
Simeon (brother of Azariah)
*Simeon b. 'Aḳashyah
Simeon b. Akiba
Simeon b. Azzai
Simeon b. Bathyra
*Simeon b. Eleazar
Simeon b. Gamaliel I.
Simeon b. Gamaliel II.
Simeon b. Gudda
Simeon b. Ḥalafta
*Simeon b. Ḥanina
Simeon he-Ḥasid
Simeon b. Hillel
*Simeon b. Jehozadak
*Simeon b. Jose b. Lekonya
*Simeon b. Judah of Kefar 'Ikos
*Simeon b. Judah ha-Nasi I.
Simeon the Just
Simeon b. Kahana
*Simeon of Ḳiṭron
*Simeon b. Menasya
*Simeon of Mizpah
*Simeon ben Nanos
*Simeon b. Nethaneel
*Simeon ha-Paḳoli
*Simeon ben ha-Segan
*Simeon ben Sheṭaḥ
*Simeon Shezuri
*Simeon of Shiḳmona
*Simeon b. Ṭarfon
*Simeon of Teman
*Simeon b. Yoḥai
Simeon b. Zoma
*Symmachus
*Ṭarfon [Rome
*Theodosius (Theudas) of
*Yannai
Zachariah b. Abkulas
Zachariah b. Ḳabutal
Zachariah b. ha-Ḳaẓẓab
*Zakkai

J. J. Z. L.

LIST OF AMORAIM.

[Babylonian and Palestinian amoraim are distinguished respectively by the initials B and P in parentheses; the figures indicate the centuries to which they belonged. For amoraim whose names are preceded by the dagger-sign, see also Jew. Encyc. s.v. Yiẓḥaḳ.]

*Aaron (B)
Aaron (B) [P)
Abba (father of Abba Mari;
Abba (father of Ḥiyya; B)
*Abba bar Abba (B)
Abba b. Abimai (B)
*Abba b. Abina (P)
*Abba of Acre (P)
Abba b. Aḥa (P)
Abba Arika (B)
Abba of Bira (P)
*Abba b. Bizna (P)
Abba of Cæsarea (P)
*Abba of Carthage (P)
Abba b. Eliashib (P)
Abba b. Hamnuna (P)
Abba bar Ḥana (P and B)
Abba Ḥanan (B)
Abba b. Ḥanina
Abba b. Ḥilefai (P)
*Abba b. Ḥiyya (P)
Abba b. Huna (B)

Abba b. Huna (P)
Abba b. Ilai (P)
Abba b. Isa (P)
Abba b. Isaac (P)
Abba b. Jacob (B)
Abba b. Jacob (P)
*Abba bar Jeremiah (B)
Abba b. Jonah (P)
Abba b. Joseph (B)
Abba b. Judah (P)
Abba b. Kahana (P)
Abba b. Levi (B)
Abba b. Lima
Abba b. Mar Papa (B)
Abba Mari (B)
Abba Mari (P)
Abba Mari (P)
Abba Mari (brother of Jose; P)
Abba b. Mari (?)
*Abba bar Memel (P)
Abba b. Mina (P)
Abba b. Naḥman (B)
Abba of Narsoh
Abba b. Nathan (P)
Abba bar Papa (P)
*Abba b. Pappai (P)
Abba b. Safra (P)
Abba b. Samuel Rabbah
Abba b. Shila
Abba b. Taḥlifa (P)
Abba Umana (B)
Abba b. Zabda (B)
*Abba b. Zabdai (P)
Abba b. Ze'era (P)
Abba Zuṭi
Abba b. Zuṭra (P)
Abbahu (P)
Abbahu (father of Samuel)
Abbahu b. Aḥa (P)
Abbahu b. Bebi (B)
Abbahu b. Ehi (B)
Abbahu b. Geniba (B)
Abbahu b. Zuṭarti (B)
Abbai (called Naḥmani; B)
Abbai b. Abbin (B)
Abbai b. Benjamin (P)
Abbai the Elder (B)
Abdima b. Ḥama (B)
*Abdima b. Hamdure (P)
Abdima b. Ḥisda (B)
Abdima b. Neḥunya (P)
*Abdima of Sepphoris (P)
Abdimi (brother of Jose)
Abdimi (father of Isaac)
*Abdimi of Ḥaifa
*Abiathar
*Abimi (B)
*Abimi b. Abbahu (P)
Abimi the Colleague
*Abimi of Hagrunya
Abimi the Nabatæan
Abimi b. Papi (B)
Abimi b. Tobi (P)
Abin (the pupil of Johanan)
*Abin (Rabin) b. Abba (P)
*Abin ben Adda (B)
Abin b. Bisna (P)
Abin b. Ḥinana (B)
*Abin b. Ḥiyya (P)
Abin b. Ḥuna (B)
*Abin b. Kahana (P)
Abin ha-Levi (P)
Abin Naggara
Abin b. Naḥman (B)
Abin of Nashikiya
Abin the Old
*Abin b. Rab Ḥisda (P)
Abin b. Samuel
Abin of Sepphoris
*Abin b. Tanḥum (P)
Abina I. (P)
Abina II. (B)
Abina III. (B)
Abram of Ḥuza (B)
Abudemi (grandson of Tobi; P)
Abudemi b. Tanḥum (P)
Abudemi b. Tobi (P)
*Adda b. Abimi (P)
Adda b. Abin (B)
Adda b. Aḥa (B)
*Adda b. Ahabah (B)
Adda of Be Zeluḥit
*Adda of Cæsarea
Adda b. Isaac (B)

Adda of Jaffa
Adda Karḥina
*Adda b. Matnah (B)
*Adda b. Minyomi (B)
Adda of Naresh
Adda b. Papa (B)
Adda b. Simi (B)
*Adda b. Simeon (P)
Adda of Sura
Afes (Efes) (P; 1)
Aggara or Agra (B)
Aḥa (brother of R. Jose)
Aḥa b. Abba (B)
Aḥa b. R. Abba (B)
Aḥa b. Abba b. Aḥa (B)
Aḥa b. Abbai (B)
Aḥa b. Abin (P)
*Aḥa b. Adda (B)
Aḥa b. Aḥa (B)
Aḥa b. Ahaba (P)
Aḥa b. Ami (B)
Aḥa b. Ashi (B)
Aḥa b. Awira (B)
*Aḥa b. Awya (B)
Aḥa b. Azza (B)
*Aḥa Bardala
Aḥa of Be Ḥusa
Aḥa b. Bebi (B)
Aḥa b. Bizna (P)
Aḥa of Carthage
Aḥa of Carthage (P)
*Aḥa of Difti
Aḥa of Galilee
*Aḥa b. Ḥanina (P)
Aḥa b. Haya (B)
Aḥa b. Hoshaiah (P)
*Aḥa b. Ḥuna (B)
Aḥa of Huẓal
*Aḥa b. Iḳa (B)
*Aḥa b. Isaac (P)
*Aḥa b. Jacob (B)
Aḥa b. Jose (P)
*Aḥa b. Joseph (B)
Aḥa b. Ḳaṭṭina (B)
Aḥa the Long (B)
*Aḥa b. Minyomi (B)
Aḥa b. Naḥman (B)
Aḥa b. Papa
Aḥa b. Phineḥas (B)
Aḥa of Porsika
Aḥa b. Rabbina (B)
Aḥa Saba
Aḥa Sar ha-Birah
*Aḥa b. Shila (P)
*Aḥa b. Taḥlifa (B)
*Aḥa b. 'Ula (B)
Aḥa b. Yeba
Ahabah b. Ze'era (P)
*Aḥadboi (B)
*Aḥadboi b. Ammi (B)
Aḥadboi b. Matnah
Ahilai (B)
Aibu (name of several Palestinian amoraim)
Alexa (P)
Alexandra b. Haga (P)
*Alexandri (P)
*Alexandri (P)
*Amemar I.
*Amemar b. Mar Yanuḳa (B)
Ammi (P)
Ammi (father of Samuel)
Ammi b. Abba (B)
Ammi b. Abin (B)
Ammi b. Ada (B)
Ammi b. Aḥa (B)
Ammi the Babylonian
Ammi b. Ḳarḥa (P)
Ammi b. Matnah (B)
Ammi b. Nathan (B)
Ammi b. Tobi
Ammi of Wadina (P; 3)
*Amram R. (B; 3)
*Amram Ḥasida (B)
Anan b. Ḥiyya (B)
Anan b. Joseph (P)
Anan b. Taḥlifa (B; 2)
'Anani b. Sason (P; 3)
Armania (P; 1)
*Ashi (B; 6)
Ashi b. Abin (B; 4)
Ashi of Awira? (6)
Ashi of Huẓal (B; 4)
Ashi the Old (B; 1)

*Ashyan bar Jakim (P; 4)
*Ashyan Naggara
*Ashyan b. Nidbak (P)
*Assi I. (B)
*Assi II. (P)
Assi of Nehor Bal (B)
*Awia Saba
*Awira (B; 3)
Babahu (B)
Bali (B; 4)
Banna'ah or Bannayah (P; 1)
Banna'ah b. 'Ula (B; 4)
Baruka of Ḥuza (B; 5)
Baruna (B; 2)
Batha (B and P; 3)
Beba b. Abba (P; 3)
*Bebai b. Abaye (B; 5)
*Bebai b. Abba (P)
Bebai b. Ashi (B; 6)
Bebai b. Mesharshiya (P; 5)
*Benjamin b. 'Ashtor (P; 3)
*Benjamin b. Giddel (P; 4)
Benjamin Ḥiyya (B)
*Benjamin b. Japhet (P; 3)
*Benjamin b. Levi (P; 3)
Beotes (P; 3)
Berechiah (P; 5)
*Berechiah (P; 2)
Berechiah b. Abba (P)
Berechiah b. Ḥamma
Berechiah ben Ḥelbo (P; 4)
Berechiah b. Judah (P)
Berechiah Saba
Berechiah b. Simeon (P; 2)
Berim (P; 2)
Berna or Bera (B; 4)
Bisa or Bisna (P; 1)
*Bisna (P; 4)
Bisna b. Zabda (P)
Budia (B; 6)
Burakai (P; 5)
*Daniel, Ḥayyata (P)
*Daniel b. Ḳaṭṭina (B)
Dari b. Papa (B)
*Dimi (brother of Rab Safra; B; 4)
Dimi b. Abba (B)
Dimi b. Abui
*Dimi b. Ḥinena (B; 5)
*Dimi b. Ḥuna of Damharia (B; 6)
*Dimi b. Isaac (B; 4)
*Dimi b. Joseph (B; 3)
*Dimi b. Levai (B; 4)
Dimi b. Naḥman (B; 5)
*Dimi of Nehardea (B)
Dimi b. Sheshna
Dosetai (father of Aftoriki)
Dosetai of Beri
Dosetai b. Maton
Elai b. Berechiah (P)
Elai b. Eliezer (B; 2)
*Eleazar b. Abina (P)
Eleazar b. Antigonus (P; 2)
Eleazar of Basra (P)
*Eleazar of Hagrunya (B; 4)
Eleazar b. Ḥagya
Eleazar b. Ḥanina (P)
*Eleazar b. Jose II. (P; 5)
*Eleazar b. Malai (P; 3)
Eleazar b. Maram (Miriam or Maron?) (P; 4)
Eleazar b. Marinus (P)
*Eleazar b. Menahem (P; 3)
Eleazar the Nabatæan
Eleazar of Nineveh (B; 3)
*Eleazar b. Pedat (P; 3)
Eleazar of the South (P; 5)
Eleazar b. Yannai (P; 2)
Eleazar Ze'era (the little)
Eliakim (B; 5)
Eliehoenai (P)
Ezekiel
Gadda (B; 4)
Gamaliel b. Elai (P; 4)
Gamaliel b. Ḥanina (P; 4)
Gamaliel Zoga (P; 2)
Gamda
*Gebiha of Argizah (B; 5)
*Gebiha of Be Katil (B; 5) Gedaliah
Geniba (B; 1)
Gershom (P; 5)
Gidal or Giddul (B; 2)
Gidal b. Minyomi
Gidal of Naresh
Giddul b. Benjamin (P; 2)

Giddul b. Menaschi (B; 5)
Giora (proselyte)
Gorion (P; 2)
Gorion of Asparak (B; 3)
Gorion b. Astion (B)
Ḥabiba (B: 1)
Ḥabiba of Huza (B; 6)
Ḥabiba b. Joseph (B; 4)
Ḥabiba of Sora (B; 6)
Ḥabiba b. Surmaki (B and P; 4)
Ḥagga (B; 4?), contemporary of R. Naḥman
Ḥagga (pupil of R. Huna; B; 4)
Ḥagga of Sepphoris (P; 2)
Ḥaggai (P; 3)
Haggai Kusmai (?)
Haggai of the South (P;?)
Hagra (Haggaria; P; 2)
Ḥalafta of Cæsarea (P)
*Ḥalafta of Huna (P; 1)
*Ḥalafta Ḳaroya (the Bible reader)
Ḥalafta of Radfa (P; 2)
Ḥalfa b. Idi (P)
Ḥama (grandfather of Raba)
Ḥama b. Adda
Ḥama b. Ashi (P)
*Ḥama b. Bisa (P)
Ḥama b. Buzi (B; 5)
Ḥama b. Gurya (B; 3)
*Ḥama b. Ḥanina (P; 2)
Ḥama b. Joseph (P; 2)
Ḥama b. Mari
Ḥama of Nehardea (B; 5)
Ḥama b. Osha'ya (P; 2)
Ḥama b. Papa (P; 5)
Ḥama b. Rabbah (P; 4)
Ḥama b. Tobia (B; 6)
Ḥama b. 'Uḳba (P; 3)
Hamnuna (B; 2)
*Hamnuna I. (B; 3)
*Hamnuna II. (B; 3, 4)
Hamnuna b. Ada b. Ahabah (B; 6)
Hamnuna of Babylonia
Hamnuna b. Joseph (B; 4)
Hamnuna b. Rabbah of Pashronia (B)
*Hamnuna Zuṭa
Ḥana b. Adda
Ḥana b. Aha
Ḥana of Bagdad
*Ḥana b. Bizna
Ḥana of Carthage
*Ḥana b. Ḥanilai
Ḥana b. Ḥinena
Ḥana b. Judah
Ḥana b. Ḳaṭṭina
Ḥana of Kefar Teḥumim
Ḥana b. Lewai
Ḥana Sha'onah
Hanan b. Abba (B; 2)
Hanan b. Ammi
Hanan of Be Zeluhit
Hanan Ḥayyaṭa
Hanan b. Ḥisda (B; 4)
Hanan of Nehardea (B; 2)
Hanan b. Rabbah (B; 2)
Hanan b. Taḥlifa (B; 4)
Hanan b. Zabdi (P; 1)
Hanana (B; 3)
*Hananeel (B; 2)
Hananeel b. Papa (B)
Hananiah (B)
Hananiah (B; 4)
Hananiah (B)
*Hananiah (P; 3, 4)
Hananiah b. Aibu (P)
Hanilai of Ḥuza
Hanilai b. Idi
Ḥanina (B; 6)
*Hanina b. Abbahu (P; 4)
Ḥanina b. Abdimi (B)
*Ḥanina b. 'Agul (P; 3)
Ḥanina of Akra
Ḥanina of Anat
Ḥanina b. Andrai (P)
Ḥanina b. Atal
Ḥanina b. Bebai (B; 5)
*Ḥanina b. Ḥama (P; 1)
Ḥanina b. Hillel (P)
Ḥanina b. Ḥiyya (B; 3)
Ḥanina of Ḥuza
*Ḥanina b. Iḳa
Ḥanina b. Isi (P; 3)
Ḥanina b. Joseph (P; 1)
Ḥanina Ḳara (the Bible reader)

*Ḥanina Katoba (the writer)
*Ḥanina b. Papa (B)
*Ḥanina b. Pazi (P)
Ḥanina b. Samson (P)
Ḥanina b. Samuel (P; 2)
Ḥanina Sholḳa (the cook)
Ḥanina b. Sisi (P; 1)
*Ḥanina of Sura
Ḥanina of Sura near the Euphrates
Ḥanina b. Tiba
Ḥanina of Tirta or Tarna
*Ḥanina b. Torta
Ḥanina b. Uri
*Ḥasa
Henaḳ
Hezekiah (B)
Hezekiah (P)
Hezekiah Akkaya
Hezekiah b. Ḥiyya
Hezekiah of Hukuk
Ḥilfa (P; 2)
Ḥilfa (grandson of Abbahu; 4)
Hilkiah (father of Minjamin; B)
Hilkiah b. Awia (B)
Hilkiah of Hagrunya (B)
Hilkiah b. Tobia (B; 3)
Hilkiah of the South (B)
Hillel (P; 3)
Hillel (B; 6)
Hillel (son-in-law of Jose; P; 6)
*Hillel b. Berechiah (P)
Hillel b. Helena (P)
Hillel of Kifra (P; 5)
Hillel b. Pazi (P; 4)
Hillel b. Samuel b. Naḥman (P; 4)
Hillel b. Vales (Valens; P; 3)
Ḥinena (father of Yanta)
Ḥinena b. Abin
Ḥinena b. Assi
Ḥinena b. Kahana (B; 3)
Ḥinena b. Rabbah (B; 4)
Ḥinena b. Shelamya (B; 2)
Ḥinena b. Shila (B; 1)
Ḥinena of Wardan
*Ḥisda (B; 3)
Ḥisda b. Abdami
Ḥisda b. Joseph (B; 4)

Ḥiyya
Ḥiyya (P and B; 4)
Ḥiyya b. Abba (B and P; 3)
Ḥiyya b. Abbahu (B)
Ḥiyya b. Abbui (B; 4)
*Ḥiyya b. Adda (P)
Ḥiyya b. Adda (P; 5)
Ḥiyya b. Adda of Joppa (P)
Ḥiyya b. Ammi (B; 4)
Ḥiyya b. Amram (B)
Ḥiyya Arika (the tall one)
Ḥiyya b. Ashi (B; 2)
Ḥiyya b. Assi (B)
Ḥiyya b. Awia (B; 3)
Ḥiyya of Ctesiphon (B; 3)
Ḥiyya of Difta (B; 3)
*Ḥiyya b. Gammada (P)
Ḥiyya b. Garya (B)
Ḥiyya of Hagra (B; 3)
Ḥiyya b. Ḥanina (B)
Ḥiyya b. Huna (B; 5)
Ḥiyya of Hurmis (B; 4)
Ḥiyya b. Isaac (P)
Ḥiyya b. Isaac (P; 5)
Ḥiyya b. Jacob (P)
Ḥiyya b. Joseph (B and P; 2)
Ḥiyya b. Joshua? (B; 4)
Ḥiyya b. Judah
Ḥiyya b. Judah (B; 3)
*Ḥiyya Ḳara (the Bible reader)
Ḥiyya of Kefar Teḥumim (P; 4)
Ḥiyya b. Lulianos (P; 5)
Ḥiyya b. Luliba (P; 4)
Ḥiyya b. Matnah (B: 3)
*Ḥiyya b. Moria (P; 5)
Ḥiyya b. Naḥman (P; 3)
Ḥiyya b. Nathan (B; 4)
Ḥiyya b. Papa (P; 3)
Ḥiyya of Parwada (B; 3)
Ḥiyya b. Rab (B; 2)
Ḥiyya b. Rabbah (B; 4)
Ḥiyya b. Shabbethai (P; 4)
Ḥiyya b. Tanḥum (P; 4)
Ḥiyya b. Tiba
Ḥiyya b. Titus (P; 4)
Ḥiyya b. 'Uḳba (P)
Ḥiyya b. Yannai (P)

Ḥiyya b. Zarnaki (P; 2)
*Huna (B)
Huna b. Abin (B; 5)
Huna b. Aḥa
Huna b. Ashi (B; 2)
Huna b. Berechiah
Huna of Damharia
Huna of Diskarta
Huna b. Geniba
Huna b. Halob (B; 4)
*Huna b. Ḥanina (B; 4)
Huna of Ḥauran
Huna b. Hillel (P)
Huna b. Hiwan (B; 6)
Huna b. Ḥiyya (B)
Huna b. Ida (B; 6)
Huna b. Iḳa (B; 6)
Huna b. Ilai
Huna b. Jeremiah (B; 5)
*Huna b. Joshua (B; 5)
Huna b. Judah (B; 4)
Huna b. Ḳaṭṭina (B; 3)
Huna b. Lewai (B)
Huna b. Manoah (B; 5)
Huna Mar b. Awia (B; 5)
Huna b. Maremor (B; 6)
Huna b. Matnah (B; 4)
Huna b. Minyomi (B; 3)
Huna b. Moses (B; 4)
Huna b. Naḥman (B; 4)
*Huna b. Nathan (B; 7)
Huna b. Nehemiah (B; 6)
Huna b. Papi
Huna b. Phinehas (B)
Huna of Porsica
Huna b. Rabbah (B; 6)
Huna b. Saḥḥora (B; 4)
Huna of Sepphoris
Huna of Sura
Huna b. Taḥlifa (B; 5)
Huna b. Torta
Huna b. Zuṭi (B; 6)
Hunya Jacob of Apretaim
Ishmael (father of Judah; P; 3)
Ishmael b. Abba (P; 2)
Ishmael b. Jacob (P)
Ishmael b. Kathriel (P; 1)
Ishmael of Kefar Yama (P; 3)
Isaac (B; 6)
Isaac (father of Samuel)
Isaac b. Abba (B; 2)
Isaac b. Abba (B; 4)
Isaac b. Abdimi I. (P; 1)
Isaac b. Abdimi II. (B; 3)
Isaac b. Abin
†Isaac b. Adda (B)
Isaac b. Aḥa (B)
Isaac b. Ammi (P)
Isaac b. Ammi (B; 4)
Isaac b. Ashi (B; 2)
Isaac b. Ashya (B; 3)
†Isaac ha-Babli
Isaac Berrabi
Isaac b. Bisna (B; 2)
†Isaac of Carthage
Isaac Dibaha
Isaac b. Elai
Isaac b. Eliashib (P; 4)
†Isaac b. Eleazar (P; 4)
Isaac of Gufta
†Isaac b. Ḥaḳola
Isaac b. Ḥalub (B; 3)
Isaac b. Ḥanina (B; 3)
†Isaac b. Ḥiyya (P; 2)
Isaac b. Jacob
Isaac b. Jonathan (P; 4)
Isaac b. Joseph (P; 2 and 3)
Isaac b. Judah (B; 3)
Isaac b. Ḳappara (P)
Isaac Kaskasa
Isaac of Kefar 'Itos
Isaac Krispa
Isaac b. Levi
†Isaac of Magdala
†Isaac b. Marion (P; 3)
Isaac b. Menahem (P)
Isaac b. Mesharshiya (B, P; 6)
Isaac b. Naḥmani (P; 3)
Isaac b. Naphtali (B; 6)
†Isaac Nappaha (the smith)
Isaac b. Ostiya (P)
†Isaac b. Parnak
Isaac Paska
†Isaac b. Phinehas (B and P; 3)

Isaac b. Rabbah b. bar Ḥana (B; 4)
†Isaac b. Redifa (P; 4)
Isaac b. Samuel (B; 2)
Isaac b. Shila (B)
Isaac b. Simeon (P)
†Isaac b. Tabla (P; 4)
Isaac b. Teradion
†Isaac b. Zeʿera or Sita (P; 4)
Jabez
Jacob (grandson of Aḥa b. Jacob)
Jacob (grandson of Samuel)
*Jacob b. Abba I.
*Jacob b. Abba II.
*Jacob b. Abbuha
*Jacob b. Abina
Jacob b. Adda
Jacob b. Adda b. Athaliah
Jacob of Adiabene
*Jacob b. Aḥa (B; 3)
Jacob b. Aḥa (P)
*Jacob b. Aḥa (P; 4)
Jacob b. Aḥa b. Idi
Jacob b. Ammi
Jacob of Armenia
Jacob b. Dosai
Jacob of Emaus
Jacob of Gebula
Jacob b. Ḥama
Jacob b. Hapiliti (Hippolytus)
Jacob b. Ḥisda
Jacob b. Idi
Jacob b. Idi b. Oshaya
Jacob b. Ise (Jose)
*Jacob of Kefar Ḥanin
Jacob of Neboria
Jacob of Nehar-Peḳod
Jacob of Rumania
Jacob b. Sisai
Jacob of the South
Jacob b. Taḥlifa
Jacob b. Yannai
Jacob b. Yoḥai
*Jacob b. Zabdai
Jehiel
Jeremiah (B; 6)
Jeremiah (B and P; 2)
*Jeremiah b. Abba (B; 3)
Jeremiah b. Aḥa (B)
*Jeremiah of Difte
Jeremiah of Gufta
Jeremiah Rabba (the great)
Jeremiah Safra (the scribe)
Jeremiah of Shebshab
Jeremiah of the South
Jeremiah b. Taḥlifa (B)
Johanan (son of the smith)
Johanan (brother of Safra; B)
Johanan Antonarta
Johanan b. Kassarta
Johanan of Maḥuka (P; 1)
*Johanan b. Meriya (P; 5)
*Johanan b. Nappaha
Johanan b. Rabbina (B; 5)
Johanan Safra of Gufta
Johanan b. Shila (P)
Joḥani (B; 1)
*Jonah (P; 4)
Jonah of Bosra (P; 5)
Jonah b. Taḥlifa (B; 4)
Jonathan (P; 1)
Jonathan b. ʿAkmai (P; 3)
Jonathan b. Amram (P; 1)
*Jonathan of Bet Gubrin (P)
Jonathan b. Eliezer
Jonathan b. Haggai (P)
Jonathan b. Ḥila (P)
Jonathan b. Isaac b. Ahor (P)
Jonathan Kefa (P; 4)
Jose b. Abba or Abai
*Jose b. Abin
Jose b. Ashyan
Jose b. Bebai
Jose of Cæsarea
Jose b. Elai
Jose b. Eliakim
Jose the Galilean (amora)
Jose b. Gezira
Jose b. Hananiah
Jose b. Ḥanina
Jose of Kefar Dan
Jose of Kefar Gufta
Jose Kuzira
*Jose b. Jacob
Jose b. Jason

Jose b. Jose
Jose b. Joshua
*Jose b. Ḳaẓrata
*Jose of Malaḥaya
Jose the Mede
Jose b. Menashya
Jose of Nahar Bul
Jose b. Nathan
*Jose b. Nehorai
Jose of Oni
Jose b. Pazi
Jose b. Petros
Jose Resha
Jose b. Saul
Jose of the South
Jose b. Tanḥum
Jose of Yodkarat
Jose of Zaitur
Jose b. Zebida
Jose b. Zemina
Jose b. Zimra
Joseph b. Abba
Joseph b. Ammi
Joseph b. Ḥabu
Joseph b. Ḥama
Joseph b. Ḥanin
Joseph b. Ḥiyya
*Joseph b. Joshua b. Levi
Joseph b. Menasya of Dewil
Joseph b. Minyomi
Joseph b. Neḥunya
Joseph b. Rabba
Joseph b. Salla
Joseph b. Samuel
Joseph b. Shemaiah
Joseph of Sidon
Joshua (brother of Dorai: P)
Joshua b. Abba
*Joshua b. Abin (P)
Joshua b. Benjamin
Joshua b. Beri (P)
Joshua b. Boethus
Joshua of Gizora (P; 4)
Joshua b. Idi
*Joshua (ha-Kohen) b. Nehemiah (P)
*Joshua b. Levi
Joshua b. Levi b. Shalum
Joshua b. Marta (B; 1)
Joshua b. Naḥman
*Joshua b. Nehemiah
Joshua of Ona (P)
Joshua b. Pedaya
*Josbua of Shiknin
Joshua of the South
Joshua b. Tanḥum
Joshua b. Timi (P)
Joshua of 'Uzza
Joshua b. Zidal (P; 1)
Josiah
Josiah of Huẓal
Josiah of Usha
Judah (brother of Sola Ḥa-[sida)
Judah b. Aḥitai
Judah b. Aibu
*Judah b. Ammi
Judah b. Ashi
Judah b. Ashtita
Judah b. Astira
Judah b. Bisna
Judah b. Buni
Judah of Difte
Judah of Diskarta
*Judah b. Ezekiel
Judah of Gallia
Judah b. Gamda
Judah b. Ḥabiba
Judah of Hagrunya
Judah b. Ḥama
Judah b. Ḥanina
Judah b. Ḥiyya
Judah b. Ḥuna
Judah b. Idi
Judah b. Isaac
Judah b. Ishmael
Judah b. Joshua
Judah Klaustra
Judah b. Levi
Judah b. Menashya
Judah b. Meremar
Judah Mosparta
Judah b. Naḥmani
Judah b. Oshaya
Judah b. Pazi
Judah b. Pedaiah

Judah b. Samuel
Judah b. Shalum
Judah b. Shila
*Judah b. Simeon
Judah b. Simeon b. Pazi
Judah of Soporta
Judah b. Titos
Judah b. Zabda
Judah b. Zebina
Judah b. Zeruya
Justa Ḥabra (the Colleague; P)
Justa b. Judah (P)
Justa of Shunem (P; 5 and 6)
Justa b. Simeon (P; 4)
Justina (P; 3)
Kadi
Kahana (B)
Kahana (B and P)
Kahana (brother of Judah)
Kahana (father-in-law of Mesharshiya)
Kahana b. Ḥanina
Kahana b. Jeremiah
Kahana b. Malkai
Kahana b. Malkiya
Kahana b. Nathan
Kahana b. Nehemiah
*Kahana b. Taḥlifa
Ḳarna
*Ḳaṭṭina
Kiris of Urmia
Krispa
Kruspedai
Levanti
Levi b. Berechiah
Levi of Biri
Levi b. Buta
Levi b. Ḥaita
Levi b. Ḥama
Levi b. Ḥini
Levi b. Ḥiyya
Levi b. Huna
Levi b. Isaac
*Levi b. Laḥma
Levi b. Panti
Levi b. Parta
Levi b. Pitam
Levi b. Rabbi
Levi Saba
Levi b. Samuel
Levi b. Samuel b. Naḥman
Levi of Sandaria
Levi b. Seira
*Levi b. Sisi
Levi of Suki
Luda
Lulianos of the South
Lulianos of Tiberias
Malkio
Maluk of Arabia
Mana of Sepphoris
Mana of Shab
Mana b. Tanḥum
Manasseh
Manasseh b. Zebid
Mani b. Jonah
Mani b. Patish
Mar b. Ashi
Mar Johanya (B; 4)
Mar b. Joseph
Mar Kashshisha
Mar b. Rabina
Mar Yanka
Mari (son of the proselyte Isar)
Mari b. Abbuh
Mari b. Bisnaa
Mari b. Ḥisda
Mari b. Huna
Mari b. Kahana
Mari b. Mar
Mari b. Phinehas
Mari b. 'Uḳba
Marino
Marinus
Marinus b. Oshaya
Marion
Matnah
Mattatya b. Judah
Matun
Menahem of Gallia
Menahem b. Nopaḥ
Menahem b. Simai
Menahem Tolomia
Menashya

Menashya of Dewil
Menashya b. Gada
Menashya b. Jacob
Menashya b. Jeremiah
Menashya b. Judah
Menashya b. Menahem
Menashya b. Raba
Menashya b. Taḥlifa
Meremar
Meremar b. Ḥanina
Meshurshiya b. Ammi
Mesharshiya b. Idi
Mesharshiya b. Dimi
Mesharshiya b. Nathan
Mesharshiya b. Paḳod
Mesharshiya b. Raba
Mesharshiya of Tosnia
Minyomi
Mona
Mordecai
Naḥman b. Ada
Naḥman b. Baruk
Naḥman b. Gurya
Naḥman b. Ḥisdai
Naḥman b. Isaac
*Naḥman b. Jacob
Naḥman b. Kohen
Naḥman b. Minyomi
Naḥman b. Papa
Naḥman b. Parta
Naḥman b. Rabbah
Naḥman b. Samuel
Naḥman b. Zabda
Nahum (brother of Ila)
Nahum (servant of Abbahu)
Naḥumi
Naḥumi b. Zechariah
Naphtali
Nasah
Nathan (father of Huna)
Nathan (brother of Ḥiyya)
Nathan b. Abba
Nathan b. Abbai
Nathan b. Abin
Nathan b. Ammi
Nathan b. Asya
Nathan b. Berechiah
Nathan of Bira
Nathan b. Mar 'Uḳba
Nathan b. Mar Zuṭra
Nathan b. Minyomi
Nathan b. Oshaya
Nathan b. Tobia
*Nathan de Ẓuẓita (exilarch)
Nehemiah
Nehemiah b. Ḥiyya
Nehemiah b. Huna
Nehemiah b. Joseph
Nehemiah b. Joshua
Nehilai
Nehorai
Nehorai b. Shemaiah
Niha b. Saba
Niḳomeki
Osha'ya (Hoshaiah)
Paddat
Paddaya
Panda
*Papa
Papa b. Abba
Papa b. Aḥa
Papa b. Hanan of Be Ẓeluḥit
Papa b. Joseph
Papa b. Naḥman
Papa Saba
Papa b. Samuel
Parnak
Pazi
*Pereda
Philippi
Phinehas
Phinehas b. Ammi
*Phinehas b. Ḥama
Phinehas b. Hananiah
Phinehas b. Ḥisda
Phinehas of Joppa
Phinehas ha-Kohen
Phinehas b. Mari
Phinehas b. Zakkai
*Raba b. Ada
*Raba b. Joseph b. Ḥama
Raba b. 'Ula
Rabbah b. Abba
*Rabbah b. Abuha

Rabbah b. Aḥa
Rabbah b. Ahilai
Rabbah b. Ahini
Rabbah b. Ammi
Rabbah b. Ashi
Rabbah b. Bar Hanah
Rabbah of Barnash
Rabbah b. Baruna
Rabbah b. Ḥaklai
*Rabbah b. Hanan
Rabbah b. Ḥanina
*Rabbah b. Ḥiyya
*Rabbah b. Huna
Rabbah b. Idi b. Abin
Rabbah b. Ihi or Iti
Rabbah b. Ilai
Rabbah b. Isaac
Rabbah b. Ishmael
Rabbah b. Isi
Rabbah b. Jeremiah
Rabbah b. Jonathan
Rabbah b. Kahana
Rabbah b. Ḳisma
Rabbah of Kubaya
Rabbah b. Lema
Rabbah b. Lewai
Rabbah b. Marion
*Rabbah b. Matnah
Rabbah b. Meḥasya
Rabbah b. Mesharshiya
Rabbah b. Minyomi
Rabbah b. Papa
*Rabbah of Parziḳi
Rabbah b. Raba
Rabbah b. Saba
Rabbah b. Safra
*Rabbah b. Samuel
*Rabbah b. Shela
Rabbah b. Shumni
Rabbah b. Simi
Rabbah b. Taḥlifa
Rabbanai
Rabbanai of Ḥuza
*Rabina I.
*Rabina II.
Rabina III.
Rafram
*Rafram I. (b. Papa)
*Rafram II.
Raḥbah or Reḥabah
Raḥmai
Rakish b. Papa
Rammi b. Abba
Rammi b. Berechiah
Rammi b. Ezekiel
Rammi b. Ḥama
Rammi b. Judah
Rammi b. Papa
Rammi b. Rab
Rammi b. Samuel
Rammi b. Tamre
Rammi b. Yeba
Redifa
Reuben
Romanus
Safra
Safra b. Se'oram
Safra b. Tobia
Safra b. Yeba
Saḥḥorah
Salla Ḥasida (the pious)
Samlai
Samlai of Bira
Samlai of Cæsarea
Samlai of Lydda
Samma b. Aibu
Samma b. Asi
Samma b. Ḥalkai
Samma b. Jeremiah
Samma b. Judah
Samma b. Mari
Samma b. Mesharshiya
Samma b. Rabbah
Samma b. Rakta
Samuel (brother of Berechiah)
Samuel (brother of Osha'ya)
Samuel (brother of Phinehas b. Ḥama)
Samuel b. Abba
Samuel (Mar) b. Abba b. Abba
Samuel b. Abba of Hagrunya
*Samuel b. Abbahu
Samuel b. Abdimi
Samuel b. Abin
Samuel b. Ada

Samuel b. Aḥa
Samuel b. Aḥitai
Samuel b. Ahunai
*Samuel b. Ammi
*Samuel b. Anaya
Samuel b. Bisna
Samuel of Cappadocia
Samuel of Difte
Samuel b. Gedaliah
Samuel b. Ḥalafta
Samuel b. Ḥananiah
Samuel b. Ḥanina
*Samuel b. Ḥiyya
Samuel b. Iḳa
Samuel b. Isaac
Samuel b. Jacob
*Samuel b. Jose b. Bun
Samuel b. Judah of India
Samuel b. Ḳaṭṭina
Samuel b. Marta
Samuel b. Nadab
*Samuel b. Naḥmani
*Samuel b. Nathan
Samuel b. Papa
Samuel Podagrita
Samuel b. Raba
Samuel b. Rabbi
Samuel Saba
Samuel b. Shaba
Samuel b. Shilot
Samuel b. Simi
Samuel of Sofafta
Samuel b. Sustra or Susreta
Samuel b. Suṭar
Samuel b. Yeba
Samuel b. Zadok
Samuel of Zarkonya
Samuel b. Ze'era
Samuel b. Zuṭra
Saul of Nawah
Se'oram
Shaba
Shabbethai
Shabbethai b. Marinus
Shabbethai of Saduki
Shalemya
Shalman of Be Zeluḥit
Shalman b. Levi
Shappir
Shayin
Shazbi
Shela
Shela b. Abina
Shela b. Isaac
*Shela of Kefar Tamarta
Shela Mari
Shela of Shalomya
Shemaiah
Shemaiah b. Zera
Shephatiah
Sherebiah
Shesha b. Idi b. Abin
*Sheshet
Sheshet b. Joshua
Sheshet of Ḳarṭiza
Sheshna b. Samuel
Sidor
Simeon b. Abba
Simeon b. Abishalom
Simeon b. Aibu
Simeon b. Bisna
Simeon b. Hillel b. Pazi
Simeon b. Ḥiyya
Simeon b. Ḥiyya of Ḥuza
Simeon b. Jacob of Tyrus
*Simeon b. Jakim
Simeon b. Jasina
*Simeon b. Jehozadak
Simeon b. Jonah
Simeon b. Joshua
Simeon the Judge
Simeon b. Ḳana or Sana
Simeon b. Ḳarsena
Simeon b. Ḳisma
*Simeon b. Laḳish
Simeon b. Levi
Simeon b. Me'asha
Simeon b. Narshiyah
Simeon b. Nezira
*Simeon b. Pazi
Simeon the Pious
Simeon the Scribe
Simeon of Shiloh
Simeon b. Simeon

Simeon b. Taḥlifa
Simeon of Tospata
*Simeon b. Yannai
Simeon b. Zachariah
Simeon b. Zebid
Simeon b. Zirud
Simi b. Abba
Simi b. Ada
Simi b. Ashi
Simi of Birtadesḥore
Simi b. Hezekiah
Simi b. Ḥiyya
Simi of Maḥaza
Simi of Nehardea
Simi b. 'Uḳba
Simi Ze'era
Sisai
Surḥab b. Papa
Ṭabala
*Ṭabi
Ṭabi (grandson of Mar Ṭabi)
Ṭabi, Mar
Ṭabut
Ṭabut Rishba
*Ṭabyome (B)
Ṭabyome (P)
Ṭabyome II. (B)
Taddai
Taḥlifa
*Taḥlifa (father-in-law of Abbahu)
Taḥlifa (father-in-law of Aha)
Taḥlifa (father of Huna)
Taḥlifa b. Abdimi
Taḥlifa b. Abimi
Taḥlifa b. Abina
Taḥlifa b. Bar Ḥana
Taḥlifa of Cæsarea
Taḥlifa b. Gazza
Taḥlifa b. Ḥisda
Taḥlifa b. Imo
Taḥlifa Ma'araba (the Palestinian)
Taḥlifa b. Samuel
Tanḥum b. Ammi
Tanḥum of Bosra
*Tanḥum b. Ḥanilai
Tanḥum b. Ḥanina
*Tanḥum b. Ḥiyya
Tanḥum b. Ḥiyya b. Abba
Tanḥum b. Ḥiyya of Kefar Agin
Tanḥum b. Ḥiyya of Kefar Akko
*Tanḥum b. Jeremiah
*Tanḥuma b. Abba
*Tanḥuma b. Judah
Tanḥum of Parwad
Tanḥum b. Skolastiḳai
Tanḥuma
Tarayya
Ṭayyefa Simmuḳa
Tobi b. Isaac
Tobi b. Ḳaṭṭina
Tobi b. Ḳisna
Tobi b. Mattanah
Tobi b. Nehemiah
Totai
'Uḳba b. Abba
'Uḳba b. Ḥama
'Uḳba b. Hiyya
'Uḳba, Mar
'Uḳba of Meshan
'Uḳba of Pashronya
'Uḳba, Rabbana
Ulla b. Abba
Ulla b. Ashi
Ulla of Biri
Ulla of Cæsarea
Ulla Ḥazzana
Ulla b. Ḥinena
Ulla b. Idi
Ulla b. Ilai
Ulla b. Ishmael
Ulla b. Menasya
Ulla b. Rab
Ulla Rabbah
Uzziel (grandson of Uzziel Rabbah)
Uzziel b. Neḥunya
*Yannai
*Yannai (grandson of Yannai the Elder)
Yannai b. Ammi
Yannai of Cappadocia
*Yannai b. Ishmael
Yannai b. Naḥmani
Yannai Ze'era (the little one)
Yeba (father-in-law of Ashyan)

Yeba Saba (the old one)
Yemar
Yemar of Difte
Yemar b. Ḥashwai
Yemar Saba (the old one)
Yemar b. Shazbi
Yemar b. Shelmia
*Yudan (father of Mattaniah)
Yudan b. Aibu
Yudan of Cappadocia
*Yudan of Magdala
*Yudan b. Phila
Yudan of Saknin
Yudan b. Shakli
Zabda
Zabda (father of Abba)
*Zabda b. Levi
*Zakkai
Zakkai of Alexandria
*Zakkai the Butcher (Ṭabbaḥa)
Zakkai the Great (Rabbah)
Zakkai of Kabul
*Zakkai of Shab
*Zebid
Zebid of Nehardea
Zebid b. Osha'ya
Zebulun b. Don (B)
Zechariah
Zechariah (son-in-law of Joshua b. Levi)
*Ze'era (P)
Ze'era b. Abbahu (P)
Ze'era b. Ḥama (P)
Ze'era b. Ḥanina (P)
Ze'era or Zera (B and P)
Zemina (P)
*Zerika
Zerika (brother-in-law of Zerikan)
Zerikan
Zuga
Zuga or Zawwa of Adiabene
Zuṭi
Zuṭra b. Huna
Zuṭra, Mar (the colleague of [Ashi)
Zuṭra, Mar (the great)
Zuṭra, Mar (the pious)
Zuṭra b. Mari
Zuṭra b. Naḥman
Zuṭra b. Rishba
Zuṭra b. Samuel
Zuṭra b. Tobia
Zuṭra b. Ze'era

J. L. G.

ṬARFON (Greek, Τρύφων; Yer. Bik. 64c): Tanna of the third generation, living in the period between the destruction of the Temple and the fall of Bethar. He was of priestly lineage, and he expressly states that he officiated in the Temple with the priests (Yer. Yoma iii. 7); in the pride of his rank he used to demand the heave-offering even after the Temple had fallen (Tosef., Ḥag. iii., end). His devotion to his mother was such that he used to place his hands beneath her feet when she was obliged to cross the courtyard barefoot (Ḳid. 61b), while his generosity made him return to the father the redemption-money for the first-born, although it was his priestly perquisite (Tosef., Bek. vi. 14). Once, in a time of famine, he took 300 wives so that they might, as wives of a priest, exercise the right of sharing in the tithes (Tosef., Ket. v. 1). On one occasion, when from his window he saw a bridal procession evidently of the poorer classes, he requested his mother and sister to anoint the bride that the groom might find more joy in her (Ab. R. N. xli., end). Although he was blessed with riches, he possessed extraordinary modesty; in one instance he deeply regretted having mentioned his name in a time of peril, since he feared that in using his position as teacher to escape from danger he had seemingly violated the rule against utilizing knowledge of the Torah for practical ends (Ned. 62b).

Although as a halakist R. Ṭarfon was an adherent of the school of Shammai, only two passages describe him as following its teachings (Yeb. 15b; Yer. Sheb. iv. 20), and he always inclined toward leniency in the interpretation of those halakot of Shammai which had not actually been put into practise (Kil. v. 6; Yeb. xv. 6; Ket. v. 2); often he decided in direct opposition to the Bet Shammai when it imposed restrictions of excessive severity (Yeb. xv. 47; Naz. v. 5). R. Ṭarfon was also the author of independent halakot, one being on the form of benediction when quenching thirst with water (Ber. vi. 8), and another on the benediction for the eve of the Passover (Pes. x. 6). The majority of his rulings, however, deal with subjects discussed in the orders Nashim, Ḳodashim, Ṭohorot, and Neziḳin. In those found in Ṭohorot his tendency is always toward severity, while in Neziḳin are found his sayings on lost objects and usufruct (B. M. iv. 3, v. 7), the payment of debts, the money due a woman when she receives a bill of divorce (Ket. ix. 2, 3), and damage caused by cattle (B. Ḳ. ii. 5, and the baraitot connected with this passage, p. 26). If he had belonged to the Sanhedrin, the death-penalty would have been abolished (Mak. i. 10; comp. Frankel, "Der Gerichtliche Beweis," p. 48, Berlin, 1846). R. Ṭarfon engaged in halakic controversies with R. Akiba (Ket. 84a; Pes. 117, 118), but the two agreed with regard to a tosefta (Miḳ. i.; Ḳid. 66; Yer. Yoma i. 1; Ter. iv. 5; Mak. i. 10; Ker. v. 3), with R. Simeon (Men. xii. 5; possibly, however, an error for R. Akiba), and R. Eleazar ben Azariah (Yad. iv. 3). Other sayings of his have been preserved which were accepted without controversy (Pes. 117a, 118a; Giṭ. 83a); and two of his apothegms are especially noteworthy as indicating his intense earnestness: "The day is short, the labor vast, the toilers idle, the reward great, and the Master urgent" (Ab. i. 15); "It is not thy task to complete the work, neither art thou a free man that thou canst withdraw thyself; if thou hast learned much, great shall be thy reward, for He that doth hire thee will surely repay thee for thy toil; yet the requital of the pious is in the future" (Ab. i. 17). In the discussion as to the relative importance of theory and practise, Ṭarfon decided in favor of the latter.

When Eliezer ben Hyrcanus was sick, and a deputation was sent to him, R. Ṭarfon acted as the spokesman, addressing him as follows: "Master, thou art of more worth to Israel than the sun, for that gives light only on earth, while thou dost shed thy rays both in this world and in the world to come" (Sanh. 101a; Mek., Baḥodesh, xi. [ed. Weiss, p. 80a]). In like manner he led a number of scholars in a visit to R. Ishmael ben Elisha, upon the death of the sons of the latter (M. Ḳ. 28b);

and when Jose the Galilean, R. Ṭarfon, R. Eliezer ben Azariah, and R. Akiba assembled to decide on the disputed sayings of Eliezer ben Hyrcanus, Tarfon was the first speaker (Tosef., Giṭ. vii.; Giṭ. 83a). He was one of those whose names occurred in the deposition of Gamaliel II., and it is expressly stated that he was addressed as "brother" by the other scholars. He is said to have dwelt at Jabneh, although it is evident that he lived also in Lydda (Ta'an. iii. 9; B. M. iv. 3; Hag. 18a).

R. Ṭarfon was accustomed to open his haggadic discourses with a halakic question (Tosef., Ber. iv. 16). In his own upper chamber at Jabneh it was decided that benevolence should be practised according to the injunction of Ps. cvi. 3 (Esth. R. vi. 2, 5). Ṭarfon held that God did not allow His glory to overshadow Israel until the people had fulfilled a task (Ab. R. N. ii.), and that death can overtake one only when he is idle (comp. Gen. xlix. 33).

On festivals and holy days R. Ṭarfon was accustomed to delight his wife and children by preparing for them the finest fruits and dainties (Yer. Pes. 37b). When he wished to express approval of any one, he would say, "'A knop and a flower' [Ex. xxv. 33]; them hast spoken as beautifully as the adornments of the candlestick in the Temple"; but when it was necessary to upbraid another, he would say, "'My son shall not go down with you'" (Gen. R. xci.), repeating the words of Jacob to his sons in Gen. xlii. 38. When he perceived that his two nephews, whom he was instructing personally, were becoming careless, he interrupted his lecture and regained their attention by saying, "Then again Abraham took a wife, and her name was Johanna" (instead of Keturah; Gen. xxv. 1), whereupon his pupils interrupted him by exclaiming, "No, Keturah!" (Zeb. 26b). His chief scholars were R. Judah ('Er. 45b; Yeb. 101b), Simeon Shezari (Men. 31b), and Judah ben Isaiah ha-Bosem (Ḥul. 55b).

R. Ṭarfon was extremely bitter against those Jews who had been converted to the new faith; and he swore that he would burn every book of theirs which should fall into his hands (Shab. 116a), his feeling being so intense that he had no scruples against destroying the Gospels, although the name of God occurred frequently in them.

BIBLIOGRAPHY: Frankel, *Hodegetica in Mischnam*, pp. 101–105, Leipsic, 1859: Brüll. *Einleitung in die Mischna*, i. 100–103, Frankfort-on-the-Main, 1876; Bacher, *Ag. Tan.* pp. 342–352; Hamburger, *R. B. T.* ii. 1196; Derenbourg, *Hist.* pp. 379 *et seq.* A list of the mishnayot which mention R. Ṭarfon is given by Schürer, *Gesch.* il. 378, note 137; of the Tosefta passages in which his name occurs, by Zuckermandel in his edition of the Tosefta; of similar sections in the Mekilta, Sifra, and Sifre, by Hoffmann, *Zur Einleitung in die HalacMscnen Midraschim*, p. 85, Berlin, 1887.

W. B. S. O.

TEḤINA, ABBA (called also **Teḥina ben Perisha** ["the Pharisee"] or **Ḥasida** ["the pious one"]): A leader of the Zealots. Together with ELEAZAR BEN DINAI, he is mentioned in the remarkable dictum of Johanan ben Zakkai concerning the Zealots: "Since the murderers have increased, the expiation ceremony of the 'eglah 'arufah [the heifer whose neck is broken for a murder the perpetrator of which is unknown; Deut. xxi. 1–9] has come into abeyance because of the many murders by these only too well-known Zealots. Such murderers are Eleazar ben Dinai and Teḥina, who was formerly called 'the Pharisee' and later on received the name of 'the Murderer'" (Soṭah ix. 9; Sifre, Deut. 205).

This Teḥina has aptly been identified by Derenbourg ("Essai sur l'Histoire et la Géographie de la Palestine d'Après les Thalmuds et les Autres Sources Rabbiniques," i. 279–280, Paris, 1867) with the Abba Teḥina Hasida of Eccl. R. ix. 7. Derenbourg, however, takes the epithet "Ḥasid" to be ironical; but he ignores the very nature of the passage to which he refers and which is as follows: "Teḥina the Essene [Ḥasid] with the title Abba [see Köhler, "Abba, Father," in "J. Q. R" xiii. 567–575], returning to his native town on Friday afternoon shortly before the beginning of the Sabbath, and carrying upon his shoulder a bundle containing the provisions for his household for the Sabbath, met a disease-stricken man unable to move, who asked him to have pity on him and bring him into the town, where his wants might receive the necessary attention. This placed Teḥina in a quandary: he was afraid if he left his bundle he might lose all his Sabbath provisions; and if he did not aid the sick man, he (Teḥina) would be accounted as guilty of death. His better impulses proving victorious, he carried the sick man to a safe place, and then went back for his bundle. Meanwhile it had grown dark; and the people, seeing him carry a bundle on Sabbath eve, wondered, saying, 'Is this Abba Teḥina the Pious?' Teḥina himself was in doubt as to whether he had really violated the Sabbath, when a miracle happened: God caused the sun again to shine forth to show that the Sabbath had not yet begun, as it is written (Mal. iii. 20 [A. V. iv. 2]): 'But unto you that fear my name shall the sun of righteousness arise with healing in his wings.'" Later the punctilious Essene became a fierce Zealot.

Eleazar ben Dinai is mentioned by Josephus several times, while Teḥina is not. He has been identified with the Alexander mentioned together with Eleazar b. Dinai by that author (Josephus, "B. J." ii. 12, § 4; see ELEAZAR BEN DINAI); but Alexander appears to be identical with Amram, cited as companion of Ben Dinai in "Ant." xx. 1, §1 (comp. Cant. R. iii. 5: "In the days of Amram [?] and in the days of Ben Dinai they attempted to bring about the Messianic time by violence"; see Grätz, "Gesch." 3d ed., iii. 431), whereas it is quite possible that Teḥina is identical with 'Αννιβας who was executed by order of Fadus (Josephus, "Ant." *l.c.*; Grätz, *l.c.* p. 278).

K.

U

ULLA (עלא; called **Rab 'Ula** in Ket. 65b and Ḳid. 31a): One of the leading halakic amoraim in Palestine during the latter part of the third and in the beginning of the fourth century. In his youth he studied under R. Eleazar II. (Tos. to Hul. 34a, *s.v.* "Man Ḥabraya"); and he transmitted nine of his teacher's halakic sayings, seven of which are contained in B. Ḳ. 11, end, one in 'Er. 21b, and one in Ket. 74a. He was greatly respected for his learning; and during his visits to Babylonia he seems to have been invited frequently by the "resh galuta" to deliver halakic lectures (Ket. 65b; Kid. 31a; Shab. 157b). He traveled repeatedly to Babylonia; and on one of his journeys he was in danger of assassination by one of his companions, saving his life only by condoning the murder of another (Ned. 22a).

Ulla rendered important decisions regarding the benedictions and the calculation of the new moon, and was accustomed to promulgate his rulings in Babylonia when he went thither (Ber. 38b; R. H. 22b; Pes. 53b, 104b). He was very strict in his interpretation of religious laws (Shab. 147a, 157b); and on one occasion, when he heard R. Huna use an expression which he did not approve, he retorted, "As vinegar to the teeth, and as smoke to the eyes, so are the words of R. Huna," applying to him the first half of Prov. x. 26 (Ḳid. 45b). Only in the presence of R. Naḥman did Ulla hesitate to pronounce his opinions, generally waiting until the former had departed (Giṭ. 11b, 12a); although he frequently sought Naḥman's company (Ket. 53a). Of his contemporaries with whom he engaged in controversies may be mentioned, besides R. Naḥman, R. Abba (B. M. 11a), Abimi bar Papa, Ḥiyya bar Ammi (Ket. 53a), and R. Judah (Ḥul. 68b, 70a); but his personal friend, with whom he associated most frequently, was Rabbah bar bar Ḥana (Tosef., Ḥul. xxxiv. 1).

In addition to the sayings of his teacher Eleazar, Ulla transmitted those of R. Hoshaiah (Ḥul. 76a), Joshua ben Levi (*ib.* 122a), R. Johanan ('Er. 67b), Rab (Shab. 143b), and Simeon ben Laḳish (Ḥag. 8b), while his own sayings were transmitted by R. Aḥa bar Adda (B. M. 117b), Hamnuna (Shab. 10b), Ḥiyya bar Abba (Ḥag. 25b), Ḥiyya bar Ami (Ber. 8a), Raba bar Ḥinena (Men. 30b), R. Ḥisda (Ber. 38b), Judah bar Ammi (M. Ḳ. 5b), and Joshua bar Abba (*ib.* 5b). Raba appears to have been his only son (Shab. 83b).

Ulla died in Babylonia, before his teacher R. Eleazar; but his remains were taken to Palestine for burial (Ket. 111a).

BIBLIOGRAPHY: Heilprin, *Seder ha-Dorot,* pp. 229–230; Bacher, *Ag. Bab. Amor.*, pp. 93–97.

E. C. S. O.

UZZIEL (עזיאל): **1.** Son of Kohath and brother of Amram (Ex. vi. 18; I Chron. vi. 2). He was the father of Mishael, Elzaphan, and Zithri (Ex. vi. 22). The first two, at the bidding of Moses, carried from the Tabernacle the bodies of Nadab and Abihu, their cousins (Lev. x. 4). Elzaphan, moreover, was chief of the family of the Kohathites during the wandering in the wilderness (Num. iii. 30). Another son of Uzziel, named Amminadab, was one of the Levite chiefs selected to carry the Ark of the Covenant to the tent which David had pitched for it in Zion (I Chron. xv. 10). Two other sons of Uzziel were named respectively Micah and Jesiah (*ib.* xxiii. 20). His descendants were termed "Uzzielites" (Num. iii. 27; I Chron. xxvi. 23).

2. A Simeonite; son of Ishi; one of the chiefs who, during the reign of King Hezekiah, passed over the Jordan, annihilated the remnants of the Amalekites, and settled in their territory around Mount Seir (I Chron. iv. 41–43).

3. One of the eponymous heroes of the tribe of Benjamin; described as one of the five sons of Bela (*ib.* vii. 7).

4. (Called also **Azareel).** Son of Heman. He belonged to the eleventh order of those who were chosen by lot to serve as singers in leading the worship in the Temple during the reign of David (I Chron. xxv. 4, 18).

5. Son of Jeduthun; one of those who were chosen to resanctify the Temple during the reign of Hezekiah (II Chron. xxix. 14).

6. A goldsmith who repaired part of the walls of Jerusalem under Nehemiah (Neh. iii. 8).

E. G. H. S. O.

Y

YANNAI: Palestinian amora of the third century; father-in-law of Ammi. According to his own statement, he had a grandson of the same name (Ḥul. 111a). He is known as having taken part in a controversy regarding the succession of the writings of King Solomon, he himself maintaining that the book Ḳohelet is the last one written by him (Cant. R. i. 1).

BIBLIOGRAPHY: Bacher, *Ag. Pal. Amor.* ii. 145a, iii. 573–574; Heilprin, *Seder ha-Dorot,* ii. 116d.

J. S. O.

YANNAI: First payyeṭan to employ rime and introduce his name in acrostics; flourished, probably in Palestine, in the first half of the seventh century. He was apparently a very prolific poet, for reference is made to "the liturgical poems of Yannai"; he is also said to have composed "ḳerobot" for the "orders of the year" (perhaps for the weekly lessons). Most of his poems are lost; some are perhaps still extant, but they can not be recognized with certainty as Yannai's work. The following fragments alone remain to show his style:

1. אוני פטרי רחמתים: A "ḳerobah" for Sabbath ha-Gadol. It is said to include also אז רוב נסים הפלאת בלילה, found in the Pesaḥ Haggadah.

2. שיר השירים אשירה נא לידידי: A "shib'ata" for the seventh day of Pesaḥ. The middle portion is missing. It is designated as דרמושה (this reading must be substituted for the senseless לרמושה in the superscription), *i.e.*, "bolt" or "beam" (*δρόμος*, otherwise called רהיט), and forms a sort of textual variation of Canticles, following the conception and interpretation of that book in the Midrash.

3. תעו אז בפתרוס: A "silluḳ" for Sabbath Shim'u, *i.e.*, the second Sabbath before the Ninth of Ab.

Yannai, like his predecessor Jose b. Jose, is not as obscure in his vocabulary and in his metaphors as is Ḳalir, who is said to have been Yannai's pupil and to have been killed by his master out of jealousy. The extant examples of Yannai's work do not indicate any great poetic talent.

BIBLIOGRAPHY: Rapoport, in *Bikkure ha-'Ittim*, 1829, p. 111; *idem*, in *Kerem Ḥemed*, 1841, vi. 25; Luzzatto, *Mebo*, p. 10; Zunz, *Literaturgesch.* p. 28; Landshuth, *'Ammude ha-'Abodah*, p. 102; Harkavy, *Studien und Mittheilungen*, v. 106; S. A. Wertheimer, *Ginze Yerushalayim*, ii. 18b.

D. H. B.

YANNAI (known also as **Yannai Rabbah** = "the Great"): Palestinian amora of the first generation (2d and 3d cent.). A genealogical chart found at Jerusalem traced his descent from Eli (Yer. Ta'an. iv. 2; Gen. R. xcviii. 13). Yannai was very wealthy; he is said to have planted four hundred vineyards (B. B. 14a) and to have given an orchard to the public (M. Ḳ. 12b). His first residence was at Sepphoris (Yer. Ber. iv. 6 *et al.*), where he seems to have held a public office, since at the death of R. Judah ha-Nasi I. (Rabbi) he gave an order that even priests might attend the funeral of the great teacher (*ib.* iii. 1). Halevy, however, has concluded that Yannai always lived at 'Akbarah, or 'Akbari, where he established a school (see below).

Yannai was prominent both as halakist and haggadist. He was a pupil of Rabbi, in whose name he transmitted several halakic sayings (Yer. Hag. iii. 2; Yer. Ḳid. iii. 14; *et al.*). The best known of his senior fellow pupils was Ḥiyya Rabbah, who, as an assistant teacher in Rabbi's school, sometimes acted as Yannai's tutor (Yer. Dem. vii. 1; Yeb. 93a). But several discussions between Ḥiyya and Yannai (Yer. Ber. iv. 5, and Babli *passim*) show the real relationship. Their friendship was afterward cemented by the marriage of Yannai's daughter to Ḥiyya's son Judah (Yer. Bik. iii. 3; Ket. 62b). Yannai transmitted also some halakot in the name of the council ("ḥaburah") of the last tannaim (Mak. 21b). He established an important school at 'Akbarah (Yer. 'Er. viii. 4), often mentioned in both Talmuds and in the Midrash as the "debe R. Yannai" or the "bet R. Yannai," and which continued after his death. His school differed from others in that the pupils were treated as belonging to the master's family; they worked on Yannai's estate, took their share of the revenue, and lived under his roof (comp. Yer. Sheb. viii. 6). His chief pupil, of whom he thought highly, was R. Johanan, who transmitted most of his halakot (Yer. Kil. viii. 1; Soṭah 18b; Ḳid. 64b). Others of his many pupils were Simeon b. Laḳish (Yer. Yoma iii. 10; Ta'an. ii. 6; Ḥul. 82a), R. Aibu (Ḳid. 19), and R. Hoshaiah (Ket. 79a).

In regard to the Mishnah of Rabbi he shared the opinion of Ḥiyya. In fact, Yannai ascribed no greater authority to the Mishnah than to the collections of halakot or baraitot compiled by Ḥiyya and other disciples of Rabbi (comp. Yer. Pes. i. 5; Yer. Yoma iv. 2). When his pupil R. Johanan remarked that the Mishnah rendered a decision different from his, he answered, "The Mishnah gives only the decision of a single tanna, while I decide conformably to the Rabbis as a whole" (Shab. 140a). He was independent in his decisions, and sometimes had all his contemporaries against him (Yer. Niddah iii. 4; Shab. 65a). His decisions were generally rigid as regards private persons (Yer. Ber. ii. 6; Yer. Ket. i. 10; Shab. 14a), but liberal when the whole community was concerned. Yannai's disregard of R. Judah Nesi'ah (Judah II.), Rabbi's grandson, was notorious (B. B. 111a, b), and so was his attitude toward R. Ḥanina, an ardent believer in Rabbi's Mishnah (Yer. Kil. ix. 7; Ber. 30a; *et al.*). Referring to Ḥanina, Yannai said, "He who studies the Law under only one teacher sees no sign of blessing" ('Ab. Zarah 19a).

Yannai is conspicuous in both Talmud and Midrash as a prolific haggadist, and he occupies an important place among the Biblical exegetes of his time. In reference to a man who studied much but did not fear God, he said: "Wo to the man who, before he gets a house, makes the door" (Shab. 31b). He recommended submission to the government (Zeb. 102a; Men. 98a). When old age had impaired his sight he requested Mar 'Uḳba to send him some collyrium prepared by Samuel (Shab. 108b). He enjoined his children to bury him neither in white nor in black clothes, as they would not know whether his place would be in paradise or in hell (Shab. 114a; Yer. Kil. ix. 4).

BIBLIOGRAPHY: Bacher, *Ag. Pal. Amor.* i. 35–47; Frankel, *Mebo*, p. 103a, b, Breslau, 1870; Grätz, *Gesch.* 3d ed., iv.; Halevy, *Dorot ha-Rishonim*, ii. 273–282; Heilprin, *Seder ha-Dorot*, ii.; Weiss, *Dor*, iii. 50, 51.

G. M. SEL.

YANNAI BEN ISHMAEL: Palestinian amora of the third century; a contemporary of Ze'era and of Abba bar Kahana. There exist a few halakot transmitted in his name, among them one referring to the prayer "Shomea' Tefillah" (Ta'an. 14a). A question, likewise referring to the "Shemoneh 'Esreh," is addressed to Yannai by Ze'era through R. Nahum (Yer. Ber. 5a). R. Zeriḳan quotes a halakah in the name of Yannai, referring to the circumcision of slaves (Yer. Yeb. 8d). Several haggadot of Yannai's have been preserved, among which may be mentioned one treating of Adam's meeting with the angels (B. M. 86b), and a farewell address based on the verse Judges i. 15 (Soṭah 46b). Once, during an illness, Yannai was visited by Ze'era and Abba bar Kahana (Yer. Ter. 45c), with the latter of whom he engaged in a controversy relating to Solomon's plantations.

BIBLIOGRAPHY: Bacher, *Ag. Pal. Amor.* iii. 572–573; Heilprin, *Seder ha-Dorot*, ii. 117a; Frankel, *Mebo*, p. 103b; *Yuḥasin*, ed. Filipowski, p. 15b.

J. S. O.

YANNAI THE YOUNGER: Palestinian amora of the fourth generation; called "the Younger" ("ze'era") to distinguish him from Yannai b. Ishmael. When his father-in-law died Yannai was exempted from the priestly laws of purity in order that he might attend to the interment of the dead (Yer. Ber. 6a; Yer. Naz. 6i). A sentence treating of the importance of an oath and how it is to be made has been preserved in Lev. R. vi. It appears that at Yannai's funeral his pupils did not follow current customs, for which reason they were reproved by R. Mani (Yer. M. Ḳ. 82c).

BIBLIOGRAPHY: Bacher, *Ag. Pal. Amor.* ii. 442, note 5; iii. 448, 623; Frankel, *Mebo*, pp. 103b–104a; Heilprin, *Seder ha-Dorot*, p. 116d.

J. S. O.

* **YIẒḤAḲ (ISAAC):** Tanna of the early post-Hadrianic period (2d cent. C.E.); a halakic exegete whose Biblical exegesis mostly belongs to the Mekilta and the Sifre. In the Tosefta he transmits sayings in the name of Eliezer ben Hyrcanus (Ter. i. 1, 15; ii. 5). He was a disciple of Ishmael, but associated also with the pupils of Akiba, with one of whom, named Nathan, he originated a halakah (Mek., Ex. xii. 2). He was also intimate with Jonathan and with the proselyte sons of Judah

* Through a misunderstanding a number of Talmudic authorities named "Isaac" were not treated under that heading; they are here entered under the transliterated Hebrew form of the name.

in the yeshibah of Simeon ben Yoḥai (Gen. R. xxxv.; M. Ḳ. 9a; Pesiḳ. 87b). Of his non-halakic exegeses may be mentioned: on Ex. xii. 7: "The blood upon the doors at Passover shall serve the Egyptians as tortures for their souls" (Mek.); on Ex. xx. 9: "Count the days of the week after the Sabbath" (*l.c.*); on Deut. xiv. 11: "Unclean birds are called עוף, while clean are called either עוף or צפור" (Sifre); on Ezek. i.: "The paragraph treating of the chariot of God extends to the word חשמל only" (Ḥag. 13a). Another of his sayings is: "The prayer in need is adapted to all occasions" (R. H. 18a).

Bibliography: Bacher, *Ag. Tan.* ii. 387–399; Weiss, *Einleitung zur Mekilta*, p. 33, Vienna, 1865; Frankel, *Hodegetica in Mischnam*, p. 203, note 3.

J. S. O.

YIẒḤAḲ BAR ADDA: Palestinian amora of uncertain period. He interpreted Ps. xcii. 13 as meaning that even as the shade of the palm-tree extends far and wide, so shall the reward of the pious extend to the future world (Shoḥer Ṭob to Ps. xcii.; Gen. R. xl., beginning). With reference to Ps. lvii. 9, he said that David procured an eolian harp in order that its tones might awaken him for midnight prayer (Ber. 4a).

Bibliography: Bacher, *Ag. Pal. Amor.* iii. 767 and note 7.

J. S. O.

YIẒḤAḲ HA-BABLI: Palestinian amora. His period is unknown. Two haggadot of his are extant. The king Melchizedek, who went to meet Abraham, was called Salem, says Yiẓḥaḳ, because he was perfect; that is, he had early submitted to circumcision (Gen. R. xliii. 7). With reference to Jacob's promise, the amora interprets the words "Which my lips have uttered, and my mouth hath spoken when I was in trouble" (Ps. lxvi. 14) by saying that one makes a vow when in need, in order to keep the commandments of the Torah (Gen. R. lxx. 1; Midrash Shemuel ii.).

Bibliography: Bacher, *Ag. Pal. Amor.* ii. 209, iii. 768.

J. S. O.

YIẒḤAḲ B. ELEAZAR OF CÆSAREA: Palestinian amora of the fourth century. He was a teacher of law in the old synagogue of Cæsarea, where he was so loved by pupils and friends that Jacob of Kefar Nibburaya placed him as high in this synagogue as is God Himself in the Temple of Zion (Yer. Bik. 65d; Midrash Shemuel vii. 6). The following halakic decisions of his may be mentioned: one concerning sale and purchase, rendered to his pupil Hoshaiah b. Shammai (Yer. M. Ḳ. 81b); another on religious law in a case referred to him by Samuel bar Abdimi (Yer. Shab. 16d); a ruling concerning fraud (Suk. 35b); instruction in regard to the writing of a letter of divorce (B. B. 163a); halakic deduction to the effect that, although a tithe of dates need not be rendered, honey made from them must be tithed (Yer. Bik. 63d); decision concerning marital law (Yer. Ḳid. 63b); regarding signs for detecting murder upon finding a corpse (Yer. Naz. 57d); and a halakah concerning the lifting of the terumah (Yer. Dem. 26b). He appears as a traditionist of Jeremiah (Lev. R. xxxiii. 2) and of Naḥman bar Jacob (Yer. Shab. 9a), and was famed for his gastronomical art (Lam. R. to iii. 17; Yer. Ber. 61c; Yer. Ḥag. 78a). He gives examples of the ban from the Mishnah (Yer. M. Ḳ. 81a), and a prescription in accordance with them (Yer. Ta'an. 69b).

In the vicinity of Cæsarea is a cliff extending into the sea. One day as Yiẓḥaḳ was walking along this cliff he saw a large bone on the ground, and tried several times to cover it with earth, so that no one should stumble over it; but his efforts were unsuccessful, as the bone became uncovered as fast as he heaped the earth upon it. He accordingly considered the bone to be an instrument of God, and waited patiently to see what would happen. Soon afterward an imperial messenger named Veredarius came that way, stumbled on the bone, and died as a result of his fall; this messenger had been sent to Cæsarea bearing malicious edicts against the Jews (Gen. R. x. 7; Lev. R. xxii. 4; Num. R. xviii.; Eccl. R. to v. 8). In answer to a question as to how it came about that two great prophets like Jeremiah and Daniel should suppress attributes of God which had been given Him by Moses himself, he said that these prophets knew that God was a lover of truth, and that any dissimulation on their part would have been punishable (Yer. Ber. 13c; Meg. 74c). He made a comparison between wisdom and humility (Yer. Shab. 3c); and he explained the expression הלעיטני in Gen. xxv. 30 by a comparison with the insatiability of Rome, saying that Esau sat like a camel with jaws wide open and that Jacob had to fill his mouth with food (Pesiḳ. R. xvi.; Pesiḳ. 59a). Yiẓḥaḳ, moreover, connected the expression וישטם in Gen. xxvii. 41 with the word "senator," in order more clearly to express Rome's hatred of Judah (Yer. 'Ab. Zarah 39c).

Yiẓḥaḳ must be distinguished from an amora of the same name who lived half a century earlier, and in whose house Ḥiyya bar Abba, Ammi, and Yiẓḥaḳ Nappaḥa used to assemble to study (Ḥag. 26a; 'Ab. Zarah 24a; M. Ḳ. 20a). This earlier amora delivered a funeral address at the death of Johanan (M. Ḳ. 25b; but see Bacher ["Ag. Pal. Amor." iii. 718, note 4] for different version).

BIBLIOGRAPHY: Frankel, *Mebo*, p. 107a; Heilprin, *Seder ha-Dorot*, il. 238; Bacher, *Ag. Pal. Amor.* iii. 717–719.

J. S. O.

YIẒḤAḲ BEN ḤAḲOLA: Palestinian amora of the third century. He was a contemporary of Joshua ben Levi and Johanan, and belonged to the school of Eleazar ben Pedat. He transmitted halakot in the names of Abba ben Zabda, Judah II. (Yer. 'Er. 24d), Hezekiah ('Orlah i. 2), and Simeon (Yer. Suk. i., end; Ket. ii. 8). There has been preserved a haggadah by him dealing with the quarrel between the shepherds of Abimelech and those of Abraham, and with the settlement of the dispute (Gen. R. liv., end).

BIBLIOGRAPHY: Bacher, *Ag. Pal. Amor.* i. 109, ii. 206, iii. 588–589; Frankel, *Mebo*, 107a; Heilprin, *Seder ha-Dorot*, ii. 238.

J. S. O.

YIẒḤAḲ BEN ḤIYYA THE SCRIBE: Palestinian amora of the fourth century; contemporary of Mani. He was well known as a scribe, and was the author of a halakah in which he asserted that Torah scrolls might be written on various parchments, but that this rule did not apply in the case of tefillin and mezuzot (Yer. Meg. p. 71c). In the name of Johanan he transmitted a halakah relating to the marriage law (Yer. Yeb. 14a). Three other haggadot by him have been preserved: (1) on the future fate of the good and the wicked (Gen. R. lxiv. 4); (2) explaining why Saul did not consult the Urim and Thummim instead of the witch of En-dor (Lev. R. xxvi. 7; Midr. Shemuel xxiv. 6); and (3) setting forth that the Torah is compared to the tree of life (Prov. iii. 18) because it is equal in value to all living men (Midr. Shoḥer Ṭob to Ps. i. 19).

BIBLIOGRAPHY: Bacher, *Ag. Pal. Amor.* iii. 449 (note 8), 716–717; Heilprin, *Seder ha-Dorot*, ii. 241.

J. S. O.

YIẒḤAḲ BAR JOSEPH: Palestinian amora of the third and fourth centuries. He was a pupil of Abbahu and of Johanan, and transmitted almost entirely in the name of the latter. It is related that he was once about to be killed by a spirit to which he was speaking, when a cedar-tree saved him (Sanh. 101a; Rashi on the passage). It was said to be due to him that the Samaritans were declared to be a heathen people, the following narrative being told in this connection: "Yiẓḥaḳ was once sent into the Samaritan district to purchase wine, and met there an old man who told him that no one in that region observed the laws. The amora returned with this report to Abbahu, and the latter, together with Ammi and Assi, declared the Samaritans to be heathens" (Ḥul. 6a; comp. also Rashi and the Tosafot on the passage).

In his teacher's company Yiẓḥaḳ often visited Usha, by whom the taḳḳanot were enacted; and he attended lectures in a yeshibah in that city (Ḳid. 50a; Pes. 72a). It was he who brought most of these taḳḳanot to the knowledge of the Babylonians; he was in fact one of the most prominent intermediaries between Palestine and Babylonia in matters pertaining to religious decisions, and was greatly respected in the latter country, being on terms of intimate friendship with Abaye (Ber. 42b).

Thirteen halakic decisions transmitted by Yiẓḥaḳ in the name of Johanan have been preserved: regarding circumcision on Yom Kippur (Yeb. 64b); on an undecided question (Shab. 45b); on the difference between Palestine and Babylonia with reference to 'erub ('Er. 22a); on the ḥaliẓah (Yeb. 104a); on the testimony of two witnesses before a court of law (Sanh. 4a); five sentences regarding ṭerefah (Ḥul. 43a); on sexual intercourse (Niddah 65b); on sacrifices (Tem. 26a); and on the gall and liver of slaughtered animals (Ḥul. 48a). He transmitted also three halakic maxims in the name of Yannai: two on the custom of washing the hands (Ḥul. 105b) and one on Nazir (Naz. 42b).

In addition to his occasional journeys in Palestine in the company of Abbahu, Yiẓḥaḳ is once mentioned as undertaking a journey to Babylonia, where he associated with Abaye, as well as with Rabin and Pappa, the sons-in-law of Yiẓḥaḳ Nappaḥa (Ḥul. 110a). Yiẓḥaḳ relates that Judah I. had a private entrance to his yeshibah in order to spare his pupils the inconvenience of rising when he entered (Men. 33a).

BIBLIOGRAPHY: Bacher, *Ag. Pal. Amor.* i. 420; ii. 96, 211; iii. 99, 402, 520; Heilprin, *Seder ha-Dorot*, ii. 240.

J. S. O.

YIẒḤAḲ BAR JUDAH: Babylonian amora of the fourth century; a junior contemporary of Ulla. He was educated at his father's house in Pumbedita; and once when Ulla visited there the latter expressed displeasure at the fact that Yiẓḥaḳ was not yet married (Ḳid. 71b). Yiẓḥaḳ was once told by his father to go to Nehardea in order to see how Ulla pronounced the Habdalah benediction at the close of the Sabbath; but Yiẓḥaḳ sent Abaye in his place, and for so doing was severely reprimanded by his father (Pes. 104b). Yiẓḥaḳ was a pupil of various scholars. First he attended the lectures of Rabbah (Sheb. 36b), and later those of Rami bar Ḥama, whom he soon left in order to study under R. Sheshet, Rami bitterly reproaching him for the slight. Among Yiẓḥaḳ's nearest friends and companions may be mentioned Aḥa bar Ḥana; Samuel, son of Rabbah bar bar Ḥana (Sheb. 36b); and Rami bar Samuel.

BIBLIOGRAPHY: Bacher, *Ag. Pal. Amor.* ii. 299; Heilprin, *Seder ha-Dorot*, ii. 242b.

J. S. O.

YIẒḤAḲ OF MAGDALA: Palestinian amora of the third century. He engaged in various midrashic controversies. Among them was one with Levi concerning I Kings vii. 50 (Cant. R. on iii. 10), and another with Kahana concerning Joseph's abstention from wine after his imprisonment by his brothers (Shab. 139a; Gen. R. xcii., xcviii.). With reference to the saying that the curse inflicted upon the world consists in the bringing forth of gnats, flies, and other insects, Yiẓḥaḳ states that even these creatures are of use in the world (Gen. R. v. 9).

BIBLIOGRAPHY: Bacher, *Ag. Pal. Amor.* i. 443, ii. 448, iii. 588; A. Perles, in *Bet Talmud*, i. 153; Heilprin, *Seder ha-Dorot*, p. 241a.

J. S. O.

YIẒḤAḲ BEN MARYON: Palestinian amora of the third century; contemporary of Eleazar ben Pedat (Yer. Suk. 53a). He transmitted some haggadic maxims in the names of Ḥanina (Eccl. R. ix. 12) and Jose ben Ḥanina (Pesiḳ. 99a). With reference to Gen. ii. 4 and 8 he remarked that since God is proud of His creation, no one may venture to find fault with it (Gen. R. xii. on xv. 5). Commenting on II Sam. xx. 21, he states that he who offends a great man is just as guilty as he who offends the king himself (Eccl. R. on ix. 18). Other haggadic maxims of his have been preserved as follows: on Gen. xxxi. 86 and I Sam. xx. 1 (Gen. R. lxxiv. 10); on Ezek. xxi. 21 (Shoḥer Ṭob to Ps. lxxviii. 19); on Job ii. 4 (Eccl. R. to iii. 9); and on Ruth ii. 14 (Lev. R. xxxiv. 8).

BIBLIOGRAPHY: Bacher, *Ag. Pal. Amor.* i. 10, 286, 327, 427; iii. 589–591; Heilprin, *Seder ha-Dorot*, p. 241a.

J. S. O.

YIẒḤAḲ BAR NAḤMAN: Palestinian amora of the third century; a friend of Jacob bar Idi, together with whom he officiated as poor-law commissioner (Yer. Sheḳ. 49a). The two friends often engaged in halakic controversies (Yer. Shab. 14d). Yiẓḥaḳ twice transmits sayings by Joshua ben Levi on the conversion of purchased slaves, Ze'era having addressed a question to him on this point (Yer. Yeb. 8d). He had a dispute with Abdima of Ḥaifa concerning some question of religious law (Yer. Niddah 50a), and also engaged in a controversy with Simeon ben Pazzi (Meg. 23a). Jacob bar Aḥa transmits a saying in his name (Yer. Yeb. 12a).

BIBLIOGRAPHY: Bacher, *Ag. Pal. Amor*, i., ii., iii.; Heilprin, *Seder ha-Dorot*, ii. 241a.

J. S. O.

YIẒḤAḲ NAPPAḤA: Palestinian amora of the third and fourth centuries. He is found under the name "Nappaḥa" only in the Babylonian Talmud, not in the Palestinian. As a haggadist he stands in the foremost rank of his contemporaries. In the Babylonian Talmud he is identified with various other Yiẓḥaḳs (Pes. 113b), and since that was due to the arbitrary action of a later amora, the real name of his father can no longer be determined. As regards the name "Nappaḥa" (the smith), there had been an older Yiẓḥaḳ of the same name, who was rich and who is said to have owned five courts in Usha; it has not yet been possible, however, to ascertain any relationship between the two, and if the elder was an ancestor of this Yiẓḥaḳ, the latter could well have inherited the name without ever having practised the trade. In the later midrashic literature he is called Yiẓḥaḳ Nappaḥa, whereas the older works call him only R. Yiẓḥaḳ.

Although he was a pupil of Johanan, his associations with the latter are indicated in only one passage (B. M. 24b), which tells of his once appearing before Johanan. As a traditionist of the haggadah of Johanan, he appears only in the Babylonian Talmud (Ber. 62b). He was in Babylonia only temporarily, probably soon after the death of Johanan; and while there he visited in the house of the exilarch (M. Ḳ. 24b), together with Sheshet (*ib.* 24b) and Joseph (R. H. 3b; Shab. 52b). Raba quoted in his name (Ber. 32a; Tem. 15a); but sometimes tradition maintains that it is uncertain whether the sayings originated with Yiẓḥaḳ or with Raba (Sanh. 94a; Ned. 39a; Naz. 23b). Rabbin bar Adda also cites in his name (Ber. 6a; Pes. 8b). His home was originally in Cæsarea, but he afterward went to Tiberias to live. He associated intimately with Ammi, with whom he often discussed halakic questions (Soṭah 34a; Men. 11b; Ḥag. 26a; Ber. 41a; Yoma 42b); and together they sometimes rendered decisions in matters pertaining to religious law (Ḥul. 48b; Ned. 57b; Ber. 27a). Yiẓḥaḳ, Abbahu, and Ḥanina bar Pappai constituted a board of judges (Ket. 84b; ‘Ab. Zarah 39b; Ber. 38a, b; B. Ḳ. 117b; Giṭ. 29b). Ḥelbo referred to Yiẓḥaḳ two liturgical questions addressed to him from Galilee: the first question he answered immediately; the second he expounded publicly in the seminary (Giṭ. 60a). A thesis on the creation of light, formulated anonymously, was made public by R. Yiẓḥaḳ (Gen. R. iii., beginning). He also engaged in haggadic discussions with the celebrated Levi (Gen. R. xix. 14; Pesiḳ. R. xxiii., beginning; Ber. 4a; Yer. Ta‘an. 65b); with Abba b. Kahana (Gen. R. xliii. 7; Lev. R. ii. 1; Midr. Teh. to Ps. xlix. 1); with Aḥa (Pesiḳ. R. xv.; Gen. R. v. 7; Yer. Pe’ah 15d); and with Ḥiyya bar Abba (Lev. R. xx. 7; Pesiḳ. R. xxii.). Among those who transmitted in the name of Yiẓḥaḳ were the famous halakist Haggai, the latter's sons Jonathan and Azariah (Gen. R. xxii. 18, xl. 6; Midr. Shemuel xxii., end), and Luliani ben Ṭabrin (Gen. R. *passim*; Midr. Teh. to Ps. xxiv. 4; Yer. Meg. 75c).

That Yiẓḥaḳ was a great authority on the Halakah, as well as on the Haggadah, is shown by an anecdote which is told and according to which Ammi and Assi would not let him speak, because the one wished to hear Halakah and the other Haggadah (B. Ḳ. 60b). So after telling them the celebrated story of the man who had two wives, one of whom pulled out all his white hairs because she was young, whereas the other extracted his black hairs because she was old, R. Yiẓḥaḳ presented to them a haggadah with a halakic background, in order to satisfy both at the same time. Yiẓḥaḳ, however, devoted himself to the Haggadah with more zeal, because he regarded it as a necessity in the adverse circumstances of the Jews. The poverty of the Palestinians had increased to such an extent that people no longer waited for the harvest, but ate the green ears of wheat (Gen. R. xx. 24); consequently they were in need of comfort and refreshment of soul (Pes. 101b). Yiẓḥaḳ tried to make his lectures as effective as possible, and they show him to have been an unusually forceful rhetorician and a skilful exegete.

Yiẓḥaḳ's haggadic material may be divided according to contents into the following four groups: I. Proverbs and dicta: concerning sins (Suk. 52a, b; Ḥag. 16a; Ḳid. 31a; Ber. 25a; R. H. 16b; Yoma 87a; B. B. 9b; Pes. 190b); concerning the relation of man to God (Ned. 32a; Soṭah 48b; Ruth R. i. 2); on the relation of man to his fellow beings (B. M. 42a; Meg. 28a; B. Ḳ. 93a); concerning prayer (Pes. 181a; Lev. R. xxx. 3; Midr. Shemuel i. 7; R. H. 16b; Yer. Ḳid. 61b; Yer. Ned. 41b); concerning study and the Law (Pes. 193a, b; Meg. 6b; Lev. R. ii. 1; Sanh. 21b, 24a; Ḥul. 91a; Yoma 77a); concerning Israel (Pes. 165a; Gen. R. lxiii. 8); concerning the nations (Esther R. i. 10; Lev. R. i. 14; Ex. R. xxxviii. 3); concerning Jerusalem (Pesiḳ. R. xli. 1; Pes. 6a). II. Exegesis: general (Sanh. 82a, 89a, 95b; Tem. 16a; Yer. R. H. 57c; Gen. R. liii. 20; Ḥul. 91b; Soṭah 48b; B. B. 16a); halakic (Ber. 13b; Giṭ. 59b; Pes. 31b; Yoma 77a; Yer. Soṭah 17a); Biblical personages (Gen. R. xxxiv. 11, xxxix. 7, lviii. 7; Yeb. 64a); Biblical narratives (Soṭah 34a; Deut. R. xi. 2; B. B. 91a; Midr. Teh. to Ps. vii. 13; Sanh. 106b; Men. 53b; Esther R. iii. 9; Pesiḳ. R. xxxv. 1). III. Homiletics (Gen. R. xix. 6, xxxviii. 7; Sanh. 96a; B. M. 87a; Yer. Soṭah 17b; Ex. R. xliii. 4; Sanh. 102a; Ber. 63b; Eccl. R. iii. 19; Tem. 16a; Yer. Ta'an. 65b; Hor. 10b). IV. Proems (Gen. R. iii. 1, lix. 2, lxv. 7; Pes. 101b; Ex. R. xxxii. 5; Lev. R. xii. 2); maxims (Gen. R. lvi. 1; Deut. R. ii. 27; Lev. R. xxxiv. 8); similes (Yer. R. H. 57b; Lev. R. v. 6; Ex. R. xv. 16; Yer. Ber. 13a; B. B. 74b); Messianic subjects (Eccl. R. i. 11; Deut. R. i. 19; 'Ab. Zarah 3b); eschatology (Lev. R. xiii. 3; Midr. Teh. to Ps. xlix. 1; Shab. 152a; B. M. 83b).

According to the unanimous testimony of several writers of the tenth century, the gaon Hai b. David ascribed to Yiẓḥaḳ Nappaḥa the calculation of the Rabbinite calendar. The only fact known concerning Yiẓḥaḳ's family is that his daughter married the Babylonian amora Pappa (Ḥul. 110a).

BIBLIOGRAPHY: Bacher, Ag. Pal. Amor. ii. 205–295: Frankel, Mebo, pp. 106b–107a; Heilprin, Seder ha-Dorot, ii., s.v.; S. Pinsker, Liḳḳuṭe Ḳadmoniyyot, ii. 148–151; Al-Ḳirḳisani, ed. Harkavy, in Publ. Kaiserliche Russische Archœologische Gesellschaft, 1894, vii. 293; Weiss, Dor, iii. 98 et seq.

J.　　　　　　　　　　　　　　　　　　　　　　　　　　　S. O.

YIẒḤAḲ BEN PARNAK: Palestinian amora of uncertain period. He is named as the author of an apocryphal work entitled פרק ר' יצחק בן פרנך מגיהנם, which describes the events that take place at the death of a human being. When a man is dying three angels come to his bedside—the angel of death, the recording angel, and the guardian angel; and these three review his entire life. If he has been a pious man, three more angels appear; and while the struggle with death is going on one of these angels recites Isa. lvii. 1, the second *ib.* lvii. 2, and the third *ib.* lviii. 8. At last four more angels descend to the bedside; and when the dying man cries out to the earth to help him, the first angel answers him with the words of Ps. xxiv. 1; when he implores the aid of his relatives, the second angel recites Ps. xlix. 8 (A. V. 7); when he turns to his money for solace, the third angel answers him with Ps. xlix. 9 (A. V. 8); and when he appeals to his good deeds, the fourth angel recites Isa. lviii. 8. There is clearly some influence here of the Buddhist legend of "The Three Friends" (comp. "Barlaam and Josaphat," ed. Jacobs, Appendix). Yiẓḥaḳ's father, Parnak, transmitted in the name of Johanan (Gen. R. liii., end; M. Ḳ. 9a; Shab. 14a; B. M. 85a).

BIBLIOGRAPHY: Bacher, *Aq. Pal. Amor.* i. 219, note 3; iii. 767–768; Jellinek, *Bet ha-Midrash*, v. 48–49, Vienna, 1873.

J. S. O.

YIẒḤAḲ BAR REDIFA: Palestinian amora of the fourth century; the transmitter of the haggadah of R. Ammi (Lev. R. xii., beginning; Ex. R. xlii., end; Yer. Sheḳ. 48a; Ex. R. iii. to Ex. iii. 14). He once requested the amora Jeremiah to decide a question, but received only an evasive reply (Yer. Sheb. 39a). He was the author of several explanations of the stories concerning Samson (Soṭah 9b). Especial mention should be made of his interpretation of the word תעכסנה in Isa. iii. 16, which he derives from the Greek ἔχις ("serpent"), saying: "The women used to place myrrh and balsam in their shoes, and when meeting young men in the streets they stamped their feet so that a strong odor arose which awakened evil impulses in the youths, as though they were under the influence of a serpent's poison" (Shab. 62b).

Yiẓḥaḳ transmitted dissertations on the salvation of the tribe of Benjamin, with reference to Judges xxi. 7 (B. B. 116a); on the list of idolatrous priests referred to in Hosea xiii. 2 (Sanh. 62a); on the pronunciation of the words "Praised be the name of His glorious kingdom" (ב"ש"כ"מל"ו) after the "Shema'" (Pes. 56a); on the act of rising when the name of God is uttered, as deduced from Judges iii. 20 (Sanh. 60a); and on the assumption of the sex of an expected child, with reference to Lev. xii. 2 (Ber. 60a; Niddah 25b, 31a).

BIBLIOGRAPHY: Bacher, *Ag. Pal. Amor. i.* 518, note 1; ii. 151, note 6; iii. 719–720; Rabbinovicz, *Diḳduḳe Soferim*, ix. 169; Heilprin, *Seder ha-Dorot*, ii. 241; Frankel, *Mebo*, pp. 90a, 107b.

J. S. O.

YIẒḤAḲ BEN SAMUEL BEN MARTA: Babylonian amora of the third and fourth centuries. He was a pupil of R. Naḥman, to whom he directed questions relating to sacrifice (Men. 81a) and to differentiation between sanctified and unsanctified things (Ḥul. 35a). In the name of Rab he transmitted sayings relating to the presentation of letters of divorce (Giṭ. 13a, 63b), and to Rab's method of pronouncing the Sabbatical benediction (Pes. 166a). Rabbah transmitted sayings of Yiẓḥaḳ's (Meg. 16b); Ze'era addressed him as "Rabbenu" (Ḥul. 30b); and Rami bar Ḥama directed a question to him (*ib.* 35a). Yiẓḥaḳ once met Simlai in Nisibis, where he heard the latter denounce the free use of oil among the Jews; and he later furnished a report of this denunciation ('Ab. Zarah 36a; comp. Yer. 'Ab. Zarah 41d).

BIBLIOGRAPHY: Bacher, *Ag. Pal. Amor.* i. 569; Heilprin, *Seder ha-Dorot*, ii. 239–240.

J. S. O.

YIẒḤAḲ BEN ṬABLAI: Palestinian amora of the fourth century; a contemporary of Jacob ben Zabdai and Ḥelbo, together with both of whom he was called upon to decide a question of religious law (Yer. Niddah 50a). When asked whether the law of Demai applied to the Syrian leek, he was unable to decide the question by himself, and had to seek the advice of R. Jose (Yer. Dem. 22d); and on another occasion, when a question relating to the divorce law was addressed to him, he had to refer it to Eleazar (Yer. Ḳid. 63c). A tradition handed down from the above-mentioned Eleazar was differently transmitted by the amoraim Jonah and Jose (Yer. Sheb. 33d).

In the Babylonian Talmud (Pes. 113b) Yiẓḥaḳ has been identified with five other amoraim of similar name, but this has been refuted by Bacher, who disproved also the allegation of S. Krauss that the names חקלא and טבלא are identical. The Babylonian Talmud (Ned. 81b) mentions Yiẓḥaḳ as the transmitter of an interpretation of Mal. iii. 20. To him is ascribed also the haggadic explanation identifying the name לבנון with the Temple, with reference to the paronomasia on לבנון and מלבין, which latter word, meaning "to make white," has been used with regard to the Temple in the sense of "atone." Yiẓḥaḳ was the author, moreover, of haggadot on Deut. xxix. 10 and Josh. x. 4 (Midr. Tan. to Deut. xxix.) and of a haggadah comparing Israel to the stubborn princess (Pesiḳ. R. xxviii.; Midr. Teh. to Ps. cxxxviii. 5).

BIBLIOGRAPHY: Bacher, *Ag. Pal. Amor.* iii. 720–722; idem, *Ag. Tan.* i. 26, note 2; S. Krauss, *Lehnwörter*, i. 77, 246; Frankel, *Mebo*, p. 107; Heilprin, *Seder ha-Dorot*, pp. 237–238.

J. S. O.

YIẒḤAḲ BEN ZE'ERA: Palestinian amora of the fourth century. He interpreted the word ארח in Ps. xix. 6, in connection with Gen. xviii. 11, as signifying that the descending sun resembles a drop of blood not larger than a mustard-seed (Lev. R. xxxi. 9). He is credited also with an interpretation of a verse of the Song of Solomon (vii. 10); but some confusion exists with regard to the name, that of Bar Nazira occurring instead of his in some passages (Yeb. 97a; Bek. 31b).

BIBLIOGRAPHY: Bacher, *Ag. Pal. Amor.* i. 121, note 1; iii. 722; Heilprin, *Seder ha-Dorot*, p. 242.

J. S. O.

YUDAN: Palestinian amora of the fourth century. His name does not occur in the Babylonian Talmud, whereas it is often mentioned in the older Palestinian midrashim, as well as in the Jerusalem Talmud, where he is repeatedly referred to as a halakist (Pe'ah 16b; Dem. 25d; Kil. 29b; Ma'as. Sh. 52c; 'Er. 20d; etc.). He was a pupil of Abba (Yer. Soṭah 16c), and became a colleague of Jose, the principal of the school at Tiberias, with whom he often engaged in halakic controversies (Yer. Pe'ah 16c; Sheb. 36d; Suk. 52a; etc.). He appears to have held the office of judge simultaneously with Jose, it being stated (Yer. Ket. 34b) that the latter once rendered alone a decision on a question of civil law at a time when Yudan had fled to Nawe. This statement concerning Yudan's flight from Tiberias to Nawe, in Peræa, is the only biographical datum known with regard to his career, no mention being made of his family relations, of his native place, or even of the name of his father. His own references to older contemporaries throw but little light upon his personality. Mention is made of an objection relating to a halakic thesis which Yudan personally brought to the attention of Ze'era (Yer. Sanh. 24d); and several comments which Yudan made upon Ze'era's halakic maxims have been preserved (Yer. Suk. 54a; Yer. R. H. 57d; Yer. Ber. 61b). Of his pupils, Mana, the son of Jonah, is the only one known (Yer. Pes. 33a; Ta'an. 66a). On a certain day Yudan did not visit the school, and Mana referred to him the halakic questions which had been brought up during the session (Yer. Giṭ. 47a).

This amora is one of the best-known transmitters of haggadic literature, he having handed down maxims of many of the older amoraim, as Ḥanina, Johanan, Ḥama ben Ḥanina, Simeon b. Laḳish, and Joshua ben Levi. He often transmitted also tannaitic maxims. In many instances maxims originating with older amoraim have been ascribed to him (comp. Bacher, "Ag. Pal. Amor." p. 242, note 8): and he often places transmitted maxims side by side with his own (Yer. Ber. 13a; Gen. R. ix. 1). Together with his own haggadic maxims there are often handed down the divergent expositions of other haggadists on the same subjects. Among the haggadists whose opinions are thus given by Yudan may be mentioned Huna, Berechiah, Phinehas, and Azariah (comp. Bacher, *l.c.*). His maxims extend to all branches of the Haggadah, and include exegetic and homiletic explanations of Biblical passages, as well as comments on Biblical personages and narratives, sentences relating to the study of the Law, and eschatological and Messianic sayings.

Some of Yudan's haggadic maxims may be mentioned here. With reference to the atoning power of suffering, he remarks that if a slave is liberated because of pain inflicted upon a single member of his body (Ex. xxi. 20), how much more entitled to liberty in the world to come is a man who has been afflicted with sufferings in his whole body? (Gen. R. xcii. 1). He who publicly teaches the Torah shall be found worthy to have the Holy Spirit rest upon him, even as it rested on Solomon, who, because he had preached the Torah, was thought worthy to write the books of Proverbs, Ecclesiastes, and the Song of Solomon (Cant. R., Introduction, § 9). The words "the law of the Lord" in Isa. v. 24 refer to the written law, while "the word of the Holy One" in the same verse means the oral law (Pesiḳ. 121b). To "the nations"—by which term the Christians are probably meant—the Sabbath has been given with the word "Remember" (Ex. xx. 8), because, although they remember that day, they do not keep it; but to Israel it was given with the word "Observe" (Deut. v. 12; Pesiḳ. R. xxiii. 115b). The visit to Seir promised by Jacob (Gen. xxxiii. 14) is meant for the future, when the "saviors shall come up on Mount Zion" (Obadiah, verse 21; Yer. 'Ab. Zarah 40c). The words "and man became a living ["ḥayyah"] soul" (Gen. ii. 7) are explained by Yudan as meaning that man was originally created with a rudimentary tail, so that he resembled an animal ("ḥayyah"); later, however, God removed this appendage in order that man's dignity should not suffer (Gen. R. xiv., where the name "Judah" occurs erroneously for "Yudan").

Yudan often interpreted Biblical words according to their consonantal formation, without referring to their vowel-sounds (Gen. R. xxxv. 1, xxxviii. 8); and he also used the numerical values of the letters as a basis for explanations (*ib.* xxxix. 11, lxxix. 1). He interpreted numbers in other ways, asserting, for instance, that the fact that the name of Barzillai occurs five times in II Sam. xix. 31–40 (corresponding to the five books of the Torah), teaches that he who supports the pious with the necessaries of life, as Barzillai sustained David (II Sam. xvii. 27), is regarded as having kept all the precepts of the five books (Gen. R. lviii.). With regard to the sentence "I saw your fathers as the firstripe in the fig-tree at her first time" (Hosea ix. 10), he remarked that even as one plucks first one fig from the fig-tree, then two, then three, and at length a whole basketful, so at first "Abraham was one"(Ezek. xxxiii. 24), then there were two (Abraham and Isaac), then three (Abraham, Isaac, and Jacob), and at length "the children of Israel were fruitful, and increased abundantly" (Ex. i. 7; Gen. R. xlvi. 1).

Many of Yudan's exegetic interpretations give the correct and simple meanings of the words or passages to which they refer. Thus he explains, with regard to Ps. ix. 18, that the word לא in the first part of the verse refers to the word תאבד in the second part: "For even as the needy shall not always be forgotten, so shall not the expectation of the poor perish forever" (Midr. Teh. to Ps. ix.). In I Sam. xxiii. 27 the word מלאך denotes a messenger, and not an angel (Midr. Shemuel xvii. 2); and the word עפאים in Ps. civ. 12 is to be interpreted "leaves" in analogy with the word עפיה in Dan. iv. 9 (Midr. Teh. to Ps. civ. 9). Yudan also frequently employs parables, the following being a representative example: "Every one has a patron; and when he is in need he may not suddenly enter into the presence of his benefactor to ask for aid, but must wait at the door while a slave or an inmate of the house carries his request before the master. God, however, is not such a patron; when man is in need he shall call neither upon Gabriel nor upon Michael, but upon God direct, who will hear him without any mediators" (Yer. Ber. 13a).

BIBLIOGRAPHY: Bacher, *Ag. Pal. Amor.* iii. 237–272.

J. J. Z. L.

YUDAN BEN ISHMAEL: Palestinian amora of the third century; probably a brother of Yannai ben Ishmael. He solved the question whether instructors in the Law should be paid for their services, by declaring that they ought to be remunerated for the time during which they might have earned something by other work (Yer. Ned. 38c). The words "he weigheth the waters by measure" (Job xxviii. 25) were interpreted by him as implying the law of God, which is compared to water. The words of the Law are given to each individual by measure; one is accorded a knowledge of the Bible, another of the Mishnah, a third of the Halakah, and a fourth of the Haggadah, while many are learned in all (Lev. R. xv. 2, where "ben Ishmael" should be read instead of "ben Samuel").

BIBLIOGRAPHY: Frankel, *Mebo*, p. 95a; Bacher, *Ag. Pal. Amor.* iii. 603–604.

J. J. Z. L.

YUDAN BEN MANASSEH: Palestinian amora of the third century. One of his halakic maxims has been preserved in the Jerusalem Talmud (Kil. 27a), and the Babylonian Talmud contains two haggadic sayings by him, both based on the interpretation of a Biblical word with varied vocalization, and both referring to I Sam. ii. 2 (Meg. 14a; Ber. 10a; see "Diḳduḳe Soferim" on both passages). In emphasizing the decorous mode of expression adopted in the Bible, Yudan declared that "even those passages which enumerate the characteristics of the unclean animals first give the marks of their cleanness" (comp. Lev. xi. 4–7); and this aphorism is frequently quoted in midrashic literature (Lev. R. xxvi. 1; Pesiḳ. iv. [ed. Buber, p. 31a]; Num. R. xix. 1).

BIBLIOGRAPHY: Bacher, *Ag. Pal. Amor.* iii. 604.

J. J. Z. L.

YUDAN BEN SIMEON (called **Judah ben Simeon** in the Babylonian Talmud): Palestinian amora of the third century; a contemporary of Johanan, who in his name transmits a ruling relating to the law of inheritance, as well as a discussion which took place between them (B. B. 114b–115a). Reference is often made to a controversy between Johanan and Yudan ben Simeon concerning written and oral law (Yer. Pe'ah 17a; Meg. 74d; Ḥag. 76d).

Several haggadic interpretations of Yudan's have been preserved; and of these many are of cosmogonic and cosmological content, while others refer to questions of natural history. Among the latter may be mentioned the following explanation of Job xxix. 18: "The phenix lives a thousand years; and at the end of that period its body shrinks, its feathers fall off, and only a kind of egg remains. From this egg new members grow, and the phenix returns to life" (Gen. R. xix. 5). The giant animals behemoth and leviathan, according to him, were created in order to serve as quarries for the pious in the future world. Those who have not seen the hunts and animal contests among the heathen peoples in this world will be found worthy to view the chase in the world to come (Lev. R. xiii. 3). In his haggadic interpretations Yudan employs parables also, explaining, for example, Hosea xii. 4 by a beautiful allegory (Lev. R. xxvii. 6; Num. R. x. 1). Moreover, he made use of the system of NOṬARIḲON, interpreting the first word of the Decalogue, לא, by decomposing the letters, so that it read למד אלף, *i.e.*, "learn thousands," that is, "study the numberless words of the Law" (Pesiḳ. xxii.).

BIBLIOGRAPHY: Bacher, *Ag. Pal. Amor.* iii. 604–607.

J. J. Z. L.

Z

ZABDAI BEN LEVI: Palestinian amora of the first generation (third century). He belonged to the scholarly group of which Hoshaiah Rabbah was the chief (Yer. Dem. vii. 26a), and his halakot were transmitted by R. Johanan (Zeb. 28b; Ker. 5a). Zabdai was particularly prominent in the Haggadah and in Biblical exegesis, in both of which he disputed with Rab, Joshua b. Levi, and Jose b. Petrus. Thus the words "le-ruaḥ ha-yom" (Gen. iii. 8; A. V., "in the cool of the day") are explained by Zabdai to mean "the side of the setting of the sun," in opposition to Rab's interpretation, "the side of the rising of the sun" (Gen. R. xix. 8). The phrase "Ka-'et ḥayyah" (Gen. xviii. 14; A. V., "At the time appointed") is explained by Zabdai as meaning "in a year from hence." God made a scratch on the wall, saying that when a year later the sun should arrive at that mark Sarah would bear a son (Pesiḳ. R. 6 [ed. Friedmann, p. 24b]; Tan., Wayera, 36; see also Pesiḳ. xxv. 158a; Gen. R. lxxiv. 11; Lev. R. vii. 2).

Two proems to Lam. R. (Nos. 29 and 30) are by Zabdai; in the second of them he contrasts the different prayers of four kings with regard to their enemies. David prayed to God that he might overtake his foes and defeat them (Ps. xviii. 38); and his prayer was granted (I Sam. xxx. 8). Asa prayed to God that he might pursue the enemy, but that God would smite him; and it was so (II Chron. xiv. 12). Jehoshaphat said that he was too feeble to pursue the enemy, and prayed God to exterminate the foe while he would sing the praises of his divine helper; and his prayer was satisfied (*ib.* xx. 22). Finally, Hezekiah said that he had no strength even to sing the praises of God, but he prayed that his enemy might be routed while he himself would lie in his bed; and it so happened (II Kings xix. 35). It is related that Zabdai, having survived Joshua b. Levi, wished to see him in a dream. Joshua accordingly appeared to him, and showed him people with faces raised and people with faces cast down. When Zabdai asked the reason for the difference in posture, Joshua answered that those who arrived there with the study of the Law in their memories had their faces raised, while those who had forgotten it had their faces cast down (Eccl. R. ix. 10).

BIBLIOGRAPHY: Bacher, *Ag. Pal. Amor.* iii. 640–642; Heilprin, *Seder ha-Dorot*, ii.

J. M. SEL.

ZADOK: **1.** A priest, perhaps the high priest during the reign of David. He was the son of Ahitub (II Sam. viii. 17), but the attempt to trace his genealogy back to Eleazar, the third son of Aaron, as opposed to Abiathar, his contemporary and colleague, who was regarded as a descendant of Eli and considered a member of the house of Ithamar, was first made by the Chronicler (I Chron. v. 30–34 [A. V. vi. 4–8]; comp. vi. 35–38 [A. V. vi. 50–53]), thus assuring the preeminence of the Zadokites over the descendants of Eli. In the beginning of his career he was associated with Abiathar (II Sam. xx. 25) and with his son (*ib.* viii. 17; I Chron. xxiv. 3, 6, 31). The hypothesis has accordingly been advanced that Zadok officiated in the Tabernacle at Gibeon (I Chron. xvi. 39; comp. I Kings iii. 4), while the sons of Eli were stationed as high priests at Jerusalem or, more probably, at Shiloh (comp. Keil on I Kings i. 8). Such a division of functions is very doubtful, however; and it is more plausible to suppose that Zadok gradually won equality of rank with the sons of Eli by his good fortune in gaining the favor of David.

According to the somewhat improbable statement of the Chronicler, a certain Zadok, as a young man, had been one of those who joined David at Hebron and helped him win the crown of all Israel, his house then including twenty-two captains (I Chron. xii. 29); and Josephus expressly identifies this Zadok with the high priest of the same name ("Ant." vii. 2, § 2).

During the rebellion of Absalom, Zadok gained still greater prominence. He and the Levites wished to accompany the fleeing David with the Ark of the Covenant, but the king begged them to remain at Jerusalem, where they could do him better service (II Sam. xv. 24–29; comp. 35), so that it actually happened that Ahimaaz, the sou of Zadok, and Jonathan, the son of Abiathar, brought the king an important message (*ib.* xvii. 21). In all these passages Zadok is mentioned before Abiathar. According to the Hebrew text of II Sam. xv. 27, David addressed the priest with the words "ha-ro'eh attah," and the Vulgate consequently regards Zadok as a seer, although this interpretation is incorrect. These two difficult words are emended by Wellhausen to הכהן הראש אתה, thus implying the promise of the high-priesthood to him. On the suppression of the rebellion, the king sent Zadok and Abiathar to the elders of Judah, urging them to hasten to bring the monarch back (*ib.* xix. 12). Zadok again manifested his loyalty to the king when he espoused the cause of Solomon against Adonijah (I Kings i. 8 *et seq.*), and in his gratitude the new king appointed him sole high priest (*ib.* ii. 35). In his account of this event Josephus states ("Ant." viii. 1, § 3) that Zadok was a scion of the house of Phinehas, and consequently a descendant of Eleazar.

Reliable historical data show that the high-priesthood remained in the hands of the Zadokites from this time until the rise of the Maccabees. The descendants of Zadok increased in rank and influence, so that his son Azariah was one of the princes of Solomon (I Kings

iv. 2), and the Ahimaaz who married a daughter of Solomon was probably another of Zadok's children (*ib.* iv. 15). Either Zadok himself or his grandson was the ruler of the Aaronites (I Chron. xxvii. 17), and Jerusha, the mother of Jotham, is apparently termed the daughter of Zadok to emphasize her noble lineage, since her father may have been a descendant of the first Zadok (II Kings xv. 33; II Chron. xxvii. 1). A Zadok is also mentioned in the genealogy of Joseph, the father of Jesus (Matt. i. 14).

G. S. KR.

2. Sadducean leader. The only data concerning the origin of the Sadducees are based on certain deductions drawn from their name, for a late rabbinical source alone appears to be founded on actual knowledge. Two pupils of ANTIGONUS OF SOKO are said to have misinterpreted their teacher's statement that God should be worshiped without hope of reward as meaning that there is no recompense, either for good or for evil, in the world to come. These two scholars, Zadok and Boethus, are accordingly regarded as the founders of the heresies of the SADDUCEES and the BOETHUSIANS (Ab. R. N. recension A, 5; recension B, 10). This statement is devoid of historicity, however, since it incorrectly postulates denial of the future life as the cardinal doctrine of the Sadducees, while it betrays also its lack of authenticity by making the origin of the Boethusians synchronous with the rise of Sadduceeism, although the former sect derived its name from the high priest Boethus, who flourished during the reign of Herod.

The only historical portion of this legend is the part which connects the origin of each of these heresies with a personal name, for the Hebrew צדוקים is derived from צדוק just as are ביתוסים from ביתוס and אפיקורסים from אפיקורוס, while Herod was the eponym of the party of the HERODIANS.

Geiger's theory of the derivation of the name of the Sadducean party from the Biblical appellative "Zadok" is, therefore, the most probable one. This name צדוק, which occurs ten times in Ezekiel, Ezra, and Nehemiah, is transliterated Σαδδούκ throughout by the Septuagint in these books, as well as in other passages in Lucian's version of the Septuagint. The same form appears in Josephus; and even a manuscript of the Mishnah (Codex De Rossi No. 138) vocalizes the name of the rabbi Zadok צַדּוּק (= "Ẓadduḳ"). The only moot point is the problem whether the appellation of the sect is to be derived from a Zadok who is no longer known or from the priestly family of the Zadokites. An unknown Zadok was assumed to be the founder of the Sadducees by Kuenen (though he later adopted the opposing theory), Graetz, Montet, and Lagarde; while the second hypothesis, which is the more probable, was maintained by Geiger and Schürer, and is now confirmed by the Hebrew Ben Sira (see Schechter's note in "The Wisdom of Ben Sira," 1899, p. 35). A third conjecture, deriving the word from the adjective צדיק, which was advocated in ancient times by Jerome and Epiphanius, and was defended more recently by Joseph Derenbourg and Hamburger, is untenable both on linguistic and on historical grounds.

From the days of Solomon the descendants of the priest Zadok were regarded with great reverence, which must have been much increased by the Deuteronomic legislation concentrating all cults at Jerusalem. In Ezekiel's prophetic vision the "sons of Zadok" are described as the only priests worthy to discharge their holy office (Ezek. xl. 46, xliii. 19, xliv. 15, xlviii. 11); and although in the Second Temple certain prerogatives were allowed the sons of Ithamar, the Zadokites alone formed the priestly aristocracy, so that the Chronicler assigns twice as many priestly divisions to the Zadokite descendants of Eleazar as to the Ithamarites (I Chron. xxiv.). In Ecclesiasticus (Sirach), in like manner, the Zadokites alone receive praise (li. 12 [9], Hebr.). Despite the fact that those members of this powerful family who adopted the Sadducean doctrines were but few, they gave the teachings such support that the entire sect bore their name, and Josephus expressly states that scions of the priestly aristocracy, *i.e.*, the Zadokites, were preeminently adherents of Sadduceeism. See SADDUCEES.

BIBLIOGRAPHY: Geiger, *Urschrift*, pp. 20, 102; Wellhausen, *I. J. G.* 4th ed., p. 294; idem, *Pharisäer und Sadducäer*, Göttingen, 1874; Schürer, *Gesch.* 3d ed., ii. 408–411.

J. S. KR.

3. Tanna of priestly descent; father of Eleazar. He flourished in the years preceding and following the beginning of the common era. According to an account which must refer to him in the prime of life, he was taken as a captive to Rome, where he was sold to an aristocratic house. Its mistress attempted to force him to marry one of her beautiful slaves, but Zadok refused, claiming that not only did he belong to one of the most influential families of Jerusalem, but that he was of priestly lineage, whereupon his mistress gave him his freedom (Ab. R. N., ed. Schlechter, p. 32a and note 11; Ḳid. 40a). A historical account dating from the time of the Temple vouches for the fact that he was a priest. During a sacrifice a strife broke out between two priests, perhaps brothers, because one had taken precedence of the other at the altar, and one of them was stabbed. There was great excitement among the congregation, whereupon Zadok ascended the steps of the "ulam," from which the priests were accustomed to give the benediction, and there calmed the people by an address based on Deut. xxi. 1 *et seq.* Since, however, it has been proved that only priests were allowed to mount the ulam, Zadok must have been a priest (Yoma 23a; Tosef., Yoma, i. 12; Yer. Yoma ii. 39d).

Together with Eliezer b. Hyrcanus and Joshua b. Hananiah, Zadok was present at the marriage of the son of Gamaliel II. in Jabneh. On that occasion Gamaliel II. himself poured out the wine and handed it round. Joshua and Eliezer began to praise Gamaliel, whereupon Zadok became angry, declaring that they should not turn away from the worship of God, who had created everything for man, and worship a mortal (Ḳid. 32a). According to Bacher, however, this incident occurred not at a wedding, but at another feast, which Gamaliel gave to the scholars of Jabneh.

The whole life of this tanna fell within the period of the dissolution of the Jewish state, and he declared that he had fasted forty years in his endeavor to prevent the destruction of the Temple. When this took place, however, Zadok had become so weak that Johanan b. Zakkai was obliged to appeal for him to Titus, who had him treated by a physician (Giṭ. 56b; Lam. R. i. 5). Zadok moved to Jabneh together with Johanan b. Zakkai and other scholars, and his few halakot, found in 'Eduy. vii. 1–5, date from this period. He was the most influential personality in Gamaliel's tribunal, and always sat at the right of the latter (Yer. Sanh. 19c), while on one occasion he was present at the eating of the sacrificial lamb in Gamaliel's house (Pes. 74a). Together with Johanan b. Zakkai and Gamaliel, he rendered a decision on the conditions under which food might he eaten outside the Tabernacle during the Feast of Weeks (Suk. 26b). Although he was theoretically an adherent of the principles of the Bet Shammai, in practise he always made his rulings in accordance with the Bet Hillel (Yeb. 15b). His motto in ethical matters was, "Do not make learning a crown to make thyself great thereby, nor a spade to dig with it" (Ab. iv. 5). The thirtieth chapter of the Tanna debe Eliyahu Rabbah relates that Zadok once came to the place where the Temple had formerly stood. In his grief at the desolation he reproached God Himself, whereupon he fell into a sleep in which he saw God and the angels mourning over the destruction of Zion. The Pirḳe de-Rabbi Eli'ezer ascribes to Zadok haggadic sayings concerning the descendants of the giants (ch. xxii.), the sacrifices of Cain and Abel (ch. xxi.), the Flood (ch. xxiii.), and Noah's prayer in the ark (*ib.*).

BIBLIOGRAPHY: Bacher, *Ag. Tan.* i. 43–46; Derenbourg, *Hist.* pp. 342–344; Zacuto, *Sefer Yuḥasin ha-Shalom*, ed. Filipowski, pp. 32a, 76a, b; Frankel, *Darke ha-Mishnah*, pp. 70–71; Heilprin, *Seder ha-Dorot*, ii. 319–320; Büchler, *Die Priester und der Cultus*, p. 126, note 1, Vienna, 1895: Neubauer, *G. T.* p. 375.

J. S. O.

ZAKKAI: **1**. Palestinian tanna of the second century; contemporary of Judah ha-Nasi I. and apparently a pupil of Simeon b. Yoḥai. He is mentioned as having transmitted a halakah of R. Jacob and one of Simeon b. Yoḥai (Tosef., Yad. ii. 9; Shab. 79b); and he had a halakic controversy with Simeon b. Gamaliel and Simeon b. Eleazar, the former being the father and the latter the companion of Judah ha-Nasi (Ber. 25b). Zakkai was prominent in the Haggadah, where he is styled "Zakkai Rabbah" (Zakkai the Great). He interpreted the words "we-yidgu la-rob" (Gen. xlviii. 14) as referring to the haggadic statement that 600,000 children were once thrown into the river by command of Pharaoh, but were saved through the merits of Moses (Gen. R. xcvii. 5; comp. Cant. R. vii. 5; Yalḳ. Isa. 472). Zakkai attained to a very great age, and when his pupils asked him through what virtue he lived so long, he said that he never called his neighbor by a nickname and never neglected to buy wine for the Ḳiddush of the Sabbath. His aged mother even once sold her cap to purchase wine for him, and when she died she left him 300 kegs of wine, while he himself bequeathed to his children 3,000 kegs (Meg. 27b).

2. Babylonian amora of the third century. He emigrated to Palestine, where he was the chief lecturer in R. Johanan's school ('Er. 9a; Yeb. 77b; Sanh. 62a; and elsewhere). In Sanh. 62a and in Yer. Shab. vii. 2, R. Johanan calls him "the Babylonian." The press-house (מעצרתא) which he left in Babylon was the meeting-place of certain rabbis ('Er. 49a; B. B. 42b). From Palestine he sent a halakah to the exilarch Mar 'Uḳba (Ket. 87a), who transmitted a haggadah of Zakkai (Sanh. 70a). The latter seems to have been a good preacher; and in one of his sermons he gives an interpretation of Micah iv. 10 (Yer. Suk. 54c).

BIBLIOGRAPHY: Bacher, *Ag. Pal. Amor.* iii. 642–643; Heilprin, *Seder ha-Dorot*, ii.

J. M. SEL.

ZECHARIAH BEN ABḲILUS (Amphikalos): Palestinian scholar and one of the leaders of the ZEALOTS; lived in Jerusalem at the time of the destruction of the Second Temple. According to the Talmud, the authority which he enjoyed among the rabbis of Jerusalem was the cause of the downfall of the city. Zechariah was present at the banquet famous for the affair of ḲAMẒA and BAR ḲAMẒA (comp. Josephus, "Vita," § 10); and though his influence might have prevented the disgrace of Bar Ḳamẓa, he did not exercise it. Again, when the emperor sent a blemished calf as an offering to the Temple, the Hillelites would have accepted it to frustrate Bar Ḳamẓa, had not Zechariah, acting in the interest of the school of Shammai, given a casting vote, or (according to Lam. R. iv. 2) refrained from voting, and thus rendered the decision negative. The people wished to kill Bar Ḳamẓa so that he should not be able to tell the emperor of the refusal, but Zechariah once more restrained them from carrying out their design. R. Johanan, on the other hand, or, according to another source, R. Jose, declared that the humility of Zechariah b. Abḳilus, in refusing to cast his vote, caused the destruction of the Temple (Giṭ. 56a; Tosef., Shab. xvi. [xvii.] 6; Lam. R. iv. 2). He is recorded as following neither the Bet Hillel nor the Bet Shammai with regard to holding date-stones on the Sabbath (Shab. 143; Tosef., Shab. *l.c.*). He is probably referred to by Josephus ("B. J." ii. 17, §§ 2–3).

BIBLIOGRAPHY: Grätz, *Gesch.* iii. 458, 509, 817–819; Derenbourg, *Hist.* p. 257.

E. C. M. SEL.—K.

ZECHARIAH BEN JEHOIADA.—Biblical Data: A reforming priest who lived under King Joash of Judah. He reproved the idolaters, announcing God's judgment against them; and a conspiracy was formed against him that resulted in his being stoned in the court of the Temple at the command of the king, who "remembered not the kindness which Jehoiada his father had done to him" (II Chron. xxiv. 22). Zechariah's dying words were: "YHWH look upon it, and require it" (*ib.* verses 20–22).

E. G. H. B. P.

——**In Rabbinical Literature:** According to the Rabbis, Zechariah was the son-in-law of the king, and, being also a priest, prophet, and judge, he dared censure the monarch. He was killed in the priests' courtyard of the Temple on a Sabbath which was likewise the Day of Atonement. Later, when NEBUZAR-ADAN came to destroy the Temple, Zechariah's blood began to boil. The Assyrian asked the Jews what that phenomenon meant, but when they replied that it was the blood of sacrifices, he proved the falsity of their answer. The Jews then told him the truth, and Nebuzar-adan, wishing to appease Zechariah's blood, slew in succession the Great and Small Sanhedrins, the young priests, and school-children, till the number of the dead was 940,000. Still the blood continued to boil, whereupon Nebuzar-adan cried: "Zechariah, Zechariah! for thee have I slain the best of them; wouldst thou that I destroy them all?" And at these words the blood ceased to effervesce (Giṭ. 57b; Sanh. 96b; Lam. R. iv. 13).

E. C. M. SEL.

ZE'ERA: Palestinian amora of the third generation; born in Babylonia, where he spent his early youth. He was a pupil of Ḥisda (Ber. 49a), of Huna (*ib.*), and of Judah b. Ezekiel in Pumbedita. He associated also with other prominent teachers of the Babylonian school, as Naḥman b. Jacob (Yer. Ber. 8c), Hamnuna (Zeb. 105b; Ber. 24b), and Sheshet, who called him a great man ("gabra rabba"; 'Er. 66a). His love for the Holy

Land led him to decide upon leaving his native country and emigrating to Palestine. This resolve, however, he kept secret from his teacher Judah, who disapproved of any emigration from Babylonia. Before leaving, he spied upon Judah while the latter was bathing, and the words which he then overheard he took with him as a valuable and instructive memento (Shab. 41a; Ket. 110b). A favorable dream, in which he was told that his sins had been forgiven, encouraged him to undertake the journey to the Holy Land (Ber. 57a); and before starting he spent a hundred days in fasting, in order to forget the dialectic method of instruction of the Babylonian schools, that this might not handicap him in Palestine (B. M. 85a). His journey took him through Akrokonia, where he met Ḥiyya b. Ashi ('Ab. Zarah 16b), and through Sura (*ib.*). When he reached the River Jordan he could not control his impatience, but passed through the water without removing his clothes. When jeered at by an unbeliever who stood by, he answered, "Why should not I be impatient when I pursue a blessing which was denied even to Moses and Aaron?" (Yer. Sheb. 35c).

Ze'era's arrival in Palestine and his first experiences there have been recorded in various anecdotes. He was small of stature and of dark complexion, for which reason Assi called him "Black Pot" ('Ab. Zarah 16b), according to an expression current in Babylonia (comp. Meg. 14b; Pes. 88a; Ber. 50a); this name probably also contained an allusion to his sputtering manner of speech. With reference to a malformation of his legs, he was called "the little one with shrunken legs," or "the dark, burned one with the stubby legs" (comp. Bacher, "Ag. Pal. Amor." iii. 7, note 2). With these nicknames is connected a legend which throws light upon Ze'era's ascetic piety (B. M. 85a). In Palestine he associated with all the prominent scholars. Eleazar b. Pedat was still living at the time (Niddah 48), and from him Ze'era received valuable instruction (Yer. Ter. 47d). His most intimate friends were Assi and Ḥiyya b. Abba. In his intercourse with Assi he was generally the one who asked questions; and on one occasion Assi made known his approval of one of Ze'era's questions by saying: "Right you are, Babylonian; you have understood it correctly" (Yer. Shab. 7c). Ze'era especially acknowledged the authority of Ammi, the principal of the school at Tiberias; and it is related that he asked Ammi to decide questions pertaining to religious law that had been addressed to himself (Yer. Dem. 25b; Yer. Shab. 8a; Yer. Yeb. 72d). Ze'era was highly esteemed by Abbahu, the rector at Cæsarea, of whom he considered himself a pupil. He was ordained rabbi, a distinction usually denied to members of the Babylonian school; and though in the beginning he refused this honor (Yer. Bik. 65c), he later accepted it on learning of the atoning powers connected with the dignity (Sanh. 14a). His insignificant appearance was humorously referred to when at his ordination he was greeted with the words of a wedding-song: "Without rouge and without ornament, but withal a lovable gazel" (Ket. 17a).

With regard to Ze'era's private vocation, the only facts known are that he once traded in linen, and that he asked Abbahu how far he might go in improving the outward appearance of his goods without rendering himself liable in the slightest degree to a charge of fraud (Yer. B. M. 9d). Information regarding his family relations is also very scanty; it is asserted that he became an orphan at an early age (Yer. Pe'ah 15c), and that his wedding was celebrated during the Feast of Tabernacles (Suk. 25b); and he had one son, Ahabah or Ahava, who has become well known through various haggadic maxims (comp. Bacher, *l.c.* iii. 651–659).

Ze'era occupies a prominent place in the Halakah as well as in the Haggadah; with regard to the former he is especially distinguished for the correctness and knowledge with which he transmits older maxims. Among his haggadic sayings the following may be mentioned as throwing light upon his high moral standpoint: "He who has never sinned is worthy of reward only if he has withstood temptation to do so" (Yer. Ḳid. 61d); "One should never promise a child anything which one does not intend to give it, because this would accustom the child to untruthfulness" (Suk. 46b). On account of his lofty morals and piety Ze'era was honored with the name "the pious Babylonian." Among his neighbors were several people known for their wickedness, but Ze'era treated them with kindness in order to lead them to moral reformation. When he died, these people said, "Hitherto Ze'era has prayed for us, but who will pray for us now?" This reflection so moved their hearts that they really were led to do penance (Sanh. 37a). That Ze'era enjoyed the respect of his contemporaries is evidenced by the comment upon his death written by an elegist: "Babylonia gave him birth; Palestine had the pleasure of rearing him; 'Wo is me,' says Tiberias, for she has lost her precious jewel" (M. Ḳ. 75b).

BIBLIOGRAPHY: Bacher, *Ag. Pal. Amor.* iii. 1–34; Heilprin, *Seder ha-Dorot*, ii. 117–120.

J. J. Z. L.

ZE'IRI: Amora of the third century; born in Babylonia. He sojourned for a long time in Alexandria, and later went to Palestine, where he became a pupil of Rabbi Johanan. In the name of Ḥanina b. Ḥama he transmitted the maxim that he who in the presence of a teacher ventures to decide a legal question, is a trespasser ('Er. 3a). He also transmitted a saying by Ḥanina to the effect that the Messiah would not arrive until all the arrogant ones had disappeared (Sanh. 98a). During his sojourn in Alexandria he purchased a mule which, when he led it to water, was transformed into a bridge-board, the water having lifted the spell which rested on the animal. The purchase-money was refunded to Ze'iri, and he was advised to apply the water-test thenceforth to everything he purchased, in order to ascertain whether it had been charmed (*ib.* 67b). When Eleazar arrived in Palestine he sought information from Ze'iri concerning men known in ancient traditions (B. B. 87a). Ze'iri was praised by Raba as an exegete of the Mishnah (Zeb. 43b). He was proffered the daughter of Rabbi Johanan for a wife, but refused because he was a Babylonian and she a Palestinian (Ḳid. 71b). Among those who transmitted in his name may be mentioned Rabbi Ḥisda (Ber. 43a), R. Judah ('Ab. Zarah 61b; Men. 21a), R. Joseph (Ned. 46b), R. Naḥman ('Ab. Zarah 61b), and Rabbah (Ned. 46a).

BIBLIOGRAPHY: Bacher, *Ag. Pal. Amor*, iii. 644; Heilprin, *Seder ha-Dorot*, ii. 123a; Blau, *Altjüdisches Zauberwesen*, p. 158, note 5, Strasburg, 1898; *Yuḥasin*, ed. Filipowski, p. 134b.

J. S. O.

ZUGOT (lit. "pairs"): Name given to the leading teachers of the Law in the time preceding the Tannaim. The period of the Zugot begins with Jose b. Joezer and ends with Hillel. The name "Zugot" (comp. Latin "duumviri") was given to these teachers because, according to the tradition in Ḥagigah, two of them always stood at the same time at the head of the Sanhedrin, one as president ("nasi") and the other as vice-president or father of the court ("ab bet din"; see SANHEDRIN). There were five pairs of these teachers: (1) Jose b. Joezer and Jose b. Johanan, who flourished at the time of the Maccabean wars of independence; (2) Joshua b. Peraḥyah and Nittai of Arbela, at the time of John Hyrcanus; (3) Judah b. Ṭabbai and Simeon b. Sheṭaḥ, at the time of Alexander Jannæus and Queen Salome; (4) Shemaiah and Abtalion, at the time of Hyrcanus II.; (5) Hillel and Shammai, at the time of King Herod.

J. J. Z. L.

ZUṬRA, MAR, I.: Exilarch from 401 to 409. He was the successor of Mar Kahana and a contemporary of R. Ashi, whose enactments he had to follow in spite of his exalted position. He was obliged to leave Nehardea and take up his residence in Sura, where he held an annual reception at the opening of the harvest season for the delegates of all Babylonian communities, the receptions being called "rigli" (ריגלא דרישי גלוותא). In addition Mar Zuṭra received various other delegations at Sura. Nothing further is known about his career.

BIBLIOGRAPHY: Gräte, *Gesch.* iv. 351, note 3; Neubauer, *Anecdota*, i. 32–33; Heilprin, *Seder ha-Dorot*, i. 167a.

J. S. O.

ZUṬRA, MAR, II.: Exilarch; born about 496; died about 520; ruled from 512 to 520. He was the son of Huna, who was appointed exilarch under Firuz; and he was born at the time when Mazdak endeavored to introduce communism in all Persia. The opposition against Mar Zuṭra, his imprisonment, and his early death have given rise to a number of legends. The following anecdote is told about his birth and the events preceding it: Mar Zuṭra's father was engaged in constant strife with his father-in-law, the school principal Mar Ḥanina, because the latter refused to obey the orders issued by the exilarch. Ḥanina was accordingly punished for his disobedience; and, being embittered and humiliated, he went into the prayer-house at night, and there shed a dishful of tears, whereupon he fell asleep. He dreamed that he was in a cedar forest, engaged in felling the trees; and when he came to the last cedar-tree King David appeared and forbade him to fell it. On awakening, Ḥanina learned that the entire house of the exilarch had perished, except his daughter, who was pregnant and had been spared. Soon afterward she gave birth to a son, whom the grandfather named Mar Zuṭra, at the same time assuming personal charge of his training. During Mar Zuṭra's infancy the exilarchate was administered by his brother-in-law Mar Paḥra, or Paḥda. The latter bribed King Kobad in order that he might remain in office; but when Mar Zuṭra had reached the age of fifteen, his grandfather presented him to the king as the legitimate ruler, whereupon the monarch installed him as exilarch. Mar Paḥda opposed this, but was killed by a fly which entered his nostril; and after that event the exilarchs had a fly on their seal.

Mar Zuṭra took up arms against the Persians, and organized an uprising to oppose the introduction of communism, although the king himself was in favor thereof. The immediate cause of the uprising, however, was the assassination of the school principal Isaac, regarding which no accurate information exists. From the fact that Mar Ḥanina took part in the struggle, it may be deduced that it was of a religious character. At the head of a company of 400 Jewish warriors Mar Zuṭra advanced against the opposing Persian forces; and the battles fought by him have furnished material for various legends. It is told that a pillar of fire always preceded his army; and it is further stated that Mar Zuṭra founded an independent Jewish state, with Maḥoza as his residence. He ruled as an independent king, and imposed heavy taxes on all non-Jews. In spite of his able government, however, immorality spread among his people, whereupon the pillar of fire disappeared. In a subsequent battle between Mar Zuṭra and the Persians the former was defeated; and both he and his grandfather Ḥanina were taken prisoners and decapitated, their bodies being suspended from crosses on the bridge at Maḥoza.

The account of Mar Zuṭra's life is based on a mixture of historic facts and legendary narratives. Thus, the description of the uprising of the Jews against Persian reforms, the statement regarding the prominent position held by Mar Zuṭra, and the account of his death are all based on historical data, whereas the stories of the extinction of the exilarchal house are legendary, as are also the dream of Ḥanina (which corresponds with that of Bostanai) and the account of the pillar of fire. All those legends, however, which tend to prove that the later rulers of Babylonia were usurpers have a basis of truth, inasmuch as Mar Zuṭra's only son emigrated to Jerusalem.

BIBLIOGRAPHY: Grätz, *Gesch.* v. 4–6, note 1; Neubauer, *Anecdota*, ii. 76; Heilprin, *Seder ha-Dorot*, i. 167.

J. S. O.

ZUṬRA, MAR, BAR MAR ZUṬRA: Palestinian scholar. On the day of his birth his father was crucified, and his mother fled with him to Palestine, where he was later appointed archipherecite. According to Brüll, he was active in causing the scientific material collected in Palestine to be gathered together and examined and the Palestinian Talmud is said to have been completed in his lifetime. During his term of office the order of Justinian in relation to reading from Holy Scripture was promulgated; and the first opposing utterance is said to have been made by Mar Zuṭra. His place of residence was probably Tiberias, and by virtue of his title he was the official leader of the Palestinian Jews.

BIBLIOGRAPHY: Brüll's *Jahrb. v.* 94–96; Heilprin, *Seder ha-Dorot*, i. 173; *Yuḥasin*, ed. Filipowski, p. 93; Weiss, *Dor*, iv. 2, 304; Grätz, *Gesch.* iii. 386.

J. S. O.

Dictionary of ancient rabbis